W9-DBK-889

THE CULTURAL DEFENSE

THE CULTURAL DEFENSE

Alison Dundes Renteln

UNIVERSITY PRESS

2004

K
5455
R46
2004

#54708622

5-26-05

c.1

OXFORD

UNIVERSITY PRESS

Oxford   New York

Auckland   Bangkok   Buenos Aires   Cape Town   Chennai
Dar es Salaam   Delhi   Hong Kong   Istanbul   Karachi   Kolkata
Kuala Lumpur   Madrid   Melbourne   Mexico City   Mumbai   Nairobi
São Paulo   Shanghai   Taipei   Tokyo   Toronto

Copyright © 2004 by Alison Dundes Renteln

Published by Oxford University Press, Inc.
198 Madison Avenue, New York, New York 10016

www.oup.com

Oxford is a registered trademark of Oxford University Press

All rights reserved. No part of this publication may be reproduced,
stored in a retrieval system, or transmitted, in any form or by any means,
electronic, mechanical, photocopying, recording, or otherwise,
without the prior permission of Oxford University Press.

Portions of this book were adapted from the following articles by Alison Dundes
Renteln, reprinted by permission: "The Rights of the Dead: Autopsies and Corpse Mis-
management in Multicultural Societies," *South Atlantic Quarterly* 100, no. 4 (2001):
1005–1027; "In Defense of Culture in the Courtroom," in *Engaging Cultural Differences:
The Multicultural Challenge in Liberal Democracies*, edited by Richard Shweder, Martha
Minow, and Hazel Rose Markus, © 2002 Russell Sage Foundation, 112 East 64th Street,
New York, NY 20021; "A Justification of the Cultural Defense as Partial Excuse," *South-
ern California Review of Law and Women's Studies* 2 (1993): 437–526; "Raising Cultural
Defenses," in *Cultural Issues in Criminal Defense*, edited by James G. Connell III and
Rene L. Valladares (New York: Juris Publishing, www.jurispub.com, 2000).

Library of Congress Cataloging-in-Publication Data
Renteln, Alison Dundes.
The cultural defense / by Alison Dundes Renteln.
p. cm.
Includes bibliographical references and index.
ISBN 0-19-515402-9
1. Defense (Criminal procedure)—Sociological aspects. 2. Actions and defenses—
Sociological aspects. 3. Culture and law. I. Title.
K5455 .R46   2003
345.73'05044—dc21   2002071523

3 5 7 9 8 6 4 2

Printed in the United States of America
on acid-free paper

FOR PAUL

ACKNOWLEDGMENTS

This book was enriched by the contributions of many individuals who generously shared their materials, insights, and time with me. Although I cannot possibly thank all of them, I would like to single out a few of those who helped me: Greg Abbott, James Brown, Doriane Lambelet Coleman, Deirdre Evans-Pritchard, John Fleming, Ron Garet, Anne McGillivray, Frank Kessel, Harvey I. Lapin, Martha Minow, Hazel Rose Markus, Noel Ragsdale, Elyn Saks, Richard Shweder, Nomi Stolzenberg, Fons Strijbosch, Alan Tarr, Rene Valladares, Kathie Walczak, Hermine Wiersinga, Deborah Woo, and Bruce Ziff. I wish to express my profound gratitude to Francesca Frey, a deputy district attorney in Los Angeles, who discussed many of the issues in the book with me. I am fortunate to have had the benefit of her expert insights.

The work of the late Sebastian Poulter was an inspiration to me. I appreciated his brilliant scholarship, collegiality, and intellectual camaraderie. His tragic early death is a great loss.

I am also indebted to my students, particularly Darya Alhambra, Ayesha Borland, Jose Gomez, Fred Hay, Andrew Kanter, James Lai, Christopher Larkins, Lana Laymon, Sylvia Maier, Nicholas Rossier, Margaret Scully, Viktoria Stamison, Leigh Turner, Linda Veazey, and Hans Wang. I very much appreciate the assistance of several outstanding reference librarians: Janice Hanks, Ginny Irving, Rosanne Krikorian, Robert Labaree, Hazel Lord, Susan McGlamery, Jennifer Murray, Brian Raphael, and Will Geeslin. I also thank the judges, lawyers, and police officers who not only sent me documents but also provided interpretations of the cases in which they had been involved. A number of journalists shared their articles with me. I am grateful to Saeed Ahmed of the *Atlanta Journal-Constitution*, Pat Alston of the *Santa*

Monica Daily Breeze, Lisa Fernandez of the *San Jose Mercury News*, Bill Morlin of the *Spokesman Review*, and Alex Pulaski of the *Fresno Bee*.

As I was writing this book, I sometimes wondered whether any of my ideas were practical enough to be incorporated into the legal system. It was a privilege to discuss the cultural defense with many fine jurists, including Philip Champlin, Ming Chin, Pat Cowett, David Garcia, Peggy Hora, Eugene Hyman, Lawrence Kay, Robert Leventer, Barry Loncke, Lillian Sing, and Robert Timlin; I benefited greatly from their thoughtful suggestions. Some of the opportunities to meet with judges were in the context of judicial education courses. I thank Kathleen Sikora, staff attorney at the California Center for Judicial Education and Research (CJER), for inviting me to teach judges at CJER-sponsored continuing judicial studies programs. I also wish to express my gratitude to Judge John Noonan for bringing some particularly interesting federal cases to my attention.

The University of Southern California (USC) provided grants that subsidized the data collection. I was fortunate to have been the recipient of awards from the Zumberge Faculty Research and Innovation Fund, the Faculty Fund for Innovative Teaching, and the Dean's Faculty Research grant program. The funding I received from the Irvine Foundation, to develop a new course, Cultural Diversity and the Law, also facilitated the completion of this study. Teaching at the USC Delinquency Control Institute (DCI) permitted me to consult law enforcement officers about their experiences with culture conflicts. I thank the officers and Garrett Capune, Don Fuller, Dan Kuhn, Doris Lar, and Mike Markulis at DCI. I am also indebted to the department of political science and especially Professor Sheldon Kamieniecki for giving me the time and encouragement to complete this project.

Special thanks to Lucy and Nicholas Weber for suggesting the image for the cover. I greatly appreciate their kindness in providing me with the Josef Albers print.

It was a pleasure to have the opportunity to work with Dedi Felman, my editor. I am grateful for her advice and counsel during the process of transforming the manuscript into a book.

It would not have been possible to complete this book without the support of my family. I thank my parents, Alan and Carolyn Dundes, for their sage advice and unwavering moral support. My husband, Paul Renteln, more than anyone else, enabled me to write this book. Paul listened as I sorted out the arguments, he encouraged me to consider all points of view, and he gave me the fortitude to finish my analysis. Our sons, David and Michael, helped, too, by vigorously defending the "When in Rome" presumption and by giving me their ideas about "where to draw the line."

CONTENTS

THE CULTURAL DEFENSE

Part I

LAW AND CULTURE

1

Introduction

In pluralistic societies ethnic minorities and indigenous groups sometimes ask the legal system to take their cultural background into account in criminal and civil cases. More often than not, courts refuse to do so. The purpose of this book is to examine the nature of the debate surrounding the admissibility of cultural evidence in the courtroom. This study analyzes the cultural defense, which, were it to be established, would require judges to consider the cultural background of litigants in the disposition of cases before them.

Most individuals, when first hearing of the cultural defense, immediately reject it for fear that it would lead to anarchy. If each person could demand exemptions from the law, then the law would be powerless to hold society together. Ethnic minorities should change their behavior so it conforms to the law of the land. "When in Rome, do as the Romans do" has been the conventional wisdom for centuries.[1] The official policies of essentially all nation-states mirror these beliefs. Indeed, most governments favor assimilation to the accommodation of cultural differences. This view, which is widely accepted by the public and government elites, has complicated efforts to raise cultural defenses in many instances.[2]

This book documents the extraordinary range of cases in which individuals have attempted to invoke a cultural defense. The legal disputes in which individuals ask that the court consider their cultural background include, for example, homicide and rape prosecutions, child abuse cases, drug use cases, the treatment of animals, custody battles, employment discrimination suits, and the treatment of the dead. In the course of surveying the various cases, I identify the intricacies of invoking cultural arguments in the diverse bodies of law under which the cases fall.

The main obstacle to the introduction of culture in the courtroom, no matter what the legal question, is the attitude on the part of judges that individuals from other cultures should conform to a single national standard, a phenomenon I will refer to as the "presumption of assimilation." Another serious problem that cuts across all the cases, and one that may be a consequence of this attitude, is that judges often exclude evidence about cultural background on the ground that it is "irrelevant."[3]

Because the practice of barring cultural evidence is so common, a cultural defense is necessary to ensure that such evidence is considered by the court.[4] The adoption of a formal cultural defense does not mean that every defendant should be exonerated, nor does it mean that every plaintiff should prevail in a quest for damages or an injunction. A formal cultural defense would simply guarantee that cultural evidence could be presented in a court of law.

In addition to offering an overview of culture conflicts,[5] this book provides a normative framework for analyzing the cultural defense. The premise of the argument is *enculturation*—the notion that culture shapes cognition and conduct. Because culture strongly influences human motivations, the legal system should take cultural imperatives into account. In pluralistic societies, it is especially vital that judges acknowledge variation in motives to better understand the behavior of individuals who come before them. In general, justice requires looking at the context of individuals' actions; otherwise, it is not possible for judges to understand what has transpired. Judges are sometimes incapable of understanding the cultural context of actions largely because they seldom come from the background of ethnic minorities and indigenous peoples, and they have not been exposed to their way of life. This suggests that another reason the cultural defense should be allowed is to protect minorities against majoritarian bias in the legal system.

In the face of substantial evidence of such bias in the legal system, we are forced to reassess the presumption of assimilation, the underlying notion that everyone should be held to a single monolithic standard. A legal system need not treat everyone identically to be fair, and it will ultimately be more fair if it recognizes the existence of different notions of "reasonableness." It is my hope that the reader will try to have an open mind in reviewing the data gathered here and in considering the often contentious argument I will advance.

SCOPE OF THE CULTURAL DEFENSE

The cultural defense is usually treated as though it were only a defense strategy in criminal cases. Although the cases mentioned most frequently in the literature are those involving homicide, the cultural defense has been raised in many other sorts of criminal prosecutions. This includes animal cruelty, arson, bribery, hunting out of season, narcotics offenses, sexual assault, and many others.[6]

Cultural arguments are raised at many stages of the legal process, not only during the guilt phase of the trial. Culture can affect pretrial decisions such as whether to arrest, prosecute, or negotiate a plea. Defendants may seek to introduce cultural evidence at trial to negate a required element of a crime, to secure an acquittal, or to support an established defense such as insanity or provocation. On appeal, cultural claims take several forms: the judge improperly excluded the cultural evidence as irrelevant, the judge declined to give a jury instruction on the proper weight to be given to culture, or the defense attorney failed to present cultural factors for consideration during sentencing.[7]

Cultural defenses are also raised in civil cases. Litigants ask judges to consider their traditions in custody battles, in decisions over whether to order medical treatment for children over parental objections, in employment discrimination cases where plaintiffs face termination because they wear symbols of their religious or ethnic identity, and in lawsuits over the negligent treatment of corpses. The common thread in all these cases is that courts are asked to take the cultural background of the litigant into account.

This study is predicated on a broader interpretation of the cultural defense than is found in the usual debates among scholars and practitioners. Our understanding of this pervasive phenomenon ought not hinge on the same few U.S. homicide cases involving Asian defendants, as virtually every ethnic group has invoked the defense.[8] Furthermore, we should not treat it as a purely criminal strategy, because it arises in so many varied contexts. It also affects many more stages of legal process than just the guilt phase of the trial.

METHODOLOGY

Over a period of many years I have amassed a large set of cases in order to discern patterns in the use of cultural defenses. It was a tremendous challenge simply to identify the cases in which a cultural issue was central. Standard tools for legal research did not index cases of this kind in any systematic way. Moreover, there were no obvious key words: searching for "culture" on computer databases often led to cases on art or mold. The *Index to Legal Periodicals* listed relevant articles most often under the heading of "culture conflict," whereas the *Index to Foreign Legal Periodicals* used the term "criminal culpability."

The most fruitful results, obtained via computer searches, employed keywords such as "culture" in close proximity to "crime," "background," "excuse," "defense," "evidence," or "sentence." A few scholars used the term "cultural evidence" in their analyses, and sometimes court decisions used the phrase "cultural differences." Another profitable strategy was to look for articles, both scholarly and journalistic, about particular groups known to have clashed with the dominant legal system— for example, the Hmong, Rastafarians, and Sikhs. Many items appearing under "customary law" and "legal pluralism" were worthwhile because the articles

addressed the question of whether the dominant national legal system ought to recognize the customary law of minority groups. Once the citations to cases were
found, it was not always a simple matter to locate the cases, as foreign case reports
were not available in most U.S. law libraries.

In the course of carrying out this research, I reviewed court decisions, briefs,
transcripts, press clippings, and other documents. As often as possible, I interviewed
the lawyers handling the litigation to find out how the cultural evidence influenced
the outcome of the particular case. Although it was not feasible to do this in every
instance, given the number of cases and jurisdictions involved, I tried to employ the
extended-case method as a general rule.[9] When cases were not taken on appeal,
there was no published decision, and my characterization of them was based primarily on newspaper articles and interviews. In some instances, the most interesting
cases were those that did not result in published decisions.[10] Even written decisions
were sometimes "unpublished," which meant that the courts that rendered the decisions did not want them to be cited as precedents. "Unpublished" decisions, I would
argue, reflect the ambivalence or possibly the antipathy of judges toward cultural
claims.

This study is not based on a scientific sampling of cases. There is no way to
accomplish this and provide an overview of the subject, which was my intention in
undertaking this project. I hope that this study will nevertheless shed some light on
a subject that has been largely ignored.[11]

This book includes examples taken mainly from the U.S. legal system, although
it also includes decisions from other countries. As it is inevitable that multiethnic
societies will experience similar culture conflicts, the analysis here will be suggestive
for the resolution of conflicts in other jurisdictions. Part of the impetus behind this
work was to document the range of disputes in which cultural factors are relevant.
At the very least, I trust that this project has succeeded in demonstrating the ubiquity of the phenomenon.

It is my view that before one can decide about the validity of the cultural
defense, one needs to review the empirical evidence. Furthermore, an inductive
approach is preferable because it means that the data are not gathered for the purpose of advocating a particular position. The researcher analyzes the data to discern
patterns and, having taken stock of the situation, is then in a position to make policy recommendations.

ORGANIZATION OF THE BOOK

To avoid the trap of ethnocentrism I have tried not to use the categories of any official legal system and have taken a thematic approach to the material in Part II. I have
used themes as an organizing principle partly because the cultural defense is not
unique to any legal system and in order to make the analysis more relevant for aca-
demics and policymakers around the world. I have also attempted to incorporate
the characterization of the phenomenon by the group rather than by the legal sys-

tem under whose jurisdiction the conflict was adjudicated. For instance, I place the discussion of dog-eating under the consumption of animals rather than under animal cruelty. Instead of statutory rape or sexual assault, I refer to the cases under the rubric of child marriage.

Some of the cases analyzed here could have been placed in more than one chapter. For instance, I decided to analyze child marriage and spiritual custody in the marriage chapter, even though they could have been considered in the chapter on the treatment of children. The phenomenon of honor killings, which is discussed in the chapter on homicide, could also have been examined in the chapter on marriage, as the unmarried woman's behavior is seen as problematic by her family largely because they believe she is not fit to be wed after the incident.[12]

I begin chapter 2 with an overview of the concept of culture, the relationship between culture and cognition, and some examples of how culture affects perceptions and behavior. Next I turn to some of the epistemological problems associated with the concept of culture. Despite the difficulties with the analysis of cultural traditions, I defend the view that culture should at least be presented in court, although the relative weight it is assigned will vary from case to case. Culture should influence the disposition of cases subject to certain limits, which I discuss in the penultimate chapter of the book.

Part II constitutes the main body of the work. In chapters 3 through 9 I present the remarkable range of cases in which culture is central to the outcome of the dispute. In chapter 3 I delineate the main types of homicide cases in which cultural defenses arise, many of which focus on honor, mental health, and self-preservation. In subsequent chapters I examine the defense in the context of decisions concerning the treatment of children, the use of illicit substances, the slaughter of animals, and marriage and divorce rituals. In the final chapter in Part II I investigate the sorts of conflicts that arise from the treatment of the dead, including autopsies, the preparation of corpses for disposal, and burial law.

In Part III I take stock of the arguments for and against the cultural defense. After responding to critics who object to the use of the cultural defense in criminal proceedings, I consider how the cultural defense could be implemented and offer some policy guidelines governing its use. In the last chapter I take up the reasons why, as a normative matter, courts must take culture into account in adjudication. I show that the human right to culture[13]—as well as other fundamental principles of law, such as equal protection, freedom of association, effective assistance of counsel, religious freedom, and the right to a fair trial—all militate in favor of the adoption of a formal cultural defense.

Requiring that individuals change their identities is problematic in a democratic society that purports to allow individuals the right to choose their own life plans. A forced assimilation, or melting pot, model is inherently coercive insofar as it requires individuals to give up traditions that are crucial for maintaining their cultural identity. Individuals should have the right to follow their cultural traditions unless they involve irreparable harm to others.

2

Why Culture Matters for Justice

In this chapter I explain the rationale for having a cultural defense. The entire argument hinges on the idea that culture shapes the identity of individuals, influencing their reasoning, perceptions, and behavior. I begin with the concept of culture and some of the problems associated with the analysis of culture. This is followed by a brief discussion of some of the scholarship by anthropologists and social psychologists concerning the manner in which culture affects individuals, especially the concept of enculturation. Next we consider the implications of culture for law: if culture affects motivations,[1] what does this mean for the functioning of the legal system?

THE PROBLEM OF CULTURE

In this study I am not concerned with high culture (as in opera, museums, and so forth) or mass or popular culture (as in comic books, films, etc.). Instead, when I refer to culture, I mean traditional culture, a synonym for a way of life.[2] As a working definition, we may use a formulation of the Canadian UNESCO Commission:

> Culture is a dynamic value system of learned elements, with assumptions, conventions, beliefs and rules permitting members of a group to relate to each other and to the world, to communicate and to develop their creative potential.[3]

Culture differs from society inasmuch as culture is an abstraction, whereas society is the collection of individuals in the community. This means culture is invisible and society is visible.[4]

The entire discussion of "culture" has become highly politicized. The postmodern tendency to deconstruct culture, so that it is treated as nothing more than a social construction, is symptomatic. According to this line of thought, cultural differences are virtually meaningless because they are designed to serve the interests of those in power. Hence, any cultural differences that work against women's rights are automatically held to be invalid. According to this view, culture is by definition "male culture" because it was created by men; therefore, culture is illegitimate.[5]

The problem with this type of reasoning is that it ignores reality. Empirical evidence shows that cultural characteristics of groups that have nothing to do with gender bias per se—such as language, folk medicine, and music—do exist, even in patriarchal societies, and these cultural traits endure.[6] It is quite clear that culture is not as malleable as postmodern critics maintain. Although culture is not static, many of the core aspects of it endure over time. Scholars who dislike aspects of cultures engage in wishful thinking when they deny that traditions are "cultural" in order not to have to address the value conflict.

A more serious difficulty with the idea of culture is the uncertainty surrounding the authenticity of certain cultural practices. To what extent is a "practice" a "tradition"?[7] It is unclear who is entitled to say whether or not a practice is "genuine." The practice may never have been part of the culture, or it may have fallen into desuetude. Expert witnesses play a crucial role in cultural defense cases by verifying the existence of traditions and by helping to show whether the tradition actually influenced the individual in particular situations. Without the benefit of their expertise, courts are often incapable of making sense of the cultural arguments advanced in specific cases. It would also be possible to consult leading members of the community about the significance of a practice. Even within the group there may be a lack of consensus as to whether or not the tradition is part of the culture.[8] Assuming one could persuade critics that consensus exists within ethnic groups on some practices, there is still a concern that discussing cultural traditions ignores the fact that some individuals deviate from the norm. "Essentializing" culture is objectionable, so the argument goes, because it borders on stereotyping. This makes discussions of group traits presumptively invalid.

These are important issues, and I deal with them more thoroughly in Part III. But they only serve to reinforce my argument rather than detract from it. The mere fact that culture is not monolithic does not deny the fact that all individuals are subject to cultural imperatives. It only emphasizes that determining the extent of the influence may be difficult. As we shall see in Part II, the validity of the cultural claims is not contested in the majority of cases. For instance, there is no doubt that the Vietnamese have traditionally used "coining" as a form of folk medicine, that the Hmong have religious objections to the performance of autopsies, or that customary law has permitted plural marriage for some groups. The denial of the existence of cultural traditions on the grounds of a lack of unanimity is manifestly absurd.

ENCULTURATION

Granted that cultural traditions exist, the more salient question remains: To what extent does culture affect individuals? Anthropologists, social psychologists, and other scholars have devoted much attention to the precise manner in which culture shapes perceptions and influences behavior. While this body of research is interesting and important, it is not my intent here to carry out a thorough review of the cultural psychology literature. The relationship between culture and psyche is a complex one, but there is no question that culture strongly influences human thought processes and behavior.[9]

Every person learns from the society in which he or she is born about the culture, and this process of acquiring the values of the group is known as enculturation (or socialization). This process takes place, by and large, on a subconscious level.[10] The basic idea of enculturation is that individuals are brought up a certain way, and this conditioning affects both cognition and behavior. A famous anthropologist, Ralph Linton, explains enculturation this way:

> No matter what the method by which the individual receives the elements of culture characteristic of his society, he is sure to internalize most of them. This process is called enculturation. Even the most deliberately unconventional person is unable to escape his culture to any significant degree. . . . Cultural influences are so deep that even the behavior of the insane reflects them strongly.[11]

Some of the clearest examples of enculturation manifest themselves in such things as oral communication, gestures and body language, color and number symbolism, food taboos, and humor. For example, in many Latin American countries, the "A-O.K." sign (in which the thumb and index finger are joined in a circle) has insulting and obscene connotations. Another classic example of cultural difference in interpretation is number symbolism. Whereas the unlucky number in American culture is 13, for the Chinese it is 4. This is because the word for four in Chinese is a homonym for the word for death. Color symbolism also varies by culture. White is worn by the bride during a marriage ceremony in the United States but is worn at funerals in China. Culture also influences legal processes in subtle ways, for example, in courtroom space. These examples should suffice to show the degree to which "givens" in a society are contingent upon cultural context.[12]

This is not to say that individuals are programmed by their culture in such a way that their behavior is predetermined. If this were true, there would be no notion of guilt or innocence, as individuals who lack free will cannot make moral choices.[13] If enculturation were so strong as to preclude independent thought and action, the law would have no meaning, because individuals would lack the capacity to make their behavior conform to its dictates. Cultural conditioning, in and of itself, does not render humans incapable of making moral judgments. The point is simply that cultural conditioning predisposes individuals to act in certain ways. The values inculcated by a person's culture strongly influence but do not determine his or her actions.

ASSIMILATION, ACCULTURATION, AND CULTURAL PLURALISM

While every person is subject to enculturation, the acquisition of the cognitive categories of his or her society, only those who move from one culture to another are subject to acculturation. Essentially, acculturation refers to the various phenomena that result from the contact of at least two autonomous cultural groups. Assimilation refers to the process by which individuals adopt the value system of the new culture.[14]

While acculturation and assimilation may go hand in hand and are often used interchangeably, they are not synonymous. For instance, a person may be exposed to a new culture by watching television but not become assimilated. Consider, for example, an older woman who lives in Chinatown speaking only her native language and seldom leaving the community. She is not assimilated, that is, could not pass in the mainstream, although she may be regarded as acculturated, at least to some degree. Sometimes even those who have become highly acculturated are unable to become fully assimilated because of insidious social forces such as racism.[15]

Members of ethnic minority groups struggle to pass on their traditions to their children. Indeed, Frederik Barth's famous analysis suggests that cultural practices are important insofar as they serve to define the parameters of the ingroup as opposed to the outgroup, "us" versus "them." Some scholars emphasize the importance of recognizing that patterns of assimilation and acculturation vary by ethnic group, by segments within an ethnic group, and particularly by generation. Whereas ethnic identity is more or less taken for granted by first and second generations, for third generations the pursuit of ethnic identity becomes a conscious activity. Herbert Gans refers to this as "symbolic ethnicity."[16]

Acculturation leads to some degree of assimilation, but rarely is the process complete. In reality, many of the newly arrived are bicultural, just as they are bilingual. Even though they appear to have adjusted to life in the new country, they retain strong commitments to their traditions.[17] Consequently, it may be unrealistic to expect people to become entirely assimilated—that is, to adopt the national identity of the new country and to set aside any loyalty to their prior ethnic identities. Even though individuals may appear to be assimilated, meaning they are able to "pass" in the mainstream, this does not imply they have completely forgotten their original way of life. The reality is that many individuals are bicultural or multicultural, operating with more than one identity.

When ethnic minorities encounter pressures from the government to conform, they develop strategies for dealing with the dominant culture. The attempt to maintain these traditions in the face of great pressures to conform to the folkways of the new society can be very stressful. These data suggest that a model of cultural pluralism, in which many cultures exist side by side, is not only more realistic insofar as it reflects the actual experiences of immigrants but also is more humane, because it takes as its premise the notion that accommodation should be the goal.[18]

CULTURAL PLURALISM VERSUS LEGAL PLURALISM

When immigrants and refugees travel to a new country, they carry with them both their cultural traditions and their legal traditions. These legal traditions are commonly referred to as *folk law* or *customary law*. The resulting confluence of customary law and the laws already present in the new country is known as *legal pluralism*. Legal pluralism can be distinguished from *cultural pluralism*, although the former is obviously predicated on the latter.[19] There cannot be diverse legal traditions without diverse cultural traditions, but the connection between the two is often more subtle. When does custom leave off and law begin?[20] For example, it is a custom to shake hands in Western culture by way of greeting. Although it is considered impolite not to offer one's hand, it is not legally required. But in some groups custom may require that a male avenge a death or kill a female relative who has been sexually active. This response may be required by customary law, carrying serious penalties for the man or woman who fails to comply. Similarly, religious law typically ordains that adherents wear religious garb on pain of expulsion from the community. Orthodox Jewish men must wear a yarmulke, and baptized Sikhs (those who have taken amrit) must wear a kirpan, or ceremonial dagger. In cases such as these, the law of the new land often prohibits a certain custom, while customary law demands it.

It can also happen that a custom is illegal in the new land, although it is permitted under customary law. Among Muslims, for example, multiple wives are permitted (but not required) by customary law. Is this a conflict of laws or of customs? It is sometimes difficult to tell. For this reason, I will use the terms *cultural pluralism* and *legal pluralism* more or less interchangeably.

IMPLICATIONS OF ENCULTURATION FOR LAW

The basic issue is the following: Given that all individuals are psychologically predisposed to act in accordance with the norms and precepts of their culture, to what extent should the dominant system make allowances for this when conflicting customs give rise to legal actions?[21] It is my position that, at the very least, justice requires that cultural evidence be admitted into the courtroom. Legal actors cannot comprehend the situation giving rise to the cultural conflict without an under-standing of the cultural background and motivations of the litigants. The failure to apprehend the significance and importance of various traditions often leads to an unjust outcome.

This is not to say that a person should always be excused on the basis of his or her culture. As I have explained in detail elsewhere, this confusion lies at the heart of the philosophical debates surrounding the notions of descriptive and prescriptive relativism.[22] Just because there are, as a factual matter, different moral codes, does not require that we accept them all; we could just as well reject them all. The mere existence of disparate cultural motivations is in no way determinative of outcome.

Nevertheless, to ignore the truth of enculturation is to bias the result from the beginning. In many jurisdictions, for example, courts generally adhere to a legal fic-tion known as the "objective reasonable person" standard when adjudicating these types of claims. Judges and juries are asked to weigh a person's actions in the light of what such an "objective" person would do under similar circumstances. Part of the aim of this study is to "deconstruct" this notion and make it patently obvious that there is no such person. The "objective reasonable person" is merely a person from the dominant culture. Naturally, if a member of an ethnic group is judged against the standards of the dominant culture, his or her traditions are likely to be con-demned as unreasonable. If the traditions are considered in the context of the ethnic minority's standards of reasonableness, however, the result may be quite the oppo-site.

To ensure that they render just decisions, courts should consider the culturally specific reasoning of litigants in all cases. This means not only that cultural evidence should be admitted into the courtroom, but also that the cultural logic must be taken seriously. Unfortunately, it is simply not possible to say precisely how much weight culture should be given in all cases. Instead, it will be necessary to use a case-by-case approach to determine how much mitigation, if any, is justifiable in a partic-ular criminal case and how much influence cultural factors should have in a civil case. As a general principle, one can say that when the cultural claim can be shown to be true, then culture should affect the disposition of the case, unless this would result in irreparable harm to others.

In the absence of any real threat, ethnic minorities should, in general, have a right to follow their cultural traditions, free from any governmental interference. The right to culture, though seldom found explicitly in domestic legal systems, is a fundamental right that is guaranteed under international law and finds its strongest formulation in Article 27 of the International Covenant of Civil and Political Rights, a key human rights treaty. My view is that where the exercise of this right does not clash with other human rights, it should be protected. Where this right is in tension with others, a careful analysis of the relative importance of the rights will be neces-sary. In some instances the right to culture will be superseded by other rights. To reiterate, where there is no such conflict, governments should follow a principle of maximum accommodation.

OTHER WORK ON THE SUBJECT

There exists no book that addresses the question considered in this work—namely, what is the proper role of cultural evidence in legal systems? The literature has simply not addressed the subject of the cultural defense adequately. As more and more cases have attracted public attention, it has become increasingly apparent that there is a need for analysis of this critical issue.[23]

Although there is relatively little written on the cultural defense, there is some empirical scholarship that bears on the question of the proper use of cultural factors in the legal system. A few criminologists have addressed the need for a more relativistic approach to the study of law. For instance, in his classic monograph *Culture Conflict and Crime* (1938) Thorsten Sellin argues that when divergent cultures come into direct contact, conflict is inevitably the result.[24] His purpose was not merely to delineate the consequences of group interactions but to establish how cultural differences affect behavior.[25] Another important part of his analysis is the notion that rule violations should be studied rather than violations of criminal statutes. This is because the distinction between criminal and noncriminal rule violations is itself culturally based.[26]

Although many assume that the cultural defense is a term which should apply only to criminal matters, relying on Sellin's broader approach to culture conflict, I reject that narrow view. In fact, as we shall see, in many "civil" cases, parties are asking the court to take their cultural backgrounds into account. After all, the distinction between criminal and civil matters is a culturally peculiar one, and the same set of facts can give rise to both criminal and civil actions. The common aspect of all the cases is the desire of litigants to be treated equally under the law by being treated differently.[27]

The cultural defense relies on a relativistic view of law.[28] This sort of interpretation is crucial to the analysis of the cultural defense, of course, since one of the main questions is whether a tradition constitutes a violation of a rule of the dominant legal system. The idea that categories of crime are social constructs forces one to confront the question of what justifies a particular form of punishment. The question here is the degree to which a person, shaped by his or her own cultural definition of normalcy, ought to be forced to modify his or her behavior to accord with that of another culture. Should immigrants, refugees, and native peoples be judged according to the legal standards of the new society (those of the dominant culture), even if they differ markedly from those of their own culture?

Although there is a vast literature on multiculturalism, this literature usually does not directly address the question of the cultural defense.[29] The discussion of multiculturalism is of some relevance because this intellectual movement is usually interpreted as promoting respect for different ways of life. It is important to note, however, that the cultural defense was used for many decades, well before multiculturalism or the "culture wars" emerged. Equally significant is that countries which are officially multicultural—including Australia, Canada, and Sweden—have not adopted the cultural defense.[30] This means that even advocates of multiculturalism may not favor the cultural defense, though the logic of their arguments should require it.

Philosophers have addressed the question of cultural rights—the question of whether individuals have a right to follow their cultural traditions—and, if so, under what circumstances. Their reflections might have led them to take up the cultural defense policy. Surprisingly, however, there has been virtually no proponent of the cultural defense in this scholarship, and even the most prominent advocates of cultural rights have championed only a narrowly circumscribed right to culture. Foremost among them is Will Kymlicka, whose scholarly works have received considerable attention.[31]

In his writings Kymlicka defends the right to culture only for groups that he characterizes as being structured along liberal lines. That is, only liberal democracies that follow the proper principles can afford to protect cultural rights because they will presumably not allow them to trump other important competing rights. However, Kymlicka is not prepared to allow cultural rights for immigrants, or voluntary minorities. If individuals leave one society by choice and move to another, they should expect to change their behavior to conform to the law of the new country. Furthermore, Kymlicka does not think immigrants have "culture." Given his predilections, it is unlikely he would endorse the cultural defense. In fact, he has explicitly rejected accommodating ethnic minorities when their traditions clash with the criminal law.[32] It is remarkable that philosophical discussions of cultural rights are extraordinarily negative, focusing mainly on the threat posed by such rights.[33]

Those who question Kymlicka's theory are not willing to defend a much more generous version of cultural rights. For example, Chandran Kukathas takes the view that cultural rights should be protected as long as individuals have the right to leave or "opt out." This is in part because of his worry that toleration of diverse practices "condones the oppression of internal minorities (minorities within minority communities)."[34] If the theory emphasizes the need to ensure that people can escape from culture, it has an underlying view of culture that is extremely negative. Another critic of Kymlicka, Bhikhu Parekh, favors the protection of cultural practices for immigrants unless they conflict with the values of the majority society, in which case they must be prohibited.[35]

For the most part, philosophers who do analyze the cultural defense reject it either because they do not regard culture as relevant to agency or because they think it would jeopardize women's rights.[36] One of the most sophisticated arguments that accommodating cultural rights would undermine gender equality is found in the work of Ayelet Shachar who says:

> Proponents of multicultural accommodation policies have been concerned primarily with the relationship among different cultures and between a given minority community and the state. Yet, they often overlook an equally important multicultural dilemma concerning the potential injurious effects of intergroup accommodation upon intragroup power relations.[37]

For the most part, theorists have been preoccupied with how to limit cultural rights, rather than empowering ethnic minority groups. On the whole, there has been little effort to urge greater acceptance of diverse cultural traditions in their normative treatises.[38]

Researchers in the fields of medicine and psychiatry have already recognized the important influence of culture on mental processes in their primary reference works. It is striking that jurists have hardly acknowledged the manner in which cultural imperatives affect human behavior.[39]

One reason the cultural defense has not attracted much scholarly interest may be that researchers have mistakenly assumed that the subject does not merit investigation because such cases are rare. Of course, the frequency of the type of the case is not necessarily an indication of its importance. In any event, the claim that cultural defense cases are an uncommon occurrence is simply wrong. In fact, numerous cases involving cultural factors have taken place in the legal system.

TOWARD A POLICY OF MAXIMUM ACCOMMODATION

As the data presented here will show, national legal systems tend to evaluate cultural traditions in an ethnocentric manner. Because of the presumed superiority of the dominant legal system, authorities demand conformity with a monolithic legal code. This ensures that the dominant culture is imposed on all who reside within its borders, a phenomenon known as *cultural hegemony*.[40] In the legal system the enforcement of the code is accomplished in various subtle ways: most judges are from the mainstream culture and have little acquaintance with diverse cultures, the judges adhere to the fiction of "objective" standards, and they refuse to recognize the customs and folk law of ethnic minority groups. The unwillingness of judges to acknowledge the internal rules of ethnic minority groups under virtually all circumstances is a function of what scholars have called *legal centralism*, or the tendency to view only state law as valid law.

In innumerable cases ethnic minorities must suffer the indignity of having to justify their traditions. Not only must they prove that the traditions exist, but, more important, they must present what the majority considers to be good reasons for following "bizarre" traditions. In the absence of a sufficient justification they may risk forfeiting the right to continue their way of life. Naturally, no such requirement exists for traditions followed by members of the dominant culture. Indeed, many Americans would have difficulty explaining why the bride throws her bouquet at a wedding, why dogs are allowed inside the house, and other customs. The use of this double standard should make us all the more wary of forcing individuals to give up their traditions. If members of the dominant culture are unable to justify their cultural traditions, why should they demand this of others? What we shall see in the cases examined here is that while individuals want to show the courts what motivated their behavior, they do not anticipate having to convince courts of the legitimacy of their folkways.

In democratic political systems individuals expect to have basic rights such as religious liberty, freedom from government intrusion in the family, and freedom of association. But they should also have the right to follow their cultural traditions, unless these traditions cause irreparable physical harm to others. In the absence of any threat of serious harm, liberal democracies should not interfere with cultural traditions. The presumption should be that governments ought not intervene unless failure to do so would result in death or irreparable physical harm to members of the ethnic minority group.

It is crucial that both elites and ordinary citizens guard against unconscious fears they may have of customs with which they are unfamiliar. Simply because another way of life seems outlandish is not a justification for ignoring its inner logic. Ultimately, governments should find ways to allow greater freedom for all by adopting policies that favor accommodation over forced assimilation.

Part II

CULTURE CONFLICTS
IN THE COURTROOM

3

Homicide

The cultural defense cases that have attracted the greatest attention are those involving killing. Individuals lose self-control for different reasons, which sometimes, unfortunately, leads to violent acts. What precipitates the loss of control can vary from one society to the next. This chapter presents an overview of homicide cases in which defendants raised cultural defenses. Despite the lack of a formal cultural defense, in a surprisingly large number of cases, courts have been willing to entertain arguments based on culture.

Even though taking a life is certainly a most reprehensible act, it is necessary in many cases to consider cultural factors to determine the appropriate level of culpability and corresponding punishment. In homicide cases prosecutors must decide upon the charge, judges must evaluate proffered defenses, accepting only those for which the defense can lay a proper foundation, and juries must decide of which offenses, if any, the defendant is guilty. The point is that criminal justice is not an exact science, and the cultural information enables legal actors to make wise judgments about responsibility and punishment. This kind of analysis requires the consideration of context, and culture is one part of the equation.

One major obstacle to the consideration of cultural defenses in homicide cases is that judges frequently consider culture to be "irrelevant." Although most of the time they could admit cultural evidence without difficulty, they exclude it instead. Evidence codes specify that anything relevant is admissible, provided it is not prejudicial. Nothing stipulates that culture is not relevant. The real difficulty defendants have faced in Western legal systems has been how to link culture to the legal categories of crimes, each of which has its own particular elements. In homicide cases, the question generally is what sort of intent was present—that is, whether the defendant had the requisite intent to be convicted of the crime.

This chapter shows how cultural arguments are incorporated into existing criminal defenses such as insanity, provocation, and self-defense.[1] I also discuss cultural defenses that do not fit existing categories very well, such as culture-bound syndromes and witchcraft killing. Also considered are cases in which the question was whether cultural evidence ought to have been presented during the sentencing phase, evidence which might have persuaded the jury to choose life imprisonment instead of the death penalty. In all of the disputes discussed here, defendants are asking for the right to present evidence in court about the cultural imperative that motivated their actions.

EXCUSE DEFENSES

Insanity

One of the most important excuses is the insanity defense, which is based on the proposition that a defendant with a mental defect should not be held criminally responsible. Jerome Hall explains that "the principle of mens rea requires the voluntary commission of a harm forbidden by penal law."[2] The notion that a person must voluntarily commit an act serves as a cornerstone of the criminal justice system. When an individual suffers from a cognitive or volitional impairment, his act may not be voluntary, and hence punishment is inappropriate. The insanity defense exists in various forms, including the M'Naghten right-wrong test, the irresistible impulse test, the Durham test, and the American Law Institute (ALI) test.[3] When a defendant wins an insanity defense, he is usually found not guilty by reason of insanity. The result is ordinarily commitment to a mental institution, but theoretically it could also be acquittal and outright release.

Two basic concepts are embedded in the different tests for the insanity defense: cognitive impairment and volitional impairment. The first type focuses attention on whether an individual perceived the nature of his act or that his conduct was wrong. This inquiry deals with the individual's cognitive function. The other form, by contrast, is volitional; the question is whether, regardless of his perception of the act (i.e., even if he knew it was wrong), the defendant was unable to control his behavior and make it conform to the law. This analytic distinction between cognitive and volitional types of cases provides a useful framework for categorizing certain cultural defense cases.

In some cases attorneys have advanced a defense that combines both mental illness and cultural considerations. Under some circumstances this approach may be necessary, because the defendant suffers from some sort of mental trauma related to his or her culture. When immigrants and refugees have difficulty with cultural adaptation, they may claim that cultural reasons led to mental problems. In such cases, culture is part of a traditional insanity defense. Insanity defenses come in various forms based on both cognitive and volitional impairments. Sometimes defendants will argue temporary insanity, automatism, and the battered woman syndrome. This section presents examples of these types of culturally based insanity arguments.[4]

THE COGNITIVE INSANITY DEFENSE   The case of *People v. Kimura* (1985) is an example of a defense combining psychological and cultural factors. It provides an illustration of a case in which a defendant successfully employed the cognitive insanity defense.[5] When Fumiko Kimura, a Japanese American living in Santa Monica, California, learned of the infidelity of her husband she attempted *oyako-shinju*, or parent-child suicide, by wading into the Pacific Ocean with her two children. The two children died, but she survived and was charged with first-degree murder with special circumstances which could have brought the death penalty. Oyako-shinju, while illegal in Japan, is not unheard of as a means by which a family can avoid an otherwise unacceptable social predicament.[6] The Japanese American community gathered a petition with over 25,000 signatures appealing to the Los Angeles County district attorney not to prosecute her, arguing that her actions were based on a different worldview. According to this worldview, it is more cruel to leave the children behind with no one to look after them than it is for the mother to take them with her to the afterlife.

Six psychiatrists testified that Kimura was suffering from temporary insanity. Some based their conclusion on her failure to distinguish between her own life and the lives of her children.[7] Through a plea bargain, her homicide charge was reduced to voluntary manslaughter, and she was sentenced to one year in county jail (which she had already served), five years probation, and psychiatric counseling. She was subsequently reunited with her husband (!).

Though her attorney claimed that the favorable plea bargain relied on psychiatric testimony, commentators believe that cultural factors played a role in the process.[8] It is worth pointing out that Kimura appears to have benefited from a cultural defense though she had resided in the United States for several years. As she had remained culturally isolated, she had not become assimilated. This suggests that assimilation often does not occur as rapidly as many believe, and a court may allow culture to affect the disposition of a case, regardless of the length of time a defendant has lived in a new country.[9]

Another important point is that the children's rights dimension of this case has hardly been discussed in the literature. While the court may have been correct in considering the cultural aspects of the case, it is arguable that probation was an unjustifiably light sentence to impose.

THE VOLITIONAL INSANITY DEFENSE   *People v. Metallides* (1974) is an illustration of the use of the volitional insanity defense. In Miami, Florida, a Greek immigrant, Kostas Metallides, killed his best friend when he found out that his friend had raped Kostas's daughter. His attorney used a temporary insanity argument based on culture. Though it was not recognized as a defense in Florida, the attorney relied on the "irresistible impulse" test. He constructed an argument around the cultural idea that the "law of the old country" is that "you do not wait for the police if your daughter has been raped." Even though the jury was given temporary insanity as the official issue to decide, apparently it recognized that honor was a cultural concept. Kostas was acquitted because the jury technically found him not guilty by reason of temporary insanity, but those involved say it was because of arguments based on Greek culture.[10]

The outcome in this case hinged on a technicality. Had the judge been unwilling to consider the irresistible impulse test, in the absence of statutory authorization, or to interpret the cultural evidence as relevant, Metallides would not have had the benefit of a cultural defense. Moreover, the accuracy of the claims made concerning Greek culture could have been questioned, considering that no expert witness was consulted on this point.[11]

While it was appropriate to allow the cultural argument to be heard, one could argue that the jury gave excessive weight to it. Although one can only speculate about the jury's reasoning, it may have been that the jury felt that a vote to convict would lead to an excessive punishment under the circumstances, and so the preferred option was acquittal. One of the reasons for instituting the cultural defense as a separate defense is to avoid such artificial dichotomies.[12]

Under the current system, a defendant's fate would appear to rest upon the attitude of the judge to the relevancy of the cultural evidence and on the availability of particular insanity tests. Although Metallides was able to escape punishment by relying on the irresistible impulse test, other defendants may not be able to do so. Another reason for adopting a cultural defense is to achieve a greater degree of uniformity in the handling of such cases.

Automatism

The automatism defense is sometimes regarded as a type of insanity defense, but it is different in character. Automatism refers to the behavior of an individual who acts either unconsciously or by reflex or spasm. The concept includes such things as somnambulism but not, say, irresistible impulse. The standard view of the automatism defense is that it does not relate to mens rea but to the actus reus. The notion is that a person who acts while unconscious should not be held responsible for illicit conduct, not because he failed to form the necessary intent but because the act was not a voluntary one.[13]

This defense would not be useful to most defendants in cultural defense cases because generally they do not argue that they are not conscious of their actions. Reliance upon such an argument would certainly do violence to our notion of free will. Defendants voluntarily act in accordance with their culture, so the automatism defense does not fit the circumstances of most cultural defense cases. As a practical matter, relying solely on the automatism defense might not guarantee the consideration of cultural data essential for the defense. Furthermore, the defense, if successfully pleaded, results in "outright acquittal."[14] If the case is more accurately characterized as a cultural defense, then, as argued later in this chapter, a partial excuse is generally more appropriate than a complete excuse.

One cultural defense case in which automatism was argued was *People v. Wu* (1991).[15] In 1989 Helen Wu, a native Chinese woman living in Palm Springs, strangled her son and then tried to commit suicide by slashing her wrists. She was distraught over the fact that her lover did not return her affection and that he was treating their son poorly. Her attorney presented an automatism defense and a cultural defense, although the two were clearly linked. The success of the former is predicated on an understanding of the cultural context of the events central to the case. The defense argued that she was in a state described by psychiatrists as a "fugue" state of consciousness, and the experts in transcultural psychology testified that Wu's emotional distress could only be understood by reference to her cultural background. The defense argued that she acted in a culturally motivated fashion to save her son and herself from shame and abuse and to be reunited in the afterlife.

The jury convicted her of second-degree murder, and she was sentenced to a prison term of fifteen years to life. Her appeal was based on the trial judge's failure to give jury instructions on the automatism and cultural defenses. Apparently the lower court did not want to allow an instruction telling the jury it could consider evidence of cultural background, because this might appear to be endorsing the cultural defense and give the jury the impression that the cultural defense was legal. Furthermore, the trial court worried that giving the instruction would condone the defendant's action.

The Court of Appeal found that the failure to instruct the jury on unconsciousness was reversible, but that it was unnecessary to decide whether failure to do so with respect to her cultural background was reversible error. However, the court stated that if the defense requested an instruction on culture, the trial court should give it. It seems that the appeal court was sympathetic to a cultural defense: "There is no reason why defendant's requested instruction, simply pointing out that the jury may consider evidence of her cultural background in determining the presence of absence of the relevant mental states, should not have been given."[16] The Court of Appeal commented on the relevance of her cultural background to the provocation/heat of passion defense.

The California Supreme Court declined to review the case on the merits but ordered the depublication of the opinion by the Court of Appeal. According to Wu's attorney, Gary Scherotter, it was "absolutely the cultural aspect" which was responsible for the decision to depublish.[17] Another factor in the court's decision making may well have been a desire to stem the proliferation of criminal law defenses.

Despite the depublication, Helen Wu was entitled to a new trial. On retrial she was convicted of voluntary manslaughter.[18] If the jury had accepted the automatism defense, Wu would have been acquitted. Thus, given the sentence reduction from murder to manslaughter, it would appear that culture served as a partial excuse, even if not formally acknowledged as such. Part of the motivation for wanting to introduce a formal cultural defense is to make this accommodation explicit.

Battered Woman Defense

Nguyen v. State (1998, 1999) shows how a battered woman defense is combined with a cultural defense. Thu Ha Nguyen, a woman from Vietnam, claimed that her husband and her stepdaughter were verbally abusive and disrespectful toward her. Nguyen shot her husband and stepdaughter when her husband informed her that he intended to divorce her. At the trial her attorney, Thomas Herman, wanted to present a battered person defense with a cultural component.[19] The cultural argument was that the defendant felt trapped in the marriage because divorce would have made her a pariah in her culture. Further, the defense argued that the defendant's fear was culturally based because the verbal abuse of her husband and stepdaughter incited fear in her which a person born in the United States might not have experienced.

The trial court refused to allow the presentation of expert testimony in support of this defense. The jury convicted Nguyen of aggravated assault, and she appealed. The Court of Appeals affirmed because she had been subjected to verbal abuse and not physical abuse. As for the evidence on differences between Asian and American cultures, the court thought it unnecessary for the jury to understand the defendant's reaction to her family's demeaning behavior. In principle, the court objected to the idea that Vietnamese notions should influence its analysis.[20]

The Georgia Supreme Court, however, disagreed with the notion that verbal or emotional abuse cannot give rise to a battered person defense. If the abuse is extreme enough that it is accompanied by a "reasonable belief in the imminence of the victim's use of unlawful force," that is sufficient to justify invoking the defense. In this case, however, the Georgia Supreme Court found that the evidence of psychological abuse did not rise to that level. The court also disagreed with the implication of the appellate court's ruling that "evidence of a criminal defendant's cultural background is never relevant," but found again that in this particular case the cultural evidence was not relevant.[21] It is significant that the Georgia Supreme Court left the door open to the use of cultural evidence about a defendant's background, provided defense counsel can make a powerful showing of the authenticity of the claim and the relevance of the cultural pattern to the accused's behavior.

Implications

Even assuming that the facts of a cultural defense case were to make it appropriate to use the insanity defense, there are disadvantages to taking this approach. Given the narrowly circumscribed meaning of "morally wrong," defendants who wish to raise a cultural defense will have difficulty trying to introduce cultural arguments through the cognitive insanity defense given existing doctrine.[22] Immigrants and refugees in most cultural defense cases are, in fact, perfectly sane according to the standards of their own culture, and, indeed, according to Western clinical standards. Giving them no option other than an insanity defense to present the cultural dimension of the case would require a gross falsification of the facts.

Furthermore, comparing the logic of immigrants with that of the insane is, at the very least, insulting. Just because someone has a worldview that differs from the mainstream surely does not justify suggesting that that worldview is insane. Such a comparison, even if successful as a strategy for avoiding incarceration, would require ethnocentric assessment of the perspectives of other peoples. Forcing cultural arguments into the insanity defense would symbolically denigrate the way of life of others. The logic of another culture is not "irrational" when it is judged from their point of view. To rely on an insanity defense would require distortion of the worldview of other groups.

If the defendant were willing to misrepresent himself and his culture in order to avoid being held criminally responsible, success might not be particularly desirable. He would be subject to commitment to a mental institution for an undetermined period of time where he would be treated.[23] But trying to "cure" someone of having been raised in a different culture is cultural genocide.

Culture-Bound Syndromes

Sometimes a defendant acts as a result of extreme mental or emotional disturbance, which may only be understandable in a particular cultural context. In some cases the defense depends on the recognition of a culture-bound syndrome.[24] A salient example of an attempt to raise such a defense was the Hawaii Supreme Court decision of *State v. Ganal* (1996). A Filipino man, Orlando Ganal, shot his relatives and set fire to a home, killing several people. At the trial he argued that he had "run amok."[25] *Amok* is defined as:

> A dissociative episode characterized by a period of brooding followed by an outburst of violent, aggressive, or homicidal behavior directed at people and objects. The episode tends to be precipitated by a perceived slight or insult and seems to be prevalent only among males. The episode is often accompanied by persecutory ideas, automatism, amnesia, exhaustion, and a return to premorbid state following the episode. Some instances of amok may occur during a brief psychotic episode or constitute the onset or an exacerbation of a chronic psychotic process.[26]

In this case, the defense was that Ganal suffered humiliation in the context of his failing marriage with his wife. Distraught because of his wife's infidelity and her taunting, he was described as experiencing severe emotional distress and depression. This profoundly affected his sense of self- esteem, precipitating his fit of rage. He went on a rampage, killing his wife's parents and injuring his wife and their son. He also set on fire the home of the brother of his wife's lover, and two young children perished in the flames. Expert witnesses testified about the concept of "amok" to explain his actions.[27]

Ganal was convicted of first-degree murder and first-degree attempted murder. On appeal, he challenged his conviction on several grounds, one of which was that the prosecutor made sarcastic comments trivializing the amok defense. The

Supreme Court rejected the argument that prosecutorial misconduct required reversal of his conviction.[28]

The use of the "amok" defense provoked criticism. Commentators suggested that the defense put the culture on trial. Some denied that it was part of Filipino culture and that even if the syndrome exists, violent behavior is not condoned in the Philippines. Whether or not the "amok" defense was properly used in the *Ganal* case, it is clear that culture-bound syndromes are important in some criminal cases.[29]

In *People v. Rev. Chung and Rev. Choi* (1997), it was the victim rather than the defendant who had a culture-bound syndrome. A Korean woman, Kyung Chung, who was suffering from "possession by demons," underwent a five-hour spiritual exorcism to rid her of "evil spirits." This ritual healing ceremony involved applying pressure to various parts of her body. Unfortunately, the treatment resulted in her death. When her husband and two ministers were prosecuted for murder, they argued that their goal was to exorcise her demons. After a three-week non-jury trial, they were convicted only of involuntary manslaughter; the husband received a two-year sentence and the two ministers the harshest possible, four years each. Evidently, the judge was willing to take the cultural and religious factors into account.[30]

DURESS   The basic notion of duress is that a person is compelled to commit a crime by forces external to himself or herself. For example, a person who is compelled to rob a bank under threat of severe bodily harm by another person could claim duress.[31] One of the main requirements that usually has to be met in order for the defense to be raised is that the individual must face an imminent or immediate threat of bodily harm.

Culture can be employed as part of duress in some instances. A defendant may claim that he was under a cultural imperative to commit an act and that failure to act will result in punishment within his community in accordance with customary law. For instance, in the Australian case of Chimney Evans, two young Aboriginal men were assigned the responsibility of strangling a man who had stolen important "corroboree" stones and sold them to a white man. The court acknowledged that their refusal would result in serious consequences and decided to mitigate the punishment as a consequence. The judge sentenced the four older men to only two years imprisonment and the two younger men to one year. Perhaps because of their age, or perhaps because of the fact that the younger men would have been subject to severe tribal sanctions had they not carried out the determination of the elders, the trial judge handed down light sentences for them.[32]

The case shows how cultural considerations figure into legal processes at different stages; here customary law was taken into account once when the prosecutor decided to charge the defendants with conspiracy instead of murder, and again when the judge imposed sentence. Moreover, while it shows that the cultural factors can be unavoidable, the case was adjudicated according to national standards. Cultural factors led to a reduction in punishment only. As Elizabeth Eggleston observed, "It is noteworthy that no one connected with the case suggested that tribal law should be a complete defence to the charge."[33]

DIMINISHED CAPACITY   One case where a defendant invoked the diminished capacity defense[34] is *People v. Poddar* (1972, 1974). Prosenjit Poddar was a member of the Harijan (untouchable) caste who was attending graduate school in naval architecture at the University of California at Berkeley. He was rejected by a nineteen-year-old woman, Tanya Tarasoff, with whom he believed he had a romantic relationship. Because of cross-cultural misunderstandings, he was convinced that she was committed to him. After she rejected him, he killed her.

At the trial Poddar's attorney sought to have an anthropologist testify about the cultural stresses experienced by Indian students who study at American universities, particularly about the difficulty of establishing relationships when arranged marriages are the norm in India. However, the judge excluded the testimony of an anthropologist who would have explained the cultural stresses that Poddar had suffered in adjusting from life as an untouchable to life at a major university.[35]

It was important that the jury understand his cultural background. Even casual interaction was significant to someone whose culture stipulated strict segregation. In addition, because he was a member of the Harijan caste, the untouchables, rejection was particularly painful. Poddar had been suffering from cultural disorientation and was severely emotionally distressed. The clinical psychologist under whose care Poddar was at the time of the killing had diagnosed him as paranoid schizophrenic and dangerous.

Poddar was convicted of second-degree murder and sentenced to five years to life in the California Medical Facility in Vacaville, but the conviction was overturned on appeal. The reversal was not based on the exclusion of the anthropologist's testimony but on the failure of the trial judge to instruct the jury properly on the meaning of diminished capacity. Although a new trial was ordered, apparently the court agreed to release him on the condition that he be deported to India. Thus, even though the defendant was not permitted to have cultural information introduced at the trial, his defense of diminished capacity tied to his cultural background indirectly prevailed in the end.[36]

Provocation

One of the most ancient doctrines in the criminal law is the provocation defense, also known as the heat of passion rule. It is found both in common law and in most homicide statutes. The "provocation/passion" formula, which can reduce a murder charge to one of manslaughter, is based on the idea that a person who is provoked to kill does so without the malice aforethought required for the crime of murder and is, therefore, less culpable.

The idea that the law should excuse those who lose self-control is not accepted by all theorists. The argument against volitional sorts of defenses is that the law should encourage individuals to comply with the rules. If individuals who have weak self-restraint know that the law will excuse their conduct, this might tend to undermine deterrence.[37]

The justification for volitional defenses seems relatively weak as compared with other defenses. In fact, a strong argument can be made for its abolition. One of the primary arguments against the provocation defense is that, by and large, the beneficiaries seem to be men who kill their spouses out of jealousy. Time and time again men get significantly reduced sentences by claiming they "lost control" when confronted with evidence, real or imagined, of their wives' infidelity. One of the principal objections to the cultural defense is that, by admitting more excusing conditions, women's lives will be further devalued.

The primary counterargument is that many individuals have no cognitive impairment but are truly unable to control themselves in the face of (what they obviously view as) incendiary actions on the part of others. The killing did not occur with malice aforethought and so does not count as first-degree murder. It should be emphasized that in most provocation cases the defendant is still convicted of manslaughter, which can carry a long sentence.

In many homicide cases defendants invoke cultural arguments, many of which turn on the question of provocation. The provocation test has two prongs, both of which must be proved: (1) that the reasonable person would have been provoked and (2) that the defendant was actually provoked. The first test relies on the "reasonable" or "objective" person test, the fictitious person against whom all conduct is to be judged. By its very nature, the reasonable person is "objective," so cultural evidence is irrelevant to the first test. For the second test, however, cultural evidence is admissible.[38]

The major obstacle to the use of the provocation defense by defendants in cultural defense cases is judicial adherence to the "objective" reasonable man standard. Critics contend that it is absurd to judge whether an "objective" reasonable man would have been provoked, when the reality is that this "objective" being is simply the persona of the dominant culture. Their position is that the court should modify the standard, so that the application of the test evaluates whether the reasonable person from the defendant's culture would have been provoked. Whether or not the cultural defense can be effectively raised through the provocation defense depends entirely on the judge's interpretation of the reasonable person standard: if the test is "objective," almost invariably no provocation will be found; if the test is "subjective," then ordinarily provocation will be found.

Retention of the "objective" reasonable man standard is grossly unfair because it means that the provocation defense, which is supposed to be available to all, is a defense only for those who belong to the dominant culture. There are two reasonable responses. Either the provocation defense should be abandoned altogether, or else the standard should be that of the culture to which the defendant belongs. After all, different things provoke different people. The purpose of the provocation defense is to hold less culpable those individuals who cannot control their actions. If the reasonable defendant from another culture cannot control his actions in the face of a certain provocation, what is the basis for holding him guilty of first-degree (premeditated) murder?

This controversy is well illustrated in cases that involve spousal jealousy killings. There has been considerable variation in courts' reactions to cultural evidence in such cases. While courts sometimes rely on this information to reduce a sentence, or even to grant probation, most often courts exclude it as "irrelevant." There are other provocation cases in which the defendant was enraged by some sort of gesture or word that, in his culture, is considered to be a great insult. These decisions collectively demonstrate the cultural bias in the interpretation of the reasonable person standard.

In 1982 May Aphaylath, a Laotian refugee residing in Rochester, New York, stabbed his wife to death in a jealous rage when she received a phone call from a former boyfriend. The public defender tried to argue that Aphaylath's loss of self control was culturally based: "Under Laotian culture the conduct of the victim wife in displaying affection for another man and receiving phone calls from an unattached man brought shame on defendant and his family sufficient to trigger defendant's loss of control."[39] Defense counsel sought to introduce expert witnesses to establish that (1) Aphaylath was suffering from culture shock[40] or extreme disorientation and (2) the infidelity of one's wife brings great shame on the family. The public defender attempted to construct an argument that in Laotian culture the combination of the disgrace of Aphaylath's wife's conduct and the stress of resettlement could have triggered his disproportionate rage.

The judge disallowed the testimony of experts on the cultural issues because they had not evaluated the defendant and could, therefore, only testify about Laotian culture and refugee problems generally. The court took the view that jealousy was not a subject beyond the comprehension of the jury for which expert evidence was needed.[41]

Aphaylath was convicted of murder in the second degree. The Supreme Court, appellate division, rejected the appeal based on the exclusion of expert evidence because it found the trial court's judgment appropriate with respect to excluding cultural evidence. The dissenting judge would have granted a new trial because the excluded testimony would have been "highly probative of whether there was a reasonable explanation for defendant's conduct from the perspective of his internal point of view." In his view, the evidence might have established extreme emotional disturbance that could serve as a mitigating factor.

The Court of Appeals of New York held that it was reversible error to exclude the testimony of expert witnesses concerning culture shock suffered by Laotian refugees. As a result the court ordered that the lower decision be reversed and the case be remanded for a new trial. This was not necessary because the prosecutor negotiated a plea bargain whereby an admission of guilt would lead to a conviction of manslaughter. Since the reduction in sentence from fifteen years to life to eight and one-third years to twenty-five years in prison was precisely what the public defender sought, the plea bargain was arranged.

Although this might have been a major breakthrough for advocates of the relevance of culture for judicial decision-making, the opinion left much to be desired. Only four paragraphs long, the memorandum of the court gives little guidance as to when culture is relevant and how the ascertainment of culture should proceed.[42]

In another case Dong Lu Chen, a Chinese-born man living in New York, bludgeoned his wife to death after she confessed to adultery. Burton Pasternak, professor of anthropology at Hunter College, testified that in China women are sometimes severely punished for adultery. He said that it is viewed as an "enormous stain" that reflects not only on the husband but "is a reflection on his ancestors and his progeny." Pasternak did observe that adultery rarely ends in a wife's murder in China. When irate husbands confront wives suspected of infidelity, the community normally intervenes to prevent any acts of violence. In fact, Pasternak could not cite any cases where Chinese men had killed adulterous wives, though he did know of beatings. Nor did he present evidence to show that a jealousy killing would go unpunished under either customary or modern Chinese law.[43] It seems that no effort was made to discover what punishment would be imposed in the case of a husband who murders an adulterous wife, either under traditional or modern Chinese law. Some commentators have pointed out that, at least under modern law, such a husband would be punished.

Nevertheless, after a non-jury trial in 1989, the judge (New York State Supreme Court Justice Edward Pincus) relied heavily on Pasternak's testimony when he found Chen guilty of second-degree manslaughter and decided to sentence him to only five years probation. This "sentence" of five years probation essentially represented a complete defense rather than mitigation.

Women's organizations, Asian American groups, and Elizabeth Holtzman condemned the decision.[44] They even went so far as to file a complaint with the State of New York Commission on Judicial Conduct asking for an investigation into the judge's decision.

In some cases defendants claim that a verbal insult or gesture provoked them to commit violent acts.[45] In the unpublished case of *Trujillo-Garcia v. Rowland* (1992, 1993, 1994) Eduardo Trujillo Garcia was playing poker with Jose Padilla. Padilla lost $140 to Trujillo-Garcia and returned four days later, demanding his money back. When Padilla said "chinga tu madre," Trujillo-Garcia's reaction to this challenge to his honor was to grab a gun from his waistband and shoot Padilla.[46] At the trial, Trujillo-Garcia argued that the phrase was so offensive that he was provoked to commit an act of violence. Those who do not speak Spanish have difficulty comprehending the seriousness of the insult. The phrase is considered "fighting words" and conjures up images of violation of the mother (associated with the Virgin Mary). It has an obscene connotation, as well as a blasphemous one.[47] He was convicted of second-degree murder and received a sentence of fifteen years to life.

On appeal in state court, Trujillo-Garcia argued the failure of the trial court to consider the words in their cultural context as part of the analysis of reasonableness constituted unconstitutional discrimination based on national origin and ethnic characteristics. The argument was specifically that a person's reaction to a particular insult depends upon his or her cultural upbringing.[48] At least two issues had to be decided: first, whether words constitute adequate provocation and, second, whether to substitute the average reasonable Mexican for the average reasonable person to satisfy the "objective" prong of the provocation test. With regard to the first requirement, California law allows verbal provocation as adequate.[49] The second argument was the more difficult one. The notion was that the failure of the trial court to apply a culturally specific reasonable persons test constituted a violation of equal protection:

> Equal protection requires that similarly provocative insults be similarly treated, without regard to their ethnic origin or cultural derivation. If certain insults are sufficiently offensive in American culture to mitigate murder to manslaughter . . . then insults that are equally offensive in another culture should be treated as equally mitigating.[50]

The district court rejected his habeas petition, noting that even though the state trial court did not take his cultural background into account, his provocation defense would have been "inadequate," even if his cultural background had been considered. The court emphasized that it refused to authorize use of a culturally specific reasonable person test. Although the court noted that the equal treatment argument was "not without merit," Judge Patel declined to elaborate because she concluded that Trujillo-Garcia "did not respond as an ordinary, reasonable Mexican male would have responded." The U.S. Court of Appeals for the Ninth Circuit affirmed, concluding that even if the failure to consider the cultural background was erroneous, it was harmless because it did not "substantially or injuriously" affect the outcome of the trial."[51]

Unfortunately, the judges did not perceive the offensiveness of the insult. This is apparent because they assumed that the average Mexican would not be provoked. In order to persuade judges and juries, defense counsel will have to argue that the proper standard is the average person from the defendant's culture. Although this standard might be characterized as "subjective," it could also be regarded as the "objective" standard of the cultural group in question. If a jury instruction focuses on a person in the circumstances of the defendant, this might allow for contextual analysis.[52] This type of framework will be crucial for the potential success of this defense.[53]

HONOR KILLING   Some provocation cases involve so-called honor killing. Male relatives kill young women who have acted in such a way as to dishonor their families. In the Australian case of *R. v. Dincer* (1983) a traditional Turkish Muslim father stabbed his sixteen-year-old daughter, Zerrin Dincer, because of her sexual relationship with a man who was considered unacceptable. The father sought to raise the provocation defense, but the question was whether the jury could use the ordinary person test with the attributes of the accused. Because the father went to the man's house to confront the daughter, the prosecution argued that the provocation was "self-induced," but the court rejected this without argument. The debate over the proper interpretation of the ordinary person part of the provocation defense continues in Australia.[54] Honor killings have also been controversial in the United States and in certain European countries.[55]

The "objective" test of what an ordinary person believes masks the subjective biases of the culture of the dominant group: the "objective reasonable person" standard is culturally biased because it is simply the persona of the dominant legal culture, namely the Anglo-American.[56] Having seen the difficulty cultural defendants have using the "objective" versions of the provocation defense, we must ask whether the law on provocation should be changed. Defendants who wish to raise cultural defenses via the provocation defense will only be able to do so if the first part of the test is modified to a subjective or culturally specific reasonable person test. Although it would be relatively easy to make this change in the law, there is likely to be considerable opposition to doing so.

There is the argument that the criminal law is designed to be a uniform set of laws applicable to everyone, irrespective of a person's particular characteristics. According to this perspective, accepting a subjective reasonable person standard would lead to anarchy, inconsistent results, and injustice.

Many object particularly to the use of provocation defenses in cases where men kill women.[57] This seems odd, given that mainstream defendants are entitled to invoke provocation defenses under these circumstances. Though it might be morally preferable if the law did not excuse any individuals who commit acts of violence after being provoked, if the law permits the provocation defense to serve as a partial excuse, it should not do so selectively. From a jurisprudential point of view, it is problematic if the provocation defense, which is theoretically available equally to all defendants, in fact cannot be used by people who come from other cultures. Though technically they can raise the provocation defense, the refusal of judges to permit a culturally specific reasonable person standard to be used is unfair.

Whatever objections one may have to the uses of the provocation defense, there is a powerful argument that it is unfair to limit the use of a criminal defense, theoretically available to all defendants, to those who are provoked by what is considered offensive by the dominant culture. Failure to consider the cultural background of the accused in assessing his or her reaction to provocation violates the principles of equal protection and fundamental fairness.[58]

JUSTIFICATIONS

Self-Defense

The most basic human instinct is the instinct for self-preservation. The criminal law recognizes this impulse and authorizes its use in the justice system via the doctrine of self-defense. When the individual who argues self-defense acts reasonably, he will have the benefit of a complete defense to a number of crimes. For the most part, self-defense will succeed only if a defendant has a reasonable belief that the use of force is necessary. Hence the critical question in cultural defense cases will be how to judge whether a person has such a "reasonable" belief.[59]

Another feature of self-defense is that the strategy only wins provided the defendant can demonstrate that he exercised a "necessary and proportional response." It is possible that the proportionality requirement would limit its utility for defendants in cultural defense cases. The reason for this is that the determination of what constitutes a proportionate response would depend upon the cultural background of the person making the assessment.[60] Presumably, the judge from the dominant culture would not view the act as a proportionate response, even if members of the defendant's cultural community agreed that it was. For example, a defendant might construct an argument based on fear of divine retribution as the motivation for the act. The idea would be that the act was culturally required and therefore necessary. From the cultural vantage point, the act was a lesser evil than the violation of the law.

Among the cases in which cultural considerations were raised via a self-defense argument is the celebrated case of *People v. Croy* (1990). Patrick "Hooty" Croy, a Native American of part Karuk and part Shasta ancestry, lived in Yreka in northern California, an area where there had been long-standing conflict between the white and Native American populations. Croy and two relatives were chased by twenty-seven police officers after a dispute over the amount of change in a liquor store. During the chase Croy killed a police officer in what he claimed was self-defense, but he was convicted of murder in 1979 and sentenced to death. The California Supreme Court overturned his conviction in 1985.[61]

At the new trial Croy's attorney presented a cultural defense in the context of self-defense. The cultural argument was that because Croy had suffered discrimination and had been conditioned not to trust white authorities (because white settlers had massacred Indians in the nineteenth century), he was predisposed to perceive that his life was in jeopardy. His main attorney, Tony Serra, introduced testimony from expert witnesses concerning "racism, genocide, and discrimination against American Indians." In his memorandum arguing for the admissibility of evidence, Serra describes Croy's fear as "objectively reasonable under the circumstances" but actually insists on the consideration of subjective factors: "the jury must be informed and educated about the factors that affected defendant's perception of danger and his ability to defend himself, including any physical, psychological, historical or cultural characteristics he may have possessed." Serra characterizes the California rule on self-defense as "something of an 'individualized' objective standard of reasonableness which includes the individual's perception of both apprehension and imminent danger from the individual's own perspective, but involves an objective view by the jurors of those circumstances." In essence, Serra argued for a culturally relative reasonable person test.[62]

As is clear from the way in which the defense characterized the central issue, the *Croy* case is not properly considered a cultural defense case. While the strategy of raising cultural genocide and discrimination against Native Americans may have been entirely appropriate, the case did not deal with any issue of culture conflict as much as it dealt with race relations. Native Americans do not believe that homicide is justifiable; the conflict was not about divergent perceptions of reality as in other cultural defense cases. Nevertheless, the jury must have been persuaded by the cultural defense because it acquitted Croy of all charges.

Crucial to the outcome of the case was the interpretation of the reasonable person test. The jury had to understand how a person in the defendant's position would have reacted. Any attempt to introduce cultural considerations via self-defense will require a "subjective" interpretation of the reasonable person. In the absence of a formal cultural defense there is no guarantee that judges will take this approach. Thus, self-defense is unlikely to be of much use to defendants in culture conflict cases. The major obstacle to its use in cases where it might be appropriate is that self-defense is only properly raised as a defense when the reasonable person would feel in jeopardy.

In *People v. Romero* (1999) the California Court of Appeal rejected a culture-based self-defense argument, holding that the trial court properly excluded evidence concerning the role of street fighters defending family honor in Hispanic culture.[63] A confrontation occurred when Michael Romero, his younger brother, and several friends were walking on the street at midnight and were almost hit by a car driven by Alex Bernal. Following the near collision, Michael Romero and Alex Bernal offered to fight. Bernal kicked off his shoes and started kicking in the air. During the altercation Romero stabbed Bernal in the heart, and he died shortly thereafter.

At the trial Romero testified that he felt that he had to protect his younger brother. He wanted to introduce the testimony of Martin Sanchez Jankowsi, a professor of sociology who specialized in the sociology of poverty, including street violence and Hispanic culture. The expert would have testified that the Hispanic culture is based on honor, and for a street fighter in the Hispanic culture, there is no retreat. Likewise, the expert would have testified that since the defendant was the eldest male in his family, he was culturally expected to assume a protective role toward his younger brother.

The testimony would help show his subjective belief in the need to defend as part of an imperfect self-defense, or an objectively reasonable belief for a claim of perfect self-defense. The trial judge ruled that the evidence was "clearly irrelevant." On appeal the court affirmed, concluding that the exclusion was harmless.[64]

The California appellate court regarded the evidence as irrelevant because it would not shed light on the question of whether the defendant actually believed he or his brother was in imminent danger or whether the belief was objectively reasonable. The court rejected the cultural argument, concluding that "the evidence regarding honor, like the evidence of street-fighter mentality, is not relevant to whether deadly force was warranted under the circumstances." According to the court, "the question of defendant's honor was irrelevant to whether defendant was in actual fear of death or great bodily injury, and whether his fear was objectively reasonable." The court expressed concern about the implications of recognizing a separate street fighter standard. If one could show that street fighters are expected to kill every person with whom they fight, then the logical implication might be that the court would have to relax the standard that the use of deadly force requires that a person actually fear imminent death or great bodily injury.

Witchcraft killings have occurred for centuries, and those who kill witches also often say their actions were motivated by self-preservation. According to some African belief systems, witches deserve capital punishment. In former colonies, the defense that a killing was motivated by a belief in the supernatural and a desire to break a spell was frequently rejected in court because "the reasonable man" does not believe in witchcraft. Attempts to introduce the defendant's belief in the supernatural via an insanity defense also proved unsuccessful because many sane individuals believe in witchcraft. Defendants found themselves in a dilemma: the witchcraft defense failed because the belief in the supernatural is unreasonable, but it was not unreasonable enough to warrant the use of the insanity defense. Some have pointed out that this bias against indigenous belief systems remains in formerly colonial legal systems. Even when courts took defendants' indigenous backgrounds into account, they were often patronizing.[65]

Modern witchcraft killing cases continue to take place throughout the world. Defendants raise variations of the witchcraft defense in modern contexts. For example, outside of Chicago, Celerino Galicia, a man from Mexico, stabbed his girlfriend, Roberta Martinez, forty-four times because he believed she was a witch (*bruja*) who had placed a spell (*embrujada*) on him. When he could not find a healer to dispel the embrujada, he killed her. Although the judge did not bar the witchcraft defense entirely, she refused to allow a professor of intercultural psychology to testify about *curanderismo*, saying the evidence was more appropriate at sentencing. After the judge ruled that the evidence was irrelevant at the guilt phase, the defense attorney dropped the witchcraft defense. The jury subsequently convicted Galicia, and the judge sentenced him to fifteen to fifty years in prison. Although Galicia's attorney advanced arguments resembling temporary insanity or provocation, Galicia's primary motivation for the act was to protect himself against the bruja. It is possible that Galicia was actually influenced more by jealousy or intoxication.[66]

In another case, Hagos Gebreamlak, an Ethiopian refugee living in Oakland, California, attempted to kill a woman, Ketema Redda, whom he claimed was a *bouda*, an Ethiopian witch with "the power to cause pain." Since he met her, he had suffered from aches and pains all over his body. At the trial, Professor William Shack testified that those from Ethiopia's central plains have a superstitious belief that "budas are evil spirits with the power to make people ill or irrational." The prosecutor claimed that Gebreamlak "invented" the buda defense after he was "caught red-handed" and maintained his motive was anger over being rejected as a suitor.[67]

The jury found Gebreamlak not guilty of attempted murder, but convicted him of the lesser charge, assault with a deadly weapon. The judge, Richard Hodge, disagreed with the jury's decision as he considered the "voodoo" defense "preposterous" and imposed the maximum possible for the assault conviction, seven years. He did not, however, recommend that Gebreamlak be deported as he thought that would be "tantamount to a death sentence."[68]

The main problem with analyzing self-defense in a cultural context is that the courts will have difficulty perceiving the situation from the point of view of the defendant. The challenge for defense counsel is to convey the cultural imperative, so that the court can perceive the reason for the action.[69] Even if the imperative is clear, the court may refrain from accepting the defense for fear of promoting social unrest. For example, in *Kumwaka Wa Malumbi and 69 Others* (1932), a Kenyan case, seventy defendants admitted beating to death an old woman who was believed to be a witch. The court rejected a self-defense argument because of concern over vigilantism. In other cases such as *Erika Galikuwa* (1951) the self-defense argument has proved unsuccessful as well. Self-defense has not worked where the defendant killed to preserve others in his family. For instance, in *Konkomba v. R.* (1952) a man killed a man he believed had killed one of his brothers by witchcraft and was in the process of killing another brother. An appellate court dismissed the appeal of his conviction.

SENTENCING: CULTURE AND THE DEATH PENALTY

In some capital cases the issue on appeal was whether the failure of defense counsel to present cultural factors during the sentencing phase constituted a constitutional error.[70] In these cases, the defendants were convicted of hideous crimes. Their guilt is not at issue. The question is simply whether the law requires that cultural evidence be presented during the penalty phase, at which time a defendant may receive the death penalty. The effect of the evidence would prevent the imposition of the death penalty.

The first published decision, to my knowledge, which addressed this question is *Kwai Fan Mak v. Blodgett* (1991, 1992, 1993). Kwai Fan Mak, an immigrant from Hong Kong who was twenty-two at the time of the crime, participated in the "Wah Mee Massacre" along with two other men of Chinese ancestry. They entered the Wah Mee Club, a gambling establishment in Washington state, tied up and robbed fourteen patrons, and then shot them. Thirteen died, and the one who survived testified as a key witness for the prosecution. One defendant, Tony Ng, fled to Canada and was only extradited to the United States on the condition that he not receive the death penalty. The other defendant, Benjamin Ng, was sentenced to life in prison. When Mak was convicted of the murder of thirteen people and aggravated assault, the jury decided he should receive the death penalty. After he exhausted his appeals in the Washington state system, he filed a habeas petition arguing that the failure of his lawyer to present mitigating evidence was an error of constitutional import. The failure to explain his difficulty in cultural assimilation and the significance of his stoic demeanor represented a Sixth Amendment violation of his constitutional right to effective assistance of counsel.[71]

Mak's lawyers presented virtually no mitigating evidence at sentencing, such as the fact that Mak had been an exemplary student before turning to illegal activities.

They did not ask family members to testify about Mak's "human qualities," nor did they have an expert witness, Dr. Graham Edwin Johnson, attest to the conflicts young Chinese immigrants experience when they immigrate to the United States. Dr. Johnson's deposition would have afforded insight into the nature of the difficulties associated with Chinese immigrants' cultural adaptation to life in the United States:[72] "But clearly for immigrants from Britain who have—who happen to be white, who happen to be Christian, who perhaps happen to be well educated, their adaptive process will be much easier than those who are racially different, who are linguistically different, who are religiously different."[73] Dr. Johnson would also have explained the cultural norm regarding the display of emotion:

> There's a strong sense that Chinese males should not express emotion in a public context or to put it another way there is a strong sense that appropriate behavior is to maintain a great deal of control. That people who lose—who become very emotional, who shout and scream and demonstrate their emotions—somehow have lost control of themselves, and that is considered to be inappropriate behaviour in a Chinese cultural context. That you can beat your wife but have to beat your wife behind closed doors. You don't beat your wife out in the open. In other words, you don't express strong emotions in a public context.[74]

The prosecutor tried to refute the culture conflict argument by pointing out that Mak had excelled in school, rendering questionable the claim that he had a "difficult time adjusting to life in America."[75] Another way the prosecutor attacked the culture conflict testimony was by suggesting it "might have been unfavorably perceived by the jury as an argument for cultural exemption from the death penalty." Finally the state put forward the argument that testimony that all immigrant groups face problems of cultural adaptation undermines the claim that Mak experienced "unique cultural circumstances."

The prosecution arguments rely on unwarranted assumptions. First, initial academic success does not prove that subsequently Mak could not have problems of adaptation. Second, with regard to the jury argument, the implication is that a request for a cultural exemption is prima facie invalid, and it is not clear that this is so. Even if the jury interpreted the defense strategy as a request for a cultural exemption from the death penalty, it would not necessarily have been viewed "unfavorably." The fact that more than one immigrant group experiences a problem does not rob it of its "cultural" aspect.

After taking stock of all the arguments, the district court held that the defense counsel rendered deficient performance by failing to present evidence showing the difficulties experienced by some Asian immigrants in cultural adaptation and evidence explaining that the defendant's apparent lack of emotion is culturally expected behavior and not a manifestation of an absence of remorse. In short, the lawyers did not offer any evidence at all that might "humanize" Mak, who had been portrayed as a "killing machine" by the prosecution. The district court concluded: "There is a reasonable probability that, but for the deprivation of counsel's effective assistance at the penalty phase, the result would have been different."

The appellate court agreed that the defense attorneys rendered inadequate representation at the sentencing phase of their client's trial by neglecting to present mitigating evidence regarding his family and cultural identity. But, given the circumstances, the court was unconvinced as to whether it prejudiced the outcome. Since there were other significant errors, such as the exclusion of evidence indicating that other men were responsible for planning the crimes of which Mak was accused, the court thought there were sufficient grounds to warrant resentencing.[76]

There is no denying that Mak was implicated in a most dastardly crime. Nevertheless, the decision about the death penalty should not hinge on something as trivial as one's body language, particularly when that may be culturally misunderstood.[77] Mak did not receive equal treatment under the law inasmuch as defendants from the dominant culture would not be subject to misinterpretations of their body language. The manner in which the trial unfolded may also offend Eighth Amendment notions: defendants are supposed to have the opportunity to have mitigating evidence presented, but Mak did not. These are among the legal issues at stake in capital cases involving cultural factors like *Mak v. Blodgett.*

Failure of an attorney to try to avoid cross-cultural misunderstanding could have fatal consequences. Because "death is different," Eighth Amendment jurisprudence requires that mitigating factors be considered.[78] One of the key points in *Mak v. Blodgett* was the question of whether Mak had a constitutional right to present all mitigating evidence concerning his character or the circumstances of his offense. The appellate court agreed that he did.

Another issue is the hypocritical policy of allowing mitigating factors to be considered, but in reality limiting their consideration. Officially, courts may consider any factor that might save a defendant from death, and yet the apparent authorization of the consideration of culture does not result in its presentation in court.

Another case in which cultural factors were not considered during the death penalty phase is *Siripongs v. Calderon* (1998). Jaturun ("Jay") Siripongs, a Thai national, participated in a robbery of a convenience store, the Pantai market, during which two clerks were killed. Convicted of two murders with special circumstances, he received a death sentence in 1983. Although he admitted to being present at the robbery, he professed that he was innocent of the murders and that his accomplices were responsible for the killings. He was unwilling to name the accomplices, however. Because he would not furnish information about them, the court did not find his account credible. His lawyer, a public defender, did not present psychological or cultural evidence that might serve as mitigating factors during the guilt or sentencing phases of the trial.[79]

After the California Supreme Court affirmed the judgment, Siripongs filed a petition for the writ of habeas corpus in the federal district court alleging, among other things, that his lawyer's failure to present mitigating evidence constituted a violation of his Sixth Amendment right to effective assistance of counsel. The district court declined to allow Siripongs to present evidence and ruled on summary judgment for Calderon. The first time the Court of Appeals heard the case, it concluded that Siripongs should have the opportunity to have the court decide his ineffective assistance of counsel claim, based on a complete factual record. The court therefore remanded the case for an evidentiary hearing on the question of whether Siripongs's attorney had failed to provide adequate legal representation during both the guilt and penalty phases of the trial. After hearing evidence for eight days, the district court ruled against Siripongs. The Ninth Circuit Court, the second time it heard the case, did not decide whether the lawyer's failure to develop the expert testimony constituted deficient performance, but simply concluded that the lawyer made a reasonable choice to forgo the testimony of Siripong's mother because of a fear her testimony would be impeached.[80]

The cultural argument central to this case was whether the refusal to name the accomplices was culturally motivated. An expert in Thai culture, Herbert Phillips, professor of anthropology at the University of California, Berkeley, explained that the reluctance to "snitch" was "consistent with deeply embedded Thai cultural values, including cultural concepts of shame and dishonor, and with Thai religious beliefs." Siripongs did not "snitch" because it would interfere with the duty to make amends for his wrongdoing in the next life. Ostensibly saving face, Siripongs avoided bringing even greater shame on his family by refusing to implicate others in the wrongdoing. There was also the possibility that his family might have experienced retaliation had he divulged names of others involved in the crimes.[81]

In his affidavit Professor Phillips explained the multifaceted cultural argument, emphasizing particularly the important Thai concept of shame:

> The Thai concept of merit and de-merit arises from a strong belief that if a Thai commits a bad or evil act, he must work extremely hard in doing good things to compensate for what he has done. The Thai notion is not to be punished for the evil act, because it is done and cannot be reversed. Rather, the Thai notion is that you have to make up for the evil act by compensating for it with merit. There is a cash register notion of merit and de-merit known as "boon" and "baap." "Boon" means goodness and "baap" means sin. There is a constant dialectic between boon and baap throughout life for all Thais, as they struggle continually to compensate for the baap they have made with more and more boon....
>
> I understand that Mr. Siripongs has refused to identify his accomplices. Such behavior makes sense from a cultural perspective even if ultimately it leads to Mr. Siripongs' death. From a Thai perspective, it would have been a useless act for Mr. Siripongs to identify the actual murderer. Making known his accomplices' identities would not reverse what had happened. The two people who had been killed would remain dead. From a cultural perspective, therefore, identifying his accomplices would have served no purpose for Mr. Siripongs. Thus, Mr. Siripongs' refusal to identify the accomplices does not necessarily mean that Mr. Siripongs killed either victim or intended death to result. Such behavior in fact is culturally appropriate under these circumstances.
>
> The cultural notion at work here is that assignment of blame is not the critical issue. The critical issue, from the perspective of Thai culture, is that the robbery got out of control. In Thai culture, "khwaan" refers to an individual's soul, which is the source of an individual's identity in the most profound sense of the term. In periods of extreme

emotional stress, a Thai's "khwaan" leaves his body, causing him to be out of control. In this case, Mr. Siripongs' behavior appears to demonstrate that he believed he had lost his "khwaan" when the robbery got out of control and his accomplice committed the homicides. With the two victims already dead, from Mr. Siripong's perspective, it made no sense to assign blame for the homicides to the actual murderer. Importantly, even if he had done so he could not have regained his "khwaan." This could only be done by regaining a state of personal and social equilibrium and by compensating for the evil or "baap" that he had committed. . . . This is exactly what he did by creating a trail that resulted in his quick arrest and punishment.[82]

Professor Phillips pointed out another cultural factor, namely the Thai concept of supernatural moral justice. According to the Thai worldview, a Thai person, if not punished in this life, will receive his due in future lives. Phillips also speculated that if the accomplices were relatives, he might have declined to identify them. Because of the Thai notions of deference to authority and of reciprocal obligations, from the Thai perspective, Siripongs's actions made some sense.

Another important cultural difference pointed out by Phillips concerns the display of emotions. In Thai culture, it is considered inappropriate to express emotion. Phillips suggested that those during the trial who observed Siripongs's "stoical demeanor" might misconstrue this body language: "To be 'ning,' or free of emotional demonstration, in the context of a criminal trial in which a Thai is accused of committing two murders is completely appropriate behavior. In fact, any outward expression of emotion would be culturally highly improper."

The appellate court was skeptical of the cultural arguments because Siripongs seemed too Americanized. The court noted that he had cooperated with law enforcement, that he was no longer a practicing Buddhist, and that he preferred the American value system.[83]

Another basis for the Sixth Amendment challenge was that Siripongs's lawyer, Spellman, had not pursued his client's interests energetically, to say the least. Not only was this his first capital case, but he was simultaneously running for Congress. The political campaign had distracted him from preparing properly for the trial. Spellman never gathered any evidence about Siripongs's background from Thailand. His investigators planned a trip to Thailand, but canceled it. No explanation for this was ever provided. Some aspects of his background might have influenced the jury—for example, that he was apparently raised by an uncle who ran a prostitution business, that he may have been sexually abused as a child, and that he was an ex-Buddhist priest. His lawyer even allowed the prosecution to present evidence he knew to be false. During the penalty phase of the trial, the jury never heard any mitigating evidence concerning his life in Thailand. He also never called Siripongs's mother to testify on his behalf, even though she sat in the courtroom on a daily basis.[84]

In 1995 Siripongs's new lawyers presented evidence showing that his trial attorney's performance fell below the standards required by *Strickland v. Washington* (1984). They argued that the failure to develop "potentially meritorious defenses" constituted deficient representation. Because this was a capital case, the attorney's duty to investigate was particularly crucial. Since death is final and irreversible, it is imperative that the lawyer find any potentially mitigating evidence.

Ultimately, however, the appellate court did not find the lawyer's performance deficient. It concluded that the system had operated correctly: "Our decision is made with the confidence that must accompany a decision that upholds a sentence of death."[85] The court thought not only that Siripongs was responsible for the killing but also that the crime must have been premeditated. Since he knew the store clerks and realized that if left alive they would be able to identify him, he must have planned to rob the store and murder the clerks. The defense response was that because that the owner of the store was apparently involved in selling stolen jewelry, this would deter the owner from reporting the robbery for fear of being arrested.

Siripongs's lawyers filed a petition for the writ of certiorari whose main argument was that Siripongs should have had an opportunity to resolve the Sixth Amendment argument and that the district court failed to conduct adequate investigation to made this determination. Siripongs's attorneys also argued that the appellate court misinterpreted Supreme Court precedent, putting its ruling in conflict with other circuits on the duty counsel have to investigate mitigating evidence. Despite these arguments, he was executed in 1998.[86]

It is impossible to know whether the evidence relating to a defendant's cultural background would have influenced the jury's decision regarding the imposition of the death penalty. There is, of course, a chance that it might have. Even those who support the death penalty will be troubled by the possibility that a defendant could be sentenced to death merely because of his body language. Given that there is nothing in the legal system which formally prohibits the consideration of cultural factors, this information should be presented to prevent any potential miscarriage of justice.

Failure to consider cultural evidence can be challenged on various grounds. It can lead to the imposition of excessive punishment—that is, a disproportionately harsh penalty. Another possible line of argument is that a court's refusal to consider it violates a defendant's right to freedom of expression. The defense attorney's failure to present the evidence could be considered malfeasance, a violation of the defendant's right to effective assistance of counsel. The emerging norm seems to be that lawyers should go some lengths to discover the background of the clients, to the extent that it might mitigate their sentences. Ignorance of other cultures will no longer be accepted.[87]

Some commentators might object to culture even at sentencing as a matter of principle, because it offends notions of equal justice. Defendants should be treated equally under the law. The problem with this argument is that the motivations and demeanor of the average defendant from the dominant culture will be understood, not subject to misinterpretation. To avoid misunderstandings, justice requires the consideration of the cultural background of defendants at all stages of legal process, and most certainly during the sentencing phase of the trial.

Jurisprudential Considerations

I turn to the normative arguments concerning the relevance of culture to the culpability of defendants in criminal cases. The main argument is that the defendant's motive is relevant to the analysis of his relative blameworthiness. Historically, mens rea included both legal guilt (or intent) and moral guilt (or motive). In Anglo-American jurisprudence it became standard practice for mens rea to refer solely to intent. The notion that a person's motive was not germane to the question of guilt became widespread in legal systems of this kind. Consequently, it has been difficult at times, as we have seen, to introduce evidence concerning a defendant's cultural background in some cases. In order for cultural motivations to be admissible in court, it is first necessary to see why motive is relevant to blameworthiness.

It stands to reason that if a person commits a crime with a beneficent motive rather than a malevolent one, the defendant is less blameworthy. If we consider the example of a mother who steals a loaf of bread to feed her starving children, she is less culpable than the person who takes it on a whim. Certainly understanding the context of the person's action and how that led to her action should be part of the assessment of the act in question.

If motive is relevant to guilt, then cultural motives should be considered. This would mean that a mother who commits parent-child suicide in order to be sure the child receives proper care is less blameworthy than a mother who kills because of anger or revenge. A person who kills a witch in order to protect his family may deserve special consideration as well.

This is not to say that individuals whose motives are better deserve no punishment. According to this line of argument, they deserve less punishment. Cultural evidence is part of a jurisprudence that would reduce the level of moral blameworthiness and therefore the severity of the punishment. The cultural defense should function as a partial excuse.[88] This means a cultural defense could result in any sentence, from a full one to none at all. The cultural information influences the determination of what constitutes just punishment.

Although the idea that culture should be considered during the guilt phase of criminal trials is highly controversial, introducing cultural factors during sentencing seems much less objectionable. At sentencing, many fewer evidentiary requirements apply than during the guilt phase of trials. Consequently, courts could permit the presentation of evidence concerning cultural differences that may serve as mitigating factors.

There is a concern that sentencing policies that prohibit the consideration of ethnicity, national origin, and race would also bar the consideration of culture. For instance, to date, U.S. courts have not made a determination as to whether the 1987 Federal Sentencing Guidelines prohibition of national origin encompasses cultural differences. There is nothing to suggest that the guidelines were intended to forbid cultural considerations. The reason the Federal Sentencing Guidelines absolutely prohibit courts from taking race, national origin, and ethnicity into account is to avoid discrimination. The concern was that prejudice might lead judges to impose unjustifiably longer sentences, more than defendants deserved. But when the reference to the cultural identity of a defendant is made in order to help him, by lessening the sentence, this objection does not apply.

There are those who would argue that it violates equal protection to treat people differently based on their heritage. The flaw in this logic is that the law is not neutral. The legal system contains cultural biases that are invisible to those who belong to the dominant cultural groups. Members of different groups are treated unequally when their folkways are misunderstood. Equal protection sometimes requires treating people differently.

Culture and Violence

Although those who take the life of others deserve some punishment, the question is how much punishment is proportionate, given the circumstances. Consideration of the cultural imperatives that may have influenced the defendant is necessary to ensure that justice is done. While there may be instances when the judge or jury may decide that culture should not mitigate, the cultural arguments should at least be presented.

Despite their inclination not to acknowledge culture, judges have seen the necessity of admitting cultural evidence in the courtroom. These decisions also make clear that defendants cannot explain their conduct without making reference to their cultural background.

We have seen that sometimes judges exclude the evidence about culture as irrelevant. In others they take it into account, sometimes even imposing virtually no punishment, as in the *Chen* case. Because it is unacceptable for a legal system to have such disparate results, this is one reason why some formal policy on the cultural defense should be adopted. The absence of a formal cultural defense can result in judicial obstruction of efforts to introduce cultural evidence and to the imposition of unjustifiably lenient penalties.

Yet individual justice requires that we examine the particular circumstances surrounding each case precisely because individuals differ. Whereas some defendants deserve full punishment for the crimes they commit, others do not. This does not mean that they deserve no punishment at all, however. The retributive principle of justice requires that individuals be punished proportionate to their degree of moral culpability. This means that it may be appropriate to accept the fact that a given offender may be somewhat less guilty morally but not acquit that individual altogether.

The relevance of motive will be seen in other chapters that contain criminal cases. The same challenge there is to persuade the court to take cultural motives into account. Without a formal cultural defense, defendants are at the mercy of judges who may or may not see the relevance of culture.

4

Children

It is generally agreed that parents should be punished if they maliciously inflict serious harm on their children. It is far less obvious what to do with parents who may inadvertently cause their child harm through actions they sincerely believe are in the child's best interest. The outcomes of such cases invariably turn on the questions of the degree of harm and the reasonableness of the parent's belief that the action would be beneficial for the child. Deciding these kinds of questions is rarely easy. It becomes particularly problematic when the parents involved belong to a cultural or religious minority group, because different peoples have such vastly different conceptions of what constitutes acceptable child-rearing practices.[1] Nevertheless, courts are sometimes confronted with cases such as these, requiring them to balance the safety and welfare of the child against the cultural autonomy of the parents.

In many such cases the question arises as to whether intervention by the state on behalf of children is justified. There is, of course, no clear-cut answer. One must weigh the competing interests of the child, the parents, and the state. Historically, the state has been reluctant to intrude into family matters and has, for instance, ordinarily interceded to order medical treatment only when the life of a child was at stake. In modern times, however, courts have become increasingly willing to invoke their power of *parens patriae* to guarantee that children enjoy a better "quality of life."[2] As a consequence, parents find their actions increasingly subjected to state scrutiny. This is especially true for those parents who belong to cultural and religious minority groups, for it is in those cases that the values held by the parents and the values promoted by the state most often conflict.

Two sorts of cases can be distinguished, which the official legal system would broadly classify as "abuse" and "neglect." In abuse cases the parent actively engages in a certain form of behavior that is considered by the state to be deleterious to the health of the child; by contrast, in neglect cases the state asserts that the parents fail to act in such a way as to maintain or restore the health of the child. These categories are, of course, ethnocentric.[3] For instance, parents may actively apply folk remedies or faith healing to cure an ailing child, but because the child is not taken to a Western medical doctor, this is interpreted as neglect by the state.

The first category to be discussed involves parents who act according to tradition where the act in question is viewed as a crime: ritual scarification, female circumcision,[4] discipline, folk medicine, and touching. The second category is a set of cases in which parents refuse to authorize medical treatment. They may prefer alternative remedies such as folk medicine or faith healing, or they may be opposed to any intervention because they believe the child was intended to have the condition in question. An important distinction will be drawn between life-threatening and non-life-threatening conditions, as the legal standards are much more firmly established for the former than the latter. Of particular interest will be the attempt to identify legitimate criteria for legal intervention.

The common thread that unites all these cases is the interplay between culture and culpability. In response to the charges brought against them, the parents in these cases typically invoke some sort of cultural defense, asserting that their actions are consistent with, and in some cases required by, their cultural traditions.[5] Cultural defenses are used in civil proceedings as well to determine custody of the child.

These divergent approaches to justice are reflected in the disputes concerning proper child-rearing practices. The United Nations has taken a strong, absolutist position condemning traditional practices.[6] Others, for example, Jill Korbin, take a position diametrically opposed to that of the United Nations. Provided individuals treat their children in accordance with their own rules, Korbin's view would not support intervention. In this chapter I argue that an intermediate standard offers the best solution to this challenging problem. It is my hope that through the analysis of the categories of conduct discussed in this chapter I will be able to provide a justification for a standard that proscribes traditional practices only in certain extreme cases.

WHEN PARENTAL ACTION IS CONSTRUED AS CRIMINAL CONDUCT: ABUSE CASES

Scarification

The much publicized unreported English case of *R. v. Adesanya* (1974) concerning the interpretation of ritual scarification illustrates well how courts typically contend with culture conflict. Mrs. Adesanya, a Yoruba woman from Nigeria, claimed to be following custom when, during the New Year celebrations, she made small incisions with a razor blade on the faces of her two sons, aged nine and fourteen. Apparently, she decided to place the traditional marks on their faces in order to ensure that her boys perceived themselves as Yoruba.[7] The boys were said to be more than willing participants. The foster parents with whom the boys had been living reported the markings to the police.

Adesanya was charged at the Old Bailey, the Central Criminal Court in London, with assault occasioning actual bodily harm under section 47 of the Offences against the Person Act 1861. She pleaded not guilty to the charge of assault and offered a cultural defense. From her cultural viewpoint, failure to make the facial scars would be condemned: "Without such markings, her boys would be unable to participate as adults in their culture. A failure to assure one's children of such scarification would thus be viewed as neglectful or abusive within the cultural context of her tribe."[8] Judge King-Hamilton QC held, however, that "the existence of the Nigerian custom was no defence to the charge brought." The judge contended that scarification differed from the piercing of girls' ears and the circumcision of young boys, noting the great danger posed by the razor on the face(!).[9] Since the cutting of the skin was a wound under the law, the judge instructed the jury that it had no choice but to convict her. Because the judge understood that Mrs. Adesanya did not realize she was breaking the law and because it was the first case of its kind, the judge granted her an absolute discharge. But he offered a warning at the same time:

> You and others who come to this country must realise that our laws must be obeyed. . . . It cannot be stressed too strongly that any further offenses of this kind in pursuance of tribal traditions in Nigeria or other parts of Africa . . . can only result in prosecution. Because this is a test case . . . I am prepared to deal with you with the utmost leniency. But let no one else assume that they will be treated with mercy. Others have now been warned.[10]

This situation illustrates several important features of culture conflict cases. First, although ignorance of the law is generally no excuse, judges seem to feel compelled to make exceptions for immigrants and refugees who are as yet unassimilated. The Nigerian High Commission testified that the Nigerian community in England was not aware that scarification was against the law. Another point is that in the absence of legislation which explicitly forbids a practice, judges may feel that an awkward application of a general statute cannot be fully rationalized. In any case, Adesanya did not argue that she was unaware of the English law on assault.

Second, even when judges are willing to consider cultural practices, they still clearly expect assimilation as a matter of course, demanding that immigrants shed their prior cultural identities. Scholars also make this assumption. A. S. Diamond, for example, contends that even if the boys were eager to have the marks, they would later resent having "facial disfigurement indicating a tribal background."[11] Implicit in this approach is the assumption that the scarification is not consistent with the best interests of the child standard because children will want to become assimilated. So, due to the irreparable nature of ritual scarification, the court tries to discourage the practice by characterizing it as being against public policy.

Third, the court failed to ascertain the validity of the cultural claim put forward. In what has been written about the case there is no indication that anyone involved in the case studied Yoruba folkways to determine the cultural imperatives for the complex facial designs. An anthropologist has pointed out that Mrs. Adesanya's conduct deviated from custom in two respects: the scarification usually takes place shortly after birth, and it is not associated with New Year festivities. In addition, the incisions were "very small by traditional Nigerian standards" and had not even drawn blood.[12] But even though they might not be permanent, the fact that charcoal was rubbed into the cuts suggests that she intended to make them permanent and was thus trying to adhere to tradition as best she could under the circumstances.

There were other problems with the ascertainment of the validity of the custom in this matter. In the case and also in the literature it is not made clear whether Yoruba scarification customs differ from Nigerian customs. Furthermore, there is an assumption that scarification is still traditional. Yet it is unclear to what extent scarification remains accepted practice in Nigeria. No one bothered to research how prevalent this practice was at the time of the *Adesanya* adjudication. Commentators assert that the custom is vanishing. Korbin stated that the practice is "dying out" in Nigeria and is performed only by traditional Yoruba in rural areas. Poulter wrote that "the traditional custom is observed far less today than it was in the past and may soon disappear altogether among those families who live in the urban centres and lead the most sophisticated lives."[13]

Fourth, the outcome of the case is typical of many culture conflict cases in which the judge officially upholds the criminal law but actually recognizes cultural imperatives in mitigating the sentence. In this way, he simultaneously preserves the rule of law and sees to it that justice is done. The fact that she received an absolute discharge means that ignorance of the law may indeed be an excuse, at least for the first offense.[14]

Female Circumcision

A quite different type of surgery required by some cultures is known variously as female circumcision, female genital surgery, or female genital mutilation (FGM). The custom involves removal of some or all of a woman's external genitalia. The practice has existed for thousands of years and approximately 85 to 114 million women in the world have been circumcised. The practice is prevalent in Africa and the Middle East, but has also been documented in Islamic Indonesia, South America, and Australia. It exists in more than forty countries, and the number is growing because of migration. European nations have had to come to grips with this custom, which was previously unknown within their national boundaries. While some countries have adopted new laws targeting the practice, others apply existing general laws.[15]

Anthropologists have explained the cultural justifications for the practice. Though religion (Islam) does not require the surgery, many cultural reasons are given for it.[16] Among the reasons most often cited are (1) it guarantees the virginity of girls before marriage and chastity afterward; (2) it is a rite of passage, and without it a girl will be unable to marry; if unmarried, she will be ostracized; (3) if the clitoris touches the baby's forehead during the delivery, it will harm or kill the baby; (4) the clitoris would otherwise grow to the size of a penis.[17] The crucial point is that the cultural logic dictates that the surgery be performed. Without it the uncircumcised girl will be a social outcast.

Feminists view women's support of the practice as a consequence of their having been victims of patriarchal systems and hence cite their attitude as an example of "false consciousness." But although many contend that this custom is the ultimate form of female oppression, women in many cultures favor its continuation. Educated women seem to be opposed to it, but some evidence indicates that even they succumb to social pressures to have the surgery performed.[18]

It is important to point out, however, the growing number of critics of the practice within the countries where it is prevalent. Many governments have banned it, for instance, Sudan in 1945 and Kenya in 1982. There have also been consciousness-raising programs coordinated with the help of nongovernmental organizations and the United Nations. Even where the custom persists, it may be performed among the same people in certain areas and not in others. Though it remains widespread, there is growing opposition to it.[19]

The international strategy has been to condemn female circumcision as unhealthy. Indeed, it may be a classic example of a "traditional practice prejudicial to the health of [female] children." The manner in which the surgery has traditionally been performed has led to many severe health complications. One difficulty with the health critique, however, is that with the dissemination of Western medical techniques, the operations can be carried out under thoroughly antiseptic conditions. This is certainly the case when Africans migrate and have their daughters circumcised by well-established surgeons in Europe.[20]

In some countries, the parents or women who perform the surgery have been prosecuted under general sexual mutilation laws and then sentenced to lengthy prison terms. More prosecutions have occurred in France than in any other country. The cultural defense has been raised as a discrete argument in these cases. Although defense attorneys claim that "ignorant Africans" were unaware that excision was prohibited in France, courts reject this based on the principle that ignorance of the law is no excuse. One French attorney argued against allowing the custom on equal protection grounds: "We accept for the little African what we would violently refuse for our own children. . . . In France customary laws should in no case pretend to substitute the enforcement of national law."[21]

As of 1999, twenty-six cases had been prosecuted, resulting in twenty-five convictions. Relatives prosecuted in France originally received suspended sentences; this followed the pattern of discouraging the practice without imposing punishment. Although punishment in the only two cases brought to the criminal court as of May 1990 were suspended sentences of three years imprisonment each, since then, defendants have been sentenced to actual jail time.[22]

Where specific laws disallowing the practice have been enacted, various issues have arisen. First, some contend there is no need for additional legislation on female circumcision because existing statutes can be utilized. The counterargument is that new laws serve to clarify the status of FGM by making it clear that neither custom nor consent can serve as defenses to the cutting. Sponsors of legislation insisted that the consent of the victim should not be a defense to the charge because the purpose of the law is "to protect the individual from his own folly and to maintain standards of behaviour in society."[23]

Finally, FGM statutes vary as to whether they make reference to the possibility of raising a cultural defense. The U.S. federal law criminalized the practice and explicitly forbade any consideration of whether FGM is required by cultural imperatives: "No account shall be taken of the effect on the person on whom the operation is to be performed of any belief on the part of that person, or any other person, that the operation is required as a matter of custom or ritual." Although this provision might be construed by courts as forbidding cultural considerations, this interpretation would be inappropriate as the cultural belief is directly relevant to the mens rea of the defendant. Laws that expressly forbid cultural defenses are questionable, and it remains to be seen whether these policies survive challenges in court.[24]

Female circumcision has also been an issue in political asylum cases. In the United States, for example, a gender asylum case—*In re Fauziya Kasinga v. U.S. Department of Justice* (1996)—received massive publicity. While the controversial *Kasinga* case was on appeal, President Bill Clinton authorized the issuance of new guidelines to allow the granting of political asylum on the grounds of persecution based on gender. Although it remains unclear what traditions other than FGM will be considered serious enough to justify asylum, this has been a significant change in U.S. law.[25]

The change in gender asylum law has an important implication for the possible use of the cultural defense. In some ways, it seems illogical to allow women to escape from their traditions via political asylum only to allow their relatives, who continue practices, to raise cultural defenses in criminal proceedings. In the final analysis, however, cultural evidence must be admitted in court because it relates directly to the state of mind of the relatives who committed the acts in question.

The new laws have been subject to criticisms. One major problem with the laws criminalizing the tradition is that they drive the practice underground. Families may take their children to their countries of origin to have the surgery performed. If they do perform the surgery in the new country and there are complications, relatives are likely to be reluctant to seek medical assistance for fear of prosecution.[26] It is also probable that girls will be disinclined to testify in court against their relatives, particularly if the consequence will be the incarceration of those relatives.

Another issue has been the symbolism associated with the policy. As there have been virtually no prosecutions under the new U.S. federal law, the policy is primarily a symbolic statement against the tradition. In view of its largely symbolic status, some have criticized the anti-FGM campaign in the United States as yet another racist attempt to condemn "barbaric" African customs.[27]

Discipline

The issue of corporal punishment of children is a highly divisive one. Some sort of punishment seems to exist in all cultures; the difficult question is what constitutes "excessive force." This is because there is considerable cultural variation in interpreting this notion. So, parents sometimes discipline their children and then find, much to their surprise, that their techniques are "unacceptable" in their new country. Most often, courts reject the cultural defense and insist that immigrants adhere to the standards of the dominant culture.[28]

In the British case of in *R. v. Derriviere* (1969) the judge had to grapple with the problem of how to balance the requirements of law with justice.[29] A West Indian father was charged with assault that led to actual bodily harm. This was the result of a family altercation: when his son misbehaved and refused to apologize to his mother, his father punched him several times, leaving him with bruises, swellings, and lacerations. The issue was whether other views of child discipline would be allowed to be practiced in England.

The judge accepted as true the claim that standards of parental correction differ in the West Indies but concluded that this was an unacceptable "savage attack":

> There can be no doubt that once in this country, this country's laws must apply; and there can be no doubt that, according to the law of this country, the chastisement given to this boy was excessive and the assault complained of was proved.
>
> Nevertheless, had this been a first offence, and had there been some real reason for thinking that the appellant either did not understand what the standards in this country were or was having difficulty adjusting himself, the Court would no doubt have taken that into account and given it such consideration as it could. The really outstanding fact in this case is that this was not the first offense.[30]

Under other circumstances, the court might have been lenient. However, no such consideration was possible as there had been a serious prior offense. Just a year before he had beaten his eleven-year-old daughter so hard that he had fractured both of her wrists. At that time the court had been more sympathetic, suspending his sentence but warning him not to repeat the behavior. Judge Widgery clearly took a dim view of the second offense, within months of the original assault. The court affirmed the decision of the lower court and dismissed the appeal, leaving intact a prison sentence of six months.

One commentator asserted that the approach taken in this case "may well be the standard method of dealing with this class of case."[31] The judge surreptitiously accepts a cultural defense if it is a first offense by convicting the defendant but then giving a suspended sentence. As this was not a first offense, however, the father could no longer allege that he was unfamiliar with English law and customs. Consequently, there was no problem with lack of notice. Since neither mistake of law nor mistake of fact applied (because he had been previously warned), he could only challenge in principle the requirement that he comply with English parenting standards.

Interestingly, even though the Court of Appeals rejected the appeal of Derriviere's sentence, the court reporter cites the principle as "immigrant parents must conform to English standards in the correction of their children, although some regard may be had initially to their different background."[32] This suggests that at least for first offenses, it is entirely appropriate for judges to consider the cultural background of the defendant as a defense. As stated, the principle articulated by the judge might also allow the consideration of culture during the determination of guilt as well as sentencing. But Poulter disagrees:

> It would appear from this decision that while the different standards of the accused and his native society may in suitable circumstances lead to a more lenient sentence being imposed, they will not afford any defence to the charge itself. The central question of guilt is decided according to a uniform standard applicable to all members of the community and ignorance of English law can afford no excuse.[33]

That judges convict and then impose suspended sentences seems to confirm Poulter's observation.

Implicit in the court's decision is a standard of reasonableness for judging the propriety of child-rearing practices, which would limit the sorts of cultural arguments that may be accepted. Yet the problem with such a standard is that it is unclear precisely what constitutes "unreasonable" parenting.

In the United States judges take differing views of the relevance of culture in adjudicating child abuse cases.[34] Sometimes a court purports to take it into account, as in *Dumpson v. Daniel M.* (1974), a case that took place in family court in New York City. A Nigerian father allegedly used excessive corporal punishment, and the issue was whether the court should affirm a lower court decision to remove the children from their parents' home. During a meeting with an assistant principal to discuss his son's misbehavior at school, the father hit his seven-year-old son, Ekenediliz, repeatedly. He explained his conduct saying

> he struck his son because according to his culture pattern this type of punishment was necessary and appropriate. In Nigeria . . . if a child misbehaves in school and causes shame to the family, the parent has the duty to punish immediately and in any manner he sees fit.[35]

The court acknowledged that there are diverse child-rearing practices but concluded that it had to decide the neglect issue according to the applicable legal standards of the dominant culture: "While recognizing individual and cultural differences, this court has the obligation to apply the law equally to all men." But the court, in reality, disregarded cultural factors: "The sole issue for determination here is whether the respondents' conduct constitutes excessive corporal punishment as would warrant a finding of neglect under the statute. We think it does." The challenge of interpreting "the best interests of the child" standard in this context seemed unproblematic to the court:

> Any reasonable man knows that it is not in the best interests of a child for its parents to punish in the manner we have seen here. While we are sympathetic and understanding of the respondents' motives, we must conclude that motive is irrelevant when we are confronted with the type of punishment this seven-year-old boy has received.

Thus, the court, denying the relevance of cultural motivation, decided to endorse the order authorizing temporary removal of the son.

Dumpson is instructive because it illustrates the standard judicial approach in cultural defense cases. There is a clear presumption that the reasonable man thinks like a member of the dominant culture. In addition, the court explicitly disregards motive, the cultural justification for the action under scrutiny. It also demonstrates how cultural defenses arise in legal proceedings other than criminal prosecutions.

This case suggests that we ought to be concerned with the impact judges' decisions will have on the ethnic community affected by the adjudication. Here the court states that its finding of neglect "is not meant to cast any negative overtones on the respondent's ability to function as a parent in any other respect." Nevertheless, the ruling could well humiliate the family. The father commented that "he was ashamed just to have to be in the courtroom." It is hard to imagine how the finding of neglect would not be interpreted as a judiciary casting aspersions on Nigerian child-rearing.[36] Even if the decision was justifiable, it is sheer nonsense to assert that the outcome has no broader implications.

Cases involving Southeast Asian methods of discipline have reached American courts. Traditional practices such as beating a child with a bamboo rod are regarded as child abuse by American authorities. In some cases the claim that the physical abuse is part of the culture may be false. Moreover, even if the harsh discipline was once allowed, the tradition may have been discarded. In other instances it is possible that the discipline is traditional, but when it results in potential irreparable harm, it must be prohibited, nevertheless.[37]

Even if the public policy of the state is to intervene when parents use what is considered "excessive" force, it is crucial that the intervention be handled with care.[38] In Oakland, California, social workers removed four children, including a five-week-old baby, from a Laotian home after a teacher reported seeing bruises on a child. The social service authorities suspected that the father, Jio Saephan, had "inappropriately" disciplined his son.[39] Kouichoy Saechao, a spokesperson for the Lao Iu Mien Culture Association, explained that his group accepts some forms of physical punishment. The Department of Social Services, however, was opposed to any discipline that leaves marks and favors intervention. Apparently the social worker removed the children while two police officers stood guard. The baby died while in foster care, apparently of sudden infant death syndrome, and one can only imagine what the Laotian community must think of the U.S. government. It is likely that removing the children from the home was an overreaction on the part of the social workers who may have feared that they would be sued if they failed to take the children out of the house.

Even if one favors intervention to halt corporal punishment among ethnic minority communities, there are unintended consequences worth considering. For example, by conveying to children the message that parents cannot use traditional discipline, the parents are emasculated and the children are empowered. If children engage in deviant behavior, parental authority has been shattered. Furthermore, failure to intervene as zealously in nonminority families will be viewed as a sign that a double standard is operating.[40]

Folk Medicine: Coining and Cupping

A number of cases have been reported in which parents have been accused of child abuse when they have attempted to use traditional healing techniques on their off-spring. Two folk remedies that have given American officials cause for alarm are coining, or *cao gio* (meaning "scratch the wind"), and cupping. Coining, practiced among Southeast Asians, particularly the Vietnamese, involves massaging the back and chest with a medicated substance, an ointment or oil, and then rubbing the serrated edge of a coin (or spoon) into the back of an individual—a procedure that leaves red marks. The purpose of the abrasive rubbing is to rid the body of "bad winds" that are considered responsible for a wide range of physical ailments such as fever, chills, and headaches. In the medical literature it has been called pseudo-battering.[41]

The other remedy which has been controversial involves using a heated cup and placing it on the body—a practice that also leaves marks. It is reported to be prevalent among the Mexican American community in the United States and is also still used in the former Soviet Union and Eastern Europe.[42] Two medical school professors explain the treatment and their view of it:

> A cup, in which a small amount of alcohol has been ignited, is inverted over the affected part. As the heated air in the cup cools, suction is produced, leading to localized conges-tion of the skin. . . . It is our feeling that the adverse effects of folk remedies are always unfortunate but they do not constitute child abuse and should not be managed as such.[43]

According to the law in many jurisdictions, if a child has physical marks, then it is legally required that the authorities be notified. Failure to do so can result in a jail sentence or a fine. It is important to emphasize that regardless of the parents' inten-tions, there is a duty to report the "injury." It does not matter that the parents intended to heal their children; all that matters is the (nonaccidental) physical sign of what is presumed to be child abuse. The prevalent belief is that the determination of the parents' state of mind is better left to law enforcement officials, child protec-tion agencies, and the courts.[44]

In a couple of instances reported in the literature parents faced legal conse-quences for using traditional remedies. In one tragic case a Vietnamese father took his three-year-old son to the hospital to check for possible influenza. The child died, and because of the marks on the child caused by coining, the father was jailed. He subsequently committed suicide. Some believe this occurred because of a lack of cultural understanding. Another Vietnamese family had to endure a trial for using coining "only to be vindicated by the expert testimony of a well-read physician."[45] Not surprisingly, many Vietnamese living in the United States are said to distrust physicians and worry that legal actions will be brought against them for coining. These anxieties may have the unfortunate effect of discouraging them from seeking medical advice in more serious cases.[46]

In the United States there is a reported case involving cupping. Parents nearly lost a daughter because they followed their own child-rearing practices. *In re Jertrude O.* (1983)[47] is an appeal from the district court's decision that three children from the Central African Republic were "in need of assistance" and that the eldest be removed from her parents and placed in a private home. The Maryland Court of Special Appeals agreed that it was correct to use American parental standards rather than those of the Central African Republic "so long as they elect to live with us" and that children raised by the latter standards were not receiving ordinary and proper care and attention. It is interesting that although the judge was genuinely trying to be culturally sensitive, the inevitable conclusion was that alternative cultural practices must be rejected:

> The reports and testimony frequently excused the contrasting practices by suggesting that while they were apparently not in accord with our standards of child rearing, the practices or lifestyles were acceptable in Central Africa. . . . The practices that caused injury to Jertrude, even as explained by the parents—such as lack of supervision resulting in falls causing bruising and fractures, as well as the "cupping" procedures leaving oval scars—are simply not acceptable treatment or care of children in America.

Although the court affirmed major parts of the lower court's decision, it held that it was inappropriate to take the eldest child from her parents' home on the basis of conjecture about future abuse. Noting that the standard for removing a child from his or her home is much more stringent than the standard for finding a need for assistance, the court remanded the case to give the judge an opportunity to provide factual support for his decision to remove Jertrude from her parents.

When judges are confronted with cases such as these, it is important that they become familiar with the folk medicine of the groups involved. They should be aware of the possible consequences of accusing parents of child abuse when the parents believe they are trying to help their children recover from illness. As one British pediatrician has said: "To make a diagnosis of child abuse when it has not occurred may be as disastrous as to fail to make it."[48]

Touching

Another cross-cultural misunderstanding involves differing interpretations of touching children. There are several publicized cases in which relatives accused of sexual abuse claim that their behavior is innocent. These "fondling" incidents have been documented in various ethnic communities, including Albanian, Afghani, Cambodian, Eskimo, Filipino, Pakistani, and Taiwanese cultures.[49] The legal question in these cases is whether or not the adults are touching the children for the purpose of sexual gratification. Ordinarily, it is only if adults have this motivation that the touching is illegal. In these cases the key notion is that the behavior is a form of expressing affection and is not intended to be erotic.[50]

In a Texas case, Sadri (Sam) and Sabahete (Kathy) Krasniqi, Muslim immigrants from Albania, lost their two children in 1989 when Mr. Krasniqi was accused of sexually molesting his four-year-old daughter in a public school gymnasium during a martial arts event. After the Texas Child Protective Service initially took the children out of the parents' home, the Krasniqis appealed. When Mrs. Krasniqi took the children to see their father, in violation of the court order, the court terminated their parental rights; the Texas Supreme Court affirmed the termination. According to the program aired on *20/20*, the parents claimed the touching was entirely innocent and a part of Albanian culture. An anthropologist at the University of Massachusetts, Amherst, Barbara Halpern, explained the cultural aspects of the behavior.[51]

Although Dr. Halpern's expert testimony was decisive in winning an acquittal in the criminal case against Mr. Krasniqi, this had no bearing on the family court decision terminating the Krasniqi's parental rights. The two children were legally adopted by their foster parents and forced to convert from Islam to Christianity. This case demonstrates an almost unbelievable abuse of state power. Termination of parental rights should be reserved for the most serious cases only.[52]

In some jurisdictions a defendant from another culture can successfully use de minimis statutes. Statutes of this kind, often modeled after the Model Penal Code, are designed to avoid unjust outcomes. They represent legislative authorization for judges to monitor prosecutorial discretion. In *State v. Kargar* (1996), an Afghani refugee, Mohammad Kargar, was convicted of two counts of gross sexual assault for kissing his eighteen-month-old son's penis. The court sentenced him to two concurrent terms of eighteen months in prison, then suspended the terms and placed him on probation for three years on the condition that he learn English. On appeal he argued that the trial court erroneously denied his motion to dismiss under the state de minimis statute. The Maine Supreme Court agreed and vacated the lower court's judgments.[53]

At the de minimis hearing testimony was presented from many Afghani people familiar with the practice of kissing a young son. They explained that "kissing a son's penis is common in Afghanistan, that it is done to show love for the child, and that it is the same whether the penis is kissed or entirely put into the mouth because there are no sexual feelings involved."[54] Kargar's attorney submitted written statements from Professor Ludwig Adamec, University of Arizona's Center for Near Eastern Studies, and from Saifur Halimi, a religious leader in New York. Kargar himself testified at the hearing that by kissing the penis, which is not the cleanest part of the body because of urination, a father demonstrates how much he loves his child.

Maine's de minimis statute is based on the Model Penal Code. The section central to the case was section 12(1)(C). The question in this case was whether the behavior was envisaged by the legislature when it defined the crime. The Maine Supreme Court evaluated the definition of gross sexual assault, which did not include specific intent. The Maine Supreme Court was careful to state that the application of the de minimis statute to Kargar did not nullify the effect of the gross sexual assault statute, nor did the court condone the behavior. The court said simply: "The issue is whether his past conduct under all of the circumstances justifies criminal conviction." Even though Kargar's conviction was vacated, the court implied that he knew he should no longer continue the practice.[55]

De minimis statutes provide the possibility of overturning unjust convictions when it would be against the interests of justice to proceed with the prosecution, at least in cases of first instance. They do not, however, address the more fundamental problem of accommodating culturally diverse practices in the long run.

All of these examples involve a type of behavior that at first glance seems obviously to be child molestation. Upon closer examination, however, it may be that the touching is not sexual in nature, in which case officials should not assume that the conduct is criminal. When the incidents occur in public, it seems more likely that the act is nonsexual. Context is important for an evaluation of the conduct; if it appears that there is a cultural basis for the action, then prosecutors will have a difficult time proving all the elements of the crime of sexual abuse, particularly that the adult acted for the purpose of sexual gratification.

It is my view that the touching behavior, even if it does not constitute molestation, should be disallowed. It is probably advisable to discourage touching that is deemed inappropriate in the United States because children who are at least partly Americanized will feel humiliated if they are touched in this manner. Even though they realize that the conduct is acceptable in their original cultures, they also know that it is proscribed in the United States. This puts the child in a difficult situation, having to experience stigma in the United States in order to satisfy a parental wish to preserve tradition. It is not as though the cultural tradition is required; it is simply permitted. Hence, while it is admittedly ethnocentric for authorities to try to restrict this behavior, it should not have a devastating effect on the culture.

If the touching behavior is required or necessary for a rite of passage, then it might be more difficult to stop the practice. But since children do not choose their cultures, it is essential that state intervention remain an option, at least for those children who are bicultural. Most of the time, decisions will have to be made on a case-by-case basis.

One further complexity is the ethnicity of the "victim." If the child who is touched is not from the same culture as the defendant, then it may seem more justifiable to intervene. But from the point of view of the defendant, the behavior is "normal," and therefore it is understandable that for him there is no reason to distinguish between children of his own culture and those belonging to other cultural groups.

It is wrong to imprison a person who has engaged in culturally motivated behavior and who is unaware of the prohibition of the conduct. If the touching is considered socially unacceptable, rather than incarcerating the individual, it is preferable to inform him that the behavior is not allowed in the new country. Even if forcing assimilation is the only option, it is certainly more humane to rely on education rather than imprisonment whenever possible.

WHEN PARENTS REFUSE TO AUTHORIZE WESTERN MEDICAL TREATMENT: NEGLECT CASES

In some neglect cases parents do not provide Western-style medical treatment because their religion or culture forbids it.[56] While in some instances they opt for "alternative" or traditional techniques that are compatible with their worldview, in others they prefer not to have any treatment whatsoever. The failure to ensure that children receive medical care can lead either to dependency proceedings to remove a child from a home on a temporary or permanent basis or to criminal prosecution of parents; under all state child abuse and neglect laws, parental failure to provide "adequate" medical care is a criminal offense.[57]

Traditionally, courts would not intrude in family decision-making regarding the health care of children unless the child had a life-endangering condition. In the past few decades they have gradually moved toward an approach that has been described as ad hoc. Intervention in non-life- threatening cases has become easier to justify and can be authorized to ensure "quality of life." The crux of the issue, of course, is deciding just what constitutes a life of quality. The presence of divergent views on this issue among the peoples of the world virtually guarantees that conflict will occur.

Finally, I turn to a consideration of Christian Science faith-healing cases. Although the parents in these cases are not immigrants and refugees, they are members of a group whose worldview differs substantially from that of the majority. Furthermore, many of the culture conflict cases considered in this chapter are in essence religious conflicts, so it is instructive to consider how these conflicts are dealt with when the defendants are in every other respect part of the American "mainstream." As will be seen, the way in which faith-healing cases are handled reveals serious biases in the legal system.

Non-Life-Threatening Conditions

The child neglect statutes permit the state to intervene and order medical treatment when children are seriously ill. If a child has a life-threatening condition, there is generally a consensus that intervention is justifiable. While in the past courts would not authorize forced medical treatment for non-life-threatening illness, increasingly they are doing so. American judges have compelled children to submit to medical treatment, even though their health problems were not life-endangering.[58]

A fascinating case that has received relatively little attention is that of Kou Xiong. In a Fresno, California, case a court ordered a six-year-old Hmong boy by the name of Kou to have surgery to correct a club foot, despite the vehement protestation of his parents. The Fresno County Social Services Department wanted Kou to have surgery because physicians said without it he would eventually lose the ability to walk and become "wheelchair-bound." The petition stated that he came within the provisions of Welfare and Institutions Code section 300(b) because his parents had failed to obtain surgery to correct his "congenital deformities"—a dislocated right hip and clubfeet. The physicians in the case testified that there was no guarantee that the surgery would ultimately be successful. Moreover, several operations would be required over a period of years. Even though Kou's own attorney argued his interests should supersede those of his parents, he stated that it was "not clear at all what course of conduct [would be] in the minor's best interest."[59]

Evidence was presented to the court to show that the Hmong believed the surgery would interfere with the natural order; misfortunes might well befall other members of the family or community. The family believed he was born with clubfeet as punishment for wrongs committed by an ancestor.[60] In fact, the family was convinced that this had already happened—after surgery in a Thai refugee camp his mother became violently ill, and the Xiongs' next two sons were born with cleft palates. The Hmong Council also informed authorities that in another case where surgery was performed against the advice of the shaman, the child's father died. The parents' objections to surgery were based on sincerely held religious and cultural beliefs. It was not apparent what compelling state interest outweighed these constitutional rights, as Kou had a disability and not a life-threatening condition.

There was some question as to whether the surgery was immediately necessary to enable Kou the ability to walk. It seems that it was already considered late to perform the surgery and that the longer he waited to have it, the more radical the medical approach would have to be. But even if it was medically advisable to have the surgery sooner rather than later, it is not at all obvious that the court should authorize surgery over the parents' religious and cultural objections. Kou himself said both that he did not want surgery and that he did not want to be in a wheelchair. He was concerned that were he to have surgery, he might be ostracized afterward. The psychologist attested to this fear on his part in his description of how Kou played with dolls during the evaluation.

The family's attorney attempted a series of appeals all the way to U.S. Supreme Court Justice Sandra Day O'Connor, but lost at every level. Interestingly, however, despite the legal outcomes, as of 1992 no doctor was willing to perform the surgery without the parents' cooperation.[61] After all the litigation, the original judge decided to vacate his earlier ruling ordering the surgery. What changed his mind was a psychiatric report which concluded that Kou would be at "grave psychological risk" if the operation were performed over parental objections. Kou said he was afraid of being separated from his parents if the surgery took place. He was also fearful that something bad would happen to his siblings (and that he would be responsible). Basically, he would be rejected by the community—he would be a social outcast. So, in spite of the protracted litigation, which appeared to disregard the cultural objections for the most part, the Hmong family, in the end, succeeded in avoiding the surgery.

What is striking about this case is that the court ordered the surgery even though the boy's condition was not life-threatening. With only a couple of exceptions, courts generally have not intervened in family decision-making concerning children in cases that were not life-threatening.[62] One can only speculate as to why the court felt the urgent need to depart from the standard doctrinal approach.

Here again it is worth pointing out the tremendous effect the court order had on the Hmong community, where the case was the source of much consternation. The Hmong Council, representing the eighteen Hmong clans, wrote a letter to the Department of Social Services imploring its director not to force the surgery on the boy. It seems likely that the Hmong learned that they could not expect justice, from their point of view, from American courts. American courts, in their eyes, ceased to be credible institutions.[63]

It is also important to realize how the disabled community might view the court's treatment of the issue. Though it was certainly not a conscious suggestion, the lawyer for Kou implied that life in a wheelchair was unacceptable: "The parents' right to raise their child in the way they see fit must give way to the child's right to have an opportunity to live a productive and pleasant, or at least bearable life." An explicit presumption was that it is sufficiently important for children to walk that even surgery with uncertain results can be ordered over family objections.[64]

Life-Threatening Conditions

Although it may be problematic to justify intervention in non-life-threatening cases, courts are more than willing to intercede on behalf of a child whose life is in immediate danger. In the process, courts sometimes run roughshod over the parents' cultural beliefs, resulting in greater suffering by the family.[65]

In 1984 a Hmong family in Columbus, Ohio, refused to authorize surgery for their four-month-old boy, Franklin Kue, who had been diagnosed as having cancer in both eyes (malignant retinoblastoma). As Hmong, the parents had extremely serious reservations about the surgery. The Hmong fear surgery for several reasons, one of which is that people will remain forever in the afterlife as they are at the time of death. Thao, a Hmong medical student, explains: "When the person dies, he will not be recognized by his ancestors in the 'spirit'world, he will not be reborn as another human being in the next life, and his soul will bring sickness to the living family members." Another reason for their apprehension is "the belief that cutting open the body allows good spirits to leave and bad spirits to enter." There is also fear that they will be used as experimental subjects. Because they were distraught about the surgery, the parents in this case supposedly even contemplated a murder-suicide.[66]

American officials intervened because doctors said the child had a 90 percent chance of survival if they removed his eyes before the cancer spread. So, when the

hospital's emergency order granting custody of the child to the county failed to produce the desired result, the public officials involved in the case returned to court.
This time Judge Clayton Rose Jr. ordered immediate hospitalization of the infant for
the purpose of surgery. He was reported as saying, "The only exception in the law is
if the child is treated by prayer from a well-recognized religion. That is not the case
in this instance." Mr. Kue, who attended the hearing, became visibly angry after the
judge issued the order and argued vehemently through an interpreter with the doctor who had requested the surgery. A police officer then escorted the baby to the
Children's Hospital.[67]

The lack of cross-cultural understanding prompted the family to spirit the
infant away from the hospital and transport him to Detroit to see a shaman. Apparently, they fled Columbus to avoid arrest and the enforcement of the court order
requiring surgery. Meanwhile, they became the objects of a multistate search by the
police and FBI. After receiving counseling in Detroit through the intervention of a
refugee resettlement organization (aided by Tou-Fu Vang, a bilingual Hmong
refugee resettlement expert), the parents consented to surgery. The prosecutor
dropped the felony charges of endangering a child, but threatened to refile them if
the child was not returned for treatment by a certain date. A social worker who
aided the family said that "having the pressure of prosecution off their backs"
helped them decide to have the operation performed.[68] It is thought that a major
factor in their decision was their recognition that the infant was already blind.

The surgery proved successful in averting further cancer, but Hmong confidence in American justice may have been permanently undermined. The father
explained his actions: "They came to the door and took our baby away. That never
happened in our country."[69] Mr. Kue also said he felt rushed and frightened by the
authorities.

The judge in this case might have played a crucial role in facilitating cross-cultural understanding but missed the opportunity to handle this culturally delicate
situation with care. While Americans may view a breach of the law (here the failure
to comply with the court order) as a serious offense, the Hmong believe that no
institution can usurp parental authority. If this transpires, it shames the parents.
Had the officials been more aware of Hmong attitudes and practices, they might
have handled this case more sensitively.

Fatalities: Faith-Healing Cases

Having considered cases involving judicial intervention to authorize medical treatment for children with non-life-threatening and life-threatening conditions, I now
turn to cases in which parents choose to treat their children according to spiritual
means and are subsequently prosecuted for manslaughter when their children die.[70]
There are several reasons why it is appropriate to consider faith-healing cases here.
First, the Christian Science parents, in refusing to consent to "conventional" medical
treatment, are acting on the basis of religious motivations that are part of their
worldview, just as, for example, the Xiongs were. Second, because of this, the reli-

gious arguments put forward as a defense in these cases are strikingly similar to the cultural arguments put forward in the cases involving immigrants.

The faith-healing cases arise because, according to the Christian Science world-view, disease is simply an illusion created by God, often as a result of sin. The tenets of their religion require that "cosmopolitan" medicine not be consulted. In fact, Christian Scientists are told that by seeking medical help, they will undermine the efficacy of faith healing. Thus, faith healing and modern medicine are, at least according to official dogma, mutually exclusive. Consequently, they believe they cannot seek medical help for their children when they are ill.

Despite similarities between faith-healing cases and other cultural defense cases, however, there is one significant difference: religious exemptions in all but a few states protect Christian Scientists from prosecution;[71] ethnic minority groups have not benefited from any similar sort of legislative exemption relating to their culture. The existence of these exemptions accounts for the differential treatment by courts of faith-healing cases and other culture conflict cases. In particular, a large number of faith-healing cases revolve around the issue of which takes precedence, the exemption or the manslaughter law.

When parents whose children died for lack of medical treatment have been prosecuted for manslaughter in the United States, the cases have turned on the question of due process.[72] For instance, in Minnesota, Kathleen and William McKown were indicted for second-degree manslaughter when they relied on Christian Science spiritual healing for their eleven-year-old son, Ian, who died of diabetic ketoacidosis. The defendants won a dismissal in the lower court, basing their argument on the due process fair notice requirement. That is, because the relationship between the neglect law exemption and the homicide law was ambiguous, they had not received notice as to the requirements of the law. The parents were, therefore, unable to make their conduct conform to legal standards:

> Respondents contend the child neglect statute misled them in that it unequivocally stated they could, in good faith, select and depend upon spiritual means or prayer without further advising them that, should their chosen treatment method fail, they might face criminal charges beyond those provided in the child neglect statute itself. In short, respondents argue that the child neglect statute does not go far enough to provide reasonable notice of the potentially serious consequences of actually relying on the alternative treatment methods the statute itself clearly permits.[73]

The state appealed, but lost. Both the Minnesota of Court of Appeals and the Minnesota Supreme Court accepted the fair notice claim and affirmed the lower court's decision to dismiss:

> The exception is broadly worded, stating that a parent may in good faith "select and depend upon" spiritual treatment and prayer, without indicating a point at which doing so will expose the parent to criminal liability. The language of the exception therefore does not satisfy the fair notice requirement inherent to the concept of due process.[74]

Commentators note that religious defenses are rejected specifically in cases where parents withhold medical treatment from dependent children: "Courts have long recognized that religion affords no defense to a statutory obligation to provide medical care for dependent children." Thus, from constitutional decisions one infers that there is little sympathy for a free exercise defense in criminal prosecutions, especially those involving children. Consequently, faith healing has only been possible because of the existence of statutory exemptions.[75]

Statutory exemptions have been challenged on constitutional grounds. One argument has been that they violate the Establishment clause because they effectively promote Christian Science. Another claim is that the exemptions deny equal protection to parents because parents of some religions are favored over others. For example, although there exist religious exemptions for faith healing, which often leads to death, there are no "religious" exemptions for coining or cupping, which never leads to death. It seems as though only members of "organized" religions benefit from exemptions, which suggests favoritism inherent in the law. More serious is the contention that exemptions deny equal protection of the laws to children, because the state fails to protect the health of children without regard to their religious affiliation.

Of all the objections to exemptions (religious or otherwise), the strongest one is the equal protection argument vis-à-vis the children. The real issue in the faith-healing cases is whether the state should permit parents to risk the lives of their children in the name of religion.[76] From the children's point of view, the legal requirement that necessary medical treatment be provided them should not depend on the group to which one's parents belong. In order to institute exemptions, children's rights may be sacrificed, including their right to religion. After all, without medical treatment to save their lives, they cannot choose to follow any religion.[77]

In most of the cases the children are too young to be competent to decide what is in their own best interest. If, however, an older child wanted to forego medical treatment and have faith healing instead, such a case might present a different issue. It might be that a mature minor's right to refuse treatment would have to be treated no differently from other cases in which there is no religious objection. For the younger children it is questionable whether parents should retain the right to choose faith healing to the exclusion of medical treatment when the children have life-threatening conditions. Certainly the exemptions deny the children their rights to medical care.

It is a sad irony that the only formal cultural defense that has been established to date is the statutory religious defense used in faith-healing cases. Surprisingly, not only are parents whose children die for lack of medical treatment charged with manslaughter instead of murder, but their convictions have, for the most part, been overturned. While I support the consideration of the parents' motive—that is, to heal their children—the appropriate punishment should be that assigned to manslaughter rather than simply probation.[78] To allow their religious worldview to reduce their culpability any further would be unjust. Until the faith-healing exemptions are repealed, it seems probable that the courts will continue to quash the convictions of parents based on the due process argument.[79]

The statutory exemptions seem to be based on a recognition that parents intend to heal their children rather than to harm them. But this method of accommodating the benificent motive of parents may suffer from constitutional defects and may also jeopardize the health of children. For these reasons religious exemptions must be subject to the closest scrutiny by the judiciary.[80]

INTERVENTION

In the faith-healing cases just discussed the children died, and the question was what to do with the parents.[81] Much of the discussion about these matters centers around the exemptions and the question of whether religiously motivated conduct constitutes a defense. But what about the case in which a child has not yet died? It is important to note that the faith-healing exemptions do not preclude child welfare authorities from reporting cases of children who are in need of medical treatment. If someone detects a problem in time, it is possible that courts could authorize child protective services departments to order medical treatment. There is no question that preventative intervention is preferable to prosecution after the fact, as the child's life might be saved. It is to the question of intervention that we now turn.

Under what circumstances, if any, should the state be empowered to intervene to protect children from cultural or religious practices that are regarded as deleterious to their health? Scholars take varying positions—supporting practically no intervention to intervention any time the health of the child might be perceived to be at risk.

The important work of Jill Korbin best exemplifies the view that intervention is never justified as long as the parents are complying with the rules of their community. Her position on traditional practices is that intervention by a national legal system should only occur if several criteria are met. Ellen Gray and John Cosgrove summarize the elements of her framework succinctly:

> If the following conditions are satisfied in Korbin's scheme, the behavior should not be considered abusive: (1) the behavior in question actually reflects a sanctioned practice of that culture; (2) it falls within the limits of (behavior and) deviation acceptable in that culture; (3) the intent of the responsible caretaker is consistent with the cultural "rules" governing the practice; (4) it is the perception of the child that this is an appropriate practice in the situation; (5) the practice is important in the development of the child as a member of the culture.[82]

This theoretical position does not allow for criticism of a practice provided that there is apparent consensus supporting its continuation. Even if the internal standard conflicts with the external standard, she assumes, without justification, that the internal one takes precedence.

Although Korbin is to be commended for her culturally sensitive analysis, she conflates two distinct scenarios. One situation exists when outsiders invade another society and then try to outlaw many aspects of the indigenous way of life, as for example, in colonialism. The other situation is where a group migrates and wants to preserve its traditions despite the fact that they violate the law of the new country. While Korbin may be right with respect to the first situation—that it is unwise to criticize customs in foreign jurisdictions (at least in the absence of domestic dissent)—the second situation poses a different question, and it is not self-evident that all traditions must be permitted in this context.

If we assume that some degree of intervention is justifiable, then the question becomes one of finding the appropriate standard. Those who fear that the state will abuse its power argue that minimal governmental intrusion in the family is the most defensible public policy.[83] Judith Areen, after noting that "there is little consensus about when a court should find that a particular child is neglected or abused" offers the following principles:

1. Standards for court intervention in a family should focus on the emotional and physical needs of the children rather than on parental fault.
2. Decisions on whether and how to intervene in a family should serve to enhance the social and emotional bonds of that family.
3. Courts should require a permanent placement for any child who has been removed from his family and who cannot be returned safely within a period of time that is reasonable in view of the age and needs of the child.[84]

The principles are intended to limit intervention by promoting family autonomy and by using the least intrusive methods of addressing intrafamilial conflict.

Other approaches to intervention are based on concepts such as irreversible or irreparable harm, serious bodily harm, and so forth. The difficulty with these standards, of course, is determining the scope of their application. In some cases, as with scarification and female circumcision, an irreversible or irreparable harm standard would require that immigrants discontinue these practices.[85] However, discipline and folk medicine do not ordinarily cause irreversible or irreparable harm. Thus, children's rights advocates might find such a standard inadequate because it is too narrow to prevent practices they view as detrimental. Serious bodily harm might be preferable because it is more inclusive, and yet it may outlaw practices which are not harmful.

The United Nations decided to adopt an extremely broad standard in the Convention on the Rights of the Child: any practices that are "prejudicial" to the health of the child are to be abolished. This gives the greatest latitude to those who seek to eradicate cultural practices that harm children in some way, whether the harm is permanent or not. Such a standard may appeal to those who want to protect children from repressive customs, but it also runs the risk of authorizing excessive public intrusion into private family affairs.

If some of the traditions that I have analyzed under the category of "abuse"— such as female circumcision, discipline, and folk medicine—endanger the lives of children, then intervention would be easily justified. However, intervention is unlikely to occur because cultural practices and their consequences ordinarily do not come to the attention of the authorities in time. Furthermore, there is a danger in intervening too early inasmuch as the parents would effectively be punished in advance for contemplating the practice of tradition.[86]

In abuse and neglect cases courts tend to use a case-by-case approach, which seems appropriate given the wide variety of situations that courts must evaluate. In abuse cases they consider the seriousness of the harm and the likelihood of repetition. If it were known in advance that children were to have scarification or female circumcision, intervention might be permissible given the seriousness and permanence of the harm. The repetition criterion seems influential: because authorities are concerned that children will continually undergo folk medicine techniques and corporal punishment, they intervene to halt the practices.

Sometimes children may initially want a permanent mark or surgery because it signifies their cultural identity, but then because of the powerful forces toward assimilation may later opt for a "mainstream" lifestyle and wish the physical change had not been made. Of course, assimilation may not always be desirable, but the national system should preserve choice. When the child is considered sufficiently old to consent, the permanent change can be made. This position is based on a Western notion of consent and on the value of choice. But Westerners are skeptical of the idea that children can consent before they reach a certain state of maturity. To ensure that there is true consent, at least according to Western notions, there will have to be a delay before the traditional practice can be performed where it involves permanent physical change.

In the medical neglect cases in which the child's condition is not life threatening and parents have religious or cultural objections to treatment, there is usually an appraisal of key factors. They include (1) whether the medical procedure is nonexperimental, (2) the likelihood of a successful result, and (3) whether the need for surgery is immediate. Despite the well-intentioned efforts of those involved in the case, it is regrettable that a family such as the Xiongs should be subjected to constant harassment by the legal system for opting not to have elective surgery. While nonlegal attempts at persuasion, provided they do not constitute harassment, might be desirable, it seems wrong to bring the full force of the legal system into motion against an impoverished immigrant family which believes that the action they will be compelled to take will disturb the natural order, as they understand it.

Since the courts disregarded the criteria normally employed in non-life-threatening medical neglect cases, one must inquire as to what standard they did use. It seems that they were using a "quality of life" standard. This may be a dangerous development inasmuch as the state is imposing its conception of "quality of life" on peoples whose value systems diverge significantly from that of the dominant culture. Why not wait until the child is old enough to decide to have the surgery rather than forcing unwilling families to have their children submit to the knife?

It has been argued that the court should not have to wait to authorize medical treatment until a child is at death's door. One commentator recommends the application of two requirements: the severity and irreversibility of the physical condition. Therefore, in the non-life-threatening cases courts should be vested with the power to intercede to protect children when they have a *potentially* life-threatening condition.[87]

As a general argument I take the view that the legal system should sanction intervention when the parental action will lead to irreparable physical injury. Although there will be debate about what conduct is encompassed by the standard, it would authorize intrusion into the family to prevent scarification, female circumcision, and some types of corporal punishment, but not necessarily for the practice of folk medicine.

In neglect cases courts should authorize surgery over parental religious or cultural objections if there is a *potentially* life-threatening situation. In the absence of a threat to life, there is time to try to persuade a family of the benefit of medical intervention. There is no need to intimidate families with the law unless the child is in jeopardy.

PROSECUTION

In many cases the discovery that a parent has followed tradition to the detriment of a child comes too late for intervention to be of any use. The question, then, is whether the parent should be prosecuted for having acted in a culturally motivated manner. At this stage the police and prosecutors may decide not to pursue the matter further if they are convinced of the parent's benevolent cultural motive and that a warning will be sufficient.[88] If the case goes to trial, however, a decision must be made as to what degree of culpability is appropriate. In order to determine whether cultural defenses can be justified theoretically, one must first ask whether motive is relevant to the determination of a defendant's moral blameworthiness.

If cultural motives are admissible in court, then this would allow for the creation of a formal cultural defense. A decision must be made whether the cultural defense should exonerate the defendant entirely or only partially. In cases where parents jeopardize the health of children in the name of culture, it would be inappropriate to excuse the parents altogether. However, the fact that the parents are not trying to harm their children is an important and highly relevant point. Hence, I would argue that in many instances the cultural motive demonstrates that the parents who act in accordance with culture are less culpable than parents who deliberately try to harm their children.

It is often assumed that a defendant who raises a cultural defense is arguing that he should be excused because he was ignorant of the law. In reality, however, the defendant usually does not claim that he was unaware that there was a law proscribing the conduct in question. His argument is that his action is not properly characterized as a crime. For example, Mrs. Adesanya stated that she was embellishing her sons' faces with powerful Yoruba symbols indicative of their cultural identity. Although she knew there was such a thing as assault, she claimed her action had nothing to do with assault. Similarly, parents who use coining do not claim that they are unaware of laws prohibiting child abuse, but would say that folk medicine is not child abuse. Likewise, the parents who touch their children affectionately have no idea that this is considered illegal behavior.

If the cultural defense is based on motive, rather than ignorance of the law, the question might arise as to whether it should be a partial excuse in all cases. But even in cases where the cultural practice victimizes someone—for example, children—cultural motivations are germane to the question of guilt. Just as the person who kills because of provocation is considered to be less culpable than one who commits murder with malice aforethought, so, too, the parent must not be convicted of a crime more serious than is warranted by the circumstances. The fact that the parents were trying to adorn, socialize, or heal a child is extremely relevant and must be taken into account. It is not that culture will permit one to commit a crime with impunity but, rather, that the offense and punishment should be adjusted to reflect the appropriate level of blameworthiness.

Where the tradition is handled through general criminal categories, there may be a lesser included offense with which the defendant can be charged. But where the penal code explicitly prohibits the practice, presumably the concept of lesser-included offenses will be inapplicable. The point of having lesser-included offenses is to ensure that the defendant who acts with a cultural motive not be charged with a crime that carries a connotation of being excessively blameworthy and that has associated with it overly severe punishment. Assuming that the legislature is culturally sensitive in drafting provisions to address coining, female circumcision, and other practices, the fear that the punishment will be disproportional will be unfounded. It is not obvious how to guarantee condign penalties, but the U.K. Female Circumcision Act of 1985 might serve as a model for drafting laws proscribing traditions.

There may be instances in which legislatures decide that the appropriate punishment for a tradition that affects the health of children is not criminal in nature. For example, until there is incontrovertible evidence that coining lacks any therapeutic benefit, legislatures might choose to discourage the practice but authorize a warning the first time it is reported and then later impose only a fine. In some cases the sanction appropriate to the offense may be minimal.

If assimilation is the goal, then at least the process of "educating" parents should be done as humanely as possible. In general, extralegal solutions should be sought in order to discourage the perpetuation of traditions that adversely affect children, thereby avoiding the intimidation of immigrant communities by the strong arm of the law. In some cases it may be possible to convince immigrants that folk medicine and Western medical treatment are not incompatible. Indeed, commentators have indicated that such an approach is most likely to yield successful results. Respect for the religious and medical folkways of others is more likely to encourage acceptance of Western health-care practices. If parents do not feel that they have to abandon their own traditions and instead can simply try two approaches simultaneously, they might be more willing to consent to Western medical treatment for their children.[89]

BALANCING CULTURAL RIGHTS AGAINST CHILDREN'S RIGHTS

The challenge is to decide how a national legal system should handle culture conflict cases involving children. Although the state must be culturally sensitive, it must, at the same time, strive to uphold fundamental human rights standards. There is a particular need to enforce the law when children's rights are implicated because children are vulnerable and unable to act as their own advocates.

In order to strike the proper balance between children's rights and cultural autonomy, I have argued for intervention to prevent irreparable harm. It is my view that the legal system should try to preserve choice for children. Thus, courts should intervene when a child's life is at stake because otherwise the child cannot decide whether or not to remain a member of the cultural group or to opt for a different cultural identity. Likewise, in cases where parents plan to make irreversible physical changes, the state should act to prevent it.

Where the issue is medical neglect because parents object to medical treatment on religious or cultural grounds, I favor a return to the life-threatening/non-life-threatening standard. I would, however, amend the rule to authorize state intervention when children have potentially life-threatening conditions. The current trend toward use of a "quality of life" standard permits excessive intrusions into family life. The notion of irreparable harm may be pertinent here as well since in some cases the question is whether delaying surgery until the child reaches the age of majority may mean that it can never be successfully performed. In general, intervention is unwarranted if the decision to withhold medical treatment will not be permanently devastating for the child. Otherwise, family and cultural autonomy will be unjustifiably undermined.

If the state discovers the abuse or neglect after it has already occurred, however, the question is how cultural arguments should figure into decisions concerning the guilt and punishment of the parent defendant. An understanding of a defendant's culture is crucial to determining whether or not criminal motivation underlies his or her actions. Indeed, it seems hard to imagine how courts can avoid cultural factors in determining the guilt or innocence of parents.

5

Drugs

Drugs are used in different cultures for various purposes, and often the substances are "integral to the constitution of culture." When immigrants continue to use drugs from the old country in their new homeland, they may be subject to criminal penalties because the drugs whose use was taken for granted in the country of origin are now considered illegal "controlled substances."[1] People using the drugs may have no idea that their use is illegal, as in the case of khat and kava discussed in this chapter. In fact, they may view the legal intervention as a form of harassment based on their cultural background.

In this chapter I present an overview of the ways in which cultural arguments are presented to courts to mitigate punishment in cases involving drugs. I begin by considering decisions in which individuals use substances accepted in the country of origin but that are regarded as unacceptable in the new homeland. Next I turn to the issue of exemptions from drug laws for medicinal and religious purposes. Here the question is whether exemptions for Native Americans are justifiable, when other groups are denied similar exemptions, and whether the exemptions have, in fact, protected Native Americans from prosecution. In the next section the focus is on individuals who carry drugs, apparently without being aware of it, and the question of whether they should be allowed to raise cultural defenses concerning the nature of their relationships with those who have asked them to carry the illicit substances. The penultimate section deals with immigrants' fear of the police and whether their consent to searches was truly voluntary, in light of their experiences with police in their countries of origin. In some of the cases, those who are subject to searches claim they did not believe they could refuse to allow the police to conduct searches. Finally, I examine the pleas of Westerners abroad, found with drugs in their possession, who seek to avoid the death penalty in nations which impose it for this offense.

Many of the assumptions about substance use and abuse are unfounded. There appears to be little data proving the dangerousness of some of the drugs discussed here. Hence, the government classificatory schemes are not based on logical criteria and, instead, reflect ethnocentric attitudes. In addition, some of the law enforcement raids of immigrant communities to deter the use of traditional herbs seem motivated by less than noble motives. In the face of doubts about the propriety of the prosecutions in many of the cases analyzed in this chapter, it is time to reconsider the enforcement of drug policies as they relate to ethnic and religious minorities, the subject to which I now turn.

CULTURAL DIFFERENCES IN DRUG CONSUMPTION: WHICH ARE ILLEGAL SUBSTANCES?

Some substances are classified as "drugs," though this category is not unproblematic. The determination of which ones are drugs and, moreover, the determination of which are illegal or controlled substances vary from one society to the next: "The boundary between illicit and licit is a shifting and negotiable one, historically and cross-culturally." Drug policies vary from one society to the next because they are "culturally and historically framed."[2] Those who move between societies are often unaware that a substance legitimate in the former place of residence is no longer considered so in the new homeland.[3] The following cases reveal the somewhat arbitrary nature of drug policies.

Khat

Khat exemplifies the problem of cross-cultural misunderstanding about which substances constitute illicit drugs. Khat is chewed like tobacco, has an amphetamine-like effect which some compare to that of a double espresso, and causes a state of euphoria.[4] The usual dose is a half-pound, which is absorbed though an individual's cheeks. It sells for approximately $40.00 per branch in the United States, enough for one person to chew for an afternoon. Grown in countries such as Yemen and East Africa where it is widely used, it is smuggled into Canada, New Zealand, and the United States, sometimes via England where it is not illegal. There has been concern because khat use appears to have increased among some immigrant communities, beyond what was typically used in their countries of origin.[5]

Khat users deny it is harmful, often comparing its effect to that of coffee. They also mention its various benefits such as increased energy, uplifting low spirits, and enhancing sensations.[6] The Deputy Minister of Culture and Tourism in Yemen, Motaher Taqy, explained: "Chewing khat has the same effect as drinking a very heavy cup of tea. It's perfectly legal here." Khat is so central to social existence in

Yemen that "most of the business and politics of Yemen take place in qat sessions." Though khat is "a fundamental part of everyday life" there, it is said to be used more often by men than women.[7] A whole set of cultural practices has evolved around the consumption of khat, including the creation of special rooms in many houses for the purpose of chewing khat.

The World Health Organization has lobbied to have khat classified in the same category as cocaine since it is convinced that its use can lead to serious addiction.[8] Because khat contains cathonine, the U.S. federal government considers it a Schedule I controlled substance along with heroin, LSD, and ecstasy. Those worried about its use compare it to amphetamines, which produce "hyperactivity, appetite loss, elevated heart and respiration rates—and when used in excess, manic behavior and hallucinations." One study mentioned trouble sleeping, mood swings, anxiety, and irritability, while another emphasized anorexia. Those who chew a substantial amount typically have a "staring look" or "pseudoexophthalus." There are also concerns about its dental implications.[9] Ultimately, the main objection is probably that it is addictive.[10]

Although khat is widely used in Yemen, in 2000 the president of Yemen, Ali Abdulah Saleh, tried to discourage this practice because of its effect on the productivity of workers and because it depletes family resources. The poorest families allegedly spend up to 50 percent of their income on the leaves. It affects the economy as well; khat occupies over 40 percent of irrigated farmland. It is banned in government offices and in the army. The government added an hour to the six-hour workday so that workers would have less time to chew khat. The president apparently announced that he himself would chew only on weekends.[11]

U.S. federal agencies such as the U.S. Drug Enforcement Administration (DEA) began to focus on khat in the 1990s. The U.S. Attorney General also undertook an investigation of it. Inspectors at the airports across the United States have confiscated khat leaves from surprised Yemeni visitors. Sometimes immigrants are subject to raids in local restaurants. For instance, when three Yemeni men were arrested in a Brooklyn cafe for chewing khat, they were stunned to find that it was illegal in the United States. Evidently they faced up to seven years in prison if convicted of felony drug charges. A man was also arrested for growing one-thousand plants in the "first khat plantation" in the United States.[12]

One issue is the question of how much khat is necessary for there to be criminal action. In Minnesota, six defendants, originally from Somalia, who were charged with one count of fifth-degree possession of khat, challenged the prosecution to prove that they possessed enough khat to justify the charge. The question in State v. Ali was whether the khat contained enough cathinone, the controlled substance, to violate the Minnesota statute. The trial court judge ruled that "the testing did not need to distinguish between positive and negative chemical components of cathinone, because both have a stimulating effect." The Court of Appeals' statutory interpretation was that the prosecution need not prove this point. The court rejected the defendants' claim that khat had unique properties and said, therefore, that there was no greater need for proof of its components than other drugs.[13]

Some think the targeting of khat chewers represents a form of cultural bias. Indeed, some consider the prosecution of khat users to be part of "culture wars." Dr. Andrew Weil commented on the use of khat by African and Arab men: "It is a symbol of their culture which we are projecting our fears on. There is a long history of people doing that with other peoples' drugs." Dr. John Kennedy also considers the targeting of khat users to be ethnocentric. Lee V. Cassanelli argues specifically that the "scientific" research on khat was politically motivated to justify banning its use.[14]

If, as Kennedy argues, human beings feel a need for stimulants, it would make sense to identify the safest ones possible, some of which might turn out to be natural stimulants rather than caffeine, tobacco, and amphetamines. His advice to undertake more research before reaching any definite conclusions is prudent.

Kava

Immigrants from Tonga have occasionally clashed with legal authorities after drinking kava tea, a beverage made from the powdered root of a South Seas pepper plant. *Piper methysticum*, which is found in Polynesia, Melanesia, and Micronesia, "has been used ceremonially for thousands of years." Kava tea is still imbibed in the South Pacific and in immigrant communities across the United States. It causes drowsiness as it is a central nervous system depressant and analgesic, and is commonly sold in the United States as a natural remedy for anxiety and insomnia.[15] Those who drink it feel quite relaxed: "When drunk in moderation, kava is a fundamentally friendly drug, promoting a state of tranquillity, happiness, and contentment." One major study gives an insider view of kava: "The most general presumptions about the effects of kava throughout the Pacific are those of peace, sociality, and camaraderie." While it used primarily for its mood-enhancing qualities, it also has medicinal uses. Because of its popularity in the United States, it has been described as an "herbal superstar."[16]

For expatriates, the kava ceremony assumes a greater importance than it did originally because it represents a link to their homeland. It provides a way of maintaining cultural identity and seems to play a significant role in immigrant communities. Political deliberations invariably take place at the "kava circle," or *faikava*. Moderate use of kava among expatriates seems be culturally integrated in their way of life.[17]

The rules associated with kava drinking are quite involved. According to scholars, participants in the ritual attach "considerable importance" to the seating arrangement, which reflects unequal hierarchical relations in society. The beverage is served in order of seniority. For the most part, kava-drinking is limited to men and women of high status. This is one of a number of strict limits on the consumption of kava.[18]

It has been known for quite some time that excessive use of kava can affect people. As early as 1932 Joseph Deihl commented that excessive use "leads most certainly to a loss of control over the muscles of the legs. One thus affected walks with a staggering gait, while the mind is clear." According to another study: "The most common side effect of heavy kava consumption is a skin rash known as 'kava dermopathy.'" This same study denies claims that kava is addictive. In the South Pacific there is some evidence that it is associated with poison and death.[19]

While its use has not been terribly controversial, on occasion kava tea has been in the news. In July 2000 a consumer group, the Center for Science in the Public Interest, condemned the food industry's spiking drinks with medicinal herbs including kava and called for the government to halt the practice.[20] Snapple, for example, sells Moon Tea Drink with kava "to enlighten your senses." The Food and Drug Administration responded with a statement indicating it would check beverages to be sure they comply with truth-in-labeling requirements.

While the government tries to determine the relative merits of kava, some immigrants from the South Pacific have been prosecuted for behavior attributed to it. In San Mateo, California, Taufui Piutau was charged with driving under the influence of kava. He had eight cups of kava tea before driving home at 3 a.m. from his church's kava circle. The California Highway Patrol stopped him because he was weaving between the lanes of the freeway. Though he failed a sobriety test, he tested negative for alcohol and drugs. After researching the effects of kava for nine months, the prosecutor, Jim Fox, decided to file a misdemeanor charge against him. One issue was whether kava was a drug which was covered by the law. If convicted, he would have been subject to a maximum of six months in jail and a $500 fine. He already suffered the consequence of the arrest, having been suspended without pay by Federal Express. Considering how little is known about kava tea, there is some question as to whether a prosecution was justifiable. As it turned out, there was a hung jury, resulting in a mistrial.[21]

It might be that Americans presume that imbibing substances leads to disorderly conduct. Immigrants from the South Pacific, by contrast, think it leads to tranquillity. The reaction by law enforcement officers to those who drink kava may stem from divergent cultural expectations about reactions to the brew. If stimulant drinks such as cola, coffee, and tea are acceptable in the world market, it is not obvious why a "relaxant beverage," kava tea, should be criminalized.[22]

Historically, religious institutions sought to prohibit the drinking of kava. In the twentieth century, despite the lack of scientific evidence of serious risks, some governments have continued to discuss legal bans. Although there is no documented threat and there may be potential therapeutic benefits, kava use continues to be subject to close scrutiny by various governments around the world.[23]

EXEMPTIONS: MEDICINAL AND RELIGIOUS USES OF DRUGS

Sometimes drugs, which are otherwise illegal, are permitted for special reasons. In the 1990s, for example, there was a debate about "medical marijuana" for AIDS patients.[24] Immigrants and refugees argued that they should not be punished, or at least not as severely, if they were using illicit substances for medical purposes.

Medicinal Use of Illicit Substances

Mr. Hojatollah Tajeddini, an Iranian citizen, was convicted by a jury of conspiracy to import and importation of heroin into the United States. Tajeddini claimed that he thought he was carrying "an herbal cancer medicine," or *shireb*, to Parviz Parvan, a friend with liver cancer, and did not realize that it was heroin. He challenged his conviction on the ground of ineffective assistance of counsel: his attorney failed to seek a continuance, which would have given him enough time to gather evidence in support of the "herbal cancer medicine" contention.[25]

A number of cases involve Laotian refugees, caught with opium, whose defense is that the opium was intended to be used as medicine. In fact, opium is known to be taken for this purpose. In *U.S. v. Koua Thao* (1983), a Hmong man received a package by mail containing 154.74 grams of opium. Federal and state law enforcement authorities searched his apartment; they found opium in the closet, some of which was inside his shoe. Mr. Koua Thao argued that "the use of opium is common in the Hmong culture, and that heavy users may smoke up to two grams per day and even more for medicinal purposes." Although he claimed that the opium was for his own personal use, the jury concluded that he intended to distribute it, a conclusion which the appellate court did not find unreasonable.[26]

In *U.S. v. Khang* (1994) two Hmong half-brothers, Lee Khang and Say Pha Khang, were convicted of importing opium to the United States. They said that the opium was medicine for their ill, aging father and submitted a letter from a "Hmong cultural consultant" to substantiate this claim. They also said they did not realize opium was illegal in the United States when used for medicinal purposes. Although their strategy was to win a sentence reduction, the district judge did not believe them. Instead of lowering their sentence, because of inconsistencies in their testimony, he raised their sentence "for obstruction of justice." Had the judge believed the argument, he indicated that he would have mitigated the punishment.[27]

A central legal issue is often whether it was proper for the court to exclude evidence concerning the use of opium in the culture. In the United States, courts have repeatedly ruled that it is not an abuse of discretion to exclude evidence from a cultural expert concerning drugs. In fact, in some cases court have reversed convictions because testimony based on ethnic stereotypes was allowed to be presented.[28]

Religious Uses of Drugs: Peyote and Marijuana (Ganja)

In addition to decisions in which defendants argue for the medicinal use of drugs, there are many in which they claim a religious need for the drug. Native Americans have litigated numerous cases to try to vindicate their right to ingest peyote in religious ceremonies. Rastafarians likewise have filed lawsuits to use marijuana, or *ganja*.[29]

Peyote is a hallucinogenic drug long used by indigenous peoples, and one that has invariably been subject to much regulation. Tribes generally eat the peyote button because it "produces a distinctive sensation of spiritual exaltation." Found only in limestone soils of the Chichuauan desert of southern Texas and northern Mexico, peyote has played a crucial role in religious life of Mexican indigenous peoples for thousands of years· During the nineteenth century it spread from Oklahoma to many tribes throughout the United States. It is difficult to find much information about health risks associated with the use of peyote, but that has not dissuaded government officials from trying to ban it. The U.S. government classified peyote as a Schedule I substance, along with heroin, which means it is considered to have a high potential for abuse.[30]

Many tribes in the United States began to use peyote in the late nineteenth century. The peyote religion, or Peyotism, became established when the U.S. government set up reservations. Peyotist beliefs sometimes combine Native American and Christian elements, and Peyotism has been described as "a religion of the oppressed . . . a response of a defeated people overwhelmed by waves of white settlers." The Native American Church (NAC), a pan-tribal institution, was formed in 1918 partly to facilitate the use of peyote as a sacrament. Members believed that ingesting peyote had physical and spiritual healing powers that would enable them to communicate with God and the spirit world. Eating the peyote cactus also created opportunities for social gatherings of various sorts, it promoted Native American political solidarity, and it provided an alternative to alcohol.[31]

Colonial authorities have consistently sought to abolish the sacramental use of peyote. When the Spaniards arrived in Mexico, they tried to do so. Since the nineteenth century, officials in the United States have also tried to prohibit its use. Anti-Peyotists argued not only that peyote would "shackle" Native Americans to an inferior position, but they also claimed that Peyotists participated in "all-night 'debaucheries.' " When efforts to lobby Congress for a ban failed, the political movement turned to state legislatures. Even though fifteen states enacted legal limits, few Indians were prosecuted because it was understood that state law did not apply to Indian reservations and that peyote was used for religious purposes; thus, the state laws were seldom enforced. Although Congress eventually authorized the use of peyote by the NAC through federal regulations, there have continued to be numerous controversies over its use.[32]

In litigation, although courts have been mostly reluctant to protect the right to sacramental use of peyote, there have been a few acquittals. Perhaps the most famous triumph was *People v. Woody* (1964), which addressed the question of whether the government interest in regulating dangerous drugs outweighs the right of indigenous peoples to the free exercise of religion. In this case the Navajo defendants were convicted of unauthorized possession of peyote at a non-jury trial and were given suspended sentences. The California Supreme Court acknowledged that peyote was a hallucinogen, and therefore subject to government regulation, but held that the California statute "most seriously infringes upon the observance of religion" without a sufficiently powerful countervailing state interest.[33] In weighing the relative harm to religion against the compelling state interest, Justice Matthew Tobriner eloquently concluded:

Since the use of peyote incorporates the essence of religious expression, the first weight is heavy. Yet the use of peyote presents only slight danger to the state and to the enforcement of its laws; the second weight is relatively light. The scale tips in favor of constitutional protection. . . . The varying currents of the subcultures that flow into the mainstream of our national life give it depth and beauty. We preserve a greater value than an ancient tradition when we protect the right of the Indians who honestly practiced an old religion in using peyote one night at a meeting in a desert hogan near Needles, California.[34]

Native Americans have also won the right to use peyote in the military. New military guidelines issued in 1997 were designed to allow peyote use by members of the NAC. The regulations require that they stop using it at least twenty-four hours before returning to active duty, notify their commanders afterward (and sometimes beforehand), and not carry it on military vehicles or bases.[35]

Sometimes religious institutions other than the NAC have sought the right to use peyote, usually by arguing for broadening the scope of application of the federal exemption. But the courts have rejected the proposition that other churches such as the Peyote Way Church of God, Inc., should be exempted from drug laws because the exemption for religious use of peyote by the NAC was a grandfather clause designed only for the NAC. In other cases, non–Native Americans who belonged to the NAC argued (unsuccessfully for the most part) that they should be entitled to the same rights as other members. Courts have been unwilling to expand the protection afforded by the federal exemption.[36]

Employment Division, Department of Human Resources of Oregon v. Smith (1990), one of the most important U.S. Supreme Court cases in recent years, revolved around the issue of peyote use. This case involved Alfred Smith and Galen Black, who were dismissed from their positions in a drug rehabilitation clinic when it became known that they ingested peyote in religious ceremonies.[37] After the state denied their request for unemployment compensation, they filed suit, alleging that the policy violated their right to the free exercise of religion. The Oregon Court of Appeals reversed the denial of employment benefits, relying on the federal exemption for sacramental wine used during Prohibition. The U.S. Supreme Court reversed, holding that the Free Exercise clause did not prevent Oregon from prohibiting peyote as a controlled substance.

The *Smith* decision altered the constitutional standard of review for evaluating free exercise claims.[38] Prior to *Smith,* a neutral law that affected a religious minority had to be justified by a compelling state interest. Justice Antonin Scalia's opinion for the majority discarded this standard, requiring only application of the so-called rational basis test. Part of his reasoning was that the notion that religious freedom merited the greatest protection was fallacious. It was based on a misunderstanding about earlier precedents; those cases involved at least one other fundamental right, which explains why religious liberty was protected. This "hybrid" analysis removed protection for litigants whose claims were predicated on religious freedom only.

The significance of *Smith* for the cultural defense is that it has become exceedingly difficult in the United States to challenge general laws that do not specifically target religious minorities. *Smith* is generally cited to support the proposition that "the right of free exercise does not relieve an individual of the obligation to comply with a valid and neutral criminal law of general applicability on the ground that it proscribes or requires conduct that is contrary to that individual's religious practice."[39]

Following the *Smith* decision, a coalition of religious organizations and civil liberties groups successfully lobbied Congress to reinstate the more protective standard. The Religious Freedom Restoration Act (RFRA) of 1993 only empowered religious minorities temporarily, as it was struck down by the U.S. Supreme Court in *City of Boerne v. Flores* (1997) because its passage violated separation of powers. Evidently, Congress lacks the power to dictate to the Supreme Court how best to interpret particular constitutional provisions.

Congress enacted the American Indian Religious Freedom Act Amendments in 1994 to ensure that Native Americans would be able to continue to use peyote in their religious ceremonies. This policy was intended to protect them from federal and state drug laws, but it did not prevent reasonable regulation and registration of peyote growers.[40]

Although members of the NAC may still use peyote in some jurisdictions, a Native American whose religion requires the use of a different drug has no right to use it. For example, in the unpublished case of *U.S. v. Carlson* (1992), Margaret Carlson appealed her convictions for possession and manufacturing of marijuana. Although the court allowed her to present evidence that she was an American Indian whose family was "involved with Yurok medicine and religious ceremonies" and that ceremonial use of the drug is "a central precept of the Yurok religion," the judge declined her request to instruct the jury that her religious use of marijuana was a complete defense to the drug charges. On appeal she claimed the refusal violated her right to the free exercise of religion. The Court of Appeals, relying on *Smith*, affirmed the lower court's decision, denying her claim. It also rejected her argument that the exemption for the NAC for sacramental use of peyote violated the Equal Protection and Establishment clauses. The NAC and the Yurok tribe were not considered to be "similarly situated," and the court emphasized the relatively greater risk associated with marijuana as compared with peyote.

The peyote litigation reveals at least two problems with the approach taken to regulating drugs used for religious purposes. The fact that the drug should be controlled is taken for granted by the authorities. In many cases the government's assertion that peyote is dangerous is presumed to be true, though no documentation is provided. The second difficulty with religious defenses is that it is hard to figure out which groups "traditionally" used peyote. To avoid this question, courts have simply inquired whether the defendant belonged to the NAC. As the exemption was designed only for Indians, non–Native Americans are not entitled to raise religious defenses. To settle this question, the court had to resort to the infamous blood quantum rule to decide whether the defendant could be considered a Native American. Needless to say, this approach is hardly satisfactory.

Finally, given that peyote appears to pose no threat,[41] particularly when it is typically used under carefully controlled circumstances, it is odd that it remains on the DEA list of Schedule I drugs. Native Americans may continue to use peyote to a limited extent through the existence of the federal exemption. The exception has given rise to claims of discrimination by other groups that seek to use illegal substances in their religious experience.

Another group that has clashed with legal authorities over the sacramental use of drugs are Rastafarians who use marijuana (or ganja) in their religious life. According to Barry Chevannes, "Ganja is considered a panacea." Timothy Taylor explains: "With the use of the 'holy herb,' Rastafarians seek spiritual unity and believe they experience the deity, Jah Raastafari." They cite passages in the Bible, including Psalms 104:14, to justify their use of the "herb." Rastafarians have faced constant threats from the legal order regarding their use of this drug. In fact, the main source of conflict between this religious minority and the police has been the smoking and possession of ganja.[42]

One of the difficulties for Rastafarians is establishing that their belief system constitutes a "religion" for purposes of legal protection. Because it is a relatively new religious movement that began in Jamaica only several decades ago, some have questioned whether it counts as a religion. Even when courts accept that it is a religion, they may nevertheless reject the proposition that they should allow sacramental use of drugs. Some predict that judicial attitudes will vary according to societal attitudes toward drug use in general.[43]

The question of whether Rastafarians' sacramental use of marijuana is protected by the principle of religious freedom has been considered in a few cases. In *Whyte v. U.S.* (1984) the court squarely addressed this question in the context of the Rastafarian religious practice. When police searched Lawrence Whyte's home, they found an envelope containing marijuana and a jar of marijuana seeds. The trial court ruled that the government interest in regulating marijuana outweighed the defendant's right to the free exercise of religion. The D.C. Court of Appeals agreed with this reasoning.[44]

In *U.S. v. Bauer* (1996) Rastafarians from Montana appealed their convictions of conspiracy to manufacture and distribute marijuana, distribution of marijuana, and simple possession. The court reversed the conviction for possession, noting that under the Religious Freedom Restoration Act of 1993 the defendants should have had the opportunity to raise a religious defense. The court left open the possibility that the government could justify prosecution because of its interest in universal enforcement of marijuana laws. With regard to the other convictions, the court affirmed, apparently unconvinced that the Rastafarian religion requires commercial marijuana establishments. If there could conceivably be a basis for using marijuana for religious purposes, the court avoids the question of how

Rastafarians can legitimately obtain it for this use. The court also mentioned but declined to analyze in depth whether or not the defendants were, in, fact, Rastafarians. With the demise of RFRA, the analysis in *Bauer* is less likely to influence other similar cases.[45]

In *State v. McBride* (1998), a case decided after the Religious Freedom Restoration Act was overturned, the Kansas Court of Appeals ruled that the trial court's rejection of a religious defense to criminal charges of cultivation of marijuana was correct. The defendants, Rastafarians for at least fifteen years, had numerous marijuana plants in their garden. The trial court was skeptical about whether their religion required that much marijuana: "Unless the McBrides could show that 86 plants were required to practice their religion, the issue of whether they were bona fide Rastafarians was moot." Even if the defendants could show that their cultivation of marijuana was supported by genuine religious tenets, and even if the law clearly burdened their free exercise of religion, the judge concluded that the public interest in regulating drugs took precedence.[46] They were convicted of cultivation and tax stamp violations, acquitted of drug paraphernalia charges, and sentenced to probation. In their appeal, the McBrides argued that the court abused its discretion by precluding the religious freedom defense. The Kansas Court of Appeals rejected this argument, largely because the U.S. Supreme Court struck down RFRA as unconstitutional because the standard reverted to the one established in *Smith,* according to which a state can pass a law of general application that burdens religious practice without running afoul of the First Amendment.

On appeal the McBrides advanced an argument based on equal protection and establishment ideas. Comparing their situation to NAC members who have exemptions, they argued that they should also be allowed to use a controlled substance in religious practices. The court interpreted the challenge as depending upon whether the Rastafarians were "similarly situated" to Native Americans. The court concluded that they were not for three reasons: (1) because they used marijuana much more frequently than Native Americans used peyote, (2) marijuana is more likely to lead to abuse than peyote, and (3) the federal government and Kansas enacted exemptions based on the federal trust responsibility. Other jurisdictions have also held that because Rastafarians and NAC members are not similarly situated, Rastafarians should not receive the exemption.[47]

In England judges have not been consistent in evaluating religious considerations during sentencing.[48] In *Rex v. Williams* (1979) the defendant, a Rastafarian from Jamaica, was caught attempting to smuggle marijuana into England in a false suitcase-bottom. Distinguishing the case from typical drug trafficking cases, the court explicitly explained its rationale for leniency:

> There are however some special circumstances relating to the appellant. He belongs to a sect in Jamaica called Rastafarians. There are persons in this country who profess whatever beliefs Rastafarians have. The court was informed and accepted, that Rastafarians make an extensive, and indeed spectacular use of cannabis [in] a form of religious rite.

... In those circumstances, the court is prepared to accept that this is not the ordinary case of commercial importation of cannabis.[49]

In the litigation concerning Rastafarian use of marijuana, it may turn out that judicial responses depend on the amount the defendants have in their possession. If they have only a small amount for their own use, they may receive more sympathy than will those who have large amounts that they intend to sell to others. For the most part, it seems unlikely that even those who sincerely follow Rastafarian tenets will be granted exemptions in the United States. As long as a "war on drugs" is a dominant part of the U.S. political agenda, the interest in regulating drugs will outweigh defendants' claims of religious freedom.

Marijuana is classified as a Schedule V substance in the law, meaning that it is among those substances with the lowest potential for abuse. Given its relative lack of dangerousness, there might be more room for accommodation with regard to this substance than for others considered in this chapter.[50]

Since RFRA was overturned, the status of religious defenses in the United States remains somewhat in question.[51] The ease with which defense counsel can invoke religious defenses may depend on the test used in constitutional cases. If the compelling interest test is restored for policies that burden religious practices, then, in theory, this should facilitate the use of religious defenses. The reality, however, is that even with heightened scrutiny, the state often persuades judges that it has a compelling interest to justify the policy with no less restrictive alternative to achieve the objective. In other countries the degree to which religious minorities vindicate their rights to the sacramental use of controlled substances may turn on the scope of protection afforded the constitutional right to religious liberty.

The question of whether the accommodation of one group—for example, the NAC—logically requires the accommodation of others deserves greater attention. It strikes one as arbitrary that only members of the NAC are entitled to use peyote, not other organizations such as the Church of Peyote or Native American individuals and not other religious minorities who seek to use other types of drugs. As long as there is no abuse of a substance and its use does not interfere with an individual's obligations, it is not obvious why the government should impose sanctions. The presumption that marijuana is more problematic than peyote may not be warranted. Even if it is true, there still might be some basis for reconsidering the enforcement of harsh drug laws that fail to take defendants' cultural and religious backgrounds into account.

Some may worry that expanding the list of substances which are permissible will be dangerous. The slippery slope argument may turn out to be based on false assessments of the degree of risk posed by the use of substances less well known to "mainstream" Americans.[52] Another concern may be that individuals will pretend to be members of religious organizations to evade drug laws, so that they may use drugs for recreational purposes. As with any law, there are those who will try to circumvent it. This argument does not justify the absolute refusal to consider more flexible policies.

RELATIONSHIPS: PRESSURES ON INDIVIDUALS INDUCE THEM TO PARTICIPATE IN DRUG OPERATIONS

In some of the cases involving drugs, individuals claim that they had no knowledge that they were carrying drugs. For example, in a Canadian case, *R. v. Mingma Tenzing Sherpa* (1986), the court held that although the accused, a Nepalese from the Sherpa people, knew he was smuggling, he did not realize he was carrying a narcotic: "The accused's cultural background did not make it overly unreasonable for the accused to fail to respond suspiciously when he was asked to carry the substance."[53] Expert testimony presented by anthropologist Sherry Ortner focused on the relationship with the friend, Wangdy (not a Sherpa), who had asked him to carry the package:

> Dr. Ortner's evidence is that the relationship is one which traditionally leads to duty and trust and I'm satisfied that trust would include faith that Wangdy would not ask the Defendant to do anything dangerous or harmful to others. The duty would carry with it the obligation to render unquestioning assistance to the other. I accept this to be the state of facts upon the evidence of Dr. Ortner and of the defendant himself.[54]

The court accepted the notion that smuggling is part of life in Nepal because border-crossing customs officials make bringing items across the border a bureaucratic nightmare. The judge seemed quite convinced that he was a naive villager who had little idea that he was carrying heroin, and so he acquitted him.[55]

In the United States, some Nepalese, arrested for bringing heroin into the country, have won reductions in their sentences based on a similar argument. For instance, in *U.S. v. Sherpa* (1996) a Pemba Rita Sherpa agreed to carry a suitcase from Thailand to the United States for Pujung Grun. Though he would be paid $6,000 for transporting the case, he testified that after he had tea at the man's home, in the presence of his wife, "he was sure that the man's intentions were honorable."[56] The trial judge considered the defendant a "relatively unsophisticated man . . . from a relatively unsophisticated culture." Sherpa had no prior involvement in the narcotics trade and did not know he was carrying heroin. The Court of Appeals affirmed the trial judge's conclusion that "Sherpa was culturally sheltered in such a way as to prevent his awareness of the questionable nature of his task." Although the trial judge was lenient in sentencing Sherpa, during the trial he denied the defendant's motion to present cultural evidence "concerning Sherpa's religious beliefs and Nepalese culture, including Buddhist beliefs in reincarnation and punishment for sinful acts, lack of knowledge of Western culture or of drug trafficking among the Nepalese and neighborly obligation in Sherpa culture." The expert would also have explained that the small spoon (a *naptul*) Sherpa was carrying was not for narcotics but was used for cleaning the ears. The appellate court found no abuse of discretion by the district court but commented that the information not heard by the jury may have influenced the judge in sentencing.

Technically, a "safety valve provision" in the federal sentencing guidelines permits a judge to "depart from the mandatory minimum sentence" if the defendant played a "minor" role in the offense and also made a good faith effort to cooperate with the government. In these cases the appellate courts affirm the decisions by lower courts to apply the safety valve.[57]

In *U.S. v. Vongsay* (1993), Todd Linh Vongsay arrived in Los Angeles International Airport with eight tubes of toothpaste and two rice cookers containing approximately 2200 grams of opium.[58] She testified she was asked to carry toothpaste tubes and rice cookers as gifts to the United States and that she did not realize they contained opium. Had she been allowed to present cultural evidence, the expert on Mien culture would have explained that delivering gifts for others is not only customary but that a request to do so is considered obligatory.

In another case an apprentice prosecuted for transporting drugs said he had no choice but to do what his master asked of him. In the unpublished case *U. S. v. Chau Hai Do* (1994) the apprentice was convicted of importation and possession with intent to distribute opium after he brought 2458 grams from Vietnam to the United States. The apprentice had only been told that he was carrying "Chinese medicine, placed in his suitcase by his 'master.' " The defense attorney tried to introduce evidence concerning the "master-apprentice relationship"—that it involves blind obedience and trust—and the tendency of Vietnamese immigrants to speak English whether or not they fully comprehend the conversation. During the trial, Judge Harry Hupp decided to exclude the cultural evidence. The issue on appeal was whether or not the district court had abused its discretion by refusing to allow expert testimony on the master-apprentice relationship and on the language issue. The Ninth Circuit Court of Appeals found no errors. Even though Do had no prior drug record or knowledge of precisely what he carried, he was, nevertheless, sentenced to a six-year prison term.[59]

Judge Hupp did not perceive a need for the introduction of evidence on the cultural background of the defendant because the issues in the case were narrower than what the expert would address. He said the testimony would not bear on "the precise issue . . . Mr. Do's knowledge and Mr. Do's state of mind."[60] The defense maintained that it is improper to exclude expert testimony that would corroborate the defendant's claim of lack of knowledge or intent. The crux of the argument was whether it was an abuse of discretion by the district court to exclude proffered testimony because of its "overbreadth."

In the United States, the Federal Rules of Evidence section 702 deals with expert testimony. The question is whether the expert has "specialized knowledge" that will help the jury understand the facts. According to the prosecution, even credible expert testimony may be inadmissible if irrelevant. The prosecution argued that the testimony had little bearing on the question of the defendant's knowledge, though it might be relevant to a duress or coercion defense. For whatever reason, the defense did not present either duress or coercion as a defense theory at the trial. It is plausible that the apprentice was not explicitly pressured to carry the "Chinese medicine"; rather, it may have been a subtle form of cultural pressure that stemmed from the type of relationship. This might have led Do not to request information about the substance, which relates directly to the question of knowledge.

The government convinced the court that the evidence on the "relationship" and on language ability had marginal relevance to the issues in the case at hand. The jury could effectively evaluate these matters on its own.[61] So the court failed to appreciate the cultural context of the apprentice's action. An American jury would have difficulty understanding why a man would agree to carry something known to be prohibited. Without knowing something about Vietnamese culture, it could not ascertain the validity of the claims. Even if the court admitted the evidence, it might not have affected the disposition of the case. In *Chau Hai Do* the defense did not argue duress or coercion, even though the prosecution seems to have thought this might have been a better strategy.

Based on the limited empirical data mentioned in the decisions discussed here, one cannot evaluate the veracity of the claim that it would have been inappropriate for the defendants to question those who asked the defendants to carry packages for them. Furthermore, it is not possible to determine from the court opinions whether or not the defendants were really unaware of what they were carrying or not.

A defendant sometimes argues that while he was aware he was involved in a drug operation, he felt obligated to help a fellow countryman or a person to whom he was indebted. In *U.S. v. Carbonell* (1990), Ruben Ceballos, a Colombian, with no prior history of drug activity, reluctantly agreed to drive an acquaintance to deliver drugs. The court lowered his sentence in light of the circumstances:

> While Ceballos' actions cannot be condoned, he did not act with what one would usually consider criminal intent. Ceballos was motivated wholly by a sense of *obligation* [my emphasis] toward a person from the same town as he, who was experiencing financial hardship in a foreign country. The cohesiveness of first generation immigrant communities in the United States engenders loyalty, responsibility and obligation to others in the community, even if they are strangers. It is these sentiments that prompted Ceballos' misguided behavior. . . . The court regrets the necessity of having to impose such a harsh punishment on a defendant who was motivated only by feelings of compassion for a person in need.[62]

Judge Jack Weinstein felt he had to impose punishment because of the importance of the "war on drugs."

People v. Manurasada (1985) is an entrapment case that involves a similar sense of obligation. A nineteen-year-old Thai man, Palrat Manurasada, was befriended by law enforcement officers. They helped him after a confrontation with other Thai individuals humiliated him, causing him to "lose face." When they obtained apologies from the individuals who had hurt him, Manurasada felt extremely indebted to the officers. Subsequently, after they put considerable pressure on him, he agreed to purchase fifteen pounds of marijuana for them. Though he had no prior record of involvement in drug trafficking or drug use, he was convicted of selling marijuana to undercover police officers. He was sentenced to three years in prison and three years probation. With the assistance of a new lawyer, Manurasada appealed his conviction.[63]

Although evidence about Thai culture was available, it was not presented during the trials as part of the entrapment defense.[64] The expert, Herbert Phillips, professor of cultural anthropology at the University of California, Berkeley, would have explained "how the concept of saving face affects Thais and how it differs from our concept . . . the importance of reciprocity to a Thai and the concept of 'bungkun,' or long-term obligation. Finally he would offer the opinion that Mr. Manurasada's conduct was consistent with and explicable by these cultural factors." The argument was that the Thai concepts of saving face and reciprocity motivated Manurasada to sell the drugs for his friends.

The question here is how to interpret "the normally law-abiding person" in this situation.[65] The basic notion is that "such a person would normally resist the temptation to commit a crime presented by the simple opportunity to act unlawfully." Manurasada's argument was that individuals brought up in different cultures react differently to police pressures, in light of their enculturation. His lawyer put it succinctly:

> Since persons brought up in two different cultures may be subjected to very different amounts of pressure arising from a single action by law enforcement officials (because of the differing significance of those acts as perceived from their respective cultures), the law should take cultural differences into account. To attain an equal application of the laws, the trier of fact must look through cultural lenses in deciding whether particular actions by law enforcement officers generate sufficient persuasion, pressure or cajolery to constitute entrapment.[66]

The gist of the argument was that the entrapment defense should be modified to consider how a normally law-abiding Thai would behave.

Unless courts are willing to consider the state of mind of the "normally law-abiding" citizen from the cultural group in question, it may prove difficult to introduce cultural considerations in entrapment defenses. Since it is usually necessary to admit the crime in order to argue entrapment, this method of raising a cultural defense may be of limited utility.

Sometimes women argue that they should not be punished as severely because in their culture women cannot refuse to do the bidding of their husbands or male relatives. In the British case, *R. v. Bibi* (1980), a Muslim widow, a forty-eight-year-old Kenyan Indian, who was living with her brother-in-law, was convicted of "being concerned in the fraudulent evasion of the prohibition on importation of a controlled drug [cannabis]" and sentenced to three years' imprisonment. In her appeal, she argued that the sentence was too severe because she had been

> well socialised into the Muslim traditions and as such has a role subservient to any male figures around her. . . . Because she has assumed the traditional role of her culture any involvement in these offences is likely to be the result of being told what to do and the learned need to comply.[67]

The court was persuaded by this line of argument, quashed her three-year sentence, and substituted a term of six-months' imprisonment. Sebastian Poulter comments that the court substantially reduced her prison sentence "once it became clear that she had been so completely socially isolated through the doctrine of purdah and so dependent upon her brother-in-law, who had organized the import of the drugs, that she bore little moral responsibility for the offense."[68]

In *U.S. v. Ezeiruaku and Akiagba* (1995) a similar argument failed to convince a district court in New Jersey. Mildred Akiagba and Vincent Ezeiruaku were prosecuted for running a heroin operation. Initially, Akiagba tried to present expert testimony on Ibo culture and on the battered woman syndrome as part of an argument that her estranged husband, Okuzu, had coerced her to sell heroin. The court denied the motion to introduce expert testimony of this kind, and she subsequently pled guilty to the crimes with which she was charged. Akiaga sought a downward departure of her sentence because she was a "minimal" or "minor" participant in the drug operation and because of duress.[69]

The gist of Akiaga's position was that she had been subjected to physical and psychological abuse at the hands of her husband, Okuzu. Because of this, she suffered from the battered woman syndrome and post-traumatic stress disorder. She claimed that she believed Okuzu would kill her if she disobeyed him. This explanation was buttressed by testimony from the cultural expert, Dr. Okechukwu Ugorji, who said that "within Igbo culture, the man plays the dominating role, and the Igbo marital relationship often contains physical abuse of the wife and forced sex."[70]

Although she tried to present the image of being a submissive wife controlled by her husband, the court rejected this characterization:

> By the age of 25, she had defied both her father and her cultural upbringing by becoming pregnant out of wedlock, had moved to a foreign country with her first husband, defied that husband and moved out on her own, obtained a job, and then remarried, and defied that husband by having an affair. These are hardly the earmarks of a dependent and easily manipulated woman.

The court also commented that the expert witnesses had only "theoretical knowledge" and were seemingly unfamiliar with Akiagba's situation. Perhaps most significantly, her drug activities began after she started her relationship with Ezeiruaku, which made it unlikely that her husband, Okuzu, coerced her into selling drugs. Moreover, the court explicitly rejected the proposition that women from patriarchal societies can invoke culture to mitigate sentences:

> Finally, we find Akiagba's argument based on her cultural upbringing unconvincing. . . . Almost any non-Western culture, and many Western cultures, may be characterized as one where women are traditionally subservient to men. We do not believe that women from such cultures are less blameworthy for sentencing purposes than other defendants, male or female, absent proof that a particular defendant was exploited or coerced to par-

ticipate in the commission of a crime. We hold that Akiagba has not proven such exploitation or coercion by a preponderance of the evidence.[71]

The court rejected the argument largely because of the absence of proof regarding coercion and duress. This seems to leave open the possibility that such an argument might be effective in U.S. courts under the correct circumstances.[72]

Even if courts are willing to consider cultural factors, they may think the prohibition against considering national origin precludes this. This was the issue, for example, in *U.S. v. Natal-Rivera* (1989), where the defendant challenged the constitutional validity of the guidelines because they prevented the trial court from taking her Puerto Rican heritage into account. The trial court erred by not considering "the fact that her Puerto Rican heritage socialized her since childhood to follow her husband's every command." The appeals court rejected her argument that this violated due process partly because "historically, a difference in cultural background has consistently been rejected as an excuse for criminal activity."[73]

Although this issue has not yet been resolved by the U.S. Supreme Court, some courts have concluded that national origin is not the same as culture. If this interpretation is followed, then when cultural factors are relevant, courts are not prohibited by the sentencing guidelines from considering them. This position remains extremely unpopular, with even those in support of the consideration of cultural factors at sentencing arguing for it under extremely limited circumstances.[74]

Fear of Police

Defendants sometimes claim that their different experience with police in their countries of origin should be taken into account in the United States. They argue that they come from societies in which deference to authority figures is required. This leads them to comply with requests by law enforcement to allow searches or to answer questions. In some cases they claim that their consent to searches or questioning was involuntary because they did not really believe that they could refuse. Consequently, they contend that the physical evidence and statements should be excluded from the trial because they were obtained illegally.[75] At least in the United States "the government bears the burden of establishing that consent to search was freely and voluntarily given." These cases raise the important question of whether cultural factors should influence the interpretation of standards in criminal procedure. These issues are of particular significance in narcotics cases.[76]

U.S. v. Zapata (1992, 1993) exemplifies the issue well. The defendant, Jorge Zapata, was in a public compartment on an Amtrak train with his wife and infant son en route from Los Angeles to Chicago. When DEA Special Agent Kevin Small boarded the train in Albuquerque, identified himself as a police officer, blocked Zapata's egress from his seat, and asked if he could search Zapata's bags, Zapata seemed to agree. Zapata stood up, took down the bags, and opened them. Inside Agent Small and his assistant found several kilograms of cocaine. When Zapata was prosecuted for possession with intent to distribute cocaine, Zapata argued that the initial encounter between himself and the narcotics agent was "an involuntary and non-consensual seizure" in violation of the Fourth Amendment. His attorney argued that because of his Mexican background, he had a different perception of the police. "He believed that police in Mexico strike or hit people if they don't answer their questions." Not only was he intimidated by law enforcement, but he had only been in the United States for a few years and was not fluent in English. Because his consent to search was not voluntary, he argued that the "fruits" or evidence obtained from it should be excluded from the trial.[77]

District court judge Santiago Campos granted Zapata's motion to suppress the physical evidence and statements:

> Because of his upbringing in Mexico, Defendant believed that he must acquiesce to all police requests because failure to do so could result in dire consequences, including physical harm.
>
> A reasonable person in these circumstances with Defendant's background would not have felt free to ignore Agent Small's presence, to decline Agent Small's requests, or to otherwise terminate the encounter and go about his business. When Agent Small began to question Defendant, the Defendant reasonably believed that he was not free to leave or to refuse to answer questions. Defendant reasonably believed that he was required to produce his ticket and identification and to allow the agent to search his luggage.
>
> Under the circumstances of this case, Defendant reasonably felt intimidated by the presence of the officers, and reasonably interpreted Agent Small's "requests" as commands or demands.[78]

The appellate court strongly disagreed with the lower court's analysis. It thought the objective reasonable person test had to be applied, meaning that Zapata's "own subjective attitudes toward the police encounter . . . are irrelevant." It reversed the trial court, saying it had erred by taking his background into account. The encounter was not a seizure as a reasonable person would have felt "free to decline the officers' requests or otherwise terminate the encounter."[79] The appellate court also emphasized the absence of any physical coercion on the part of the agents. The court concluded:

> Because we hold that the encounter between the officers and Mr. Zapata was consensual, and did not constitute a seizure in violation of the Fourth Amendment, and because we hold that Mr. Zapata voluntarily consented to the search of his luggage, we reverse the district court's grant of the motion to suppress.

Among the objections that might be raised to shifting to a culturally specific reasonable person test in this context is that it would impede police investigations. The police could not determine in advance whether their conduct would violate the constitutional standards if it were to depend on the subjective perceptions of others. Another possible criticism is that the new standard might promote stereotypes: it might create a presumption that anyone from Mexico could not conceivably consent to a search.[80]

The chief difficulty with this line of argument is that it relies on the illusion of "objective" reasonableness. Naturally, individuals who have grown up in other countries have widely divergent views of the police.[81] Those who have experienced the terror of death squads are bound to react differently to law enforcement officers than those who have been raised in the United States. As in other areas of law, this steadfast adherence to the so-called objective reasonable person test ignores the reality of many peoples' experiences.

Execution of Westerners

While some may remain unconvinced that immigrant drug couriers and users should raise cultural defenses, they may feel differently about the plight of Westerners caught with drugs in other countries. In Malaysia and Singapore, for instance, the law requires that those convicted of drug trafficking receive a whipping and the death penalty, whether natives or foreigners. When Westerners are caught with heroin or marijuana, their embassies and families try, usually to no avail, to intervene to prevent the imposition of capital punishment. Should the cultural defense be established as a valid policy, it would benefit not only minorities in Western countries, but also Westerners who are abroad.[82]

Although there is little question that trafficking in illicit drugs is considered a crime in many nations, the relative severity of punishment imposed for transgression varies. It is quite unlikely that those who violate the law are unaware of the policies in Malaysia and Singapore because customs officials distribute forms marked with the penalties. Nevertheless, given that all justice systems do not afford adequate due process and that the death penalty is irreversible, in this context it would be desirable to take the defendants' cultural background into account to mitigate the punishment at least from death to life imprisonment. Another way to handle the situation would be to extradite the individuals to their countries of origin to stand trial there.[83]

RELATIVE MERITS OF PROSECUTING
DEFENDANTS IN DRUG CASES

In this chapter I have shown the ways in which cultural arguments are put forward in cases involving defendants caught with drugs traditionally used in the societies from which they came. In essence, their contention is that "every society has its own forms of chemical escape." Defendants also point out the benefits of substance use, one of which is that it often promotes a sense of community. Furthermore, the substances in question have traditionally been used in moderation as societies have their own internal restraints on excessive use of drugs.[84]

Nevertheless, the use of powerful substances, which are imbued with symbolic meanings, will inevitably be controversial, outside a "medical" context. Even drugs for medicinal purposes may be suspect when used by minority groups. While excessive dependence on any substance may be problematic, one must guard against the tendency to assume that unknown substances are automatically harmful, no matter how they are used. More information is needed to ascertain the degree of harm associated with each substance.[85]

Even if drug regulation is necessary, some of the arbitrary distinctions drawn among different substances merit reconsideration. Why is caffeine allowed, when khat is not? Why is alcohol legal, when kava apparently is not? Considering the vast number of people involved in alcohol-related fatalities, it might make more sense to regulate alcohol use more stringently rather than substances with less devastating effects.

I have tried to demonstrate the lack of cross-cultural understanding about drug practices in the cases discussed. In some instances, however, it was not possible to determine whether the cultural claim was true, especially in some of the "relationship" cases. In those cases when individuals were truly unaware that the substances were illegal, a more humane approach might be desirable.

When the danger associated with an herb is beyond question, so that regulation is necessary, it is not obvious that those who violate drug policies should be subject to penal sanctions. As Virginia Berridge argues, there are other models that are less punitive and which do not create a backlash or black market.[86]

Ultimately, the question is whether the resources necessary to try to eliminate drug use are justified. To the extent that drug crimes are deemed "victimless" crimes, there is less reason for society to intervene. Punishing those in possession of illicit substances takes its toll. The coercive effects of this type of social control should give one pause.[87] If the limiting principle for determining when to allow or disallow cultural traditions is irreparable harm, then unless societies are prepared to punish harm to self, for the most part, intervention cannot be justified.

6

Animals

The treatment of animals represents a classic example of the manner in which enculturation affects moral intuitions. For instance, in some societies cows are sacred and may not be eaten, whereas in other societies beef is a popular food. One's sense of which animals may be eaten and which are not to be eaten is a reflection of one's enculturation. It is crucial to acknowledge that the consumption of certain foods can be symbolic of membership in a "civilized" or "uncivilized" group. The uses of animals generally reflect this type of evolutionary, dichotomous thinking. There is no question that animal metaphors relate to group identity. Quite often, because an animal is the totem of a group, members do not eat it. Certainly, one should be attentive to the symbolic aspects of the animal disputes. In general, there is a tendency to personify animals—to ascribe human characteristics to them—and this provides a justification for giving them legal protection. The main question considered in this chapter is what practices constitute cruelty to animals. Although many traditions disallow cruelty to animals, what constitutes cruelty varies from one society to the next.[1]

In this chapter I discuss a wide range of cultural clashes about animals, which raise such questions as which ones may be eaten, how they may be killed, for what purposes they may be slaughtered, and when they may be hunted. These examples should suffice to demonstrate a pervasive bias against ethnic minorities and indigenous peoples in their uses of animals. Although many uses of animals are arguably inhumane, the fact that the dominant legal system focuses on practices by marginalized groups reflects ethnocentrism.[2] The legal question is how much punishment ethnic minorities deserve when they treat animals differently from what the mainstream considers appropriate. The culpability may depend on knowledge that the act was forbidden. In some instances, the newly arrived may be unaware that the manner in which they treat animals is unacceptable.[3]

In these cases, how ought one to weigh the human right to culture against animal rights? In the past, animals were treated as legal beings: they were held responsible for criminal acts and were even placed on trial.[4] If animals have duties under the law, it is certainly worth considering whether they have any rights. What is peculiar in the present context is that there seems to be a common presumption that the protection of animals trumps the right to culture. This is odd, considering that few defend the proposition that animals have rights.[5] The question remains, then, why the dominant culture reacts so strongly to what it considers mistreatment of animals. It appears that humans personify animals so much that they regard particular ones as members of the family. In some instances this will account for the visceral reaction by those in the "mainstream" to some uses of animals.

USE OF ANIMALS IN RELIGIOUS CEREMONIES

In numerous cases groups clash with the dominant legal system when they seek to use animals required for religious ceremonies. When prosecuted for violating the law, they attempt to invoke religious defenses. That it is extremely difficult to raise a cultural defense through a religious freedom defense is evident in the Canadian Supreme Court case of *Jack and Charlie v. the Queen* (1985). Two members of the Coast Salish Indian people were charged with violating a provincial Wildlife Act by hunting and killing a deer out of season.[6] The reason for the hunt was the need to burn deer meat as part of a religious ceremony. An anthropologist explained the significance of the practice to the court:

> This is a very ancient traditional practice among all Coast Salish people and the essence of the ceremony is to provide food for deceased relatives by burning it and the essence of the food, as I understand it, is transmitted through the smoke to the essence of the deceased person.[7]

Failure to burn deer meat as is required may result in some form of divine retribution.[8]

The court dismissed the appeal for two reasons. The first was that "the prohibition of hunting deer out of season by the Wildlife Act does not raise a question of religious freedom or aboriginal religion." The peculiar reasoning was that the killing of the deer was not itself part of the religious ceremony and that the Indians should have foreseen their religious need for deer meat and have frozen some for that purpose. Second, the court objected to the idea that the reason the defendants had violated the law should be deemed germane to the determination of their culpability. The court agreed with the Crown that "the intention of the Appellants that the deer meat be used for the burning ceremony was their 'ultimate intention' or 'motive.' As such, it is irrelevant to legal responsibility for the commission of the offence."[9]

Jack and Charlie v. the Queen shows how courts can manipulate the interpretation of religious freedom so that its scope is quite narrow. This case also suggests that some courts remain opposed to the idea that motive is relevant to the assessment of blameworthiness.[10]

In the preceding example, the question involved weighing the state interest in wildlife management against the religious rights of the Native Americans. The balance is much more delicate if the animals involved belong to an endangered species. In many cases, Native Americans are prosecuted for hunting eagles because they need to use their feathers in religious ceremonies. The conflicts occurred after the U.S. government enacted laws protecting some types of eagle because their numbers had diminished and because of the bird's importance as a national symbol. Courts were divided over the validity of a treaty rights defense—that is, that Indians had a nineteenth-century treaty right to hunt and fish on their reservations. The crux of the issue was whether congressional legislation protecting eagles as endangered species abrogated earlier treaty rights. Some commentators assumed that Congress had the power to abrogate, but only if Congress made its intention to do so explicit.[11]

The Supreme Court decided to hear *U.S. v. Dion* (1985), a case concerning the taking of eagles and the treaty rights defense. In district court, Dwight Dion Sr., a member of the Yankton Sioux, was convicted of shooting four bald eagles and of selling eagle carcasses and parts in violation of the Bald Eagle Protection Act (Eagle Protection Act) and Migratory Bird Treaty.[12] The federal appellate court reversed the shooting convictions. The Supreme Court, in turn, reversed the appellate court's decision and let all of Dion's convictions stand.

The central question was whether the Eagle Protection Act and the Endangered Species Act violated the treaty right of Yankton Sioux to hunt bald and golden eagles on their reservation for noncommercial purposes.[13] The 1858 treaty clearly authorized the Yankton to hunt on their own reservation and placed no limits on the hunting rights. While the court acknowledged such rights, it considered them subject to congressional revision:

> As a general rule, Indians enjoy exclusive treaty rights to hunt and fish on lands reserved to them, unless such rights were clearly relinquished by treaty or have been modified by Congress. . . . Those treaty rights, however, little avail Dion if, as the Solicitor General argues, they were subsequently abrogated by Congress. We find that they were.[14]

The court required that Congress's intent to abrogate a treaty be "clear and plain," and thought that in the case of the Eagle Protection Act that it was. Because Congress included in the law a provision allowing the taking of eagles for religious purposes by Indians, the court inferred that Congress must have intended the law to ban, in other circumstances, the shooting of eagles. Furthermore, the court denied that the law was biased against all Indians, as only "individual Indians who are authentic, bona fide practitioners of such religion" would be issued permits to hunt eagles.[15]

Some critics think that the court failed to adhere to its own policy because it interpreted congressional silence as an intention to abrogate Indian treaty rights.[16] The *Dion* case shows the ease with which the U.S. government derogates from its obligations under treaties negotiated in good faith with Indian peoples. It also shows a paternalistic attitude insofar as exceptions will be made to "real Indians" provided they use them for religious and not for commercial purposes. Considering that capitalism is the American way of life, it is odd that despite pressure to force assimilation, Indians are actually punished for adapting to the commercial way of life. As long as they remain "traditional," then they may get a few feathers.

In general, public policy in the United States prohibits the taking of eagles under all but the most narrowly circumscribed conditions. It is extraordinarily difficult for Native Americans to receive permission from the government to take eagles as the relevant laws fail to provide an exemption for religious use. Although the Eagle Protection Act makes some provision for religious use, it requires navigating an involved permit system. According to the Eagle Protection Act, the director of the Fish and Wildlife Service must issue a permit for any person who plans to take an eagle, alive or dead.[17] Although Native Americans have tried to comply with the system, sometimes the system has proved to be too cumbersome, forcing them to choose between adhering to U.S. law and following their own religious law.

Because some Native Americans continue to require eagle feathers for use in ceremonies, the U.S. government has tried to formulate a policy which would be a compromise. On April 29, 1994, at a meeting with more than three hundred American Indian leaders, as a military band played "Hail to the Chief" in the background, President Bill Clinton issued an executive memorandum on the distribution of eagle feathers for Native American religious purposes.[18] The memorandum ordered the establishment of a National Eagle Repository. The idea was to salvage eagles which were found dead from natural causes, harvest their feathers, and then dole out the feathers to Indians.

While this effort to facilitate the collection and distribution of eagle fathers was well intentioned, policymakers did not consider the possibility that the process of hunting the eagle is an important part of the ritual. Merely obtaining eagle feathers from a store is not always sufficient from the Indian point of view. Furthermore, having to submit a request to the government is considered demeaning. Many Native Americans regard the permit system "an unreasonable imposition of 'white tape.'"[19] Basing their argument on their status as sovereign nations, some contend that their own tribal governments should act as eagle repositories and distribute the feathers themselves.

From the repository's point of view, a major problem has been scarcity. In 1996 with approximately nine hundred birds at their disposal, the repository received three thousand requests for birds. Partly because of the shortage, there continues to be a thriving illegal market.[20]

A major flaw with the permit system has been the length of time it takes before the bird finally arrives. This presents a serious problem if a ceremony must take place immediately. When the birds are finally delivered, they may be in "deplorable shape"—with broken tail or wing feathers, with missing or burnt parts; on occasion, it is the wrong type of bird altogether.[21]

When Frank and William Hugs were prosecuted for killing eagles without permits, they emphasized the bureaucratic problems with the permit system. They tried to raise a religious defense, but the district court refused, telling the jury that "it is no defense to the charges against the defendants that they took or purchased or sold the eagles, eagle feathers or eagle parts for religious purposes without a permit. In other words, Native Americans cannot legally kill, sell, or purchase eagles, eagle feathers or eagle parts without a permit." Because the law contained no exception for religious use without a permit and because there was no less restrictive alternative to achieve the compelling interest of protecting eagles, the court of appeals affirmed in a per curiam decision.[22]

A philosophical objection to the permit system is that it places a disproportionate share of the burden for environmental protection on the shoulders of Native Americans. The fact that few non–Native Americans are prosecuted for illegal possession of eagle feathers is another indication of discrimination. In future eagle feather litigation, arguments like these might form the basis of equal protection claims.

In some cases, courts are willing to entertain religious defenses but require that the tradition is "central" to the way of life in order to rule in favor of the cultural community. The *Billie* (1986, 1987) panther litigation, which also involved the abrogation of Indian treaty rights, exemplifies this judicial practice. James Billie, a Seminole Indian and chairman of the tribe, was charged with violating a Florida law after he hunted a panther on the Big Cypress Seminole Indian Reservation, which he claimed was necessary for a religious healing ceremony. The Florida panther, or *Felis concolor coryi*, is a subspecies of the panther on the list of endangered species. The first *Billie* decision by the Florida Court of Appeal held that state law could protect endangered species more than federal law and therefore that it was permissible for the state to prosecute Billie under the law. Although Seminole Indians had a right to hunt on their reservations, that right could be limited to protect a species, as held in *Dion*.[23] The court effectively avoided analyzing the religious defense because its decision focused on whether Billie could be prosecuted, rather than on the proper defenses that might be raised at trial, but it strongly implied it would reject a religious defense.

Subsequently, Florida commenced prosecution of Billie in federal district court for violating the Endangered Species Act. The federal district court noted that Indian treaty rights to hunt " do not extend to the point of extinction." In response to Billie's request that the court clarify the requisite mens rea to sustain a conviction, the court concluded the government need only prove the defendant acted with general intent.[24] Most important was the court's treatment of the religious freedom argument. The court rejected his religious defense because it concluded that the use of panther was not central to the religion and that the state interest in preserving panthers outweighed his right to religion:

In this case, Billie has not adequately shown that the possession of panther parts is regular and material to any important religious ceremony or ritual. Although there was testimony that panther parts are important to healing, after having viewed the witnesses, the court is not convinced that panther parts are critical or essential.[25]

Although panther parts might be "preferable," they were not "indispensable."

As is often the case, the court of the dominant culture makes a determination as to whether or not something is "indispensable" to the minority group's religion. From the group's point of view, this is patronizing. Of course, even the requirement itself that something be "indispensable" is a value judgment. One might argue that even preferred practices should be protected under the right to religious freedom.

It would have been far better if the court had acknowledged the religious significance of the panther parts, and then discussed an appropriate compromise. Obviously, if panthers are important to Seminole religion, they would not want the species to become extinct. The court might have suggested the establishment of a breeding program on the Seminole reservation to increase the panther population.[26]

Even where animals are not subject to wildlife conservation or endangered species policies, conflicts arise. Some cases involve the ritual sacrifice of ordinary animals during religious ceremonies. In a case in Fresno, California, a Hmong shaman had tried the usual offerings—burning paper money, sacrificing a chicken and pig—and even Western medical techniques, but his wife remained very ill. In desperation, Chia Thai Moua decided to sacrifice a three-month-old German shepherd because the dog's night vision and keen sense of smell enabled him to track down spirits.[27] A neighbor called the police. When Moua pleaded no contest to felony animal cruelty, he explained his action in this way:

We burned the paper money. We did the chicken and the pig. But still my wife gets no better. What was I to do? I am a shaman, and this is what we believe. So I bought this dog for $5 and did the ceremony right here. . . . We are not cruel to animals. We love them. Everything I kill will be born again.[28]

The judge did not allow him to raise a religious freedom defense. The Hmong community, upset by the prosecution, urged him to appeal the judge's decision disallowing the religious freedom defense. The community seemed to have interpreted the judge's decision as an assault on their culture. In the end, Moua received probation, community service, and a small fine.[29]

The U.S. Supreme Court considered the Santería practice of ritual animal sacrifice in the landmark case, *Church of Lukumi Babalu Aye v. City of Hialeah* (1993). The Santería religion is considered a New World African-based syncretic religion consisting of parts of traditional African religion (orisha worship of the Yoruba of Nigeria), Kardecan spiritism (which originated in France and spread through the Caribbean and South America), and aspects of Spanish folk Catholicism.[30] In Cuba the worship of orishas led to an adaptation, worshiping them through the iconography of Catholic saints. Many Yoruba were taken as slaves to Cuba where they practiced their religion in secret, and the ritual sacrifice of chickens, goats, sheep, and other animals often occurred inside buildings. The arrival of Santería in the United States apparently begin in the mid-1940s, although most emigrants left Cuba after 1959. Although Santería practitioners have settled throughout the United States, including New York City and Los Angeles, most live in Florida. At the time of the controversy, approximately 50,000 Santería practitioners from Cuba had settled in South Florida.[31]

One main purpose of the Santería ritual sacrifice of animals is to obtain blood for the orishas. According to Joseph Brandon, only priests can sacrifice the animal victims, and the saints then drink the blood through sacrificial objects. The specific animal to be sacrificed varies from deity to deity, as does the method of sacrifice (there are four, depending on the type of animal involved). In most cases the sacrificial animals are cooked and eaten after the ceremonies. The rituals continue because, according to Brandon, they facilitate cultural adaptation. When the rituals are performed, particularly outside in public places—for example, in city parks—government officials may intervene.[32] Consequently, priests often have little choice but to sacrifice the animals in their homes.

With the influx of Santería practitioners, residents of Hialeah began to complain about the carcasses of ducks, chickens, and goats that were strewn on sidewalks, in cemeteries, and in rivers in South Florida. Because the animal debris and the idea of the Santería rituals were disquieting to Hialeah residents, the city council held an emergency public session in June of 1987. The city council adopted ordinances prohibiting their practices. The policy was based on four rationales: the protection of public health, preventing emotional injury to children who witness the sacrifices, avoiding cruel and unnecessary killing of animals, and restricting slaughter of animals to areas zoned for slaughterhouses. The Church of the Lukumi Babalu Aye, Inc., filed suit, alleging violations of the Free Exercise clause and arguing that the ritual sacrifice of animals was integral to their religion.[33]

The district court found no violation of the Free Exercise of Religion clause. As the ordinances did not target religion on their face, the effect on Santería practitioners was "incidental" to their secular purpose and effect. The court proceeded to balance what it considered four compelling governmental interests against religious freedom. Based on this analysis, the district court concluded that the laws "fully justify the absolute prohibition on ritual slaughter." The Court of Appeals for the Eleventh Circuit affirmed in a one-paragraph per curiam decision.[34]

The Supreme Court ruled unanimously that Hialeah could not ban the ritual sacrifice of animals.[35] Though the city argued its law was neutral, the Court thought it was clear that the ordinances had as their objective the suppression of religion. The Supreme Court insisted that the determination of whether a policy targeted a religious minority did not end with an analysis of the text of the laws in question: "Official action that targets religious conduct for distinctive treatment cannot be shielded by mere compliance with the requirement of facial neutrality." The Court concluded that: "the record in the case compels the conclusion that suppression of the central element of the Santeria worship service was the object of the ordinances." Furthermore, the Court noted that the legitimate government interests in protecting public health and preventing cruelty to animals could be achieved by policies "far short of a flat prohibition of all Santeria sacrificial practice." The city could simply require proper disposal of organic garbage.

The Court found several of Hialeah's claims unpersuasive. First, the Court was struck by the arbitrary interpretation of "unnecessary" killing, which resulted in a double standard. While sacrificial killing of animals was "unnecessary," the city apparently did not consider other secular killings of animals unnecessary, such as "hunting, slaughter of animals for food, eradication of insects and pests and euthanasia." Second, the Court was not convinced that the method of killing animals used by the Santería religion was inhumane. If there was concern about the technique, however, it could be handled by a slaughter law that would not be based on a religious classification.

The Supreme Court struck down the ordinance because it was not neutral or of general application, and the governmental interests asserted were not compelling so as to justify the targeting of religious activity.[36] Since the ordinances were neither neutral nor of general application, the Court applied strict scrutiny and concluded that the "ordinances cannot withstand this scrutiny."

The decision was not widely supported. The Humane Society of the United States condemned the ruling for sanctioning animal cruelty. Some religious organizations also questioned the merits of the opinion. Those sympathetic to animal rights arguments were naturally displeased. In Miami, a Santería priest and president of International Yoruba Rights, Rigoberto Zamora, was charged with cruelty to animals for fifteen animal sacrifices. He was prosecuted for a public sacrifice on June 26, 1993, which was supposed to be a celebration of the *Lukumi* decision handed down two weeks earlier. Prosecutors denied that religious freedom was at stake, claiming the case was about torturing animals.[37]

Other attempts to outlaw Santería practices demonstrate its unpopularity in the United States.[38] Critics of these policies often point out the hypocrisy of disallowing animal sacrifice but allowing Kentucky Fried Chicken to use so many chickens. After all, from the chicken's point of view, participating in a religious ceremony is more dignified than winding up in a bucket of fried chicken!

Although some laws in the United States forbid ritual sacrifice, they generally permit ritual slaughter. The United States, like other governments, permits religious minorities to kill animals in accordance with their religious beliefs, so that they will be able to eat the meat. In the United States, some policies provide exemptions from animal welfare laws to permit Jewish individuals to slaughter animals in order to obtain kosher meat.[39] England has authorized exemptions from the 1974 Slaughterhouses Act for Muslim and Jewish slaughter because they are based on clearly delineated religious principles. The two religious techniques, *halal* and *shechita*, respectively, are not wholly uncontroversial, though. The Royal Society for the Prevention of Cruelty to Animals has attacked the ritual slaughter methods as involving greater cruelty than ordinary methods. As it is not possible to prove which techniques are more or less painful, some (for example, Sebastian Poulter) argue that religious minorities should be permitted to use their techniques. However, in cases where the killing can be shown to involve cruelty, the courts may impose sanctions.[40]

In Western Europe there has been considerable debate about ritual slaughter. In the Netherlands, the Jewish community had managed to secure the right to do this, and the Muslim community asked for the same privilege. The Muslims faced two particular questions: (1) whether they could use meat slaughtered by Christian and Jewish butchers and (2) whether stunning animals before slaughtering them was consistent with Islamic precepts. Although the Dutch government was reluctant to allow ritual slaughter by Muslims, it began to allow it in 1975, in part because of pressure from the large influx of Muslims to Holland. Legislation was formally adopted in 1977, permitting Muslims to slaughter animals ritually, but only in government-designated public slaughterhouses. The matter was not altogether settled, however, as animal protection organizations mobilized to try to reverse the policy with some help from right-wing extremists. Despite considerable opposition, ritual slaughter gradually became "a widespread (though not generally accepted) phenomenon in the Netherlands."[41]

In France a dispute over who was empowered to perform ritual slaughter eventually led to a ruling by the European Court of Human Rights. The controversy began when an ultra-Orthodox Jewish organization, Cha'are Shalom Ve Tsedek, was denied access to slaughterhouses to perform ritual slaughter because France had empowered only the Joint Rabbinical Committee of the Jewish Consistorial Association of Paris (ACIP) to authorize slaughterers; France considered the ACIP to be the main representative of the French Jewish community. After losing domestic challenges to the policy, Cha'are Shalom Ve Tsedek filed an application against France with the European Commission of Human Rights, alleging religious discrimination in violation of Articles 9 and 14 of the European Convention for the Protection of Human Rights and Fundamental Freedoms.[42]

The gist of the case was that although France permitted ritual slaughter by one organization, Cha'are Shalom Ve Tsedek claimed a violation of religion freedom because it did not consider the ACIP to be representative of its interests and therefore wanted to have its own ritual slaughterers:

> What the Jews who belonged to the applicant association were asserting was the right not to consume meat if they could not be certain—because it was not from animals slaughtered and, above all, examined by their own ritual slaughterers—that it was perfectly pure, or "glatt."[43]

To be sure that the kosher meat was "glatt," members of the organization claimed that they had to either slaughter animals illegally or obtain supplies from Belgium. France's main contention was that there is a general interest in avoiding unregulated ritual slaughter unsupervised by public authorities. France also questioned whether

Cha'are Shalom Ve Tsedek should be considered a religious organization, as France considered it primarily commercial in character. The fact that it was a relatively small organization seems to have been an influential factor as well.[44]

After the European Commission on Human Rights concluded, by a vote of fourteen to three, that there had been a violation of Article 9 taken together with Article 14, France appealed to the European Court of Human Rights. Although the European Court of Human Rights thought ritual slaughter was protected under religious freedom, it accepted France's argument that there was a benefit in avoiding unregulated slaughter. In the end, the court found no violation of religious freedom largely because it was not impossible for ultra-Orthodox Jews to find "glatt" meat; it was available in some places in France and in Belgium. The court also failed to see the significance of any difference in techniques used by the ACIP and the applicant: "The only difference is the thoroughness of the examination of the slaughtered animals' lungs after death."[45]

The court explicitly said that the great majority of Jews accept the ACIP kosher certification system. The implication is that the dominant part of the minority should speak for the rest of the minority: that religious pluralism includes pluralism within a single religious tradition. This controversy exemplifies well the concern of those who worry about oversimplifying religious practices. Obviously, divergent practices exist within the same group. Despite the variation with the group, however, one can say that ritual slaughter is part of Jewish customary law. Perhaps the real problem is that the dominant legal system decides which group to designate as the spokesperson for the minority group.

Since many cultural claims have no underlying religious basis, a religious freedom defense alone will not address the concerns of many cultural defendants. In some of the cases discussed, the right of immigrants to their traditions could not be framed in terms of religious freedom. Even where ethnic minorities and indigenous people have advanced arguments based on religion, they have encountered biases: their traditions are not considered religious, the practice is not deemed central or indispensable to the religion, or the government interest based on the values of the dominant group outweighs the right to religious freedom.

CONSUMPTION OF ANIMALS

A number of disputes revolved around the question of whether it is acceptable to eat particular animals—for example, whether horsemeat should be consumed. When food preferences are viewed as unacceptable, there may be legislative attempts to forbid them. Although some food habits are explicit, others are only implicit. It is only when a foodway rule is violated that an implicit attitude becomes explicit.[46]

If it is arbitrary which animals are eaten, then this raises the question as to whether individuals from other places should be punished for their behavior. In some places a creature is eaten, whereas in others that would be unthinkable. Even if an animal is eaten, some parts of the animal may not be considered edible. In Spain, for instance, the testicles of the bull are eaten, though in other beef-eating countries, it is unlikely that one would expect to have this served at a meal.

Many culture conflicts involve consumption of animals, a number of which are dogs. In a case that received considerable media attention, two Cambodian men, Sokheng Caea and Seng K. Ou, were prosecuted for attempting to eat a four-month-old German shepherd–Doberman mix puppy that had been given to them as a gift. When the prosecutor realized that there was no law in California prohibiting the eating of dogs, she focused instead on whether the dog had been killed in an "inhumane" fashion.[47] If convicted, they would have been subject to up to a year in the Los Angeles County jail and a fine of up to $2,000 each. The immigrants' lawyers argued that they were following their own "national customs" and did not realize their conduct was offensive to "American sensibilities." Ultimately the judge dismissed the case because he did consider the manner in which the defendants killed the dog different from the state-approved method of slaughtering animals.[48]

Because the judge's decision to dismiss the case led to a tremendous public outcry, the Cambodian Association approached Assemblywoman Jackie Speier (San Francisco). At their request, she agreed to sponsor what became known as "the Pet Law" bill. In its original form it prohibited the consumption of "animals traditionally kept as pets," which were defined as dogs and cats. Some members of the Vietnamese community objected to the definition, claiming that the law targeted them and was "racist." Consequently, the final version of the law deleted any definition of a pet. The law prohibited the killing for food of "any animal traditionally or commonly kept as a pet or companion," making this act a misdemeanor, punishable by six months in jail or a $1,000 fine, or both.[49] Governor George Deukmejian asked for a follow-up bill that would substitute civil penalties for the criminal misdemeanor ones. He signed the law, issuing a letter saying:

> Although I am signing this bill, I do not believe it is appropriate to impose criminal penalties for a violation of this law. If the killing of pets for food is a cultural practice that new arrivals to our country have as a custom, their assimilation to accepted practices can be accomplished with more sensitivity.[50]

The controversy is important for several reasons. It shows how the reaction by the majority to a single incident can lead to the passage of anti-minority policy. It also demonstrates the tremendous pressure on ethnic groups to become assimilated as evidenced by the Cambodian Association denial that Cambodians ever ate dogs and by its decision to seek legislation banning the consumption of pets. Furthermore, the debate over passage of the law generated interethnic conflict between Cambodians and Vietnamese in the area.[51]

One of the points of contention was whether, in fact, Cambodians traditionally ate dogs. Newspaper reports indicated that it was rare in Cambodia until the starvation during the Pol Pot regime. Both the judge and the prosecutor acknowledged that the defendants were ethnic Chinese who had moved to Cambodia. One was known to have eaten dog in Cambodia.[52] Though it is unclear whether dog is eaten in Cambodia as a delicacy or out of necessity, the consideration of the cultural tradition in this case was not deemed inappropriate by the prosecutor or the judge.

Regardless of whether Cambodians do or do not eat dogs, the point was that Americans consider dogs as pets, members of the family, and "man's best friend." It is unacceptable to eat one's pet, something which various theories have attempted to explain.[53]

The crux of matter is that not all cultures keep animals as "pets," and even those that do may not keep dogs as "pets." The notion that dogs would be members of the family, while taken for granted in some societies, is foreign to many other societies. In fact, in many places it would be considered indecent to have a dog in the house and permitted to eat from a human fork. Dogs are considered filthy in many parts of the world. So, the case forces one to reconsider the presumption that some animals are necessarily "pets." It is possible that Americans are hypersensitive to the possibility of dog-eating. By contrast, it is doubtful that one would have witnessed the same sort of overreaction if French immigrants had been discovered eating horse or rabbit.[54]

Let us turn to another culture conflict over the consumption of an animal: here the issue was whether the display of Peking duck (Chinese style roast duck) would endanger public health. The controversy over Peking duck in Chinese restaurants raises questions of cultural sensitivity and the possibility of accommodating an ethnic minority. Public health inspectors challenged the practice of hanging Chinese ducks in the windows of Chinese restaurants because the ducks were not at the required temperature. Under California state health code regulations, all perishable foods must be maintained at 40 degrees or lower, or 140 degrees Fahrenheit or higher. Adhering to this regulation would impair the flavor of the duck, which is prepared especially to ensure its crispiness.[55]

Even though there was not a single account of any problem associated with the eating of Peking duck for the thousands of years it has been part of the diet in China, public health inspectors undertook a vigorous campaign against the hanging roast ducks. This, in turn, prompted responses by Chinese groups such as the United Chinese Restaurant Association, which considered the campaign a form of harassment. A task force on Chinese food was established to respond to the enforcement.[56]

In response to the aggressive inspectors, Assemblyman Art Torres sponsored legislation in the California legislature to exempt Chinese restaurants from public health regulations for Peking duck. The major opposition to the bill came from the health department and from the scientific community. The health argument was that bacteria such as salmonella can proliferate and that the food item will attract flies. In one letter to the editor, a microbiologist argued that the emergency legislation was an ill-advised, dangerous "political faux pas." To disprove the health claim, Michael Woo, a legislative assistant to Assemblyman Torres, drove a duck from Los Angeles to Sacramento for tests.[57]

Assembly bill no. 2603 sponsored by Torres passed both houses in July 1982. On July 6, 1982, Governor Jerry Brown signed the Peking duck bill, an emergency statute. The law provided an exemption from the health and safety code for a period of up to four hours after the duck is prepared. It also exempts raw duck in restaurants for periods not to exceed two hours if the food is subsequently to be cooked at or above 350 degrees Fahrenheit, for at least sixty minutes. The policy has, apparently, not led to any health difficulties whatsoever.[58] One ought to be wary of claims that different ways of displaying food necessarily put public health in jeopardy.

This Peking duck dispute differs from the Pet Law because here an exemption was granted to enacted legislation. Although there was an attempt to use existing policy to disallow the consumption of an animal traditionally eaten, this failed. It could be that the public was prepared to let Chinese eat ducks because they are not regarded as pets, and if the Chinese were willing to undertake the health risk, the public would not interfere. In the case of the Pet Law, the safety of a family member, the proverbial Fido, was at stake.[59] Surprisingly, even though the Peking duck debate was framed as a human welfare matter, the attempt to block the cultural tradition failed. In the Pet Law controversy, the issue was animal welfare, and the policy to disallow consumption of an animal eaten elsewhere succeeded.

Another debate focused on the conditions under which living animals were kept. This highly publicized controversy was over the sale of live animals for food in Chinatown markets in San Francisco, a practice that has been going on since the late 1800s. In 1996 animal activists condemned it on the basis of animal cruelty (partly because of the number in a single cage) and the potential for the spread of disease. They also expressed concern about ensuring the humane death of the animals since customers can take the animals home alive. In their defense Chinese merchants contended that they obey state regulations and take proper care of the animals. After all, their livelihood depends on keeping the animals alive and healthy. Another point of contention was whether the markets affected tourism. The real issue was that Chinese prefer to have fresh meat. From their point of view, if the animal is dead, one never knows how long it has been dead.[60]

One Chinese homemaker testified, her voice quavering with emotion, and pleaded with the commissioners not to ban the sale of live animals for food: "No matter what effort it would take ... even if I have to go out into the country and buy a live chicken, I will do it," vowed M. J. Lee. who had prepared fresh-killed birds, frogs, and turtles for her family for thirty-seven years. "These people have no business coming into Chinatown and telling us how to buy and prepare food. We don't interfere with them, why should they interfere with us?"[61]

After a two-year debate described as pitting "culinary and cultural traditions against animal rights," the Commission of Animal Control and Welfare decided by a vote of seven to three (with one abstention) to recommend a ban on live animal markets. The Board of Supervisors had to make the final decision and was disinclined to consider or support the ban. The California Fish and Game Commission also considered banning the importation of these foodstuffs.[62]

Chinese Americans denounced the proposed ban as culturally insensitive and discriminatory. Some denied that the practice was cruel, pointing out that it preserved the animal's life until a customer is ready to purchase whereas slaughterhouses kill vast numbers of animals based on projected needs, which leads to the unnecessary death of animals when there are miscalculations.[63] Critics of the policy argued that policymakers failed to consider compromises and to study the potential impact of the ban.

Some were hostile to the Asian American community's position. There were those who made the mistake of conflating race and culture, accusing Chinese Americans of playing the "race card." Critics also implied that allowing the live animal markets would require allowing all traditions, including, perhaps, opium dens. Others assumed that what they regarded as cruel practices should be changed as traditions are not "fixed." Still others failed to understand how the ban would affect Chinese Americans' eating practices.[64]

When the Board of Supervisors did not take action, a coalition of ten animal rights group activists filed a lawsuit to stop twelve Chinese American merchants from selling live animals for food but did not name any Fisherman's Wharf merchants as defendants. Paul Wartelle, the San Francisco attorney for the merchants, publicly accused the activists of "cultural arrogance." In Superior Court, Judge Carlos Bea said the animals rights groups failed to show that the Chinatown merchants violated animal cruelty laws or unlawful business practices.[65] Judge Bea found no proof that the animals suffered unnecessary harm or that other methods of killing them than those used by the merchants were more humane.

In the aftermath of the litigation some animal rights groups publicly stated that they intended to appeal the decision. The San Francisco SPCA worked with the Chinese Consolidated Benevolent Association to draft a voluntary set of guidelines concerning the treatment of animals. It is conceivable that the lawsuit was necessary to put pressure on the groups to forge a compromise.

Cultural differences sometimes arise in civil suits as well. In one publicized case a Hindu, Mukesh K. Rai, filed a suit against Taco Bell for serving him a beef burrito. Because he mistakenly ate an animal prohibited by his religion, his contention was that he was entitled to damages for the trauma he suffered. His attorney explained that the mental impact was "the equivalent of eating his ancestors." The public did not appear to find his case sympathetic. Taco Bell settled the case just before it went to trial.[66]

ANIMALS IN SPORTING EVENTS

Although mainstream society permits the use of animals in sporting events such as horse racing, western-style rodeos, and dog races and shows, some uses of animals in ethnic minority competitions have been questioned. One controversy was over the *charreada*, or classic Mexican-style rodeo. The rodeo has three events that involve tripping the horse. The charreada is a national sport in Mexico and is said to date back to sixteenth-century Spain. After the Spanish conquest of Mexico in 1520, many horseman would show the superiority of Spanish military strength compared to that of the indigenous people. It remains popular in the United States, although animal rights groups have criticized the tradition.[67]

The animal welfare movement persuaded Assemblyman John Burton to sponsor legislation to ban horse tripping, the traditional events at the charreada. Because it was difficult to prosecute charros under the general cruelty to animals statute (California S597), the animals rights groups preferred a law that would avoid this problem. The first attempt to pass a law failed because of pressure from the American rodeo organizations which feared the regulation would eventually target their sport as well. The next year the Pro Rodeo Cowboy's Association decided to remain neutral. In 1994 the legislature banned the practice in California based on claims that some horses were hurt in the event. Also in 1994 the attorney general of Texas issued an advisory opinion, concluding that horse tripping was illegal in that state as well.[68]

The Charro Federation publicly stated that experienced charros know how to trip the horse without endangering it. Considering the charreada part of their heritage, charros apparently also regarded the legislation as discriminatory. It is also noteworthy that the California law was passed at the time when voters enacted a major anti-immigrant policy. Another question is why the welfare of horses in other sporting events received so little attention. Legislators like Assemblyman Richard Polanco (Democrat, Los Angeles) publicly stated that the law creates a double standard by outlawing charreadas events but "preserving" the right of cowboys to rope calves and steers at western-style rodeos: "Tripping and roping of a horse is no different than what is done to steers and calves in the Anglo rodeos. It's a double standard. The same standard should apply to all." In essence, the criticism is that the policy violates the principle of equal protection.[69]

Animal rights activists, including Latinos, deny the charge of discrimination, arguing that the charros were merely trying to justify cruelty. Another denial of discrimination is based on a claim that the event is not part of Mexican culture. The debate about the charreada led to claims by non-Mexicans and Mexicans alike that the event was not "traditional."[70]

During the debate in the California legislature one organization directly addressed the right to culture. The California Equine Legislative Council presented the argument as follows:

> The few Charreada Federations opposing this bill see this issue as a "cultural right." The sponsors and endorsers of this bill perceive it as a "cruelty issue." The question is: does culture supersede cruelty in the State of California? There is no constitutional protection of culture. Both Cesar Chavez and the Mexican-American Political Association oppose the tripping of horses and see the practice as a cruel cultural anachronism. As a society, we cannot encourage our children to be indifferent to cruelty and not reap consequences later.
>
> This is not an attack upon Mexican-American culture. The purpose of AB49X is not to ban charreadas. There are, however, several events in the charreadas that have cruel consequences for the horse.[71]

To its credit, the organization acknowledged that there is at least an argument concerning the right to culture that must be answered. The basic points made here are that (1) even if the practice is part of the culture, the right to culture may be trumped by animal rights; and (2) the implicit concern is that children will learn to accept cruelty if the events are allowed.[72]

It is possible that a compromise could be reached where the Mexican-style rodeo evolves, so that other events replace the horse tripping. As far back as the mid–twentieth century, the movie industry had to change its attitudes toward animals when it came under pressure from animal rights groups. Now every movie using animals must issue a statement to the effect that no animals were harmed in the making of the film. Other sports competitions have accepted compromises, such as bloodless bullfighting in California.[73]

Another example of a culturally based sport involving animals is cockfighting. The cockfight is one of the oldest forms of animal competitions, and its meaning has been subject to many interpretations. Cockfighting raids have been reported across the United States. In Monterey, California, thirteen men were arrested and forty-one fighting birds were taken in a raid. The men were charged with attending an animal fighting event, cruelty to animals, gambling, and possession of cockfighting paraphernalia. In New York, a 1995 campaign against the sport led to the arrest of nearly two hundred people and the seizure of 1,450 fighting birds. Most of the people arrested were Spanish-speaking immigrants from countries where cockfighting is legal and occurs in public. The participants expressed concern about what they perceived as an unfair double standard. In 1995, cockfighting was legal in five states—-Missouri, Oklahoma, Louisiana, New Mexico, and Arkansas. States that forbid it say the justification is not only concern with animal cruelty but also a desire to discourage the gambling associated with it.[74]

Although it is true that the treatment of animals in these sporting spectacles is considered by some to be inhumane, one cannot help wondering why certain other fowl practices continue without much criticism. For instance, Pennsylvania has a tradition of pigeon shooting. Each Labor Day in the Schuylkill Country Hegins pigeon shoot, shooters gun down thousands of pigeons. It has been argued that anti-cockfighting policies violate equal protection.[75] More generally, the targeting of particular animal competitions conveys the impression that only some uses of animals merit state intervention. It is the double standard that appears to be particularly offensive to minority groups.

ANIMALS AS EXOTIC PETS

Some cases involve smuggling of animals which some ethnic groups like to keep as exotic pets. In the mid-1990s the Justice Department and the U.S. Fish and Wildlife Service launched Operation Chameleon, a four-year sting operation aimed at the black market in endangered lizards, tortoises, and snakes, estimated to be a $6 billion business.[76] When the smugglers are prosecuted in federal court, they sometimes ask the court to mitigate their sentences because of cultural differences in the uses of the animals.

U.S. v. Tomono (1998) is an example of judicial treatment of cultural factors in sentencing. Kei Tomono was accused of violating U.S. laws concerning wildlife and smuggling. A national of Japan, twenty-six-year-old, college-educated Tomono ran an import/export business known as Amazon International based in Chiba, Japan. On one trip to the United States in April 1996, he had sixty "Pignose" or "Fly River" turtles, and 113 "Irian Jaya Snake-Neck" turtles in his luggage, which he intended to sell. Later in August 1997 he made another trip from Japan to San Francisco to attend a reptile breeders conference, this time carrying with him six "Red Mountain Racer" snakes and two "Mandarin Rat" snakes in his luggage. On both occasions, he filled out the standard Customs Declaration Form, denying that he was carrying any "fruits, plants, food, soil, birds, snails, other live animals, wildlife products, farm products." Government agents had searched his luggage in San Francisco, without his knowledge. Although he was permitted to fly on from San Francisco to Orlando, once he reached Florida, a Fish and Wildlife agent asked to search his luggage. He consented, the snakes were found, and he and his traveling companion were taken into custody. The creatures were said to be worth approximately $70,000.[77]

A grand jury indicted him for violations of the federal anti-smuggling act and the Lacey Act which forbids the import, export, sale, or possession of fish or wildlife taken in violation of federal, state, or foreign law. The violations dealt not only with the possession and intended sale of the creatures but also with the failure to declare them to customs.

Charged with violations of the Lacey Act and the federal anti-smuggling act, Tomono decided to plead guilty. Tomono argued for a downward departure under Sentencing Guidelines section 5K2.0. His position was that due to cultural differences between Japan and the United States, he "was unaware of the serious consequences of his actions, and that these actions constituted a factor not considered by the Sentencing Commission that should be taken into account in calculating his sentence."[78]

Taking his cultural background into consideration, the district court lowered his sentence.[79] At the sentencing hearing, Judge Ann Conway stated:

> Basically, the court agrees with the defense that the cultural differences in this case give the court a basis to depart downward that is not otherwise available or covered by the Sentencing Guidelines. . . . The court finds that Mr. Tomono's not declaring [the animals] to the U.S. Customs could well be the result of the cultural differences and his misunderstanding of the laws and the forms. The court is departing three levels downward because the cultural difference would be demonstrated by the difference in the market value in Japan versus the difference in the market value in the U.S.[80]

The judge explicitly distinguished between cultural differences and national origin: "Even though culture might be related to a person's origin, not every person who has the same national origin has the same culture and background. Culture extends beyond just national origin and includes factors such as beliefs, religion, laws, morals, and practices."

The court made it clear that it based the sentence not on national origin, but on cultural differences. In particular, the court referred to the fact that the turtles in question were not endangered species in Japan and that Tomono would not have been arrested there. The court also made a special point of the "unique" place of reptiles in Japanese culture and that Tomono is widely respected for his work in the field of herpetology. Furthermore, the court was influenced by Tomono's apparent ignorance of American law. Since Tomono had only been to the United States on two or three occasions and ostensibly was unfamiliar with the laws, the court was sympathetic to his argument.[81] Based on the specific facts in this case, the court sentenced Tomono to five years' probation (unsupervised, provided he leave the United States), a $5,000 fine, and another "assessment" of $200.

The government appealed the downward departure of his sentence, presenting arguments that provided the basis for the Court of Appeals decision. The government argued that departures downward for factors not adequately considered by the guidelines should be an uncommon occurrence. The offense at the center of this case, namely foreign nationals smuggling wildlife into the United States, is routine. Since defendants generally come from different cultures, a downward departure in a case such as this would lead to rampant misuse of the guidelines. Downward departures based on culture would be a common occurrence, something not anticipated by the policy.

Another part of the prosecution's argument was that the motivation for smuggling was economic and not cultural. This motivation applies also to smugglers of drugs, contraband, and other substances. The basic point the government wished to make was that the guidelines are only to permit departures for rare or unique circumstances. The prosecution emphasized what it regarded as a contradiction. Tomono claimed ignorance of the law, but admitted knowledge of U.S. policy during the plea negotiation.[82] He also was aware of U.S. regulations on trade in wildlife and federal health regulations prohibiting the importation of turtles under four inches in carapace (shell) length.

The government argued that following the logic of the district court's decision would result in two different sets of sentencing guidelines, one for U.S. citizens and one for foreign nationals. The government's brief rejects, in principle, the notion that the norms in other legal systems should influence the disposition of cases in the United States:

> The fact that a defendant's country of origin does not prohibit or penalize conduct that constitutes a criminal offense in the US does not justify a downward departure. . . . This circumstance is all too common and would result in routine downward departures, not the highly infrequent occurrence contemplated by the Sentencing Commission.[83]

On appeal, the court rejected all strands of the cultural differences argument. The court found that the endangered status of turtles was also taken into account by the guidelines, there was no evidence in the record supporting the "unique" place reptiles occupy, that counsels' arguments alone were usually not enough to justify departures from the sentencing guidelines, and that Tomono showed familiarity with U.S. policies during the plea negotiation.[84]

The Court of Appeals concluded that there were insufficient grounds for a downward departure and therefore that the district court had abused its discretion when it took the case "out of the heartland" of the guidelines. The court, remarked in a footnote that "considering 'cultural differences' attributable solely to a defendant's country of origin comes uncomfortably close to considering the defendant's national origin itself, in contravention of the guidelines." The court was reticent about the question of whether, in principle, cultural differences may be used in sentencing: "We need not decide whether 'cultural differences' may ever be an appropriate ground upon which to depart from the guidelines." The court vacated the sentence and remanded it for resentencing.[85]

Judge Paul Roney, writing in dissent, began with the proposition that the Sentencing Commission had not prohibited the consideration of culture. Since it is permissible to base a downward departure on cultural differences, according to Judge Roney, the crucial question is whether or not the sentencing court abused its discretion. Emphasizing that the trial court is in a "preferred position" to understand what justice requires in particular circumstances, he eloquently defended the use of discretion by the district court. After explaining that discretion means a decision either way is not wrong, he concluded that the district court judge in *Tomono* did not abuse her discretion.

In the United States it remains unclear whether cultural differences may legitimately be referred to in sentencing. The decisions thus far are from the circuit courts and, as a consequence, are binding only on the states in their jurisdictions. The appellate decisions, in any event, have not resolved the question of whether the prohibition against considering national origin encompasses cultural differences.

GREATER ACCOMMODATION OF CULTURAL MINORITIES' USE OF ANIMALS

The culture conflicts discussed in this chapter reflect varying attitudes toward the proper uses of animals. Judges have preconceived ideas about the value of animals, which lead them to discount arguments about the importance of the animals to minority groups. Insofar as there are no objective criteria to delineate correct versus incorrect uses of animals, many of the decisions are strikingly arbitrary.

Many traditions involving the use of animals are seemingly cruel.[86] The problem is that the legal system often appears to be more concerned with the unacceptable practices of minority groups than with those of the dominant culture. This appearance of a double standard calls into question the fairness of the system for groups that lack political power. That is why it is essential that judges explicitly recognize differing perspectives about the humane treatment of animals.

If a principle of maximum accommodation is to be applied, it would require judges to take cultural and religious claims more seriously in this area. In cases where the taking of one animal will hardly jeopardize the species, an exception to policy should be made. Not only should cultural and religious considerations influence decisions about criminal responsibility, but also the principle would encourage legislatures to create exemptions for such practices as ritual slaughter based on clearly delineated religious principles and for the sale, preparation, and display of animals, such as Peking duck and live animal markets, so that prosecutions would be altogether unnecessary.

Given the strong pressures to assimilate, it is highly unlikely that many will try to eat or sacrifice dogs, have public cockfighting competitions, or hunt eagles. In those few rare cases where the rules of the dominant culture are contravened, courts should try to weigh the rights of human beings to culture and religious freedom against animal rights or the government interest in deterring animal cruelty. The presumption should be in favor of the right to culture unless a significant demonstrable harm can be shown to exist.

7

Marriage

There are different cultural conceptions of marriage. In some societies marriage is based on the individual choice of a mate and depends on love or romantic attachment. In others a marriage is designed to permit an alliance between groups. In some instances, when immigrants and refugees attempt to follow marriage rituals required in their countries of origin based on a group-oriented conception, this conflicts with the law of the new nation.[1]

Societies have varying rules that specify the appropriate age for marriage, the proper methods for getting married, the number of permissible marriage partners, the ways of divorcing and remarrying, and the principles governing child custody. In this chapter I present examples of the sorts of culture conflicts associated with marriage. While most of the cases considered here would ordinarily be classified as family law issues—for example, marriage, divorce, and child custody—sometimes the disputes are handled as criminal matters. For instance, if a man marries more than one woman, in those jurisdictions in which monogamy is standard practice, this would be considered the crime of bigamy. Some of the cases could be analyzed under more than one category—child marriage and forced marriage could have been considered in chapter 4, for instance—as the categories are not entirely discrete.

Because there are various motivations behind marriages, it may, at times, be difficult for judges in North America and Europe to ascertain the "validity" of unions contracted in immigrant communities.[2] What is accepted as a legitimate way of marrying within the community may appear to an outsider to be a violation of an individual right to choose one's marriage partner. Indeed, this issue is a topic of some concern in the international human rights literature. In several major conventions there are articles stipulating that every person has a right to choose his or her own marriage partner. Of course, this does not really settle the question because the human right to practice one's culture and follow one's religion are equally well established. Hence, the conflict has not been resolved as of yet. Although the human right to choose one's marriage partner seems intuitively correct to those raised in countries where choice is highly valued, those who have grown up in systems where their parents and other relatives make the match think otherwise. They say in the West "you marry the one you love"; in the East "we love the one we marry." If duration of marriages is any indication of the degree to which the marriage is successful, it may be that the latter is superior to the former.

Relatively little scholarship exists documenting the sorts of culture conflicts surrounding marriage practices. The most important works are those by Sebastian Poulter and David Pearl, which focus on case law in England. Of all the marriage rituals considered here, plural marriage, or polygamy, has apparently received the most attention. This chapter has two objectives: to identify the types of culture conflicts that result from marriage traditions and to address some of the legal problems that can be expected to occur. Marriage law reflects well how adherence to a single standard results in the deprivation of rights for those coming from other traditions.[3]

TYPES OF CULTURE CONFLICTS INVOLVING MARRIAGE

Child Marriage

In many parts of the world—for example, in Africa, Asia, and Latin America—girls under the age of sixteen enter into marriages. In fact, there is often no minimum age prescribed by the customary law concerning marriage. Parents usually make the decision as to when their children are ready for marriage. If there were a minimum age, it might be difficult to enforce the rule as some societies do not have the capacity to administer a system of birth certificates, so there is no way to determine the precise age of those who are getting married. The difficulties arise when the couples emigrate and arrive in countries that adhere to minimum age rules. There can be quite serious consequences: men who are married to girls may find their marriages considered void or voidable, and they may also stand accused of child sexual abuse or statutory rape.[4]

Societies that have established a minimum age for marriage—such as the United Kingdom and the United States in the early twentieth century—base their policies on several concerns about child marriage. First, if children are not considered to have the capacity to choose, then the marriage will violate the individual right to choose.[5] This means that the marriage violates the child (usually the girl's) right to give free and informed consent, a key value in European and American political thought. Second, girls who marry will be less likely to complete formal education. Third, marriages of teenage brides more frequently result in divorce, which is considered socially undesirable.

In some countries, such as India, efforts to abolish child marriage have failed.[6] India adopted the Child Marriage Restraint Act in 1978. Despite the law, child marriage has remained extremely popular in India, where in some regions girls marry before the age of fifteen. Villagers are aware of the law but disregard it, considering it a "paper law" (a derogatory term for written law).

Alhaji Mohamed v. Knott (1968) illustrates well the difficulty judges have had in untangling conflicting laws concerning child marriage.[7] Here a twenty-five-year-old Nigerian student went through a potentially polygamous Muslim marriage ceremony in Nigeria with a young girl, Rabi Mohamed Musi. Both were Muslims belonging to the Hausa tribe, and this was unquestionably a valid marriage according to Nigerian law.

Three months after the wedding, she accompanied him to London where he was studying medicine. She was removed from their home five months after their arrival by an order of the Southwark North Juvenile Court. A female police constable named Knott filed a complaint (under sections 2 and 62 of the Children and Young Persons Act of 1933) alleging that Rabi was not receiving "such care, protection, and guidance as a good parent might reasonably be expected to give and was exposed to moral danger."

The justices of the juvenile court, horrified by the promiscuous conduct of the man, determined that the complaint was substantiated by the facts. The girl was ordered to be committed to an institution as "a fit person."[8] Their decision was based on two grounds: first, because the marriage was potentially polygamous, it was not recognized in England, and in the absence of marriage she was exposed to moral danger in the relationship. Second, even if the marriage were valid, it would be wrong to leave the girl in such a condition: "In our opinion a continuance of such an association notwithstanding the marriage, would be repugnant to any decent-minded English man or woman. Our decision reflects that repugnance."

The man's appeal to the Divisional Court proved successful. The court held that the fact that the marriage was potentially polygamous did not mean that it was not recognized in England. In fact, she was as much a wife in England as in Nigeria. The court further ruled that even though a fit person order was possible for husband-wife relationships, there were no grounds for such an order in this case. A source of confusion was the existence of the Sexual Offences Act of 1956, which forbade sexual intercourse with girls under sixteen years of age. But the court took the view that intercourse within marriage was lawful, no matter what the spouse's age.

One of the justices, Lord Parker, rejected completely the lower court view that the relationship was offensive, saying:

> I would never dream of suggesting that a decision by this bench of justices with this very experienced chairman, could ever be termed perverse; but having read that [the lower court memorandum], I am convinced that they have misdirected themselves. When they say that "a continuance of such an association notwithstanding the marriage, would be repugnant to any decent-minded English man or woman," they are, I think, and can only

be, considering the view of an English man or woman in relation to an English girl and our Western way of life. I cannot myself think that decent-minded English men or women, realising the way of life in which this girl was brought up, and this man for that matter, would inevitably say that this is repugnant. It is certainly natural for a girl to marry at that age. They develop sooner, and there is nothing abhorrent in their way of life for a girl of 13 to marry a man of 25. Incidentally it was not until 1929 that, in this country, an age limit was put on marriage.[9]

Even though the juvenile court may have been somewhat ethnocentric in its attitude, as pointed out by Justice Parker, it did make some effort to ascertain the applicable customary law. Noel Coulsen, professor of Islamic law at the University of London, informed the court that while there is no minimum age for marriage, it is unlawful for the bridegroom to cohabit with the bride or consummate the marriage until "there are decisive indications of pubertal maturity in the bride." It is assumed that a girl cannot attain puberty before the age of nine and that she has attained it by the age of fifteen. The difficulty was that her age was not known. One doctor assessed her age at between ten and twelve, while another doctor thought she might have been as old as fourteen and a half.

Ultimately, the interpretation of the case turned on whether the court was willing to accept diverse folkways. The juvenile court concluded that public policy required intervention to rescue the child wife, regardless of her cultural background. By contrast, the divisional court concluded that justice required a more culturally sensitive attitude toward the institution of child marriage.

The English immigration law was changed in 1986, so that child brides under the age of sixteen could no longer enter the United Kingdom. Because sixteen was the minimum age for consent in lawful sexual intercourse and for marriage, Poulter explained, "it was felt to be intolerable to have these child brides performing their wifely duties here."[10]

Those who reside in the United Kingdom as nonimmigrants have complained about the minimum marriage age. In 1986 a Muslim who wanted to marry a fourteen-year-old in accordance with Islamic law submitted a complaint to the European Commission on Human Rights. The commission rejected the argument that his religious freedom was violated because English law prevented marriage of girls under the age of sixteen.[11]

Although no systematic data appear to exist on such practice in the United States, there are accounts of what are arguably child marriages from time to time. One policy to promote child marriage led to considerable controversy in Southern California: the Orange County Social Services Department, concerned about teenage pregnancies, helped at least fifteen girls marry their adult male sex partners instead of treating them as victims of child abuse or statutory rape. The criteria were whether the couple were willing to marry and raise their child together, whether the sex had been consensual, and whether the girl needed the man's financial support. When the media exposed the policy, there was sharp criticism of the approach taken to "a cultural issue." Under pressure, the Social Services agency stopped recommending marriage as a solution to the problem of teenage marriage to juvenile court judges.[12]

At issue in a New York case was whether a person who arranged for a child's marriage could be charged with endangering the welfare of a child. In *State v. Benu* (1978) the father, Ibrahim Morris Ben Benu, claimed that his thirteen-year-old daughter "Fatima" asked him to help her elope with seventeen-year-old Richard Springer. The father enlisted the help of El Hadi, a poet who, though not an imam or Muslim religious leader, claimed he was authorized to perform the marriage rites (he was apparently not authorized by the city clerk to do so). El Hadi confirmed that "Fatima" wanted to marry Springer. A witness wrote a contract in which the groom gave a sewing machine to the bride as a gift.

Despite all of this, the court was skeptical about the validity of the marriage under Islamic law, concluding that at best the marriage was a voidable relationship. Regardless of the question of Muslim religious law, the marriage was voidable, said the court, because "Fatima" was thirteen years old. The judge explained that the "public policy of this State is to discourage early marriage, or at best, to demand that the parents of certain underage children consent to their assuming the responsibilities of matrimony."[13] Perhaps because she was pregnant, the court concluded that the marriage was voidable rather than void.

The father was convicted of contributing to the endangerment of his daughter's welfare because he had played an active part in the wedding ceremony.[14] Although the court's opinion does not discuss any actual harms to the daughter, the court finesses this point by saying that it was not necessary to establish that her welfare was endangered, just that there was a potential for endangerment. The court held that the fact that the marriage was not void was no defense, and that the consent of the daughter was irrelevant. From the published decision one gets the impression that the judge wanted to take an opportunity to condemn child marriage in the strongest terms possible.

Much of the debate about child marriage hinges on the notion of individual choice. If, however, the purpose of marriage, according to many societies, is to forge an alliance between groups, this objection based on individual choice seems less compelling. Individuals do not get to choose—but they are not supposed to have a choice, as that is not the purpose of marriage. Moreover, because they lack choice, opponents of child marriage presuppose that girls will be unhappy in their marriages.[15]

The entire discussion also presumes that there a clear distinction between childhood and adulthood. If young individuals work, serve in the military, and have other responsibilities, it is not obvious that they should not be able to marry. The cultural assumptions about children's roles at particular ages lie at the center of the controversy.

This is not to suggest that child marriages should be considered presumptively valid. The question is where to draw the line. One commentator proposed that a minimum age should be based on puberty because of physical and psychological considerations.[16] If cultural sensitivity requires lowering the minimum age for marriage, this might mean doing so not just for immigrants but for everyone.

It is noteworthy that the child marriages with which we are concerned involved young girls. Some argue that defending the institution of child marriage based on culture simply reinforces patriarchy. While many might prefer that girls pursue other options besides marriage, it seems odd for the government to handle child marriage as a crime.[17] It is peculiar that it is only when the frustration that the "victim" will not testify properly that social workers and prosecutors resolve to treat the phenomenon as a valid marriage.[18] The complexity of this issue requires much more careful consideration.

Marriageability

One of the motivations parents have for marrying off their daughters at an early age is to ensure their virtue. If parents wait too long, there is a greater risk that the girls will not be considered suitable for marriage in the eyes of their community. In some court cases the cultural concern was damage to a girl's potential marriageability. A few examples will suffice to show how this cultural preoccupation with the ability of a girl to marry is presented as part of the litigation.

For example, in one case, *Friedman v. State* (1967), a sixteen-year-old girl, Ruth Friedman, an Orthodox Jew, sued the state of New York for negligent operation of an aerial ski lift. In the late afternoon, after a picnic with a male friend, Friedman tried to ride the chairlift down the mountain. The ski lift company negligently stopped the lift while she was halfway down the mountain, leaving her stranded in the chair with a young man, twenty-five feet in the air. As it was apparently contrary to religious law to be alone with a man (certainly overnight), she threw herself off the ski lift and suffered various serious physical injuries that required medical attention. In addition, because of the accident, she suffered a post-traumatic convulsive disorder.

In her lawsuit for damages, she wanted the court to take into account the religious motivation for her behavior. Unless the court understood this "moral compulsion" for jumping off the lift, she had no hope of recovery. An expert witness, Rabbi Stahl, testified that

> under the Hebrew Law, the Shulchan Arukh, there is a specific law, the Jichud, which absolutely forbids a woman to stay with a man in a place which is not available to a third person. To violate this jichud would be an overwhelming moral sin which would not only absolutely ruin this young girl's reputation but also the reputation of her parents.[19]

Although there was some question as to whether this interpretation of Jewish law was "absolutely correct," the court thought the real issues were "whether there is a branch of Judaism which believes in this interpretation; and whether Miss Friedman is a member of this group. We answer both in the affirmative."[20] After the court rejected the state's arguments that Friedman had not proved negligence on the part

of the state and that she had been contributorily negligent, it awarded the Fried-
mans nearly $40,000.

In another case involving the honor of young girls, Grover Marks sued the city
of Spokane after the police searched two Gypsy homes to determine whether there
were any stolen goods on the premises. Although the officers had obtained a search
warrant, they executed the search earlier than was authorized. During their investigation they seized numerous items, including $500,000 worth of jewelry and $1.6
million in cash, some of which was sewn into sacred quilts. They also conducted
body searches of thirteen family members of all ages, including of young, unmarried Rom girls. Afterward, the Gypsy families claimed that because the girls had
been touched, they were *marime*, or polluted. The girls' families were shunned by
their own community. In response to what they claimed was an egregious offense,
they, along with the Gypsy Church of the Northwest, filed a civil rights lawsuit for
$40 million. The city of Spokane admitted liability, acknowledging the illegality of
the search. This meant that the only issue in the litigation was the proper size of the
damage award.[21]

To increase the damages, the Gypsies had to demonstrate what effect the search
had on the Gypsy girls. This depended largely on showing the relevance of the
notion of marime. A crucial dimension of the Gypsy worldview is their ideology of
defilement, which divides Gypsies from non-Gypsies (or Gaje).[22] The latter group is
unclean because of their ignorance of the rules concerning purity and impurity:

> Gypsy society relies heavily on distinctions between behavior that is pure (vujo) and pol-
> luted (marime). The marime concept has powerful significance for Gypsies. Marime has
> a dual meaning: it refers both to a state of pollution as well as to the sentence of expul-
> sion imposed for violation of purity rules or any behavior disruptive to the Gypsy life.
> Pollution and rejection are thus closely associated with one another.[23]

This division between clean and unclean is represented symbolically in their
view of the human body with the waist as the "equator or dividing line." According
to the Rom belief system, there should be no contact between the upper and lower
parts of the body. Ritual separation preserves the purity of the upper body by "containing" the impurity of the other. One scholar explains: "Any contact between the
lower half of the body, particularly the genitals, which are conceptually the ultimate source of marime, and the upper body is forbidden." The consequence of
improper sexual contact is "to spread shame and defilement through the kin
group." The Rom believe that non-Gypsies convey venereal disease, not only
through sexual contact. Gypsies who eat with or work for gaje will be considered
marime by some members of the Rom community. As the stigma of marime constitutes "an official state of social disgrace" and as men are more active in public,
the marime sanction applies mainly to men, and it affects the entire household,
which can expect to be treated with contempt by the rest of the community. It is
also important to protect the home because it is regarded as the "last bastion of
defence against defilement."[24]

When used in the sense of a penalty, marime or banishment is the most severe Gypsy punishment.[25] It results in the complete social ostracism of the wrongdoer:

> Marime stigmatizes all wrongdoers as polluted and justifies their expulsion from the community. No one will eat with them. If they touch an object it must be destroyed, no matter what the value. Nobody will even attempt to kill them, for fear of contamination. When they die, no one will bury them, and they will not have a funeral. They will soon be forgotten. No marriages are arranged for those stigmatized as marime, and without marriage in Gypsy society one's economic and social life is over. In other words, permanent banishment is the equivalent of social death.[26]

However, this punishment is only used for the most serious crimes such as murder. It is considered to be a "drastic sanction."[27]

Although there is no doubt as to the existence of the Gypsy ideology of defilement known as marime, it was unclear whether the marime sanction is permanent or whether it can ever be removed. Each side had an expert witness who offered a different interpretation of the folk law on this point. It is worth noting that even when the customary law requires a sanction—for example, Gypsy parents are supposed to disown daughters who marry non-Gypsies—parents may not comply with the law. If the defilement was permanent and truly rendered the girls "unmarriageable," it was hard for the court to determine the monetary value of the taint to the girls and their families.[28]

In the end, a settlement was reached which gave the Marks family $1.43 million to end the eleven-year legal battle. So, while the cultural argument clearly influenced the litigation, the lawsuit provides no clear guidelines as to the proper weight to be given culture in assessing damage awards.[29]

Incestuous Marriages

While most societies disallow "incestuous" marriages, they have differing rules on how closely individuals may be related and still be permitted to marry. In some jurisdictions, first cousins may marry, while this is illegal in others. A relationship considered too close is designated "incest," which is "a particularly atrocious crime, involving a much higher degree of moral depravity than murder or highway robbery."[30]

Although all states in the United States prohibit uncle-niece and aunt-nephew marriages, Rhode Island had religious exemptions from the law, permitting marriages for Jewish individuals.[31] *In re May's Estate* (1952, 1953) is a case concerning the status of such exemptions. In this case Alice Greenberg, the daughter of an uncle and his niece, challenged the validity of the marriage after her mother died. The New York court had to decide whether the marriage, consummated in Rhode Island, was valid in New York. After deciding that the constitutions of the state and the United States prohibited marriages between an uncle and a niece as incestuous, the court noted that the Old Testament did not forbid the relationship. Finally, the court concluded that it was void and criminal: "Incestuous marriages are crimes."[32] The complexity was the general rule that the validity of marriage contracts has generally been determined by the place where they were contracted. But the court justified its decision, finding that exceptions were necessary for polygamy, incest, and other marriages prohibited by positive law. The decision was, however, reversed on appeal.

Arranged and Forced Marriages

There have been several highly publicized controversies in the United States and abroad over what are either arranged or forced marriages involving girls under the age of eighteen.[33] One of the main problems in these cases is whether or not there should be a presumption of a lack of consent, considering the age of the girls. If one disregards the question of whether young girls can legally consent, then there may be a question of whether the girls "agreed" to marry under duress. It is often hard to tell from the facts whether or not the girls were willing participants in the marriage, as the following example reveals.

In 1996 the San Francisco district attorney's office had to decide how to handle a case involving a seventeen-year-old Iraqi girl whose family was arranging her marriage to a thirty-year-old man, Mohammed Alsreafi. Police investigators said that the relationship began when she was eleven years old. Prosecutors filed two charges of lewd and lascivious conduct against Alsreafi in municipal court, but one month later a deputy district attorney, Susan Breall, dropped the charges after consulting an expert on Iraqi culture. She had some concerns: the girl's precise age was in dispute, her marital status was unclear, and she would give conflicting testimony. Breall explained her decision:

> Do we want to spend a lot of time and money prosecuting a person and putting on trial this particular culture when the victim is uncooperative and when I and many other San Franciscans pride ourselves on being sensitive to someone's culture?[34]

The public outcry against the prosecutor's decision not to proceed appeared in the *San Francisco Chronicle*. One letter to the editor, "Politically Correct 11-Year-Old Brides?," compared child marriage to slavery and female genital mutilation, concluding that it was obviously wrong. Another reaction suggested that taking cultural factors into account would lead to xenophobia: "Using the 'cultural difference' excuse to sidestep our laws only exacerbates the differences of immigrants from non-Western countries and increases anti-immigrant sentiment."[35]

As is often the case, the precise age of the girl was in dispute. Her conflicting statements about her age would have made the case difficult to prosecute. Her attitude toward her marital status was unclear until a video of the ceremony was produced in which she appeared radiant. Given that her status as a "victim" might be difficult to prove in a court of law, the prosecutor decided not to proceed. Since statutory rape does not require any particular attitude on the part of a victim inasmuch as it is a strict liability crime, it is interesting that the female district attorney was persuaded by cultural arguments not to prosecute.

In a couple of instances, parents evidently accepted money from men who wanted to marry their young daughters. For instance, Gypsy parents ostensibly sold their fourteen-year-old daughter twice to other families. The first time she was sold for approximately $11,000. After she had a miscarriage, the family returned her to her family for a partial refund. Newspapers describing the case quoted a woman purporting to be her grandmother who claimed that selling a child is a Gypsy custom.[36] In a very odd turn of events, the Arizona Attorney General's office concluded that it is not illegal in Arizona for parents to sell their child provided it is not for sex, slavery, or servitude. In these cases there is some question about the validity of the claim that selling daughters into marriage is or ever was an authentic part of the culture.

Interesting conflicts occur when immigrants accustomed to more control over choice try to impose the traditional matchmaking method on their children. The children may prefer to exercise the right to choose, a right taken for granted by citizens in the new country, sometimes rejecting an arranged marriage. In some cases if the girl declines to marry the person chosen by her family, there can be lethal consequences. Sometimes families will take their daughters to their countries of origin where they are forcibly married. Families may also kill their daughters. When a Pakistani woman, Tasleem Begun, refused the Pakistani partner her family had selected for her, her brother-in-law killed her by driving his car onto the sidewalk and running over her. Although he escaped to Pakistan that day, he was eventually returned to England where he was convicted of murder and sentenced to life imprisonment.[37]

The question of arranged or forced marriage has received some attention in Norway where there have been numerous cases. The highly publicized case of Nadia demonstrates the tragic circumstances of such conflicts. Nadia's parents were Moroccan immigrants, devout Muslims, living in Norway who were concerned about the identity of their daughter. When she appeared to be rejecting the Muslim way of life, preferring instead the Scandanavian lifestyle, in October 1997 her parents apparently kidnapped her and took her to Morocco to be married against her will. Supposedly, her parents drugged her, forced her into a van, and drove her from Europe to Morocco.[38]

While in Nador in her aunt's home, Nadia managed to call her employer in Oslo, who immediately contacted the police. This led to consultations between the police and the Foreign Ministry, and between the Ministry and the Norwegian Embassy. The ambassador spent three weeks trying to locate Nadia, but was unable to persuade local authorities to intervene. The difficulty was the difference in the legal age of adult between Norway and Morocco: Nadia was eighteen, technically an adult according to Norwegian law, but in Morocco a girl is a minor until the age of twenty. As Unni Wikan put it: "And so Nadia, a Norwegian adult, became Nadia, a Moroccan child." Various negotiations between the Norwegian ambassador in Morocco and Nadia's father and between the Norwegian foreign minister and his

Moroccan counterpart produced no result. Although her parents promised several times to take her to the embassy in Rabat, they failed to appear. The father only relented when he was threatened with the immediate loss of his social welfare benefits in Norway.[39]

Eventually Nadia returned to Norway where initially she retracted her story, denying the allegations she had made. She explained that she decided to travel to Morocco to see her sick grandmother. Although she claimed she concocted the abduction story when she thought she would have to stay longer in Morocco than she wanted to, she reverted to the original story shortly afterward.[40]

At the direction of police, she phoned her parents. In the conversation the father admitted that she was coerced to leave Oslo, and the phone call was recorded for use in court. The police recommended charging Nadia's parents and her younger brother with violations of the Norwegian Criminal Code, sections 223 and 224.[41]

In the fall of 1998 the Norwegian state decided to prosecute her parents under the two sections, much to Nadia's dismay. Nadia was so distraught during the trial that she asked that her parents leave the courtroom while she testified. After a one-week trial, the parents were found guilty and received sentences much lower than the usual minimum of a year in jail. The father received one year and three months and the mother one year, both as suspended sentences. In addition, Nadia's father had to pay court expenses, which were approximately $10,000. The court's decision to mete out a light sentence was influenced by Nadia's plea for leniency. Despite this, however, the court noted that "traditions cannot supersede Norwegian law," particularly if parents rely on violence and kidnapping as means for the transmission of folkways.[42]

The case shows how children can be caught between two traditions. While they may prefer the worldview of the new country, they do not wish to have their parents punished for adhering to a traditional one. The Norwegian legal system in this case indicated that while it would show compassion in a case of first instance, the right of children to become assimilated had to be vindicated. The court emphasized the need for the newly arrived to let their children become "Norwegian." Unni Wikan's interpretation of the case emphasizes this point:

> The verdict against Nadia's parents is an historic one in Norway. For the first time, the court declared that the law applies equally to all parents irrespective of ethnic background. Kidnapping is a crime even when it is done with the best of intentions—as to raise one's child in one's own traditions. The verdict went even further: it stated in plain language that when people choose to live in Norway, as Nadia's parents have, they must be prepared to let their children be influenced by their surroundings, that is, Norwegian society. To refuse children the right to be or become "Norwegian" in that respect, is not their right. In the case of Nadia's parents, it was even noted (in the several page long verdict declaration) that they have chosen to remain in Norway with their two young children; it must mean that they cherish the good that Norway has to offer over and above the benefits of Moroccan society: this entails a choice and the choice has consequences, some of which may be unwanted, but are unescapable by Norwegian law.[43]

The Moroccan community in Oslo expressed great displeasure with the verdict. They regarded the decision as sanctioning interference with parents' rights to bring up their children as they see fit. The actual concern was with the sexual freedom of women. When Nadia's mother was quoted as saying to the Norwegian ambassador: "All Norwegian women are whores, and I don't want my daughter to become one of them," this highlighted the worry of Muslim parents.[44]

The difficulty with cases like this one is that it can be hard to tell whether coercion has been used. Indeed, families may employ different types of pressure. In this case the government did not have sufficient evidence to charge the parents with attempting to force Nadia into marriage with someone in Morocco, despite the father's remarks on the phone about protecting the honor of the family. Furthermore, it is unclear whether the parents' actions would have been considered legitimate in Morocco. Evidently, leaders of Muslim organizations in Norway throughout the trial claimed that such marriages were no longer accepted in Morocco. Ironically, it is sometimes immigrant parents who adhere to traditions more strictly than those in the country of origin.

England has had considerable experience with the legal analysis of arranged marriages. The question that British lawyers have faced is how to deal with unhappy marriages. What are the grounds for "nullity"? According to English law there are at least three: duress, incapacity to consummate the marriage, and willful refusal to consummate the marriage.[45] The case of *Hirani v. Hirani* (1983) illustrates the difficulty courts have had in interpreting duress.

A nineteen-year-old Hindu woman had a relationship with an Indian Muslim. Her parents immediately tried to arrange for her to marry a Hindu, Mr. Hirani, who was from the same caste and spoke the same language. Although neither she nor her parents had met Mr. Hirani, she was pressured to marry him:

> You want to marry somebody who is strictly against our religion; he is a Muslim, you are a Hindu. You had better marry somebody we want you to—otherwise pick up your belong[ing]s, and go. If you do not want to marry Mr. Hirani and want to marry Mr. Husain, go.[46]

She and Mr. Hirani went through a civil marriage ceremony and the following day a religious one. After living with Mr. Hirani for six weeks, she left him and went to Mr. Hussain's house. She claimed the marriage with Hirani had never been consummated, and she never returned to his house. She petitioned for a decree of nullity on the ground of duress. The judge dismissed the duress petition because "the duress allegedly exerted by her parents was not sufficiently grave to place her in fear for her life, limb, or liberty."[47] The decision by the Court of Appeal seemed to take a more "subjective" approach:

> The crucial question in these cases . . . is whether the threats, pressure or whatever it is is such as to destroy the reality of consent and overbears the will of the individual. It seems to me that this case . . . is a classic case of a young girl, wholly dependent on her

parents being forced into a marriage with a man she has never seen in order to prevent her (reasonably from her parents point of view) continuing in an association with a Muslim which they would regard with abhorrence. But it is as clear a case as one could want of the overbearing of the will of the petitioner and thus invalidating or vitiating her consent.[48]

Despite the sympathetic treatment of the wife's claim in *Hirani,* English courts have generally been "reluctant" to find duress in these cases. If children are simply being obedient to their parents, this does not constitute duress.[49]

One of the concerns of the British legal system with refusals to consummate the marriage is that it may indicate that the marriage was a sham, arranged only to permit a person to immigrate to England. Although the law did not prohibit the entry of spouses in arranged marriage, the primary purpose of the marriage cannot be to facilitate entry into the United Kingdom. The leading case was *R. v. Immigration Appeal Tribunal ex parte Bhatia* (1985). A citizen of India, Vinod Bhatia, applied for entry clearance to be allowed to go to Great Britain to marry Vinjay Kumari, a Hindu divorcee with a child. The entry clearance officer was not satisfied that the primary purpose of Bhatia was not to gain entry to the country. Apparently his statement that his father would probably not have agreed to the marriage had his bride not been in England was problematic. He appealed the decision unsuccessfully.[50]

The technical legal argument in these cases is whether parents have pressured their daughters to marry. If this can be established, then the wife may have a basis for annulment because of duress. The notion is that the wife did not give valid consent to the marriage.

Ultimately, cases of forced marriage will have to be resolved by girls who learn how to use the legal system of the country. If they challenge their parents' authority, they will find their rights vindicated. There may well be a cost associated with the legal victory; they may find they are ostracized by their own communities.[51]

Marriage by Capture

Marriage by capture might be regarded as a type of forced marriage, and it is found in many parts of the world. In some cases, girls as young as twelve or thirteen are abducted by much older men who claim this was a marriage ritual. When the men are prosecuted in American courts, they are charged with statutory rape, sexual assault, kidnapping, or false imprisonment. In cases when the woman is older, it may be difficult to determine whether or not she consented to the match.[52]

There have been many reports of marriage by capture, or *zij poj niam,* among the Hmong communities in California, Colorado, Minnesota, and Wisconsin.[53] After a Hmong man and woman exchange gifts, on a certain night, the man carries the woman off from her parents' home. In order to prove that she is virtuous, she is supposed to engage in a ritualized protest, crying "no, no, no; I'm not ready," even if she, in fact, wants to marry the man. The man, to demonstrate his virility, has to forcibly take the woman. They are supposed to go to his family's home where they spend three days together to consummate the marriage. Afterward there are marriage negotiations between the two clans.

A marriage by capture case—one of the most frequently cited cultural defense cases, *People v. (Kong) Moua* (1986)—dramatically illustrates the problem of disentangling the facts in cultural defense cases.[54] Twenty-one-year-old Kong Moua carried off eighteen-year-old Xieng Xiong as part of a traditional Hmong marriage ritual. When the first attempt failed because the parents prevented Xieng from leaving their home, Kong and two friends took her from the Fresno City College campus, throwing her into a station wagon. Her American friends observed her being taken in this fashion and naturally called the authorities. When the police arrived a few days later at Kong's family's home, they asked her who the man was with her and whether she wanted to leave with them. She responded that he was her husband and that she preferred to stay with him.

Shortly thereafter the woman decided to file kidnapping and rape charges against the man. The judge had to decide whether to admit evidence concerning Hmong marriage rituals, though it would have been difficult to understand the course of events without this information. The prosecutor was disinclined to take the case to trial because it would have been difficult for the jury to understand why the woman declined to leave with the police.[55] Her testimony also contained inconsistencies that might have undermined her credibility. The public defender did not want to have his client go to trial because he said he did not want to admit that his client had made a mistake. In reality, he was wary of invoking a mistake-of-fact defense, given the requirement of objective reasonableness.

In the end, the judge dropped the kidnapping and rape charges, and Moua pleaded guilty to false imprisonment, the lesser included offense under kidnapping. He received ninety days, with credit for time served, and was fined $1,000.[56]

Journalists and legal scholars referred to the case as "marriage by capture" even though the Hmong community did not consider it to be one. The woman's family considered the incident to be rape, not a marriage at all. The man's family thought the woman had consented to marry him, making it a marriage by elopement. Since she claimed that this was rape, and he insisted that this was marriage by elopement, it is unclear why it is has always been described as a marriage by capture case. Since the public defender basically argued that the case involved Kong's mistake of fact as to her consent, it should not be treated as a mistake of law case.[57]

The difficulty was establishing whether or not the woman had consented. An American jury would not have thought the woman, under the circumstances, was consenting. Indeed, feminists have educated American men that "no" means *no*. The problem in this case is how could the woman have said "no," given the cultural context.

The appropriate legal argument would have been mistake of fact as to consent. Even though commentators erroneously characterized the case as one involving a claim of ignorance of the law, which is no excuse, the case actually involved mistake of fact. Moua thought, apparently incorrectly, that Xiong was consenting to marry him when she engaged in the ritualized protest (since that is what she is expected to say). The problem Moua would have had with any attempt to argue mistake of fact as to Xiong's consent is that the law requires that the mistake be an objectively reasonable one. The objective reasonable person would not have thought that she was consenting, even if the average reasonable Hmong person would have thought so.

This highlights an obstacle to the use of the cultural defense, namely the continued adherence to objective reasonableness. Inasmuch as the objective person is the persona of the Anglo-Saxon, or European, it will be virtually impossible for a defendant to avail himself of a defense in the criminal law which is theoretically available to all. The interpretation of the mistake-of-fact defense seems to violate the principle of equal protection.

It may be that from a feminist perspective the mistake-of-fact defense in rape cases is offensive. Indeed, legislators might see fit to abolish such a defense generally. Until such time as the defense is rejected altogether, it is troublesome that it cannot be used by defendants who come from different cultures. One's cultural background ought not preclude the use of defenses that are supposed to be able to be invoked by all defendants.

The legal actors who were involved in the cases often show ambivalence to the culture conflicts. With reference to marriage by capture cases one prosecutor commented: "We want to acknowledge background as a mitigating circumstance, but we can't ignore the crime. . . . We shouldn't try to change their culture, but they should understand the limits."[58] The district attorney in a Colorado case also said: "We recognize cultural diversity here. That's what prompted our recommendations. But we also feel we need to tell the Hmong or any culture that when their culture conflicts with the laws of this country, that can constitute a crime. We can't just ignore that."[59]

The capture cases are problematic for several reasons. The girls are often underage, which means they cannot consent. Even when they are technically old enough to make a choice, the marriage ritual makes it virtually impossible to tell whether or not there is actual consent. Since this method is used rarely, only when the man is so poor or so ugly that no one will marry him, and other methods of marrying exist, it should not be used. Given the likelihood that a man will wind up with kidnapping, false imprisonment, or rape charges, he is better off finding an alternative method.

Those opposed to the use of the cultural defense tend to argue that girls prefer freedom of choice and prefer to be liberated from oppressive, patriarchal traditions. Although many may be "Americanized," one cannot assume that they entirely reject the way of life of their communities. They, too, may be somewhat ambivalent about the marriage ritual, which will make it difficult for district attorneys to prosecute.

Polygamy

Polygamy is a term used to refer to plural marriage, usually a husband who has multiple wives. The precise term for this is *polygyny*, whereas the term for a wife with multiple husbands is *polyandry*. Most of the cases that lead to culture conflicts involve polygyny. There are several legal consequences of attempts by immigrants to continue plural marriages or even enter into a potentially polygamous relationship in jurisdictions that allow only monogamous relationships, such as prosecution for bigamy, prosecution for statutory rape, and complications in the implementation of policies such as taxation, health insurance, and immigration.

Among the better known culture conflict cases are the early Mormon polygamy cases. In *Reynolds v. United States* (1878) the U.S. Supreme Court held that a religious freedom defense to a bigamy charge was properly rejected because to do otherwise would lead to anarchy, with each person deciding for himself with which laws he would comply. Despite this ruling in the nineteenth century, in Utah a controversy remains over the legitimacy of plural or "celestial" marriage. The American Civil Liberties Union in Utah unsuccessfully lobbied the national board to win a change in policy concerning plural marriage by appealing to its commitment to religious freedom.[60]

The Church of Jesus Christ of Latter-day Saints (Mormon) officially rejected polygamy, excommunicating polygamists for over a century. The notion was that a true Mormon could attain the highest level of heaven by conceiving as many children as possible. Statehood came in 1896 after the president of the church, Wilford Woodruff, formally disavowed polygamy in the "Polygamy Manifesto." In 1895 Utah approved a state constitution with the following clause: "polygamous or plural marriages are forever prohibited."[61]

Although polygamy remained against the law, no one was apparently prosecuted in Utah for over forty years.[62] Authorities attribute this to the lack of a specific statute outlawing polygamy; they would have to use the state bigamy laws. Most Utah polygamists, however, are not bigamists. They marry only one wife officially and take the others in church ceremonies, so that technically they have not committed bigamy. Because the state does not recognize the religious law concerning marriage ceremony, they are beyond the reach of the state law. Another problem faced by law enforcement is that the "victim" wife will rarely want to confront members of her extended family by testifying against them. Taking polygamists into custody has proven to be dangerous for the police, as well.[63] Instead of using bigamy laws, Utah officials instead rely on related crimes to go after polygamists such as child abuse, statutory rape, welfare fraud, and incest.

In 2000, Tom Green, an admitted polygamist, was to stand trial for four counts of bigamy, one count of criminal nonsupport for twenty-five of his twenty-nine children, and one count of child sexual assault. Although he divorced each wife before marrying the next one, after he appeared on national television programs boasting to 500 million people about his marital status, Utah prosecutors decided to press charges. Authorities considered his relationships as common law marriages and decided to proceed with prosecutions. In May 2001 Green was convicted of four counts of bigamy and one count of failing to pay child support. He received one five-year sentence for bigamy and later a concurrent sentence of five years for child rape. His lawyer filed an appeal with the Utah Court of Appeals on September 18, 2002.[64]

On occasion, immigrant polygamists have also been prosecuted in the United States. For example, in 1992 in the Bronx, a Nigerian national, Dr. Gregory Ezeonu, was prosecuted for the rape of his second or junior wife, Chiweta, who was thirteen years old.[65] His defense was that he was legally married to a living wife under both New York and Nigerian law. The court had to evaluate the status of the second marriage and second wife in New York. Although generally a marriage is recognized if valid where consummated, the court concluded that where recognition would be "repugnant to public policy," the general rule does not apply. The court thought it was obvious that polygamy was against public policy. In what was apparently a case of first instance for New York, the court held that bigamy was no defense to the charge of rape. Furthermore, the court explicitly said it was not interested in hearing witnesses from Nigeria who observed the marriage ceremony or expert witnesses to discuss marriage customs:

> While Nigerian law and custom may permit a "junior wife," New York does not recognize such status. Since at the time of his "marriage" to complainant, Dr. Ezeonu was married to his living wife, his "marriage" to her is absolutely void even were it legally consummated in Nigeria. Consequently, this court holds, as a matter of law, Dr. Ezeonu is not married to Chiweta for purposes of criminal liability for rape in the second degree, pursuant to Penal Law S130.30. Accordingly, he cannot raise the purported marriage as a defense to that crime.[66]

Temporary Marriage

Another type of marriage that has led to some controversy in legal systems unfamiliar with it is the temporary marriage. By this, I mean not a marriage that fails, resulting in divorce, but rather a union that is established for a limited period of time. Islamic law provides for a temporary marriage known as a *mut'a*. The practice originated in pre-Islamic Arabia and was outlawed by the Calipha Omar in seventh century a.d. It continues to be practiced only by Shi'a Muslims who reside mainly in Iran. Some criticize the tradition, comparing it to prostitution. The purpose of mut'a marriage is "sexual enjoyment for men and financial return for women." According to Haeri, although mut'a is considered a legitimate arrangement, both legally and morally, it never won much support.[67]

There are at least three requirements for mut'a: (1) it must take the form of a contract, (2) the contract must specify the precise duration of the marriage, and (3) the contract must indicate what consideration the husband will pay to the wife. There is no requirement that there be witnesses or that the contract be registered. Temporary marriage is said to have advantages: it discourages extramarital relations, permits relationships that would otherwise lead to punishment, and ensures that children resulting from temporary unions are legitimate and have inheritance rights. Mut'a also has disadvantages such as that it is difficult to prove the existence of the relationship in the case of a dispute, and it gives women fewer rights than are available in permanent marriage.[68]

In one Canadian case, a judge had to decide to whom to give custody of a child conceived in a temporary marriage. Farhat, a young Shi'a Muslim woman from South Asia, contracted eight mut'a marriages with Salman with whom she had a daughter, Fawzia.[69] Although Salman and his wife adopted the child, and Farhat was willing to have her live with them, she objected to their plans to leave Canada, taking the child with them. The legal dispute between the couple and the young woman forced the Canadian legal system to confront preconceived ideas about what constitutes a valid marriage.

In the litigation Farhat wanted to distance herself from the social constraints of Islamic culture.[70] When she underwent a psychiatric exam as a required part of the custody dispute, she insisted that she wanted a non-Muslim psychiatrist, but this was problematic because none of them knew about mut'a. The white male psychiatrist's report "portrayed Farhat as an eighteen-year-old woman who had knowingly had an affair with a married man, and who, after giving up the child for adoption to the biological father wanted to disrupt the life of what was "a happy family." Because Farhat's lawyers were dissatisfied with the report, they contacted Khan, a known expert on the status of Muslim women in Canada. The expert testimony was, according to Khan, misinterpreted by the judge who concluded that because Farhat would be socially ostracized as a consequence of the mut'a marriage, the child was better off with the father. The flaw in the judge's reasoning was to assume that Farhat and Fawzia could not have a life outside their family and community. Ultimately, it seems that the case shows the failure of the Canadian judge and other legal actors to understand the nature of mut'a.[71]

Another case where the judiciary had to grapple with the interpretation of mut'a, this time under California law, was *In re Marriage of Vryonis* (1988).[72] According to Fereshteh Vryonis, an Iranian citizen and a visiting professor at the University of California, Los Angeles, she and Speros Vryonis Jr., the director of the Near Eastern Studies Center, entered into a temporary marriage. When the relationship disintegrated, she filed for dissolution, attorney's fees, spousal support, and a determination of property rights. Speros denied that a marriage existed.

The trial court ruled that Fereshteh had a good faith belief that a valid marriage existed between them based on a finding that the private marriage ceremony in her apartment "conformed to the requirements of a Muslim Mota [sic] marriage." Speros appealed, challenging the finding of a "putative spouse status," arguing the ruling "resurrects common law marriage, contravening public policy" and contending that "it was an error to allow Fereshteh to testify as an expert regarding Islamic custom and practice and the Mut'a marriage." The appellate court held that even if Fereshteh had a good faith belief that she was "validly married" under California law, the ruling was in error because the requisite good faith belief must have an objectively reasonable basis. The fact that the couple had not attempted to comply with what the court considered the usual "indicia of marriage" made her belief, although sincerely held, unreasonable and therefore lacking in good faith.[73]

The difference in approach was that the trial court focused on the meaning of the ceremony for the parties under Islamic law, whereas the appellate court thought the proper analysis was whether the ceremony constituted a valid marriage under California law. The appellate court concluded that the trial court erred because a good faith belief that a valid marriage exists must be "objectively reasonable," which was not the case here. As Lona Laymon put it: "Thus, the less the custom "looks like" it complies with California law, the more "unreasonable" the belief in a valid marriage is."[74]

TYPES OF CULTURE CONFLICTS INVOLVING DIVORCE

When marriages disintegrate, rules differ as to whether divorce is allowed, and, if so, in what manner this should occur. Some religious law systems empower only men to make a divorce happen. This section considers the controversy over the *get* in Jewish law and the *talaq* in Islamic law as illustrations of the complexity involved in trying to correct inequalities in customary law systems.

Get

Under Jewish law the husband can refuse to grant a bill of divorce, or a *get*, leaving his wife unable to remarry. This meant that the Jewish wife was an *agunah*, the Hebrew word for a chained woman. Although it was not necessary that Jewish law be interpreted in this way, the fact remains that traditional Jewish wives have had no legal recourse within their own religion. Various forms of social pressure that had been used previously ceased to be as effective because people were increasingly mobile. As more Jewish women joined the women's rights movement in the 1970s, greater attention was focused on this issue. While some legal systems tried to liberate the agunah, this has been highly problematic.[75]

One problem is that a Jewish divorce cannot be imposed by the Jewish court, or Beth Din. Divorce is considered to be a two-way transaction between the husband and the wife, with the court playing only a "supervisory" role. The "recalcitrant spouse" is a challenge for U.S. orthodox and conservative Jews and for British reform communities where a get is necessary to end a marriage. Even in Israel, where a husband's failure to deliver a get when ordered by a rabbinical court is theoretically punishable by imprisonment, the rabbinical courts seldom find the facts merit such an order.[76]

The agunah has faced a number of difficulties because of her status. She could not remarry in the Jewish religion, any children born of civil marriages were considered illegitimate in the eyes of the Jewish community, and she remained indefinitely in a limbo state. Furthermore, some husbands, taking advantage of the plight of the *agunot* (plural of agunah), have wielded their exclusive power to grant a divorce for economic coercion. They pressured their wives to give up property and other assets in order to obtain a divorce. It was not unknown for wives to pay exorbitant sums of money and to forego child support in order to obtain a get. In *Segal v. Segal* (1995), for instance, Israel Segal refused to consent to a get unless his wife, Shirley, conveyed one residential property to him, waived child support and alimony, disclaimed any interest in martial assets including his business, and paid him $25,000. In such cases, the husband's pressures exerted on the wife seeking a get may be construed as duress.[77]

There have been attempts to rescue the chained wife through legislation and prenuptial agreements. New York, for example, enacted a law that required husbands to give their wives a get. This policy, while well-intentioned, was arguably unconstitutional as it led to an excessive entanglement of church and state. Indeed, the Reform movement opposed the law not only because it imposed religious obligations on American citizens in violation of the Establishment clause but also because it thought the Jewish community should solve its problems from within. The law has been criticized as being incomplete because it requires that parties suing must have removed all barriers to the other party's remarriage.[78]

In numerous U.S. cases, courts have been asked to interpret Jewish divorce law. Judges initially had difficulty understanding its complexities. Sometimes courts have ordered the enforcement of Jewish marriage contracts, while others declined to do so, citing constitutional and other impediments to this action. Where civil enforcement has been "successful," some rabbis may claim that, in any event, the get given by the husband is void. On occasion courts have used remedies to punish husbands who failed to deliver the get, such as awarding all the marital assets to wives. They have also denied visitation or custody rights on the grounds of moral turpitude.[79]

Courts have sometimes condemned economic blackmail by husbands in harsh terms. For example, in *Giahn v. Giahn* (2000) a court held that an agreement to deliver a get in exchange for assets was null and void, saying: "The State of New York has made painfully clear that it will not tolerate the perversion of the Jewish Get process into an unconscionable instrument of coercion by husbands who have the sole power to cause delivery thereof, a situation putting wives at the mercy of unscrupulous, often sadistic husbands."[80] In 1992 a wife was granted a divorce on the grounds of cruelty, and the court divided the assets equally between them. Three months afterward, the husband promised to deliver a get in exchange for a deed to her interest in their former domicile. The husband failed to deliver the get, after which the court ruled that the agreement was null and void and awarded all the marital assets to the wife.

The issue remains unresolved in Europe, Israel, South Africa, and the United States. The main concerns are that government interference in the divorce process is unconstitutional, that it is unwise for the state to make the get problem its responsibility, and ultimately that a secular policy will not be accepted by those within the religious communities. One must recognize that if the state fails to take a position on the get, this "neutral" position leaves the Jewish wife in her predicament. The dilemma is that even if the state intervenes and the get is considered invalid, the agunah is no better off than she would have been had she simply abandoned her faith or remarried in the Reform movement. Intervention is invalid according to the external constitutional standards and results in a divorce that is invalid according to internal religious principles, all of which perpetuates a self-imposed system. The precise method for reconciling civil and religious law continues to be hotly debated.[81]

Talaq

Whereas the Jewish wife in the cases just described had to contend with a husband who refused to end the marriage by granting a get, the Muslim wife sometimes faces precisely the opposite problem: namely, the ability of the husband to divorce her without her consent.[82] The institution of *talaq*, or unilateral divorce by the husband, creates special legal problems for wives residing in countries which are unsure how to interpret their marital status. According to religious law, a husband can pronounce the required formula—"I divorce you, I divorce you, I divorce you"—which instantly dissolves the marriage. Because recognizing this tradition reinforces a patriarchal custom, courts are disinclined to do so.

This issue has received attention in England where the relevant policy was a 1971 law, the Recognition of Divorces and Legal Separations Act, which specified that if a divorce was obtained by "judicial or other proceedings" outside the United Kingom and valid in the country where it was obtained, English court would accept the divorce. Sometimes the analysis is complicated by "transnational talaqs." In England, Pakistani women wanted to enter the U.K. as fiancees of men who had tried to dissolve previous marriages with wives by pronouncing the talaq and sending a letter to their wives in Pakistan. In *Fatima v. Secretary of State of the Home Department* [1986], a Pakistani husband pronounced a talaq in England and sent home the required notice to his wife. The House of Lords affirmed the decision of the lower courts that the divorce could not be recognized in England, and hence he was not allowed to bring another woman, his fiancée, into England. In general, the English courts have not wanted to facilitate talaq divorces. Occasionally, this might disadvantage women. Evidently, Muslim women have not felt that they could remarry in England with only a civil law divorce. As of 1990, it was apparently an open question whether a British judge could force a Muslim husband to pronounce a talaq.[83]

Another case where the crux of the issue was the proper interpretation of the talaq was the *Radwan* litigation. In *Radwan v. Radwan* (1972) an Egyptian national married an English woman at the Egyptian consulate in Paris; she was his second wife. After the couple moved to London, the husband entered the Egyptian consulate there and used the talaq to divorce her. Several years later, the wife filed for divorce in the English court. The wife's lawyer argued that the talaq performed in the consulate should not be recognized under English law as it was not performed "outside of" England. The judge eventually agreed with the wife's position that Mr. Radwan had not legally divorced his wife in a place "outside of" England. However, in *Radwan v. Radwan* (No. 2) (1972), the same judge ruled in the wife's action for divorce that France also did not recognize the extraterritoriality fiction, and therefore that the marriage performed in the consulate in Paris was void.

Child Support

Yet another cultural question arises when a couple divorces and the court has to make a determination as to whether the children should receive support. This was contentious in *Uboh-Abiola v. Abiola* (1992) where Gloria Uboh-Abiola, a thirty-four-year-old physician living in New York, and one of Chief Abiola's twenty-five wives, filed for divorce as well as child support for their three children.[84] Chief Abiola claimed to have married only four times in accordance with Islamic law and that Uboh-Abiola was one of his eighteen concubines.

The status of their relationship was not considered important as the court was unwilling to recognize a polygamous marriage. All that mattered to the court was that Mr. Abiola was legally married more than once and that Uboh-Abiola was not the first woman he married. Because they were Yoruba from Nigeria, the court was unwilling to recognize the marriage, as this was considered to be against public policy.[85] Nevertheless, the court ordered Mr. Abiola to pay $15,000 a month in child support as well as the children's other medical insurance expenses.

Spiritual Custody

Another cultural conflict resulting from divorce occurs when courts must decide on the custody of children who are born to parents of differing religious faiths. The number of interreligious marriages increased dramatically in the 1990s. As a consequence, when these unions disintegrate, there is a question about the religious upbringing of the children.[86] Sometimes one parent will convert during the marriage—for example, the Catholic mother will convert to Judaism—and the parents will raise their children in accordance with the one religion. When the couple divorces and the mother returns to Catholicism and receives physical custody of the children, the issue is whether she must raise the children in the Jewish tradition. In some cases the courts will award mothers physical custody but award the fathers so-called spiritual custody. One legal issue is whether courts must enforce agreements to give the noncustodial parent control over the religious upbringing of the child.[87]

Courts are sometimes asked to determine the religious identity of children, in the presence or absence of written religious upbringing agreements.[88] There are serious concerns about judicial enforcement of these agreements. Even where there is no pre-existing agreements, the idea that courts should regulate the practice of religion in the home is cause for alarm. The argument in favor of having judicial determination of the child's religion is that it is too confusing for the child to have to contend with two worldviews. Religious individuals also worry that the exposure to two religions will cause the child to opt for secular humanism or no religion. In addition to ensuring that the child is securely committed to one faith, adjudicating spiritual custody may minimize the number of conflicts between the father and mother.

In a comprehensive discussion of the arguments associated with spiritual custody, Martin Weiss and Robert Abramoff emphasize a few key arguments in support of enforcing religious upbringing agreements: they argue (1) that children will be torn between pleasing one parent and upsetting the other parent, (2) that adults adhere to only one religion and therefore it is unrealistic to expect children to cope with more than one, and (3) that while it is fine to belong to many cultures, religion is something quite distinct from heritage or culture.

There are several arguments against having state intervention in matters religious. One is that this represents excessive encroachment into private, familial decisions. It is overly intrusive to have the government monitoring the religious practices in the home to guarantee that a child is exposed to only the agreed-upon traditions. Furthermore, spiritual custody will violate the free exercise and privacy rights of the custodial parent.

The central question is often what determination would be in the best interests of the child. Unfortunately, this standard is nebulous and cannot provide much guidance as to the proper resolution of many of these conflicts. In some cases such as religions that use snake-handling, judicial orders to protect children from ceremonies may correspond to the best interests standard. Often, however, it will not be clear-cut, as for example, in the cases where Jehovah's Witnesses have taken children with them during door-to-door solicitations and courts have intervened to forbid this.

With virtually no empirical evidence demonstrating harm to the child from exposure to two religions, the case for allowing judicial intervention in spiritual custody disputes is remarkably weak. Despite the lack of a justification for this sort of involvement, judges have sometimes taken it upon themselves to require adherence to one religion or another. This kind of intervention may be deleterious.[89]

An example of a "neutral" approach is that of the California Court of Appeals in the case of *Weiss v. Weiss* (1996). Although Martin and Marsha were adherents of different religions—he was Jewish and she was Baptist—during their marriage they practiced Judaism; Marsha converted one month before their wedding. When they divorced, they were awarded joint physical and legal custody of the children. Martin appealed the trial court's decision not to enjoin Marsha from having the children participate in non-Jewish religious activities. The court held that the prenuptial agreement, according to which the children were to be raised as Jewish, would lead to judicial entanglement and was also unenforceable:

> In view of Marsha's inalienable First Amendment right to the free exercise of religion, which includes the right to change her religious beliefs and to share those beliefs with her offspring, her antenuptial commitment to raise her children in Martin's faith is not legally enforceable for that reason as well.[90]

REFLECTIONS

Cultural variation in marriage traditions has led to numerous clashes with the law. As presented in this chapter, courts have often had considerable difficulty trying to figure out how to approach the traditions in light of formal legal requirements. Although one might have expected courts to be disinclined to intervene in disputes of this kind because marriage is a private familial matter, they have nevertheless often been willing to scrutinize the relationships and the rules governing them.

In some of the cases, when courts tried to figure out whether marriages were contracted with the full and free consent of both parties, it often proved challenging to do so because of the different cultural context in which the marriage was negotiated. After the fact, it is exceedingly difficult for a judge to determine whether or not legal consent existed. Did the woman or husband agree to the union only because of duress? It is often hard to say. As a consequence, judges appear reluctant to declare marriages of ethnic minorities null and void.

When it is clear that a husband or wife was coerced into marrying a person, courts have the power to conclude that no marriage ever occurred by invoking the legal doctrine of duress. This legal principle provides a means of rescuing women from relationships not of their choosing and represents an alternative to the notion of irreparable harm for deciding when to limit cultural traditions. Duress may also be employed to restore marital assets to the Orthodox Jewish wife who was compelled to surrender her claims to property through economic coercion in order to obtain the get from her recalcitrant husband. While duress may be an effective principle, it can only influence the outcome if judges are willing to interpret it in the cultural context in which the relationship existed.

Some may think that those who travel from a society in which the group selects a mate to one in which the individual has the say-so will prefer the later. However, even though many of the defendants and plaintiffs in the cases considered in this chapter were highly educated, they still preferred to marry in accordance with the traditional law. This suggests that it is naive to assume that assimilation will occur on its own and that it is simply a matter of time before immigrants will shed their traditional practices. It is likely, therefore, that ethnic minorities will continue to follow different marriage customs for quite some time.

Where courts regard marriage rituals as repugnant, they have intervened. Despite these well-intentioned efforts, often to rescue women or girls from apparently unacceptable situations, the courts have either made matters worse or simply failed to solve the problem, as with the agunah. In the case of judicial treatment of the get, courts have arguably violated the rules of the dominant legal system and have also rendered a decision which is almost certainly incompatible with Jewish law.

In many instances judges will have to be more open-minded about the broad range of social relationships that exist in the world. Failure to grasp the significance of family bonds and unwillingness to understand the rules by which others operate can often lead to the miscarriage of justice. This is not to say that courts should decline to intervene to protect women from oppressive practices in all circumstances, but before doing so, courts should ascertain whether there is truly an irreparable harm posed to the spouse by the marriage practice, or whether the relationship was established under duress. In the absence of any actual threat or coercion, intervention should be impermissible.

8

Attire

Dress codes often generate significant culture conflicts. In this chapter I concentrate on disputes involving ethnic or religious garb. Individuals may challenge rules regarding attire either because they are required by religion to don a symbol or because they choose to dress in an ethnic fashion. The central question is whether individuals should be permitted to wear symbols linked to their cultural identity in various contexts including the workplace, the courtroom, public transport, schools, the military, and prisons. This chapter examines court cases involving ethnic minorities who wish to wear ethnic or religious garb[1] but are denied the right to do so by one of these institutions.

In many cases the plaintiffs base their legal arguments on the constitutional right to the free exercise of religion and sometimes to freedom of expression; in other cases they allege discriminatory conduct under a civil rights statute—for example, in the United States on Title VII. Regardless of what legal framework is utilized, the justifications for disallowing attire are usually aesthetics, public health, public safety, and solidarity. In the vast majority of cases, courts uphold dress code policies, despite their negative effect on ethnic minorities and despite the absence of evidence of any threat of harm to society. Through the close analysis of a set of cases it will be possible to determine whether the law should be more flexible and make exceptions to permit attire with cultural or religious significance. The degree to which accommodation is feasible may depend on the nature of the institution, the type of symbol, and the sort of justification offered for the dress restriction.[2]

In virtually all of the culture conflict cases considered in this chapter, the symbols are either hair or headgear. For instance, many lawsuits are concerned with

hairstyles such as beards, braids, cornrows, and dreadlocks. The headgear controversies involve the kufi, the turban, the veil or headscarf, and the yarmulke. It is
important to try to ascertain the reasons why these symbols generate so much litigation. Part of the explanation hinges on the symbolic meanings conveyed by different
types of clothing.[3]

It must be noted at the outset that as ethnic minorities are usually in positions
of relative powerlessness, they themselves rarely determine dress codes. Consequently, they do not decide what the "image" of the establishment or institution
should be. Because of this power imbalance, it is crucial that those in positions of
power within the legal system evaluate their cultural assumptions regarding the
threat of harm to society posed by particular symbols. I wish to challenge the pre-
suppositions evident in many of the cases examined here.

In what follows I provide an overview of culture conflicts in which dress codes
are in dispute. I will examine selected cases in depth as a way of getting at the
broader theoretical implications of allowing culture in civil litigation. By studying
this type of litigation, we should gain insight into the ways in which the law handles
symbols that are crucial for the maintenance of the identity of ethnic minority
groups. We can then determine whether contemporary legal approaches to culture
in attire cases are jurisprudentially sound.

INSTITUTIONAL SETTINGS

Workplace

Generally, the presumption is that if an employee chooses to work for an employer
whose uniform is clearly specified, then the employee should be prepared to comply
with the required dress standards. The underlying assumption is that a business
establishment should have the right to control its image. Obviously, however, there
are limits to this. For instance, a restaurant may not hire only men because they prefer to have a "European" ambiance.[4] Moreover, it would clearly be illegal to hire only
members of one race because of a desire to have, for example, an Aryan image.

Dress codes involve more subtle interpretive questions. Is it racially discriminatory not to permit an African American woman to wear a cornrow hairstyle as a
badge of ethnic pride? Is it a violation of religious freedom not to allow a Sikh man,
who seeks employment in a pizza parlor, to wear the beard or kesh required by his
religion? The question is when a restriction on attire is actually a subterfuge for discrimination.

Hotels

In several cases African American women have challenged hotel grooming policies
that prohibited the wearing of cornrows, a hairstyle worn predominantly by black
women to celebrate their cultural heritage. In 1987 Pamela Mitchell, a hotel reservations phone operator, after being threatened with termination if she refused to

remove her cornrows, decided to challenge the Marriott hotel's policy which prohibited "extreme faddish hairdos." The hotel apparently "sought to eliminate all 'grooming fads' from the workplace." Considered in the same category as spiked hair and purple hair, braided hairstyles were also deemed to be "fads" and hence "unacceptable." Ms. Mitchell was told that she had to either remove her cornrows or cover them with a relaxed/European style wig. Failure to do one or the other would result in termination of her employment. Despite these warnings, Ms. Mitchell continued to wear her cornrows because "to wear a wig under these circumstances . . . would be shamefully hiding a part of her cultural identity."[5]

Mitchell initially filed a complaint with the Equal Employment Opportunity Commission (EEOC), asking for an injunction to prevent Marriott from terminating her job.[6] Eventually, it was the more expeditious D.C. Office of Human Rights which, in its determination, found probable cause to believe that Marriot's policy constituted discrimination on the basis of race and personal appearance. According to the settlement of June 29, 1988, Mitchell was allowed to keep her part-time job and to wear cornrows to work. She reportedly received $40,000 in compensatory damages (and $15,000 in attorney fees), and Marriott was required to modify its policy to allow multibraided hairstyles and to notify its employees of this change in policy. As a condition of the settlement Mitchell "agreed to withdraw her discrimination complaint and to refrain from pursuing the issue in court."[7] Since the amount of the damages represented a mere pittance to a major corporation, some downplayed the significance of the decision. There was some reason for celebrating the victorious outcome inasmuch as Marriott did change its policy and the result could affect decision-making in other cases.[8]

In a case raising similar issues, Cheryl Tatum and Cheryl Parahoo, employees of the Hyatt Hotel coffee shop, challenged Hyatt's policy: "Hairstyles must not be extreme or unusual and should be appropriate for the health, safety and grooming standards of your department and the hotel." Although the general corporate policy did not explicitly state that cornrow hairstyles were prohibited, it was apparently Hyatt's interpretation of the policy that cornrows were "extreme or unusual." Parahoo said "she was forced to wear a wig over her cornrow hairstyle," and Hyatt admitted that both women were "instructed to wear wigs over their cornrow hairstyles." In their complaint the women alleged that the Hyatt company policy against "extreme or unusual hair styles," which was interpreted to include cornrows, was racially discriminatory.[9]

The Hyatt case received national media attention. The publicity surrounding the dispute led to a national boycott campaign against Hyatt, protest rallies at Hyatt hotels, and an attempt at mediation by the Reverend Jesse Jackson. Like Marriott, Hyatt eventually decided to overrule local managers and accept cornrow hairstyles, provided they were "neat" and "conservative."[10]

Hyatt defended its appearance policy, maintaining that it was "intended to enhance its image and provide a professional, high-quality atmosphere."[11] There was a special need for image control where women are "front-of-the-house" employees because of their direct contact with hotel guests. Interestingly, however, other women, not "front-of-the-house" employees—for example, those in the housekeeping and security departments—were also subject to the anti-cornrow policy.

Another difficulty with Hyatt's position was that the hotel allowed employees to wear "European-inspired" hairstyles that could be considered "extreme or unusual," such as "spiked" hair, hair that was several feet long, and "hair dyed decorative shades at the tips." It also permitted Latino men to wear small ponytails. Thus, it was, in reality, only black women who were sanctioned for choosing to wear a particular hairstyle.

On May 4, 1988, the EEOC ruled against Hyatt in what was hailed as a landmark decision. That the EEOC found Hyatt's policy to be in violation of section 703(a) of Title VII was highly unusual because seldom are employers' dress codes found to be racially discriminatory. On August 26, 1988, the Hyatt Hotels Corporation dropped its ban on cornrows and announced the initiation of a new program to encourage more minorities to enter the hotel and resort management industry. In light of these developments, the D.C. Office of Human Rights decided not to pursue it investigation of discrimination complaints against Hyatt.[12]

The EEOC ruling that Hyatt had discriminated against black female employees did not lead to a successful conciliation. Consequently, in May 1987 the plaintiffs filed a lawsuit in the Superior Court of the District of Columbia, alleging that Hyatt violated federal and local antidiscrimination laws. The court dismissed the suit, but the Court of Appeals reversed. Then in a pre-jury settlement, the complainants recovered damages comparable to those received by Mitchell.[13]

While it is certainly true that the damages might have been more substantial, the cornrow cases were significant. First, legal institutions finally acknowledged that the dress codes were racist. Second, major hotels actually changed their policies. The plaintiff's attorney, Eric Steele, stated that as many as one thousand women may have been "victims" of the Hyatt ban on cornrows.[14] In addition, many other employers enforced anti-braid policies,[15] which were called into question by the EEOC ruling. Third, national media coverage served to raise public consciousness about ethnocentric practices and the need for greater cultural sensitivity.

The plaintiffs advanced two main legal arguments: disparate treatment and disparate impact. Because the policy was enforced only against African American women, the hotels were treating employees in cornrows differently, in violation of civil rights law. A disparate treatment claim will succeed even if not all members of the group share the characteristic that is at issue and as long as there is no defense of bona fide occupational qualification as there is for religion, sex, and national origin.[16]

The second argument was that since braids are worn predominantly by African American women, the policy, though apparently neutral, has a disproportionate impact on them. Moreover, there was no manifest relationship between the braided hairstyle and job performance, and hence the business necessity defense had no effect.[17] In the context of dress codes that have a disparate impact on African American women, one wonders what business necessity would serve as a justification. An aesthetic claim for image control based on customer preference should not be able to legitimize racially discriminatory policies as customer preference is normally not a legitimate basis for accepting an employer's discriminatory practices. Another conceptual difficulty with the image control argument is that no evidence was presented by either Hyatt or Marriott to prove that cornrows were inconsistent with the hotel image.

It is hard to tell from the decisions which argument was more compelling and whether each provided a discrete and independent basis for deciding in favor of the complainants. In general, it seems that the disparate impact argument is stronger because an employer might enforce an anti-braid policy consistently, in which case the disparate treatment argument might fail. Regardless of which argument was more persuasive, the end result was that the anti-cornrow policy was determined to be a form of invidious racial discrimination, and the hotels had to change their policies.

The successful outcome was somewhat unexpected because in past court cases—for example, *Renee Rogers v. American Airlines* (1981) and *Carswell v. Peachford Hospital* (1981)—the plaintiffs had failed to convince courts that policies forbidding cornrow hairstyles were racially discriminatory. Their attorney, Eric Steele, distinguished the precedents, arguing that the flight attendant in *Rogers* had been given the option to wear a bun, whereas the hotel employees were given no such alternative. *Carswell* evidently differed from the more recent cases because it was the beads in the cornrows that were impermissible and not the cornrow hairstyle itself.[18]

One of the key arguments in the earlier litigation was that cornrows are worn as a matter of choice. Unlike the "Afro" or "natural" styles, cornrows are not a necessary or immutable trait but are instead deliberately worn: "It is not the product of natural hair growth but of artifice."[19] The fact that the hairstyle is created seems to imply that it is not a racial trait but rather a cultural one. Given current doctrine, it is, therefore, a more subtle question as to whether the anti-cornrow policy was clearly racist. However, it is not obvious why traits chosen by ethnic groups should be less privileged than immutable traits. Whether innate or not, they are part of the cultural identity of the group in question. Ethnicity need not be interpreted in racial terms.[20]

One might have expected the complainants to argue that the dress code violated Title VII's provision regarding discrimination based on national origin. Although Title VII does not define "national origin," it is unlikely that transnational groups can use this part of the law. For several reasons, it would have been difficult for Mitchell and Tatum to argue national origin discrimination. An African American aesthetic standard is not "national," and it would not be feasible to prove that the anti-braid policy was adopted because of prejudice against any particular African nation. Of course, using national origin as opposed to race would have made the bona fide occupational qualification defense available to the employer.[21]

It is noteworthy that the cases involved double claims of discrimination. Mitchell argued that she was discriminated against on the bases of her race and personal appearance, and the D.C. Office of Human Rights agreed. In addition, the office found that the policy adversely affected black females. When Tatum argued that the hotel grooming policy had an impact on black women in particular, the EEOC found discrimination against black women based on both race and gender. Some scholars have criticized the analysis in similar earlier cases, claiming that it ignores the interactive effect of race and sex.[22]

In their defense, the hotels tried to claim that the national headquarters never proscribed cornrows and that local hotels mistakenly interpreted the national policy to prohibit this hairstyle. In fact, the national policies allegedly prohibited only "extreme" or "faddish" hairstyles, a policy that was interpreted by some local hotels to forbid cornrows. But it was the contention of the complainants that the national office knew about the "misinterpretation" of the policy and did nothing to correct it. Since the anti-cornrow policy was an unwritten one, it was, therefore, not inevitable that the hairstyle would be considered impermissible.

Another issue raised by the hotels was whether employees worked in high- or low-visibility positions. This distinction is legally irrelevant unless cornrows are considered to be repugnant. The point is that no matter where employees work, they should be permitted to wear cornrows.

It is somewhat puzzling that a hairstyle should spark such a controversy. Why are cornrows objectionable? Cheryl Tatum noted that personnel director approached Tatum's hairstyle "like those braids were something that horrified her." The personnel director reportedly exclaimed: "I can't understand why you would want to wear your hair like that anyway. What would our guests think if we allowed you all to wear your hair like that?"[23] What is so threatening about cornrows that hotels and other employers disallow them and are willing to litigate to defend this policy?

The hotels claimed they had to engage in image control. In the case of Marriott, however, this is suspect, considering that Mitchell's contact with the public was almost exclusively conducted by phone. The director of corporate relations for Marriott defended the policy, claiming that having two separate grooming standards "would cause resentment among workers in public positions."[24]

There seems to have been something particularly objectionable about cornrows. One possible interpretation is that this hairstyle was simply not compatible with European aesthetic standards. Unfortunately, however, the enforcement of a Eurocentric dress code worked to the detriment of black women. For example, in *Mitchell v. Marriott* (1988), counsel argued that Marriott did not threaten "to discharge any other employee notwithstanding how outlandish their appearance or dress, as long as the appearance or dress was European-inspired. Their actions in this regard were motivated by arbitrary, ethnocentric, and racist considerations."[25] The corporate world, despite affirmative action, seems unwilling to accept culturally different aesthetic standards:

> It seems that although white establishments are forced, by law, to seek an integrated workforce, many employers nonetheless insist that their Black female employees appear as white or "European" as possible. Thus, often when a sister wears cornrows, another braided artstyle, or any other chemical-free natural hairstyle, this seems to strike a racist

"nerve" in her white supervisor who cannot stand to see something inherently African in the workplace. . . . It appears that for many whites, integration is, at best, only a one-way street of assimilation for blacks.[26]

Some whites associate the African style with the uncivilized "jungle." This effort to protect European civilization from the threat of other images is perceived to be crucial for the maintenance of white power structures.[27]

Another reason some European Americans dislike cornrows may stem from an erroneous perception that the braids are not clean. The style was, in fact, developed because it promotes healthy scalps and good hygiene. Those wearing the hairstyle wash their hair at least once a week, and after six to eight weeks have their hair completely unbraided, washed, and conditioned. Maintenance of cornrows requires that they be oiled almost daily.[28]

Whites are, for the most part, are generally unaware of most aspects of the braiding enterprise. Although there is a so-called cottage industry in braiding, there is virtually no legal protection for braiders because they may not be considered official cosmetologists under the law. Some contend that they earn less as a result.[29]

These arguments hardly seem serious enough to warrant prohibition of cornrows. It would appear that the concern about cornrows has something to do with their symbolic power. As a badge of African pride, the hair conveys a strong pro-black and perhaps activist message, which may be viewed as threatening by whites. In a number of articles, cornrows are described as being part of a "militancy" (or there is a denial that they project this attitude) or as "anti-business"[30] One explanation was that those frightened of cornrows have confused the hairstyle with dreadlocks. Another suggestion is that an association between cornrows and slavery creates "a negativity toward braids." It is conceivable that the style evokes feelings of white guilt.[31]

Drawing on psychological interpretations of hair symbolism, one might gain insight into the symbolic dimensions of cornrows that give whites cause for alarm. According to some scholars hair is linked to sexuality and may have phallic connotations, whether it belongs to women or men. One study of cornrows suggests that they may conjure up imagery of "snakelike locks" associated with Medusa, the goddess whose glance turned viewers to stone. These braids, unconsciously linked to Medusa, inspire fear: "Female phallicism constitutes terrorism to male authority." Although it may be dangerous to interpret an African hairstyle by means of Western mythology, it seems appropriate, as here we are interested in the misperception of cornrows by whites. Whether or not a psychological interpretation of cornrows is compelling, it seems likely that the choice to wear cornrows is perceived by the dominant system as an expression of female power.[32]

Whites may also view cornrows as sexually provocative. They may associate cornrows with Bo Derek who wore cornrows when she appeared as a sex symbol in the film *Ten*. Even though Bo Derek was probably not responsible for the increased appearance of cornrows, she may have given whites the impression that the hairstyle was seductive.[33]

Regardless of why cornrows have proven to be controversial, there is no aesthetic justification for prohibiting them.[34] Only extreme cultural arrogance leads employers to deny African American women the right to wear the magnificent braids as a way of recognizing and preserving their cultural identity.

It is intriguing that Tatum and Mitchell prevailed even though the attire was cultural, as opposed to religious or racial (in the usual sense of an immutable characteristic). It may, of course, be easier to justify accommodation where the justification for the dress restriction is purely aesthetic.[35] These cases demonstrate that it is politically possible for institutions to accommodate ethnic minorities. Legally, however, the reality is that the anti-cornrow policy is still permissible as *Rogers* has never been overruled.[36] Since the EEOC decision in *Tatum* has no value as a precedent, employers can still cite *Rogers* in their defense as persuasive authority.

Restaurants

Restaurants often have strict rules governing appearance, which are ostensibly based on a public health rationale. Among those who have challenged dress codes in the food industry are Sikhs. Because baptized Sikhs are required to wear the "five K's," including *kesh* (uncut hair), their religion prevents them from shaving their beards. This led to a conflict in December 1987 for Mr. Prabhjot Kohli, a Sikh from India, who sought employment as a manager in a franchise of Domino's Pizza, Inc. (DPI). Although initially impressed with Mr. Kohli's credentials, which included eighteen years of experience as a salesman, the franchise decided not to hire him because he would not remove his beard.[37]

Kohli filed a complaint with the Maryland Commission on Human Relations under a state civil rights law, alleging that he was unlawfully denied employment because of his religion. Although the Administrative Law Judge (ALJ) decided in his favor, awarding him $6,000 in back pay and ordering him appointed to the next available manager position, the appeals board of the Maryland Commission on Human Relations did not agree with the ALJ decision. After the state trial court in Maryland also ruled in favor of DPI, Kohli appealed to the Maryland Court of Appeals. The case was eventually settled out of court for a small sum, thousands less than Kohli spent on litigation. Domino's changed its no-beard policy but denied that it was related to the lawsuit, saying it was "changing American fashions."[38]

The Maryland law mirrors the provisions of Title VII, which makes it useful to consult Title VII decisions on this matter. The statutory framework for analysis developed from Title VII and the 1972 amendments to it led to the following statutory framework for analysis:

> First, a conflict must exist between an employee's religious practices and her employer's rules; second, that conflict then triggers a duty for the employer to reasonably accommodate the employee; unless, third, all accommodations cause undue hardship on the employers's business.[39]

The statute requires that the employee make a prima facie showing of religious discrimination, after which the burden shifts to the employer. The question becomes the scope of the employer's duty of reasonable accommodation, which has been interpreted to mean a duty to accommodate, provided it requires no more that a "de minimis cost." Even if an accommodation requires more than this cost, it may not necessarily constitute a hardship.[40]

The central legal question in this dispute was whether or not DPI had made a reasonable accommodation. Based on one precedent, *EEOC v. Sambo's of Georgia, Inc.* (1981), DPI argued that where the accommodation would have been too burdensome, it did not have to make any attempt to accommodate. However, the ALJ ruled in favor of Kohli, finding that Domino's Pizza had failed to make any effort whatsoever to accommodate him, in the absence of convincing evidence of a costly burden.[41]

DPI tried to prove that modifying its no-beard policy would jeopardize its business. Two beard studies were presented to demonstrate the cost of accommodation, and so, one issue was how much weight to give them. According to the beard study, customers were more unlikely to purchase pizzas from employees with beards or facial hair because they "associate cleanliness with clean shaven employees." The beard snood study was designed to measure customers' attitudes toward employees wearing a beard snood, a type of beard restraint. According to this study customers "reported negative feelings toward such employees."[42]

The ALJ took a skeptical view of the studies. She questioned the scientific validity of the beard study and noted that the beard snood study was conducted for use in the litigation. Neither study could establish whether customers would object to employees with beard nets.[43]

Whether or not the studies provide an accurate characterization of customers' perceptions of employees with beards is ultimately irrelevant. The justification for a no-beard policy was supposed to be public health, but in the end it turned out be image control. Domino's Pizza was concerned with customers' perception of cleanliness based on prejudice toward beards, not with any actual health threat such as contamination of food by hair. Domino's justification conflates the public health argument with an appearance argument.[44]

When customers' preferences are based on bigotry, they should be given no weight. If customer preferences could justify discriminatory employment practices, public accommodations might still be segregated. If attitudes are obviously repugnant and irrelevant in cases involving racial discrimination, then it is unclear why these prejudices should matter in cases involving religious discrimination.[45]

A few other legal arguments deserve mention. First, DPI did not raise any question about either the authenticity of the Sikh religion or the sincerity of Kohli's commitment to the Sikh religion.[46] Second even though he was prepared to compromise by wearing either a beard snood or net, Domino's Pizza expected him to assimilate completely.

Another issue was whether the precedent of *EEOC v. Sambo's of Georgia* should influence the disposition of this case. The fact pattern in Sambo's was strikingly similar. A Sikh applied for a manager position in Sambo's restaurant but was not hired because he would not shave his beard. However, the ALJ distinguished Sambo's because it was a restaurant, whereas Domino's was primarily a pizza delivery service. Moreover, the ALJ was impressed by the failure of the court to consider possible accommodations.

It is worthwhile considering the implications of this dispute. First, the stated justification for the dress code may not be the actual one. The rationale for a no-beard policy was not public health but appearance! Since, as seen in the cornrow cases, the control of image often involves bias, there is reason to question the policy. Even if it could be empirically shown that the majority is more "comfortable" buying pizzas from beardless employees, the public may simply have to adjust to avoid religious discrimination.[47]

The legal standard involved in this case—namely, the duty of reasonable accommodation—has consistently been interpreted in a manner detrimental to religious minorities. Unless the courts rethink the "de minimis" requirement, virtually no protection will be afforded members of these groups.

Let us consider the proposal that customer preferences be considered irrelevant in all discrimination cases, including religion. Further, we must change the obvious pro-business bias that persists because of the minimal burden notion and because the employer chooses the type of accommodation among the possible options. Whether or not accommodation is required should be decided by weighing the burden of the dress policy to the religious employee against the burden to the business. This means that burden should not be understood solely in monetary terms. In addition, the religious employee should be empowered to select the type of accommodation most appropriate for his or her religion.

The significance of shaving the beard can be understood in religious and psychological terms. When a Sikh cuts his hair, he may be excommunicated. According to the psychological interpretation of hair symbolism, the shaving of the beard, as a form of haircutting, means castration. Charles Berg has amassed considerable data to support this argument. One of the most interesting pieces of information is that religious figures who take a vow of celibacy often shave their heads. In symbolic terms, therefore, requiring a man to shave symbolically means his emasculation.[48]

It is possible that at the conscious level the general public simply views the beard as "a gesture of rebellion" or the locus of bacteria. But as with the cornrows cases it is intriguing that something as seemingly mundane as an exemption from a dress code should give rise to expensive litigation.

Industries

In the industrial context, dress and grooming policies are often justified on public safety grounds. In *Bhatia v. Chevron* (1984) the Federal Court of Appeals for the Ninth Circuit affirmed a summary judgment ruling against a Sikh who would not remove his beard to comply with the employer's safety policy. In order to comply with California's Occupational Safety and Health Administration (OSHA) standards, Chevron adopted a safety policy requiring employees whose work exposed them to toxic gases to shave facial hair that "prevented them from achieving a gas-tight face seal when wearing a respirator."[49]

After Bhatia informed Chevron that he could not shave his beard as required by the policy, Chevron suspended him from his machinist position without pay while the company looked for another job for him. Chevron subsequently offered him lower-paying clerical and janitorial positions.

The court found that there had been a reasonable accommodation. The court noted that while Bhatia was suspended without pay, his coworkers who refused to shave were simply terminated. Particularly persuasive was the fact that granting Bhatia an exemption would have put Chevron out of compliance with OSHA standards. Furthermore, retaining Bhatia as a machinist who could not use a respirator would have been an "undue hardship" because it would have been administratively inconvenient for Chevron and might have imposed additional hazardous burdens on his coworkers (to complete the work he could not do). The court concluded that Title VII did not require such a burdensome accommodation.

It is interesting that court mentions in passing that Chevron "promised to return Bhatia to his old job if a respirator were developed that would be safe for him to use." This suggests that creating a respirator for use by men with beards was at least in the realm of possibility. If the majority were sufficiently concerned with safeguarding the rights of religious employees, such a device might already have been in existence.

Another key point is that, in the past, the federal OSHA authorized exemptions for the Sikhs and the Amish, so there is no reason Chevron could not have requested an exemption for its Sikh employee. The fact that this was not even considered by the court may indicate that religious bias was involved.[50]

Although the justifications in the cases discussed here are not sufficiently compelling to legitimize religious discrimination, religious employees are sometimes unable to perform certain jobs:

> There are obviously some jobs which individuals, because of their religious beliefs, are not able to perform. Without intending to be facetious, a Sikh obviously could not be employed as a male fashion model for a hat manufacturer. A Sikh would encounter real problems working as a scuba diver or a deep sea diver for a marine salvage company since the wearing of a turban would be incompatible with such work.[51]

Unless we are confronted with such an extreme case, the employer should facilitate the religious way of life of employees in the absence of any proven harm to society.

Courtroom

In several fascinating cases judges have refused to allow attorneys or defendants wearing religious or ethnic garb to appear in court.[52] Ordinarily, the justifications for the dress code include the need for the judge to maintain dignity, decorum, and order in the courtroom and the need to ensure the proper administration of justice, including the need to avoid jury bias and prejudice to guarantee a fair trial. These cases rest on two assumptions: that the judge can control the courtroom proceedings and that it is possible to limit bias.

In *La Rocca v. Lane* (1975, 1976) a Roman Catholic priest, who was the defense attorney for a criminal defendant, appeared in court before the jury in his clerical garb. After the judge ordered him to change, he initiated a proceeding to prohibit the judge from requiring him to remove his clerical collar. The court ruled that the judge was justified in limiting the defense counsel's right to free exercise of religion to ensure a fair and impartial trial. The basic argument was that

> a clergyman is accorded high status by most members of our society. Whatever the character of the man or woman who wears the cloth, the cleric is accorded a measure of respect and trust unlike that which is given to those of other vocations. Consequently, it is understandable, but not condonable, that a jury might view differently statements made by a member of the clergy than those made by others, and might ascribe a greater measure of veracity and personal commitment to the rightness of his client's cause.[53]

In addition, the court expressed concern that some jurors might be biased against religious figures. The New York Court of Appeals held that the trial court was correct in requiring the attorney's change of garb to ensure "the right of both the defendant and the People to a fair trial."

Subsequently, La Rocca was granted the right to appear with his collar.[54] The New York Supreme Court concluded that the risk of prejudice was not supported by empirical evidence. Moreover, *voir dire* (the process of selecting a jury through questioning) could help identify unbiased jurors, and jury instructions could help ensure the integrity of the process. The court argued that it was not obliged to follow precedent because much had changed in the four years since *La Rocca*. In particular, an increasing number of men and women of the cloth had entered secular activities. Despite its persuasive reasoning, the decision was subsequently reversed.[55]

In *Close-It Enterprises, Inc. v. Weinberger* (1978) a trial court ordered the defendant, an Orthodox Jew, to remove his yarmulke. When he refused, the court required him to wait outside the courtroom for the duration of his trial. The appellate division unanimously reversed the lower court and ordered a new trial:

> The defendant should not have been placed in the situation of having to choose between protecting his legal interest or violating an essential element of his faith. . . . In any event, any potential prejudice could have been taken care of through the voir dire and the court's instructions to the jury.[56]

The court distinguished *La Rocca,* noting that it involved an attorney as opposed to a defendant. It is unclear whether this distinction is valid. If voir dire and jury instructions would "cure" any bias for defendants in religious garb, then why would they not be effective for attorneys in religious garb? There is also the question of whether prosecution witnesses should be permitted to wear clerical attire.[57]

Another issue is whether ethnic garb should be allowed in court. In Washington, D.C., attorney John Harvey III was wearing his usual attire, a business suit and a kente cloth scarf, when he entered the court of Judge Robert M. Scott. The judge refused to allow him to continue representing his client, a criminal defendant, unless he removed his kente cloth scarf.[58] The judge said he was concerned that the kente cloth, associated with Afrocentrism, would bias the predominantly black jury in favor of his client, a black defendant. When Harvey filed a lawsuit challenging the ruling on his ethnic garb, the judge asked him to submit a statement explaining the cultural significance of kente cloth.[59] Harvey also claimed that the cloth had a religious aspect because he belonged to a church that required members of the congregation to wear it as an expression of religious faith and ethnic solidarity.

Kente cloth is worn by many African Americans as a way of acknowledging their ancestry. It is probably no accident that this cloth, which comes from the Asante people in Ghana, was originally worn only by royalty. Since the civil rights movement there has been a concerted effort to raise the self-esteem of a people that endured slavery. Wearing the cloth of kings would seem to be an appropriate symbol. As with cornrows, traditionally there were many variations, each with its own meaning. Although some of the cloth sold in the United States is "authentic" and conveys proverbial sayings, much has been lost in the process of moving the cloth from Africa to the United States.

One question that is raised by the case is whether cultural symbols should receive less legal protection than religious ones. Another question is whether a religion can adopt a cultural form and endow it with religious significance. These issues were not resolved because the judge died, and the action was then dismissed as moot.

In the courtroom attire cases since *La Rocca* the assumption is that the court should rely on voir dire to weed out biased jurors. While this is a valiant attempt to safeguard religious freedom, it may not be possible to determine whether prospective jurors harbor any prejudices relevant to the case. Many jurors may not want to admit to racism or religious biases, or they may not be conscious of their bigotry.

In the end it may not be realistic to try to control bias in the courtroom. Social psychologists have demonstrated the effect of all sorts of nonverbal cues and behavior, none of which can be controlled. Nowadays, jury consultants are hired in cases where the stakes are high to ensure that jurors have the correct bias! It may be that the concern with jury prejudice masks religious discrimination. Ultimately, it is unclear whether dress codes in court really have much effect on jurors.

In some cases the justification for the dress code is not bias, but is instead public safety. In the Canadian case of *Hothi et al. v. Regina* (1985), the judge refused to allow a Sikh defendant to wear his *kirpan*, a ceremonial dagger, in the courtroom.[60] The judge may have had cause for alarm since this particular defendant was charged with assault. However the defendant presumably did not use his kirpan (assuming he was guilty), as it is as preposterous to suggest to a Sikh person that a kirpan, a religious symbol, would be used as a weapon as it would be to suggest to a Christian that the crucifix would be used in that way.

Some of the results in these cases seem to trivialize the importance of the worldviews of ethnic minorities. Judges should not have unfettered discretion to exclude attire in the absence of any threat of harm. In none of the cases discussed here was there any empirical data to demonstrate the presence of such a threat.

Public Places and Transportation

Some reported cases involve restriction on dress in public places. The Commission for Racial Equality in England litigated a case involving a Muslim woman, Mrs. Farida Patel, who was asked to remove her veil by a launderette attendant. Apparently, the veil frightened children in the launderette, and it was important for the staff to be able to recognize customers in case their clothes became mixed up.[61] These justifications for the undress policy were obviously absurd. There was no evidence that children were afraid of her. Even if they had been, that would be irrelevant because prejudice cannot justify discriminatory practices. As for the identification point, it is hard to see how the staff could fail to identify her if she wore traditional religious garb.

The case was settled by a court order: the owner of the launderette apologized and agreed not to attempt to restrict the use of their launderette by veiled women in the future. Although the outcome was favorable insofar as the launderette promised to change its practices, the case has no precedent-setting value.

When ethnic minorities use public transportation while wearing religious garb, they may encounter some difficulties. For instance, in *People v. Singh* (1987), a Sikh priest was arrested in a subway for violating a New York City ordinance that prohibited wearing an exposed or unexposed knife in a public place. Mr. Singh was required by his religion to wear his kirpan at all times. To him, this was a religious symbol, but to the state it was a weapon.[62]

The judge did not dispute the defendant's claim that his religion required him to wear the kirpan. Indeed, Mr. Singh would be socially ostracized and subject to divine retribution for failure to comply with religious law. The judge reasoned that Mr. Singh's right to the free exercise of religion did not protect this religiously motivated action. Nevertheless, the judge decided to dismiss the case because the prosecution would not be in the interest of justice. It seemed unjust to subject Mr. Singh to either a possible maximum fine of $300 or imprisonment not exceeding fifteen days, or both.

While the judge did not question the sincerity of Mr. Singh's commitment to Sikh religious principles, he felt that it would be too cumbersome for law enforcement officials to have to figure out whether a person claiming to be a Sikh with a kirpan really was one or not. In legal terms the judge felt that the First Amendment right at stake had to yield to the compelling state interest of protecting the health and safety of its citizens. Though the judge noted that sometimes less restrictive alternatives may not exist, here he proposed that Sikhs wear a symbolic kirpan encased in plastic or lucite. Whether this would be acceptable to Sikhs was not considered.

The case is of interest because it involves a criminal prosecution, whereas most of the dress code disputes are civil law cases. More important is that the judge, despite some culturally biased assumptions, does recognize that enforcing the dress code would result in injustice.[63] However, the implication is strong that if Mr. Singh were to appear in his courtroom again, he would not be so lenient, as the expectation is that once informed of the public policy, Mr. Singh will have to conform to it. Finally, it also demonstrates the common practice of judges of upholding the law technically but avoiding having to impose punishment. Judges often give suspended sentences to achieve this result.

In the past, airlines permitted passengers carrying Swiss army knives aboard planes while refusing to allow Sikhs to fly if they were wearing kirpans. In Canada the Air Transportation Association allowed small kirpans as carry-on items, but some airlines depart from this policy.[64] In 1996 Balbir Singh Nijjar was refused permission to board his flight on Canada 3000 because he was wearing his kirpan. He filed a complaint with the Canadian Human Rights Commission alleging religious discrimination. In a fascinating decision, the commission concluded that "there is no standard within the airline industry with respect to kirpans on aircraft." On the one hand, there was concern about the appropriate level of risk that the airline should have to bear. On the other hand, the airline provided eating utensils that could do bodily harm. Ultimately, the decision handled the risk analysis, noting that the airline's policy "only prohibits those kirpans with a greater potential for injury than that of Canada 3000 eating utensils," and this represents a form of accommodation. To allow larger kirpans would constitute an undue hardship.[65]

Sikhs have been asked to remove their kirpans when they ride on Amtrak trains. In one case a Sikh man was questioned by an Amtrak conductor and then forcibly detained for wearing his eight-inch kirpan on the train. Ultimately, the prosecutor decided not to charge him.[66]

When the ethnic minority is not the passenger but the employee, there may be conflicts as well. For instance, a Muslim woman was discharged as a bus driver for wearing her turban instead of a garrison-type cap. A Sikh man was told he could not lease a taxicab unless he removed his turban. In England a Rastafarian man, Trevor Dawkins, applied for a job as a van driver with a government van service. When interviewed for the position, his hair was in dreadlocks and the interviewer told him in no uncertain terms that he would have to cut his hair to be hired (though Dawkins was willing to put his dreadlocks up under a hat). The Industrial Tribunal ruled in favor of Dawkins, finding his complaint persuasive. The Employment Appeal Tribunal reversed because it was wrong to consider the Rastafarians, a religious sect, as an "ethnic" group. The Court of Appeal upheld the ruling that Rastafarians do not constitute an ethnic group for the purposes of the Race Relations Act; consequently, an individual who is refused a job because he would not cut his hair was not discriminated against on account of his race.[67]

Schools

School dress codes have generated much litigation. In many of the cases, the issue is whether compliance is essential to ensure the safety of students and whether this is the only means of accomplishing this objective.[68] A number of cases involve the kirpan, including *Cheema v. Thompson* (1994, 1995). In 1994 the Livingston Union School District adopted a "no weapons" policy and then applied it to prevent Sikh students wearing kirpans from attending school. At the center of the dispute were three young Khalsa Sikh children, Rajinder, Sukhjinder, and Jaspreet Cheema, who were faced with a choice between going to school without their kirpans or taking them to school with the likely consequence of expulsion or criminal prosecution. Under the circumstances, the students opted to stay at home where they remained for several months, while their parents filed a lawsuit in federal court under the Religious Freedom Restoration Act with the assistance of the American Civil Liberties Union of Northern California.[69]

A key question was whether the kirpan was dangerous. There was allegedly no incident of violence involving a kirpan in any school in the United States or Canada. There have been reports in the press of adult Sikhs drawing their ceremonial daggers during brawls.[70]

The district court judge upheld the school board's policy, but the ruling was reversed on appeal. The Court of Appeals for the Ninth Circuit insisted that the children have their right to religious liberty respected and ordered that they be permitted to attend school wearing their kirpans. The appeals court found that the school district had not shown that the "no knives" policy was the least restrictive means of ensuring student safety. But the court also thought it was reasonable to expect the Sikhs to render the blades blunt or to have the daggers sewn into their sheaths. Although it took three years of litigation to resolve the conflict, the case demonstrates the possibility of reaching a compromise. Such accommodations may be less likely in the United States, after the demise of the Religious Freedom Restoration Act.[71]

Orthodox Jewish high school students wearing yarmulkes are sometimes barred from participating in interscholastic basketball competitions ostensibly because the bobby pins that hold their skullcaps are thought by some to constitute a danger to other students. There are no headgear policies, but exceptions are usually made for medical or religious reasons. In one California dispute even though the students had letters giving special permission to wear the skullcaps, some referees refuse to accept the exemptions. Indeed, officials ordered the Valley Torah students to remove the yarmulkes or risk forfeiture on two occasions. During one game a referee called a technical foul against a Torah senior when his yarmulke fell off.[72]

In *Menora v. Illinois High School Association* (1982), Jewish basketball players sued to challenge the no hat or headgear policy. The rule was based on a concern that "the headwear might fall off in the heat of play and one of the players might trip or slip on it, fall, and injure himself." The court considered the conflict between the interscholastic association policy and the right to don religious garb as a false conflict:

The parties have argued this case to us as if the religious obligation that was in conflict with state regulation was an obligation while playing basketball to wear a yarmulke fastened to your hair by bobby pins. But that is not what the stipulation says, and while we are not Talmudic scholars we are reasonably confident, and the plaintiff's counsel acknowledged at oral argument that the precise nature of the head covering and the method by which it is kept on the head are not specified by Jewish law. . . . The affixing of the yarmulke to the head (more precisely to the hair) by bobby pins is even more obviously a convention than a religious obligation, and it happens to be an inherently insecure method of keeping the yarmulke attached during basketball play.[73]

The judge concluded by saying that the students "have no constitutional right to wear yarmulkes insecurely fastened by bobby pins and therefore they cannot complain if the Association refuses to let them do so because of safety concerns which, while not great, are not wholly trivial either." The court asked the plaintiffs to devise some more secure method of fastening the yarmulke to the head. In the final analysis the court did not think the "no-headwear rule" burdened the free exercise rights of the students.[74]

Little evidence exists to show that yarmulkes put other players in peril. Jewish players in high school and college have played thousands of games with no reported injuries from a yarmulke or bobby pin.[75] Even if one were persuaded that the pins or clips endanger other players in the court, there appears to be a double standard. Eyeglasses are much more likely to cause injury, and yet this headgear is allowed.

Students have also been penalized for wearing ethnic symbols to graduation ceremonies. For example, in 1996 a student from the Dakota tribe who wore an eagle feather on her mortarboard and two African American students who wore kente cloth with their graduation robes to the Muskogee High School graduation in Oklahoma were informed that they would not receive their high school diplomas or transcripts until they completed twenty-five days in summer school as punishment.[76] School officials defended the dress code as a measure intended to remove the "carnival quality" of recent graduation ceremonies. The American Civil Liberties Union of Oklahoma agreed to represent the students.[77]

In other cases the issue is not physical safety but, rather, the symbolic message conveyed by the religious garb. One of the most famous controversies was the "Affaire des Foulards," or the "great kerchief controversy." The controversy began in Creil, France, an industrial city thirty miles north of Paris, in 1989 when the principal applied a 1937 law prohibiting all religious symbols in school. Young Muslim girls were told they could not attend school wearing their headscarves. Eventually the girls decided to take off their headgear in class.[78]

This discrete local problem became a full-blown national one later on. Subsequently, the Minister of Education issued instructions to principals of all public schools to start enforcing a ban on the wearing of Muslim headscarves. The government was concerned that allowing religious garb ran afoul of the principle of secular education. Permitting girls to dress in a way that made them appear different also undermined the French goal of assimilation. Not only did the hijab challenge national French unity, but it also was thought to symbolize the inferior status of women. After litigation and international media coverage, the Minister of Education reversed the policy, allowing the girls to attend school in their headscarves.[79]

Sometimes teachers, rather than students, have challenged dress codes on the basis of their right to religious liberty. In *Cooper v. Eugene School District* (1985, 1986) a teacher, Janet Cooper, who had become a Sikh, challenged a statute prohibiting the wearing of religious dress while teaching in a public school. When she wore her religious garb, she was suspended from teaching and faced revocation of her teaching certificate. The school defended its policy based on the Establishment clause requirement that schools maintain religious neutrality.[80] The Oregon Court of Appeals thought that, despite this concern, revoking the teacher's certificate was a greater sanction than was necessary for accomplishing their objective. As there were less restrictive alternatives, the appellate court set aside the revocation as an excessive sanction under the First Amendment. The Supreme Court of Oregon reversed, holding that the religious dress statute did not violate state or federal guarantees of religious freedom.

Police

Some grooming policies are imposed for safety reasons. Law enforcement officers are usually expected to cut their hair so that criminals cannot seize it. Challenges to regulations requiring short hair have been unsuccessful. A number of officers have objected to no-beard policies; for some shaving the beard would offend religious beliefs, while for others it would result in a skin condition prevalent among their ethnic group.[81]

In some cases plaintiffs want exemptions from hat requirements. In 1990 the Royal Canadian Mounted Police (RCMP) began to allow Sikhs to wear their turbans as part of its recruitment policy. However, the Royal Canadian Legion was unwilling to allow Sikhs to wear their turbans in lieu of the Mounties' traditional headgear.[82] They filed a lawsuit, *Grant v. Canada* [1995], seeking an order preventing the Commission of the RCMP from allowing religious symbols as part of the RCMP uniform; they wanted a declaration from the court that the exemption was unconstitutional. The trial division of the federal court dismissed the complaint, finding that the RCMP policy of trying to recruit more "visible" minorities by allowing them to wear religious symbols as part of the uniform violated no constitutional principle in the Canadian Charter of Rights and Freedoms. The Federal Court of Appeals dismissed the appeal.

Military

The military has often been sued for religious accommodations. In this institutional context the claim is that uniformity is necessary to ensure solidarity. The leading U.S. case is *Goldman v. Weinberger* (1985). S. Simcha Goldman was an Air

Force captain who was a clinical psychologist, an Orthodox Jew, and a rabbi. Although he wore a yarmulke during his first four years of active duty, after he testified as a witness at a court-martial, a complaint was filed. Goldman was told he could not wear the yarmulke in uniform outside the hospital. When he refused, he was told his active duty might not be extended, and he was threatened with a court-martial.[83]

The district court ruled in Goldman's favor, issuing orders prohibiting the Air Force from enforcing its uniform regulations to prevent him from wearing his yarmulke while in uniform. Subsequently, in a trial on the merits, the court found that the uniform regulations violated the right to the free exercise of religion. On appeal, the U.S. Court of Appeals for the District of Columbia reversed. This was the first time the U.S. Supreme Court considered a free exercise claim of a service member.[84] As is standard practice, the Court deferred to the military, relying on the doctrine of military necessity.

The decision, giving almost complete deference to the military, sparked tremendous controversy. In the aftermath, Congress considered legislation on religious apparel. During the discussions it was noted that service members in countries such as Canada, India, Israel, New Zealand, and the United Kingdom are allowed to wear religious headgear, and that this did not undermine "military readiness." After three years Congress adopted an accommodation statute that gave discretion to the Department of Defense to formulate the precise manner in which accommodation should occur.[85]

Prison

Another institutional context in which individuals challenge dress codes and grooming policies is prison. Some have suggested that the numerous suits are partly a reflection of the time that inmates have at their disposal. Generally speaking, the justification for denying exemptions is security, which includes ensuring that prisoners can be easily identified. Sometimes courts find that the prison is not using the "least intrusive means" of ensuring prison safety by easy identification. It was not that religious freedom was clearly deemed more important than prison security, but that alternate means of achieving the same goal were available. In addition to identification, haircuts are sometimes justified on the grounds that it will protect prisoners from being victims of homosexual rape (because long hair makes them more attractive to other inmates).[86]

Native American prisoners have challenged policies requiring haircuts and disallowing them medicine bundles. Rastafarian inmates also object to cutting their dreadlocks. Orthodox Jews refuse to cut their beards or earlocks. Other litigation is concerned with religious headgear that may be prohibited because prison officials worry that inmates can hide contraband inside it. Most of the time the plaintiffs lose their suits, as courts tend to accept the penological rationale for the policies.[87]

QUESTIONING CONFORMISM

Challenges to dress codes lose in most cases. Considering that wearing the symbol involves no threat of harm to society, the tendency of courts to uphold these restrictions on attire is puzzling. At the outset I wondered whether there was any difference in judicial responses to ethnic or religious garb. Although one might have expected that individuals who want to don religious symbols would receive more legal protection than those seeking to wear ethnic or cultural symbols, there turns out to be little difference. In the dress code cases based on the free exercise of religion, the results have been "less than adequate protection of constitutionally guaranteed, free-exercise rights."[88]

In the vast majority of cases the conflict was over hair or hats. It is intriguing to consider the symbolic implications. Both relate to the head, which in some cultures represents the "seat of power."[89] Clearly, bowing one's head often means showing deference to those in power. This may be related to judges' enforcement of no headgear policies in the courtroom.

The basic objection to ethnic and religious garb presumably is that it accentuates the differences among different peoples. Since the policy in the United States has been assimilation, that would explain why institutions require compliance with dress codes. Conformity is the rule. But not only do Americans insist that ethnic minorities become assimilated, they are also suspicious of those who are different. The American tendency toward xenophobia has been noted by scholars, including Richard Hofstadter in his famous essay "The Paranoid Style in American Politics."[90] Since "American" national identity is ill-defined, anything that is different is considered threatening.

In the cases considered in this chapter the symbols were considered to be "militant" or "divisive." The courts have tended to accept the interpretation of the hairstyle or garb provided by individuals from the dominant culture. For instance, instead of treating a Sikh kirpan as a religious symbol, courts regard it as a "weapon." It is disturbing that even in the absence of empirical proof of any threat of harm to society, courts uphold dress code policies.

The most fundamental point to be made here is not limited to symbols that people wear. It is quite clear that many types of symbols have tremendous evocative power. One need only consider the controversies over flag desecration or those involving nativity scenes on public property. It may be that symbols will generate culture conflict when a symbol elicits different responses in different groups. This suggests that conflicts will arise until such time as members of the mainstream deign to learn about the folkways and worldviews of ethnic minorities. The disputes over dress codes reveal how ethnocentrism pervades many institutions.

9

The Dead

There have been many culture conflicts over the dead, despite the widespread belief that the dead deserve to be treated with respect. Culture conflicts over corpses give rise to lawsuits because there are myriad beliefs about the proper methods for the disposal of dead bodies based on different conceptions of "the body" and of the afterlife. In this chapter I examine legal disputes in which different folk laws concerning dead bodies are at issue, and I explain why failure to comply with these rules is distressing to members of the community in question.[1] The central argument is that the law ought to permit diverse cultural groups to follow their way of death to as great an extent as possible. This is consistent with the approach I have defended throughout—the principle of maximum accommodation.

In the process of advancing this argument, I discuss a series of cases in which the treatment of the dead leads to conflict with the dominant legal system. The plaintiffs in these cases are religious and cultural minorities, as well as indigenous peoples.[2] First, I analyze disputes involving religious objections to the performance of autopsies and the question of whether unauthorized autopsies should result in the payment of damages to the decedent's relatives. Next, I focus on cases in which the preparation of the corpse or its transportation was inconsistent with the customary law of the group to which the dead person belonged. Then, I review conflicts related to burial.

In the cases to be discussed, the plaintiffs seek various remedies, depending on the nature of the problem.[3] For the most part, they seek exemptions from existing statutes, damages for emotional distress, or injunctions to enjoin actions that violate folk law. In general, judges seem to find plaintiffs in these dead bodies cases to be relatively sympathetic. They are, however, more inclined to grant motions in some situations than in others. It is important to speculate as to the possible reasons why plaintiffs are most successful in some lawsuits as this insight may permit us to exploit the reasons and suggest their use in other kinds of multicultural lawsuits.

The notion that the dead should be treated with respect seems to be such a widespread notion that it may turn out to be nearly universal. Despite the wide acceptance of this value, the ways in which the dead are to be treated varies from one society to the next, partly because of divergent conceptions of the afterlife. In some cultures the dead have rights which the living are obligated to protect. It is precisely this relationship between the dead and the living that requires close examination. To determine whether the courts have handled the cases correctly, one must first come to terms with the question of whether the dead have rights. In philosophical terms, one might ask whether the dead have "personhood," are autonomous in any sense, and have juridical status in their own right.[4]

In the cases analyzed in this chapter there is a tendency to resolve disputes by reference to the wishes of the surviving spouse, next of kin, or decedent's express wishes while alive. The implication is that only the living have the authority to make decisions concerning human remains.[5] This may be a matter of practicality because it is difficult to ask the dead their preferences after they have "passed on."

The law in the United States generally has not regarded the corpse as the relatives' property. The traditional view was that it was *nullius in bonis*, or no person's property. It is also an established principle of law that the living relatives ("next of kin") have what is called a "quasi property" interest in the disposition of the dead body. The relatives have this right because of their duty to bury the dead. When they sue for damages for unlawful mutilation of the corpse, the action is based not on harming the corpse but on causing psychic injury to the living relatives: "The basic interests in the surviving spouse, children or next of kin of the deceased are emotional interests connected with the dignity of the disposition of the body and their own peace of mind."[6]

It is my view that the cultural rights of the dead must be protected, as well as those of the living relatives. In the disposition of cases in which families challenge decisions made regarding the dead, the utmost care must be given to cultural factors. Certainly the diverse cultural traditions concerning the treatment of the dead deserve more respect than they often receive.

PROHIBITION AGAINST AUTOPSIES

The autopsy, also referred to as a postmortem examination or necropsy, is an ancient practice. The term is derived from the Greek word *autopsia*, meaning "seeing with one's own eyes." Early civilizations may have carried out dissections—as, for example, the early Egyptian embalmers—but they did not engage in a scientific study of the process. In 300 B.C. Erasistratus is considered to have made the connection between organ dysfunction and disease through dissections.[7]

Although the Roman Catholic Church generally disapproved of dissections, the pope authorized autopsies to determine the cause of the plague. In the thirteenth century a treatise "Hsi Yuan Lu," containing instructions for coroners, was published in China, but it was not until the fourteenth and fifteenth centuries that the autopsy became established in medical science. The first reported case of a postmortem examination in the "New World" was in Haiti in 1533, where it was performed to determine whether Siamese twins had one or two souls. Subsequently, other reported autopsies included a French explorer ordering dissections of deceased members of his party in 1605 who had developed scurvy, and an autopsy in Hartford, Connecticut, in 1665 of a girl to determine whether she had died from witchcraft. In the eighteenth century, studies began correlating symptoms of diseases with autopsy findings.[8]

The autopsy is used in forensic medicine, a field that involves the scientific application of medical techniques to legal investigations. *Medicolegal* deaths must be investigated because of particular circumstances. Those authorized to conduct the investigations of the cause of death in the United States are from the medical examiner's office. In some jurisdictions the coroner, a person without medical training and often an elected official, is in charge of death investigations rather than a medical examiner.[9]

Autopsies are performed for several reasons. The most obvious is to establish the cause or causes of death. The most commonly mentioned, more specific justifications are (1) criminal investigation, particularly where there is a suspicion of foul play and (2) medical investigation, when there is a threat to public health, sometimes to prevent a contagion. In addition to these, other rationales are mentioned in the literature. One is the quality control of official health institutions, including hospitals and mental institutions. Autopsies may confirm the accuracy of clinical diagnoses. Another purpose of autopsies is the documentation of disease rates and the identification of new diseases. The autopsy also has pedagogical benefits for medical school for research and training.[10]

The performance of an autopsy may yield insurance and other benefits. Ruling out suicide permits families to receive life insurance benefits. To obtain workman's compensation or to proceed with a lawsuit it may be necessary to establish that the relative actually died of a certain cause, such as asbestosis. An autopsy report confirming this cause of death may strengthen the family's case. Postmortem examinations enable investigators to detect environmental and occupational hazards and sometimes to prevent an epidemic. They may help identify product tampering in over-the-counter drugs.[11]

Another argument advanced in favor of necropsy is that it helps families assuage any guilt they may feel in connection with the death of a relative. A similar point is made in reference to political and religious leaders. Some analysts have recommended autopsies to help rule out "phantasmagorical" theories about assassinations, such as that of John F. Kennedy, and recommend them for all heads of state. An autopsy of Pope John Paul I "would have put a large number of concerned minds to rest." Overall, the medical community in the published literature on the subject takes an extremely pro-autopsy position.[12]

Despite the generally positive view of autopsies in the medical community, some legal systems have traditionally maintained limits to its usage by requiring consent. In the United States the general rule is that the surviving spouse or the "next of kin" is legally empowered to "grant or deny authority for an autopsy." In some cases families may have religious objections to autopsy, and the question is whether or not their refusal to authorize one will be respected.[13]

Mutilation of the dead is proscribed by many groups including the Hmong, Jews, Mexican Americans, Muslims, and Navajo (Dine).[14] The worldview of these groups often includes a belief in the afterlife and the idea that a person enters the afterlife with his or her body in its condition at death. There are other notions associated with the idea that the dead should not be disturbed. For instance, Mexican Americans believe that

> the soul resides in or near the body and can feel pain for as long as several days after bodily death. If an autopsy is performed, the soul suffers either physical pain from cutting of the flesh (if the soul resides in the body) or psychological pain from observing the desecration of the body (if the soul resides outside the body).[15]

Even educated members of minority groups may continue to support a prohibition against autopsy.[16]

For those groups that disallow tampering with the dead, the performance of autopsies is unacceptable under most ordinary circumstances. In cases where relatives contend that an autopsy ought not to have been performed because of religious objections, the question is whether the state had a sufficiently compelling interest that outweighs the right to religious freedom. Normally, the autopsy may be conducted only under statutorily designated conditions such as when there is a suspicion of foul play as part of a criminal investigation or where there is a perceived threat to public health.[17]

STATE JUSTIFICATIONS FOR AUTOPSIES

In many of the lawsuits for wrongful autopsies, coroners and medical examiners claim that, as public officials, they are protected by immunity. This claim may be unjustified as many jurisdictions will not grant immunity for acts that are completely without authority.[18] Evidently, this immunity argument is seldom raised for this reason, although on occasion courts have accepted the claim. Hence, the crucial issue is whether the performance of the autopsy is within the scope of authority— that is, authorized by statute.

Thus, even if the autopsy impinges upon the right to religious freedom, the examination is permissible, provided the state has a strong enough justification to warrant the infringement.[19] Because the legal system in the United States does not provide constitutional or statutory protection for a person or a group's right to culture, plaintiffs have no choice but to argue that the state treatment of the dead body violates their right to religious freedom. Although this may be an accurate characterization of what transpired, in instances where we might be tempted to consider the belief "cultural" rather than "religious," the plaintiff will not have the luxury of arguing that the practice is culturally based.

Not only must the claim be framed in the language of religious freedom, but there is also a question as to the appropriate constitutional test to be employed. In some cases the degree to which the state must justify its policies may affect the disposition of the case. Even though it is easier for courts to justify autopsies while the standard of review is lower—while the *Employment Division, Department of Human Resources of Oregon v. Smith* (1990) decision was in effect—even under the compelling state interest standard, the autopsy can proceed as long as there is a sufficiently compelling state interest.[20] At this point I turn to a consideration of the state interests offered in selected autopsy cases.

Criminal Investigation

Relatives often object on religious grounds to the performance of an autopsy when the state wants to conduct one as part of a criminal investigation. *Albareti v. Hirsch* (1993) provides an apt illustration of this conflict. Dafir Albareti was shot to death in a Manhattan grocery store where he was employed. Although the external exam indicated that he died from two gunshot wounds to the torso, an internal exam was deemed necessary. The Albareti family was Muslim, objected to the autopsy, and consented only to the removal of a blood sample from Mr. Albareti's chest. The family sued to enjoin the medical examiner from performing an autopsy.[21]

The court found it obvious that New York law authorized the medical examiner to proceed:

1. Notwithstanding any other provision of law, in the absence of a compelling public necessity, no dissection or autopsy shall be performed over the objection of a surviving relative or friend of the deceased that such procedure is contrary to the religious belief of the decedent, or, if there is otherwise reason to believe that a dissection or autopsy is contrary to the decedent's religious beliefs.

2. For the purposes of this section: (a) 'compelling public necessity' shall mean:. . . (2) that the dissection or autopsy is essential to the conduct of a criminal investigation of a homicide, as defined in section 125.00 of the penal law, of which the decedent is the victim . . . (Public Health law 4210-c).

The language suggests that an autopsy can be performed, religious objections notwithstanding, if it is "essential" to complete a criminal investigation of a homicide. Whether the additional information garnered was in any sense necessary is unclear, but the court takes for granted that the state can seek to obtain the maximum information in the name of public necessity.

Not only did the court rule that the compelling public necessity to investigate a homicide superseded the right to religious freedom, but it also concluded that the statute did not actually violate Islamic law. The court cited the director of the local Islamic Cultural Center in New York, who stated that Islamic law allows an autopsy in the case of suspicious death. This interpretation is not unanimously shared. The traditional view was that no cutting of the body was permissible, but relatively little is written about autopsy. Over time the Muslim view has changed and may permit autopsies for the investigation of crime, although the sentiment is not universal. At least two conferences dealt with the subject and considered them legitimate if benefits were derived:

> If medical students learn from postmortems, if justice prevails through them and if contagious diseases can be controlled through them, then benefits indeed outnumber damages, provided that these examinations are performed only when necessary.[22]

It appears that the religious position has been modified in light of new circumstances. But while the Islamic demonstration of good faith is evident, one observes no similar flexibility on the part of the American legal system. The crux of the issue is whether or not the examinations are "necessary" and therefore required in the name of the "public interest." From the facts given in the *Albareti* case (the autopsy had not been performed yet), there is no way to determine whether the information from the exam would be necessary for the successful prosecution of this case.

Threat to Public Health

Another justification for necropsy is to avoid a threat to public health. In *You Vang Yang v. Sturner* (1990) the medical examiner, Dr. William Sturner, performed an autopsy on a twenty-three-year-old Hmong man, Neng Yang, who had died suddenly of undetermined causes. The doctors at the hospital had been unable to figure out the cause of his death, so they sent the body to the Rhode Island Medical Examiner's office where the autopsy was conducted, without obtaining the permission of the family. His parents, the Yangs, filed suit against Rhode Island's chief medical examiner, alleging that the performance of the postmortem examination violated fundamental religious principles.[23]

The Hmong object to any cutting of the body, including both surgery and autopsy. They fear mutilation as they believe that surgical incision allows the soul to leave the body and also permits evil spirits to enter the body. The postmortem exam may affect a person's reincarnated form as the Hmong think that the autopsy "will preclude reincarnation or result in an incomplete reincarnated being." Probably the most frightening consequence of the autopsy is the possibility of divine retribution. One religious belief is that the removal of a body part may cause the individual to be re-born with the "deformity," but this may also cause descendants to be born with the same "deformity." When Hmong are interviewed about their belief systems, they report instances in which mutilations have led to divine retribution. The Yangs' argument was that because of the autopsy, "the spirit of Neng [their son] would not be free, therefore his spirit will come back and take another person in his family."[24]

Rhode Island law authorizes the medical examiner's office to conduct an autopsy only under specific circumstances.[25] The court surmised that Dr. Sturner felt the autopsy was "necessary to protect 'the health, safety, and welfare' of Rhode Island residents by making sure Neng Yang had not died because of an 'infectious agent capable of spreading an epidemic within the state.'"[26] The court was not persuaded that there was sufficient evidence of a potential epidemic to warrant the postmortem examination and concluded that Yang's death did not fit any of the categories justifying an autopsy. The court ruled that Dr. Sturner had violated their First Amendment right to religious freedom and found no compelling state interest in performing the autopsy which outweighed the religious beliefs. Hence, the court concluded that the medical examiner was liable for damages, granted summary judgment on the issue of liability to the Yangs for emotional distress caused by the First Amendment violation, and ordered a hearing to determine the amount of the damages to be awarded.[27]

In a remarkable passage of its opinion, the court took the position that a "reasonable" medical examiner ought to be familiar with the deathways of minorities and ought to have known

> that certain people and religions abhor autopsies as a violation of their deeply held beliefs. Such an examiner would know which religions and people hold those beliefs. Such an examiner would realize that the Hmong population in Rhode island has grown, particularly in the last ten years. Such an examiner would know that the Hmongs prohibit autopsies; public officials should be knowledgeable of, and sensitive to, the many beliefs held by Rhode Island's citizens. Therefore, it is reasonable to believe that when a medical examiner receives the body of a person who might be a Hmong, he should realize that an autopsy would violate the religious beliefs of the decedent's next of kin. This conclusion is strengthened if the Yangs' uncontested allegation that they expressed their opposition to an autopsy to the doctors at Rhode Island Hospital is true.
>
> Given the Yangs' clearly established rights and the specific facts of this case, this Court denies Dr. Sturner's request for qualified immunity.[28]

Shortly after Judge Raymond Pettine's ruling in favor of the Yangs, the U.S. Supreme Court handed down the *Smith* decision, which lowered the standard of review to be used in religious freedom cases. Only months later Judge Pettine withdrew his opinion. Although he concluded that the state law governing autopsies did "profoundly impair the Yangs' religious freedom," after *Smith* he could not rule that "the impairment rises to a constitutional level." The judge regretted having to change his ruling and expressed the deepest sympathy for the Yangs.[29]

It is unclear whether even the existence of the most demanding constitutional test will ensure that autopsies are performed only when they are consistent with the family's religious beliefs. If the state can demonstrate a compelling interest for conducting the autopsy and can meet additional constitutional requirements—for example, the least restrictive alternative—then the autopsy may still be able to be performed, despite religious objections. In the case at hand, the mysterious disorder among Hmong refugees was, in fact, a public health issue. Considering, however, that the syndrome was limited to the Hmong community and that the Hmong community preferred not to have autopsies, even at the expense of information which would potentially be gleaned from the examinations, one could argue that the decision ought to have been left to the cultural group. Another reason not to insist on postmortem exams in this context is that thus far "they have revealed little significant evidence."[30] If this lethal syndrome began to be documented among other segments of the population, then that would be a different case, which might require the performance of autopsies.

There is a real question about the legitimacy of forcing postmortem examinations on unwilling groups unless we are certain that the amount and quality of information which they yield justifies the imposition. In many cases the cause of death is readily apparent, and the autopsy simply confirms the fact of the gunshot or the drowning. While it is possible that the exam may in rare instances reveal surprising information—for example, that the drowned person was actually poisoned or that the gunshot victim actually died of a heart attack— it is not obvious that these infrequent discoveries justify the relative lack of concern for religious freedom.[31] If it is patently obvious why a person has died, then it makes little sense to burden a grieving family further with a useless exam that offends cherished religious beliefs.

Violent Accidental Death

State justifications for autopsies include the investigation of a violent accidental death. The case of *Montgomery v. County of Clinton, Michigan* (1990, 1991) involved a sixteen-year-old boy, Sannie Montgomery, who died during a high-speed chase with the police. Although a deputy sheriff immediately notified the parents of his death, he "apparently neglected to inform them of the impending autopsy." The medical examiner ordered an autopsy under a statute requiring exams in the case of violent deaths.[32] Afterward, the mother objected on two grounds: that the cause of death was patently obvious and that the exam violated Jewish law.

In its decision the district court referred to interpretations of Jewish law according to which autopsies are permissible under limited circumstances and commented that the mother's understanding of her own religious law was "perhaps somewhat confused." But the court concluded that it was inappropriate to "question the validity of one's interpretation of religious beliefs or practices, or to determine the plausibility of a religious claim." Denying that the autopsy violated Jewish religious law, the court held that even if it did, the performance of the autopsy "was a necessary or at least reasonable means of ascertaining death" and "was reasonably related to a legitimate governmental purpose." The court concluded that the autopsy did not violate her religion.[33]

There is no consensus among scholars on Judaic law with respect to the circumstances under which autopsies are justified. Some maintain that the exam can be performed to save the community or to save an individual's life.[34] Interestingly, the court assumes that there is a single correct interpretation of Jewish law and that Mrs. Montgomery may have been "confused" about her own religion. The court might have taken a more tactful and sensitive approach of suggesting that alternative interpretations exist. This would have avoided having the government ridicule the mother for apparent ignorance of her own religion. The court's disdainful approach to the mother[35] and the question of whether the autopsy would disclose any additional information make one wonder about the appropriateness of legally requiring the examination.

It is not obvious that governmental curiosity about the cause of death should take precedence over religious freedom. If the state can justifiably force autopsies on unwilling families, then the constitutional right to free exercise is, at best, a weak one. Whereas Jewish law can make exceptions to save the community or another person's life, the secular law seldom allows exceptions from the autopsy rule.[36]

In some autopsy cases judges are confronted with another cultural difference—namely, how to interpret the "next of kin" rule, given varying kinship systems. The legal question is who has standing to file a lawsuit challenging the decision to conduct an autopsy, and a case which illustrates this issue is *Smialek v. Begay* (1986). George Nelson, a sixty-year-old Navajo, was found in an alley behind a bar in Farmington, New Mexico, with his wallet missing. The police discovered his identity and notified his family a few hours later. Relatives arrived from the Navajo Nation early the next day, but the body had already been sent to Albuquerque for an autopsy. The cause of death was determined to be pancreatitis, related to alcoholism.[37]

The litigation involved relatives of the deceased who attempted to sue the state and state medical investigator for the performance of an autopsy because it was contrary to their Navajo religious beliefs. The investigator was charged with negligence, "not in the performance of the autopsy, but in deciding to perform an autopsy."[38]

The defendants argued that the plaintiffs only had standing to assert a federal constitutional claim if they had a quasi-property right in the decedent's body. They further claimed that since the brothers and sisters of Nelson did not possess this quasi-property right, they lacked standing to assert their own constitutional right to practice their religion. The trial judge granted the state's motion to dismiss the case, but the Court of Appeals of New Mexico ruled that although the state was not liable, the state medical investigator could be sued for the violation of their First Amendment rights under section 1983. The Court of Appeals of New Mexico reached a somewhat different conclusion. Judge Garcia's interpretation of the precedents was

that "religious or moral objections by a family member to an autopsy will be sufficient to override a medical examiner's decision to autopsy unless that autopsy is
'necessary' under the relevant statutes."[39] The court granted all the relatives standing to sue and determined that the only question for the trial court would be
whether the state interest, on balance, outweighed the free exercise right.

The Supreme Court of New Mexico chose to decide only one issue on appeal,
which was whether the decedent's siblings could join their mother in the lawsuit for
damages. The court took a different view of the standing question, concluding that
only "next-of-kin" could sue:

> We hold, therefore, that since, in the absence of a surviving spouse or child of the dece-
> dent, the mother was the only proper remaining survivor to claim and bury her son's
> body, she was the only proper remaining survivor with standing to assert an alleged vio-
> lation of the free exercise of her religious beliefs.[40]

The Supreme Court reversed the Court of Appeals, reinstating the lower court order
to dismiss the siblings as plaintiffs.[41] The reasoning was based on the fact that the
mother had a quasi-property right in Nelson's body which the petitioners lacked.

This logic depends on a specific cultural assumption about ownership of property. The reasoning in the case also reflects a Western interpretation of family. It is
not clear why the mother should be the only relative to be permitted to sue. The
harm caused by the autopsy may have affected not just the siblings but the entire
community. The Supreme Court was unwilling to consider this possibility.[42]

POLICY APPROACHES TO AUTOPSIES

Should autopsies be performed on a routine basis? The assumption in these cases is
clearly that the state has a compelling interest in gathering whatever information
may be available from the examinations. It is doubtful that this is a valid policy in a
pluralistic society. In a pluralistic society it should be incumbent upon medical
examiners to know the belief systems of groups that may have objections. Careful
scrutiny of cases on autopsies gives one the distinct impression that the exam rarely
provides additional insight and that governmental officials are simply using the
examination to harass religious minorities.[43]

Three policy approaches aimed at accommodating religious differences have
been tried, and they merit consideration. The first of these is California's system of
distributing certificates of religious objection to autopsy. In California individuals
can obtain a certificate of religious belief, which prevents the coroner from performing an autopsy. The autopsy is still allowed if the coroner "has a reasonable suspicion that the death was caused by the criminal act of another or by a contagious
disease constituting a public health hazard."[44] Other exceptions include allowing
autopsies if the cause of death is not evident and the public interest in ascertaining
the cause outweighs the religious convictions of the decedent and relatives.

Although the implementation of a certificate system might appear to show sensitivity to diverse religious groups, the reality is that there are so many exceptions permitted that the protection given by the certificate is minimal.[45]

Another proposal is the establishment of a committee to review autopsy decisions and to assist with populations that are unwilling to permit the examinations. In Florida where there is a large Jewish community, the Florida State Medical Examiners Commission formed an ethical advisory committee to recommend approaches to death investigation that would be sensitive to religious minorities. The committee devised a distinction between mandated autopsies and nonmandated autopsies, initiated training about other religions as part of the orientation of forensic pathology residents, and created a consulting council of rabbis who can monitor the postmortem exam and reassure the grieving family. Most helpful are the instructions on how to perform the autopsy in a manner least offensive to the Jewish family.[46]

This approach was criticized on several grounds: (1) The distinction between mandated and nonmandated autopsies was unhelpful because some of the nonmandated autopsies should be mandated, (2) physicians do not need ethical training from others, and (3) laypersons such as rabbis should not be allowed in the autopsy room.[47] Some argued that any such plan should require waiver forms, signed by relatives objecting to autopsies, to shield the medical examiner from liability for not performing the autopsy. In addition, families should be informed that failure to allow the autopsy might result in the forfeiture of insurance benefits. Despite these reservations, Florida implemented this policy.

The real impetus for establishing advisory committees on death may not be to safeguard the religious rights of minorities. The advocates of the ethical advisory committee approach make a revealing statement to the effect that recalcitrant medical examiners wind up with "onerous" laws like the one enacted by the New York State legislature.[48] The compromise position in Florida has had the dual benefit of avoiding a restrictive law and of not reducing the autopsy rate. Although advocates of the Florida policy purport to be concerned with respect for religious differences, the reality is that the policy facilitates autopsies. The rabbi's role is to convince the family of the necessity of the autopsy and to console the family afterward. As it stands, the policy does not actually give the objecting family the means to refuse to consent.

Some jurisdictions have adopted policies that minimize the number of autopsies performed. For instance, the New Jersey state legislature passed a law that requires the medical examiner to honor a religious objection that is expressed or to be inferred from the clothing or hairstyle of the deceased.[49] Where such an objection is evident or implicit, the medical examiner must wait forty-eight hours before deciding the disposition of the case. If the autopsy is considered "necessary," the examiner must obtain a court order based on a compelling state interest. Although medical examiners found this policy objectionable, the state interest loophole makes it relatively easy, if bureaucratically cumbersome, to procure authorization to undertake an autopsy.

Since there is such a firmly entrenched presumption in favor of autopsies, they continue, in most cases, to be performed over religious objections. Even policies designed to exempt religious minorities have not successfully protected them from the majoritarian desire to dissect the dead. It appears that the only way religious groups can avoid autopsies is if they are in power. If we consider the policy of Israel, for example, a state in which the Jewish community (a religious minority in the United States) is the majority, we observe the type of policy that takes religious objections seriously.

In Israel the autopsy issue was a major public controversy beginning in 1944, at which time autopsies could be performed under specific circumstances. The conflict started after the autopsy was regulated by law. In principle, "the dissection of the dead without explicit consent of the family is viewed as a serious infringement of human rights." In practice, religious people avoided going to the hospital for fear of being dissected after death.[50]

In 1977 the government announced it would revise the law to make autopsy contingent on the consent of the family, but evidently did not take the steps necessary to implement the policy. Even though there was no change in the written law, there have been discernible changes in policy. While the law apparently was not changed, the health authorities interpreted it in such a way as to forbid postmortem exams unless the family consented: "The Minister of Health issued directives to all hospital directors to refrain from performing autopsies in the event of an explicit objection by the family."[51] It seems that this strict policy has been the only one that actually ensures respect for the wishes of religious groups opposed to postmortem examinations.

Obviously, this policy would be challenged by the elites in the United States, or at least by medical professionals who are largely unconcerned with religion[52] and who insist that autopsies serve the public interest. From the viewpoint of religious minorities, however, these mundane rationales for cutting seem unpersuasive when a person's immortal fate is in question. Whether or not a particular crime is solved, for instance, seems, to the group, relatively unimportant in comparison with the condition of a person for eternity.

The United States could adopt the policy that no autopsies could be performed without the consent of the family. This would not prevent the performance of all autopsies. Indeed, there would be nothing to prevent medical, religious, political, and other officials from trying to persuade the family of the value of the exam. The change would simply mean that the legal system would not compel families already bereft of a loved one to observe the mutilation of the deceased's body.

The autopsy often provides little or no information, in which case the justification for it seems particularly weak. But even if it could establish crucial facts, it might be better to rank religious freedom over crime detection or public health. Except for an exigent circumstance like a life-threatening epidemic, the autopsy is unlikely to be of vital importance. If the policy remains one where the state can force an autopsy regardless of the family's consent, this may have the unfortunate effect of discouraging minorities from seeking medical attention for fear they will be dissected if they expire while institutionalized.

It is worth noting that some minorities interpret their customary law in a way to permit exceptions. This enables them to have their behavior conform to official public policies. For instance, although Jewish and Muslim persons disapprove of autopsies because they are considered desecration of the dead, when there are compelling legal or medical reasons, they allow the examinations. No similar good faith effort is observed on the part of the dominant legal system. Seldom are exceptions made, as it is virtually always claimed that the need for the autopsy is compelling. If the minorities are willing to make exceptions under their customary autopsy laws, then the majority should also make a good faith effort to grant exceptions as well.[53]

PREPARATION OF BODIES

Funeral directors, also known as undertakers, are sometimes asked to prepare human remains for disposition according to customary laws with which they are not familiar. When they err, families sometimes file lawsuits for emotional distress. Compared to the number of lawsuits for unauthorized autopsies, there are relatively few challenges to the so-called death industry. Those that do arise involve embalming, cremation, and transportation.[54] Although courts have been disinclined to award monetary damages for only mental distress, they are increasingly willing to do so.

Embalming

Sometimes families suffer emotional trauma when the body of a loved one is prepared in a religiously inappropriate manner. For example, in *Kohn v. United States* (1984) a soldier, Marc Kohn, was accidentally shot to death by a fellow soldier, after which an autopsy was performed without informing his relatives or obtaining their consent. Some of his organs were removed, and others were cremated. His parents and sister filed a lawsuit alleging the government's actions violated Jewish law. Although the federal district court declined to find the U.S. government liable for performing the autopsy, the court did award damages of $105,000 to each parent for the mental distress caused by the embalming of the body and for the cremation and retention of parts of his body. The court was persuaded that the family reacted with genuine "shock" and "horror" upon learning that his body "had been dealt with in violation of their Jewish beliefs and buried other than in its entirety" and found no reason for the immediate embalming.[55]

On some occasions it is the hospital that makes the mistake. In the case of *Lott v. State and Tumminelli v. State* (1962) the bodies of two woman of different religions, Rose Lott, an Orthodox Jewish woman, and Mary Tumminelli, a Roman

Catholic, were mixed up in the hospital mortuary (probably because they died within an hour of each other), each being prepared for the other's death ritual. Because of the emotional harm caused by the mix-up, the relatives of each won a monetary damages for mental anguish, an award of $1,000 for each family.[56] The court was not concerned with physical damage to the dead body but with the mental suffering caused by the mismanagement of the corpse.

In *Doersching v. State Funeral Directors Board* (1987), funeral director Philip Doersching shipped a body to a Mexican funeral home for an open casket presentation, but failed to ensure that the embalming incisions and head wound were properly closed. As he did not clean or prepare the body properly, when it arrived at the Sanchez Funeral Home in Nuevo Laredo, Mexico, the body showed signs of decomposition. Because he engaged in such outrageous conduct and gross negligence, including having "badly botched a funeral," the Funeral Directors Examining Board revoked his license. The conduct exceeded "all bounds usually tolerated by decent society."[57] After the circuit court reversed the revocation, the board appealed. The Court of Appeals of Wisconsin had to resolve two issues: (1) whether there was substantial enough evidence to support the board's findings and (2) whether the board's decision represented a proper exercise of its discretion. The appellate court reversed the lower court, affirming the board's decision. In the dissenting opinion, the judge expressed his disagreement with an issue not discussed in the majority opinion, namely Doersching's cultural insensitivity:

> The board's conclusion that Doersching's action exhibited willful disrespect for the feelings and welfare of the Rocha family impute to Doersching a knowledge of Mexican culture. The Mexican funeral director, Sanchez, testified as to the importance of viewing the body in Mexican culture. He said that it is important for the Mexican family members to be with the deceased until the last possible minute and that is why it is important to be with the body. This evidence came out at the time of the hearing but there is no evidence that Doersching was aware of these aspects of Mexican culture at the time he was retained.
>
> The gist of this case is that the deceased's body did not arrive at the funeral home in Mexico in the condition expected by the family. However, the body had suffered severe trauma as a result of the auto accident in which the deceased was killed. Doersching was admittedly negligent in failing to suture the embalming incisions, wash the hair, and close the head wound. Yet there was uncontradicted testimony in the record that there were no steps Doersching could have taken which would have insured that the body would arrive in Mexico in the kind of condition the family obviously hoped for. Drainage of the wounds and purging in air flight, and lack of cosmetic makeup all contributed to the poor appearance of the body when it arrived in Mexico.
>
> The board is entitled to find that Doersching was negligent in not knowing that the family wanted an open casket funeral and was grossly negligent in not preparing the body accordingly. But on the question of whether Doersching flouted the family's wishes, or acted in reckless disregard of those wishes, the testimony is inconclusive.[58]

The need to view the body is documented in the literature.[59]

The question here is whether funeral directors have any obligation to be knowledgeable about the folkways of different cultural groups.[60] Not all would share the sentiment expressed by the dissenting judge in this case. Part of civic responsibility is, arguably, some level of knowledge about the traditions of other groups.

Cremation

Another technique of disposing of the dead body is cremation, which was known to have been used in antiquity. It has become increasingly popular in modern times because it permits a tremendous saving of space and is less expensive than other methods like burial. Although cremation was not popular in Europe until the late nineteenth century, it has come to be widely used there. The country where cremation was practiced most widely was Germany.[61]

While cremation is required by some groups such as Hindus, it is prohibited by others. Although the Catholic Church has not always been opposed to burning human remains, there is a widespread belief on the part of Catholics that cremation is unacceptable. Sometimes when the funeral director cremates a Catholic person by mistake, the family sues. For instance, in *Leonard v. Kurtz* (1992), a Roman Catholic woman was unsuccessful in her lawsuit against the Park Crematory for cremating her husband without her consent. In other cases the cremation may not be performed expeditiously, as for example when Jewish law requires disposition of the body with twenty-four hours and the mortuary fails to do this.[62]

Transportation

In a remarkable case, *Onyeanusi v. Pan Am* (1990, 1992), an Ibo man from Nigeria sued Pan Am for mishandling his mother's corpse while transporting it from the United States to Nigeria. Olamma Onyeanusi died on October 1, 1986, during a visit to her son who resided in Philadelphia. Her son Onyebuchim arranged to have her body flown from New York to Port Harcourt, Nigeria, via Paris. Her body was scheduled to leave New York on October 15 and arrive in Nigeria on the 17th. In the meantime, twenty thousand members of the Ibo tribe gathered in the village of Uzuakoli waiting for the body to arrive, so that they could perform a traditional funeral. There was a nine-day delay, and when Mr. Onyeanusi went to get the corpse from the airport in Port Harcourt, he received the remains of a stranger. When he finally received the correct body, it was in a burlap sack. This error caused special trauma to him and his people because her body arrived in a burlap sack, which meant to the Ibo that her death had been by suicide, and her body was face down, which meant to the Ibo that the death was under dishonorable circumstances.

The legal question was whether or not the Warsaw Convention applied. That depended on a determination of whether the mother's body was a "person, goods, or baggage." If her corpse fit one of the three categories, then the Convention applied. If the Convention applied, then the statute of limitations barred the son from bringing the lawsuit. In the end the court ruled that the dead body was "goods."

Of course, from the cultural viewpoint the human remains was still considered a "person," but making this argument would not have helped win the lawsuit. So, even if the cultural interpretation of the body had been employed, it would not have changed the disposition of the case.[63] But the real point is that airlines could traumatize people in unforeseen ways if they negligently transport corpses. Even with the delay the airline could still have avoided putting the mother in a burlap sack and placing her face down.

In *Singh v. Air Illinois* (1988), another suit against an airline, the relevance of the deceased's cultural background was at issue. After Jasbir K. Singh, a Sikh man, was killed in a plane crash, his estate sued, arguing that the calculation of the damages take into account the religious custom of sons taking care of their parents in their old age. After the jury awarded $400,000 to the administrator of his estate, the defendant challenged the relevance of expert testimony indicating that Mr. Singh, as a dutiful Sikh son, was required by custom to care for his parents. However, the appellate court in Illinois concluded that the testimony concerning "religious custom" was relevant to "the value of the loss of support and society suffered by decedent's parents and siblings."[64]

Another legal dispute involving the transport of a dead body involved an eighty-nine-year-old Orthodox Jewish woman, Mimi Goldberg, who died in Hawaii where she lived with her son. After her death, her son arranged to have her remains sent to Oakland, California, where she had spent the better part of her life, so that she could be buried next to her husband. When the burial group opened her casket in Oakland, a pig was discovered next to her body. This "error" was particularly offensive because Orthodox Jews do not eat pork, and the pig has historically been used as an anti-Semitic symbol. Because of the defilement, her son filed a lawsuit against the Nuuanu Mortuary, which, in order to avoid adverse publicity, settled the case for $750,000. As part of the settlement the defendants had to print an apology in leading West Coast newspapers.[65]

Another instance in which a body did not arrive as requested occurred in 1997. In the middle of a funeral Mass the church received a call from the MacDougall Family Mortuary indicating that the wrong body had arrived. The correct casket finally did show up, but the husband was distraught and filed a lawsuit for emotional distress. He was worried that because his wife had missed the first blessing, she might not get to heaven.[66]

Sensitivity to Diverse Cultures

Having considered some of the known cases in which funeral directors have been sued by religious minorities because of what we might call "multicultural" malpractice, one ought to consider why there are relatively few suits of this kind. Several explanations are possible. First, funeral directors perceive their role as wanting to comfort families, so naturally they want to do whatever is requested, provided it is within the law.[67]

Second, besides normative arguments about the value of multiculturalism, there are economic benefits to be gained, and funeral directors recognize the tremendous business opportunities. There is a huge market incentive to cater to families from diverse cultures, considering that the funeral industry is a multibillion-dollar business. To take advantage of the market, homes are beginning to attract different groups by learning about multicultural death practices. The larger mortuary companies are looking for diverse clients, and some mortuaries actually become known for specializing in one ethnic group. For example, the Douglass Family Mortuaries in Paramount, California, became known as "the Gypsy mortuary."[68]

A third key reason why funeral directors strive to be sensitive to diverse cultures is their strong desire to avoid adverse publicity. Some litigation is prevented because religious minorities take their dead to funeral directors from their own cultural background who will prepare the bodies properly. When that is not possible, they seek out funeral directors known to be acquainted with their folk laws.[69]

The funeral industry disseminates information about diverse funeral rites. The National Funeral Directors Association (NFDA) has published one book that delineates the practices—Habenstein and Lamers, *Funeral Customs the World Over* (1994)—and distributes another: Irish et al., *Ethnic Variations in Dying, Death, and Grief* (1993). In 1997 the NFDA's main trade journal *The Director* devoted an issue to "Cultural Differences in the U.S." The National Association of Colleges of Mortuary Science published an overview of different death rituals in *Funeral Services and Ceremonies* (1994). Although there is increasing interest on the part of the funeral industry and although the subject of multiculturalism is considered in the forty-eight mortuary science colleges in the United States, it is not a required subject.[70]

The fact that courts award monetary damages in the funeral director cases implies recognition that relevant error is regarded as significant. It suggests that plaintiffs ought to prevail in lawsuits against the medical examiners as well. Furthermore, the funeral directors often make mistakes because the medical examiner misidentifies the body. The funeral directors may resent this because they can be sued, whereas the medical examiner may be shielded from suit by immunity.[71]

Another difference between the first two sets of cases is that the medical examiner deliberately acts in a way that violates the religious law of groups. Funeral directors' errors are often accidental. To the extent that the law punishes intentional infliction of harm, it is actually the medical examiners who should be sanctioned rather than the funeral directors.

BURIAL

There are numerous burial disputes that reflect different cultural conceptions regarding the proper treatment of the dead. Sometimes the question is what law applies, as in the celebrated *Otieno* case (1991) in Kenya. At the center of the sensational dispute was the body of a prominent Nairobi attorney, Mr. Silvanus Melea

Otieno, originally from the Luo tribe. Mr. Otieno and his wife, Wambui Otieno, a Kikuyu, had a modern Kenyan marriage across ethnic lines; they married under the Christian Marriage Act, rather than customary law. During his lifetime the Otienos clearly renounced tribal folkways. After he died intestate of heart failure on December 20, 1986, Mrs. Otieno wanted to bury him on their farm outside Nairobi. The Luo people argued, however, that he could not change his ethnic identity: once a Luo, always a Luo. Otieno's younger brother, Joash Ochieng Ougo, and four hundred members of the Umira Kager clan of the Luo intended to bury him next to his father's grave in Luoland. Moreover, unless he was buried as required by tradition, the Luo would suffer divine retribution. The court had to decide whether to apply Luo customary burial law over the objections of Mrs. Otieno.[72]

According to Luo customary law, when a man marries, he must follow certain traditions to establish a "home" as distinct from a house. It is crucial that the father give his blessing to the house to render it a "home." Although Otieno and his wife built several houses, because they did not follow tradition, none were recognized as a "home" by the Luo. Failure to establish a "home" as required by customary law means a man must be buried at his father's "home." It is of the utmost importance that the Luo be buried at "home" because if the body is not returned, the spirit will haunt his family and tribe:[73]

> The Luo, like many of Africa's tribes, take their burial customs seriously. Mr. Otieno's brother, Joash Ochieng Ougo testified that unless he was allowed to bury the body on the ancestral farm, the dead man's angry spirit would sabotage his life, pester him in his sleep, and make his Luo clansmen spit on him.
>
> The Luo attribute car accidents, birth defects and house fires to the restless ghost of a clansman buried in violation of tribal law.[74]

Mrs. Otieno filed suit against Johash Ochieng Ougo and Omolo Siranga, her brother-in-law and the chair of the burial committee of the Umira Kaga clan. On January 5, 1987, the trial judge in the High Court, Mr. Justice Frank J. Shields, a white Kenyan, issued an injunction, which prevented the Luo clan from removing Otieno's body from the Nairobi City mortuary, and declined to issue one requiring that Otieno be buried on Luo land. He based his decision on the definition of "next of kin" in the Law of Succession. His view was that nothing in the Kenyan legal system required the person having custody of the body to bury it in accordance with "tribal custom."[75]

The Luo lawyer, Richard Kwach, appealed to the Kenyan Court of Appeal (the court of last resort). Before a three-judge panel, Kwach argued that the judge erred by ignoring Luo folk law and not allowing him to adduce evidence in support of their claims. Mrs. Otieno's lawyer's response was that English common law applied rather than customary law.[76] On January 8, 1987, the court set aside Judge Shield's order, issued an injunction restraining her from taking possession of the body, and remanded the case for a trial before a different judge. On February 13, 1987, after hearing evidence for three weeks concerning Luo customary law and Mr. Otieno's wishes, the trial judge, this time Justice Samuel Bosire, ruled in favor of Otieno's brother, Ougo and the Luo tribe. Though Judge Shields had ruled that the deceased's wishes were irrelevant, Justice Bosire thought they were. He accepted the claim of the gravedigger over that of Mrs. Otieno and witnesses who testified in support of her position. Apparently he found that Otieno had not renounced Luo law. Public reaction to the decision was remarkable: "The High Court building was roped off and guarded by hundreds of Kenyan police carrying billy clubs and riot shields and wearing helmets with Plexiblas face guards." Mrs. Otieno appealed the decision.[77]

On appeal the court had to resolve apparently conflicting laws. Kenyan law gave preference to the wife for inheritance, but it did not address burial. The constitution allowed for the application of customary burial law. According to the evidence code, those invoking folk law have the obligation of proving it. Under the Judicature Act, in order to be admissible, the customary law had to satisfy two requirements: it could not be inconsistent with existing statutes, and it could not be repugnant to justice. The burial law seems incapable of satisfying either. Although the burial law might appear to be repugnant, judges seldom use the Repugnancy clause because of abuses of it during colonial times. In this case, the tradition also seemed to conflict with the Married Women Property Act of 1882, an English law incorporated into the Kenyan legal system. This law gave the wife the right to administer her husband's estate without his consent.[78]

The court disposed of the argument that a conflict existed, arguing that the Succession Act gave the widow preference to handle the deceased's estate but did not address burial law. Although the court took judicial notice of Otieno's nontribal lifestyle, it regarded this as irrelevant:

> It matters not that the deceased was sophisticated, urbanised and had developed a different life-style. It seems to us quite unsustainable on the grounds suggested by Mr. Khaminwa [Mrs. Otieno's lawyer] that a different formal education, and urban life style can effect adherence to one's personal law. . . . At present there is no way in which an African citizen of Kenya can divest himself of the association with the tribe of his father if those customs are patrilineal. It is thus clear that Mr. Otieno having been born and bred a Luo remained a member of the Luo tribe and subject to the customary law of the Luo people.[79]

The court concluded that where "there is a conflict between Common Law and Customary Law, the latter must prevail." With respect to the argument that the law was unjust, the Court said: "We are persuaded . . . that there is nothing in the Luo customary law which a reasonable man in Kenya would find repugnant to justice and morality." The gist of the argument was that the new Kenyan jurisprudence had to be based on African customary law.[80]

The court chastised Mrs. Otieno's lawyer for shirking his professional duty by failing to study Luo customary law as it related to the case. Mrs. Otieno's appeals were unsuccessful, and the final decision was that the customary law of the Luo applied. The Court of Appeal ordered that the body of the late S. M. Otieno be released to his younger brother.

While many viewed the case as involving a tension between state law and folk law, there have been other interpretations. The outcome has been criticized principally for erroneous legal analysis that condones the violation of women's rights. Stamp argues that the house/home distinction said to be part of folk law was invented as a strategy to win the case. Another critic of the decision focuses on the "neo-colonial misrepresentation of our customs and traditions." Interestingly, Mrs. Otieno explicitly acknowledges the existence of the custom but dismisses it as "primitive." Goldfarb, noting that Kenya ratified the Convention on the Elimination of All Forms of Discrimination against Women, contends Kenya failed to meet its treaty obligations. Others see the conflict as one of tribal politics between the Kikuyu and the Luo. Yet another interpretation of the case focuses on the role of class bias. While a major issue in the case was women's rights, it did not mobilize women in Kenya. Indeed, one feature of the case was that it heightened tensions among women. The case also epitomized the tendency toward politicization of burials in the African context.[81]

Otieno is a significant culture conflict for at least three reasons. First, this case, like other burial disputes, involves a conflict between customary law and national law, but unlike most decisions considered in this work, the folk law takes precedence. Second, the case illustrates how for some groups, there is no way to opt out, as group rights trump individual rights. The court said that "a man cannot change his tribal origin." Third, as sometimes occurs, the result leads to the protection of cultural rights at the expense of women's rights.[82]

The repatriation of human remains of indigenous peoples for burial has also engendered much controversy. In 1990 the U.S. Congress enacted the Native American Graves Protection and Repatriation Act (NAGPRA), which requires museums and other institutions to return the human remains and grave goods to individuals who can prove their relationship to these items. There are many problems confronting those seeking to return these cultural objects. First, the identification of the items is difficult, as museums have often commingled the bones of numerous peoples. Second, there is a possibility that some museums may challenge the constitutionality of NAGPRA as a "taking," despite language in the law attempting to avoid this matter.[83]

A third type of burial dispute focuses on sacred sites. When the government builds a road or when a business plans to develop an area that encompasses sacred burial grounds, this may spark a controversy. In the case of *Lyng v. Northwest Indian Cemetery Protective Association* (1988) the government prevailed, whereas in Hawaii hotel developers were persuaded to build hotels in a different location.[84] Although there is some concern with the desire of indigenous peoples to protect their ancestors from being disturbed, where land is involved, indigenous peoples face considerable difficulty protecting the dead.

Another set of cases deal with reinterment. It is widely thought that Jewish law prohibits moving bodies, except under extraordinary circumstances. In one case a

Jewish cemetery was sued for moving a body from one grave to another without the consent of the family. The cemetery moved the body because it had mistakenly placed it in a grave outside the family's plot. But the decision to reinter the body in its originally intended place occurred in consultation with the family.[85]

THE LEGAL STATUS OF DEAD BODIES

In much of the litigation surrounding the dead there is ambivalence about the corpse. Judges generally treat it as something not quite a person, yet not quite an object, either. This accounts for the tendency since the nineteenth century to interpret the legal relationship between the living and the dead as one in which the living have a quasi-property interest in the dead relative in order to determine proper disposition of the remains. It is not ownership but, rather, possession.

Although one might have thought the dead had rights not to be maltreated, this notion has little currency in Anglo-American jurisprudence. The only reason lawsuits against those who mismanage corpses are possible is because the living have legal rights with respect to the bodies of their relatives, provided they are related closely enough. It is clear, after reviewing the case law on the subject, that in the absence of living relatives prepared to sue on their behalf, the dead would not have standing to challenge policies that result in their desecration. Likewise, those who are not "next of kin" would be unable to bring suit.

The dead cannot be said to have a right to autonomy in the sense used by bioethicists. To what extent should the living have to adhere to wishes of the dead person if they were expressed while he or she was alive? Because there is an aversion to the dead, the denial of death results in an unwillingness to classify dead bodies as persons. Hence, it may strike some as odd that lawsuits for harm to the dead are possible (only if they adversely affect living relatives).

Presumably, the living are motivated to sue when their deceased relatives are subject to corpse malpractice. The standard explanation would be that they want to ensure that the dead are treated with dignity and that they will rest in peace. In many societies these ideas are firmly established. Another possible reason why the living strive to protect the dead from indignities is that they fear retribution. Michel Ragon argues that respect for the dead is actually fear of the dead: "At the origin of funeral rites, one observes not so much respect of the dead as fear for their survival and a desire to prevent their return. Whether we realize this or not, this fear is still apparent in our beliefs and practices."[86] He says that putting heavy stones over a corpse does serve to mark a burial place, but it also serves to prevent it from rising. The traditions of placing the dead in coffins in cemeteries reflect a desire to protect the living from the dead. Because modern societies dread the dead, this feeling is transformed to one of respect through the psychological mechanism known as "reaction formation."[87]

In the autopsy cases, the conflict is between the religious minorities and the state which claims that public necessity requires the performance of the postmortem examination. In the corpse mismanagement suits concerning embalming, cremation, and transportation, the claim is that the family suffered emotional distress as a consequence of the mismanagement. In order to sustain the claim, the relatives have to show that the error was of a sufficient magnitude because of their religious background. Hence, the cultural dimension is the effect on the family, which gives rise to the claim for damages. Were the relatives not of a different religion, the mistake might have been somewhat troubling, but it might not have caused as much emotional distress.

The law, in general, has difficulty with the concepts of psychic injury, emotional distress, and mental suffering. Judges have trouble calculating the monetary value of such claims. They also worry that courts will impose excessive liability on the defendant and about the filing of fraudulent claims. In the area of corpse mismanagement, the problem sometimes is whether the law allows suits for emotional distress.[88] Where suits are possible, the plaintiff must show that a physical injury occurred simultaneously. The real point is that the harm has to be to the living relative; the harm to the dead body is insufficient in and of itself to provide a cause of action. It is not obvious why the lawsuit should serve only to vindicate the rights of the living.

The litigation in the United States is predicated on the notion that living persons have the right to see that their relatives are disposed of as they see fit. The lawsuits presuppose that the dead person would prefer to be disposed of in the manner required by his religion or culture. When relatives sue because the religious beliefs attributed to the dead body have not been respected, the courts may award damages.[89]

One of the problems with the litigation is that the dominant society is in the position of evaluating other peoples' conceptions of the afterlife. If judges challenge the worldviews of others, this may call their own conceptions into question. In reality, there is no way for judges to determine whether, in fact, the desecration will or will not result in divine retribution. If the beliefs are sincerely held by plaintiffs, that ought to suffice for the purposes of the lawsuits considered here.

TOWARD CULTURAL RIGHTS FOR THE DEAD

The disputes concerning cadavers suggest that on one level culturally different disputants win sympathy because the notion that the dead deserve respect is a widely, if not universally, held belief. Despite the possible universality of this value, numerous conflicts arise over the treatment of the dead. This stems, at least in part, from different cultural interpretations of the corpse. As seen in many of the examples in this chapter, cultural minorities and indigenous groups regard the dead body as a person in contrast to the dominant legal system in the United States, which considers it to be a piece of property in which certain relatives have a "quasi-property" interest. Because historically it was necessary to characterize the body as "some form of property" to protect it from theft and other harms, early American cases treated the dead body as "quasi-property."[90] Hence, the status of the cadaver in different worldviews accounts for the numerous and varied conflicts examined in this chapter.

What makes these cases particularly fascinating is the judicial reaction to them. On the one hand, judges express great sympathy for the plaintiffs because they, too, regard disturbing the dead as a serious desecration and worry about their own mortality. On the other hand, judges may rule against them because the state interest takes precedence over religious freedom, because they do not share the plaintiffs' beliefs about the afterlife, and, most of all, because they have a fundamentally different view of the corpse.

For many reasons, it is vitally important that courts respect the folk laws of groups concerning the dead. It is necessary to protect the dead because, if the belief system is correct, mutilating the body or preparing it improperly for burial will prevent the person from reaching the afterlife or make his or her existence miserable there. Moreover, the dead are in no position to vindicate their own rights.[91]

Ensuring that the treatment of the dead is consistent with the customary law of ethnic and indigenous groups is also crucial for the living. After all, most death rituals serve the function of consoling the bereaved family members who are struggling to come to terms with the loss of a loved one.[92] The insensitive handling of a corpse is particularly traumatic, considering the time at which it occurs. The emotional consequences can be devastating, and this may explain why judges, even if they do not share the plaintiffs' views about the afterlife, will nevertheless, award damages in some cases. They recognize the harm done to aggrieved families.

If the legal system fails to recognize the folk law of grief-stricken individuals in a time of emotional crisis, then it is unlikely they will ever take seriously the commitment of the larger society to cultural pluralism. Constitutional values like equal protection and religious freedom will seem to be empty or inapplicable to them. The reaction could be severe, leading large numbers of individuals to feel alienated and to avoid contact with the dominant system. For instance, groups that fear autopsies may not seek medical care when they really need it. By forcing American medical practices on ethnic minorities, the law may inadvertently put the health of some at risk. Furthermore, individuals who feel that their folkways are not respected will feel alienated and may become disinclined to report criminal wrongdoing to law enforcement authorities. This is hardly an ideal situation, and it is one that can be easily remedied. A greater attempt to be culturally sensitive to relatives of the deceased would promote intergroup harmony.[93]

Public policies should establish the principle that the dead should be treated with respect, and that treatment should be dictated by the group to which the person belongs. This, of course, will not guarantee that public officials will be culturally sensitive,[94] but it will ensure that minorities and indigenous peoples have some recourse. Paying monetary damages after an act of desecration cannot repair the injury and can, at best, only provide some degree of deterrence. Hence, injunctions should used to prevent the harm from taking place.

The number of culture conflicts that relate to dead bodies is quite astonishing. The conflict in worldviews seems to reflect fundamentally different assumptions about corpses, namely the property approach versus the personhood approach. But since the idea that the dead are sacred is a cross-cultural belief, it ought to be relatively easy to ensure that the dead are handled in a culturally appropriate manner. The expectation should be that death investigators should be familiar with the ways of death of groups in their communities. They should not invoke "ignorance of the law" with regard to the customary law of other peoples. Failure to show concern for the traditions of others will result in widespread alienation, a dangerous situation. Furthermore, if pluralistic societies cannot accommodate diverse groups with respect to the dead, how can they realistically expect to show sensitivity toward the living?

Part III

TOWARD A PRINCIPLE OF MAXIMUM ACCOMMODATION

10

The Cultural Defense
in Theory and Practice

The material in Part II demonstrates both the ubiquity and extraordinary variety of disputes involving diverse cultural traditions. One of the most striking features of many of these cases is the arbitrary treatment of cultural minorities in the legal system. Cultural evidence may be found admissible or inadmissible. Either way, the decision to exclude or not is sometimes upheld and sometimes overturned on appeal. There is no uniformity in the way culture is handled by the courts, and this variation leads to dissimilar outcomes, sometimes for similar offenses.

More importantly, the cases also reveal a profound ignorance of the folkways of ethnic minorities, which often leads to bias, or what may be called cultural discrimination. This bias is revealed in the disparate way in which fundamental legal principles such as equal protection of the laws, a right to a fair trial, and religious freedom are applied in criminal cases involving cultural minorities. Although murder is reprehensible and ought never to be condoned, when the court refuses to admit that persons of a different culture might be provoked by different words or gestures, as was the case in *Trujillo-Garcia v. Rowland* (1994) and *State v. Trakulrat* (1990), it denies equal protection of the laws. When Kong Moua is prevented from raising a mistake of fact defense, because according to modern legal doctrine his mistaken belief that Xeng Xiong consented to go with him was not "objectively reasonable," he is denied equal protection of the laws. Charreadas are declared illegal, but Western-style rodeos are not, even though both involve the tripping of animals. When a defendant such as Siripongs is executed because his attorneys do not introduce cultural evidence concerning the significance of Thai body language at sentencing, he is denied the right to a fair trial.[1]

When Native Americans are prosecuted for hunting deer, moose, and eagles, sometimes even when treaty rights authorize it, they are denied their right to religious freedom. Adherents of the Santería faith are prevented from sacrificing animals according to their religious dictates. Although we profess to believe in religious liberty, cultural minorities are unable to wear hats, beards, or ceremonial daggers. Autopsies are performed contrary to the deeply held religious beliefs of the decedent's relatives, and sometimes despite the deceased possessing a certificate of religious objection. Many Native Americans are punished for using peyote in religious ceremonies, despite the existence of a statutory right to do so.

If a government purports to protect the religious liberty of all who reside within the borders of the country, then even religious minorities apparently can assert this right. Were this principle to be enforced uniformly, in many instances, cultural defenses would be unnecessary. As we have seen in many cases, because of the belief-action distinction, courts have been unwilling to allow religiously motivated actions where the state interest is thought to outweigh the right to religious freedom.

Cultural discrimination is also found in civil cases where it manifests itself as an unwillingness to accommodate diverse cultural traditions. Because of the power of enculturation, we are often shocked by some of the practices of other cultures. This visceral reaction leads to oppressive responses such as removing children from their parents' homes. Mr. and Mrs. Krasnqi and Mr. Kargar are separated from their children, even though when the cultural evidence was finally considered in criminal prosecutions, it was clear that their actions were motivated by love and affection. This lack of flexibility on the part of judges and other civil authorities is incompatible with the values of a liberal democracy.

Even in cases where the legal system could be more understanding, ethnic minorities are generally coerced into conformity. So, for example, Pacific Islanders are harassed for drinking kava and Middle Easterners are arrested for chewing khat, even though the precise effects of these substances are unknown, and these traditions have existed for centuries. Sokheng Caea and Seng K. Ou are arrested and jailed for attempting to eat a dog, even though there was no law against it at the time. The cultural minorities who experience the legal system often consider the treatment to be a form of harassment.

The children of immigrants are legally compelled to have surgery against the wishes of their families and communities despite the fact that surgery holds no guarantee of success. Sometimes, as in the case of Franklin Kue, the parents are so desperate to avoid the operation that they flee with their child. When we contrast these cases, in which reasonable accommodation is possible, with the Christian Science manslaughter cases, in which entirely unjustifiable accommodation is made in the name of religious liberty, the double standard is clear.

I am not saying that every cultural tradition ought to be tolerated. As I have emphasized throughout this book, the consideration of cultural evidence does not necessarily require that courts permit the continuation of all cultural practices. But the preponderance of the data belies the commitment of liberal democracies to the value of cultural diversity. Assuming that culture is constitutive of identity, in a pluralistic society government policies should support the flourishing of multiple identities. In order to ensure that ethnic minorities are accorded the dignity and rights which are their due, some kind of formal cultural defense is essential.[2]

In practice, a cultural defense is grounded and implemented in very different ways, according to the manner in which the legal issue underlying the dispute is evaluated. Modern legal systems classify disputes as criminal or civil. In this book I have made a deliberate attempt to survey the range of culture conflicts in as unbiased a fashion as possible, and this accounts for the thematic organization of the cases in Part II. At this stage, however, the legal issues must be sorted out. In order to be as clear as possible as to the legal subtleties involved in the adjudication, this chapter divides the cases into criminal and civil. The resulting framework is intended to facilitate the discussion of precisely how to ensure that culture be considered at all stages of the legal process.

THE CULTURAL DEFENSE IN CRIMINAL LAW

Arguments for the Cultural Defense

In this section I offer arguments in favor of the establishment of an official "cultural defense" in the criminal law. The purpose of a cultural defense is to allow defendants to introduce evidence concerning their culture and its relevance to the totality of circumstances surrounding their case. A successful cultural defense would permit the reduction (and possible elimination) of a charge, with a concomitant reduction in punishment. The rationale behind such a claim is that an individual's behavior is influenced to such a large extent by his culture that either (1) the individual simply did not believe that his actions contravened any laws, or (2) the individual felt compelled to act the way he did. In both cases the individual's culpability is lessened.

The reason for admitting a cultural defense lies not so much in a desire to be culturally sensitive, although that is surely a large part of it, but rather in a desire to ensure equal application of the law to all citizens. By equality I mean not merely the desire to treat all culture conflict cases in a more uniform manner but also the desire to treat all individuals in society as equals.[3] As I shall argue, individual justice demands that the legal system focus on the actor as well as the act, and on motive as well as intent. This, in turn, necessitates the introduction of cultural information into the courtroom.

As we have already seen to some extent in chapter 3, cultural information is sometimes brought into the courtroom by defense attorneys in the context of a preexisting defense, such as provocation or insanity. For many reasons, however, this strategy is unsatisfactory for the generic culture conflict case. The most salient drawback is that the standards against which a defendant's actions are judged are those of "the reasonable person." But it is precisely this idea of reasonableness that lies at the heart of the conflict. As I argue here, the actions of defendants should be judged against behavioral standards that are reasonable for a person of that culture in the context of this culture. This would balance the requirements of individual justice and cultural accommodation with the competing demands of social order and the rule of law.

The balance is best achieved by the establishment of a cultural defense as a partial excuse. In this way, juries could decide whether cultural factors were determinative in a defendant's behavior, and, if so, whether that is sufficient to warrant a lesser charge.[4] That is, employing the cultural defense as a partial excuse would enable courts to better fit the punishment to the crime, which is surely one of the goals of the criminal justice system.

I first provide a philosophical justification for a defense based upon culture. I argue that retribution, with its associated concept of proportionality, provides the true justification for punishment. I then give a brief discussion of the relevance of motive to the determination of guilt within the context of the retributive theory. Finally, I contend that one cannot understand the motive of a defendant without an understanding of his culture.

Before one can judge whether culture is properly considered in the determination of guilt, it is essential that the purpose of punishment be made clear. The three principal theories of punishment are deterrence, rehabilitation, and retribution. The focus of each is somewhat different. Deterrence theorists believe the primary reason for punishment is to prevent other crimes. Rehabilitationists believe that punishment is only valid as long as its principal aim is to reform the criminal so that he becomes a more law-abiding citizen. Retributionists focus on the moral blameworthiness of a defendant, arguing that an individual should be punished only as much as he deserves (the just deserts doctrine).[5]

There is no doubt that punishment may be legitimized by appeal to some combination of these, but I believe the fundamental justification for punishment to be retribution.[6] Deterrence cannot stand alone, because general deterrence could be achieved by punishing individuals irrespective of guilt. Unless the individuals are those who deserve punishment, punishing them would not be justifiable, even for the sake of deterrence. Deterrence is only valid if others are deterred by the punishment of one who is deserving of it. By like token, rehabilitation only succeeds if the prisoner accepts that he is blameworthy. Thus, the concept of just desert underlies the other theories of punishment insofar as it is a tacit assumption for their legitimacy.

Intrinsic to retribution is the concept of proportionality: the punishment should fit the crime. That is, it should not be disproportionately severe or lenient. There are various types of proportionality, the most famous of which is perhaps the *lex talionis,* or "an eye for an eye." In contrast to this identical or strict type of proportionality is a more flexible sort of scaling that might be called *general proportionality.* Of course, it is a challenging analytic problem to determine just how much punishment a given defendant deserves. Even within the same society, there is often disagreement over what constitutes condign punishment. Nevertheless, retributivists all agree on the idea of proportionality.[7]

It is this idea that provides the justification for a cultural defense. A defendant whose act is culturally motivated is less blameworthy, and, therefore, he deserves a lesser punishment. To see why this is so, we must consider the relevance of motive to criminal liability.[8]

MOTIVE AND INTENT   The primary motivation for wanting to admit cultural evidence in the courtroom is to attempt to bridge the gap that currently exists in the law between moral and legal guilt. The gray area that separates these two concepts owes its existence to the confusion surrounding the distinction between motive and intent, and the roles which each of these play in establishing legal guilt.[9]

As is well known, the role of intent is a long-standing problem in criminal jurisprudence. In the criminal law it is construed narrowly to refer to whether the individual intends to commit the act that is defined as a crime. If so, the mens rea requirement is satisfied. Officially, motive is not germane.[10] The standard example is that the robber is culpable even if he steals from the rich to give to the poor; his motive for theft is inconsequential.

Yet, motive is critical in establishing blameworthiness. There is certainly a difference between the robber who steals for his own personal gain and the robber who steals to feed his children. Whereas both are guilty legally, the latter is in some sense less guilty morally. Insofar as the law derives its legitimacy from morality, it should accommodate this distinction. The law should officially recognize the role motive plays in adjudicating the guilt of a defendant.

The reason courts have been loath to allow any consideration of motive probably stems from a desire to maintain deterrence. There may have been a fear that allowing considerations of motive would increase the crime rate. Those who appear to have a reasonable motive might then fail to be convicted, and this would undermine deterrence. A further objection is that some might fraudulently manufacture an expedient motive.

Yet, for a long time it has been recognized that justice is not served by ignoring motive entirely. Motive is currently considered at many different stages in the legal process. The police and district attorneys exercise their discretion in deciding not to arrest or to prosecute the offender who acts with a good motive. Judges adjust sentences, depending on the motive of a defendant.

Motive can play an important role in trials as well. The classic examples where motive is considered relevant in the guilt phase are self-defense and necessity.[11] The person who kills in self-defense has certainly committed the act, and has done so intentionally, but was motivated to do so to preserve his life. If this motive can be demonstrated, it may serve to acquit the defendant completely. The motive of necessity functions similarly.

Motive is relevant here because the law recognizes that justice requires its consideration. Justice requires that there be exceptions to rules. Killing is wrong, but may be justified if one's life is threatened. Breaking into a house is wrong, but may be justified if one would otherwise die of hypothermia. Of course, these are somewhat extreme examples; in both cases the defendant finds himself in a situation in which he was essentially compelled to take the proscribed action. Nevertheless, they demonstrate that an understanding of the motive of the defendant is necessary in some cases to bridge the gap between legal and moral guilt.

PARTIAL EXCUSES: THE RELEVANCE OF MOTIVE   It is a common feature of these sorts of cases that possessing the relevant motive does not automatically exculpate a defendant. In many of these cases the defendant is actually convicted, but then given a suspended sentence. This is done to preserve the illusion of the blanket illegality of the action (and thus presumably to deter others), while tailoring the punishment to the defendant's moral culpability. Sometimes the defendant is charged with a lesser offense, as when murder is reduced to manslaughter.

In these instances, motive serves as a partial excuse. Partial excuses can function either to reduce a charge or reduce a sentence. The classic examples of defenses acting as partial excuses are provocation and diminished responsibility.[12] The key idea of the provocation defense is that the defendant lacks the mens rea required for murder, namely malice aforethought. His culpability is less, and therefore he should be held responsible only for manslaughter.

The advantages of partial excuses are clear. They allow the law to accommodate the motivation of the defendant without requiring inappropriate conviction or complete acquittal. The current binary choice between guilt or innocence is much too simplistic to accommodate the subtleties of the real world. By providing alternatives, partial excuses would allow more flexibility. More importantly, they would allow the jury, after hearing all the evidence, to determine the appropriate degree of culpability.

Partial excuses are a double-edged sword. On the one hand, allowing the jury to take motive into account would permit them to acquit a defendant with reason instead of "perversely."[13] On the other hand, by giving the jury more options for conviction, the partial excuse would enable the jury to convict more easily, though for a lesser charge. That is, the defendant may be convicted of the lesser charge when under the old system he might have been acquitted. But, if the defendant is convicted of the lesser charge, then presumably it is because he is guilty of this lesser charge. The goal is to achieve the proper proportionality between the punishment and the crime.

It has been argued that to extend the purview of partial excuses to crimes other than murder, one would have to duplicate all known laws, including for each one a lesser included offense with which the defendant could be charged in the event his partial excuse was accepted by the court. Of course, this is an overstatement, as many laws have lesser included offenses. For example, kidnapping and false imprisonment are one such pair.[14] One could also argue that not every crime needs to have a lesser included offense. Perhaps creating such a categorization is only necessary for the most serious crimes, those that carry either great moral stigma or heavy sentences. At the very least the cultural defense as partial excuse could be used to mitigate sentences.

The concern that defendants be punished as much as they deserve requires that motive be considered. One might argue that if the concern is merely that the punishment should fit the crime, then that could be handled at the sentencing stage. However, even if the person receives a lesser punishment, he must still suffer the stigma of having been convicted of a crime of greater opprobrium. Wasik agrees that "some criminal law excuses are so morally and legally significant that they must be considered prior to the verdict." In the interests of fairness, the defendant should be found guilty of a lesser charge rather than manipulating the sentence ex post facto.[15]

THE CULTURAL DEFENSE AS PARTIAL EXCUSE   If motive may legitimately be considered in criminal prosecutions, then, because of the power of enculturation, courts should take cultural motives into account. If cultural motives are admissible in court, then this would allow for the creation of a formal cultural defense. A decision must be made whether the cultural defense should exonerate the defendant entirely or only partially.[16]

My position is that the cultural defense should function as a partial excuse. The fundamental issue here is the retributive theory of punishment whose basis is proportionality. The key idea is that the punishment must fit the crime. The crime with which a defendant is charged must correspond to the nature of the act. Without a cultural defense as partial excuse two possible egregious errors will be made: individuals will receive no punishment because the choice is between full punishment and no punishment; juries will simply acquit if they feel conviction will lead to an unduly harsh penalty or because judges will impose no punishment. In many of the cases considered in Part II a consistent pattern emerges: judges convict and then impose probation or suspended sentences. In such cases defendants arguably receive less punishment than they deserve because they intended to commit the act that is defined to be a crime and they committed the act. Since they satisfy the legal requirements (mens rea and actus reus), the reduction in sentence may be excessive, considering that some of these crimes are not victimless.

The other error will be the imposition of full punishment. For example, in some cases the judges exclude cultural evidence as irrelevant to the case, which may result in excessive punishment.[17] If motive is relevant to the determination of guilt, then it is arguably unfair to exclude consideration of the cultural motive, leaving the defendant subject to the most severe punishment.

Even assuming that cultural defenses should be allowed in principle to aid in the assessment of culpability, it is not obvious whether the cultural defense as partial excuse should exculpate at trial or whether the effect of the culturally motivated act should influence sentencing. Some might distinguish between the trial and sentencing in order to argue that cultural considerations should be allowed at sentencing, but not at trial. In reality, this argument depends on an artificial and somewhat misleading distinction. It is well known that juries may refuse to convict individuals if they are opposed to the punishment, for instance, the death penalty, that will be imposed. This suggests that the trial and sentencing stages are far too interconnected for the distinction to make much sense.[18] Furthermore, failure to consider the cultural dimension at the trial in some cases will lead to a tremendous distortion of the facts. If justice is to be done, it is inconceivable that culture not be admitted in the courtroom.

So, the question becomes how much less culpable is a person who commits a culturally motivated crime. While it would be convenient if we could establish a "bright line" or clear-cut rule to make this determination, there is no way to do so. The magnitude of the punishment will have to be arrived at on a case-by-case basis.

Arguments against the Cultural Defense

There are several key arguments advanced by those who oppose the use of the cultural defense, some of which are principled and others of which are practical. Many of the specific critiques in the cultural defense literature are variations on the deterrence argument.

One of the dominant justifications for punishment is deterrence. The core idea is that the law must sanction deviant acts to uphold the social order. This view of the penal function is sometimes referred to as the crime control model. There are two types of deterrence: specific and general. Specific deterrence means that punishment is warranted if it will prevent the defendant himself from committing another crime.[19] General deterrence signifies the imposition of penal sanctions on a defendant to deter others in society from committing crimes. The central question is whether a cultural defense that reduces culpability and, therefore, lessens a sentence would undermine the deterrence function of the criminal justice system. A worry commonly expressed in the literature is that the cultural defense will undermine both types of deterrence. If a person is not punished for a culturally motivated act, he may continue to follow the tradition. Members of the ethnic community likewise will observe that they may perpetuate the tradition with impunity.

Not only is there concern that the tradition will persist but also that this will lead to a weakening of the criminal justice in general. It is simply too confusing to have separate legal codes for different groups within the same national political system. One major practical concern is the fear that the absence of a uniform legal code will lead to anarchy. If individuals and groups could decide on their own with which laws they would comply, there would no longer be any certainty or predictability in the legal system. This anarchy argument is prominent in the scholarship on the cultural defense.[20]

While some express concern over widespread anarchy, others worry about the impact of the policy on particular groups. Some critics focus on the possibility that the cultural defense would be employed so as to undermine the rights of vulnerable groups such as women and children. They believe that this will be the most common use of the defense and that this will undermine the deterrent function of the law.[21] If members of the ethnic community learn that particular types of behavior such as domestic violence will go unpunished, this will not deter future misconduct, and might even encourage it.

Foremost among the principled objections is the "When in Rome" assimilation argument. There is a tacit assumption that, as a matter of principle, everyone should be held to the same, single standard. Hence, the cultural defense is objectionable because it violates the principle of equal protection. These commentators contend that equality means identical treatment under the law. Accordingly, they regard the cultural defense as an illegitimate form of affirmative action or unequal preferential treatment insofar as any departure from the single standard is unacceptable.[22]

As the cases make clear, there is widespread acceptance of the "When in Rome" philosophy—that is, the presumption is that individuals should become assimilated. This means that the cultural defense is illegitimate because it would undercut one goal of punishment, namely rehabilitation (or reformation). According to the theory of rehabilitation, the justification for meting out punishment is that it will reform the character of the defendant. The process of being punished will lead the criminal to the realization that he deserves his punishment. Having reached this understanding, he will change his behavior, and thus he is on the road to recovery.

If the cultural defense is used exclusively or principally to excuse men in cases of domestic violence, then the policy may violate equal protection of the law with respect to victims.[23] It appears to condone violence against women and the maltreatment of children. According to the logic of this position, if the legal system mitigates punishment for those who commit culturally motivated crimes but not for those who commit the same crimes in the absence of the cultural imperative, the victims of the former receive less protection than victims whose perpetrators happen to be from the mainstream community.

Many critics allege that the use of the cultural defense promotes stereotypes. As one scholar put it: "Creation of a formalized 'cultural defense' will result in fossilizing cultures as a reductive stereotype, and lead to inquiries into whether a defendant's identity sufficiently matches that stereotype to merit expert testimony." Opponents generally assert that the defense is used mainly by Asians whose culture is misrepresented in court. The vast majority of these arguments focus on representations of mainly Asian women as "exotic" and contend that acceptance of these images by courts will be detrimental to women who seek to change their cultures. To the extent that the defense reinforces false, anachronistic stereotypes, it seems objectionable to many commentators. Some go so far as to question whether it is even possible to characterize a "culture."[24]

Even if one could justify the use of the cultural defense on normative grounds, many would still object to the defense because of difficulties they anticipate with the implementation of the policy. A frequently mentioned criticism of the cultural defense is that it will be impossible to draw the line between legitimate and illegitimate uses of it. This is partly because some claim it is hard to prove the existence of specific customs.[25] They also question whether second- and third-generation offspring of immigrant parents are sufficiently influenced by traditions to justify their use of the cultural defense. Some refer to the cultural defense as opening a Pandora's box, while others use the metaphor of the "slippery slope." Other concerns are that some will pretend to be members of ethnic groups, others will falsely claim that practices are traditional, and even if some can prove that belong to a particular group and the custom is traditional, they may lie, saying that their actions were motivated by cultural factors, when they were not. Those with criminal tendencies might be encouraged to commit crimes because they would be able to rely on a fraudulent claim of group membership.

Another argument against establishing a formal cultural defense is that the legal system can incorporate cultural evidence via existing defenses such as provocation, insanity, and mistake of fact. In the many provocation cases considered here in chapter 3 it was clear that culture could have been considered if judges had been willing to consider how the average reasonable person of the culture or the ordinary person under those circumstances would have reacted. Were courts prepared to modify the so-called objective reasonable person standard that constitutes one prong of the provocation test, culture could be considered in homicide cases where individuals lose self-control. It is also possible for defendants to introduce cultural factors when they raise an insanity defense. In cases such as *People v. Wu* (1991), *Nguyen v. State* (1999), and *State v. Ganal* (1996)—which involved the automatism defense, battered woman defense, and the "amok" defense, respectively—we observed how culture can be combined with the established insanity defense.

Another objection to a formal cultural defense holds that culture is more appropriately considered during sentencing, so there is no need to have a cultural defense during the guilt phase of the trial. As virtually anything can be considered during the sentencing phase of a trial, unless it is inflammatory or prejudicial, there is prima facie no reason why defendants should not be able to introduce cultural evidence at the final stage of the process.

Counterarguments to Criticisms

Many of the arguments against the cultural defense were based on the notion of deterrence, which even in the abstract has shortcomings. There exist at least two objections to deterrence theory: (1) empirical data does not prove that punishment deters crime; usually the issue is whether more severe punishment creates a greater deterrent, but it is the causal relationship that is in question; (2) punishing the innocent is consistent with deterrence theory. That is, if the sole objective of punishment is deterrence, then it makes no difference who is punished—guilty or innocent.

The deterrence argument is problematic for several reasons. To the extent that criminal conduct is motivated by cultural differences, general deterrence may not be affected by the introduction of a cultural defense. The number of culturally motivated acts is a fraction of the total number of crimes. It also seems unlikely that a cultural defense, whether a complete or partial excuse, would have much effect on the crime rate of the society allowing it.

As for specific deterrence, depending upon the type of culturally motivated act, a reduction of a sentence might well have no effect whatsoever. Punishment, no matter how severe or light, would provide notice to the ethnic minority community that the conduct is not permissible. In many cases, the fact that the act is condemned may be sufficient to achieve specific deterrence. The severity of the punishment is inconsequential to deterrence.

If the concern is that the penal sanction should deter others who belong to the ethnic group in question, rather than all members of society at large, then the issue is more difficult to settle. If men from a particular culture realized they could kill their wives with impunity, merely by employing the cultural defense, then other husbands might be encouraged not to try to control themselves when provoked. It is less clear, however, that a sentence reduction, as would be achieved by allowing the cultural defense to operate as a partial excuse would provide the same incentive. That is, if a husband is convicted of manslaughter instead of murder, the general deterrence function of the law would still exist.

It should be noted, however, that if the cultural defense were to be established as a complete defense, then that might be altogether different. While severity may not be critical for specific deterrence, some type of punishment is probably necessary. Thus, if specific deterrence is a legitimate aim of the justice system, then a cultural defense is permissible, so long as it is partial and not complete. In those rare cultural defense cases where the defendant poses a threat to society, incapacitation might be necessary. The cultural defense is not incompatible with incapacitation.

The real reason why general deterrence would be unaffected by the establishment of a cultural defense is that the type of crime involved is completely different from most crimes. Reducing the punishment for an immigrant because of the cultural context of the act has no connection to crimes committed under ordinary circumstances. The only individuals who could conceivably be influenced would be those inclined to commit culturally motivated acts. As long as they are entitled to use a cultural defense only as a partial excuse, this objection would seem to be met.

In the case of so-called heat of passion crimes, the cultural defense would not affect deterrence. In contrast, acts perpetrated with deliberation could conceivably be affected. But even culturally motivated acts that are not precipitated by an emotional crisis of some sort may not be able to be deterred by the law. If a member of a particular ethnic group believes strongly in the efficacy of folk medicine or the importance of traditional marriage practices, it stands to reason that he will try to preserve his way of life wherever he goes. So, even where the act is a more deliberate one, the attempt to buttress general deterrence by rejecting a cultural defense may prove unsuccessful. In the event that refusing to allow a cultural defense fails to deter other members of the group anyway, there seems to be no principled reason for rejecting a cultural defense on the basis of deterrence.

Even if the adoption of the cultural defense were to undermine deterrence to some degree, that does not necessarily mean that the policy should be rejected. If proportional justice requires the consideration of culture, one could argue that the cultural defense should be adopted even at the expense of deterrence.

It is not obvious that individuals, once having been informed that they may not follow tradition, will continue to do so. If they were unaware that their conduct violated the law, then the trial might serve the function of informing them of the rules of the dominant culture, without the necessity of incarcerating them. In other words, even if culturally motivated defendants are unpunished, this will not necessarily undermine deterrence.

The argument that the cultural defense will undermine the capacity of the law to deter future crimes presumes that the defense would function only as a complete excuse—that is, by leading to acquittals. If, instead, a cultural defense served as a partial excuse, thereby reducing the charge or level of culpability rather than excusing the defendant altogether, this argument loses some of its force.

There is no empirical support for the anarchy rationale. It is important to observe that legal systems have always made special exceptions for specific groups, and these exemptions have not led to the demise of the political order. In any event, this argument is highly speculative as there is no legal system, to my knowledge, that has been flexible enough for one to test the anarchy claim.

Likewise, the presumption that the cultural defense would endanger vulnerable groups appears erroneous. Critics who advance the deterrence argument usually rely on a mistaken assumption that the defense is invoked principally by jealous husbands who kill their wives. In fact, most critiques of the cultural defense in law reviews make the unfortunate mistake of only using examples in which men harm women. While this bolsters their argument, it is contrary to reality, as we have seen in Part II.[26]

The tendency to treat the defense as anti–women's rights ignores two aspects of reality: the defense also benefits women, and there are many more cases not concerned with women in which cultural defenses are raised than there are cases involving jealous husbands. Furthermore, just because a defense is available does not, of course, guarantee that it will succeed. If one thinks of the insanity defense, for example, it is obvious that juries oftentimes reject it. It is my view that defendants should be entitled to raise the cultural defense, even it does not or should not affect the ultimate disposition of a case.

Then there is the argument that allowing the cultural defense violates the equal protection rights of victims. This criticism misses the purpose of the criminal law, which is to ensure just punishment for the defendant by focusing on the mental state of the defendant, or mens rea.[27] If there is any equal protection violation, it occurs when courts fail to consider cultural evidence, thus rendering them unable to assess accurately what has transpired in a given case. Whereas courts require no additional information for "mainstream" defendants, as the motivations for their behavior are apparent, the lack of information for defendants from other cultures virtually guarantees that courts will be unable to evaluate fairly the situation of defendants whose motivations cannot readily be understood.

Another flaw in the reasoning is that, generally speaking, defendants do not receive identical sentencing, even under mandatory sentencing laws designed to minimize disparities in sentencing. Individualized justice is widely accepted, and the notion that defendants should have sentences appropriate to their particular circumstances is a principle that is broad enough to encompass the cultural background of defendants.[28]

With respect to rehabilitation, the notion is that the criminal can be reformed, so that he or she may return to society. The difficulty with using this rationale in the context of culture conflict cases is that rehabilitating defendants means forcing them to become assimilated. It is doubtful whether a defendant can be "rehabilitated" without having to alter, quite dramatically, his or her ethnic identity. Rehabilitation, which is normally considered to be a progressive approach to punishment, takes on a different meaning if we mean compelling a defendant to shed his or her cultural identity in order to be released from prison.

The most profound objection to using rehabilitation as a theoretical justification for denying the cultural defense concerns its very premise. This position assumes the validity of rehabilitation, or in this case assimilation. But is it justifiable to force a person to transform his identity? Some will argue that the person is being asked only to give up one tradition that the dominant system regards as offensive. If that custom is central to his way of life, however, then his entire worldview or cultural identity will be in jeopardy. It is at least worth asking whether it is desirable to force the assimilation of culturally diverse members of a given society.

A more serious concern is whether, in fact, punishment is even capable of forcing assimilation. Since every individual has been subject to enculturation, it may not be possible to discard deeply rooted, closely held beliefs. If it can be empirically proven that rehabilitation is virtually impossible for the defendant who acts in accordance with cultural imperatives, then this theory fails to provide a rationale for opposing the cultural defense.

Rehabilitation seems to be an odd policy if all members of the cultural group, except those who have had the misfortune to be incarcerated, retain their group identity. Assuming what may be impossible—namely, that it is possible to rehabilitate a defendant so that he will no longer commit any culturally motivated act— what effect will this have in general? If the goal is to "rehabilitate" all of those belonging to culturally diverse groups, since they may be predisposed to commit culturally motivated acts, then it would be strange to employ such a piecemeal approach. Rather than forcing the assimilation of the few who end up in prison, it might be more effective to wage a major "educational" campaign.

The "When in Rome" objection is problematic inasmuch as there is little recognition that legal standards are not culturally neutral—that they reflect the values of the dominant culture.[29] There is little discussion of the possibility that the single standard might be unjust because it is biased against ethnic minorities. Moreover, it is not obvious why the law must be applied in a uniform fashion to all individuals and groups, who, after all, do not have equal power or status and are not "similarly" situated.

Some object to having a formal cultural defense on the grounds that putting the culture on trial may have adverse consequences for members of the group. There is a fear that decisions based on group characteristics will lead to the reinforcement of social stereotypes.[30] But this worry that the cultural defense will reinforce stereotypes, especially of Asians, is unwarranted. As is clear from the examples in this book, many different groups, including European Americans, have raised the defense, so it is simply false to claim that it is limited to any one group.[31]

As for the more general point that the defense reinforces stereotypes, several points must be considered. First, the stereotypes exist whether or not the defense is used. Second, patterns of culture are not equivalent to racist stereotypes, even though in the debate about the cultural defense there is an unfortunate tendency to conflate race and culture. Third, some stereotypes are true or at least contain a kernel of truth, if by stereotype we mean one group's perception of another group.[32]

It is important to recognize that members of groups do share common characteristics,[33] and the desire to obliterate prejudice and hatred should not lead to the unfair treatment of individuals. That is, individualized justice based on group traits may be necessary to safeguard the rights of individual defendants and thus be more important than the promotion of a progressive social policy. Furthermore, since the cultural defense will only serve as a partial, rather than complete, excuse, this will ensure that the rights of children and other vulnerable groups are not violated in deference to culture.

Although the concern about stereotypes may be an overreaction to the policy, it is certainly important that the cultural defense not be implemented in such a way as to disseminate false stereotypes. This depends on judges requiring that evidence meet high standards. The stereotype objection is not one of principle but, rather, one of practice. If the defense could be invoked carefully, then this problem might be avoided or at least minimized.

The final point about group traits is that courts do allow them to be presented in many cases. Oddly enough, when legal actors make reference to negative cultural characteristics in the form of ethnic slurs, it is rare that this results in a reversal of a conviction. Given that courts are disinclined to avoid pejorative reference to ethnic traits that may influence juries to convict, it seems even more unfair that if parties seek to make reference to their cultural background to mitigate a sentence or to obtain a larger damage award, that this is not allowed because it is considered detrimental to ethnic minority groups. It would be better to more effectively prevent negative references to ethnicity rather than to foolishly reject all information about cultural identity.[34]

The practical difficulties with the evidence are not insurmountable. As I discuss later in this chapter, under implementation, there are mechanisms for determining the existence of specific traditions. Those who make this objection generally lack any knowledge of the extensive research that has been undertaken of ethnic groups. Ethnic community centers in many areas are also a resource for this matter.

The intergenerational issue is a red herring. There is no reason to suppose that second and third generations will necessarily want to cast off their traditions. The Jewish community has not abandoned male circumcision, the dietary practices of many groups remain largely unchanged, and marriage rituals continue in the new country. Although the question of whether an individual was influenced by a cultural imperative is a matter of fact, which will have to be determined by the court, this is hardly a reason for abandoning the defense altogether.

As for those pretending to belong to particular ethnic groups, it seems doubtful that individuals would, in reality, convert to a new religion or embrace a radically different worldview for the sole purpose of committing a crime. Even if criminals were to go to such extraordinary lengths, courts would be able to assess the sincerity of their commitment to the groups in question. It is unlikely that the number of fakers would be significant.

Finally, there is the argument against establishing a formal cultural defense based on the claim that existing defenses are adequate for the consideration of culture. While, in principle, there is nothing which prevents courts from admitting cultural evidence, using a culturally specific reasonable person test, or giving jury instructions on culture, this often does not happen. Because of the bias built into many legal systems, it is often impossible for defendants to introduce evidence related to their motivations in such cases.

Another difficulty, at least in the United States, is that federal court judges have been leery of allowing the consideration of culture during sentencing. They fear that the prohibition against considering national origin and other attributes also, by implication, encompasses culture. Because they want to avoid discrimination, they frequently reject attempts by lawyers to present the cultural background of defendants where it might have the effect of mitigating their sentences. While it may be permissible for defendants to raise cultural arguments during sentencing, the legal system has not found that this is necessary for defendants to receive a fair trial. Although in principle culture might be influential in these cases, courts generally exclude the evidence as irrelevant.[35]

Those who purport to argue against a formal cultural defense accept the proposition that cultural evidence should be considered.[36] These commentators contend that this information should be incorporated into existing defenses in the law mainly to disprove an element of a crime—for example, to show the absence of specific intent. They say they reject the proposal for a separate defense, usually because they think it would constitute a violation of the principle of legal equality.

I find their position quite peculiar chiefly because I regard the consideration of cultural evidence in the context of an existing defense to be a cultural defense. There is no reason to limit the use of the term to cases in which culture is invoked as an affirmative defense to attack the characterization of the act as a crime. According to this line of argument, it is preferable to bring in the evidence surreptitiously rather than to acknowledge the use of the cultural defense. Even if one concedes that in many instances culture evidence could be used simply to negate an element of a crime, thereby obviating the need to establish a formal cultural defense, those who subscribe to this view should admit that they actually support the use of cultural defenses.

Why a Formal Cultural Defense Is Necessary

Much of the analysis focused on the question of whether culture can be considered adequately under the status quo. While it might appear that the legal system has the flexibility to allow for the evaluation of cultural claims, the reality is that courts are disinclined to admit cultural evidence into the courtroom, as in the cases of *People v. Aphaylath* (1986), *People v. Estep* (1977), *People v. Poddar* (1974), and *R. v. Ly* (1987). Therefore, even if it is theoretically possible for cultural defenses to be raised at trial, this will not occur if judges consider culture irrelevant.

Although there is nothing inherent in the rules that would preclude the consideration of culture, as we have seen judges are disinclined to allow culture in the courtroom. One of the main reasons for their reluctance to admit such evidence is that they subscribe to the widely held philosophy of "When in Rome, do as the Romans do." Because they believe that those who move to a new country must conform to a single code of conduct, they do not allow much latitude for newcomers. In those rare cases where they have held in favor of ethnic minorities, it has more often than not been a case of first instance. In the *Adesanya* case where the Yoruba mother put tribal markings on her sons' faces, the judge clearly stated that his leniency was attributable to the fact that this was a case of first instance. Presumably in the *Singh* case where the Sikh priest was prosecuted for carrying the kirpan required by his religious law, the judge was compassionate because Mr. Singh did not realize that his behavior was "criminal" in New York.[37]

Another attitudinal barrier to the use of the cultural defense is the judiciary's view of its role. Judges are often socialized to believe that their role is to interpret the law, not to make it. As there has been essentially no discussion of the cultural defense as a matter of public policy, and officially there is no such thing, it is awkward for judges to allow cultural defenses. During judicial education seminars, judges have expressed the sentiment that they would be much more comfortable allowing the consideration of cultural evidence if legislatures were to authorize this.

One solution to the conundrum of culture conflict might be to have legislatures consider each controversial tradition. The problem with this approach is that when legislatures have considered cultural practices, such as the consumption of dogs and female genital cutting, they almost invariably prohibit them.[38] If courts have the power to counter discriminatory acts of the majority, it is more likely that the judiciary will be in a position to vindicate cultural rights.

This raises an interesting problem. Suppose the legislature were to enact a law supporting a cultural defense while simultaneously outlawing a particular practice. Which would take precedence? Could a cultural defense be invoked even if the law against the practice includes a clause to the effect that no consideration of culture is allowed?[39]

The position I wish to defend is that courts should consider cultural evidence in all cases. It should not be excluded as irrelevant and should be admissible in the courtroom. Although I contend that defendants should have the right to explain the motivations behind their behavior, I do not think that all defendants should necessarily be exonerated. Acknowledging the existence of different moral codes does not require that courts endorse all traditions.[40] In my view it is wrong to pretend that cultural background is irrelevant as it most certainly is relevant to understanding the context of an individual's behavior. But that in no way means that, having understood the cultural imperative, it is improper to impose any sanction whatsoever.

Some support the policy of treating cultural data as inadmissible because they regard it as irrelevant to the question of guilt. Instead, they favor the consideration of cultural factors during the sentencing phase. As explained earlier, I object in principle to this contention because cultural motivations are essential to any judgment concerning a defendant's culpability. Even if one were to accept their position, it appears that the present system is oftentimes unwilling to consider cultural issues even during sentencing. Thus, whether culture is considered in a given case is a matter of fortuitous circumstances. The existence of a formal cultural defense would ensure the admissibility of evidence pertaining to the defendant's cultural background.

In actuality, the cases that do not fit any existing defense are the ones in which one's sympathy lies with the defendant. If we consider Mrs. Adesanya and her desire to ensure the maintenance of her sons' cultural identity, parental use of folk medicine such as coining, and the hunting of deer out of season, the dilemma is clear. The law simply refuses to recognize that these individuals act with a beneficent motive.

Without a formal cultural defense the rights of ethnic minority groups will not be respected. Seldom do courts seem willing to allow cultural arguments to be advanced in the courtroom. As a result, the pattern we have discerned is that courts convict individuals who have acted on cultural imperatives but then impose little or no punishment. If we were to adopt a formal cultural defense, then we would be able to avoid the widespread manipulation that runs rampant in the legal system. Instead of ruling that the cultural evidence is admissible and then rejecting the argument based on it, courts pretend that the evidence is simply not relevant. It would be far better if judges would, in a straightforward manner, admit the evidence as relevant and then decide on the merits of the claim presented.

CULTURE IN CIVIL LITIGATION

Although cultural defenses in civil law receive less attention in the literature, there are many cases in which culture is invoked in civil litigation involving family law, employment discrimination, civil rights violations, and ordinary tort actions. With respect to family law, courts are asked to determine whether individuals are "fit parents" when the government seeks to remove children from the home, enforce prenuptial contracts that specify the religious identity of children, and order child support payments for wives in polygamous relationships.

In these lawsuits plaintiffs' arguments often take the form of requesting an exemption from a policy, such as parental objections to medical treatment.[41]

Although doctors would otherwise perform surgery, the parents opt not to let the child have the operation because of religious objections. Another example would be employees or prisoners who ask to be exempted from dress or grooming policies because their religions require that they wear particular symbols. The specific remedy sought in these cases is an injunction requiring that the institution not subject the individual to the policy, thereby effectively granting an exemption.

In some of the other cases the plaintiffs seek monetary damages. This was the object of relatives who sued when medical examiners performed unauthorized autopsies, of the young Roma girls when police conducted a search with an invalid warrant, and of the teenage Orthodox Jewish girl who jumped off the ski lift. The argument is predicated on the notion that because of their background, the particular incident was more traumatic than for the person of the dominant culture. Hence, the plaintiff is entitled to a larger damage award than the ordinary plaintiff would receive.

In civil cases ethnic minorities also ask that courts give special consideration to their cultural background. When institutions, including public agencies and private employers, try to prevent them from following their traditions, courts are asked to ratify their decisions. Not only must courts address the question of when state intervention in the private realm of the family is justified, but they must also decide when private employers may enforce policies that conflict with the customary law of the ethnic minority employee. The following sections look at the various ways culture should influence decision-making as to the proper remedies courts provide.

Intervention

We must consider what constitute just criteria for intervention in the family. Although liberal democracies generally favor nonintrusion in the private realm, governments have an obligation to intervene to save children's lives, and they must exercise their power of *parens patriae* to do so. They also intrude to prevent irreparable harm to family members. As was seen in the controversies over the health of children, the state intercedes to remove children from the home when they have a life-threatening condition and parents fail to obtain medical treatment. Intervention in this circumstance is deemed justifiable as parents should not have the right to deny their children life because of the parents' deeply held cultural or religious beliefs.

Much more complicated is the question of intervention when children seemingly require medical attention, though their condition is not life threatening. If a child's life is not in jeopardy and the family has genuine objections to the medical procedure, intervention is considered wrong. In the case of *Kou Xiong* (1990), the state tried to force the boy to submit to surgery to "correct" his clubfeet, despite the strenuous objections of his family and the entire Hmong community in Fresno, California. The decision to order the surgery was not justified by legal doctrine, as there was no life-threatening condition or even medical emergency and no guarantee that the operation would be a success. The ruling had the unfortunate effect of alienating a minority group from the medical and legal establishments. Although authorities may be well intentioned, as was surely true in the Kou Xiong case, intervention should be limited to the most extreme cases only, where the lives of children are in peril.

In some of the other cases considered such as *Krasniqi, Kargar,* and others, social workers broke up families because of their ignorance of traditions. It was simply a disgrace in the *Krasniqi* case when the Texas Department of Child Protective Services disregarded the guidance of an expert on Albanian customs. This suggests that even the availability of information will be insufficient to prevent ethnocentric reactions to ethnic minority customs. Even though the touching was innocuous, according to the criteria of the dominant legal system itself, the families were destroyed.

To allow intervention simply because a child-rearing practice differs from standard practice, where the tradition involves no threat of harm to anyone, contradicts a basic principle in liberal democracies that the state should not supplant the parents in family matters. This is not to say that courts should refrain from inquiring into the nature of cultural practices with which they are unfamiliar. Courts should certainly distinguish between traditions that involve irreparable harm such as scarification, female genital surgeries, and moxibustion and those that are innocuous such as affectionate touching and coining.

If we apply the principle of irreparable harm, then this would preclude the use of cultural arguments to defend wife beating, many types of corporal punishment of children, and other practices using violence. Intervention to protect family members from domestic violence, according to this principle, is entirely appropriate. This is one of the clear limits on the legitimate use of cultural defenses.

With regard to animals, intervention can be justified under much more limited circumstances. If vegetarianism is not legally required, then the state should not interfere with the dietary practices of minority groups, even if their menu deviates from mainstream etiquette. Although virtually none of the traditions encountered in the process of conducting research for this book involved cruelty to animals, if they did, the state could intervene to remove the animal.[42] In addition to cruelty, if the killing of animals—for instance, in Santería religious ceremonies—could be shown to pose an actual imminent public health threat to the lives of a community, then that would justify limiting the practice.

The extent of power wielded by government agencies to intervene should be sharply curtailed. When, for instance, child welfare agencies decide to take a child into protective custody, it is exceedingly difficult for a family to appeal that decision. Indeed, it is rare that mechanisms exist which are accessible to them to challenge decisions. The absence of adequate due process standards should make government authorities more chary of intervening. It would behoove them to become more acquainted with the folkways of groups in their regions. The discretion these agencies have has led to the fragmentation of families in the name of the best interest of the child.

Yet another family law issue is the proper role for judges in divorce and custody decisions. As we saw in the controversy over the agunah, courts were asked to intervene in religious law and force the Orthodox Jewish husband to grant the get. Not only was this questionable from a constitutional standpoint, as it may have violated the principle of separation of church and state, but it was ineffectual. The divorce is only considered valid within the Orthodox community if the husband granted it of his own free will. Quite simply, judicial intervention in religious divorces may be inadvisable.

In the spiritual custody cases, judges had to decide whether to enforce prenuptial agreements that were designed to determine the religious identity of children produced by parents of different religions. Judges enter their lives for an hour and may not be of either faith. This, too, appears to be an improper role for judges to play as it is overly intrusive. The prospect of a judge forcing a particular religious observance on a family is unacceptable. Unless failure to intervene will result in irreparable harm, courts should exercise restraint in this type of conflict.

Exemptions

In many cases cultural groups seek exemptions from policies.[43] For instance, because they are required to wear religious symbols, they ask not to be subject to dress codes. Religious minorities who must kill animals in a manner stipulated by religious law may request exemptions from animal welfare laws, so that they will be shielded from prosecutions. Cultural minorities have lobbied for exemptions from public health statutes,—for example, Chinese restauranteurs who serve Peking duck.

Various methods exist for creating exemptions. These issues are handled in courts through the issuance of injunctions, which enjoin institutions from subjecting them to the dictates of the policies. When groups anticipate culture conflicts, they may lobby for legislative protections through official statutory exemptions.

In *Cheema v. Thompson* we saw how the court enjoined the school board from enforcing a no-weapons policy that prevented the Sikh children from attending school. The children had to be allowed to go to school with their kirpans, provided they had rendered the kirpans safe by making them blunt or gluing them into the sheath. Although the case shows the potential for successful use of an injunction to vindicate the rights of ethnic minorities, it also demonstrates how long this approach can take; the lengthy process of litigation meant the children were out of the school for almost a year.

The power of courts to issue injunctions is one way to protect the rights of minority groups. However, considering the requisite time for a judicial resolution, a more systematic approach is preferable. Rather than relying on a case-by-case approach for Sikhs who encounter policies denying them the right to wear a kirpan, legislative enactment of a statutory exemption is a more efficient way to settle this question.[44]

Exemptions have long been used as a way to mediate culture conflicts, but they have been attacked for various reasons, including equal protection. For instance, an exemption permitting members of the Native American Church to use peyote in religious ceremonies, but not allowing others—for example, Rastafarians—to use ganga for their religious rituals is prima facie unfair. This equal protection challenge can be easily met by granting exemptions for other groups that are similarly situated, provided they have genuine religious grounds for needing a substance that is not dangerous.

Where exemptions are allowed for religious minorities (as opposed to purely cultural minorities) the state risks excessive entanglement in the affairs of religious institutions. One example of this arose in France in the context of a dispute over which institution was recognized by the government as the official representative of the religion for the ritual slaughter of animals for consumption.[45] The question is whether religious exemptions inevitably violate the principle of the separation of church and state.

Clarifying the scope of ethnic minority rights through legislative exemptions is highly desirable. It is unlikely to occur, however, if legislators do not wish to appear to favor "special treatment" for groups. Where the political climate does not support affirmative action measures, it will be difficult to find the necessary political support for exemptions. Furthermore, many groups, particularly the newly arrived, tend to lack the necessary resources to mobilize support for legislative exemptions.[46] So, although exemptions can be achieved through various political institutions, courts will still play a critical role because of their duty to protect minority rights.

Damages

The techniques for securing rights considered thus far can be used if the harm has not yet occurred. If the individuals have already suffered the injury and the mistake cannot be rectified—for example, the autopsy has been performed—then the question is how much, if at all, the cultural background of the plaintiffs ought to affect the calculation of damages.[47] The argument is that, because of the plaintiff's cultural background, he or she was more adversely affected by the error and hence is entitled to a larger award. Though often any plaintiff would be entitled to recover some damages—for example, for an unauthorized autopsy or an illegal police strip search—the ethnic minority plaintiff argues that given the greater magnitude of the injury, the damage award should likewise be correspondingly greater. The trauma caused by the "cultural offense" warrants more restitution. This argument was advanced in the case of the Orthodox girl who leapt off the ski lift, the Hindu man who was mistakenly served a beef burrito, and the families whose deceased relatives were improperly prepared for funeral rites.

In all of these cases members of ethnic minority communities ask courts to take their cultural backgrounds into account. For courts to evaluate these claims effectively, litigants must be allowed to introduce cultural evidence. The way in which this is done, and the difficulties encountered in the process, are similar in both criminal and civil cases. It is to these more practical considerations that I now turn.

IMPLEMENTATION

If a formal cultural defense were to be established, certain practical matters would have to be addressed. In what follows I provide an overview of what I regard as some of the key policy questions that would need to be formalized to facilitate both civil and criminal litigation.

Ascertainment of Cultural Information

First and foremost, there would need to be statutory authorization of the admissibility of cultural evidence in the courtroom.[48] Legislative authorization would protect judges from appeal on the basis that it was an abuse of discretion to consider cultural evidence.

Where the court must base its decision on the interpretation of a cultural tradition, verifying information about the tradition will be key. The tendency is generally to identify an expert witness on the subject, sometimes in a haphazard fashion.[49] In order to guarantee the caliber of expert witnesses, lists of appropriate experts should be established that are easily accessible. An effort should be undertaken by professional associations such as the American Anthropological Association, including, particularly, organizations whose membership specializes in specific regions—for example, the Association for Asian Studies and the Latin American Studies Association—to compile lists of experts on different groups.

Because there may be concern about the ethical conduct of expert witnesses who appear to be "hired guns" for lawyers on either side, a code of ethics for expert witnesses would be advisable.[50] Not only would this ensure that the information presented to the court is accurate, but it would also help preserve the reputation of the expert witness as a researcher. To protect the integrity of the legal process, some careful consideration should be given to the role expert witnesses play in cultural defense cases.

Some may think, upon reflection, that experts should not be consulted in cultural defense cases. After all, they are usually not members of the groups in question. In lieu of "experts," leaders of ethnic communities could explain the significance of traditions to courts.[51] But while it is probably more politically palatable to have insiders explain their traditions, there is no guarantee that they will not succumb to pressures to misrepresent their culture in order to save a relative or friend from prison. It is also possible that an expert will be more likely to persuade the court, whose judges and jurors are comprised of nonmembers, of the importance of the tradition. In the end it may not matter so much who presents cultural evidence to the court as much as the fact that it is presented at all. As we have seen, the main problem in the cases was the proclivity of judges to exclude cultural information as irrelevant.

Courts may have legitimate fears that it will be difficult to ascertain the validity of the practice in question. Invoking a cultural defense might be unjustifiable because the practice may never have existed, may be considerably different from that described by a defendant (as may have occurred in the *Adesanya* case), or may have ceased to exist (as may be true of traditional Nigerian child discipline). One real danger of allowing cultural defenses might be the unwarranted assumption on the part of lawyers and judges that traditions do not change. Of course, cultures evolve, and so courts must guard against basing decisions on information that is anachronistic.[52]

We must consider the possibility that the information, once introduced, shows that the tradition is contested. Some members of the group may wish to halt the practice. What difference should it make to a court of law that there is not unanimity with regard to the custom at the center of the dispute? There can be no hard and fast rule regarding contested traditions, but it is surely a factor that courts should consider in deciding how much weight to give the cultural argument in the disposition of the case.

It may be useful to delineate what issues courts must decide when they adjudicate cultural defense cases. We may call the following issues the *cultural defense test*; its use should ensure appropriate use of cultural imperatives:

1. Is the litigant a member of the ethnic group?
2. Does the group have such a tradition?
3. Was the litigant influenced by the tradition when he or she acted?

This test clearly applies to criminal behavior, but it could also be employed in civil cases. For example, when Friedman sued for damages after jumping off the ski lift, the same queries could be made:

1. Was she an Orthodox Jew?
2. Can Orthodox Jewish law be interpreted to disallow a young girl from being with a man after dark?
3. Was she influenced by this belief when she catapulted off the lift?

The law must make many difficult determinations, such as those involving questions of insanity and causation. There is no reason to suppose that cultural evidence is any more difficult to interpret than any other data. If it turns out to be the case that the process of verifying the cultural claim demonstrates its falsity, then it should obviously be rejected.

Limitations on the Use of the Cultural Defense

One of the most vexing questions is how to limit the use of the cultural defense to bona fide ethnic minority groups and to prevent its use by subcultures. The reason subcultures should not be entitled to use it is that their worldview is not radically different from the rest of society. Gang members do not believe in witchcraft, coining, or other customs integral to a markedly different conceptual system. It may well be that the social and economic background of subcultural defendants should be raised in some cases. The suitable defense for this purpose is not the cultural defense but what has been called the "rotten social background defense."[53]

The subcultural defense has more to do with class differences than with cultural differences. If individuals who come from lower socioeconomic backgrounds were to rely on the cultural defense, then there would be nothing to prevent aristocrats from raising a "Great Gatsby" defense when they drive while intoxicated. Use of the rotten social background defense ensures that only those who have experienced life in the ghetto, or something akin to it, are entitled to this criminal defense. In reality, it may not be possible to thwart the use of the cultural defense by subcultures.[54] But just because a cultural argument is advanced does not obligate a judge or jury to accept the argument.

Often the question arises as to the period of time during which an individual could avail himself of the cultural defense. But it is inappropriate to limit its use because any time limit would be arbitrary.[55] There is no evidence indicating that cultural adaptation and assimilation occur within any finite time period. Even those immigrants who have lived in the United States for a long time, for example, may not have shed their culturally divergent outlooks. Consider such traditions as male circumcision, arranged marriages, food taboos (e.g., avoidance of pork) or preferences (e.g., Peking duck), or religious practices such as death rituals. Once having acquired a value system from one society, an individual may be disinclined to reject a specific value, especially if it plays an important role in his belief system as a whole. Consequently, cultural defenses may be particularly appropriate in cases where individuals have clearly acted upon cultural assumptions that constitute an important component in their worldview, no matter how long they have resided in the new country.[56]

Some take the view that only first-generation immigrants should be entitled to raise the defense, as they assume that subsequent generations will not adhere to traditions. It seems incorrect to make that assumption as many groups have continued to follow traditions, despite living in a new country for many decades. It is unrealistic to expect that individuals will shed their cultural identities by any particular point in time, and it may be unjust to require them to do so in the absence of any harm posed by the tradition to others in society.

There is also the question of whether it matters if the defendant is charged with violating a general law like assault or with violating a law that specifically forbids the cultural practice. This matter is the question of whether cultural defenses could be raised where statutes explicitly forbid any consideration of culture. Some of the laws that prohibit female genital cutting state clearly that no consideration is to be given to any cultural beliefs by the defendant. Disallowing cultural defenses for individuals prosecuted under laws that explicitly prohibit them might be rationalized on the ground that legislatures have evaluated the traditions and found them unacceptable.

There are some difficulties with the argument that statutes could disallow the cultural defense. From the perspective of the defendant it makes little difference whether his conduct is prosecuted under a general law like child abuse or under a specific one like female genital mutilation. Regardless of the particular formulation of the policy, the defendant's act was motivated by a cultural imperative. The criminal law requires an analysis of mens rea, which may be impossible if courts fail to take the defendant's cultural background into account. This suggests that legislative attempts to preempt cultural defenses may be illegitimate insofar as they go against fundamental precepts in the criminal law. Therefore, even if legislatures modify their penal codes to prohibit traditions expressly, this would not preclude the use of a cultural defense.[57]

Some wonder whether the cultural defense should be allowed in cases where the victim is not from the defendant's culture. The question is whether the cultural defense should carry much weight in cases, for instance, where the victim was unaware that her conduct constituted a provocation. In the *Poddar* case it is arguable that Tanya Tarasoff would not have accepted the sari had she fully understood the symbolic connotations of doing so.

Yet it is not obvious why the cultural background of the victim should matter. Poddar's culturally motivated act was the same, irrespective of the cultural identity of his victim. Some might argue that it was unreasonable of him to be provoked by the conduct of woman who was not from his culture and hence was not cognizant of the extent to which her conduct was a provocation. It is unclear why he should have assumed that she was making a commitment to him by accepting the gift and paying attention to him since he knew she was not Indian.

Since most of the cultural defense cases involve defendants and victims from the same culture, this issue may not often arise. But when it does, it will be necessary to determine whether the relative culpability of the defendant should be adjusted in light of the victim's culture.

Another practical question is whether legal systems that have juries should modify the composition of the jury for cultural defense cases. If even one juror were to belong to a member of the ethnic group, there would be a greater likelihood that the jury would give serious consideration to the cultural arguments. In some cases, such as provocation, if the standard were the average reasonable person of the culture, then having a jury composed of members of the group would make it more feasible to evaluate the defendant's behavior in light of the standard. While from the point of view of the cultural minorities, it might be preferable to have a jury made up of members of their group, it is unlikely that legal systems will be willing to make this accommodation.[58] It might actually be in the interest of legal systems to do so as the presence of jurors from the litigant's culture will guard against misrepresentation of cultural traditions.

To promote greater cultural sensitivity on the part of lawyers, judges, and law enforcement officers, some have called for "cultural competence" training. The desire for greater cross-cultural understanding is admirable but is unlikely to be sufficient to resolve many culture conflicts so long as the training is elective and the course is a matter of hours.[59] To become a police officer, lawyer, or judge should be contingent upon significant knowledge of other folkways. This could be accomplished by required courses, homestays in other countries, or cultural questions on exams like the bar examination. It is only when actors receive a signal that their governments are serious about cultural pluralism that they will have the incentives to overcome their own ethnocentrism. Another crucial step is to open access to these key professions. Until there is a much more diversified legal system, it is unlikely that culture conflicts will be minimized.

CONTEXTUAL ANALYSIS

I have advanced an argument that in criminal cases culture should serve as a partial excuse. In such cases punishment could range from none to almost complete punishment. With regard to civil cases the extent of trauma will likewise have to be determined with a contextual examination of the facts in the case at hand. There can be no "bright line" rule according to which we determine how much weight should be given to culture in cases. A case-by-case approach will be necessary. I have outlined some of the questions that should be posed to reach a just conclusion.

As culture conflicts are unavoidable and courts will inevitably be forced to adjudicate cultural claims, it would be far better to have a coherent, uniform approach to these issues than is currently the case. Instead of pretending that there is no such thing as a cultural defense, it is time to acknowledge the problem and decide upon its proper use. Insofar as cultural conditioning shapes human motivations, the law should acknowledge this. To do otherwise would be unjust.

11

The Right to Culture

CULTURAL RIGHTS AND TOLERANCE

In the preceding chapter I examined the ways in which culture can figure into legal decision-making. I argued that courts should admit cultural evidence to contextualize the actions of individuals in disputes, but I did not address the question of how much weight ought to be given to those traditions. An often expressed concern is that simply by admitting cultural evidence, courts will have to give it weight, and that this will require a particular result.[1] As I have tried to show, acknowledging the existence of cultural imperatives does not compel any specific disposition. There will be cases in which courts should be lenient or accommodating, and others in which they should not. This will depend upon the nature of the tradition and the context of the action.

This chapter provides a philosophical consideration of the different sorts of cultural traditions central to the cases considered in this book. I ask whether it is possible to decide where to draw the line with regard to specific customs. If there were a list of unacceptable traditions, then courts would know, in advance, when to give weight to cultural evidence and when not to. There has been some important work done on the scope of cultural rights, which analyzes traditions according to abstract criteria. Much of it revolves around the idea of tolerance.[2] In this final chapter, I devote some attention to the theoretical debate over how much tolerance we should expect from liberal democracies with regard to diverse cultural practices.

In liberal democratic systems, governments generally allow individuals to follow their own conceptions of the good life. Governments are not supposed to legislate morality; even if individuals choose ways of life that seem ill advised, it is not considered appropriate for the state to exercise its power to intervene. Choice is a supreme value guaranteed in systems of this kind. When, however, choices are made that appear to challenge other core values, the government is faced with a dilemma. The question then becomes: how much intolerance should be tolerated?[3] What are the limits of tolerance? Because they fear the consequences of intolerance, many theorists underscore the importance of protecting minorities within minorities. Frequently, this means protecting women and children from seemingly oppressive traditions, sometimes by arguing for a right of exit from their cultural communities.[4]

Tolerance, as a concept, is somewhat unappealing, however, because it is predicated on the notion that those who are tolerating are having to put up with things they do not like. The word has distinctly pejorative connotations. Nevertheless, it stands to reason that liberal democracies, if they are true to their own principles, should tolerate a great deal. The notion that tolerance is a corollary of liberty is often expressed under the rubric of cultural rights. This formulation means that, in general, ethnic minorities have a right to follow their traditions.[5]

Cultural rights are similar but not identical to other types of rights.[6] We should distinguish them from group rights or collective rights. An individual or a group may have a right to culture, so the right does not necessarily have to be conceptualized as a group right. Furthermore, there are many types of groups that are not cultural in nature.

What remains to be considered is whether or not there is any principled argument in favor of allowing groups to pursue their own life plans. In other words, do individuals belonging to different types of groups have a right to their culture? If so, what are the parameters of such a right? Under what circumstances will they have this right? And, most importantly, what is the relative weight of cultural rights as compared with other human rights?[7]

Most of the time individuals have no need to assert a right to culture. It is only when they are punished for following their cultural traditions that they must invoke such a right to show the reasons for their conduct. Because I think that the right to culture is properly interpreted to include the cultural defense policy, I devote some attention here to the jurisprudential foundation of the right. The right to culture should mean, at the very least, that individuals have the right to present evidence in court concerning traditions that are important for the maintenance of their cultural identity.[8]

CULTURAL RIGHTS IN INTERNATIONAL LAW

The idea that cultural minorities have a right to follow their traditions has been codified in international human rights law. International law guarantees the right to culture in various provisions. For instance, Article 15 of the International Covenant on Economic, Social and Cultural Rights guarantees the right to participate in the

cultural life of one's community, but it has been criticized for "a highbrow bias"—
that is, for being applied mainly to "high culture."[9]

The strongest statement of a right to culture is found in Article 27 of the International Covenant on Civil and Political Rights (ICCPR) which provides:

> In those states in which ethnic, religious, or linguistic minorities exist, persons belonging
> to such minorities shall not be denied the right, in community with the other members
> of their group, to enjoy their own culture, to profess and practice their own religion, or
> to use their own language.

Article 27 has been interpreted to require affirmative steps on the part of governments to protect culture, and it contains no limitations clause (in contrast to Article
18, the religious freedom provision). Some object to the negative formulation of "no
one shall be denied" and wonder what groups can invoke the right.[10] The main
problem is that Article 27 has been applied in a relatively small number of decisions
of the Human Rights Committee, the body that enforces the ICCPR, and, consequently, the scope of its potential application remains unclear.[11] The scope of protection for cultural rights under international law remains indeterminate as the pertinent rights have so far been limited to narrow contexts to such as disputes over
sacred sites and exclusive membership rules.

One might have expected that Article 27 would often be invoked in litigation
because virtually all nations have ratified the ICCPR, with only one nation trying to
evade responsibility for enforcing Article 27. This has not been the case, however,
and the right to culture remains controversial.[12] Although other types of basic
rights are "self-evident," the right to culture seems to require additional philosophical justification.[13]

Philosophers have attempted to map out what practices are covered by a right
to culture. Some of the analysis revolves around Charles Taylor's argument for a presumption that all cultures deserve equal respect.[14] Even if one agrees with the argument in favor of recognition, the premise that culture should be recognized does not
indicate how much weight it ought to be given in concrete cases. With few exceptions, the philosophical debate about cultural rights takes place at a level of abstraction that fails to provide much guidance to institutions as to the proper role culture
should play in legal disputes. Some of the more thoughtful analyses, however, clarify
the issues at stake by applying the cultural rights principle to specific policies, but
they do not elucidate the question of whether cultural rights justify the use of the
cultural defense.[15] This policy is not mentioned in their schema as their focus is on
the question of the proper limits on cultural traditions in liberal democracies.

As I have argued throughout this work, cultural evidence should be considered
in all cases, even if it is ultimately not used as the basis for mitigation, damages, or
other remedies. With respect to the broader question of limits, my own view is that
individuals should have the right to follow their cultural traditions without interference, unless the traditions pose some great risk to members of the ethnic group or to
society at large. The risk must be extremely grave, so as to threaten irreparable phys-

ical harm. This version of the "no harm" principle should be broad enough to cover most traditions that liberal democracies should legitimately discourage.

LIMITATIONS ON CULTURAL RIGHTS

If we may assume that there is such a thing as cultural rights, one of the key points in the debate is who may invoke the right to culture. Whereas many political theorists do not hesitate to endorse cultural rights for groups that have resided in an area for a long time—such as indigenous peoples and long-established communities such as the Gypsies, the Amish, and others—some of them reject the proposition that immigrants are entitled to cultural rights.

As we have noted throughout the book, the "When in Rome" presumption of assimilation leaves immigrants without any legitimate claim to the preservation of their culture. This presumption can be challenged on a number of grounds, including the fact that their decision to leave their country of origin may not have been voluntary.[16] Even if an immigrant's movement was based on a truly voluntary decision, it would be wrong to equate voluntary departure with a decision to renounce his or her culture.[17] Immigrants who move to a new place may wish to continue to follow cultural traditions, and it is wrong to deny them cultural rights on the basis of their birthplace. In terms of liberal theory, a person's birthplace is arbitrary, something over which he or she has no control, and, therefore, it would be unjust to deny cultural rights to immigrants on this basis.

Even if it can be shown that immigrants deserve cultural rights, the status of immigrants' children remains unclear. It is difficult to know whether the children will identify more strongly with the national identity of the new country, or whether they will prefer to retain the cultural identity associated with their parents' country of origin. Since one cannot know in advance what children's preferences will be with regard to identity, governments should preserve choice for children to the greatest extent possible. Consequently, the children of immigrants (and their grandchildren as well) should also have the benefit of cultural rights.

There is no reason why membership in a group or any particular generation should have any bearing whatsoever on the question of who is entitled to exercise cultural rights. If the right to culture is a human right, it is illogical to deny these rights to individuals, depending upon the group to which they belong, since human rights are by definition supposed to be available to everyone. Why should a newly arrived Sikh who is compelled to don a kirpan not be entitled to wear it, when an observant Jew, part of a long-established community, is allowed to wear his skullcap? A taxonomy that distinguishes between newly arrived immigrants and long-established communities is incompatible with the concept of human rights. The assumption that second or third generations will necessarily be less attached to cultural traditions is also indefensible.

It is often said the right to culture, as it is formulated in Article 27, is a minority rights provision. This is also erroneous, because all individuals, including those in the mainstream, have a right to their culture.[18] The reason for this claim is most likely the fact that only minorities have to struggle to preserve their traditions in the face of policies that require conformity with majoritarian standards. While the original purpose of the right may have been to prevent cultural discrimination against ethnic minorities, there is no reason why it ought to be so narrowly construed.

While theorists have been concerned with the matter of who can legitimately claim cultural rights, the more elusive issue has been which traditions should be protected by the right to culture. Even the staunchest advocates of cultural rights do not defend any and all customs. The challenge has been to identify criteria according to which one may distinguish acceptable traditions from those which are unconscionable. Though most would concede that there can be no foolproof criteria, there have been some inspired efforts to draw the line, most notably the human rights framework of Sebastian Poulter and the dialogue device of Bhikhu Parekh.

In an important article Poulter relies on universal human rights standards as the basis for determining when cultural traditions should be allowed.[19] His theoretical position is as follows: if a cultural tradition violates a human right, the tradition should not be permitted; if not allowing a cultural tradition would violate a recognized human right, the tradition should be permitted. His analytic framework provides a useful way of classifying ethnic minority customs but is ultimately unsatisfactory.

There are a number of difficulties with this position, the most important of which is that he finesses the point that the right to culture is itself a human right. By asserting that when a cultural tradition conflicts with another human right, the tradition may legitimately be prohibited, he assumes, implicitly, that cultural rights are superseded by other rights. This is not necessarily a valid assumption, considering the fact that the formulation of cultural rights in international law, Article 27 contains no limitations clause.

In his analysis, Poulter overlooks the complex tensions among rights. This is clear in his treatment of cultural traditions, which if prevented would violate various human rights. When he discusses the Muslim girls whose parents want them to go to single-sex schools, to illustrate the situation when he would allow cultural rights, he ignores the possibility that the girls may wish to attend a coed institution, in which case they would regard their parents' victory as a violation of their human rights.[20]

One might also challenge Poulter's presupposition that international human rights standards are culturally neutral. Many scholars have, in fact, questioned the philosophical foundations of international human rights law, charging that they are Eurocentric. If human rights are considered Western, then it would not be surprising if these standards were interpreted to forbid cultural traditions such as arranged marriages, something which Europeans have always disliked. During colonial times, the European powers enacted repugnancy clauses according to which practices that were "repugnant to natural justice" were forbidden. To members of diverse ethnic groups, human rights standards might appear to be neocolonial repugnancy clauses and therefore unacceptable criteria.[21]

There are other objections to using human rights as the limiting principle. The universal principles are too vague to permit decisive resolution of conflicts, in part because they will be subject to multiple, potentially conflicting, interpretations. Inevitably there will also be those who claim not to accept particular human rights. Others think that although cultural rights are significant, it is dangerous to elevate culture to the status of a universal human right.[22] This gives cultural rights too much importance.

Basing cultural rights on treaty provisions has also been criticized for being too positivistic. Relying on conventions makes it seem as though the validity of the right depends on whether or not it is contained in an international instrument. If there were no Article 27 in the ICCPR, would that mean that there was no right to culture? It might be the case that the right to culture was an unwritten norm, part of customary international law, or that it constituted a fundamental right, or *ius cogens*. With respect to the former, there is little evidence indicating that the right to culture is part of customary international law.[23] With respect to the latter, there is little reason to suppose that the right to culture has attained the status of being a fundamental right.

Poulter's brilliant analysis highlights the "hierarchy" problem, the reality that the right to culture must necessarily be limited in some circumstances. Even if one can show that cultural traditions deserve legal protection, it is unclear what the limits are. Rights conflicts abound both within treaties and between treaties. For example, Article 30 of the Convention on the Right of the Child guarantees the children of ethnic minorities and of indigenous peoples a right to culture. But Article 24(3) of the same treaty mandates that children be protected against traditions that are "prejudicial" to their health. Although the provision was drafted with female genital cutting in mind, it applies to a broader range of customs. The resolution of the tension between the two provisions is not clear.[24]

In international human rights law also one finds rights conflicts between instruments. For example, the Convention on the Elimination of All Forms of Discrimination against Women also prohibits traditions that interfere with gender equality in Articles 2 and 5.[25] The international community has not clarified the conflict between these provisions and Article 27 of the ICCPR. Until such time as rights conflicts are addressed and there is a good-faith effort to harmonize these conflicts among principles, international human rights law will be unequal to the task of solving the question concerning the scope of cultural rights.

This discussion is not intended to denigrate the invaluable contribution of Poulter's admirable scholarship on ethnic minority customs. Indeed, his work paved the way for others to investigate these issues. There is much that is useful in his analyses. In addition, it is important to point out that the right to culture is clearly regarded as a human right in the international community, although the precise content of the right remains open to debate.

Another provocative analytic device for identifying limits to cultural traditions can be found in Parekh's work. In his elaborate scheme advocating "a principle of dialogical consensus," Parekh proposes having a minority spokesman who will engage in a dialogue with representatives of the majority about cultural practices that clash with "operative societal values." It is the duty of the spokesperson to explain how the tradition is authoritative, central to the way of life of the ethnic minority group, and, in general, desirable. His treatment of the subject is admirable for its eloquence, incisive analysis and use of concrete examples.[26]

While there is much with which I agree in his lucid analysis of the issue, in the end I part company with him. For, if it is not feasible to persuade the majority representatives of the value of the tradition under debate and if it offends an "operative societal value," the ethnic minority must give it up.[27]

My approach to culture conflicts differs from Parekh's in that I would ask ethnic minorities to surrender their traditions in fewer circumstances. Whereas Parekh bases his analysis on offense to majority values, I favor use of the no-harm principle, construed as prohibiting irreparable physical harm. This is a narrower principle than Parekh's because there are bound to be customs that seem offensive to the majority in a political system, but which involve no irreparable harm. For instance, whereas Parekh rejects polygamy because it offends the principle of gender equality, I would not.

The irreparable harm principle has, to be sure, difficulties of its own. The most obvious problem is that what constitutes a "harm" will vary from one community to the next. It is a matter of one's cultural background whether a tradition is interpreted as involving a harm. The use of coining as a form of folk medicine, which results in temporary bruises, does not involve irreparable harm as the child suffers no permanent physical injury. By contrast, female genital cutting would be disallowed. Although female genital cutting would be impermissible under the principle of no irreparable harm, individuals in the traditions who believe that the surgery is a necessary rite of passage for girls to ensure their marriagability (and avoidance of social ostracism) would take issue with my interpretation.

In deciding what counts as a harm, I would begin with traditions that cause death. If a tradition involves the loss of life of a person who does not wish to die, it should be prohibited. Though valuing life is not universal, insofar as sacrificing one's self for the larger society is a value in some societies, in liberal democracies, a premium is placed on the preservation of life.[28] I would also include as harmful those traditions that cause permanent disfigurement. This would seem to preclude male circumcision, ritual scarification, and cosmetic surgery. Many of these operations are controversial in large part because they are performed on children.

Many cultural conflicts involve children. Their fate depends on whether their parents are permitted to shape their cultural identity or whether the state has the final say. As there are strong pressures to conform, one cannot assume that children will choose to remain within their cultural communities. To the extent that one protects their choice, traditions such as ritual scarification and female genital cutting would be incompatible with that. Of course, it may be less likely that children will opt to have these surgeries when they become adults as they are supposed to be performed as rites of passage.

This argument that children should be protected from cultural traditions involving permanent bodily change is ethnocentric. It relies on an individualistic notion that children are separate from their parents, a viewpoint not shared by more group-oriented societies. This line of reasoning also assumes that children cannot make choices or consent to surgeries before they have reached the age of "majority." Although some may object to this analysis because of a cultural bias, at least it does not entirely prevent the practice of traditions, but merely delays them.

If we turn to less extreme examples, we can evaluate the possibility of irreparable harm by studying the record of countries that have allowed the traditions without incident. Governments would be well served by examining the example of others. For instance, if England has experienced no difficulties after creating an exemption allowing Sikhs to don the kirpan, this provides some empirical proof of the absence of harm.

Although my own preference would be for limiting traditions that involve irreparable physical harm, I must admit that the principle will not solve all questions. For instance, forced marriages should be disallowed, though they do not necessarily lead to violence. In modern legal systems they would be dissolved on the basis of duress.

In the end there is no one analytic framework which is capable of solving all rights conflicts.[29] Therefore, the resolution of culture conflicts can only take place on a case-by-case basis. One hopes that this discussion of general principles has illuminated at least some of the conflicts legal actors encounter in their work.

REASSESSING THE MONOCULTURAL PARADIGM

As we have seen, the dominant culture often perceives unfamiliar cultural traditions as ominous. The threat is often illusory, as with kirpans in school, the use of coining as folk medicine, affectionate touching in families, and the cornrows hairstyle. The beliefs and traditions are not dangerous, and the misperceptions surrounding them stem from cross-cultural misunderstanding and even xenophobia. In general, intellectuals and the wider society seem to overreact to the prospect that cultural pluralism might be allowed. Liberals and conservatives alike fear recognizing divergent cultures because they worry that acknowledging differences will undercut the foundations of the system.[30] It is precisely the fear of "balkanization," or the disuniting of the nation, which is the paramount concern.[31]

National governments are fearful of multiculturalism because it exposes the fiction of any national identity.[32] If there is uncertainty about the national identity, then the presence of different ethnic groups causes anxiety because it may call the national identity into question. The ambivalence and unease of legal actors demonstrate this deep-seated fear of the consequences of recognizing diverse ways of life. That unconventional lifestyles seem so threatening should give us pause.

Where traditions involve no threat of any harm, liberal democracies should let people choose their own life plans. It is highly coercive to force people from other parts of the world to change what they eat, wear, how they raise their children, how they heal their relatives, how they react to particular gestures and insults, and so on.

It is incomprehensible that individuals should have to reinvent themselves to such an extent in countries that claim to protect religious liberty, freedom of association, and other fundamental rights.

If there is such a thing as a right to culture, which governments are obligated to protect, then this necessitates a reconsideration of what I have called the *presumption of assimilation*. We should not assume the validity of the notion that individuals who move from one culture to another should be expected to conform to the new law in all respects. There has to be greater flexibility in the enforcement of legal standards to give space for ethnic minorities in democratic societies. If governments move in this direction, then we will have taken a large step toward reevaluating the monocultural paradigm.

It is shortsighted, in my view, to deny fundamental rights in the name of nationalism. To the extent that cultural minorities have a vested interested in the survival of the state, they will be more inclined to lend their support to it. Rather than denying cultural rights with the likely result of alienating minorities, it would be a far more prudent strategy to adopt more inclusive policies such as allowing individuals to follow their cultural traditions.

Culture shapes individual identity in crucial ways. The failure of the law to recognize this has resulted in injustices. Until the right to culture is understood to be a basic human right, individuals will continue to be told that they must become assimilated, that their background is "irrelevant," and that there is only one correct way to behave. In a culturally diverse society, it is necessary that individuals be permitted to pursue their own life plans without interference from the government. Unless the cultural traditions at issue involve irreparable harm, they should be allowed.

NOTES

CHAPTER 1

1. This proverb is attributed to Saint Ambrose. Bartlett, *Familiar Quotations*, 113; Ehrlich, *Amo, Amas, Amat and More*, 235; Partington, *Oxford Dictionary of Quotations*, 10, 679: Si fueris Romae, Romano vivito more; / Si fueris alibib, vivito sicut ibi [When in Rome, live as the Romans do; when elsewhere, live as they live elsewhere]. Ojoade gives many examples of proverbial analogues. For instance, the French say, "You must howl if you are among wolves." A Bantu proverb expresses this sentiment: "The visitor of the monkey eats what the monkey eats. A Sudanese proverb is "In the village of the one-eyed, close one eye."

2. National policies that promote a single national identity, i.e., assimilation, are generally referred to as "melting pot," whereas those that support cultural pluralism, as in the case of Canada, use the "mosaic" metaphor. Even countries that are officially multicultural still reject the cultural defense. For the historical background of the melting pot metaphor, beginning with Israel Zangwill's play by that title, see Sollors, *Beyond Ethnicity*, 66–101. Australia, Canada, and New Zealand considered adopting an official cultural defense policy, but all decided against it. After completing a comprehensive study of aboriginal customary law, the Australian Law Reform Commission rejected the proposal for a general cultural defense but acknowledged the need for some special exemptions. Law Reform Commission, *Recognition*, 214, and *Multiculturalism*, 170–172; see also Bronitt and Amirthalingam, "Cultural Blindness," and Garkawe," Cultural Relativism." Canada briefly considered establishing an official cultural defense in 1994 when the Department of Justice circulated a consultation paper that included a section "Culture as a Defence." See Anon. (1994d), "Should Culture." For background, see Carlson, "Culture"; Fisher, "Rock Solid"; Wong, "Good Intentions." The Justice Minister in New Zealand rejected an advisory group proposal that "cultural differences" serve as a defense to crimes: "There should be one law for all, but cultural factors can be taken into account in sentencing." Anon. (1994b), "Today's Briefing." In the Netherlands, there has been considerable interest in the cultural defense as well. See van Dijk, "Democracy," 154, and Wiersinga, *Nuance in benardering*.

221

3. Bernard Diamond also considers the key issue to be the admissibility of evidence. "Social and Cultural Factors." He defends the use of evidence concerning social and cultural background to negate specific intent crimes rather than limiting the presentation of such evidence only if it can be subsumed under a medical model of mental illness.

4. When I first began to conduct research on the cultural defense, I believed that the law, at least in the United States, was flexible enough to accommodate arguments based on culture. Renteln, "Culture and Culpability." I also thought there were reasons to be concerned about the abuse of the cultural defense. After reviewing numerous cases in which judges excluded cultural evidence as "irrelevant," I have changed my position.

5. This term was made famous by Thorsten Sellin in his classic study *Culture Conflict and Crime*, published by the Social Science Research Council in 1938.

6. For a sexual harassment case, see *People v. Jaechoel Yi* in Anon. (1995c), "Sociologist's Testimony," 25.

7. The only empirical study of cultural factors during sentencing is Winkelman, "Cultural Factors." A few articles address the question of whether the 1987 Federal Sentencing Guidelines policy statement S5H1.10, which prohibits the consideration of national origin, should be interpreted so as to exclude the consideration of culture as well. See Olabisi Clinton, "Cultural Differences"; Matsumoto, "Plea"; Murray, "Battered Woman Syndrome"; Jon Sands, "Departure Reform." For elaboration on this issue, see the discussion of *U.S. v. Tomono* (1998) in chapter 6, "Animals."

8. Critics often make the inaccurate claim that the defense is invoked primarily by Asian defendants. See, e.g., Chiu, "Cultural Defense," 1055, 1096, 1100; Roberts, "Why Culture Matters," 94, 96; Sams, "Availability," 350–351.

9. This theoretical approach is described by Max Gluckman as the "extended case-study method" in "Ethnographic Data" and by J. van Velsen as "situational analysis" in "The Extended-Case Method."

10. After commenting on one case in which a court mitigated the sentence of a Puerto Rican defendant, Bernard Diamond speculates that "similar mitigations of sentence because of sensitive consideration of ethnic and cultural factors probably are not uncommon, but go unreported in law case books." "Social and Cultural Factors," 203.

11. Some have suggested reviewing all the cases in one courthouse over a specific period or searching for all the cases having a few specific foreign names. None of these approaches would have been effective for my purposes. There is relatively little written on the cultural defense apart from law review articles authored by mainly female commentators who mostly reject it. Some criminologists have advocated taking a more relativistic approach to the study of deviance; e.g., Hinch, "Cultural Deviance," and Sellin, *Culture Conflict*. Although their empirical scholarship bears on the question of the proper use of cultural factors in the legal system, it does not focus on the cultural defense per se. There is a vast literature on multiculturalism, but it also does not directly address the question of the cultural defense. The most illuminating work is that of Sebastian Poulter, which concentrates on the protection of ethnic minority customs in the English context.

12. This is explicit in the Australian case *R. v. Dincer* (1983) discussed under honor killings in chapter 3.

13. International law guarantees this right, which is discussed in chapter 11. For a splendid overview, see Symonides, "Cultural Rights."

CHAPTER 2

1. For a book focusing on the relationship between culture and motivation, see Munro et al., *Motivation and Culture*.

2. An attempt to delineate all elements of culture can be found in Murdock et al., *Outline of Cultural Materials*, i–x. For a survey of definitions, see the classic work by Kroeber and Kluckhohn, *Culture*. See also Malinowski, "Culture," and Smelser, "Culture."

3. Canadian Commission for UNESCO, "A Working Definition of 'Culture,'" 83.

4. While scholars sometimes distinguish culture from custom, tradition, and customary law, these nuanced distinctions are not necessary for my purposes. The specific cultural traditions at the center of the court battles in my study are generally well established within the ethnic groups in question. See also Kluckhohn and Kelly, "Concept of Culture." Although culture is an abstract notion which is invisible, obviously it is possible to witness a group following cultural traditions.

5. For politicization, see, e.g., Abu-Lughod, "Against Culture." For an example of this type of cultural critique, see Smith, "Culture as Explanation."

6. I will refer to the groups following traditions as ethnic or cultural minorities. *Ethnic* refers to identity based on socially defined characteristics, whereas *racial* groups have historically been considered to be groups whose shared identity is based on biological or genetic traits. For in-depth analysis of the race/ethnic distinction, see Simpson and Yinger, *Racial and Cultural Minorities*. Yinger defines an ethnic group as "a segment of a larger society whose members are thought, by themselves and/or others, to have a common origin and to share important segments of a common culture and who, in addition, participate in shared activities in which the common origin and culture are significant ingredients." "Ethnicity in Complex Societies," 200.

7. Some of the literature on tradition focuses on the "invention" of traditions such as the Scottish tartan. This debate is about the authenticity of so-called traditions in social life but does not address the question of the veracity of cultural claims in court. See, e.g., Hobsbawm and Ranger, *Invention of Tradition*, and Handler and Linnekin, "Tradition," 273–290. Although a distinction is made between traditions (which are fixed, whether "authentic" or "invented") and customs (which can change), I use the two terms interchangeably in this work. Some literature on the invention of ethnicity examines phenomena such as the fact that the Chinese American laundry has nothing to do with a Chinese heritage. Sollors, *Invention of Ethnicity*, xvi.

8. Of course, if there is a lack of consensus as to the validity of the practice within the group, that does not prove the tradition is nonexistent but, rather, that a society may be in the process of discarding it.

9. An entire subfield in psychology has developed to demonstrate the manner in which culture influences cognitive processes. See, e.g., works by Fiske et al., "Cultural Matrix"; Kitayama et al., "Collective Construction"; Markus and Kitayama, "Culture and Self" and "Cultural Variation"; Markus and Lin, "Conflictways"; Shweder, *Thinking*; Shore, *Culture in Mind*. An important early essay is Shweder and Bourne, "Concept of the Person?" One of the major themes in the work of cultural psychologists is the way in which individuals from different cultures conceptualize the relationship between "the self" and "the group." Douglas Allen, *Culture and Self*. For instance, Markus and Kitayama distinguish between two styles of reasoning, or "construals of the self"—the independent view of the self that is associated with many Western cultures, and the interdependent construal of the self that is found in many non-Western cultures. "Culture and the Self." This subtle difference in cognition has important implications for some criminal cases involving parent-child suicide, such as *People v. Kimura* (1985), discussed in chapter 3.

10. Enculturation and socialization are not identical in that the former affects all individuals who absorb the values of their communities by a process almost by osmosis, whereas the latter presumes that an agent—that is, some institution such as the family or the state—is directing the formation of identities. For one attempt to draw a distinction, see Mead, "Social-

ization and Enculturation," 187. For an essay explaining enculturation, see Shimahara, "Enculturation." Other insightful works include Shweder and LeVine, *Culture Theory*, and Bohannan, "Rethinking Culture."

11. Linton, *Tree of Culture*, 39. For other work on the subject, see D'Andrade, "Cultural
Cognition," 809. For a critique of D'Andrade's formulation, see Shore, *Culture in Mind*,
45–46.

12. With regard to oral communication, culture affects the manner in which a language
is spoken. For instance, even where all members of a group speak English, they will speak it
with different accents. Within societies there are hierarchies according to which some accents
have higher status. Matsuda, "Voices of America." Nafziger makes the point that judges express
themselves differently even if they speak the same language, because they come from different
linguistic backgrounds. "Some Remarks," 337. With respect to humor, misunderstandings also
occur. For example: Dodger pitcher Chan Ho Park felt humiliated when his teammates cut up
his clothes as a practical joke, and a sports psychologist attributed this to cross-cultural misunderstanding. Gustkey, "Team of Cut-Ups." In regard to the A-O.K. sign: In the 1950s Vice-
President Richard M. Nixon made the wrong impression when he landed in South America
and emerged to greet a crowd with his hands in a double "A.-O.K." In France the same sign
means zero, while in Japan it means money. Anon. (1996j), "What's A-O.K." With regard to
numbers, a controversy raged in Monterey Park, where a predominantly Asian American
community in Southern California protested when the state Public Utilities Commission
announced it would change the area code from 818 to 626. The numbers 626 add up to 14,
which means guaranteed death. Kang, "They've Got Luck." This was a terrible change from the
number 8, which is considered to be very lucky. After Pacific Bell rejected the complaint,
claiming it could not consider the "cultural impact" (Dresser, "Luck"), in response, many business people put in toll-free lines with the prefix 888. In regard to space: The scientific study of
spatial relations is known as *proxemics*. Hazard's perceptive analysis "Furniture Arrangement"
contains an argument for the study of legal symbolism.

13. Regarding determinism, some misconstrue the cultural defense argument. See, e.g.,
Torry, who says that "culture defenses rest on principles of compulsion, implicated in the
defendant's emblematic excuse, 'my culture made me do it.'" Although Torry stresses that "the
concept of cultural dictation (cultural compulsion) forms the nucleus of the theory," he later
contradicts the premise of his essay when he says, "No one, however, is proclaiming that all
culturally motivated behavior is compelled." "Culture and Individual Responsibility," 68.
Regarding free will and moral choices, see, e.g., Moody-Adams, "Culture," and Barry, *Culture
and Equality*, 252–291.

14. While *acculturation* is the term used by American anthropologists, their British
counterparts preferred *culture contact*. Spicer, "Acculturation," 21. See also the important
study of cultural dynamics by Herskovits, "Acculturation." For an overview of different for-
mulations of acculturation, see the lucid analysis of Berry, "Acculturation." Some have
argued for a more complex understanding of the processes. See, e.g., Teske and Nelson,
"Acculturation and Assimilation"; Margaret Clark et al., "Explorations"; Szabad and Rubin,
"Newest Americans."

When ethnic minorities move to a new culture and face the challenge of acculturation,
many responses are possible. One is *assimilation* (also called the melting pot model), which
Berry defines as "relinquishing cultural identity and moving into the larger society." "Acculturation," 13. Yinger distinguishes four subprocesses of assimilation: amalgamation (biological), identification (psychological), acculturation (cultural), and integration (structural).
"Toward a Theory," 249. See also Kolm, *Change of Cultural Identity*. Another is "integration,"
which "implies the maintenance of cultural integrity as well as the movement to become an
integral part of a larger societal framework." Berry, "Acculturation," 13. Other responses to cul-

ture contact are segregation by the host culture or self-imposed withdrawal. Many of the cases discussed in this book involve situations in which the dominant legal system is attempting to force ethnic minorities to abandon their cultural traditions. Consequently, the model of integration, which stresses preservation of folkways, is not really the relevant one for my purposes here. One famous analysis suggests that traditions serve as a vehicle for boundary maintenance insofar as they help define the parameter of us versus them. Barth, *Ethnic Groups*. For a study of ethnic groups' strategies of dealing with the dominant culture, see Royce, *Ethnic Identity*. Some scholars have emphasized the importance of recognizing that patterns of assimilation and acculturation vary by ethnic group, by segments within an ethnic group, and particularly by generation.

15. Broom and Kitsuse advance this argument in the context of their data on Japanese American immigrants. "Validation of Acculturation." They demonstrate that acculturation may or may not lead to assimilation by focusing on social forces that impede assimilation.

16. Barth, *Ethnic Groups*. For a study of ethnic groups' strategies of dealing with the dominant culture, see Royce, *Ethnic Identity*. Gans, "Symbolic Ethnicity." Because of these complexities, some scholars caution against trying to give an "authentic" account of a culture. MacCannell advances an argument of this sort in his essay "Ethnosemiotics."

17. Szapocznik and Kurtines explain that "biculturalism implies that the individuals can participate in two cultural contexts." "Acculturation," 155. Their analysis suggests that the process leading from acculturation to assimilation varies, depending on the cultural context. For a discussion of bicultural individuals who experience divided loyalties and multiple consciousness, see Goldberger, "Cultural Imperatives."

Following cultural traditions is important for perpetuating value systems and maintaining group identity. Because immigrants often have to struggle to preserve some semblance of their way of life, they may cling to their traditions more strongly than do individuals in the country of origin. For instance, two Moluccan immigrants were prohibited by their communities in the Netherlands from marrying because they were from clans that were considered to be too closely related. When the man returned to his homeland, however, he found the village elders were much more willing to countenance exceptions to the rules: "You in the Netherlands apply the rules more strictly than in Indonesia. With us the pela system has weakened." The elders gave the boy permission to marry. Strijbosch, "Concept of Pela," 192–194.

18. For instance, "transculturation" is an example of a strategy by ethnic minority group to guard itself against pressures of acculturation and assimilation. Ervin, "Acculturation Approach," 49. See also Eaton, "Controlled Acculturation."

Padilla suggests that biculturalism may be a more healthy alternative to acculturation. He observes that there is less stress in multicultural societies than in unicultural societies. *Acculturation*, 8, 21. On accommodation, see Poulter, *Ethnicity, Law, and Human Rights*; Raz, "Multiculturalism"; Anon. (1986a), "Cultural Defense"; Milton Gordon, *Assimilation*.

19. Renteln and Dundes, *Folk Law*. A vast literature exists on legal pluralism. See, e.g., Chiba, "Legal Pluralism"; Galanter, "Justice"; Hooker, *Legal Pluralism*; Merry, "Legal Pluralism." The phrase *legal pluralism* is not meant to necessarily imply that each of the various legal systems operating within the same geographic area carries equal weight. Clearly, minority groups are most often in subordinate positions of power. The idea of legal pluralism has also been criticized, from a positivist perspective, for denying the reality that only state law should count as law. See Tamanaha, "Folly." In a classic essay John Griffiths states that legal pluralism is a corollary of cultural pluralism. "What Is Legal Pluralism?," 38. The term *cultural pluralism* was coined by the psychologist Horace Kallen in a 1924 essay, *Culture and Democracy in the United States*. See Jiobu, *Ethnicity*, 8.

20. This has been the source of much debate in legal anthropology. Bohannan, "Differing Realms."

21. Some have acknowledged the ramifications of culturally divergent reasoning processes for the law. See, e.g., the last chapter of Tyler et al., *Social Justice.*

22. Renteln, "Relativism."

23. Articles have begun to appear, but many address only a narrow aspect of the problem. They generally conclude that the newly arrived should become assimilated as quickly as possible. Pertinent articles include those by Anon. (1986a), Brelvi, Cardillo, Chiu, Choi, Olabisi Clinton, Coleman ("Individualizing Justice"), Bernard Diamond, Fischer, Gallin, Taryn Goldstein, Holmquist, Kanter, Kim, Nicole King, Koptiuch, Anh Lam, Li, Lyman, Ma, Maeda, Magnarella, Maguigan, Matsumoto, Moody-Adams, Murray, Renteln, Rimonte, Jenny Rivera, Roberts, Rosen ("Integrity of Cultures"), Sacks, Sams, Sheleff ("Right"), Sherman, Sheybani, James Sing, Suri, Tim Taylor, Thompson, Tomao, Torry, Volpp, Wanderer and Connors, Wong, and Deborah Woo.

24. Sellin interprets culture conflicts as conflicts of cultural codes and his use of the term differs from that of other sociologists. See Shoham, "'Culture-Conflict' Hypothesis"; Sutherland, *Principles*; Zubrzycki, "Immigration"; and contributions by Allport, Maurice Price, Todd, and Wirth in *Social Forces.*

25. Hinch, "Cultural Deviance," 178.

26. Sellin, *Culture Conflict,* 86.

27. In the field of political theory there is a large debate about the relationship between equality and difference. See, e.g., Benhabib, *Democracy.*

28. Beirne argues that contemporary criminological studies are ethnocentric. His contention is that comparative criminology ought to take cultural relativism into account: "Firstly, criminal behavior cannot ultimately be understood apart from the cultural context in which it occurs. Second, generalizations about criminal behavior must refer to the cultural and subjective values of those who engage in it." "Cultural Relativism," 373.

29. Some of better known works are by Gutman, Parekh, and Raz. For a discussion of culture and power in the context of India, see Sarah Joseph, *Interrogating Culture.* The debate surrounding Huntington's *Clash of Civilizations* is also tangential to the central questions of the cultural defense. His thesis does suggest that differences in worldview merit some consideration. The literature on U.S. constitutional theory, identity politics, and public policy never touches on the cultural defense. See, e.g., the works by Brigham, Coyle and Ellis, Ellis and Thompson, Hart and Bauman, Howenstein, Karst, Mazur, Rutherford, Brett Williams, and Iris Young.

30. Wayland, "Immigration," 33.

31. In fact, a voluminous literature on cultural rights emerged in the past two decades. Charles Taylor, for instance, argues that minorities' cultures be "recognized" (more than tolerated) because of his presumption of equal worth. "Politics of Recognition," 199. Some defend cultural rights in general, though none of these authors suggests a method for implementing the right to culture in a legal system. Baubock, "Cultural Rights"; Deveaux, *Cultural Pluralism*; Raz, "Multiculturalism." For the most part, the analysis of cultural rights in international law has paid little attention to the scholarship on the subject in political theory.

32. In attempting to reconcile liberalism with minority rights, Kymlicka imposes two limitations on minority groups, one of which is freedom within the minority groups. This is to ensure that women and children can revise traditional practices. In fairness to Kymlicka, I must note that he admits his theory may be a "Pyrrhic victory." *Multicultural Citizenship,* 153. One critic construes his theory as follows: "Cultural minorities are given protection—provided they mend their ways." Kukathas, "Any Cultural Rights?," 123. Minow argues that because cultural minorities invoking cultural rights emphasizes their subordinate position, they may not wish to do so. "Rights and Cultural Difference."

Regarding voluntary minorities, see Kymlicka, *Multicultural Citizenship*, 94–101. Because immigrants "choose to leave their own culture," he says "the expectation of integration is not unjust ... so long as immigrants had the option to stay in their original culture" (95–96). On the lack of "culture" Kymlicka says that "immigrants may associate with each other to pursue their ethnic preferences, but such groups are not nations and do not constitute cultures." "Liberalism," 239. See also Kymlicka, "Ethnic Associations," 201. Kymlicka's work might also be criticized for ignoring the international law scholarship on cultural rights. He condemns minority rights provisions, saying that "human rights are insufficient for ethnocultural justice," without engaging in a careful consideration of the actual provisions. "Human Rights," 218.

33. Okin advances the argument that protecting cultural rights will undermine women's rights. See her *Is Multiculturalism Bad for Women?*

34. Kukathas, "Cultural Toleration," 87. Kukathas emphasizes that there are divisions within groups meaning that there are those within the minority culture who disagree with its practices and may not wish to preserve "cultural integrity." "Any Cultural Rights?," 114. Consequently, he argues that members of cultural communities have "an inalienable right to leave—to renounce membership of the community" (117).

35. See Parekh, "Cultural Pluralism."

36. Moody-Adams, "Culture." In her superficial treatment of multiculturalism Okin attempts to trivialize the cultural defense by associating it mainly with female genital cutting and forced marriage. *Is Multiculturalism Bad for Women?* Feminist journalists, liberal and conservative, also condemn culture in a simplistic fashion. See, e.g., McPhail, "Unacceptable," and Cathy Young, "Feminists' Dilemma."

37. Shachar, "Puzzle," 385. See also her other scholarship.

38. See, e.g., Das, "Cultural Rights." See also Baubock, "Cultural Rights"; Carens, *Culture*, 150–160; and Poulter's scholarship.

39. Major reference tools in medicine and psychiatry, such as the *Merck Manual* and the *Diagnostic and Statistical Manual* (4th ed.) (hereafter *DSM-IV*), have sections on culture-bound syndromes. See also Al-Issa, *Handbook of Culture*, and Dein, "Mental Health." On jurists, see Nicole King, "Role"; Moore, *Immigrants*; Judicial Studies Board, *Handbook*.

40. Lears, "Cultural Hegemony."

CHAPTER 3

1. Though I do not discuss the defense of necessity (as it is unlikely a cultural defense could be raised via necessity), I do analyze it in Renteln, "Justification."

2. Hall, *General Principles*, 402.

3. For a delineation of the various types of insanity defenses, see LaFave and Scott, *Criminal Law*, 304–310. I analyze these in more depth in Renteln, "Justification."

4. It is impossible to separate the psychological state of a defendant from her culture as they are inextricably intertwined. For mental problems, see Westermeyer and Thao, "Cultural Beliefs," and Suh, "Psychiatric Problems." For cognitive insanity, the test used in most U.S. jurisdictions is the M'Naghten test, which provides that "the defendant cannot be convicted if, at the time he committed the act, he was laboring under such a defect of reason, from a disease of the mind, as not to know the nature and quality of the act he was doing; or, if he did know it, as not to know he was doing what was wrong." LaFave and Scott, *Criminal Law*, 304. It is not necessary that the defendant be unable to distinguish generally between right and wrong; this distinction is required only with respect to the act in question in the specific case. For volitional insanity, the irresistible impulse test permits an insanity defense if a defendant has "a

mental disease which kept him from controlling his conduct." LaFave and Scott, *Criminal Law*, 304.

5. Information about the case describes the defense as one of temporary insanity. Instead of a cognitive insanity defense, some might think that the defense in *Kimura* was a volitional insanity defense, automatism, or diminished capacity. However, the Defense Sentencing Report contains statements suggesting that Kimura suffered a cognitive impairment: "Her severe mental and emotional illness prevented her from thinking or acting rationally. . . . Because of her mental condition and her cultural background, Defendant did not perceive her parent-child suicide as an illegal act." *People v. Kimura*, Defense Sentencing Report, 13–14.

6. See Matsumoto, "Plea"; Bryant, "Oya-Ko Shinju"; Markman and Bosco, *Alone with the Devil*, 347–348. Though it is illegal in Japan, the parent survivor is rarely punished. Dolan, "Two Cultures Collide," 3. Its occurrence has been estimated as once a day. McCaslin, "Immigrant's Suicide Attempt," and Markman and Bosco, *Alone with the Devil*, 348. Approximately five hundred cases are reported annually. Dillow, "Legal System."

7. See *People v. Kimura*, Defense Sentencing Report, 8–9

8. Deborah Woo, "*People v. Kimura*," 406.

9. A Sikh mother facing trial for the attempted murder of her two children by holding their heads under water was compared to *Kimura*. Piccalo, "Attorneys." It may be a false analogy, as it is doubtful that there is an equivalent to parent-child suicide in Sikh culture. Seng Chow SaeChao tried to commit parent-child suicide by drinking diazinon, a highly toxic pesticide, after her husband tortured a son and beat her. Gilbert, "Mother Blamed," and Leeson, "Mother."

10. See Oliver, "Cultural Defense," and Brady, "Insanity." The quotation on the "law of the old country" is from Bernard Yedlin, personal communication, 1988. Sellin mentions a similar example from the 1930s: "A Sicilian father in New Jersey killed the sixteen-year-old seducer of his daughter, expressing surprise at his arrest since he had merely defended his family honor in a traditional way." *Culture Conflict*, 68. On Greek culture, see, e.g., Moskos, *Greek Americans*, 94.

11. Nine psychiatrists testified at the trial, but no expert on Greek culture did so. Bernard Yedlin (personal communication, 1988) said that the judge may have allowed the consideration of the argument about honor because the judge's wife was Greek. Members of the community could have testified about the Greek customary law code of honor.

12. If a cultural defense were established policy, this would enable the jury to better tailor the punishment to the crime. It is possible that, were the case to have been tried using a cultural defense as a partial excuse, Metallides would have received a punishment somewhere between first-degree murder and complete acquittal. Such an outcome would, on the face of it, appear more just.

13. In *The King v. Cogdon* (1950) a woman was acquitted on the basis of somnambulism. See Morris, "Somnambulistic Homicide." It may be treated as a type of insanity defense. LaFave and Scott, *Criminal Law*, 385. The difference between irresistible impulse and automatism is that "in the case of the former, the accused is aware of what he is doing, but is unable to control his actions, whereas in the latter the accused is not only unable to control his actions but is completely unaware of what he is doing." Jayaratnam, "Irresistible Impulse," 111. Regarding voluntary intent, see LaFave and Scott, *Criminal Law*, 382. The distinction seems silly. One could equally well argue that the defendant performed the act itself (actus reus) but did not do so intentionally.

14. LaFave and Scott, *Criminal Law*, 384; Jayaratnam, "Irresistible Impulse," 111.

15. *People v. Wu* (1991), 614. For background on Wu's motivation, see Renteln, "Justification."

16. *People v. Wu*, 639

17. Gary Scherotter, personal communication, 1992. Depublication means the case cannot be cited as a precedent and is removed from official court reports.

18. Acosta, "Woman Found Guilty."

19. See Viele, "Court." It is striking that the defense invoked both the battered woman defense and the cultural defense, as the two are seemingly in tension. For a thoughtful discussion of this, see Suri, "Principle." A defense attorney advanced a battered husband and cultural defense argument in the trial of Moosa Hanoukai, an Iranian immigrant, who bludgeoned his wife of twenty-four years during a fight because she made him sleep on the floor and beg for money, even for cigarettes. See Mrozek's series of *Los Angeles Times* articles; Tugend, "L.A. Rabbis"; Ma, "Cultural Defense," 472–473. Herman said his decision to use the battered woman defense was in part because Georgia does not have perfect and imperfect self-defense. Personal communication, 1999.

20. Although a precedent required the consideration of psychological characteristics, the court rejected the notion that "her psychological characteristics include her Vietnamese upbringing" and displayed its ignorance of the field of cultural psychology and the most basic notions of anthropology: "The fact that verbal threats or verbal abuse might justify the use of deadly force in some cultures is not relevant to whether the use of such force is justified under Georgia law." *Nguyen v. State* (1998), 846.

21. "The expert testimony proffered by the defense showed the loss of status, humiliation and possible adverse spiritual consequences to appellant and her family from her husband's failure to maintain appellant's proper position in the household. However, there was no evidence that individuals sharing appellant's cultural background would believe themselves to be in danger of receiving any physical harm as a result of such loss of status and disrespectful treatment. While we can envision rare situations in which such evidence might be relevant to assist the jury in understanding why an accused acted in the way he or she did, that situation is not present in this case." Georgia Supreme Court, in *Nguyen v. State* (1999), 908

22. (a) Wrong means legally wrong; and (b) when wrong means morally wrong, it refers only to the delusional belief in divine commandments. In many instances, cultural defendants can invoke only the cognitive type of insanity defense, because the M'Naghten test is found in the majority of jurisdictions. But an explanation of a culturally motivated act may require the volitional form of the insanity test. This means that it will be a matter of luck whether the immigrant happens to commit the offense in the right state—that is, in one which has the requisite type of insanity test. Such circumstances are clearly arbitrary and unfair. Moreover, even if they do adjudicate their claims in a jurisdiction admitting a volitional insanity test, establishing such a claim is notoriously difficult.

23. Goldstein and Katz, "Abolish," 858.

24. Although Western medical experts and legal analysts sometimes discuss culture-bound syndromes under the rubric of insanity, this terminology is likely to be offensive to people whose worldview differs from the dominant one. These syndromes should be considered as a separate category for analysis. King treats the syndromes as mental illness in "Role." See, for example, Fabrega, "Cultural Relativism and Psychiatric Illness"; Leong and Silva, "Asian American Forensic Psychiatrists"; Shweder and Bourne, "Concept of the Person?" For an overview of culture-bound syndromes, see Gaw, *Culture*. They are becoming more accepted within the medical establishment. *DSM-IV* contains a special section, "ethnic and cultural considerations," and an appendix with a useful glossary. *The Merck Manual* (16th ed.) added section 275, "Cross-cultural Issues in Medicine (Folk medicine; Ethnomedicine)." For articles on particular groups, see two issues on "Cross-Cultural Medicine" published in the *Western Journal of Medicine* in 1983 and 1992. See also Al-Issa. *Handbook of Culture*.

25. An excellent detailed account can be found in Li, "Culture as Defense." Li favors the use of cultural evidence and would leave the determination of the reasonableness of the cultural explanation to the jury.

26. *DSM-IV*, 845. The description goes on to mention that the original reports of the syndrome came from Malaysia but that similar behavior patterns have been documented in Laos, the Philippines, Polynesia (*cafard* or *cathard*), Papua New Guinea, and Puerto Rico (*mal de pelea*) and among the Navajo (*iich'aa*). For more information on "amok," see Spores, *Running Amok*, and its comprehensive bibliography. Spores says commentators attributed amok to drug intoxication (opium or hemp), and he mentions infections as another cause (91, 140). European colonial authorities in Malaysia used to capture "amok runners" and then execute them (75–89).

27. The concept of self-esteem (*amor proprio*) in the Philippines is based on how one is viewed by one's group, or *barkada*. If a man's wife had an affair, this would call into question his maleness, or *paglalaki*. Li, "Culture as Defense," 792–793. The experts were Dr. Ricardo Trimillos, chair of the Asian studies program, and Dr. Anthony Marsella, professor of psychopathology, both at the University of Hawai'i at Manoa. Apparently the prosecutor did not make strenuous objections. Li, "Culture as Defense," 792.

28. The Supreme Court upheld his sentence of life without parole for murder and attempted murder. Subsequently Mrs. Ganal was held liable in a civil action: if she participated in conduct that caused an unreasonable risk of harm, she could be held responsible. *Touchette v. Ganal* (1996).

29. Criticisms included the fact that the defense "served to spread the erroneous and appalling stereotype that Filipinos are prone to run amok." Anon. (1993c), "Ganal Case Jury." Another concern was the implication that such crimes would be tolerated in the Philippines. Some charged that the "amok" defense was "racist." For putting the culture on trial, see Aquino and Miarlao, "Philippine Culture." For the denial of its part in Filipino culture, see Robert Allen, "Letter: 'Amok.'" The amok syndrome was part of the legal insanity defense in the Canadian case *R. v. Hem* (1990). Serey Sonia Hem, a Cambodian, used a machete to attack a man with whose family he was staying.

30. Judge Albracht said, "This is a murder case that involves the confluence and collision of California criminal law with honestly held Christian religious beliefs overlaid and blended with Korean pre-Christian shamanist practices." For background provided by one of the expert witnesses, see Chin, "Bearing Witness." The ritual healing, *ansu kido*, involved "laying on the hands." An autopsy revealed sixteen broken ribs, and "crushing force" pressed her heart. Pat Alston, "Verdicts." See also Kang and Corwin, "Men Charged," and Anon. (1997b), "Two Ministers Sentenced." Evidently charismatic beliefs are popular in South Korea, after having been introduced by U.S. missionaries in the 1920s. Salopek, "Korean Exorcism," and Zane, "Minister." Korean American Christian leaders denied any cultural dimension, claiming that exorcism is "almost unheard of in their community." Kang and Corwin, "Men Charged." The judge may have been influenced by the husband's demeanor, which was described as "contrite and tearful" and the pleas of his children for his release. Pat Alston, "Man Gets Four Years." "Albracht bucked the current legal trend by recognizing the cultural and religious strains in the case, even welcoming testimony from a cultural anthropologist who appeared as an expert for the defense. Despite a horrifying outcome, Albracht, found, the missionaries acted with the best of intentions." O'Neill, "Two Missionaries Guilty."

31. It is odd that courts generally do not allow a duress defense in cases of intentional homicide. Presumably this is because the law prefers that the person under duress sacrifice his life rather than kill an innocent third party.

32. The judge noted during sentencing that "the main contention is that they acted in accordance with tribal laws and that particularly the younger ones may have been in a serious

position if they had refused to agree to a decision of the elders of the tribe. This may be true enough, but there is a limit to which this Court can accept it as an excuse for what is after all a very serious crime."

33. Eggleston, *Fear*, 288–292. See also Renteln, "Justification."

34. See Morse, "Diminished Capacity." The rise of new versions of the diminished capacity defense is worth noting. Defendants have raised the postpartem defense, the intoxication defense, and post-traumatic stress syndrome defenses, including the Vietnam veteran's defense and the battered woman defense. Insofar as the law is willing to authorize the consideration of information that relates to the specific background of particular defendants, there may be new opportunities to incorporate cultural evidence in trials.

35. Poddar had interpreted her behavior to mean she was committed to him. For instance, she accepted his gift of a sari, which, according to Poddar meant in his culture that she was prepared to marry him. Students of mine from India deny that the gift has the significance Poddar claimed.

The judge thought the expert was not qualified to testify about the direct effect of the stresses on Poddar. Though he was willing to allow the anthropologist to testify about cross-cultural difficulties in general and to answer hypothetical questions, the defense attorney refused, as he wanted to have the anthropologist testify as an independent expert on the issue of diminished capacity.

36. See Blum, *Bad Karma*, 303. The question of whether Poddar's psychiatrists had a duty to inform his intended victim and her family was the center of another lawsuit. In *Tarasoff v. Regents of University of California* (1975) the California Supreme Court held that such a duty existed under some circumstances. The Court of Appeals expressed concern that the consideration of social science would distract the jury. *People v. Poddar* (1972), 84, 88. However, the court ruled that because of all the other errors, Poddar should have been convicted of manslaughter rather than second-degree murder. Poddar had an arranged marriage and pursued his studies in Germany. Blum, *Bad Karma*, 303. The defense may be of limited utility if it has been abandoned in some jurisdictions, as occurred in California. Monahan and Walker, *Social Science in Law*, 425.

37. For an example of losing self-control, see Morse, "Undiminished Confusion," 33. The existence of the provocation defense lends support to advocates of partial responsibility: "If one accepts the traditional assumption that the provoked and therefore less rational and self-controlled actor is less responsible, how can one deny similar mitigation to an actor whose problems with rationality or self-control are the product of mental disorder or defect? Indeed, a powerful argument can be mounted that the disordered person deserves mitigation more than his provoked counterpart. . . . Thus, the law already appears to accept partial responsibility for actors less deserving than the mentally abnormal." Morse, "Diminished Capacity," 30. Morse opposes most types of volitional defenses, including the volitional insanity defense (except for impulse disorders; see his "Excusing the Crazy," 813), diminished responsibility, and provocation.

38. In actual practice, cases are argued using many different defenses, of which provocation is only one. For example, in *Bui v. State* (1988) a Vietnamese defendant killed his children and then slit his own throat when he discovered that his wife was unfaithful. He argued both provocation and volitional insanity, but the death penalty was upheld on appeal. In *R. v. Parnerkar* (1972, 1974) an Indian man stabbed to death the woman he wanted to marry. His attorney raised provocation and automatism defenses, both of which were held to be improper. On the second appeal, the Canadian Supreme Court said the only appropriate defense in this case would be the M'Naghten-based insanity test. The strategy of arguing more than one defense simultaneously can lead to logical difficulties. For example, the problem in *Poddar* was that the provocation defense seemed to contradict the argument of dimin-

ished capacity. The provocation defense requires showing that an objective, reasonable person would have been provoked; but the basis of the diminished capacity defense is precisely that the defendant is not "the ordinarily reasonable man at the time of the occurrence." For more on provocation, see LaFave and Scott, *Criminal Law*, 653–664; Perkins and Boyce, *Criminal Law*, 84–88; and works by Bernard Brown, Donovan and Wildman, Colin Howard, Macklem, Marsack, O'Regan, Samuels ("Excusable Loss"), Vasdev ("Provocation"), and Glanville Williams ("Provocation").

39. *People v. Aphaylath* (1986a, b). Quotation is from 1986b, 999.

40. Nguyen, "Culture Shock"; Rutledge, *Vietnamese Experience*; Oberg, "Cultural Shock."

41. It is common for courts to exclude cultural evidence. See, e.g., *Lee v. State* (1992). Lee, a Taiwanese man, was convicted of murdering a man in a relationship with Lee's ex-wife. On appeal, he argued unsuccessfully that the trial court's exclusion of cultural evidence was an abuse of discretion. The idea here is that this emotion is universal. The court ignores the possibility that there might be cultural variation in its expression. That is, there may exist societies in which it is permissible to act on certain emotions, even though there may be others in which it is not.

42. For a similar Canadian example where, by contrast, the court upheld the exclusion of cultural evidence on appeal, see *R. v. Ly* (1987). For commentary, see Renteln, "Justification."

43. See Bohlen, "Killing of a Chinese Woman," and Cardillo, "Violence." See also Rorie Sherman, "Cultural Defenses," and Polman, "Controversial," 4A.

44. Trimarchi, "Judge Refuses"; Sing, "Sexual Bias"; Rorie Sherman, "Cultural Defenses"; Yen, "Refusal."

45. For example, Pongsak Trakulrat, originally from Thailand, was singing at a restaurant in Los Angeles, when a man in the audience put his feet up on the table, so that his soles were pointing at Trakulrat. Evidently this gesture is considered to be extremely derogatory in Thai culture. Trakulrat became enraged and shot the man to death. He was convicted of second-degree murder and sentenced to twenty-nine years to life in state prison. David Dahle, personal communication, 1991.

In *State v. Haque* (1999) words were not considered adequate provocation. Nadim Haque, a man from India, was convicted of killing his girlfriend, Lori Taylor, when she verbally rejected him. The Maine Supreme Court upheld the lower court's exclusion of psychiatric testimony that he was in a "blind rage" when he killed and the exclusion of the anthropological testimony concerning his background and how his traditional upbringing as a Muslim Indian influenced his perception of the relationships. The court noted that Haque "expressly disavowed any reliance on a cultural defense." If Haque had raised a cultural defense, the court might have considered the anthropological testimony admissible for that defense.

46. Trujillo-Garcia was a nineteen-year-old man from a traditional Catholic Mexican family with twelve children which was of lower socioeconomic status. He and Padilla had come from Mexico three years before the incident. Trujillo-Garcia had bought a gun after the house where he lived was robbed, ostensibly to prevent further burglary attempts.

47. Trujillo-Garcia's lawyer translated "chinga tu madre" literally as "Go and fuck your mother." He told his brother the victim said, "We're gonna get to the mother, and we're gonna have a fight about this, we're gonna get to the mother." And [then] he said, "You know what, I like you to go and fuck your mother." Appellant's Supplemental Brief, *People v. Trujillo-Garcia*, Ct of Appeal, California, 17.

For a consideration of the meaning of *chingar*, see Paz, "Sons of La Malinche." Paz discusses numerous interpretations of the term whose meaning is changed by tone, inflection, and context. He explains that chingar means "to do violence to another" (77). "The Chingada is the Mother forcibly opened, violated or deceived" (79), and "the Chingada is a representation of the violated Mother" (86). The word is taboo and cannot be used "casually in public. Only an excess of anger or a delirious enthusiasm justifies its use" (77).

An expert witness on the Spanish language, Robert Lozano, testified at the trial that "chinga tu madre" is different from the English expression "motherfucker": "When you say 'chinga tu madre,' you are like telling the person to exert an action against his mother. It is like you are giving a command. It's an imperative." Appellant's Supplemental Brief, *People v. Trujillo-Garcia*, Ct of Appeal, California, 18. The lawyer argued that the closest approximation of the insult would be an ethnic slur.

El Chingoles: Primer Diccionario del Lenguaje Popular Mexicano defines "chingar" as "to injure, to abuse in whatever sense, but especially in reference to women, to alter the order of things and or persons" (110). This work gives the impression that the word has become a casual word in Mexican slang. If it is part of common parlance, that might call into question its shock value.

48. The equal protection argument was based on the Fourteenth Amendment and the California Constitution, Article 1, section 7. The attorney, Richard Targow, filed a supplemental brief in the California Court of Appeals, the first time the cultural defense issue was raised. The brief emphasizes the importance of understanding the words in their cultural context. The argument was specifically that a person's reaction to a particular insult depends upon his or her cultural upbringing. See Appellant's Supplemental Brief, *People v. Trujillo-Garcia*, Ct of Appeal, California. The impressive brief mentions the Whorf-Sapir hypothesis, the notion that language structures one's view of reality.

49. The California legislature rejected the common law rule in its manslaughter rule. Prior to the adoption of this policy, courts disapproved of acknowledging verbal insults. For instance, in *People v. Natale* (1962) the court held the judge properly refused to give an instruction on *dago* because doing so "would permit a finding of adequate provocation merely because the word 'dago' may have been used by the victim of an assault."

50. Appellant's Supplemental Brief, *People v. Trujillo-Garcia*, Ct of Appeal, California, 13. The attorney clarifies his proposed standard based on cultural relativity: "If the statement 'p,' when directed to A in the context of American culture, is sufficient to constitute adequate provocation when judged by American standards of reasonableness, and the statement 'q,' when directed to B in the context of another culture, signifies the same degree of offensiveness as the statement 'p,' then A and B are similarly situated with respect to the reasonableness of their loss of self-control, and should be similarly treated" (14).

51. *Trujillo-Garcia v. Rowland*, Memorandum and Order by Judge Marilyn Patel (1992), 10. Judge Patel did not make clear on what basis she reached this conclusion. There is no indication that she made her decision with the benefit of any empirical research. According to anthropologist Stanley Brandes, under certain circumstances, the insult could be sufficiently inflammatory to incite someone to kill. Personal communication, 1998. The affirmation was in 1993 U.S. App. LEXIS 30441. The U.S. Supreme Court denied certiorari.

52. Some cases require an understanding of machismo. In *People v. Miguel Hernandez* (1994), for example, a Mexican was provoked to kill two men when they called him names such as *mujercito*, meaning little woman. On the day of the killing, Hernandez had lost his job, fought with his spouse, and been drinking. After the jury trial, he was convicted on two counts of first-degree murder and received twenty-five years to life. Personal communication with his attorney, Terrell Powell, 1993, 1994. In California the standard instruction provides the following: "The heat of passion which will reduce a homicide to manslaughter must be such a passion as naturally would be aroused in the mind of an ordinarily reasonable person in the same circumstances." *California Jury Instructions Criminal* (6th ed.), I. St. Paul: West, 1996 (8.42).

53. Yi Ching "Teddy" Chou was prosecuted for first-degree murder for killing Wen-Cheng "Roc" Hsieh, a restaurant owner who caused him to lose face. Evidently when Chou asked for medical expenses incurred from a fight he had lost with Hsieh a year earlier, Hsieh told Chou in Chinese to "roll your body out," which is apparently a profane remark, the equivalent of telling someone to "crawl out of here." Pankratz, "Jury," and Bartels, "Jury." Convicted of first-degree murder, Chou was sentenced to life in prison. Lindsay, "Killer." His appeals failed. *State v. Yi Ching Chou* (1999); *Yi Ching Chou* (1999).

Another unpublished case involving a verbal insult is *People v. Bonadonna* (1990). Giacomo Bonadonna, a Sicilian, claimed to have been provoked by Roberto Lucarini, a northern Italian. Lucarini called him *cornuto*, which means cuckold and also the passive partner in homosexual sodomy. A few days later he shot Lucarini. Despite the presentation of testimony about the cultural significance of the insult, he was convicted of first-degree murder and received a sentence of twenty-seven years to life. On appeal, in a peculiar ruling, the court held that the use of culture was appropriate to understand the insult, but that culture could not be used to evaluate the response to the insult: "Thus, consideration of cultural context may be irrelevant to the jury's determination of how the reasonable person would react to the perceived insult" (5–6). Hence the refusal of the trial court to give a special jury instruction concerning the cultural context was "properly rejected" as it was "overly broad."

54. An excellent analysis of honor killing in Arab Muslim society can be found in Kressel, "Sororicide/Filiacide." See also the commentaries and Kressel's reply. In the *Dincer* case, the court said, "Whether the ordinary man possessed of those characteristics might have acted as the accused man did is a question which could conceivably be rationally answered yes, and therefore should be left to the jury." *R. v. Dincer* (1983), 463–464. Jenny Morgan criticizes the court for "essentializing" culture, by relying on a male characterization of what a "traditional Turkish Moslem would do." "Provocation," 268. The leading advocate of the position that the test should be based on the personal characteristics of the accused is Stanley M. H. Yeo. For an overview of the controversy over whether the ordinary person should be interpreted in light of his cultural background, see Yeo's articles ("Recent Pronouncements" and "Provoking"), as well as Leader-Elliott, "Sex," and Heller, "Reasonable Man?"

55. Reaction to an FBI tape that recorded Palestinian parents killing their sixteen-year-old daughter suggests that the provocation argument will be repugnant to jurors. Anon. (1991a), "Terror." See Connelly, "Review."

In 1989 Abdul Malik, a devout Muslim, killed his sixteen-year-old daughter, Pharbin, with a knife when she refused to recite a Muslim prayer. He was distraught because she planned to become a Christian and had attended some Jehovah's Witness meetings with her Jamaican boyfriend. O'Brien, "Moslem Cut Throat," and Horowitz, "Moslem Father." The jury rejected his reasonable person test, which had been adapted to a "reasonable Muslim," and imposed life imprisonment. Anon. (1989d), "Muslim Jailed." According to reports, Malik thought Islamic law permitted him to put his daughter to death for apostasy, but experts at the Center for Islamic Studies said he was mistaken as Bangladeshi Muslims who follow the Hanassi Islamic jurisprudence did not put women to death for the crimes of apostasy or adultery. Anon. (1989e), "Life for Father." Dr. Shabbir Akhtar submitted an expert report to the judge: "In my view the Koran . . . does not prescribe any penalty" but later added: "The view is widely held that apostasy is a capital offence and this belief has been transmitted from generation to generation."

In France the parents, brother, and cousin of a fifteen-year-old Turkish girl strangled her because she dishonored the family by becoming too "Westernized." They received sentences ranging from twenty years to life. Jones, "Family Sentenced." In the West Bank and Gaza Strip such a killing is considered murder with special circumstances and results in a lighter penalty.

Curtius, "High Price for Honor." There is an international movement to outlaw this practice. Beyer, "Price of Honor," and Goodman, "Honor Killings."

56. See Saltman, *Demise.*

57. See, e.g., Littman, "Adequate Provocation," and Spatz, "'Lesser' Crime."

58. See Sing, "Culture as Sameness," who says it is problematic to argue that exclusion of cultural evidence violates equal protection because the interpretation of criminal law standards is not based on a desire to discriminate. However, the decision to adhere to the "objective" standard is arguably based on a desire to discriminate against cultural minorities.

59. If a defendant has a "reasonable" but mistaken belief that force was necessary for self-protection, some jurisdictions allow an "imperfect" self-defense, which reduces a murder charge to one of manslaughter. LaFave and Scott, *Criminal Law,* 463.

60. Paul Robinson, "Criminal Law Defenses," 216. With self-defense there is the question of whether the defendant's belief in the imminence of danger was reasonable. See, e.g., *Ha v. State* (1995).

61. For another example, see *State v. Butler* (1985), discussed in Renteln, "Justification," in which two Native Americans were tried for killing a Caucasian who had been digging up Indian graves in order to sell Indian artifacts.

62. Croy's attorney, Tony Serra, used the same strategy later in the case of Eugene "Bear" Lincoln. Anon. (1997f), "Cultural Defense." See also Ray Delgado,"Cop Killer Suspect"; Snyder, "Indian Reservation" and "Families"; Anon. (1997e), "Serra's Cultural Defense"; Snyder, "Mendocino Acquittal"; Cockburn, "Rural Justice"; Elias, "Counsel Criticized." Croy explained in court that "because there was widespread bias against American Indians in that region, he did not believe he had the option to surrender and thought the police wanted to kill him." Halstuk, "S. F. Retrial." Quotations from Bodovitz, "Indian's Defense." For discussion of the case, see Paul Harris, *Black Rage,* chap. 13.

Another case involving a challenge to the objective reasonable man standard is *State v. Wanrow* (1977). Interestingly, here the court concluded that use of the "objective" standard of self-defense violated gender equality, but ignored the effect of her Native American background on her perceptions.

63. An earlier case relying on this notion is *State v. Rodriguez* (1964) where a court reduced a manslaughter sentence in part because of the defendant's Puerto Rican background or "racial heritage."

64. "Absent evidence that defendant was in fear of imminent death or great bodily injury, the jury had no evidentiary basis from which to conclude that defendant subjectively had an actual but unreasonable fear which negated malice aforethought." *People v. Romero* (1999), 856.

65. *Witchcraft* is a crude term that is used to cover many different types of supernatural phenomenona. A leading scholar notes that the term is "notoriously devoid of precise definition." Mutungi, *Legal Aspects,* 1. In general, it is preferable to refer to the specific belief system at the crux of the case. See, e.g., Gluckman, "Logic"; Klingshirn, "Trial"; Currie, "Crimes." Regarding self-preservation, see the works by Aremu, Chukkol, David Clark, Drummond, Hogbin, Howman, Kanter, Bill Keller, Leikind, Justin Lewis, Ojo, and Vasdev. For a review of other arguments, such as mistake of fact, provocation, and insanity, put forward in witchcraft cases in the colonial settings, see especially the studies by Mutungi, Seidman, and Glanville Williams ("Homicide").

Concerning nonbelief, see, e.g., *Gadam v. R.* (1954). Where the law was governed by the common law, self-defense was only possible if retreat was impossible; that is, it was necessary that the accused act as he did. It is questionable whether "retreat" is a relevant concept for witchcraft. Colonial governments tried to stop the practice by outlawing it with explicit statutory provisions. Karibi-Whyte, "Cultural Pluralism." For a study of contradictions in the statutes, see Mutungi, "Witchcraft."

For a discussion of the insanity defense, see, e.g., *Philip Muswi s/o Musele v. R.* (1956). See also Renteln, "Justification," 872–873. Regarding colonial legal systems, see Ojo, "Supernatural Powers," and Seidman, "Witch Murder." Chukkol says in reference to witchcraft cases where courts rejected self-defense: "Yet trial courts were administering 'justice' when they sentenced the accused persons for murder, whose mind at the time of killing their assailants could not be described as blameworthy by any stretch of imagination!" "Supernatural Beliefs," 462. See also Mutungi's discussion of the predicament faced by witchcraft believers. *Legal Aspects,* 26.

With regard to patronizing attitudes, David Clark analyzes the case of a man who killed a person he believed to be a witch. He received less punishment from the Colombian Supreme Court because Indians, the "juridical equivalent of minors," were not thought to have the mental capacity to justify imposing full punishment." "Witchcraft," 683.

66. See Anon. (1997j), "Voodoo Defense," and Drell, "Killer" and "Witchcraft Murder Defense." For use of the defense in tribal courts, see Kanter, "Yenaldlooshi," and Reid, "Witchcraft." For an interpretation of an earlier case in which an Indian was prosecuted for killing a shaman in U.S. district court, see Asher, "Shaman-Killing Case." In the famous Canadian case in which an Indian (whose tribe is not mentioned) killed a person he thought was a Wendigo (or spirit), the court nevertheless upheld his conviction of manslaughter. *R. v. Machekequonabe* (1897).

The court documents equate curanderismo with Mexican "folk psychiatry and witchcraft." See Motion for Appointment of Expert Witness, *People v. Galicia,* 679. The documents make reference to intoxication, provocation, and insanity in the context of advancing a witchcraft defense. See Drell, "Witch Defense Out." Some witchcraft claims are a flagrant misuse of the cultural defense, e.g., *Guttierrez v. State* (1996).

67. The *bouda,* also sometimes spelled *buda,* are said to have the evil eye. See Coronado, "Suspect Found Guilty." Quotation from Shack in Franklin, "Man Shot Woman." Nowhere in the court documents or journalistic discussion of the case is there any mention of the specific people to which he belonged. Shack stated that the belief was widespread in that region, so the question of his tribal identity may not have been crucial.

68. Martinez, "Ethiopian"; Franklin, "'Hexed' Guilty"; Anon. (1985b), "Profile."

69. Sometimes this type of argument is linked to an insanity defense as in *State v. Blake* (1999), where the defendant used his practice of Santería to strengthen his insanity defense. McDonald, "Harvey." But the jury found the suspect guilty on all charges. R. Robin McDonald, personal communication, 2000.

70. On culture and sentencing generally, see Olabisi Clinton, "Cultural Differences."

71. *Kwai Fan Mak v. Blodgett* (1991, 1992). For another case in which this argument proved unsuccessful, see *Tuan Anh Nguyen v. Reynolds* (1997). Mak appealed his conviction and death sentence to the Washington Supreme Court, which affirmed seven to two in April 1986. *State v. Mak* (1986). Four months later the court denied a motion for rehearing. The U.S. Supreme Court denied certiorari in Dec. 1986. The lawyers' performance was flawed in other ways, largely because, as recent law school graduates, they had not previously handled a capital case. In *Strickland v. Washington* (1984) the Supreme Court established the two-prong test for analyzing inadequate legal representation: it requires a showing that the lawyer's performance was deficient, and that it was so below the required standard that it was prejudicial to the defense, meaning that it had an adverse impact on the outcome of the case. In prior cases lawyers made tactical decisions not to present mitigating evidence, but here the defense counsel did not make a strategic choice.

72. *Mak* (1992), 618, n.5 indicates what the testimony would have been: "Family members would have testified that Mak was the beloved youngest son of a traditional Chinese fam-

ily; that he had been a good student and dutiful son in Hong Kong; that after coming to this country he did well in citizenship, and in some school subjects, for the first few years; that he worked and gave money to the family; that he helped his parents in other ways; that he was kind to the other members of the extended family; and that he was a "favorite uncle" to young nieces and nephews."

"The expert testimony of Dr. Johnson would have discussed serious assimilation problems experienced by many Chinese who are moved during adolescence from Hong Kong to North America, and certain values in the Chinese culture of Hong Kong which could help to explain petitioner's involvement in criminal activities here. [The testimony] would also suggest that petitioner's apparent lack of emotion at trial did not necessarily indicate disinterest or coldness, but was consistent with cultural expectations of Chinese males" (*Mak*, 618, n.5). The issue of Asian American cultural adaptation is widely known and is the subject of newspaper coverage. For instance, the *Los Angeles Times* reported that Asian American gangs have proliferated since the 1980s. Tamaki, "Cultural Balancing Act."

Turner presents the Mak case as an example of the need to have anthropological testimony to explain the cultural context of the defendant's behavior. If a jury fails to appreciate the different cultural rules for behavior, "the misinterpretation may yield injustice." "Prolegomenon," 402.

73. Deposition of Graham Edwin Johnson, Oct. 18, 1990, 121.

74. Deposition of Johnson, Oct. 18, 1990, 59. Courts sometimes realize that failure to express remorse reflected cultural differences. See, e.g., *People v. Superior Court* (Soon Ja Du) (1992).

75. *Mak*, 620.

76. Although the appellate court ordered resentencing in July 1992, this did not occur until 2002 when he received thirteen life sentences. During that decade, Mak's attorneys were embroiled in litigation to determine the identities of the others allegedly involved in the massacre.

77. In an essay "Torn between Cultures," Thao points out that Southeast Asian immigrants avoid looking their own attorneys straight in the eye and find it "very difficult" to say no.

78. For U.S. Supreme court cases on point, see *Eddings v. Oklahoma* (1982), *Lockett v. Ohio* (1978), and *Skipper v. South Carolina* (1986).

79. *Siripongs v. Calderon* (1998). Siripongs sued the warden of San Quentin prison as is customary in habeas corpus cases. The case name changed because the previous warden was Vasquez. Afterward, Siripongs used the victims' credit cards. This may suggest that he wanted to be caught. See Affidavit of Professor Herbert Phillips, Nov. 14, 1991. One especially puzzling aspect of the case is the accomplice defense. Much of the cultural evidence pertained to the question of whether another person had committed the murders. Even if that is true, Siripongs could still receive the death penalty. Pulling the trigger is not a prerequisite to the imposition of capital punishment.

80. *Siripongs v. Calderon* (1994), denial of cert. (1995). The court had to evaluate a record consisting of thirty volumes of transcripts!

81. Phillips quotation from *Siripongs v. Calderon* (1998), 4. Siripongs never told his family about his arrest; they learned from the local Thai paper. Phillips notes that this is consistent with "the cultural expectation that an individual endeavor not to cause his family shame. By so doing, Mr. Siripongs can get on with his own death, begin to compensate for the evil, the 'baap,' with more good, the 'boon,' if not in this life, then in future lives" (27).

82. Affidavit of Professor Phillips, 25, 27–28.

83. *Siripongs v. Calderon* (1998), 4.

84. Although the Ninth Circuit found this matter "troublesome" the first time it heard the case, the second time it concluded that his campaign had not interfered with his trial

preparations (13). Evidently a rap sheet from Thailand showed Siripongs had been convicted of one crime, a nonviolent burglary. It was translated improperly in the California court, but despite having a corrected copy, Spellman did not rectify the error in the court record. The lawyer failed to notice that the court interpreter was a friend of the victim's husband, something which at the very least created the appearance of bias.

85. *Siripongs v. Calderon* (1998), 14.

86. If this petition failed, his lawyers planned to advance an argument along the lines of the *Breard* case (1998). Daniel Breard, a national of Paraguay, was convicted of murder in Virginia. While on death row, he filed a lawsuit in which he alleged that the failure of the Virginia authorities to permit him to speak with his embassy was a serious error, a violation of the Vienna Convention on Consular Relations. When a national of another country is accused of a crime, according to public international law he is supposed to have access to his consulate. The U.S. Supreme Court declined to intervene, despite an international outcry, including a plea from the U.N. International Court of Justice. Siripongs, like Breard, was tried for a capital crime without ever having the opportunity to consult his embassy. Brooks and Wright, "Deny Treaty Rights."

Many pleaded for Siripongs's life, including relatives of victims, two jurors who had recommended the death penalty, Pope John Paul II, and even the warden of San Quentin prison and a death row prison guard. Marcosi and Yi, "Friends and Foes." Neither Republican Governor Pete Wilson nor Democratic Governor Gray Davis would grant his plea for clemency. Marcosi, "Attorney" and "Siripongs"; Marcosi and Hernandez, "Convicted Killer."

87. If this trend continues, law schools will have to offer some cross-cultural instruction, which they have been loath to do.

88. The classic example of a partial excuse is provocation which, if it is successful, reduces a charge of murder to manslaughter.

CHAPTER 4

1. See, e.g., Eisenberg, "Cross-Cultural Perspectives"; Gabarino and Ebata, "Significance of Child Maltreatment"; Gray and Cosgrove, "Ethnocentric Perception"; Ima and Hohm, "Child Maltreatment"; McGillivray, "Reconstructing." The most insightful work is that of Jill Korbin.

2. Wadlington et al., *Cases on Children*, 894.

3. Even in the United States there is no clear definition of child abuse and neglect. See, for example, the range of definitions in Parke and Collmer, *Child Abuse*, 1–3. A leading journal, *Child Abuse and Neglect*, suggested a basic definition: "Any interaction or lack of interaction between a caregiver and a child which results in nonaccidental harm to the child's physical or developmental state." Besharov, "Toward Better Research," 383. Since Henry Kempe set forth the battered child syndrome, that has served as a major paradigm. But it does not cover all the situations delineated in this study. Although this chapter concentrates on child-rearing practices which Americans regard as abuse or neglect, it is important to recognize that some American practices are considered cruel by others. For example, in one study Hawaiian women were shocked to find that white mothers put their infants in a separate bedroom. Korbin, "Cross-Cultural Perspective," 10. Interestingly, another study suggests that Sudden Infant Death Syndrome (SIDS) may occur at a higher rate in societies where infants sleep in separate rooms or separate beds. McElroy and Townsend, *Medical Anthropology*, 106.

4. Although female circumcision is not an accurate characterization of the surgery, it is a term used widely in the literature. Feminists refer to the practice as female genital mutilation (FGM). Since the purpose here is to argue for culturally sensitive legal interpretation, I will use

the more neutral terminology, though as a Western woman I do not favor the perpetuation of this custom.

5. Few articles consider the cultural defense in the context of child abuse and neglect cases. The two essays that do focus on this topic both question its validity; see Terhune, "Cultural and Religious Defenses," and Todd Taylor, "Cultural Defense." There is a growing literature on requiring "cultural competency" for professionals who work with children, but it does not discuss the cultural defense per se. See, e.g., Veronica Abney, "Cultural Competency"; McPhatter, "Cultural Competence"; Tharp, "Cultural Diversity." Textbooks on child abuse and law hardly mention the subject, e.g., Sagatun and Edwards, *Child Abuse*, 18–20, 27.

6. The absolutistic approach is reflected in the Convention on the Rights of the Child. Article 24(3) provides that "states parties shall take all effective and appropriate measures with a view to abolishing traditional practices prejudicial to the health of children." The phrase "prejudicial to the health of children" is ambiguous, and it remains unclear how broadly this clause should be interpreted.

7. There may be reason to wonder about her identity. Before marriage she had been a Muslim and afterward had become a Christian. If she was able to change her religious affiliation, it might have appeared to the court that her commitment to Yoruba tradition was not deeply rooted.

8. See Poulter, *English Law*, 150. See also Anon. (1974a), "Mother"; Anon. (1974b), "Discharge"; Hayter, "Female Circumcision," 327. The quote is from Poulter.

Quotation from Korbin, "Cross-Cultural Context," 24. It is generally true that scarification traditionally is an important part of initiation rituals. It conveys the symbolic message that an individual has become part of the social group. See Polyhemus, *Body Reader*, 151.

9. Quotation from Poulter, *English Law*, 150. Poulter explains what the judge meant by this remark: "There was a very great risk involved because the slightest movement of the child's head could result in serious injury to the eye or eyelid." "Foreign Customs," 138.

10. Poulter, *English Law*, 151. Commentators have taken different views of the case. For instance, Samuels regards the case as correctly decided ("Legal Recognition," 242), whereas others have been more critical: "We in this country [England] are supposed to believe in people from other cultures who come to live here preserving their own traditions, and to regret it when the children of such cultures abandon the old ways, in favour of a proto-plastic regime of pop, coke, and denims." Harper, "Travellers' Tales," 708. Poulter wonders whether "this was a case where the police should have used their discretion merely to caution the mother rather than prosecute her" or whether it was appropriate to take the opportunity to issue a public warning to the Nigerian community about the "criminal nature of the scarification of children in England." *English Law*, 152, and "Significance," 127.

11. A. S. Diamond, "Case of Mrs. Adesanya," 2.

12. Lloyd, "Case of Mrs. Adesanya," 2, and Poulter, *English Law*, 150.

13. The court treated Nigerian and Yoruba customs as if they were synonymous, despite the fact that there are many different peoples in Nigeria. See Favazza and Favazza, *Bodies under Siege*, 128; Korbin, "Anthropological Contributions," 7; Poulter, *English Law*, 151.

14. In a New York scarification case, grandparents cut the face of their six-year-old grandson, Akinbohun Moore, against the wishes of his mother (their daughter), who preferred to wait until he was thirteen for the marks; 120 stitches were needed to close three vertical slashes. Gearty, "Arrested," 6, and Rayman, "Grandma Jailed." According to the grandparents, they descended from the Yoruba tribe in Nigeria, and their relatives continued the tradition in Buford, South Carolina. After investigating the matter, the prosecutor decided to press charges. The grandparents pled guilty to assault in the second degree, received probation, and had to sign a court order promising not to cut children younger than age seventeen again. Jennifer Clegern, personal communication, 2000.

15. There is a voluminous literature on this subject. See, e.g., Lane and Rubinstein, "Judging the Other." Three different types of female circumcision are distinguished, varying in their degree of severity. For a more detailed description, see Huelsman, "Anthropological View." Women may have to endure surgery throughout life, for example, to permit sexual intercourse or childbirth. Sometimes husbands want them to be sewn up after delivery to enhance their own sexual pleasure. See also McLean and Graham, *Female Circumcision*, 6; Boulware-Miller, "Female Circumcision," 156; Toubia, "Female Genital Mutilation," 224. Information on prevalence comes from Brennan, "Cultural Relativism," 373, and Lyons, "Anthropologists," 500. One of the first laws specifically outlawing the custom was England's Female Circumcision Prohibition Act (1985). For background, see Renteln, "Cultural Defense Detrimental?"; Poulter, *English Law*; Sochart, "Agenda Setting." For information concerning U.S. laws, see Hughes, "Criminalization." For a synopsis of statutes, see Maguigan, "Prosecutions," 397–402.

16. McClean and Graham, *Female Circumcision*, 7–8; Koso-Thomas, *Circumcision of Women*, 5–14; Lyons, "Anthropologists." For a famous defense of clitoridectomy by Kenya's first president, see Kenyatta, *Facing Mount Kenya*. See also Funder, "De Minimis," and Gunning, "Arrogant Perception." Female genital surgery was an acceptable medical procedure in the United States during the nineteenth century. It was considered to be a cure for various ailments, including female masturbation, which was thought to cause insanity. Scull and Fabreau, "Clitoridectomy Craze."

17. Slack, "Female Circumcision," 445–450.

18. For a psychological analysis of their motivations, see Cathy Joseph, "Compassionate Accountability." See also Slack, "Female Circumcision, "472. Kenyatta claimed elites supported the practice.

19. For banning, see Rule, "Female Circumcision," and Favazza and Favazza, *Bodies under Siege*, 163. See also *Koykoy Jatta v. Menna Camara* (1964). International organizations were initially reluctant to intervene because of the deeply rooted cultural attitudes that would be challenged, and they were criticized for their silence. Slack's essay ("Female Circumcision") describes regional and national strategies. The Inter-African Committee on Traditional Practices Affecting the Health of Women and Children was created to support national efforts to abolish female circumcision and is an exemplar for human rights intervention.

20. Boulware-Miller, "Female Circumcision," 172. I have argued elsewhere (Renteln, *International Human Rights*, 56–58) that the people whose culture is being challenged on health grounds realize that the actual basis for Western criticism is one of moral superiority. See also Savane, "Against the International Campaign," 37, 39. Article 24(3) of the Convention on the Rights of the Child was drafted with, among others, female circumcision in mind. While the article does not explicitly mention female circumcision, the *travaux preparatoires* reveal that the article was intended to apply to it. Brennan, "Cultural Relativism," 394, n.135. See also LeBlanc, *Convention on Rights*, 85–89.

Some wealthy African families had their daughters circumcised by private surgeons in London. Favazza and Favazza, *Bodies under Siege*, 163, and Hayter, "Female Circumcision." Some commentators realize that the health argument is weakened if superior medical facilities are employed. They then shift to the argument that the operation is "unnecessary," at least from their point of view! Boulware-Miller, "Female Circumcision," 174, and Slack, "Female Circumcision," 466. Their other response is that health includes both physical and psychological harm. So, even if the adverse physical consequences can be avoided, they contend that the psychological effects remain. This argument assumes that this psychological harm is more damaging than failure to take part in a socially required rite of passage.

21. Information on France comes from Maguigan, "Prosecutions," 401. The defendants in France have typically been the parents, usually the mother, although the practitioner was

charged in three trials. The mothers may be "acting at the direction of the fathers, though not in their presence." Winter, "Women," 942. Sometimes parents were charged as accomplices. See Simons, "Prosecutor Fighting," "Mutilation," and "Eight-Year Sentence." Maguigan refers to the cultural defense as a "free-standing" defense. "Prosecutions." The French attorney is Weil-Curiel, "France," 9. "French authorities, meanwhile, defend their stand against excision on the grounds that ethnic heritage is no valid defense for those who maim children on French soil." Tempest, "Ancient Traditions," A10.

22. Weil-Curiel, "France," and Maguigan, "Prosecutions," 402. Some note a trend away from suspended sentences and toward "real jail time." Tempest, "Ancient Traditions."

23. The laws used the term "female genital mutilation," or FGM. There was even a controversy over a policy that authorized a hospital to make a symbolic cut. See Coleman, "Seattle Compromise." In the United States some members of Congress questioned whether a law was necessary in the absence of any evidence the custom was being followed within U.S. borders. To demonstrate the potential threat, the Centers for Disease Control and Prevention issued a report indicating the number of girls from countries that had the tradition; it then extrapolated the number of girls at risk of having the surgery performed. Wanda Jones et al., "Female Genital Mutilation." Some state laws were also enacted in the absence of empirical data, e.g., California where the justification for the law was an article in the *San Jose Mercury News* saying five women per year were treated at a hospital in San Jose for FGM. Jung, "Female Circumcision." The objective was to convey the message that "you cannot plead in aid as a defence that you did the operation for ritual or customary reasons." Baroness Jeger (debate in)Parliamentary House of Lords, 1985, HL vol 464, col 587). For a consideration of the consent defense in this context, see Cranfield and Cranfield, "Female Circumcision." The quotation is from Cranfield and Cranfield, "Female Circumcision," 816. The authors compare the practice to ritual scarification: if the consent of Adesanya's boys was no defense to that less serious bodily injury, then it should not serve as one in the case of female circumcision. The gist of their position seems to be that in the absence of a "medical" justification for a surgical procedure, consent should not be accepted as a defense. See also Hayter, "Female Circumcision," 327.

24. For a compilation of U.S. provisions, see Maguigan, "Prosecutions." For commentary on the law, see articles by Bashir, Crossette, Lenihan, Sharif, and Sussman. Commentators who take the view that it forbids cultural considerations are Messito, "Regulating Rites"; Edward Morgan, "Defence"; Terhune, "Cultural and Religious Defenses." The information on mens rea is from Maguigan, "Prosecutions," 408. One analyst argues that culture should mitigate punishment for a first offense only. Lori Larson, "Female Genital Mutilation," 248.

25. Kasinga fled Togo to avoid FGM and an arranged marriage (she would have been the fourth wife to a man three times her age). For background, see articles by Dugger. Although the immigration judge did not believe her story, she won her appeal. *In re Fauziya Kasinga v. U.S. Department of Justice* (1996). For her account of events, see Kassindrja and Bashir, *Do They Hear You?* See also Robert Jackson, "Unusual Asylum Case"; Coven, "Considerations"; Coyle, "Case."

In another case a court granted an asylum petition based on the fear of an individual being subjected to FGM. In *Abankwah v. INS* (1999), a twenty-nine-year-old women from the Nkumssa tribe of central Ghana sought asylum in the United States, but both the immigration judge and the Board of Immigration Appeals denied it. After the federal appellate court ruled that she had established a well-founded fear of FGM, it granted her petition. One issue was whether FGM was imposed as punishment for lack of virginity. Although the Board of Immigration Appeals noted the absence of written documentation on this point, the court accepted the applicant's testimony as sufficient. Subsequently Abankurah's petition was exposed as a hoax, and Regina Danson (who stole Abankwah's identity) was convicted of immigration fraud. See Geaberson, "Perjury Conviction." For general analyses, see Kelly, "Gender-Related Persecution," and Kelson, "Granting Political Asylum."

Aminata Diop from Mali sought asylum in France because her parents intended to have her circumcised before her arranged marriage. Talton, "Asylum," and Weil-Curiel, "Courageous Girl."

26. Winter, "Women," 957, and Maguigan,"Prosecutions," 394.

27. Maguigan, "Prosecutions," 406. The issue was raised in a case in which a husband sought an annulment because the circumcision made it impossible for the couple to consummate the marriage. Hansen and Scroggins, "Female Circumcision," and Kellner, "Under the Knife," 124. A district attorney in Georgia prosecuted a Somali woman for performing a clitoridectomy on her two-year-old niece. Lacayo, "'Cultural' Defense." A couple from India were charged for possible female genital mutilation. Abraham and Ellement, "Parents Charged." For criticism of the U.S. policy, see Dawit and Mecuria,"West." Some women of color both abroad and in the United States were offended that white Congresswomen took credit for the campaign, when African women had worked for decades to stop the tradition. Congresswoman Pat Schroeder anticipated this objection when she sponsored the bill. A member of her staff called the author to ask how to present the anti-FGM policy so that it would not be perceived as "cultural imperialism." For the legislative rationale, see Schroeder, "Female Genital Mutilation."

28. In the United States there are different views about its justifiability. See Roan, "Spank Your Kid?" and Gurza, "Spanking." As some groups customarily use harsh punishment to discipline their children, the question ultimately is how much is too much. The question about "when spanking ends and child abuse begins" remains "one of the central cultural clashes." Dugger, "Immigrant Cultures." In a Canadian case parents from Trinidad were prosecuted for assault causing bodily harm after they beat their fifteen-year-old daughter. The court explicitly said that in deciding whether the force was excessive, it would make reference to "the customs of the contemporary Canadian community" and that the standards of Trinidad "were not, therefore the appropriate test." *R. v. Baptiste and Baptiste* (1980).

29. For a similar U.S. example involving Michael Francis, a Jamaican immigrant, convicted of felony child abuse for disciplining his fourteen-year-old son with excessive force, see Louisna, "Discipline."

30. The judge assumes the validity of the claim, even though the use of physical punishment in the West Indies has been called into question there. See, e.g., Arnold, "Corporal Punishment." Quotation from *R. v. Derriviere* (1969), 639.

31. Shyllon, "Immigration," 139.

32. *R. v. Derriviere* (1969), 637.

33. Poulter, *English Law*, 148.

34. For a consideration of other discipline cases, see Renteln, "Cultural Defense Detrimental?"

35. *Dumpson v. Daniel M.* (1974). All quotations in this section are from the case. In addition to the shame caused by misconduct at school, the father said he was irked by his son's disrespect. Ekenediliz looked at the principal's face while they discussed his behavior.

36. It is surprising how little effort seems to have been made to ascertain what child discipline practices actually are in Nigeria. Articles on the subject suggest that such traditions are being reconsidered.

37. See Hugh Wright, "Father Sentenced." For a Canadian case where a Swiss father gave a cultural explanation for beating his daughters with a fishing rod, see Renteln, "Cultural Defense Detrimental?" In a Buffalo, New York, case a father (ethnicity unspecified) killed his son by beating him with an electrical cord. His attorney planned to raise a cultural defense based on "disciplinary methods used in the minority community." Simon, "Man Convicted."

For the discarded tradition, see Watanabe, "Sparing the Rod." When Young Lee, a Korean immigrant, was sentenced by a judge in Georgia to two years in prison for beating her stepdaughter, her supporters claimed canings "are a cultural tradition in Korea." A Korean-born police officer commented, "Even in Korean culture, it is beyond reasonable." Anon. (2000f), "'Tradition.'"

38. For instance, when child welfare officials mistakenly removed several children from an Iraqi family, the entire Arab community was outraged. Jeter, "Arab Family."

39. According to the father, his son Vourn was playing with a kitchen knife and stabbing the walls. In order to teach him not to be reckless, his father slapped the son's left hand with the dull end of the knife. Pimentel, "Culture Clash" and "Grieving Laotian Family."

40. Immigrant children learn quickly to call 911 to control their parents. Dugger, "Immigrant Cultures." Experts say that the emasculation of fathers is one reason why boys join gangs. It is remarkable that while courts reject the use of corporal punishment by families from different cultures, they countenance its use in public schools. In *Ingraham v. Wright* (1977), the Supreme Court held that paddling by a principal which led to severe bruises was not unconstitutional because the Eighth Amendment prohibition of cruel and unusual punishment does not apply to educational institutions.

41. Incidents have occurred throughout North America and England. See Hubler, "Foreign Customs"; Slonim, *Children*, 97–100; Griffin, "Coin Cure"; Barker, "Bad Circulation?"; J. A. Black, "Misdiagnosis"; McCullough, "Medical Conditions." On coining and cupping, see Sandler and Haynes, "Nonaccidental Trauma." Other types of folk medicine that might be interpreted as child abuse include spoon-scratching, nose-rubbing and skin-pinching, moxibustion, and lesions caused by the hot-cold theory of disease found in Latin American cultures. Leung, "Ecchymoses"; Kenneth Feldman, "Pseudoabusive Burns"; Lock, "Scars"; Nunez and Taff, "Chemical Burn." See also Primosch and Young, "Pseudobattering," and Yeatman et al., "Pseudobattering."

42. J. A. Black, "Misdiagnosis," 49.

43. Sandler and Haynes, "Nonaccidental Trauma," 921–922. Other physicians agree that the use of traditional remedies should not be treated as a form of child abuse, e.g., Gellis and Feingold, "Cao Gio"; Keller and Apthorp, "Folk Remedies," 1173; Primosch and Young, "Pseudobattering."

44. Those involved in these institutions do not always agree on how to interpret these methods of folk medicine. Although police do not always regard these practices as child abuse, they often take a noncriminal report and then admonish the family not to continue to use the techniques. If there is a second report for the same family, it could be treated as a criminal matter.

45. For these incidents, see Nguyen, "Culture Shock"; Leung, "Ecchymoses"; Yeatman and Dang, "Cao Gio."

46. In the 1970s the refugee press advised its readers not to use coining on persons they intended to take to the hospital. Tung, *Indochinese Patients*, 25.

47. *In re Jertrude O.* (1983). Quotations in this section are from the case.

48. J. A. Black, "Misdiagnosis," 48.

49. In a classic essay Weston LaBarre analyzes cultural variation in what constitutes unacceptable touching: "Even more striking, from our point of view, is that among the same Manchu who regard public kissing with such horror, it is quite customary for a mother to take the penis of her small son into her mouth and to tickle the genitals of her little daughter in petting them in public." "Obscenity," 266. See also Konker, "Child Sexual Abuse," 148.

A controversy surrounding Elian Gonzalez, the Cuban boy whose mother died while taking him to the United States, involved a grandmother who unzipped his pants. She reportedly said, "Let me see, let me see . . . if it has grown." Anon. (2000a), "Grandma's Report." His relatives denied this was a Cuban custom. Anon. (2000b), "Cuban Boy's Relatives." Anon. (2000c), "Elian's Miami Relatives." Though some deny that this is acceptable in the Latino culture, this argument has influenced the disposition of cases. See Gurza, "Concocting," and Lacayo, "'Cultural' Defense," 61.

For Albania, see Downs and Walters, "Want Our Children Back." For a detailed account of the Afghani case co-authored by his attorney, see Wanderer and Connors, "Culture and Crime," arguing for the adoption of de-minimis type statutes at the state and federal levels to avoid injustices in exceptional situations. The Cambodian case is discussed in Booth, "Culture Clash." The executive director of the Cambodian Association of Philadelphia explained: "It is very common among Cambodian males to touch each other's genitals. . . . There is nothing sexual to it. It is an ancient custom and a way of greeting. It's a way of being nice and friendly. This does exist in Cambodian tradition, and I'm sure the man was not doing anything sexual." That the boy was Caucasian and not a member of the defendant's ethnic group did not seem to concern the prosecutor, Ms. Liccardo. Chom pled guilty and was admonished not to do this again. The Eskimo case is in Toomey, "Eskimo Erotica?" After two anthropologists testified that the touching behavior was consistent with traditional Eskimo culture, the judge acquitted a defendant, Jack Jones, of all charges. A man from the Philippines was accused of illegally touching a child. Oscar Campomanas (1993, Oct. 28), Professor of English, University of California, Berkeley. *People v. Paule* (1993), Partial Testimony. In Seattle, a Pakistani father was accused of touching his young sons' genital areas when they were naked and clothed, blowing on their penises, and kissing their behinds and possibly their penises, all openly in front of the rest of the family. The prosecutor, Nicole MacInnes, consulted cultural anthropologists, knowledgeable about South Asia, one of whom emphasized this practice is "so common they don't write about it." E. Valentine Daniel, personal communication, 1988. On the basis of the cultural information the prosecutor decided to dismiss the charges against the defendant. Leslie Berger describes an incident where a father from an island near Taiwan kissed the vagina of his six-year-old daughter in front of relatives supposedly as part of a rite of passage from infancy to childhood. "Learning to Tell."

50. Child sexual abuse is a specific intent crime, meaning that the prosecution must show that the touching was for an illicit purpose. If the motive were not included, then parents would not be able to bathe their children. In the case of *State of Maine v. Kargar* (1996) discussed later in this chapter, the Maine legislature had changed the law so that it no longer required specific intent. Touching in and of itself constituted a crime. As a consequence, the defense had to use a de minimis statute as its strategy.

51. For a factual account of the case with an unsympathetic interpretation concerned primarily with critical race theory, see Brelvi, "News." Brelvi thinks the cultural defense may lead to stereotyping or "essentializing" ethnic groups. Mr. Krasniqi was advised to admit wrongdoing. Child Protective Services apparently told Mrs. Krasniqi that she should divorce her husband and retain custody of the children. Although she was not charged with any crime, she also lost her children. Paradysz, "U.M. Professor Testifies." Dr. Halpern was quoted as saying, "There's lots of kissing full on the lips, lots of hugging, lots of caressing, even fondling, what people might call fondling, but the important thing to understand is that there is no sexual intent." Downs and Walters, "Want Our Children Back."

52. The Krasniqis appealed the termination of their parental rights. Their lawyer failed to file a statement of facts by the time limit. The Texas Court of Appeals concluded that the rules prevented them from reviewing a late motion. *Krasniqi v. Dallas Cty. Child Protective Services* (1991). For more detail, see Schutze, "Albanian Cleared," and Hajrizi, "Court Takes Children." The judge said that the children might be better off in a Christian home, and that it might be more damaging to move them to a new home simply because the family was Muslim. Krasniqi claimed that the Albanian community did not support him and suspected they

envied his financial success. In another case, *Edwards v. County of Arlington* (1987), a Korean mother won a reversal of a trial court ruling that terminated her parental rights partly because of its failure to consider cultural barriers.

53. On appeal Kargar also argued that the conviction violated his constitutional rights to due process, freedom of religion, parental autonomy, and privacy, all of which the Maine Supreme Court declined to address. On one occasion the Kargar family was babysitting a young neighbor. When she told her mother that she had witnessed Kargar kiss his eighteen-month-old son's penis (her mother had seen a picture of this in the family photograph album), the mother notified the police. Kargar was separated from his family for a few years during the litigation. Quotations that follow are from *Kargar*.

For an analysis of the application of de minimis statutes to culturally motivated crimes, see Pomorski, "On Multiculturalism." The Model Penal Code 2.12 (1962) provides, "The Court shall dismiss a prosecution if, having regard to the nature of the conduct charged to constitute an offense and the nature of the attendant circumstances, it finds that the defendant's conduct: (1) was within a customary license or tolerance, neither expressly negatived by the person whose interest was infringed nor inconsistent with the purpose of the law defining the offense; or (2) did not actually cause or threaten the harm or evil sought to be presented by the law defining the offense or did so only to an extent too trivial to warrant the condemnation of conviction; or (3) presents such other extenuations that it cannot reasonably be regarded as envisaged by the legislature in forbidding the offense."

54. *Kargar*, 83.

55. Maine's provision permits the court to dismiss a prosecution if the defendant's conduct "presents such other extenuations that it cannot reasonably be regarded as envisaged by the Legislature in defining the crime" (*Kargar*, 83). Before 1985 the crime included sexual gratification, but the Legislature removed that element.

"Kargar does not argue that he should now be permitted to practice that which is accepted in his culture" (*Kargar*, 85, n.5). In fact, he stated publicly that he realized the tradition is unacceptable in the United States and hoped the publicity surrounding the case would "help other Afghani refugees avoid similar problems." Anon. (1996f), "Kissing Son's Genitals."

56. There are other sorts of neglect cases like the "stroller case." When a Danish mother, Anette Sorensen, was arrested for leaving her fourteen-month-old daughter in a stroller outside a Manhattan restaurant, she raised a cultural defense. Harden, "Child Parked." After the incident, "pictures wired from Denmark later showed strollers outside cafes in view of dining parents." Ojito. "Not in Denmark." Danish parents do this because their baby carriages are "enormous" and because Danish cafes are "very smoky places." Dyssegaard, "Danes." Some publicly attacked her cultural defense saying that the crime rate in New York was too high or "When in Rome . . .," or that in Denmark this practice does not occur in urban settings, only in rural areas. McCormick, "Leaving Baby"; Haberman, "Let It Snow"; Gibbs, "Ideas and Trends." One Dane wrote to the *New York Times* to say that even though her behavior was not in accordance with Danish norms, the police would simply have asked her to take the stroller inside the restaurant; she would not have been prosecuted. Larson, "Danish Child Care." Eventually all of the child endangerment charges were dropped on the condition that she leave the United States (Anon. 1997c, "Charges Dropped,") but not before the baby spent four days in foster care, and the parents two days in jail. After the mother was acquitted, the parents filed lawsuits seeking $60 million. Rohde, "Court Ruling." The jury awarded $66,000 for the strip search and the police failure to notify her of her right to contact the Danish Consulate. Bone, "41,000 Pounds," and Weiser, "Danish Mother's Claim." Some considered it gauche for her to sue, after she was treated leniently. David Chen, "City Is Sued." For a case in which a Korean woman argued that leaving children unattended is customary, see *State v. Chong Sun France* (1989) and commentary in Tomao, "Cultural Defense," and Volpp "(Mis)identifying Culture."

57. Although a dependency proceeding is not technically a trial, effectively the parent is on trial for having acted in a culturally motivated fashion, and the court can decide whether, because of that conduct, the child should be removed from the home. For this reason the analysis in the two situations is similar. Information on "adequate" medical care is from Holder, *Legal Issues*, 101.

58. In the past American courts did not authorize medical treatment in the absence of a life-threatening condition. That courts have moved away from a strict life-threatening standard is evidenced in a number of decisions. See Renteln, "Cultural Defense Detrimental?" For a discussion of *Cheng v. Wheaton* (1990), where the court ordered surgery for a child afflicted with severe juvenile rheumatoid arthritis, see Renteln, "Cultural Defense Detrimental?"

59. Kou's physician, Dr. Brian Shaw, was very much in favor of surgical intervention. Interestingly, his father, Dr. Anthony Shaw, was a member of the Bioethics Committee of the American Academy of Pediatrics. This committee issued a policy statement calling for the repeal of religious exemptions for parents who rely on faith healing to the detriment of the health of their children. Quotation from *In re Kou X.* (1990, Oct. 16), Minor's Brief, p. 11

60. Ethnographic studies confirm that some cultures often attribute illness to the transgressions of social norms. See, e.g., Rubel and Hass, "Ethnomedicine," 117.

61. The fact that no physician was willing to perform the surgery, even with the support of the legal system at every level, was proof to the Hmong of the validity of their position. Verla O'Donovan, personal communication, 1992.

62. Of course, in many cases the threat of legal action may, in fact, compel parents to consent to medical treatment. Korbin and Johnston cite a case in which a mother from Belize objected to treatment of her daughter who was diagnosed with meningitis, or sepsis. Although the mother initially took her daughter to the hospital, she "resisted the child's admission until threatened with legal action." "Resolving Cultural Conflict," 260. The law may be an effective tool, if an oppressive one.

63. It is noteworthy that the medical treatment of Xiong was such a divisive issue in Fresno. Normally, in Hmong society the effect of shamanistic healing rituals is to promote social cohesion. Chindarsi, "Hmong Shamanism," 191. For a moving account of another culture conflict involving a Hmong child with epilepsy, see Fadiman, *Spirit Catches You.* Information on the Hmong Council from Cha, letter to Mr. Ernest Velasquez, director of social services in Fresno. In the case of the Hmong the conflict over court orders for medical treatment is but one of many clashes they have had with American law. T. Christopher Thao, "Torn between Cultures."

64. See, e.g., Salsgiver, "Editorial." Quotation from *In re Kou X.* (1990, Oct. 16), Minor's Brief, p. 9.

65. For a case involving a teenage Hmong woman diagnosed with ovarian cancer who refused medical treatment, see Renteln, "Cultural Defense Detrimental?," and Arax, "Cancer Case." The mature minor doctrine sometimes allows older children to make their own decisions about treatment, even when the outcome is likely to be death.

66. See Bliatout, "Hmong Attitudes"; Deinard and Dunnigan, "Hmong Health Care"; Tou-Fu Vang, "Clash of Cultures"; Kraut, "Immigrant Attitudes." From the Hmong perspective all traditional methods of healing should be tried and only after they fail should Western physicians be consulted. On the afterlife, see Westermeyer and Thao, "Cultural Beliefs." Quotations from, respectively, Xoua Thao, "Cultural Beliefs," 3302, and McInnis, "Ethnic-Sensitive Work," 578. Information on murder-suicide from Berens, "Laotian Parents," and Tou-Fu Vang, "Clash of Cultures."

67. Quotation from Stratton, "Ailing Baby." See also Grabmeier, "Tot's Dad."

68. Kehres, "Laotian Baby."

69. Grabmeier, "Surgeons."

70. There is a large literature on this subject. See, e.g., Renteln, "Cultural Defense Detrimental?" Ordinarily faith healing is associated with Christian Scientists, but other groups also rely on it. For instance, Mexicans who practice *curanderismo* will seek the assistance of the *curandero* (folk healer) instead of a physician. See, e.g., Graham, "Role of Curandero"; Krajewski-Jaime, "Folk-Healing"; Marsh and Hentges, "Mexican Folk Remedies"; Charles Williams, "Persisting Cultural Values."

71. The statutory exemptions were enacted in 1974 initially by all states in response to a federal policy formulated by high-ranking Christian Scientists in the Nixon administration, which required states to adopt a religious exemption in order to receive federal funding for their state child abuse programs. Because of the federal policy many district attorneys were reluctant to prosecute parents, and appellate courts have been predisposed to overturn convictions. Gathings, "When Rights Clash," 591.

72. Florida and Massachusetts also reversed on due process grounds (in *Hermanson* v. *State* [1990, 1992] and *Commonwealth v. Twitchell* [1993], respectively), but the California Supreme Court rejected the notion that the statutes were in conflict in *Walker v. Superior Court* [1988]. The court thought the misdemeanor child neglect exemption did not apply to felony child neglect and involuntary manslaughter because the laws had differing objectives. In *Twitchell* the Massachusetts Supreme Court, citing *Walker*, did not view the faith-healing exemption and manslaughter laws as being in conflict (i.e., no "mixed signal"), but accepted the parents' argument that they had read a Christian Science church publication that misrepresented an attorney general opinion; they mistakenly believed that they need not take their child to the doctor. Although reliance on wrong official information may be an exception to "ignorance of the law is no excuse" rule, it may have been improper to apply it in this context: "The Court has applied the reasonable reliance doctrine only where the defendant actually relied on an official's misrepresentation [not a private party's misrepresentation of a government position]." Rosato, "Square Pegs," 89.

73. *State v. McKown* (1991), 67.

74. *State v. McKown*, 68. Much of the opinion is concerned with the relationship between the child neglect statute and the second-degree manslaughter statute and whether they are *in pari materia*, a doctrine which holds that statutes with a common purpose must be interpreted in light of one another.

75. Quotation from Malecha, "Faith Healing Exemptions," 253. For a historical overview of religious defenses in the United States, see Trescher and O'Neill: "Where a statute is held to impose a specific duty to provide medical care there has been no difficulty in overruling a defense predicated on religious beliefs." "Medical Care," 212. See also Abraham, "Religion"; Keefe, "Failure"; Anon. (1921), "Homicide," 1146–1150; Anon. (1965), "Homicide."

Because the Free Exercise clause would not excuse criminal conduct, even if religiously inspired, defense attorneys in Christian Science cases have tried to advance an argument based on *U.S. v. Ballard*, 322 U.S. 78 (1944). There, the Supreme Court held that evaluating the "reasonableness" of a defendant's religious beliefs violates the Free Exercise clause (although a jury may decide if the defendant was "sincerely" following his beliefs). In this way, attorneys hoped to prevent jurors from deciding the case based on whether or not they felt the defendants were acting rationally.

76. The famous precedent in American constitutional law, *Prince v. Massachusetts* (1943) (though it concerns child labor), is often cited in faith-healing cases but seemingly to no avail: "Parents may be free to become martyrs for themselves. But it does not follow that they are free, in identical circumstances, to make martyrs of their children before they have reached the age of full and legal discretion where they can make a choice for themselves" (170). This quote seems particularly apt in the light of evidence that in some cases the parents allowed themselves the benefit of modern medicine but denied it to their children. An article on the

subject of religious exemptions in *JAMA* (*Journal of the American Medical Association*) questions the double standard for adults and children: "The church declines to explain its 'theological and pragmatic reasons' for allowing dental care and pain medication while denying medical care for severely ill children." Skolnick, "Religious Exemptions," 1226. Christian Scientists consult physicians for dental problems, eyeglasses, setting bones, and the delivery of babies. Shelli Robinson, "*Twitchell*," 425.

77. In many of the cases it would have been a simple matter to save the lives of the children who were visibly ill; see, e.g., *State v. Miskimens* (1984), 938.

78. In some of the best-known cases convicted parents have only been sentenced to probation.

79. The entire conflict might be avoided if Christian Scientists could be convinced that faith healing and modern medicine are not mutually incompatible. Of course, this is precisely the problem.

80. Faith-healing exemptions may be held constitutionally invalid because they constitute an establishment of religion. To date this argument has not been a salient one in the faith-healing litigation. They may violate equal protection in two ways. See *State v. Miskimens*.

Many have called for the repeal of faith-healing exemptions. This would enable parents to avoid religious pressures: "It may provide an 'easy way out' for sect members who do not want to admit to a 'lack of faith' by resorting to medical treatment for the children. If parents were legally required to seek medical treatment for their children, they could overcome the pressure to conform to the dogma of their faith by blaming their actions on secular law." Malecha, "Faith Healing Exemptions," 260. Since religiously observant parents tend to be law-abiding, if the law were clear that they must provide medical treatment to their children in addition to faith healing, it seems likely that they would comply. Moreover, most of the court opinions in the faith-healing cases make it clear that, were it not for the existence of the exemptions, most of the parents would be convicted. A useful suggestion is that the federal policy reverse its earlier damage by requiring the removal of exemption (and substituting the requirement that "all states recognize that withholding medical care from a child where death or serious bodily injury is likely to result constitutes neglect") to qualify for federal funding (262). The American Academy of Pediatrics has officially opposed the exemptions and waged a campaign to lobby legislatures to repeal them. Other interest groups such as the American Medical Association have also taken a position against them. One leading group in this campaign is CHILD (Children's Healthcare Is a Legal Duty), whose president is Dr. Rita Swan (a former Christian Scientist turned activist after her infant died of bacterial meningitis).

81. An additional question is what to do with the faith healer. Cawley called it a "glaring anomaly in the law" that parents are prosecuted while the faith healer goes free. "Criminal Liability," 74. It is striking that the parents in most faith-healing cases are either acquitted or receive probation or suspended sentences: "The failure to uphold such criminal convictions may reflect judicial sympathy for those whose religious beliefs result in tragedy." Malecha, "Faith Healing Exemptions," 257. These legal maneuvers occur despite the fact that the state's official policy is to value the life of the child over the religious freedom of parents. Anyone who investigates the literature on faith healing will be struck by the determination of most courts to avoid punishing parents too severely; losing a child is considered to be punishment enough. Even those who advocate retention of exemptions maintain that court-ordered intervention is less intrusive than criminal prosecutions subsequent to the child's death. Christine Clark, "Religious Accommodation," 580; but see *Walker v. Superior Court* (1988), 140.

82. Quotation from Gray and Cosgrove, "Ethnocentric Perception," 391. See Korbin, "Anthropological Contributions," 11–13.

83. Joseph Goldstein, "Medical Care," and Joseph Goldstein et al., *Best Interests*.

84. Areen, *Family Law*, 888, 918.

85. I recognize that those who defend the tradition will deny that the change is a "harm."

86. Although intervention is not to be judged by criminal law requirements, nevertheless there may be conceptual problems akin to those associated with inchoate crimes if the state intervenes.

87. The commentator is Probst, "Conflict," 182. See *State v. Williams* (1971) where a child died when parents neglected to obtain medical treatment for a toothache because "of fear that the Welfare Department would take the baby away from them."

88. Todd Taylor argues that motive is irrelevant in child abuse and neglect cases. "Cultural Defense," 364.

89. An alternative to the legal system exists in Seattle, where Child Protective Services hired a "cultural-relevancy" specialist whose function was to train child-welfare caseworkers and to inform parents that they must abandon traditional disciplinary methods and folk medicine. Serrano, "Cultures Clash." The commentators are Korbin and Johnston, "Resolving Cultural Conflict." Australian psychiatrists describe the case of a Cambodian adolescent with cancer whose family accepted Western treatment. Eisenbruch and Handelman, "Cultural Consultation," 1298.

CHAPTER 5

1. This chapter discusses intoxicants or "substances that alter the state of consciousness": hallucinogens (peyote and marijuana), stimulants (khat), and hypnotics including kava and narcotics (opium and heroin). Rudgley, *Alchemy*, 7–8. For purposes, see Edwards et al., *Drug Use*; Dobkin de Rios, *Hallucinogens*; Furst, *Hallucinogens and Culture*; Adrian, "Substance Abuse." Quotation on "integral" from Sherratt, "Alcohol," 34.

2. The quotation on "boundary" is from Jordan Goodman et al., *Consuming Habits*, x. See also Rudgley, *Essential Substances*. The quotation on framing is from Berridge, "Drug Policy," 301.

3. The interpreter for the Somalian defendants charged with possession of khat in *State v. Ali* (2000) (discussed later in this chapter) told the public defenders that "no one believes it is illegal." Renee Bergeron, personal communication, 2000.

4. Khat is also known as *qat*. According to John Kennedy in his erudite work, *Flower of Paradise* (12–13), *qat* is a more accurate transliteration, though *khat* is the most common spelling in the English language; other variants are *kat, cat, kaht,* or *quat*. It is known as *chat* in Ethiopia and Somalia (*tschat* or *ciat*) and in Kenya as *miraa* or *marongi*, as well as other indigenous names. The scientific name for khat is *Catha edulis*. Though it has been used for centuries, the first scientific report on it was in the eighteenth century by botanist Peter Forskal, who gave it its name. Baasher, "Use of Khat." For a popular book on khat chewing in Yemen, see Rushby, *Flowers of Paradise*. Americans may associate khat with Somali gunmen in Mogadishu. Anon. (2000d), "Police Arrest." There was some mention in the press of concern that U.S. soldiers were chewing khat. Gunby, "US Military."

"In some countries khat is considered even as the rival of coffee." Balint et al., "*Catha edulis*," 555.

For a detailed description of khat's effects ("the khat syndrome"), see Kalix, "Khat: A Plant," and "Pharmacology." See also Krikorian, "Kat"; Louis Harris, *Problems of Drug Dependence*; "Satellite Session on Khat"; Randrianame et al., *Khat Use*; Nencini and Ahmed, "Khat Consumption." One expert says khat "induces a euphoric and elated state characterized by joviality, hilarity, and garrulous behavior that may culminate in logorrhoea." In some individuals it can lead to hostile, aggressive behavior. Kalix, "Khat: A Plant," 166.

5. See, respectively, Zack, "Khat Tests," and Weir, "Drug-War Aim." In Canada six to ten branches cost 90 cents to $60, varying according to quality. Donna Abu-Nasr, "Yemenis

Addicted." More than seventy thousand tons were seized in the United States in 2000. Saeed Ahmed, "Light Buzz." Canadian customs officials seized a ton of khat in April 2000. Anon. (2000e), "Khat Bust," and Anon. (2000i), "Customs." Some have speculated that "khat usage may spread and become a problem in the Western world." Giannini and Castellani, "Psychosis," 458.

On England, see Poulter, *Ethnicity, Law and Human Rights*, 375. Legislation to limit its sale and distribution was under consideration because of the greatly increased presence of khat in the United Kingdom. Doherty et al., "Fascioliasis." It is used in Italy. Nencini et al., "Khat Chewing." On immigrant communities, see Griffiths et al., "Transcultural Pattern."

6. Some scholars deny charges of negative effects; for example, Kennedy in *Flower of Paradise*, the definitive study of the subject, disputes many of the adverse health claims. Baasher, "Use of Khat," 47. Coffee was not always mainstream. Sherratt, "Alcohol," 16 and 37 n.29. A 1999 survey of rural Ethiopians found the main incentive for chewing khat was to improve concentration for prayer. Alem et al., "Khat Chewing."

7. Taqy claimed, however, not to chew it himself. Donna Abu-Nasr, "Yemenis Addicted." Quotations from Kennedy, *Flowers of Paradise*, 90, and Kandela, "Women's Rights," 1437, respectively. According to Kandela, at least 80 percent of men, 60 percent of women, and increasing numbers of children younger than ten chew khat. See also Luqman and Danowski. "Use of Khat." See Mengel et al., "Peridontal Status." More than 50 percent of women in Yemen chew qat on a regular basis, and they have their own meeting places and qat sessions known as *tafrita*. Kennedy, *Flowers of Paradise*, 98. For an elaborate description of the traditions associated with qat use in Yemen, see Kennedy's chap. 4.

8. In 1935 the League of Nations discussed khat in its Advisory Committee on the Traffic of Dangerous Drugs. An Expert Committee of the World Health Organization (WHO) took the view that it should be treated like amphetamines, despite the drug's different effects. In 1975 the U.N. Narcotics Laboratory isolated cathinone in khat. Kalix, "Khat: A Plant," 163. In 1973 WHO put khat in the category of "dependence-producing drugs." Randall, "Khat Abuse." For the report of the WHO expert advisory group which met in 1978 in Madagascar, see *Bulletin on Narcotics* (1981).

9. Khat contains several phenylethylamines including cathine (d-norpseudoephredrine) and cathinone (1-a-aminopropiophenone). Silverman and Shargel, "Phenylpropanolamine." Quotation from Karch, *Pathology*, 193. On mood, see Paul Griffiths et al., "Transcultural Pattern." On anexoria, see Giannini et al., "Khat." On staring, see Luqman and Danowski, "Use of Khat," 249. For discussion of the manic-like psychosis, see, e.g., Giannini and Castellani, "Psychosis," and Alem and Shibre, "Khat Induced Psychosis." On dental implications, see Mengel et al., "Peridontal Status," and Hill and Gibson, "Oral and Dental Effects." Kennedy found no support for the thesis that khat chewing has a negative effect on the "oral cavity" and cites evidence that its use has a cleansing effect on the teeth. *Flower of Paradise*, 222–223.

10. Kennedy challenges this as an unfounded assumption, saying that although "outsiders have been nearly unanimous in asserting that the Yemenis are massively 'addicted to qat' . . . [a] search of the literature revealed that these statements reflect no grounding in research, but rather are founded on prejudice and on the obvious fact, apparent to any visitor to Yemen, that qat is found everywhere in the country, and that it provides a major focus of interest to a high proportion of Yemenis." *Flower of Paradise*, 189. He suggests that social pressures account for its use, a factor downplayed by other studies (210).

11. Another attempt at regulation occurred in 1972 but because of violent resistance, it was repealed shortly thereafter. Baasher, "Use of Khat," 49. For a balanced consideration of regulation, see Kalix, "Khat: Scientific Knowledge." On farmland, see Kandela, "Women's Rights." On banning for government use, see Donna Abu-Nasr, "Yemenis Addicted." On the president, see Hays, "Yemeni Drug." Officially the government supports anti-khat groups such

as the Friends without Khat association and the Society to Fight the Effects of Khat, which were established with the support of Western aid organizations. The president still chews khat, however.

12. Early in 1992 the DEA placed it into Schedule 1 of the Controlled Substances Act. Goldstone, "'Cat.'" On the attorney general, see. Pine, "Local Hedges." On the Brooklyn case, see Hays, "Yemeni Drug." The attorney for one of the defendants said that if the case went to trial, he would not raise a "cultural defense" because it is not recognized at law. He would, however, argue that (1) khat is relatively harmless, (2) it is widely used in Yemen, and (3) it is not generally known to be an illegal substance. This would be part of an appeal for jury nullification. Though the arguments form the basis of a cultural defense, he was reluctant to designate it as such. James Palumbo, personal communication, 2000.

On the plantation, see Hays, "Yemeni Drug." There have been other prosecutions, some in Georgia and one federal case in Michigan. Saeed Ahmed, "Light Buzz."

13. The case was *State v. Mohamed Galony Ali et al.* (2000). In this opinion the court notes that khat contains both cathine and cathinone, both of which are controlled substances under Minnesota law. The precise question was, "Must the state prove that the amount of cathinone possessed by a defendant is in a quantity 'having a stimulant effect' in order to support a charge for possession of cathinone, a controlled substance under Minn. Stat. S 152–02, subd. 2(6) (1998)?" This "certified" question had to be answered before the trial could take place.

Quotation from Zack, "Khat Tests." Also: "We conclude that the district court properly denied defendants' motions to dismiss because the statute prohibits the possession of cathinone regardless of whether the amount present is sufficient to produce a stimulant effect." *State v. Mohamed Galony Ali et al.* (2000).

In 2000 a Connecticut appellate court affirmed the conviction of a defendant for possession and sale of khat. It rejected his arguments that the state law did not apply to khat and that he had not received adequate notice that the law was interpreted as applying to khat. State regulations mentioned cathinone and cathine, chemical constituents of khat, but not khat itself. *State v. Gurreh* (2000). For a similar argument on the question of whether a defendant knew he possessed a controlled substance, see the decision of a federal district court in Maine. *U.S. v. Hussein* (2002).

14. Although the argument of cultural bias was not advanced in the pretrial motions, it is conceivable that a cultural defense might be presented at trial. The defendants did not realize that chewing khat was illegal in the United States, or they had been told but simply could not believe it. Renee Bergeron, personal communication, 2000. Weil quoted in Pine, "Local Hedges." Most foreigners visiting Yemen tended to view khat as a "pernicious influence—an evil habit which should be rooted out." Kennedy, *Flower of Paradise*, 13. "It is primarily foreigners who have proclaimed the harmful health effects of qat, though some Yemeni intellectuals are of the same opinion" (213). See the intriguing interpretation of the debate on "scientific" research in Cassanelli, "Qat."

15. Forster established kava in botany by calling it *Piper methysticum*, an intoxicating pepper. Deihl, "Kava." The seminal treatise on kava was published in 1886 by Lewin. It has continued to be the subject of numerous popular, medical, and anthropological works. For a popular discussion, see Kilham, *Kava*. For ethnographic studies, see, e.g., Lebot et al., *Kava*; Brunton, *Abandoned Narcotic*; Singh, *Kava: A Bibliography*.

Piper methysticum is said to be a close relative of the black pepper plant, which produced a drink with a "slight peppery bite." It is an extract of an Australasian shrub, a member of the pepper family which has been used by South Pacific islanders for over three thousand years. It is made from "the chewed, pounded, or grated root of *Piper methysticum* mixed with water.... Chewing is the most common method of preparation. This is often done by boys, uninitiated men, or young virgins (as in Samoa) to whom formal consumption of the beverage may be denied." Mac Marshall, "Drugs in Oceania," 23. Brunton explains that the requirement that a virgin prepare the kava derives from the belief that "once a man had had sexual contact with a woman, he should never directly touch anything that would be consumed either by himself or by others." *Abandoned Narcotic*, 98.

Regarding ceremonial use: "Four lactones from kava (kavain, dihydrokavain, methysticin, and dihydromethysticin) have been found to possess significant analgesic effects in animal studies." Anon. (1998b), "*Piper methysticum*." It is used for anesthesia, but too high a dose can lead to temporary paralysis. It contains kawain, yangonin, and methysticin, known as kavalactones. Ives, "Make Mine Kava."

Kava drinking has been found throughout Polynesia except for New Zealand (the Maori had trouble growing it but used an alternative). The most important centers of kava drinking have been Fiji, Samoa, and Tonga. Singh and Blumenthal, "Kava: An Overview." It is consumed in Hawaii where it is known as 'awa. Titcomb, "Kava." See also Enge, "Few Cups."

Lindstrom, an anthropologist, described kava as being "like a folk Valium." Quoted in Enge, "Few Cups." Ives also likens kava's effect to Valium, saying, "Although all individuals react differently to kava (some people feel slightly sedated, whereas others experience enhanced concentration and mental alertness), the effect also depends on which product you take, as they all contain varying amounts of kava. However, within an hour, most people tend to experience feelings of peace and contentment." "Make Mine Kava." Goodman et al. refer to kava (along with alcohol and tobacco) as a "mild intoxicant." *Consuming Habits*, 16. See also Cawte, "Psychoactive Substances," 85.

Kava is a possible treatment for depression and anxiety. McCarthy, "New Antidepressants"; Buckley, "Pharmacology of Kava"; Pittler and Ernst, "Efficacy of Kava Extract"; Pepping," Kava."

16. Quotation on "tranquillity" from Kilham, *Kava*, 64. He goes on to distinguish kava from alcohol, heroin, and prescription sedatives, noting that it does not cause violent behavior or hangover, incapacitate the user, or lead to addiction. Quotation on "peace" from Lebot et al., *Kava*, 138. The book emphasizes that Pacific Islanders never drink alone, always in a social context. Because of this, social pressures discourage abuse of kava.

On medicinal uses, see Kilham, *Kava*, 98. It has been compared favorably to benzodiazepines. It may enhance the quality of sleep and serve as a centrally acting muscle relaxant. Most of its pharmacologic effects are attributed to kavalactones. Pepping, "Kava," 957. It is also considered beneficial for the treatment of menopause. Kass-Annese, "Alternative Therapies." It has also served as a treatment for controlling pain, a diuretic, for asthma, rheumatism, headaches and fever, and bladder infections. Mac Marshall, "Drugs in Oceania.," 25. It is called an "herbal superstar" in Ives, "Make Mine Kava." Kava is served in several drinks such as smoothies in the Kava Lounge in New York where the menu says it tastes like "dirty dishwater with a hint of cloves." It has also enjoyed a resurgence of interest in the Pacific Islands. Lebot et al., *Kava*, 198.

17. For the cultural meanings of the ritual, see James Turner, "Water of Life"; Lebot et al., *Kava*, 121–138; Leach, "Structure of Symbolism"; Bott, "Psychoanalysis and Ceremony"; Collocott, "Kava Ceremonial." See the discussion of politics in Mac Marshall, "Drugs in Oceania," 24. Historically ceremonial drinking of kava was associated with royalty. Cowling, "Kava Drinking," 40. Kava has to be drunk in sufficient quantities so as to have power, or *mana*.

18. At one time in Hawaii commoners who were caught drinking kava received the death penalty. Singh and Blumenthal, "Kava: An Overview." For kava etiquette, see Holmes, "Function of Kava." On hierarchy, see James Turner, "Water of Life," 206. Tongans have three types of kava drinking: (1) *taumafa kava*, the Queen's kava; (2) *ilo kava*, nobles' kava; and (3)

fai-kava, kava for commoners. Lemert, "Secular Use," 329. Mac Marshall comments that the gender restriction on consumption is the "single most striking thing about kava use in Oceania." "Drugs in Oceania," 28. Rudgley notes that "historically, the use of kava is indeed a male prerogative." *Alchemy*, 132. This is consistent with the general point that the kava circle is based on power relations, and in kava communities, as elsewhere, women lack political power. Titcomb notes that Hawaiian women were seldom allowed to drink 'awa in the presence of men. "Kava," 128. For discussion of sexual imagery associated with kava, see Lebot et al., *Kava*, 132–138, and Bott, "Psychoanalysis and Ceremony." Mac Marshall notes that the restrictions on kava use are all the more impressive when one recognizes that other substances such as betel and tobacco are used by nearly everyone in Pacific societies, including young children. "Drugs in Oceania," 28.

19. Deihl distinguishes among different types of kava, noting that the kava plant in Hawaii is a stronger type than the Samoan kava, which is one of the mildest. "Kava," 63. The other study is reported in Anon. (1998b), "*Piper methysticum*," and Norton and Ruze, "Kava Dermopathy." Interestingly, the Tongan myth, which explains the origin of kava, involves a leprous female child. See James Turner, "Water of Life," 211. On poison and death, see Brunton, *Abandoned Narcotic*, 87–90. One effect mentioned in the literature is "the extinction of sexual desire." Lemert, "Secular Use," 333.

20. Hellmich, "Foods with Kava."

21. See de Turenne, "Kava Tea." One writer says that at a "normal session" in Vanuatu a man drinks three cups. Cawte, "Psychoactive Substances," 85. The potencies of different kava vary by type, however.

Piutau was charged with violating Vehicle Code section 23152: "(a) It is unlawful for any person who is under the influence of any alcoholic beverage or drug, or under the combined influence of any alcoholic beverage and drug, to drive a vehicle." See also Vehicle Code section 312: "The term 'drug' means any substance or combination of substances, other than alcohol, which could so affect the nervous system, brain, or muscles of a person as to impair, to an appreciable degree, his ability to drive a vehicle in the manner that an ordinarily prudent and cautious man, in full possession of his faculties, using reasonable care, would drive a similar vehicle under like conditions." The case went to trial in September 2000. The defense attorney, Scott Ennis, had experts testify as part of a cultural defense. Scott Ennis, personal communication, 2000.

Some studies have found that kava did not slow reaction time but "actually enhanced performance." Anon. (1998b), "*Piper methysticum*," 459. Dr. Samuel Benjamin, director of the Center for Complementary and Alternative Medicine at the State University of New York in Stony Brook, who gives kava to patients who are suffering bereavement and insomnia, doubts whether it is addictive. Quoted in Ives, "Make Mine Kava." See also Marshall Wilson, "Driver Busted." Ennis thought his client was a victim of a "profile stop"—that is, stopped because he fit the "racial profile" of an offender. Quoted in Enge, "Few Cups."

See Stannard, "Mistrial." In November 2000, the prosecutor was preparing for a second kava prosecution. Although the first prosecution resulted in a mistrial, it nevertheless had the effect of stopping kava klatches after services at one congregation. Marimow, "DA Targets."

22. One ethnographic study found that Tongans were surprised that kava was considered to be a drug of addiction. Cowling, "Kava Drinking," 40.

23. See Gregory et al., "Vanuatu." Kava is a "symbol of opposition." The Western Australian government limited access to kava during consideration of adding kava to the State Poison Act.

24. Anon. (2000h), "U.S. Pledges." In California, although voters passed the Compassionate Use Act to permit patients to grow marijuana with a doctor's recommendation, the Justice Department has threatened to revoke doctors' licenses to dispense medication.

25. Parvin was known as the "Al Capone of San Francisco" and key to the California heroin supply. The court said, "As for a Persian doctor, even if we were to assume that he could testify to the existence of various herbal preparations of medications used in Iran for cancer, petitioner would not be significantly aided, for it is common knowledge that different cultures use different substances for medicinal purposes." *U.S. v. Tajeddini* (1991), 466. The appellate court considered his *pro se* appeals twice, eventually rejecting all of his arguments. *U.S. v. Tajeddini* (1993).

26. For an interesting discussion of one such case, *U.S. v. Kouay and Kao Vurn Saeturn* (1992), see Olabisi Clinton, "Cultural Differences." Another opium case is mentioned in Bishop, "Asian Tradition." See also *Nhia Bee Vue v. INS* (1995) in which a Hmong shaman was convicted of importing 412 grams of opium and of possession with intent to distribute. Though he served only eighteen months of a three-year sentence, he faced deportation upon his release. The Ninth Circuit reversed, finding that the immigration judge and the Board of Immigration Appeals failed to consider his particular circumstances: "Although traditional drug use in another country does not wholly justify use of the drug in this country, the fact remains that Vue is not a garden variety opium user or dealer, a fact that would mitigate against deportation where the deportee faces certain persecution and probable death upon his return." The court was impressed that Vue understood that opium use of any kind was illegal in the United States and had promised to refrain from using it in the future. In *U.S. v. Blong Her* (1984) an elderly Hmong man and his son were charged with possessing opium for distribution. Charges against the son, Blong Her, were dropped because the judge could not determine his age; the birth certificate stating he was older than eighteen was unreliable. The father (Ya Her) pled guilty in exchange for a sentence without jail time; the plea was based partly on the belief that Ya Her would kill himself if he were jailed. Sherman, "Cultures Collide."

This does not mean, however, that opium is not addictive. Westermeyer, e.g., says that some addicts function well, at least for the first few years of addiction. *Poppies*, 283–284. See *U.S. v. Koua Thao* (1983), 369. The Court of Appeals found insufficient evidence to support the mail and importation charges but upheld the possession and intent to distribute charges.

27. The appellate court agreed that the "cultural departure" argument was a "red herring" because the defense failed to prove a factual basis for it. The appellate court also had to decide whether the Khangs could receive a downward departure for accepting responsibility at the same time as an enhancement for obstruction of justice. In the absence of authority on the question of whether a defendant is disqualified from receiving a responsibility reduction when apparently lying about motive, the court allowed the reduction for acceptance of responsibility "where the lie would not establish a defense to the crime or avoid criminal liability." *U.S. v. Khang* (1994), 80.

28. *U.S. v. Todd Linh Vonsay* (1993); *U.S. v. Rubio-Villareal* (1991, 1992) (district court excluded expert testimony in case involving Mexican defendant for drug offenses); *U.S. v. Ruelas-Altamirano* (1972) (per curiam); *U.S. v. Hoac* (1993) (district court excluded cultural evidence in case involving Chinese convicted of heroin importation because expert's limited knowledge of defendant would not aid the jury).

See, e.g., *U.S. v. Vue* (1994), where the appellate court found a violation of due process ("an insurmountable challenge") because the trial allowed "testimony concerning the likelihood of the involvement in opium smuggling of persons of Hmong descent." Even though the appellate court thought the evidence was sufficient to sustain the convictions, it reversed because the error was not harmless. Evidence linking defendants to crimes because of their background is wrong because it is either irrelevant or prejudicial. See, e.g., *U.S. v. Doe* (1990), where the court excluded evidence concerning the proclivity of Jamaicans to be involved in the drug market.

29. Foster, "Annotation." Other groups have also litigated to win the right to use marijuana for religious purposes. Mostly the courts find that the right is outweighed by the government interest in regulating the use and distribution of drugs. For cases involving the Ethiopian Zion Coptic Church, see *U.S. v. Middleton* (1982), *U.S. v. Hudson* (1970), and *Town v. State ex rel. Reno* (1979). For Tantric Buddhism, see *State v. Rocheleau* (1982).

30. *Lophophora williamsii* is the scientific name for peyote (Aztec term, *peyotl*). Peyote is made from parts of a small spineless cactus, which contains mescaline as well as more than thirty other alkaloids. Furst, *Hallucinogens and Culture*, 111. In the literature there is a debate about whether it is a narcotic. Barber, "Peyote," and Stewart, "Peyote." Indigenous groups such as the huichols have their own systems of plant taxonomy. Schaefer, "Crossing of Souls." For some of the major studies, see Edward Anderson, *Peyote*; La Barre, *Peyote Cult*; Meyerhoff, *Peyote Hunt*; Steinmetz, *Pipe*. See also the classic, Stewart, *Peyote Religion*. For a succinct overview of peyote law, see Stewart. "Peyote and the Law."

Quotation on exaltation from Lowie, "Peyote Rite." Peyote is sometimes confused with mescal bean or button, which comes from a different plant; peyote is a far milder intoxicant. Stewart surmises that American confuse the nomenclature of the two plants because they both grew in the same location. *Peyote Religion*, 4–6. See also Furst, *Hallucinogens and Culture*, 112. It is sometimes consumed as tea. Haddad et al., "Peyote and Mescaline."

Some experts have questioned whether peyote has any harmful effects: "Although chemically a narcotic, peyote is not habit-forming and as used by the Indians is not harmful." Stewart, "Peyote," 700. "Lethal overdoses of mescaline have never been reported, nor have there been any reports of medical complications with its use." Karch, *Pathology*, 244. But others assumed it is dangerous. Efron et al., *Ethnopharmacologic Search*, 21–23.

In 1965 Congress amended the Federal Food, Drug, and Cosmetic Act to limit use of depressant and stimulant drugs including peyote, except "its use in connection with the ceremonies of a bona fide religious organization." Stewart, *Peyote Religion*, 4.

31. In the scholarship there has been considerable discussion of the origin of the drug. Stewart reviews the data, concluding that "the evidence is strongly in favor of finding the Carrizo to be the originators of the peyote ceremony." *Peyote Religion*, 49. It should be noted that most Indians in the United States and Canada are not Peyotists. William Powers, *Peyote Road*, 772. On reservations, see Autumn Gray, "Effects," 774, and Edward Anderson, *Peyote*, 35. From the confluence of cultures, peyote folklore emerged. For example, James Howard, "Peyote Jokes." Although the Peyotist religion may have appealed to some because of its "Indian" character, it is replete with Christian symbolism. See Hultkrantz's excellent study, *Attraction of Peyote*, 147–158. Perhaps a conscious effort was made to include Christian motifs in order to win legal protection. See Autumn Gray, "Effects," 775.

Quotation from Bannon, "Legality," 478. With the assistance of anthropologist James Mooney, the church was established to thwart the anti-Peyotists forces, including the Bureau of Indian Affairs. Hultkrantz, *Attraction of Peyote*, 195. In 1997 the Native American Church (NAC) reported its total membership as 250,000 people from fifty tribes. Brooke, "Military Ends Conflict," and William Powers, "North American Indians."

32. Because peyote was viewed as a threat, the Inquisitors condemned its use as heretical in violation of Catholic tenets. Stewart, *Peyote*, 20–25. The Mexican government continues to interfere in peyote rituals, despite constitutional and international human rights provisions. Anon. (1998d), "Indians Jailed." Peyote was banned by government agents in 1888 and by fifteen states. One absurd strategy was to classify peyote as an intoxicant. Since Congress had prohibited anything that would intoxicate Indians, this theoretically allowed officials to ban peyote. Indians easily won the two cases that challenged this interpretation of peyote. Sometimes tribes themselves tried to outlaw the use of peyote. Stewart, "Peyote and the Law," 46. Anti-Peyotists argued that government had a responsibility to ensure the assimilation of

downtrodden Native Americans by ridding them of ignorance and superstition. They also thought peyote was a sexual stimulant whose use led to orgies. Edward Anderson, *Peyote,* 191–192.

Congress made provision for religious use when it outlawed peyote generally in the 1965 Drug Abuse Control Amendments Act. Anon. (1990a), "Must Say No." In 1971 a federal regulation exempted the NAC from the Controlled Substances Act of 1970. See Native American Church, 21 C.F.R. section 1307.31. The American Indian Religious Freedom Act in principle afforded protection but lacked real enforcement mechanisms. See Beeson, "Dances," 1163.

I will not review the entire history of U.S. hostility to Peyotism here. Those who wish more detail should consult Stewart's definitive study, *Peyote Religion.* For a case reflecting a lack of sympathy, see *Native American Church of Navajoland, Inc. v. Arizona Corporation Commission* (1972).

33. For reversal of convictions, see, e.g., *Whitehorn v. State* (1977) and *McFate v. State of Arizona* (1961). Lawsuits have challenged the constitutionality of Native American tribal ordinances prohibiting the use of peyote, e.g., *Native American Church v. Navaho Tribal Council* (1959). According to an appellate court, a company that refused to hire a NAC member who used peyote as a truck driver violated Title VII because it failed to show accommodating his religious practices would constitute an undue burden. See *Toledo v. Nobel-Sysco, Inc.* (1989).

Attorney General Stanley Mosk (later a California Supreme Court Justice) argued three state interests: (1) the need to protect the Indian community from the deleterious effects of peyote, (2) the state obligation to remove a symbol "that shackles the Indian to primitive conditions," and (3) "the threat of fraudulent assertions of religious immunity will render impossible the effective enforcement of the narcotic laws." The Court found that "the record, however, does not support the state's chronicle of harmful consequences of the use of peyote." *People v. Woody* (1964).

34. *People v. Woody* (1964). See also *In re Grady* (1964).

35. Sergeant Shaw Arnold nearly had to go through two courts-martial over his use of peyote. Brooke, "Military Ends Conflict," and Benjamin, "Justice," 11 n.81.

36. See *Peyote Way Church of God, Inc. v. Thornburgh* (1991) and *Peyote Way v. Meese* (1988). See generally Bannon, "Legality." None of Peyote Way's members were officially Indians. Moreover, Congress had ample opportunities to change the exemption when it adopted new Controlled Substances laws.

The question of whether non–Native American members of the NAC are protected under the exemptions was central in *U.S. v. Warner* (1984). The district court rejected the argument that their indictment for possession and distribution of peyote violated the Equal Protection clause because the preferential status for Indian members of the NAC was political, not racial, in nature. Despite this, the jury acquitted the Warners. Judd Golden, "Non-Indian." Frances Warner, a drug counselor who was fired after the arrest for possession of five thousand peyote buttons, then filed a million dollar civil rights suit in district court. Though she won initially, the court of appeals rejected the proposition that the Warners' right to use peyote was privileged under the Free Exercise clause, and that even if it was, the supervisors were entitled to qualified immunity. *Warner v. Graham* (1988). By contrast, in *U.S. v. Boyll* (1991) the refusal to afford protection to non–Native American peyote users was deemed racial discrimination in violation of the Equal Protection clause. In *Native American Church of New York v. U.S.* (1979) the court allowed an exemption, although the church was not a branch of the NAC, nor were most of the members Native Americans.

37. *Employment Division, Department of Human Resources of Oregon v. Smith* (1990). This was the second time the case reached the U.S. Supreme Court. In 1988 the Court remanded the case to the Oregon Supreme Court to determine whether religious use of pey-

ote is legal in Oregon, a ruling on state law that was necessary for the disposition of the federal question. For an article on the background of the case, see Epps, "Unknown God."

38. There is a vast literature on the *Smith* decision and the Religious Freedom Restoration Act. I do not review that scholarship here. Suffice it to say that it is considered a "radical departure" from precedent. Savage, "Won't Shield Religions."

39. See Bullis, "Swallowing the Scroll." In chapter 6, "Animals," I discuss a Supreme Court decision that invalidated a ritual slaughter law because it actually targeted Santería practitioners. Quotation from Smith, 880.

40. Although peyote gardens are still legal in Texas, there are stringent regulations. Access to a supply of peyote has been an issue. Sahagun, "American Album," and Anon. (1999b), "Semi-legal Drugs."

41. See Autumn Gray's summary of scientific research showing peyote is not addictive. "Effects," 791.

42. The Rastafarian movement originated in Jamaica in communities of former slaves. Members worship Haile Selassie, a former emperor of Ethiopia. The belief system dates from 1953 and was derived from individuals considered to be prophets, particularly Marcus Garvey. For a description of how ganja is prepared, see Rubin and Comitas, *Ganja.* They also describe motivations for its use: "Working class users smoke ganja to support rational task-oriented behavior, to keep 'conscious,' fortify health, maintain peer group relations and enhance religious and philosophical contemplation. They express social rather than hedonistic motivations for smoking" (166). See also Rubin, *Cannabis.*

The panacea quote is from Chevannes, *Rastafari,* 31. See also Barrett, *Rastafarians,* and Clarke, *Black Paradise.* Quotation from Timothy Taylor, "Redemption Song," 676. Jah Rastafari is a Supreme Being. On Bible passages, see Timothy Taylor, "Soul Rebels," 1609, and Clarke, *Black Paradise,* 88–89. When authorities incarcerated Rastafari, it reinforced the importance of smoking ganja for some. Chevannes says the Youth Black Faith "institutionalized ganja as an integral part of the Rastafari reform movement." *Rastafari,* 157, 219.

43. Timothy Taylor "Soul Rebels," 1629.

44. See, e.g., *Town v. State ex rel. Reno* (1979). Others have argued for the right to use marijuana for religious purposes, e.g., *U.S. v. Meyers* (1996). David Meyers, when prosecuted for possession with intent to distribute the drug, argued that as the pastor of the Church of Marijuana, he had to distribute it. Because the trial court considered his beliefs secular, it denied his religious freedom defense. The court assumed that the Twelve Tribes of Israel, another term for Rastafarians, was a bona fide religion under the First Amendment. On appeal Whyte raised for the first time an argument that his use of marijuana in his own home was protected as part of his right to privacy, which was rejected.

45. Judge Noonan acknowledged that the question of the interaction of the Religious Freedom Restoration Act (RFRA) and the Rastafarian religious defense was one of "first impression." According to one journalist, the court decision meant that "Rastafarians can defend themselves against marijuana-possession charges by arguing that they need the weed because of its sacred role in their religion." Holding, "Rastafarian Pot." The government might prevail, despite a religious defense. Here the court thought RFRA required that the government show a compelling state interest in prosecuting the defendants and that its policy was the least restrictive means of furthering the interest.

In *People v. Peck* (1996) the California Court of Appeals also expressed skepticism at the notion that the religion of the defendant (ostensibly president and priest of the Israel Zion Coptic Church) required that he distribute marijuana to others at a lower price and rejected his religious defense to the charge of possession of illegal drugs for sale. Judge Farris discussed the standard for determining when a defendant is entitled to funds for a theology expert who could demonstrate that she was a Rastafarian. In *People v. Trippet* (1997), e.g., the court dismissed RFRA as irrelevant and said *Smith* applied: "A state may prohibit religiously inspired drug use without running afoul of the free exercise clause" (565).

46. The quantity seemed to be an issue. The judge questioned whether the McBrides were "legitimate practitioners of the Rastafarian faith because the quantity of marijuana found at their residence was so large." *State v. McBride* (1998), 912. Although "sincerity" analysis was used in earlier cases involving Rastafarian defendants and sacramental use of marijuana, courts were less inclined to do this in 2000. For an overview of the issues in *McBride*, see Brendon Taylor, "Kansas."

47. From the opinion it does not appear that these arguments were made at the time of the trial. The notion is that Native Americans deserve unique *sui generis* protection because of their special trust relationship with the U.S. government. See *Morton v. Mancari* (1974). See, e.g., *Olsen v. Drug Enforcement Administration* (1989), *U.S. v. Rush* (1984), and *Olsen v. Iowa* (1986). For a critique, see Lesley Frank, "Religious Drug Use." Non-Rastafarians have also argued unsuccessfully that marijuana, like peyote, should receive constitutional protection. In *Leary v. U.S.* (1967) the appellate court doubted that Hinduism requires the use of marijuana and affirmed the lower court's decision not to instruct the jury that Leary should be acquitted if his religious practices were in good faith. The court was especially bothered by the fact that he knowingly and purposely violated the law.

48. In *R. v. Steve Joseph Dallaway* (1984) the appellate judge rejected the argument that the defendant did not intend to sell the marijuana in his possession and upheld his one-year sentence. In *R. v. Daudi and Daniels* (1982) two Rastafarians were admonished by the court that they were not entitled to differential treatment, although their sentence was "at the lower end of the bracket for the offense." Poulter, *Ethnicity, Law and Human Rights*, 361

49. *Rex v. Williams* (1979).

50. See Joy et al., *Marijuana*. Rubin and Comitas conclude that the main physical risk from ganja is from smoking per se, not from the drug, and they reject claims that cannabis has psychiatric and other deleterious effects. *Ganja*, 165. Interestingly, even though Poulter concludes that there is no justification for regulating marijuana use by Rastafarians (and others) in a democratic society, he nevertheless rejects, largely for practical reasons, exemptions for Rastafarians: "Problems in defining Rastafari, of distinguishing religious from social practice, and of verifying a person's bona fides, all militate against introduction of such a scheme." *Ethnicity, Law, and Human Rights*, 372. Cumper considers the Rastafarian's religious motive for using marijuana irrelevant as regulating it is necessary for the protection of public health. "Religious Liberty," 229.

51. Since many states have their own versions of RFRA, practitioners will need to consult their own state statutes to determine the possibility of raising such a defense. See Durham, "State RFRAs."

52. It is noteworthy that even though alcohol leads to numerous accident-related deaths, after the failure of Prohibition, there has been no serious effort to restrict its use.

53. A prominent defense attorney became convinced of the necessity of raising cultural defenses from just such a case. He describes how juries found it incomprehensible that some Mexicans would agree to drive a car across the border for a stranger for a modest sum of money. An expert witness, Dr. Gettner explained to the jury, based on research that because "Mexican culture emphasized being non-confrontational, trusting, and non-suspicious," such an offer "would not strike one as a solicitation to criminality." The testimony led to acquittal. Sevilla, "Preface." For discussion of the supposed Mexican propensity for carrying guns in the context of a prosecution for possession and sale of cocaine, see Metzger, "Exculpatory." All the people born in a particular area of Nepal have the surname "Sherpa." Sherpas are known for their mountaineering expertise. They lead trekkers on expeditions. Quotation from *R. v. Mingma Tenzing Sherpa*, 461.

54. Ortner is the author of *Sherpas through Their Rituals*. During her fieldwork, the defendant was her "cook, translator (in the initial phases), and all-around assistant" (x). A photo of Mingma Tenzing and his family appears on the second page. Quotation from *R. v. Mingma Tenzing Sherpa* (1986), 13–14.

55. There may have been cross-cultural differences in understanding motive and intent here. See Robert Paul, "Act and Intention."

56. The defendant's prosecution generated several *U.S. v. Sherpa* opinions. His conviction was affirmed in (1996b) without opinion and in (1996c) in an unpublished opinion. The disposition of the appeal of the sentence is found in *U.S. v. Sherpa* (1996a). Quotation from *U.S. v. Sherpa* (1996a), 658. Subsequent quotations are from this decision.

57. In *U.S. v. Shrestha* (1996), the court upheld a lower sentence for a Nepalese involved in drug trafficking.

58. In *People v. Nai Chanh Saeturn* (1993), a Mien woman claimed not to know packages she received by mail contained opium, but she was convicted anyway. In the mitigation statement her lawyer wrote: "During the trial the defense honored its commitment not to use a 'cultural defense.' Yet the district attorney employed a cultural prosecution to obtain a conviction against Ms Saeturn. . . . The prosecution's evidence and arguments were replete with theories that 'they' grow it, 'they' smoke it,' so therefore 'they' must know that a package coming from Thailand contains it."

59. Chau Hai Do was told not to declare it to U.S. customs because it was not allowed in the United States. This suggests that even though he might not know it was opium, he was aware that "Chinese medicine" was a controlled substance. (Appellant's brief said Chinese medicine looks exactly like opium, 7). The expert would have testified that "it was not unusual, in the context of a master-apprentice relationship, for an individual to blindly follow his master's instruction and to not question what was going on." Excerpts of Record quoted in Appellee's brief, 7. Their two-year relationship was based on an agreement that Pham Van Tu would teach Do the jewelry business.

Because the decision is only three sentences long, I derived most of the information about this case from the Appellant's and Appellee's opening briefs and from interviews with the appointed defense attorney in Ventura, Esther Sorkin, and the Assistant U.S. Attorney, Ronald Cheng.

The Court of Appeals said, "The district court did not abuse its discretion in refusing to admit expert cultural testimony. The jury was capable of determining his reasons for not questioning his master. In addition, the reluctance of immigrants to admit a lack of facility in English is not specialized knowledge." *U.S. v. Chau Hai Do (a/k/a Do Hai Chau)* (1994, 1995). The U.S. Supreme Court declined to review the case.

Do's behavior was in some respects uncharacteristic of a drug smuggler. First, he gave his actual name to government officials immediately; second, he had a round-trip ticket. Chau Hai Do received a seventy-five-month prison term, a supervised release of three years, and a special assessment of $100.

60. Appellant's brief, 9 (Excerpt of Record 3: 7).

61. The Appellee's brief cited precedents generally supporting the exclusion of cultural evidence. It also argued that even if the exclusion was improper, the error was harmless (21). "To the extent that defendant sought to establish that he was told by Tu Van Pham that there was Chinese medicine in the suitcase and that defendant felt uncomfortable inquiring further of his 'master,' he presented that assertion at trial during the course of his testimony. Additional expert testimony would not tend to make that assertion more or less likely." Appellee's brief, 18.

62. *U.S. v. Carbonell* (1990), 187.

63. *People v. Palrat Manurasada* (1985). The somewhat procedurally complex case

involved several issues, only one of which was the cultural claim. The first jury hung eight to four for conviction. Postverdict juror interviews indicated the entrapment evidence was important to the four dissenting jurors. At the second jury trial, this evidence was not presented. He was found guilty of the crime of sale of marijuana on October 16, 1985. The new lawyer, John Sink, in the petition for habeas corpus to the California Supreme Court, advanced three main arguments: (1) Manurasada had been denied his Sixth Amendment right to effective assistance of counsel because by failing to present evidence he withdrew a potentially meritorious defense. (2) He had been denied his right to due process of law because the "attorney's omissions deprived him of a meaningful opportunity to present his defense." (3) Equal protection because failure to consider the cultural motivation of the defendant meant the jury could not properly analyze the acts in question. The California Supreme Court denied the petition for the writ of habeas corpus, July 11, 1985.

64. The lawyer failed to put the expert on the stand. The judge in the first trial, though skeptical about the relevance of the information to the entrapment defense, decided to delay ruling on the question until he heard the evidence, which never happened. During the second trial the lawyer did not even contact the expert. Afterward, the defendant wanted to change lawyers, partly as a consequence of his failure to present cultural evidence as part of the entrapment defense.

65. The California entrapment standard was set forth in *People v. Barraza* (1979): "The proper test of entrapment in California is the following: was the conduct of the law enforcement agent likely to induce a normally law-abiding person to commit the offense?"

66. *People v. Manurasada*, Petition for Review of the Decision of the Court of Appeal, Second Appellate District, 17. Feb. 29, 1988.

67. *R. v. Bibi* (1980), 1196. The court quotes from a "social inquiry report."

68. Poulter, *Ethnicity, Law, and Human Rights*, 63–64. He considers the cultural and religious background of Bibi "incidental" to the offense, as compared with Rastafarian defendants whose background "lie[s] at the heart of the offense" (375).

69. The U.S. Sentencing Guidelines, section 3B1.2, permit a reduction in punishment for a "minimal" participant and a somewhat lesser reduction for a "minor" participant. In *U.S. v. Mustapha* (1998), a Nigerian, Akinola Mustapha, argued that the district court erred in refusing to find that he was a minor or minimal participant in a heroin operation. The matter turned on the interpretation of the Yoruba phrase "One door opener." Mustapha claimed this meant fifty grams, whereas the government that it was an allusion to "key," slang for a kilogram. Because the court decided to hold him accountable for at least one kilogram of heroin, his role was not deemed minor. The appellate court thought the lower court was entitled to resolve the linguistic dispute as it saw fit and affirmed the sentence.

70. This is the district court's rendition of his testimony.

71. *U.S. v. Ezeiruaku and Akiagba* (1995). Obviously the court found Akiagba was not a "minimal participant" in the drug operation. She was said to play the role of a broker in the conspiracy, facilitating transactions between Okuzu and Ezeiruaku.

72. In *U.S. v. Gaviria* (1992), a judge also rejected a culture-based duress defense, noting the difficulty of proving such a defense. Judge Weinstein still substantially reduced the sentence of Maria Gaviria, a young woman from Colombia, who was subject to domestic violence and compelled to help with her husband's drug operation. He rejected the contention that the federal sentencing guidelines preclude the consideration of culture. In *U.S. v. Villegas* (1990), one defendant, John Berrio, claimed that he only remained at Johnnycake Farm, where cocaine operations were under way, because he feared the Colombian drug cartel. His lawyer argued that because of his Colombian background, Berrio "kn[ew] that if he was [*sic*] to leave, they would kill him" (1344), and an expert witness in Latin American studies testified about the reputation and activities of Colombian cartels. Despite these arguments, the trial court

disallowed the duress defense. The appellate court affirmed. For other cases in which courts considered the duress argument, see Sungaila, "Gendered Realities."

73. Section 5H1.10, Race, Sex, National Origin, Creed, Religion and Socio-Economic Status (Policy Statement), of the sentencing guidelines lists factors not relevant in the determination of a sentence. The judge at sentencing said: "I accept counsel's statement about there being a cultural problem in that the defendant was, I will say, unduly influenced by her companion who she treats as her husband. But for purposes of deterrence, the sentencing commission has seen fit to send this sort of a message, and I will do what I believe is required by the guidelines." Appellee's brief, p. 15.

Quotation from *U.S. v. Natal-Rivera* (1989), 392. The appellant's brief explained the argument: "This type of cultural behavior has been labeled as 'machismo' and is widely prevalent in many underdeveloped countries. As a result of the defendant's upbringing, she truly believed that she had no other choice but to follow her 'husband's' orders to participate in the illegal activity of which she was convicted" (13).

74. Some, e.g., Murray ("Battered Woman Syndrome") and Holmquist ("Cultural Defense"), worry that arguments of this kind will reinforce stereotypes. For a reluctant expression of support, see Olabisi Clinton, "Cultural Differences," who seems to favor allowing its use only until the newly arrived become Americanized, and only on one occasion.

75. This is known as the "fruit of the poisonous tree" doctrine. For instance, in *U.S. v. Ochoa-Zaragoza* (2000), the defendant claimed his "limited education, unfamiliar surroundings, and cultural differences prevented him from understanding his Miranda rights" and therefore that his incriminating statements should have been suppressed. The court held that the exclusion of testimony by a linguistics expert was not an abuse of discretion and affirmed his conviction for possession of methamphetamine with intent to distribute. Because he was notified in English and Spanish, the court thought his waiver of his Miranda rights was "knowing and intelligent." For an overview of this topic, see Einesman, "Cultural Issues," especially a list of cultural factors that influence a determination as to the validity of Miranda waiver, one of which is "cultural attitude toward law enforcement authorities." See also Valladares, "Cultural Issues," esp. 3.4 and 3.5. For a comprehensive discussion of these matters, see Richard Cole and Maslow-Armand, "Role of Counsel."

76. It is, of course, true that any American citizen might also believe he or she could not refuse police requests. Sometimes, before analyzing the waiver issue, courts have to decide whether the interrogation was "custodial," so that Miranda rights were applicable. In *U.S. v. Joe* (1991), a sexual abuse case, the court grappled with the question of whether to relativize the "objective standard" to take into account the defendant's cultural background in figuring out whether he believed he was in custody at the time of the interrogation. It concluded: "Cultural heritage may be a factor in determining a suspect's subjective belief. However, having determined the suspect's subjective belief, the Court must then determine whether or not that belief is objectively reasonable."

77. For a detailed summary, see Miner, "*U.S. v. Zapata*." See also *U.S. v. Gutierrez-Mederos* (1992). Gutierrez-Mederos was stopped because, supposedly, he fit the narcotics trafficking characteristics profile. Though he consented to a search of the vehicle for weapons and narcotics, he subsequently maintained he did not freely consent: "His background [unspecified] and limited ability to speak English prevented him from voluntarily consenting to the search." The appellate court rejected this argument and upheld his conviction for possession of cocaine and a firearm in connection with a drug-trafficking offense. In *U.S. v. Yusuff* (1996) an appellate court agreed with the district court "that any cultural differences that Yusuff had did not negate the voluntariness of her consent to a search leading to heroin." Although Olufunke Yusuff claimed not to understand her rights because she was a Nigerian national, she was fluent in English.

On Zapata's agreeing, see *U.S. v. Zapata* (1993). Evidently the fact that the duffel bags were new made them suspicious; 75 percent of drug dealers use new luggage. *U.S. v. Zapata* (1993), 754. The defense attorney alleged that it was also the fact that the family was Hispanic. Appellee's answer brief, 16. Zapata had no criminal record or prior contact with the police in the United States. Zapata argued that the encounter was neither a consensual one (which does not implicate the Fourth Amendment) nor a lawful investigative detention based on reasonable suspicion. The encounter constituted an investigative detention qualifying as a "seizure" under the Fourth Amendment. A seizure is only valid if there is reasonable suspicion; if not, the "fruits" of the search should be excluded. Zapata was not told he had the right to decline to answer the questions, to leave the presence of the officer, or to refuse to have his luggage searched. Though courts have not required this, it is relevant to the "totality of the circumstances" analysis, which determines whether or not the action was indeed a seizure.

Others have argued that the police are perceived differently by individuals from different cultures. In one case, *U.S. v. Ruelas-Altamirano* (1972), a Mexican police officer claimed to have crossed the border to purchase cigarettes in a car containing concealed marijuana; the car was lent to him by a stranger. He was convicted of possession with intent to distribute marijuana. An appellate court affirmed the decision to exclude a cultural geographer's expert testimony that "favors are regularly given to and accepted by the Mexican police from strangers."

Quotation on Mexican police from Appellee's answer brief, 11. "Zapata thought that if he didn't do what the police officer said, the police officer would 'get angry or he would do something else.' During the entire encounter with Small, Zapata was feeling 'very frightened' and 'very scared.'" Appellee's answer brief, 5 quoting the transcript, 42–43. The government countered that he had not had or observed any encounters with the police in Mexico. Appellant's brief, 5–6. The brief also implied any fear of Mexican police would not affect Zapata's view of American police. Small asked him many questions, the most incriminating of which was, "You don't have any drugs in your luggage do you?" Appellee's brief, 9.

78. *U.S. v. Zapata* (1993), 755.

79. But see the powerful dissent by Judge Holloway. *Zapata*, 759. Quotation from *Zapata*, 757. The court rejected the notion that a person's subjective characteristics are relevant to consent. Even if they were, the court said: "We reject the notion that his attitude toward the police, from whatever source, can constitute such a relevant subjective characteristic" because "an intangible characteristic such as attitude toward authority is inherently unverifiable and unquantifiable" (759).

The appellate court applied the standard in *Bostick v. Florida* (1991), involving police questioning of individuals on a bus. There the Supreme Court said that when police approach an individual and ask a few questions, that does not necessarily constitute a seizure. The legal question is how this standard applies to train cars, and whether there is difference between public and private compartments.

80. In *U.S. v. Joe* (1991) (quoting *Berkemer v. McCarty*) the court said it would be wrong to make the police "anticipate the frailties or idiosyncrasies of every person whom they question.... To modify the reasonable man standard based on cultural heritage would place upon the police the burden of determining, first, every suspect's cultural heritage and second, the relevance of that heritage to the suspect's perception of the nature of the interview" (609–610). The government's brief criticized the district court judge for relying on the defendant's Mexican background, "an approach which amounts to a per se conclusion that anyone who was raised in Mexico is seized in almost every kind of police encounter." Appellant's brief, 11.

81. For instance, when the Hmong first arrived in Fresno and were stopped by the police for erratic driving, some were reported to have kneeled down in preparation for execution. This behavior was based on their expectation of what would have happened in Laos.

82. Several countries impose the death penalty for trafficking in drugs, e.g., China, Iran, Malaysia, the Philippines, Saudi Arabia, Singapore, Syria, and Thailand. Schreiber, "States That Kill," 273. Of the 2,500 Americans arrested in ninety-five foreign countries in 1994, some 880 were in jail for drug possession. U.S. Department of State, "Travel Warning."

See Nick Williams, "Malaysia," and Anon. (1986c), "Australians Hanged." In 1985 Brian Chambers and Kevin Barlow were convicted of trafficking 6.3 ounces of heroin after losing their appeals in the Supreme Court. The government rejected mercy pleas from Australia and England. Derrick Gregory was hanged for trafficking in heroin. Anon. (1989f), "Briton Hanged." In 1990 Kerry Wiley was prosecuted for possessing marijuana and faced a possible death sentence under Malaysia's harsh drug laws. Wallace, "American on Trial." Another unsuccessful plea for clemency was Dutch Queen Beatrix's for Johannes van Damme, a man who was caught in Singapore with 4.32 kilograms of heroin. Anon. (1995b), "Foreign Minister." But one Canadian, Ronald Wilson McCulloch, avoided being hanged when he was found with 3 kilograms of marijuana because the charges were changed from trafficking to possession. Anon. (1996h), "Singapore."

Some might discount this point as there is a worldwide movement toward elimination of the death penalty. Short, "Abolition." Yet even if capital punishment is eventually abolished worldwide, Westerners would still be subject to other forms of punishment, such as amputation, flogging, and stoning. See also Bahrampour, "Caning."

83. This issue involves two questions: (1) how drug offenses are handled juridically, and (2) under what circumstances, if any, the death penalty is appropriate. With respect to the first, the United Nations has attempted to develop universal standards to harmonize divergent national policies. See the multilateral Vienna Convention against Illicit Traffic in Narcotic Drugs and Psychotropic Substances. For information on the second, see Wyman, "Vengeance?" For example, the disembarkation form for visitors to Singapore conveys the information in red capital letters: "Warning: Death for Drug Traffickers under Singapore Law." The U.S. Department of State has supported extradition treaties to address transborder drug trafficking problems. See Borek, "Testimony before the Senate Committee on Foreign Relations," and Nash, "Contemporary Practice," 103.

84. Quotation from Baron, "Memorable Experience," 500. See also Dobkin de Rios, *Hallucinogens*. Plant hallucinogens had religious connotations which tended to prevent their abuse. She and co-author David E. Smith hypothesize that "in traditional societies drug rituals developed in the absence of legal restrictions on their use and that, intended or not, these rituals have served the function of controlling drug use." "Drug Rituals," 269. By contrast they say that in "modern" societies there are "maladaptive drug rituals" like the "overdose phenomenon," and in the United States some of these maladaptive responses are to the "illegality of such substances in the society in general" (273). There are also "partially protective factors," e.g., in Italy and France "where there is lifelong training to drink wine only with meals." Lolli et al., *Alcohol*. See also John Frank et al., "Historical."

85. Sherratt, "Alcohol," 16. Of course there is no way for unconventional substances to be justified medically. Those who use folk medicine can be prosecuted for practicing medicine without a license. Some traditional remedies can lead to accidental herbal toxicity. Some toxicologists have made a plea for collaboration by botanists and ethnopharmacologists focusing on the toxic, rather than the beneficial aspects of traditional medicines. M. J. Stewart et al., "Toxicology."

86. Berridge, "Drug Policy." See also Joseph Westermeyer, *Poppies*, 292–299.

87. Joseph McNamara refers to this as "the continuation of a kind of pharmacological McCarthyism." "Chief's Plea." For a thoughtful analysis, see Gilmore, "Drug Use."

CHAPTER 6

1. Simoons, *Eat Not Flesh*. Food patterns appear to be "among those most resistant to acculturation." Spiro, "Acculturation," 1249. For a study of moral codes and cuisine, see Paz, "Eroticism." Some groups are referred to by the animals they eat; e.g., the English call the French "frogs," and the French call the English "rosbif." The English have been known as "limeys" (for the citrus fruit eaten on long voyages to avoid scurvy; the Germans "krauts" (for sauerkraut). The relationship between food and national identity is explored in Murcott, "Food." In his seminal, though controversial, study of animal categories Leach contends that the abuse of animals is related to their symbolic importance to the group. "Anthropological Aspects." For an intriguing analysis of animal metaphors as a tool of social control, see Brandes. "Animal Metaphors." A poll reported in the *Los Angeles Times* said that nearly half of Americans think animals "are just like humans in all important ways." Balzar," Creatures." The fact that killing animals at the pound is called "euthanizing them" seems to imply that they are considered almost human. For a thoughtful discussion of animal cruelty in different times and places, see Passmore, "Treatment." Cruelty may be regarded as categorically wrong or as unacceptable because it leads to cruel behavior toward humans. See, e.g., Cross, "Ancient Faiths."

2. One manifestation of the prejudice is the widespread rumor that Asian immigrants eat animals in parks, despite any evidence to substantiate this claim. Bishop. "Culinary Rule." Because of this rumor, in 1981 California legislators introduced Assembly Bill 241 to outlaw the eating of dogs, but it was defeated in committee. Vu-Duc Vuong, "Position Paper." One SPCA officer told me that when dogs disappear, neighbors tend to accuse their Asian neighbors of having taken the animals to eat them. Corinne Whetstone, personal communication, 1988. In Sacramento the executive director of the SPCA said he had received five calls in which people "felt their pets may have been taken (to be eaten) by Southeast Asians. Fortunately, these claims turned out to be unfounded." Abrams, "Ban."

3. A man was questioned about his having placed rubber bands on the testicles of his dog. His explanation was that this was how a dog was neutered in the Philippines, and that he could not afford the $80 to have a veterinarian perform the procedure. Victoria Young, personal communication, 1985. He pled no contest to one count of allowing animals to go without proper care and attention, received a suspended sentence of forty days, one year probation, and a fine of $370. The dog recovered and was adopted by another family. In another case, a Japanese man tied a dog to a tree where it was dying. When told by an SPCA agent that he was obligated to have the dog treated by a veterinarian, he said: "Is that a law here? In my country there is no such thing, since the dog is going to die anyway." When the man took the dog to the vet, the dog was diagnosed with a malignant tumor on his spinal cord and was euthanized. Because the man complied with the officer's request, she recommended that he not be charged with any violation. Corinne Whetstone, personal communication, 1988.

4. Evans gives accounts of these trials in *Capital Punishment*. In a wonderful article, "Conjuring Rats," Newell discusses the practice of sending letters of eviction to rats. Superstitions continue to affect animal public policy; humane societies have refused to allow the adoption of black cats just prior to Halloween to avoid abuse. Aileen Cho, "Black Cats."

5. Instead, philosophers Regan and Singer speak about human duties not to harm animals. *Animal Rights.*

6. There are numerous cases in which indigenous peoples are prosecuted for hunting or fishing out of season. This chapter discusses only selected examples of hunting. For similar discussions about fishing, see, e.g., Chapin, "Indian Activists"; Michael Anderson, "Law and

Protection"; Mylonas-Widdall, "New Zealand." Some indigenous groups whose survival depends on hunting have claimed an aboriginal exception to the international legal policy prohibiting the taking of certain whales. This has led to some controversy because Japanese and Norwegian fishing communities contend that their way of life depends on whaling; it is unfair, they say, not to give them exemptions as well. See, e.g., Doubleday, "Aboriginal Subsistence"; Gambell, "International Management"; Hankins, "Abuse of Whaling"; Kalland and Moeran, *Endangered Culture*; Miller, "Exercising Cultural Self-Determination."

7. *Jack and Charlie v. the Queen* [1985], 91.

8. Mandell, "Native Culture on Trial," 362. Her essay discusses the case as an example of judicial bias.

9. Quotations from *Jack and Charlie*, 88, 102. The court stated: "There was no evidence that the use of defrosted raw deer meat was sacrilegious as is alleged in appellants' factum. . . . There was no evidence that the killing of the deer was part of the religious ceremony" (100). But their attorney Mandell noted: "It is significant that although the judges could envision a proper burning with stored deer meat, the Indians could not." "Native Culture on Trial," 363.

10. Frequently judges deny that the law infringes on the religious freedom of indigenous people, e.g., *State v. Berry* (1985). However, the Alaskan Supreme Court reached the opposite conclusion in *Frank v. State* (1979). The case involved an Athabascan community that was preparing a funeral potlatch for which fresh moose meat was needed for the feast after the burial. Although the lower courts' assessment of the religious needs of the indigenous group is strikingly ethnocentric, the state supreme court's decision is remarkably sensitive in its treatment of culture.

11. It is not a violation of the Establishment clause to deny non–Native Americans eagle feathers for religious ceremonies. *Rupert v. Director, U.S. Fish and Wildlife Service* (1992). Only federally registered tribes may benefit from the exemption. *Gibson v. Babbitt* (2000). Native Americans may take eagles for religious purposes only, not commercial ones. *U.S. v. Top Sky* (1976). Those who sell artifacts with feathers may be prosecuted whether or not they realized the feathers were illegal. *U.S. v. Corrow* (1997). In 1940 the federal Bald Eagle Protection Act was passed. Lawrence, "Symbol." It may not be considered endangered in the next century. Gerstenzang, "Eagle," and Edwin Chen, "Eagle." The Eighth Circuit accepted the treaty defense in *U.S. v. White* (1974). Several years later, the Ninth Circuit, in *U.S. v. Fryberg* (1980), held that the Bald Eagle Protection Act modified Indian treaty rights, so that treaty Indians could only hunt eagles for religious purposes and then only if they had permits. In 1986, however, the district court held that a member of the Isleta Pueblo could not be prosecuted for possession of golden eagle parts without a permit because the Treaty of Guadalupe Hidalgo had not been abrogated by the Bald Eagle Protection Act. *U.S. v. Abeyta* (1986). The court distinguished the earlier cases by noting the defendant was not engaged in eagle killing for commercial reasons and that this treaty was an "international compact securing religious freedom to Mexican citizens in the ceded territories" (1306). A district court reached the opposite conclusion in *U.S. v. Thirty Eight Golden Eagles* (1986), holding that protecting endangered species was a compelling interest. According to De Meo, *Abeyta*, "the one case sympathetic to Native American religious freedom, may no longer be valid or persuasive law" because the defendant lacked standing to challenge the Eagle Protection Act because he has not applied for a permit. "Access," 806. On abrogation, see, e.g., Jane Walker, "Treaty Hunting Rights," and Wilkinson and Volkman, "Judicial Review."

12. For a critique of the case, see Banks, "Birds," and Tarpley, "Law." Dion and three other Indian men were caught in a "sting" operation. Sally Johnson, "Honoring," 183.

13. Because Dion did not challenge the part of the court's decision that the tribe had no treaty right to hunt and sell eagles for commercial purposes, the Supreme Court did not evaluate that issue.

14. *U.S. v. Dion* (1985), 738.

15. Because the Supreme Court concluded that Congress, by enacting the Eagle Protection Act, abrogated Dion's treaty right to hunt bald eagles, he could therefore not assert a treaty right as a defense. The Court thought it would be illogical to allow Dion to raise a defense based on the original treaty, expressly abrogated by the Eagle Protection Act, to conduct forbidden by the Endangered Species Act, even if Congress did not explicitly declare its intention to abrogate the treaty in the second law.

16. Sally Johnson, "Honoring," 188.

17. For a comprehensive analysis of the federal permit system, see De Meo, "Access." The Migratory Bird Treaty Act and the Endangered Species Act provide no exemptions for religious use. The policy of permits applies equally to eagles and feathers acquired by gift of inheritance. 50 C.F.R. sections 13.1, 22.11 (1992).

18. Broder, "Tribal Leaders," and William Clinton, "Memorandum."

19. Policy is that "in many cases ceremonial feathers traditionally had to come from an eagle that was killed in a ritually prescribed way, for the eagle himself was considered a kind of human being." Jerome Levi, personal communication, 1998. For an example of the elaborate eagle-killing ritual and an analysis of its functions, see Bean, *Mukat's People*, 138–141. The Eagle Permit Instructions of the U.S. Fish and Wildlife Service have constraints such as that Native Americans must be eighteen years old to apply and may have only one request pending at a time. More significant, perhaps, is the requirement to submit certification of enrollment from the Bureau of Indian Affairs, i.e., that the person is a "real" Indian. Another requirement is a Certification of Participation. A recognized tribal leader (defined as an elder, medicine man or woman, or spiritual leader) has to certify the need for eagle feathers and return it to the applicant. Quotation from De Meo, "Access," 792.

20. See Brooke, "Agency Struggles." In 1997 the U.S. Fish and Wildlife Service completed a two-year undercover operation into the killing and selling of eagles by approximately thirty-five individuals. Anon. (1997a), "FWS Finds." Other raids have occurred. Brooke, "Arrested."

21. In *U.S. v. Jim* (1995), a Yakima Indian was prosecuted for killing two bald and two golden eagles (this was not a first offense). His explanation was that he acted in accordance with a "vow beyond law. . . . This is a religious duty, a tribal duty." De Meo, "Access," 800. Although the district court acknowledged the long delays in the permit system, it still found the government interest in protecting eagles to be compelling and saw the law as the least restrictive alternative means of achieving this objective. This case was one of the first to be decided under the Religious Freedom Restoration Act, which reestablished the highest level of protection for religious liberty temporarily until it was struck down.

The attorney for a man prosecuted for hunting an eagle explained the time pressure his client was experiencing: "There are initiation rites or death rites where feathers are needed on short notice. Imagine having to order a Bible from a federal bureaucracy—and then waiting three years." Quoted in Brooke, "Agency Struggles."

Quotation in text from De Meo, "Access," 791.

22. In *U.S. v. Hugs* (1997) the court said the Hugs lacked standing to challenge the constitutionality of the permit system as administered because they had not used it. The court accepted evidence showing that eagles played "a central role" in Native American religion and the proposition that the permit scheme "imposed a substantial burden on the practice" of Native American religion. The system has also led to intertribal conflicts. See *Ferrell Secakuku v. Albert Hale* (1997) for a Hopi vs. Navajo dispute over eagles.

23. *State v. Billie* (1986). The court says *U.S. v. Dion* (1985) "strongly suggests that species protection is the more compelling factor." The effect of this decision was to permit the state to go forward with the prosecution.

24. Quotation from *U.S. v. Billie* (1987), 1489. The court assumes that Congress intended to resolve the conflict between Indian treaty rights and the Endangered Species Act by abrogating the treaty rights (1491). Billie argued that the government should have to prove that he knew he shot a Florida panther and that he knew it was a crime to do so on the reservation. The court said if proof of specific intent (rather than general intent) were required, the prosecution would fail. Billie also argued that he lacked the mens rea because it was unclear whether the Endangered Species Act applied to on-reservation hunting. The court rejected this argument because intent to violate the law was not an element of the crime.

25. *U.S. v. Billie*, 1497.

26. Morin argues that the decisions demonstrate the need to formulate a policy to save the panther for the benefit of Indians and non-Indians. "Indians," 178. Such programs exist. Sometimes biologists recommend bringing in other subspecies to restore genetic diversity and to avoid problems of inbreeding. Dold, "Florida Panthers."

27. A dog is only sacrificed in the most serious cases, generally after other techniques have failed to produce a result. From the Hmong perspective, if a dog dies during a religious sacrifice ceremony, that makes the dog's life significant. Cross, "Ancient Faiths."

28. Anon. (1995e), "Sacrifice of Dog."

29. His attorney, Richard Ciummo, said that without the religious defense, he would have little chance in front of a jury. Moreover the jury would have trouble with the killing of a puppy as opposed to a chicken: "If it was a chicken, that would be one thing. But he killed a puppy. He didn't understand that to Americans, that's like family." Arax, "Hmong's Sacrifice." One question in such cases is whether any compromise is possible. A Hmong shaman used a stuffed black velveteen cat to cure an ailing Hmong boy. Cross, "Ancient Faiths."

30. Some consider *syncretism* to be a term with negative connotations because they think it implies "a mixture of religious ideas without an inner integrity." Murphy, *Santeria*, 120.

Orisha is a Yoruba word which has been roughly translated as spirit. Murphy, *Santeria*, x. From the voluminous literature, see, e.g., Murphy, *Santeria*, and Brandon, "Sacrificial Practices."

31. See Brandon, "Sacrificial Practices," 121, and Savage, "Justices Affirm."

32. Murphy contends that no part of the religion is more misunderstood than the blood sacrifice. He explains: "Their [animals] blood is offered to the orishas to show human beings their dependence on the world outside them and to give back to the invisible world something of what it gives to the visible." *Santeria*, 44. See Brandon, "Sacrificial Practices," 128. Each deity is believed to have its favorite animals, plants, and foods. The animal victims are sacrificed for particular problems, e.g., sheep against death in sickness; ram, sheep, and old cock for victory in time of war (129). On cultural adaptation, Brandon says, "It has become a system through which adjustments to exile in a foreign land and an alien culture may be mediated" (137). He also mentions that "a number of victims of sacrifice end up in the hands of sanitation departments and the Association for the Prevention of Cruelty to Animals" (136). For a survey of cases in urban centers since the late 1970s, see David Brown, *Garden*, 317–325, 362–365. He describes priests as "under siege" from the SPCA enforcement of health and animal cruelty laws.

33. The four ordinances and two city council resoluaions are appended to the court's decision. The suit was filed under 42 U.S.C. section 1983. The church sought a declaratory judgment and injunctive and monetary relief. Animals offered to orishas are not always killed: "Very often an animal is offered to an orisha without killing it. This animal then becomes a sacred object, the exclusive property of the orisha to whom it is dedicated. It must never be killed or harmed in any way unless the saint demands it." Gonzalez-Wippler, *Santeria*, 50. Murphy notes that the news media fixates on one aspect of the religion, namely the ritual sacrifice of animals. *Santeria*, viii.

34. *Church of Lukumi Babalu Aye v. City of Hialeah* (1989), 1487, and (1991).

35. *Church of Lukumi Babalu Aye v. City of Hialeah* (1993). All quotations are from this opinion, 227–233.

36. The Court found the ordinances underinclusive because they did not prohibit secular conduct that endangered the government interests at stake.

37. The mayor of Hialeah apparently stated that the city would take no further actions against the church. Murphy, *Santeria*, 13. However the janitors at the courthouse known as the "voo doo squad" collect various Santería talismans on a daily basis to ensure a "carcass-free workplace" around the exterior of the Miami criminal courthouse. Shapiro, "Cake." A dozen major church groups filed amicus briefs urging the court to strike down the ordinances because immigrants should have religious freedom, no matter how unpopular their religion is. Savage, "Justices Revisit." See, e.g., the article by Holzer, "Contradictions," based on an amicus brief filed on behalf of twelve animal rights' organizations in *Lukumi*. The two-hour ceremony, which appeared on television, showed the priest using a blunt knife for the slaughter of a goat. Correa, "Santeria Priest's Trial."

38. In 1990 the Los Angeles City Council adopted an ordinance in response to approximately one hundred complaints to the department of animal regulation about animal carcasses found in parks and trash containers. For background, see Scott Harris, "Ban Urged," and Braxton, "Challenge." A committee of the San Francisco Board of Supervisors approved an ordinance to prohibit animal sacrifices in 1992. Espinosa, "Resistance." In 1980 the houses of two Santería priestesses in New York city were raided by SPCA agents. Brandon, "Sacrificial Practices," 136–137.

39. Laycock explains the legal difference is that ritual slaughter is primarily for food, whereas ritual sacrifice is primarily for ritual and secondarily for food. "Remnants," 67. Commercial slaughtering of animals in the United States is subject to extensive regulations. Favre and Loring, *Animal Law*. In some cases the question has been how to analyze ritual slaughter for tax purposes—that is, whether this constitutes providing goods or services. See *London Board for Shechita v. The Commissioners* (1974). In *Jones v. Butz* (1974) plaintiffs argued that the failure to stun the animal was cruel, in violation of the humaneness requirement of the law, and that the exemption for the Jewish community to ensure a supply of kosher meat had the effect of promoting religion in violation of the Establishment clause. The district court ruled that the Humane Slaughter Act, including provisions allowing for ritual slaughter, did not violate the Establishment clause. However, kosher policy has run into trouble, as in *Ran-Dev's County Kosher, Inc. v. New Jersey* (1992). The New Jersey Supreme Court considered a challenge to its consumer protection regulations designed to guarantee that foodstuffs advertised as "kosher" were, in fact, "kosher." The court held that the regulations violated the Establishment clause of the federal and state constitutions because the civil enforcement of religious law involves substantial governmental entanglement in religious matters. Of course, there is a strong business incentive to accommodate the dietary needs. Indeed, fifteen four-star Los Angeles hotels have kosher kitchens. Beyette, "Keeping Kosher." Moreover, kosher meat companies are required to comply with the general provisions of law. *Commack Self-Service Kosher Meats, Inc. v. New York* (1997).

40. See Poulter, *English Law*, 278. The courts enforce the rules strictly, as in *Malins v. Cole and Attard* (1986), where the owner of a poultry slaughterhouse and his Muslim employees were unable to show all three elements necessary for an exemption (the slaughter was by the Muslim method, by a Muslim, and for the food of Muslims). As evidence did not show the bird was for the food of Muslims, the exemption was held not to apply. One report recommended reevaluation of Jewish and Muslim techniques and disallowing others, e.g., Sikh decapitation of animals. Farm Animal Welfare Council, "Report," 25.

The RSPCA put out a pamphlet questioning the techniques and challenging the right to religious freedom when such beliefs "adversely affect the welfare of food animals." *Slaughter*, 12. One issue is stunning the animal prior to killing it. Orthodox Jews reject stunning an animal because their interpretation of Jewish law is that it must be well and not injured before slaughter. Mews, "Religious Slaughter."

On pain: "There is a lack of scientific evidence to indicate at what stage in the process of losing consciousness the ability to feel pain ceases." Farm Animal Welfare Council, "Report," 20. Poulter argues, however, that if scientific evidence were to show that the religious methods of slaughter involved unnecessary suffering to animals, then regulations that restricted religious freedom would be justifiable "in the interest of the protection of public morality." *English Law*, 281. When an Iranian diplomat ritually slaughtered a sheep in his front garden, this might have been cruelty under the law, but no court ruled on this matter as he invoked diplomatic immunity. In *R. v. Efstathiou* (1984) a Greek Cypriot was fined 200 pounds for slaughtering three goats at home by cutting their throats. (Both cases are discussed in Poulter, *English Law*, 282.) A Muslim, prosecuted in Colorado for slaughtering sheep in his backyard, faced a $300 fine. Dyers, "Moslem Charged."

41. See the debate about the European Convention on the Protection of Animals for Slaughter. Council of Europe, *Explanatory Report*. For a detailed account of the ritual slaughter controversy in Holland, see Shadid and van Koningsveld, "Legal Adjustments." I draw heavily on this essay for the information in this paragraph. The Dutch Society for the Protection of Animals argued that stunning was consistent with Jewish and Muslim religious tenets. Shadid and van Koningsveld, "Legal Adjustments," 22–23. There may be an economic incentive to allow ritual slaughter without previous stunning. Some countries such as Australia, Argentina, and Uruguay permitted this practice in order to facilitate the export of large quantities of meat to Arab countries. Another flap occurred when the State Secretary of Agriculture and Fisheries decided to stop the practice of exporting ritually slaughtered meat mainly to Israel and Switzerland, but he was forced to reverse course when the new policy was attacked as anti-Semitic. Quotation from Shadid and van Koningsveld, "Legal Adjustments," 23.

In January 2002 the German Constitutional Court invalidated the ban on religious slaughter, reasoning that the policy violated the "professional freedom" of Muslims to be butchers. Homola, *Germany: Muslim*. See also Langenfeld, *Developments: Germany*.

42. The case was *Cha'are Shalom Ve Tsedek v. France* (2000) (hereafter *CSVT v. France*). The Jewish Consistorial Association of Paris (ACIP), an offshoot of the Central Consistory, is an institution established in 1808 by Napoleon I to administer Jewish worship in France. In 1905 with the official separation of church and state, Jewish congregations formed Jewish liturgical associations under the Union of Jewish Congregations of France but retained the name Central Consistory. The organization represents the main denominations within Judaism except for the liberals and the ultra-orthodox. The Joint Rabbinical Committee consists of the Chief Rabbi of Paris and the rabbis of the orthodox and traditionalist congregations. It grants authorization necessary to obtain a card to gain access to slaughterhouses. Relevant legal provisions are cited in the European Court of Human Rights decision. The power to authorize slaughterers was granted to the Joint Rabbinical Committee on July 1, 1982. The Minister of the Interior refused the request for permission to practice ritual slaughter because the group was not a religious association and was not "sufficiently representative" of the French Jewish community. In 1987 the Paris Administrative Court dismissed the appeal, and the Conseil d'Etat also did so in 1994.

43. *CSVT v. France*, 19. *Glatt* is a Yiddish word meaning smooth. For meat to be glatt, the slaughtered animal must be free from any impurity, e.g., sign of a previous illness.

44. It had approximately six hundred subscribing members and forty thousand adherents as compared with the ACIP membership of seven hundred thousand. The court disposed of the argument that the larger organization held a monopoly over ritual slaughter noting that this "was not the . . . deliberate intention on the part of the state" (21).

45. Article 9 provides: "1. Everyone has the right to freedom of thought, conscience, and religion; this right includes freedom to change his religion or belief and freedom, either alone or in community with others and in public or private, to manifest his religion or belief, in worship, teaching, practice and observance. 2. Freedom to manifest one's religion or beliefs shall be subject only to such limitations as are prescribed by law and are necessary in a democratic society in the interests of public safety, for the protection of public order, health or morals, or for the protection of the rights and freedoms of others." Article 14 provides, in pertinent part: "Enjoyment of the rights and freedoms set forth in this Convention shall be secured without discrimination on any ground such as . . . religion." Technically, the case was referred to the Grand Chamber of the European Court of Human Rights by the European Commission of Human Rights and the French Government.

On the benefit, the court said: "The Court considers, like the Government, that it is in the general interest to avoid unregulated slaughter, carried out in conditions of doubtful hygiene, and that it is therefore preferable, if there is to be ritual slaughter, for it to be performed in slaughterhouses supervised by the public authorities. Accordingly, when in 1982 the State granted approval to the ACIP, an offshoot of the Central Consistory, which is the body most representative of the Jewish communities in France, it did not in any way infringe upon the freedom to manifest one's religion." *CSVT v. France*, 22, para. 77. The court's ruling is consistent with its generally narrow interpretation of religious freedom. For an analysis of the doctrine, see Gunn," Adjudicating Rights."

The court applied the margin of appreciation doctrine, which gives governments some leeway to interpret their own laws. The court voted twelve to five that there had been no violation of Article 9, the religious freedom provision and ten to seven that there was no violation of Article 9 taken together with 14. A joint dissent by seven judges noted that "public authorities" must take "all necessary measures to ensure that the competing groups tolerate each other." *CSVT v. France*, 27, para. 1. They also thought that even if permission had been granted to one religious body, that did not "absolve" the government from considering claims by other religious bodies of the same religion.

Quotation from *CSVT v. France*, 23, para. 79.

46. Horsemeat is considered a delicacy in Europe. The U.S. Humane Society conducted an undercover investigation and reported that 250,000 horses are slaughtered in the United States for human consumption in France, Belgium, Italy, and Japan (for horse sushi). Dirk Johnson, "Last-Chance Sale." Small birds have traditionally been eaten in Italian cuisine. Root, *Cooking*. California State Senator Mike Thompson asserted that California passed a law to protect robins, considered a delicacy by Italian immigrants. Bishop, "Culinary Rule." On implicit/explicit, see Simoons, *Eat Not Flesh*, 106.

47. Dogflesh is traditionally eaten by many peoples. See Simoons, *Eat Not Flesh*, 91. Celedonio Paranada was found guilty of being an accessory to cruelty to an animal in Hawaii, when a young Labrador retriever was killed to be eaten. Tanji, "Dog's Death." With no law against eating dog, the issue was simply whether the manner in which the dog was killed was cruel. On the California case: "When dealing with one's own animal, the right to kill is not questioned, it being an attribute of private ownership." Favre and Loring, *Animal Law*, 144. Joseph Beason, a defense attorney in the case, was quoted in *Newsweek* as saying: "I don't like people interfering with what I do in the privacy of my own refrigerator." The prosecutor, Sarah Lazarus, indicated that there were a lot of jokes told during the trial, e.g., change of menu instead of change of venue.

48. The men received a death threat while in custody. Charles, "Judge Chooses." On the lawyers, see Haldane, "Culture Clash," and "Cambodians." One defendant guaranteed it would never happen again; it was not worth it. Quoted in Charles, "Judge Dismisses."

"To hold otherwise would be to subject every slaughterhouse employee or farmer to prosecution." Anon. (1989a), "Cultural Differences." The judge explains his reasoning in the excellent video documentary "Animal Appetites." The defendants' attorneys filed multimillion-dollar lawsuits against the city of Long Beach, alleging the two men's arrests violated their civil rights. Charles, "Men Charged."

49. Arguments in support of the Assembly Bill 1842 (third reading) celebrated the importance of dogs and cats: "According to proponents, dogs and cats are celebrated in history, literature, folklore and cinema as symbols of loyalty, heroism and intelligence. Proponents state that each year across America, hero dogs are recognized for their acts of bravery and devotion. According to proponents, numerous scientific studies have demonstrated that the human/animal bond significantly improves the quality of life, and is instrumental in combating loneliness and depression. Dogs and cats are viewed as among the animals most important to our society." However, the fact that dogs and cats have certain perceived benefits does not mean they might not also have another benefit, namely nutritious sustenance. Considering how many thousands of animals are "euthanized" annually, it seems incoherent to suggest that, if a few were eaten, that would interfere with the other benefits.

Letters sent to Assemblywoman Speier on behalf of Vietnamese organizations strongly objected to defining pets narrowly. Andrew Lam, a Vietnamese American journalist, was an outspoken critic of the bill: "This bill will do nothing more than perpetuate false stereotypes and heighten racial tensions." Abrams, "Ban." See also Andrew Lam, "Cuisine," who explains that many Vietnamese regard the lavish attention for dogs as "ludicrous;" nevertheless, the habit of eating dogs in the United States causes some to "feel shame" or to "deny that such practices even exist." Lam's article provoked an angry response from Nhu charging that media coverage of the incident would reinforce false stereotypes about Asian dog eaters and lead to more xenophobia. "Not Doggie Diners." The Cambodian community also expressed concern about this imagery. Corrales, "Case Shocks." See the California Penal Code, section 598b.

50. Deukmejian, "Letter." See also Jacobs, "Governor Signs." Richard Steffan, legislative aide in Assemblywoman Speier's office, said there was no legal significance to the governor's signing with an understanding. Personal communication, 1993.

51. Nil Hul, executive director of the Cambodian Association of American, said "nobody does it." Quoted in McMillan, "Pets Not Food." After doing some research, the judge in the case concluded that eating dog meat is not a "native" Cambodian custom but that it was brought to Cambodia from Vietnam by ethnic Chinese. The two defendants in the case were Cambodians of Chinese descent. Robeson, "Governor Pleads." The newspaper stated that the eating of dogs was uncommon until the 1970s during the Pol Pot regime when many were starving. Haldane, "Culture Clash." Some reports claim that dog eating has been popular in most countries throughout Southeast Asia, including Cambodia. Some groups deny that dog eating is traditional for their groups, despite evidence to the contrary. For instance, Koreans have been known to deny the eating of dogflesh, though this practice is well documented in Korea. Simoons, *Eat Not Flesh*, 96. Korean officials dislike the custom because they fear it may damage the nation's image. Wudunn, "Dog." In 1987 the International Fund for Animal Welfare launched a campaign against the practice of eating dogs in South Korea, where it still attracts media attention. Demick, "Culinary Flap." The law and incident which provided the impetus for its enactment are discussed in Randolph, *Dog Law*, 17–18, and Abrams, "Ban."

52. Joseph Beason acknowledged that the men were ethnic Chinese and that traditionally Chinese ate dogs; Cambodians are also known to eat dog, despite their denial. Personal communication, 1992. On the Pol Pot regime, see Haldane, "Culture Clash."

His wife said this, though she denied that she herself had ever eaten dog. Corrales, "Began with Gift."

53. The most widespread explanation is that animals are personified, and therefore humans should not eat them (this presumes that cannibalism is unacceptable). See, e.g., Serpell, "Pet-Keeping," 47, and Leach, "Anthropological Aspects." Another theory is that the resemblance between eating a pet and the act of sexual intercourse between close relatives makes eating a pet metaphorically akin to incest. See, e.g., Tambiah, "Animals."

54. For history of the "pet" tradition, see Rikvo, "Modern Pet-Keeping," and Serpell, "Pet-Keeping." For the significance of dogs as pets, see Rollin, *Animals Rights*. Linzey considers the proposition that keeping animals as pets may be immoral. *Christianity*, 133–138. Even artistic portrayals of dogs as food may be unacceptable. Rainey, "Banner." Chiu uses the "gastronomy lesson" ("Be American. Eat American food. If not, you will go to jail") to highlight anti-Asian and pro-European sentiments in the United States. "Cultural Defense," 1110.

55. Temperature regulations can lead to culture conflicts. See Yi, "Health Codes." Dried, salted, or otherwise preserved foods are not subject to the regulation as they will not spoil.

56. It is curious that the public health department decided to investigate the restaurants at that point in time. Octavio Paz's description of American puritanical attitudes toward the food industry may offer some insight: "The maniacal preoccupation with the origin and purity of food is the counterpart of racism and discrimination." "Eroticism," 74. Although this was primarily a California policy question, restaurants in other states expressed concern, e.g., the New York Chinatown Chamber of Commerce. The Task Force on Chinese Food contacted the USDA. A health inspector evidently supported the four-hour lead time allowance that was subsequently included in the legislation. The task force strategy was to procure a letter from USDA endorsing the time allowance to convince state and local departments. Yee, "Minutes," 1.

57. From Berquist, "Peking Duck," and Michael Woo, personal communication, 1996.

58. Audrey Noda and Senator David Roberti were instrumental in helping secure passage of the law. It was passed quickly, so as not to disrupt Chinese restaurants' business. Steve Erickson, "Ancient Art." See Health and Safety Code, section 27602: "(a) Whole Chinese-style roast duck shall be exempted from section 27601 for a period not to exceed four hours after the duck is prepared, since the methods used to prepare these foods inhibit the growth of microorganisms which can cause food infections or food intoxications. . . . (b) for the purpose of this section, "Chinese-style roast duck" shall include, but is not limited to Chinese-style barbecue duck, dry hung duck, and Peking duck."

Another culturally insensitive incident occurred in the region of Miami, Florida, known as Little Havana. The sidewalk window, an institution in Latin American, was challenged by state inspectors who regarded the open windows as a health violation. They insisted that proprietors install sliding glass or screens between the food and the customers; Cuban Americans considered this a "cultural blunder." Wells, "Coffee Windows."

59. For a discussion of the image of the dog as savior and as man's best friend, see Herzog and Burghardt, "Attitudes," 89.

60. See, e.g., Curtius, "Cultures Clash." One activist suggested that instead of stopping the practice of selling live animals, all stores should require this. If (hypocritical) Americans had to slaughter their own meat, she speculates that they might become less carnivorous. Shulman, "Letter." Chinese merchants reject the claim that tourists find the markets abhorrent. Chinatown is the second most popular site in San Francisco after Fisherman's Wharf. Ironically, the sale of live lobsters and crabs there has not attracted the attention of animal rights activists. Curtius, "Cultures Clash." Mrs. May Chang, owner of a food store in Chinatown, explains: "When I was a girl in Shanghai, my mother always told me, 'when it is dead, you never know how long it has been dead.' I have been here 20 years, but I still sell every-

thing live. It is healthier. If you offer people dead animals, they won't eat them." Tim Golden, "Cuisine."

61. Quoted in Curtius, "Cultures Clash," A21.

62. Quotation from Henry Lee, "Preliminary Ban." The commission devoted two years to studying the practice of selling live animals such as fish, frogs, turtles, poultry, and crustaceans. The commissioner from the Department of Public Health did not vote as he said there was no public health issue. Even though there are two hundred cases of salmonella poisoning per year in San Francisco and 20 percent of the poisoned are Asians, there is no data connecting the live animal markets to the infections. Tsai, "Animal Groups." See also Lynch, "Supervisors." Lynch commented that "powerful" Chinatown groups were lobbying hard, but that animal rights groups were "no pushover." No board member introduced legislation. Epstein," Animal Rights Lawsuits." The city council may have been ambivalent because it was committed to protecting minority rights and animal welfare. As Tim Golden put it: "What's an animal-respecting, multiculturally sensitive, compulsively democratic city to do?" "Cuisine." Barbara Kaufman, president of the Board of Supervisors, suggested that if the goal is to ensure the humane treatment of animals, then the focus should not be on a handful of merchants but on the entire industry, including factory farmers and slaughterhouses. Gurnon,"Messy Food Fight." The Fish and Game Commission took up the matter, and Assemblyman Mike Honda also sponsored legislation to try to prevent the ban. Bustillo, "Cultures Clash."

63. San Francisco supervisor Tom Hsieh said: "[Animal advocates] disrespect our traditions, cultures, and values. They may not be aware that their rhetoric is insensitive and divisive and perpetuates discrimination against our community." Quoted in Guillermo, "Live Food Ban." See also Le, "Letter," and Tam, "Slaughtering Practices."

64. See, e.g., Guillermo, "Live Food Ban." Critics also made this error: Supervisor Leland Yee said of the lawsuit that it was "a racial issue." Quoted in Epstein, "Animal Rights Lawsuits." On "fixed," see Ortiz, "Tradition."

"I don't understand the reaction of Chinese Americans outraged by the preliminary ban on the sale of live animals for food—this does not affect their eating practices. It just asks them to treat animals with some small degree of respect and keep their suffering to a minimum. If their culture condones needless cruelty, then I suppose it could be construed as an attack on their culture." Zwigoff is unselfconscious about condemning what she assumes is a sadistic practice. "Letter."

65. Chiang, "Suit." Seventy-five individuals joined the animal rights organizations as plaintiffs. See also Epstein, "Animal Rights Lawsuits"; Gledhill, "Rights Group" and "Restrictions"; Schwartz, "Accord."

66. After Rai bit into the beef burrito, Taco Bell refused either to give him a refund or to pay him the difference between the more expensive beef burrito and the bean burrito (they offered just to give him a bean burrito). Rai explained; "Eating the cow, it was a really devastating experience. . . . So much so that I had to go to a psychiatrist. I went to a doctor. I couldn't sleep." Quoted in MacGregor, "Faith and Food." He even went to England to perform a religious purification ritual with Hindu masters and eventually to India to purify himself by bathing in the holy waters of the Ganges River. Maharaj, "Taco Bell." Quotation from MacGregor, "Faith and Food."

On nonsympathy, for instance, one letter to the editor said: "To Mr. Rai: Cut into your burrito first if it's such a great concern. To Taco Bell: Give him 10 free bean burritos. To the lawyers: Get a real case." Beigel, "Beef."

The newspaper indicated that Rai sought $144,000 but did not say what the settlement was. Maharaj, "Taco Bell."

67. There is a large literature on this subject. See, e.g., Kathleen Sands, who says: "Charreada, the performance of competitive equestrian events, is often referred to as Mexico's num-

ber-one sport." *Charreria Mexicana*, xi. For background, see Bustillo, "Question." Charreadas were routinely held in Arizona, California, Colorado, Illinois, New Mexico, and Texas. The Mexican cowboy is the *charro*, the *charreada* is the Mexican-style rodeo, and the *charreria* is the tradition. The three events are *piales en la lienzo* (roping of the hind legs of a horse), *manganas a pie* (tipping or felling of a horse from on foot), and *a caballo* (tripping or felling a horse from horseback). For all events the point is "not to damage the mare." Kathleen Sands, *Charreria Mexicana*, 10. See also Fox, "Riders"; Meg Sullivan, "Charreadas"; Gurza, "Charro Spirit."

68. The organization worried that the animal rights groups would next launch an anti-calf roping bill. The director of administration was quoted in the *Los Angeles Times* as saying "he feels no kinship with charros, and sees no reason to look after the interests of charreria." Bustillo, "Question," A18. The governor signed the AB 49X by Assemblyman John Burton which made it a misdemeanor to intentionally trip a horse. Gillam, "Sacramento file," and Lucas, "Crime." Horse tripping was also specifically banned in Los Angeles County. Carla Rivera, "Supervisors." The Advisory Opinion said, "A finding that a person has intentionally engaged in the activity known as 'horse tripping' is sufficient to support a conviction for 'torturing an animal' under section 42.09(a)(1) of the Penal Code." Morales, Attorney General, Letter Opinion.

69. In a compelling analysis, Najera-Ramirez reveals how the debate over the charreada villified Mexican Americans. Noting that charros seldom injure horses, she explains that the "charreada functions to create a cultural landscape in which individuals can fully engage in and, indeed, nurture and preserve their Mexicanness." See her "Racialization," 505–506. On discrimination, see David Rose, "Ride 'Em." Bustillo's article states that "charro leaders, charging racism, say they are the victims of an attack on minority and rural culture that the urban majority does not, and perhaps cannot understand." "Question." I am referring to California's Proposition 187, "Save Our State," which was designed to deny basic social services to illegal immigrants and their children. On the same standard, see Lucas, "Crime." Although cruelty to horses is not unknown in western rodeos, it "makes a person subject to 'hostile gossip.'" Lawrence, *Rodeo*, 172.

70. One said: "As a Mexican American, I'm very concerned that some Mexicans use the issue of race to justify the criticism for their abuse of animals, the so-called 'tradition' of charreadas. . . . I am not against tradition, just against cruelty." Bustillo, "Question." A fifth-grade school teacher says that children discussed the contests with their parents, who "do not consider them to be part of their culture, pronouncing them instead the lowest sort of cruelty to animals. . . . As for this being a 'tradition' and therefore worthy of being taught to a new generation: This is the United States of America, and although other cultures are part of what has built this nation, deliberate cruelty and torture of any sentient being are not an acceptable "tradition" in our world." Lobsenz, "Letter." It is a common rhetorical move to deny that traditions which are objectionable are, in fact, traditions. Refusal to designate the practices as traditional implies that if they were, they might be worthy of some respect.

71. Statement (N.D.) (expanded notes AB49x) of California Equine Legislative Counsel.

72. The effect of animal cruelty on children is also a major concern in the Santería litigation.

73. The point on the movie industry was raised in a letter to the editor by the coordinator of Animals in Entertainment, Los Angeles office. She describes how the death of a horse falling from a cliff during the making of the 1939 film *Jesse James* resulted in an effort by the American Humane Association to open an office to stop such practices. Barbara Sands, "Horse Treatment."

Although bullfighting is banned throughout the United States, the bloodless form of the sport is allowed in California where it is said to be a popular pastime for the large Portuguese

American community in the San Joaquin Valley. Evidently the bullfights are allowed only if they are part of religious festivals, like the Portuguese Holy Ghost Fiesta. Anon. (1997g), "Bloodless Bullfighting."

74. For various interpretations, see Dundes, *Cockfight*. Although the birds seized in this raid were kept alive, those taken in a previous raid were euthanized and their carcasses frozen in order that they could be used as evidence. Howe, "Cockfight Raid."

On the 1995 New York campaign, see Nieves, "Blood Sport." Cockfighting is legal in Guam, Mexico, and the Philippines. Kilborn, "Rural Enclaves." "Participants say they don't understand why cockfighting is illegal here. One mentioned that it seems inconsistent where hunting is a sport, eating turkey is part of a national holiday, and throwing a lobster in boiling water is considered cooking." Nieves, "Blood Sport."

In some places cockfighting is only legal on certain dates, e.g., the annual fair in Tijuana. Manson, "Cockfighters." For a historical overview of law regulating cockfighting in the United States, see McCaghy and Neal, "Fraternity." With support from the Humane Society of the United States, ballot measures outlawing cockfighting in Arizona and Missouri passed in 1998. Kilborn, "Rural Enclaves." States that allow cockfighting generally ban it on Sundays. In 2000 it was reported that more than 180 House members and more than 40 senators were sponsoring bills to prohibit the interstate shipment of cocks. Organizations like the United Gamefowl Breeders Association (UGBA) lobby against legislation limiting cockfighting. Herzog and Burghardt, "Attitudes." The UGBA director said it is a multimillion-dollar business, and the major trade magazine *Gamecock* claims to have sixteen thousand subscribers.

One particular raid of a national championship cockfight led to the arrest of 296 people who were betting on the birds. Anon. (1995a), "Cockfight Raided." Not all cockfighting prosecutions have a cultural dimension. In *State v. Albee* (1993), e.g., a defendant challenged an Oregon law prohibiting being present at preparation for a cockfight on the grounds of vagueness and overbreadth.

75. See the Fund for Animals, advertisement in *New York Times*, May 23, 26, 1995. One court tackled the issue of equal protection in *State v. Ham* (1984). The Court of Appeals held that the failure of the law to prohibit all hunting and gaming did not render the law unconstitutional. The defendant in the case was apparently not a member of an ethnic minority.

76. Alonso-Zaldivar describes the arrest of Anson Wong, a politically connected Malaysian business man. "Agents." Evidently the United States is the largest market for exotic fauna. Creatures believed to possess important medicinal, aphrodisiac, or aesthetic qualities are highly sought after. Sometimes those bringing them into the United States claim that they were unaware of the policy, or they say the animals are not considered endangered in their countries.

77. Leusner and Jacobson, "Dealers."

78. *U.S. v. Tomono* (1998).

79. *U.S. v. Tomono* (1997). The Court of Appeals explained the lower court's behavior: "The district court granted a three-level downward departure for what it termed cultural differences." Before making the downward departure, the court had reduced his level of culpability because of his "acceptance of responsibility."

80. District court judge quoted in the Court of Appeals decision.

81. All of these points are in the court order.

82. "When he pled guilty, Tomono admitted that he knowingly sold the wildlife (though he need not have known that the sale violated the law) and that he specifically knew that the wildlife he sold had been imported into the US in violation of the law." Brief of Appellant, Dec. 1997, 27.

83. Brief of Appellant, Dec. 1997, 32.

84. "The fact that the turtles may or may not be endangered is already considered in the applicable guideline, which mandates a four-level enhancement if the wildlife in question is listed in the Endangered Species Act of the Convention on International Trade in Endangered Species. See U.S. Sentencing Guidelines Manual S 2Q2.1(b)(3)(B)." *U.S. v. Tomono* (1998), 1404. The government's brief states that the turtles are not considered "endangered" in the United States, either. Assuming that that is correct, there is a question as to why their sale is regulated (30). The government had to show the defendant knew the wildlife was illegal, not that he was aware of the existence of the Lacey Act.

85. Quotation from *U.S. v. Tomono* (1998), 1404, n.2. Tomono was subsequently deported to Japan.

86. Alan Dundes argues that humane treatment of animals in many instances is motivated by a desire to control animal instincts: "Man would like to indulge his animal desires but has been educated to deny or restrain them. Accordingly, he takes pleasure in watching animals behave like humans." *Game to War*, 30.

CHAPTER 7

1. While most of the cases are criminal in nature, some conflicts involve family law issues like custody, questions such as whether the marriage is void or voidable, and divorce. For example, in *Singh v. Singh* (1996), an Indian man living in the United States filed a suit for $4 million in damages because he had married a "defective bride." Pittman, "'Defective Bride,'" and Mowatt, "Man Sues." When Anita advertised her availability for marriage in the *India West* and *India Abroad* magazines, she described herself as having a traditional Indian background and being a vegetarian, neither of which was apparently true. Although he married her anyway, and they had a child, after they divorced, he claimed that the marriage had damaged his reputation in the Indian community. Subotnik, "Sue Me." The judge ruled that, despite the misrepresentations, public policy bars such a cause of action.

2. Of course, whether the marriage is "valid" according to the "official" law does not mean that the couple will not consider itself married. This is merely a question of whether state law recognizes customary law.

3. Watson contends that non-Western citizens experience a deprivation of their rights and uses examples from marriage law to underscore this point. "Justice," 25.

4. Over thirty countries allow child marriages under the age of fifteen. Anon. (1996k), "Child Mothers." Traditional law addresses this issue, however. For instance, although Islamic law does not prohibit marriage under a specific age, it does specify that the marriage should not be consummated before the bride reaches puberty. Poulter discusses English conflicts law: if a couple marries in England and one spouse is under age sixteen, the marriage would be void. Should the couple marry abroad, the marriage would be void even if the person under sixteen was a "foreign domiciliary." *English Law*, 18–19.

5. England enacted the Age of Marriage Act 1929, which mandated a minimum age of sixteen for boys and girls and specified that marriages with a spouse under the minimum age would be void. Evidently one motivation behind the 1929 reform was Britain's desire to raise the age of marriage overseas. Poulter, *English Law*, 18. Some human rights treaties explicitly forbid child marriage, e.g., Article 16(2) of the 1962 Convention on Consent to Marriage. For analysis of the provisions, see Askari, "Convention."

6. John Burns, "Illegal."

7. *Alhaji Mohamed v. Knott* (1968). Quotations are from the opinion.

8. This was the language used for placing juveniles in institutions in England.

9. *Knott*, 1457–1458.

10. Poulter, *Ethnicity, Law, and Human Rights*, 53. The law was modified when authorities discovered that two very young brides (aged twelve and thirteen, from Iraq and Oman) had come to the United Kingdom with student husbands.

11. Evidently there is debate about the legitimacy of child marriage. Some Muslim countries have enacted legal reforms to prohibit the marriage of young children. Poulter, *Ethnicity, Law, and Human Rights*, 233, and J. Anderson, *Law Reform*, 102–109. The case was *Khan v. UK* (1986).

12. For instance, in Texas charges were dropped against a Mexican immigrant for having sex with a minor because he was married to the fourteen-year-old. Anon. (1996e), "Marriage Dissolves." In an unpublished case in Los Angeles, *People v. Jose Isabel Panigua* (1992) a Guatemalan man, aged twenty-six, was charged with committing a lewd and lascivious act upon a child under the age of fourteen. As the couple was living together with the blessing of both families and would have been married in Guatemala, where there was apparently no minimum age for marriage and only a requirement for parental consent, he received probation and had to promise to pay child support. Francesca Frey, personal communication, 1999. Information on Orange County from Ayres, "Marriage Advised," A10. Evidently because virtually all the minors were Latinas, "some social workers and lawmakers charged that the agency was confronted with a 'cultural issue.'" Lait, "Agency's Role."

13. *State v. Benu* (1978).

14. The court did acknowledge the father's motivation: "under the tenets of his faith matrimony was a desirable alternative to fornication or adultery." *Benu*, 225.

15. Even if girls are unhappily married, ordinarily courts accept marriages if they are valid where consummated. Courts only refuse to recognize marital status on the very strongest public policy grounds. Karsten, "Child Marriages," 214.

16. Karsten, "Child Marriages."

17. On patriarchy, see McPhail, "Unacceptable." Intervention can have tragic results. In one case when officials from Child Protective Services told a thirteen-year-old Hmong "wife" to return home, the "husband" was found dead. A relative said because he was despondent over the intervention, this may have led him to commit suicide. Anon. (1995d), "Death Puts Spotlight."

18. The victim phenomenon was noted during the Orange County policy debate. See Ayres, 1986.

19. *Friedman v. State* (1967), 862.

20. The court noted that some liberal as well as conservative Jews might disagree with that interpretation, but "a 100 per cent orthodox" Jew would agree with it. *Friedman*, 862.

21. Perhaps because the word "Gypsy" can have pejorative connotations, many in the community prefer to call themselves "Roma" (singular "Rom"). Weyrauch and Bell, "Autonomous Lawmaking," 335; Lockwood and Salo, *Gypsies*, 2; Dean. "Gypsies Banding." The name is derived from their language, Romani. Originally from northern India, they are found in Eastern Europe and all over the world. More than a million Gypsies live in the United States. Dowling and Fusco, "Gypsies."

Over the years Grover Marks, a *baro* (literally, the great one or the big one, i.e, leader of the community), known as King of the Gypsies, was involved in several different legal actions, including tampering with jurors and evidence, welfare fraud, tax evasion (*Marks v. U.S.*, [1987]), and assault of officers in a cemetery. The civil rights lawsuit is the relevant one here. It involved the question of qualified immunity for the officers and whether the confiscated property should be returned. See the decisions of the Washington state supreme court, *State v. Marks* (1990) and the U.S. Court of Appeals (Ninth Circuit), *Marks v. Clarke* (1996).

There was no question that the manner in which the search was carried out was illegal. Morlin, "Searches." The courts involved in the different lawsuits made different rulings about the flaws with the search. They included that the warrant was not signed by a judge, that it did not specify precisely what stolen items were sought, that it authorized the search of only two men, that the police did not read the search warrants, and that they began to search the defendants' homes before the warrants were issued. The expert witness for the Gypsies on this question, Peter Arenella, UCLA professor of law, concluded that the police officers' conduct violated the particularity requirement of the Fourth Amendment. The warrant was deficient both because it was overly broad, authorizing the search of any person in the homes, and because there was no probable cause to support the authorization. "Deposition," 23–24. He also found that "any reasonably well trained police officer should have realized that such a provision in the context of this case was patently overbroad" (24). This means that despite *U.S. v. Leon* (1984), which prevents the suppression of evidence where the police rely in good faith on a defective warrant, here there was no good faith on the part of the police. However, a lawyer for the city said the Gypsies consented to the search, obviating the need for any warrant. Rocco Treppiedi, personal communication, 1997.

On the seizures, see Timothy Egan, "Police Raid." Because Grover was the leader of the Gypsy community, his house was the repository of church monies. Dowling and Fusco, "Gypsies," 46. The police were accused of desecrating a sacred urn and urinating on a Gypsy leader. Morlin, "Police Accused."

The girls said male and female police officers ordered them to submit to a body search in their parents' bedrooms. Morlin, "Raids Catastrophic" and "Ill Judge." According to Ruth Anderson, the Marks' expert witness on Gypsy customary law, because women "never expose their bodies to anyone other than their husbands," the body searches were the equivalent of rape. "Deposition." Quote in Morlin and Nappi, "Gypsy Daughters." This is also discussed at length in the deposition of Dr. Ruth Anderson (see esp. 62–80). For an excellent analysis of marime, including a study of six cases, see Carol Miller, "American Rom." Apparently the Gypsy tribunal known as the *kris* met after the raid and decided that Grover Marks was marime. Consequently, because it was not possible to arrange marriages under the circumstances, two of the Marks boys had to elope. Other Rom told Grover's son, Jimmy, that no one would attend their funerals: "When you or Grover dies, you'll have to rent pallbearers. No Rom is even going to be at the funerals to put you in the ground because you're so dirty and blackballed." Dowling and Fusco, "Gypsies," 54. Evidently, however, when Grover Marks died in 1997, Gypsies came from all over the country to attend his funeral. Morlin, "Celebrating."

The Gypsies filed the lawsuits after state courts ruled that the searches were conducted without legal warrants. Anon. (1992b), "Gypsies Claim." One suit requested $40 million, and the other asked for $19 million. Morlin, "Gypsies" and "City Settles." Courts have held that Gypsies constitute a discrete ethnic group. See *Saint Francis College v. Al-Khazraji* (1987), *Janko v. Illinois State Toll Highway Authority* (1989), and *Commission for Racial Equality v. Dutton* (1989). For the civil rights lawsuit see *Marks v. Clarke* (1996). See also *State v. Marks* (1990). For background, see Dowling and Fusco, "Gypsies." For a critique of Gaje definitions of who counts as a "Gypsy," see Hancock, "Roots."

On Spokane's admission of liability, see Morlin and Nappi, "Gypsy Daughters," and Morlin, "Police Accused." The plaintiffs sought both general and punitive damages. The trial was delayed because the original judge died of cancer. Morlin, "New Judge." The district court found that the searches violated the constitutional rights of twenty-seven members of the Gypsy Church of the Northwest and that both the city and county of Spokane were liable for damages. Morlin, "Searches." On appeal the city and county lost the argument that the officers were entitled to use a qualified immunity defense because they had acted in good faith. See the Court of Appeals decision (*Marks v. Clarke*, 1996) and Morlin, "City Loses Again."

22. Expert witnesses who testified disagreed over the proper interpretation of the damage caused by the search. Dr. Ian Hancock explained the devastating effect of the

search, noting that the Romani community "reacted in a culturally specific way" because of their cultural background. "Deposition," 19. See Hancock's description of marime, 44–49, 167–172. He was doubtful that the family could change its status: "right or wrong, the family is marime in the eyes of the community. Now, how the family will regain its status is hard to say, it may never do that. Some people may argue that they are marime because of an outside factor, but that doesn't carry a lot of weight. It is the end result that counts" (48–49). Hancock calls the police behavior "a two time mess up," noting that the officers not only violated American law by executing an illegal search, but also violated Gypsy law. "Deposition," 170–171. Andersen pointed out that even if the police search had been legal, the damage to the Gypsies would have been the same. "Deposition," 16. They would probably not have been able to recover any damages had the search been legal. On defilement, see Hancock, "American Roma."

23. Weyrauch and Bell emphasize that "adherence to these ritual purity laws is central in setting Gypsies apart from their host cultures." "Autonomous Lawmaking," 343.

24. Quotations from, respectively, Weyrauch and Bell, "Autonomous Lawmaking," 343, and Carol Miller, "American Rom," 43, 42. Contact of upper and lower body is also discussed in Andersen, "Deposition," 62–63. Quotation from Carol Miller, "American Rom," 45. Gypsies do not share their dishes and utensils with gaji; if visitors come, afterward they either destroy the set or save them for use by other non-Gypsies. Silverware can only regain purity by being soaked in bleach. Weyrauch and Bell, "Autonomous Lawmaking," 349–350.

Final quotations from Carol Miller, "American Rom," 51–52. Andersen explains marime this way: "[It] is that someone is so contaminated that one simply must shun him or her, not through dislike or hate, not because the person did anything to merit that status, simply out of fear of similar contamination." "Deposition," 79, 142–145.

25. The lawyer for the city seemed surprised that the Gypsy community would be considered defiled if it was not its fault that police had conducted the search. Andersen, "Deposition," 123.

26. Weyrauch and Bell, "Autonomous Lawmaking," 359. While Weyrauch and Bell describe the dire consequences associated with marime when it is permanent punishment, they acknowledge that this is used only for the most serious offenses such as murder. For less serious crimes such as Gypsy theft from another Gypsy (it is not a crime to steal from a Gaje), "familiarity with a Gaje," and failure to pay a debt on time, a temporary marime sentence may be imposed (359).

27. Weyrauch and Bell, "Autonomous Lawmaking," 391.

28. According to a lawyer for the city, Gypsies said that Grover Marks was pretending to be marime; the lawyer also said the girls did marry according to customary law. Rocco Treppiedi, personal communication, 1997. Carol Miller suggests that the sanction may not result in permanent ostracism. Based on only six cases, she concludes that the "inflexibility of pollution beliefs" may be modified in light of circumstances. The sanction's purpose is "to modify behaviour, not to outcast indefinitely." "American Rom," 53. She says the daughters may be reinstated after they leave their non-Gypsy husbands if they prove that they do not have any sexually transmitted diseases and show remorse. The family will still be barred from some communal activities, however (45).

29. Mulick, "Reach Settlement." I thank attorneys Mark Deife and Rocco Treppiedi, journalist Bill Morlin, my former student Fred Hay, and an expert witness, Ian Hancock, for providing me with documents from and insights about the case. For another case in which a court had to assess the monetary value of a sexual assault, see *Salinas v. Forth Worth Cab and Baggage Co., Inc.* (1987).

30. Storke, "Incestuous Marriage," 473.

31. Ibid., 477.

32. *In re May's Estate* (1952; reversed in 1953). The effect of the ruling was to deny letters of administration to the husband of the deceased and to give them to the daughter. Sometimes relationships are forbidden not because they are too close by blood but, rather, by socially ascribed affinities. See Strijbosch, "Concept of Pela."

33. The cases discussed in this section differ somewhat from the cases covered in the previous section "child marriages" because the girls in those cases evidently did not object to the relationships. For an analysis of several forced marriage cases from a critical race theory perspective, see Volpp, "Blaming Culture." For cases reported throughout the United States, see Dean, "Cultures"; Martin, "Cultures Collide"; Margaret Talbot, "Baghdad"; Terry, "Cultural Tradition"; Hugh Wright, "Man Gets Probation." In the late 1980s Legal Services for Children had a case involving Palestinian Muslim parents from Israel. I am grateful to Martha Mathews for giving me the background on this case.

34. Sward, "No Charges."

35. "Cultural sensitivity is a noble notion, but is not a blanket. We do not honor the Sudanese 'custom' of black slavery, and now female genital mutilation is against our law. Why is child marriage all right just because her 'community' thinks it is all right? What are we thinking of? We should rescue that child!" Farhat, "Letter." The writer makes an implicit comparison between child marriage and female genital mutilation, bride burning, cannibalism, foot binding, and animal sacrifice. Gary Cramer, "Letter: Cultural Differences."

36. A Laotian man paid $9,000 to a family so that their ten-year-old daughter would marry him. When he was prosecuted for allegedly raping her, he tried unsuccessfully to raise a cultural defense. Anon. (1989g), "Immigrant Sentenced." See also Rotstein, "Girl Tells."

37. In England there have been reported instances when Pakistani families, displeased with their daughters' conduct, "have commissioned searches by bounty hunters, kidnappings, and forced one-way trips to Pakistan. In extreme cases, the families have punished their daughters by beating them, throwing acid in their face and burning them to death." Hoge, "Women Marked." For instance, a Canadian Indian girl was forcibly married during a visit to India. Although she managed to escape, the family that assisted her was incarcerated. Anon. (1998h), "NRI Girl." On the Pakistani case, see. Hoge, "Women Marked." While in 1997 this was reported to be the only known conviction, a retired inspector stated that he had had 742 cases of Asian woman from northern England who had sought protection from their own families. Hoge, "Women Marked."

38. The story of fictional Noreen is recounted in *Izzat: For the Sake of Honour* (1996) by Nasim Karim, a Norwegian of Pakistani descent. The Norwegian government considered enacting a law against forced marriage. Allegedly, several hundred boys and girls were abducted from Norway to be forcibly married in 1996 and 1997. Wang, "Nadia Case," 6. All three, Nadia and her parents, were Norwegian citizens. Much of the information concerning this case comes from an unpublished paper "Parents' Rights, the Rights of the Child, and Citizenship: The Case of Nadia" by Unni Wikan, a prominent anthropologist who testified on behalf of the parents. Evidently in Norway an expert may be called by the court and, similar to U.S. jury duty, cannot decline to serve, even if disinclined to do so. She says that she was astonished that she was asked to be a special witness for the defense because she had publicly sided with Nadia on national television. See also Wikan, "Citizenship on Trial." The other main source is a paper, "The Nadia Case," written by Hans Wang, a lawyer and former political science student at the University of Southern California, who is Norwegian.

Nadia's mother awakened her telling her she needed to leave the house which was on fire. As Nadia left the house, she realized the house was not on fire. When she was unwilling to get into the van, her father beat her, handcuffed her, and placed her in the back of the van. Wang, "Nadia Case," 2.

39. See Wang, "Nadia Case," 3–4. During the period of negotiations Nadia was reportedly held captive and physically punished for having brought shame on her family. See also Wikan, "Parents' Rights," 1–2. Wikan expresses concern about the "value of citizenship" if one country can "simply 'undo'" the citizenship of another country (4). Wikan says the idea for the "ingenious strategy" came from the Norwegian police (2). The father received social security payments from the Norwegian government of approximately $30,000 per year since he became a citizen of Norway. Wang, "Nadia Case," 4. Nadia's mother received approximately $3,000 per year.

40. Wikan, "Parents' Rights," 2. Her parents subsequently denied the story of abduction and forced marriage, saying Nadia had made it up because she was homesick for Norway.

41. Wang explains that sections 223 and 224 both deal with holding persons against their will: section 223 is concerned with why the person is held; section 224 does not take into account the reasons for doing so. Wang, "Nadia Case," 6.

42. See Wang, "Nadia Case," 7–9. The charges against her brother were dropped. The government did not have sufficient evidence to charge the parents with attempting to force her to marry someone from Morocco. The trial was in the Oslo Byrett, which is the "entry level court" in Norway. Both of her parents decided to exercise their right to appeal the judgment. Nadia's father died six months after the trial, and though his son, Nadia's brother, attempted to appeal on his behalf, the court refused to allow this. The government decided to withdraw its charge against Nadia's mother. Wikan, "Citizenship on Trial," 138. It also appears that Nadia's father was criticized in the Moroccan community for not accepting full responsibility and making sure his wife avoided having to serve any time in jail. The court's judgment accepts Nadia's version completely and her plea for leniency.

43. Wikan, "Parents' Rights," 4.

44. The term *whore* is apparently a "usual non-dramatic swear word in Arabic and Berber," according to Wikan, "Citizenship on Trial."

45. This may occur when the wife finds the husband physically repugnant. A finding of nullity on this ground may make it impossible for the family to arrange another marriage for their daughter. The legal difficulty is that courts may find it hard to distinguish between "I can't" and "I won't," as Pearl puts it. For the third ground, situations that might be interpreted as willful refusal by the husband could be failure to carry out the religious ceremony or failure of the groom to pay the dowry. The three criteria are found in the 1973 Matrimonial Act. If one criterion is met, a marriage is considered voidable. Pearl, *Family Law*, 17–21.

46. Pearl, *Family Law*, 14.

47. Pearl explains that many immigrant communities require both ceremonies before the couple is considered married. Quotation from Pearl, *Family Law*, 15. Poulter says she "cried throughout the religious ceremony and was utterly miserable." *Asian Traditions*, 11.

48. Pearl, *Family Law*, 15.

49. In *Mahmud v. Mahmud* (1994) the Scottish Court of Session ruled in a manner similar to the Court of Appeals in *Hirani v. Hirani* (1983). For more citations, see Bradley, "Duress." In *Singh v. Singh* (1971), the court ruled that the daughter's compliance with parental choice of marriage partner did not involve fear on her part, merely a sense of duty. Poulter said courts would be unlikely to take such a "tough stand" in subsequent cases. *Asian Traditions*, 11. In *Singh v. Kaur* (1981) a Sikh son tried to have his marriage voided, but the court thought he clearly had a choice in the matter: "Through our English eyes, he is in a sad position; at the same time, he has to make up his mind, as an adult, whether to go through with the marriage or whether to withstand the pressure put upon him by his family." Pearl, *Family Law*, 17.

50. For discussion of the "primary purpose" rule, see Pearl, *Family Law*, 22–28. According to Poulter, the challenge is how to stop bogus marriages of convenience and forced mar-

riages without preventing the entry of genuine spouses of arranged marriages. *Asian Traditions*, 17. Because of the difficulty of remarrying their daughter, the parents of Vinjay advertised in the *Hindustan Times* Indian newspaper for a husband for their daughter. Bhatia responded and was selected as a suitable husband. Pearl, *Family Law*, 24, and Poulter, *Asian Traditions*, 18–19. Poulter explains that it is not enough that the marriage is shown to be genuine rather than spurious; the primary reason might still be entry into the United Kingdom. *Asian Traditions*, 19. He lost appeals to the Immigrant Adjudicator, the Immigration Appeal Tribunal, the High Court, and the Court of Appeals. Pearl, *Family Law*, 24. For a contrasting result, see *R. v. Immigration Appeal Tribunal ex parte Kumar* (1986). Here the court reversed the decision of the immigration officer. Poulter says the court was persuaded by evidence of the couple's devotion to each other during time spent in India. *Asian Traditions*, 20.

51. According to Wikan, in 1998 Nadia was living at a secret address, had a police escort, and no longer had any friends in the Moroccan community. "Parents' Rights," 6.

52. With women under age eighteen, consent is not an issue as statutory rape is a strict liability crime.

53. Anon. (1989c), "Kidnap." Another California case that received virtually no attention was *California v. Chong Pao Kue* (1989). See also Beth Goldstein, "Resolving Sexual Assault"; Titunik, "Worlds Collide"; deFiebre, "Cousins Accused"; John Cramer, "Rocky Reception"; Anon. (1991b), "Kidnapping?"; Trevison, "Sexual Assault."

54. Dershowitz, "Marriage by Capture," and Evans-Pritchard and Renteln, "Interpretation and Distortion."

55. The Hmong are frightened of police because they were frequently executed when stopped by the police. It is possible that Xeng might have been more afraid of the police than of a rapist.

56. Evidently this would have been the amount required according to Hmong folk law had the matter been handled in a traditional manner. In cases where no fines are imposed, the Hmong feel there is an injustice. Titunik, "Worlds Collide."

57. For instance, Kadish and Schuelhofer discuss *People v. (Kong) Moua* (1986) in *Criminal Law and Its Processes* (5th ed.) where they treat it as a mistake of law problem (288–289). This approach seems quite peculiar as Moua did not claim that he was unfamiliar with American law or that he did not know specifically that rape was illegal; he thought he was getting married according to Hmong tradition. In fact, it is insulting to imply, as the adoption of this conceptual framework does, that the Hmong have no concept of rape. Rape exists in Laos, though it is not common.

58. Scott Horne, La Crosse district attorney, who handled a dozen culture conflict cases, including one bride capture case. Quoted in Titunik, "Worlds Collide."

59. Bill Wise, chief deputy district attorney. Quoted in George White, "Hmong Case."

60. For a wonderful historical overview, see Firmage and Mangrum, *Zion in the Courts*. See also Sarat and Berkowitz, "Disorderly Differences." In 1998 there were approximately forty thousand polygamous families, representing 2 percent of the state's population. Brooke, "Utah Being Torn." See Cart, "Incest Trial," whose article discusses the trial of David Kingston, age thirty-three, charged with having sex with his sixteen-year-old niece. She was to be his fifteenth wife but instead ran away. See also Kenworthy, "Spotlight," and Stumbo, "Polygamists." The Utah affiliate asked the ACLU national board to revise Policy 91 to support plural marriage. A special panel was convened to conduct a broad study of the plural marriage issue, including not only Mormon experience but that of other groups as well. Parish-Pixler, "Polygamy." One group proposing legalized polygamy in Utah is the Women's Religious Liberties Union. Tapesty of Polygamy, an advocacy group of former polygamist wives, is opposed. Cart, "Polygamy Continues."

61. Brooke, "Utah Being Torn."

62. Cart, "Incest Trial." Evidently there were raids in the early 1950s, but the last major raid was badly handled. When photographs of children taken from their families were disseminated, this led to public outcry. Brooke, "Utah Being Torn." The Utah Supreme Court seems moderately supportive of polygamy, ruling in 1991 that polygamous families were eligible to adopt. The governor, Mike Leavitt, initially explained that polygamy is not prosecuted because of religious freedom concerns. His own family had practiced polygamy for four generations. When this provoked controversy, he issued a statement indicating his personal opposition to the tradition and clarifying that the lack of prosecution was due to problems of proof. Kenworthy, "Spotlight."

63. Anon. (1988b), "Police Officer Dies." The officer was trying to arrest the polygamist clan's patriarch because he had defied a court order to send his children to public schools.

64. Green conceived a child with his first wife in 1986 when she was thirteen. There was some question as to whether Green could be prosecuted for the rape charge because the statute of limitations had expired. In 1991 the law changed, requiring that the charges be filed no longer than four years after the crime was first reported. The judge ruled that "since the law changed in 1991, three years before the eight-year statute of limitations would have expired on a 1986 child rape, the statute could be applied retroactively." Vigh, "Prosecutor Rebuts." See also Anon. (2000g), "Mormon Ordered."

65. *People v. Ezeonu* (1992). The record does not reveal from which of hundreds of peoples Ezeonu came. (Polygamy is only practiced among some groups.) Dr. Ezeonu was a psychiatrist affiliated with Harlem Hospital. His children were removed from the household by the Child Welfare Administration. When detectives went to his apartment to discuss his children, he evidently invited them in and volunteered that he was interested in "giving Chiweta sex education."

66. The court denied his motion to suppress statements made to police in the absence of his attorney, concluding there was no violation of his constitutional right to counsel.

67. I am indebted to my colleague, Professor Eliz Sanasarian, and to my former student, Darya Alhambra, for providing references on the subject of mut'a. In Iran it is known as *sigheh.* Haeri, *Law of Desire,* ix. After the revolution of 1979 mut'a became more common. For a scholarly analysis, see Haeri, *Law of Desire.* See also Shahnez Khan, "Race." One cleric said "because God banned alcohol, he allowed temporary marriage." Sciolino, "Love." While 90 percent of Muslims are Sunni, only 10 percent are Shi'a. Khan, "Race." A Shi'i man may contract as many temporary marriages as he wishes, in addition to the four wives legally allowed for all Muslim men. A Shi'i Muslim woman, however, may only marry temporarily one man at a time, and in between marriages she must abstain from sex for a time in order to permit identification of the legitimate father. Children born as a result of temporary marriages have equal status with siblings born as a result of permanent marriages. Quotation from Shahnez Khan, "Race," 251. Haeri interprets the institution as a form of social control, one that minimizes the potential for divorce. She identifies a tension between religious acceptance of the practice with cultural disapproval of it. *Law of Desire,* 199. For a general discussion of the purpose of marriage in Islam, see al Faruqi, "Marriage in Islam." On legitimacy, see Haeri, *Law of Desire,* 6. The president of Iran, Hashemi Rafsanjani, apparently endorsed temporary marriage as part of a campaign to promote more acceptance of "sex and social interaction." al Faruqi, "Marriage in Islam." He endorsed the "God-given solution" to avoid being "promiscuous like the Westerners." Sciolino, "Love."

68. Such a marriage can theoretically last one hour to ninety-nine years. Ghodsi, "Slipknot," 667, and Shahnez Khan, "Race," 250. On witnesses and registration, see Haeri, *Law of Desire,* 2; Ghodsi, "Slipknot," 667. An overview is in Ghodsi, "Slipknot," 681–684.

69. This case is described in Shahnez Khan, "Race," using pseudonyms. My discussion is based on Khan's provocative essay; Khan is a scholar who served as an expert witness in the lit-

igation and who is highly critical of the ethnocentric disposition of the case. Raised in Canada from the age of five, Farhat led a sheltered life. She was only allowed to leave her house to go to school and Sunday School. Salman was her Sunday school teacher.

70. For a general discussion of problems Muslims in Canada face because of conflict between Islamic traditions and Canadian mores, see Yousif, "Family Values."

71. Quotation from Shahnez Khan, "Race," 255–256. This may be a misinterpretation of what transpired. Khan suggests that the teacher used his position of power to seduce Farhat. "Race." Another issue was the fact that a father's consent is supposed to be necessary for either a permanent or a temporary marriage. This may be a non-issue for mut'a when the woman is a widow or divorcee, but in the case of a young, inexperienced woman, one would have expected the requirement to be relevant: "Virgins . . . must always obtain their father's permission before contracting into any marriage." Ghodsi, "Slipknot," 69.

Shahnez Khan acknowledges that the judge was trying to be culturally sensitive by allowing her to testify, but he manipulated her by refusing to allow her to comment on the main issue, Farhat's access to her daughter: "He marginalized my comments to the cultural aspect or to the topic of mut'a." "Race," 258. "The judge and others within the Canadian legal system involved in this case did not understand mut'a and it appears that they did not wish to do so either" (257).

72. I am grateful to Joan Dempsey Klein, presiding justice of the California Court of Appeal, Second District, for bringing the case to my attention and for discussing it with me.

73. *In re Marriage of Vryonis* (1988), 716. The court relied on the "putative marriage" doctrine, which makes an otherwise invalid marriage valid through the reasonable expectations of one of the spouses. Laymon, "Valid," 375. *In re Marriage of Vryonis,* 717. The court found that because her belief was unreasonable and therefore no marriage existed, it declined to address the other contentions. The court said the fact that there was a private marriage ceremony at her apartment with only the two of them present—that is, no witnesses and no recording— meant that they failed to meet the statutory requirements for the formation of a valid California marriage: "Because the parties made no colorable attempt at compliance, Fereshteh could not believe reasonably a valid California marriage came into being." The court also rejected the proposition that "ignorance of the law" "could compel a contrary conclusion." *In re Marriage of Vryonis,* 721.

74. Laymon, "Valid," 376.

75. Jewish divorce law is based on the Old Testament, as well as on interpretations of biblical questions found in the Mishnah and the Talmud. The Jewish marriage contract is the *ketubah.* For a description of how Jewish divorce law evolved, see Tager, "Chained Wife," and Jessica Miller, "History of Agunah." One should also note that Orthodox, Conservative, and Reform communities differ in how they have chosen to address this issue. Although only Reform communities have allowed remarriage by women without a get, one Orthodox Beth Din adopted the controversial practice of helping women obtain Jewish "annulments" of their marriages. Leichter, "Problem." See also Anon. (1998e), "Schpiel"; Breitowitz, "Plight" and *Between.*

Agunah is also translated sometimes as a woman "anchored" to a husband who refuses to grant her a divorce, although the marriage is effectively over. Elon et al., *Jewish Law,* 30. The root is *agan,* or anchor. According to Tager: "The term Agunah applies to a married woman who is separated from her husband but cannot obtain permission to remarry because her huband is: a) unwilling to grant her a religious divorce upon the breakdown of the marriage, b) unable to do so on account of illness, c) has disappeared and cannot be traced, or d) is an apostate, and is thus outside the jurisdiction of the Jewish community." "Chained Wife," 426.

Jewish women enjoyed greater equality in terms of the right to divorce in earlier periods. Tager argues that the law, which previously was interpreted more leniently so as to enable women to escape marriages, was changed "primarily" because of the views of one Jewish leader, Rabbenu Tam, whose objective was to preserve marriage in part by minimizing the number of divorces. Tager, "Chained Wife," 436. Until the late 1970s the Orthodox community, including many of its modern rabbis, denied the agunah was a serious problem. Berger and Lipstadt, "Women in Judaism," 315.

Berger and Lipsadt describe techniques such as humiliation in the synagogue and excommunication to compel the recalcitrant husband to release his chained wife. "Women in Judaism," 313–314. Greenberg describes how twenty Canadian Orthodox women announced one sabbath morning in synagogue that none of them would go to *mikvah*, the ritual bath (required after menses before couples can resume sexual relations) until a friend of theirs received a get from her husband who had been blackmailing her. This tactic resulted in the quickest divorce in Jewish history. "Feminism," 155. In *Klagsbrun v. Va'ad Harabonim* (1999) a traditional shaming technique was employed by the Va'ad, an unincorporated association of Orthodox rabbis. After they distributed a notice explaining the circumstances surrounding Seymour Klagsbrun's failure to furnish Shulamith, his wife of nearly thirty years, with a get, he sued, alleging that the statements were false and defamatory and furthermore that they had resulted in the community shunning him and his new wife. Because of constitutional concerns about entanglement, the federal court declined to review the allegations of bigamy and defamation.

Traditional Jewish women did not join the women's movement until the 1970s. Jessica Miller, "History of Agunah," 10. The climbing divorce rate in the Orthodox community also contributed to heightening awareness of the plight of the agunah. Greenberg, "Feminism," 153.

Tager provides an excellent overview of how different jurisdictions across the globe have dealt with the problem of the agunah, including Canada, England, France, Germany, the Netherlands, South Africa, and the United States. "Chained Wife." For discussion of cases in Israel, see the work of Ayelet Shachar.

76. Outside Israel the Beth Din lacks the power to force a recalcitrant spouse to divorce. Even within Israel courts are "reluctant to use punitive measures." Tager, "Chained Wife," 437, 452, and Elon et al., *Jewish Law*, 30. On the "supervisory role," see Elon et al., *Jewish Law*, 25. On "recalcitrant spouses," see Tager, "Chained Wife," 438. To address the problem of findings, the Israeli Knesset passed a law in 1995, which provides that a husband's failure to obey a decree of divorce will result in a loss of "many important privileges." Elon et al., *Jewish Law*, 30.

77. The offspring were *mamzerim*. The term, translated "misbegotten," is defined as "offspring of an incestuous or adulterous union that is subject to capital punishment by a court of extirpation (karet) by God; often mistranslated as 'bastard,' in the sense of one born out of wedlock." Elon et al., *Jewish Law*, GL-2. See also Berger and Lipstadt, "Women in Judaism," 314. Judge Rigler in the case of *Becher v. Becher* (1997), discussed later in this chapter, said that in his twenty-two years on the bench, he saw "the withholding of Gets as a method of economic coercion by recalcitrant husbands on occasions too numerous to count." March 18, 1997, n.2. The appeals court "found that extreme pressure exerted upon Shirley constituted duress" and therefore that the deed to the property had to be invalidated. Another case in which a court voided an agreement based on coercion and duress is *Golding v. Golding* (1990). In *Weiss v. Goldfeder* (1990) the denial of a get was grounds for an emotional distress action.

78. Elon et al., *Jewish Law*, 1, and Tager, "Chained Wife." Segments of the Orthodox community have suggested use of standardized prenuptial agreements issued by the Rabbinical Council of America. This is supposed to avoid the entanglement problem, as civil courts only enforce a civil contract signed by both parties. Berger and Lipstadt, "Women in Judaism," 317. See also Greenberg-Kobrin, "Civil Enforceability." On the New York law, see Rostain, "Permissible Accommodations." According to one estimate there were fifteen thousand agunot in New

York when the law was enacted. McQuiston, "Jewish Divorce Law." As of 1998 New York was the only state with a 'Get Law.' Leichter, "Problem." See also Jacob, "Agunah Problem," and Marc Feldman, "Jewish Women."

Much has been made of this Establishment clause argument. See, e.g., Lawrence Marshall, "Religion Clauses." As of 1998 appellate courts had not yet decided whether the statutes concerning religious divorces offend the Establishment clause. Felder, "Get' Statutes." For rejection of the Establishment challenge, see the *Becher* litigation. For this reason other states have declined to adopt this type of legislation. Berger and Lipstadt, "Women in Judaism," 317. See also Jessica Miller, "History of Agunah," 12. Contrary to expectation, the more conservative segments favor civil solutions to release the agunah because it does not require a change in *halakha*, whereas the reform community tends to worry about the constitutional principle of separation of church and state. This division occurred over an Australian government measure, which eventually passed. Greenberg, "Feminism," 154.

The actual name of the get statute is "Removal of Barriers to Remarriage Statute," enacted August 8, 1983. It prohibited remarriage until all barriers, including religious inhibitions, were resolved. The law was expanded in 1992 "to permit judges of civil courts to take into consideration a husband's refusal to grant a get when deciding the distribution of marital assets."

79. Because the reform branch of Judaism permitted remarriage without having a get, American courts sometimes did not sympathize with the Jewish wife. Jessica Miller, "History of Agunah," 9. See her discussion of *In re Spondre* (1917) as an example of this complexity (4–6). Courts enforced the Jewish marriage contract in *In re Marriage of Goldman* (1990), *Avitzur v. Avitzur* (1983), and *Minkin v. Minkin* (1981) but refused to order the husband to grant the get in *Aflalo v. Aflalo* (1996) and *Victor v. Victor* (1993). Jewish law requires that the get be given willingly, i.e., with free consent. On "moral turpitude," see Leichter, "Problem."

80. *Giahn v. Giahn* (2000). In another case, the court endorsed the New York law saying its enactment "was a recognition by this state of the deplorable level of morality of those unscrupulous Jewish men who hide behind a religious facade to keep their wives in bondage by refusing to execute or deliver the religious 'get' freeing them unless exorbitant, often bizarre, demands are met." *Izsak v. Izsak* (1996).

81. Hadassah, a national Jewish organization, held a panel July 18, 1998, in New York City on the plight of agunot. Anon. (1998f), "Jewish Controversy." See also Berkovits, "Get and Talaq." On a secular policy, see M. D. A. Freeman, "Law, Religion." But see Greenberg, who argues that an agunah should not have to abandon her faith "to find personal protection from abuse." "Feminism," 173. She is ambivalent about the proper course of action. While she defends a religious community's "right to proceed at its own pace," she also says "there are instances when a community cannot be left to its own devices" and that there is no reason why human rights language (though not tactics) may not be used to "wage the internal struggle" (171). See, e.g., Greenawalt, "Religious Law," and Greenberg-Kobrin, "Civil Enforceability," for methods of reconciliation.

82. The similarity is that the husband wields the power to determine the outcome of the marriage.

83. See Pearl, *Family Law*, 68–78. The talaq in England was consistent with the Muslim Family Laws Ordinance of 1961. For elaboration, see Pearl, *Family Law*, 74–87. See also Poulter, *Asian Traditions*, 45–46. Poulter explains that the House of Lords thought "it would be contrary to legal policy to allow a Pakistani husband, resident in England, to divorce his wife merely by posting notices to Pakistan if he could not do so by the pronouncement of a talaq" in England. *Asian Traditions*, 51. According to Poulter, this meant that the husband had to travel to Pakistan to obtain a divorce. If this interpretation is correct, it appears that only wealthy men could use the talaq. See Poulter, *Asian Traditions*, 43.

84. The children were three of his seventy-nine offspring.

85. Since Ms. Uboh-Abiola had failed to establish the existence of a valid monogamous marriage, the judge said the court lacked subject-matter jurisdiction over her claims. Cerisse Anderson, "Chief." The judge said that New York courts do not recognize any polygamous marriage as valid, even if it was legal where it was contracted. This barred the wife's action for divorce. Since the usual rule courts follow is "valid where consummated," the treatment of the divorce claim may be questionable.

86. There can even be a conflict for parents of the same religion, if one parent is more observant than the other. In *J.B. v. R.M.* (1999), for example, an Orthodox Jewish father tried unsuccessfully to win custody because the mother, his ex-wife, was only Reform, though she kept a kosher home. Anon. (1999f), "Change in Custody."

87. There is a large literature on this subject. See, e.g., Mumford, "Judicial Resolution"; Jordan Paul, "House, Car, Kids"; Van Praagh, "Religion"; Wah, "Custodial Parent's Right"; Weiss and Abramoff, "Enforceability."

88. For an analysis of cases in various jurisdictions, see Ahdar, "Religion."

89. Mumford expresses concern about possible judicial bias against unorthodox religions to which parents might belong. "Judicial Resolution," 145.

90. *Weiss v. Weiss* (1996), 714.

CHAPTER 8

1. Hilda Kuper argues that it is important to use precise terminology and proposes a classificatory scheme: *clothing* as the most inclusive term, *dress* for everyday secular clothing, *uniform* for clothing prescribed for ceremonials (conventionalized secular performances), and *costume* for clothing necessary for the effectiveness of rituals. "Costume and Identity," 349. In this analysis, I will discuss most clothing as attire, garb, or dress, except for military uniforms. I also consider "grooming" and "appearance" policies under the rubric of "dress" codes.

2. See, e.g., Neely, "Conditions of Employment." Because context is crucial for the analysis of dress codes, I have used institutional settings as the basis for organizing my discussion of the issues at stake.

3. Although there is, to my knowledge, nothing in the literature which surveys various dress code controversies involving ethnic attire, there are superb studies of individual symbols. See, e.g., the exemplary analysis of the turban by Cohn, "Cloth." For general works on the symbolic aspects of clothing, see, e.g., Horn and Gurel, *Second Skin*; von Ehrenfels, "Clothing"; Nathan Joseph, *Uniforms*.

4. See, e.g., *Carole Dubniczky and Edna Proulx v. Tiffany's Restaurant* (1981). Tiffany's restaurant declined to employ two women in its dining room because the owner felt that "European service" required male waiters only. The Board of Inquiry ruled that this was sex discrimination and ordered the restaurant to cease this practice and pay damages.

5. "Cornrows" are defined as "an early African American nomenclature for patterns in braiding that resemble rows of corn planted in a field; also called 'canerows.'" Anuakan, "Hairpins," 10. See also Mercer, "Black Hair/Style Politics," 261. Peters describes the braiding technique "whereby three sections of hair are interwoven to create one straight or curved line, picking up additional strands of hair along the way . . . named for neatly planted rows of corn." "Braids," 9. For more background and pictures of various styles, see Thomas-Osborne and Brown, *Accent African*, and Sagay, *African Hairstyles*.

Regarding cultural heritage: "Traditionally, African hairstyles indicated the status of the woman: age, sex, place of birth, wealth, occupation, marital status, place of origin, and social standing could be defined by a hairstyle and its adornments. Special rites of passage—into adulthood, marriage, motherhood, or priesthood, for instance—merited special hairdos to mark the occasion." Peters, "Affirming an Ancient Aesthetic." See also Houlberg, "Social Hair," and de Negri, *Adornment*, 15. Some of the symbolic meanings were lost because slave holders did not permit blacks to groom. Anuakan, "Hairpins," 12–13. Contemporary versions are still complex, and the braids take hours to complete.

The case is *Pamela L. Mitchell v. J.W. Marriott Hotel, Inc. and Marriott Corporation* (1988). Eric Steele, Mitchell's attorney, argued that the express or implied discriminatory anti-braids policy was in accordance with national corporate policy of the Marriott corporation. Steele, "Letter Brief," 3–4. Although Mitchell filed complaints with both the EEOC and the Office of Human Rights in the District of Columbia, it was the latter which found probable cause that Marriott had discriminated against Mitchell, based on the D.C. Human Rights Act of 1977 that prohibits discriminatory practices by employers based on race or personal appearance.

It is odd that the multibraided hairstyle worn for over four thousand years by great Egyptian queens like Nefertiti and Cleopatra should be regarded as a fad. McClintock, "Cornrow Hairstyle." Interestingly, the employee manual did not specifically prohibit braids. Earlier versions did contain a cornrows restriction, but "corporate headquarters" directed its removal. The hotel and the parent corporation allegedly tried to enforce an unwritten anti-braids policy. Steele, "Letter Brief," 3. Mitchell received written notification on November 23, 1987, that if she had not removed her braided hairstyle by December 23, 1987, the hotel would terminate her. The next day, under the glare of media attention, Marriott withdrew its objection to her hairstyle. Nevertheless, the D.C. Office of Human Rights proceeded with its investigation.

Quotation in text from Steele, "Letter Brief," 3.

6. McClintock, "EEOC Asked."

7. Information in this paragraph from Barker, "Marriott." Marriott's public relations office stated publicly that "cornrows are allowed now as long as they are neat and well-trimmed in appearance." Nick Hill, quoted in Rowland, "D.C. Human Rights Office," and Anon. (1988d), "Clerk's Cornrows." Quotation on condition of settlement from McClintock, "Marriott Stung."

8. Taalib-Din Uqdah, owner of Cornrows and Co., a hair salon in Washington, D.C. that assists victims of job discrimination, said that Marriott "got off cheap" and that "they bought their way out of this." Quoted in McClintock, "Marriot Stung." Steele anticipated that the *Mitchell* decision would influence other EEOC decisions, e.g., *Cheryl Tatum and Cheryl Parahoo v. Hyatt Hotels Corporation and Hyatt Regency Crystal City* (1988). Hereafter *Tatum and Parahoo v. Hyatt*.

9. Case is *Tatum and Parahoo v. Hyatt* (1988), 1. Caldwell views the "solution" of wearing wigs as public degradation. "Hair Piece," 390.

10. See Milloy, "Centuries-Old Fad," and Schacter, "EEOC." Jackson also promised not to stay at any Hyatt hotels during his presidential campaign until the dispute was settled. Anon. (1987b), "Upbraiding"; Shipp, "Braided"; Latimer, "Union." "Neat" and "conservative" from Schacter, "Perfect Fit."

11. *Tatum and Parahoo v. Hyatt Hotels*, 3–4.

12. See Schachter, "EEOC," and Arocha and Sklansky, "D.C. Cornrow Policy." "'The Office of Human Rights did not make a finding in this case because Hyatt worked actively and closely with the office to resolve the issues, exhibiting an exemplary spirit of cooperation,' Maudine R. Cooper, director of the D.C. agency, said at a press conference with Hyatt officials." McClintock, "D.C. Drops Probe."

13. See, respectively, Anon. (1989b), "Anti-Braid Policy"; York, "Dismissal"; Eric Steele, personal communication, 1993. See also Steele, "Letter to Ms. Patricia Spinner."

14. Quoted in Schacter, "EEOC."

15. For instance, the Smithsonian Institution enforced such a policy. For details, see McClintock, "Smithsonian Retreats" and "Coiffeurs of Cornrow." Even some black institutions prohibit their employees from wearing braids and advise students not to wear cornrows. See Caldwell, "Hair Piece," 384 n.58. Other employers with anti-cornrow policies include American Airlines and the Washington, D.C., police department. James Davis, "Good Hair/Bad Hair." In 1993 Barbara Cooper filed a complaint against American Airlines with the EEOC which resulted in a change in the airline's policy. Steele, "Letter to Ms. Patricia Spinner." The American Civil Liberties Union challenged the anti-braid policy of Avis Rent A Car. Bauers, "Hair-itage." A black female television announcer who appeared on the air in cornrows was suspended. Anon. (1981, Feb. 19), "TV Reporter."

16. Schlei and Grossman, *Employment Discrimination*, 290–302. See the 1991 Amendments to Title VII of the Civil Rights Acts of 1964 for the requirements of proving disparate treatment and disparate impact. For the former, race need be only a motivating and not the sole factor in the discriminatory policy. For the latter, the employer must demonstrate that the policy is job-related and consistent with business practice.

17. A policy with a disparate impact may not be considered racial discrimination if it is justified by business necessity.

18. In this case the plaintiff, a nursing assistant, worked in the detoxification unit of a hospital that treated patients who were afflicted with psychiatric disorders and drug addiction. The court reasoned that her discharge was not based on an immutable trait and therefore the dress code was not a "subterfuge for discrimination." The court found persuasive evidence that other employees were reprimanded for wearing beads and bells and that blacks were not disciplined for wearing braids without beads. The court's conclusion was that "an evenhanded application of a reasonable grooming standard does not constitute racial discrimination." *Carswell* (1981).

19. Quotation from *Renee Rogers v. American Airlines* (1981), 232.

20. Omi and Winant, *Racial Formation*. Consistency in the enforcement of a policy does not necessarily defeat a disparate treatment challenge if the adoption of the policy was motivated by intentional discrimination.

21. In *Rogers* the court drew an analogy between the anti-cornrow policy and English-only policies. On Title VII, see Schlei and Grossman, *Employment Discrimination*, 305. Regarding prejudice against any nation: This is partly because national boundaries in Africa are arbitrary and often reflect the effects of colonialism. This conceptual problem may arise in cases where there is discrimination against Hispanics, a category broader than one nation. That is, the prejudice may be against this group generally rather than anti-Cuban feeling. Another problem is that anti-Puerto-Rican sentiment is not "national" since Puerto Rico is a commonwealth of the United States. Charles Sullivan et al., *Employment Discrimination*, 406. On national origin, see Charles Sullivan et al., *Employment Discrimination*, 407.

22. It seems possible that the case could have been argued entirely on race grounds since black men sometimes wear cornrows. Moreover, arguing sex discrimination might enable employers to raise the bonafide occupational qualification (BFOQ) defense (except that race is still involved). For a critique of *Rogers* on this basis, see Caldwell, "Hair Piece," 372.

23. Quotations from, respectively, Titunik, "Women Sues," and Shipp, "Braided."

24. See Anon. (1988a), "Pamela Mitchell." Quotation from Linda Wheeler, "Hotel Worker."

25. Quotation from Steele, "Letter Brief," 5. Also: "The application of the Respondents' grooming policy to all employees without regard to their racially different physiological and cultural characteristics tends to affect blacks adversely because they have a hair texture and historical perspective different from whites. Thus, blacks are impermissibly measured by the

Respondents against a standard which for all practical purposes exclusively assumes non-Black physiological and cultural characteristics." Steele, "Letter Brief," 7–8. Steele goes on to offer a hypothetical. Suppose the Howard Inn required all hotel employees to wear an African-inspired hairstyle such as an Afro or a braided style. Steele queries: "Is it at all conceivable that, when confronted with the inevitable law suit from a disgruntled white employee, the Howard Inn could persuasively argue that its grooming restrictions were "non discriminatory" because the rules were applied to all employees 'equally'?" (8).

26. Taalib-Din A. Uqdah, quoted in Anon. (1987a), "Hyatt Hotel."

27. On the jungle, see Yourse, "Cornrow Wearers." For an interesting analysis of white control of images as central to white hegemony, see hooks, *Black Looks*, 2–3. She discusses the potentially devastating effect of essentially white aesthetic standards on the identity of black children.

28. See Lazarus, "Ease of Care." On daily oiling, see Thomas-Osborne and Brown, *Accent African*, 67, and Sagay, *African Hairstyles*, 51. It is possible that the use of oil contributes to the mistaken belief regarding the cleanliness of the braids.

29. The case of no legal protection for braiders occurs in Maryland. Banerjee, "Ancient Style." On lesser earnings, see Mullin, "Braiding Bunch."

30. This was the case for the "Afro" (or "Natural"), the black hairstyle of the 1960s: "Although they had existed prior to these politico-cultural movements militancy gave rise to a new aesthetic in personal grooming that liberated "the Natural." Anuakan, "Hairpins," 22. See also Firth, "Hair." For a legal challenge to a dress code forbidding the Afro, see, e.g., *Jenkins v. Blue Cross Mut. Hospital Ins., Inc.* (1976). Pamela Mitchell attributed the fear of braids to an association with black militancy. Rowland, "D.C. Human Rights Office." Others said, "There is nothing militant about braids, as some hotel managers fear." Milloy, "Centuries-Old Fad." "It's not a statement of militancy, it's an aesthetic statement." Karamu Welsh, instructor in African American aesthetics, Temple University, quoted in Mullin, "Braiding Bunch." On anti-business, the Marriott spokesman is quoted in McClintock, "EEOC."

31. Banerjee, "Braids." But then why are whites afraid of dreadlocks? According to Taalib-Din Abdul Uqdah, legend has it that "a cornrow was braided into a particular slave's hair after each crop row was planted." Quoted in Mullin, "Braiding Bunch."

32. There is an extensive literature on hair symbolism, much of which focuses on its sexual meanings. Cooper, for instance, says that "a woman's head hair is to the male a symbol of her pubic hair." *Hair*, 65. Hair symbolism is complex as hair can be "a symbol of sexuality and pollution or the very stuff of sacredness." Brain, *Decorated Body*, 120. See also articles on hair by Lawless, Basu, and Firth. And see works by Charles Berg, "Unconscious Significance" and *Unconscious Significance*. See also Anuakan, "Hairpins," 10.

Interestingly, the reason Medusa endowed with "snakelike locks" was a form of punishment for her illicit sexual relationship with Neptune. It may be that the historically documented stereotyping of black women as promiscuous may partly explain the extreme reaction by whites to cornrows. See Sharp, *Black Women*. Perhaps related is the connection between cornrows and fertility.

One article on the cornrow litigation refers to Medusa. Mullin, "Braiding Bunch." See also Freud's interpretation of the fear of Medusa's head as being related to the castration complex. "Medusa's Head." For his theory that plaiting and weaving are motivated by penis envy, see "Feminity." Quotation from Anuakan, "Hairpins," 97.

33. There is no question that hair has sexual connotations, and cross-cultural data suggests braids do as well. For example, in an Eastern European context traditionally hairstyles depended on marital status. Bogatyrev describes the customs of unmarried girls wearing one braid hanging down while married women wound two braids around their head. *Folk Costume*, 68–74. If hair represents sexuality, then the braids appear to signify control of it.

There was an "outcry" following Derek's "announcement that she had invented cornrows." Peters, "Braids," 9. Indeed, many African American commentators pointed out that Bo Derek did not "popularize" cornrows; it was Cicely Tyson who "popularized" the style. Caldwell, "Hair Piece," 379. At most, Derek made whites aware of the hairstyle and may have encouraged some black women to wear the braids. Mercer observes: "It also seemed that her success validated the style and encouraged more black people to cane-row their hair." "Black Hair/Style Politics," 261. Mercer uses cornrows as an example of white appropriation of black cultural forms. See also hooks on white commodification of black culture and her claim that this limits the power of the black symbol. *Black Looks*, 14.

34. Some might argue that only "traditional" cornrow styles should be permitted. But there is no reason why new fashions should receive any less legal protection than styles originating in Africa. In some cases new braiding styles developed in the United States are taken back to Africa. This phenomenon has been called "reculturation." Anuakan, "Hairpins," 80. Because of the Diaspora, African braiding customs have been modified in the process of cultural adaptation.

35. Of course, the point of this analysis is that aesthetic judgments are inherently political. Caldwell, "Hair Piece," 393.

36. Caldwell, "Hair Piece," 367. The *Rogers* decision has limited value as a precedent because as a decision of the federal district court of New York, it is binding only on courts in that jurisdiction. It is only persuasive authority elsewhere.

37. Sikhs come from India. Approximately 300,000 reside in the United States. On the "five K's," see Uberoi, "Unshorn." One issue in the Kohli dispute was whether Domino's Pizza (DPI) could be held responsible for the dress code of its franchise, named LOOC, Inc. DPI claimed that it had not received notice of the challenge to the policy. However, since Kohli raised this question in a letter to the Maryland Commission on Human Relations, this argument carried no weight. Logically, DPI is the proper party to be sued here as the franchise was required to carry out DPI's dress code. This technical question of whether DPI and LOOC were an "integrated enterprise" appears to have been an unwarranted attempt by Domino's Pizza to evade the vital civil rights questions. See Michael Burns, "State Challenges." Although not addressed in the complaint or administrative hearing, counsel for DPI alleged that Kohli also could not have complied with Domino's uniform requirement, as his turban would not fit under the required uniform hat.

38. This case was based on Article 49B of the Maryland Annotated Code, section 16(a). The commission argued that DPI discriminated against Kohli because of his religion. *Kohli v. LOOC, Inc. D/B/A Domino Pizza, Inc.* (1992) (hereafter *Kohli v. DPI*), Provisional Order and Opinion, Administrative Law Judge (hereafter ALJ). Sally Swann, a lawyer for the commission proclaimed the case a great victory. Bock. "Domino's." Although Kohli technically won, the $6,000 damages were far less than his attorney fees up to that point, which totaled $14,000! Final quotation from Timothy Wheeler, "Domino's Pizza."

39. Charles Sullivan et al., *Employment Discrimination*, 380.

40. The U.S. Supreme Court gave this narrow interpretation to the duty of reasonable accommodation in *Trans World Airlines, Inc. v. Hardison* (1977), where the conflict was between the employee's religious practices and the employer's work schedule. For a critique of this case, see Retter, "Reasonable Accommodation." For a lucid account of the employer's duty to accommodate, see Schlei and Grossman, *Employment Discrimination*. The EEOC wanted to protect religious employees from the apparently neutral employment policies that would limit their ability to work. The accommodation was to be made unless it involved an "undue hardship," and the burden of proof fell to the employer. One issue was whether the EEOC policy, by requiring private employers to accommodate the religious beliefs and practices of employees, violated the Establishment clause. On constituting a hardship, see *Kohli v. DPI*,

Provisional Order and Opinion, ALJ, 28. The judge based this argument on the 1980 EEOC Revised Guidelines on Discrimination because of Religion.

41. Domino's argued that if the grooming policy was a business necessity, then it was relieved from any duty to accommodate. This argument that one provision superseded the other is absurd because it would render the duty to accommodate provision meaningless.

42. *Kohli v. DPI*, ALJ decision, 35, 40. Quotations are from this decision.

43. Counsel for DPI argued that the first study applied to beard nets. Since they are transparent and give the impression that the wearer has no restraint on, the study about attitudes toward bearded employees is relevant to this inquiry. *Kohli v. DPI*, Brief for Respondents, 34.

44. DPI eventually focused on image control, contending that it is critical to the enforcement of the dress code. For one thing, it would be difficult for Kohli as manager, if exempt from the dress code, to enforce it.

45. DPI conceded this point: "Respondents have never suggested, nor are they suggesting now, that under Maryland law, customer concerns, which are in any way, shape or form discriminatory . . . could or were used to justify or validate its grooming standard or any other rule or practice." *Kohli v. DPI*, Brief for Respondents, 7–8.

46. The sincerity issue is said to be "difficult" for defendants as courts are reluctant to question sincerity. Sullivan et al., *Employment Discrimination*, 383.

47. A public health justification was given for a no-beard policy in a U.K. chocolate factory: a Sikh employee lost his challenge in *Panesar v. Nestle Co., Ltd.* [1980]. Where the public health justification is the actual rationale, as in *Panesar*, there is cultural bias in the operation of the policy. If companies were truly concerned with contamination from hair, everyone would have to shave from head to toe! Of course, if the majority were Sikhs, then bearded employees would be the norm. In many countries where men wear beards, and the food industry employs them, there have been no reported health problems due to beards.

48. On excommunication, see *Kohli v. DPI*, ALJ decision, 6. Dr. Bhupinder, a Sikh surgeon who served as chairman of the Sikh Association of Baltimore, testified about the sanctions for those who cut their hair. Five holy people elected from the congregation determine the punishment, which, among possible sanctions, might simply be to grow the beard again or to excommunicate the person until his hair grows back. Transcript of testimony before the ALJ, 93–94. "He said if he could successfully operate on patients, then surely Kohli could make pizza." Anon. (1992a), "Gursikh Wins."

On castration, see works by Charles Berg. It is also curious that shaving the beard and hair generally have been forms of punishment in many cultures during many time periods. In addition, "shaving the hair of a defeated enemy was a common humiliation." Wendy Cooper, *Hair*, 44. On celibacy, see Wendy Cooper, *Hair*, 45. See also Brain, *Decorated Body*, 120.

It is fairly clear that hair often signifies strength. For this reason, totalitarian governments "are always nervous of long hair, and it may be forcibly cut by the police." Brain, *Decorated Body*, 118. As an example, Brain mentions that in 1967 the military dictators in Greece made it know that long-haired tourists were no longer welcome there.

49. *Bhatia v. Chevron* (1984), 1383. Quotations are from this decision.

50. There was some confusion following the *Smith* decision, which led to a November 4, 1990, decision to rescind an OSHA instruction authorizing hard hat exemptions. However, a memorandum dated July 24, 1991, sent to all regional administrators from the director of the Directorate of Compliance Programs, OSHA, U.S. Department of Labor, stated: "Citations are not to be issued to employers of employees who object to wearing hard hats for religious reasons in the workplace." Kohli, a highway engineer, received a hard hat waiver from the Maryland State Highway Administration.

51. *Re Aclo Compounders Inc. and United Steelworkers* (1980). Here a Sikh unsuccessfully challenged a hard hat rule. For the Canadian Supreme Court case upholding a hard hat rule against a challenge, see *Bhinder v. Canadian National Railway Company* (1985).

52. See, e.g., *State ex rel. Burrell-el v. Autrey* (1988) where the Missouri Court of Appeals ruled that the trial judge had improperly cited a defendant for criminal contempt for refusing to remove his fez while in court. For an overview of this topic, see Hopewell, "Appropriate Attire."

53. In *La Rocca v. Lane* (1975).

54. *People v. Rodriguez* (1979). Quotations in the paragraph are from *Rodriguez*.

55. *Matter of Gold* (1980), appeal dismissed (1980).

56. *Close-It Enterprises, Inc. v. Weinberger* (1978), 587. For a detailed explanation of the importance of wearing the yarmulke, see Chazin, "*Goldman*."

57. Glassman discusses casses in which defense motions to prohibit testimony by witnesses in religious apparel were denied on the same basis as in *Close-It*. "Free Exercise," 76.

58. Marriott, "Kente Cloth"; Britt, "Kente Cloth's Wiles"; Chartrand, "Dispute."

59. For an overview of the Afrocentric philosophy, see works by Molefi Kete Asante, *Afrocentricity* and *Kemet*. Some of the major works on kente cloth include Gilfoy, P*atterns of Life*, and Rattray, *Religion*. See also Shea Smith, "Motifs"; Hale, "Kente Cloth"; Herbert Cole, "Kente."

60. The defendant challenged the ruling of the provincial judge that excluded his kirpan from the courtroom, but the judge's ruling was affirmed on appeal. For background on the kirpan, see McLeod, *Exploring Sikhism*; Uberoi. *Religion*; W. Owen Cole and Sambhi. *Sikhs*; Richard Jones and Gnanapala, *English Minorities*. For additional cases involving the kirpan, see Bhachu, "Shield."

61. Gourley, "Veil."

62. In Cincinnati, Ohio, a trial ruled in *State v. Harjinder Singh* (1996) that carrying a kirpan of any size, concealed or otherwise, is a criminal act. The fact that it is a religious requirement is no defense. The Court of Appeals reversed, saying it was an error to instruct the jury that there is no religious defense to charges of carrying a concealed weapon, when the Religious Freedom Restoration Act applies. Students often comment that even if Mr. Singh would never use the kirpan as a weapon, a mugger on the subway might seize it from him and use it for this purpose.

63. Cases involving kirpans arise in diverse institutional settings such as airplanes and schools (see later in this chapter), as well as hospitals. For a ruling that hospitals should allow Sikh patients to wear kirpans while receiving treatment, see *Pritam Singh v. Workmen's Compensation Board Hospital and Rehabilitation Board* (1981).

64. After September 11, 2001, airlines prohibited any sharp objects whatsoever on board and confiscated items from passengers. See Scrivener, "Standing Tall."

65. Singh had stowed his large, eleven and one-half inch kirpan in his luggage and was wearing a smaller one purchased specifically for air travel. Quotations from *Canada (Human Rights Commission) v. Canada 3000 Airlines, Ltd.* (1999). Also: "In our view, however, the respondent has established that the presence of kirpans with a greater offensive capacity than Canada 3000 dinner knives on its aircraft would present a sufficient risk to the safety of the public so as to constitute an undue hardship." *Canada v. Canada 3000 Airlines*.

66. Henry Lee, "Contest Citation," and Charny, "No Charges."

67. The Muslim case was *In re Alameda-Contra Costa Transit District and Amalgamated Transit Union, Local 192* (1982). The arbitrator appeared to question whether she was genuinely committed to Islam. The Sikh case was *Yellow Cab v. Civil Rights Commission* (1991). The case was dismissed for lack of jurisdiction. For analysis of turbans in British trans-

portation, see Beetham, *Transport and Turbans*. The Rastafarian case was *Dawkins v. Department of the Environment Sub nom Crown Suppliers PSA* (1993). Although originally it was thought that the House of Lords would hear his appeal, this apparently never occurred.

68. In Mississippi a school prevented a Jewish boy from wearing a Star of David because it has sometimes been used as a gang symbol. Anon. (1999g), "School Board." Maya Indians won a victory in Guatemala when education officials agreed students could wear traditional dress after having threatened them with expulsion for refusing to wear the school uniform. Anon. (1999h), "Guatemala." An eighth-grade Oneida Indian student in San Diego had her medicine bundle containing sacred herbs cut open by school officials in search of illicit drugs. Barfield, "Educators." In a famous English case, *Mandla v. Dowell Lee* (1983), decided by the House of Lords, a Sikh student was not admitted to a private school because he would not cut his hair or stop wearing his turban. For commentary, see Anon. (1983), "Turban," and Saunders, "Ethnic Origins." In the Canadian case of *Sehdev v. Bayview Glen Junior Schools Ltd.* (1988), the board of inquiry found the school discriminated against a Sikh boy by refusing to admit him because of his faith and the fact that he wore a turban. It ordered the school to modify its uniform policy so minorities could attend. Many schools require that students cut their hair. Native Americans have challenged this in *New Rider v. Board of Education of Indiana* (1973).

69. Stephen Bomse from the law firm Heller, Ehrman, White and McAuliffe was co-counsel. For an overview, see Bjorhus, "Knife Ban." See also Bhachu, "Shield for Swords."

70. Bomse repeatedly made the statement about the kirpan and nonviolence in the press and in briefs. See, e.g., Bossert, "Ceremonial Knife." I found only one reference to a student wielding a kirpan as a weapon. Anon. (1994e), "Kirpan Brandishing." There are interesting Canadian cases concerning kirpans at school. In *Tuli v. St. Albert Protestant Board of Education* (1987) the Board of Inquiry dismissed a complaint of religious discrimination because Tuli obtained a court injunction preventing the school board from implementing its resolution forbidding kirpans at schools, and he wore it without incident until graduation. In *Pandori v. Peel Board of Education* (1990) the school board adopted a no-kirpan policy. Consequently, a Sikh teacher, Harbhajan Singh Pandori, could no longer teach in the region, and Sikh students were prohibited from attending classes. The Board of Inquiry found that the policy contravened the Ontario human rights code. See also Wayland, "Religious Expression." For an adult incident in Fremont, California, see Winston, "Most People." The melee was sparked by the firing of a popular priest who had long served the community. Lee and Schwartz, "Faithful Worship."

71. Initially, in an unpublished decision *Cheema v. Thompson* (1994), the Court of Appeals for the Ninth Circuit held that the district court abused its discretion when it denied the Cheemas' motion for a preliminary injunction enjoining the enforcement of the no-weapons policy as to the Cheema children. Although this ruling was not on the merits of the case, the court required that the parties find some accommodation, suggesting "for example, kirpans might be blunted and dulled, as well as sewn or locked into their sheaths" (13). According to the press coverage, the children "can wear a dulled kirpan blade no more than 2½ inches long. The blade must be sewn into its sheath and placed in a cloth pouch designed specially by members of the Sikh community to accommodate school safety concerns. In addition, the school retains limited inspection rights." Kisliuk, "In Brief." In its second decision *Cheema v. Thompson* (1995) the majority affirmed the "plan of accommodation" with one judge dissenting. For an analysis of the case, see Deb, "Kirpans." In an essay analyzing the implications of *City of Boerne v. Flores* (1997), which struck down RFRA on the grounds of separation of powers, a commentator noted: "The Cheemas were lucky, for if their case arose today, the school district would have little legal motivation to make this long over-due common-sense accommodation." Kassman, "Unfree Exercise."

72. Sometimes referees simply refuse to allow players to wear their skullcaps during play or require that they use tape instead or pins or clips. Garcia, "Team Harassed." On the Valley Torah students, see Fernas, "Sports Official." When the coach objected, the referee "issued another technical and had the coach ejected." Garcia, "Team Harassed." The incident was publicized in the newspaper, leading to criticism of the failure to respect the students' right to religious liberty. Parry, "Referee's Reaction."

73. *Menora v. Illinois High School Association* (1982). Quotations are from this decision.

74. Judge Posner, a well-known jurist in the law-and-economics camp, later co-authored an article with McConnell using a cost-benefit analysis that defends his interpretation of free exercise in this case. McConnell and Posner, "Economic Approach." The dissenting opinion disagreed with the Illinois High School Association that "mere" exclusion from basketball was only a de minimis burden on plaintiffs' religious practice; he saw this as a significant (though indirect) burden.

75. Lou Gordon, "Anti-Semitism."

76. Anon. (1996b), "Diplomas Denied," and Romano, "Diplomas Denied." I am indebted to Judge Philip Champlin for bringing this controversy to my attention.

77. Anon. (1996d), "High School Students." Evidently after the conflict received national media coverage, the school decided not to withhold the transcripts, but still required that students attend summer school in order to obtain their diplomas. Swindell, "Students."

78. Many cases revolve around the headscarf, or *hijab*. The term is *foulard* in French. For a critique of incorrect terminology, see Moruzzi, "Headscarves." Some commentators mistakenly used the term *chador*, which is a long garment. For analysis, see Leila Ahmed, *Women*, and Abu-Odeh, "Post-Colonial." Much has been written about this debate. See, e.g., Baines, "L'Affaire"; Beriss, "Scarves"; Durand-Prinborgne, "Le Port"; Gaspard and Khosrokhavar, *Le Foulard*; Johnstone, "'Great Kerchief Quarrel'"; Minow, "Identities"; Moruzzi, "Headscarves"; Tuong, "Le Port."

For the French controversy, see Anon. (1989h), "Muslim Pupils," and Tempest, "Muslim Schoolgirl." The girls came from Morocco and Tunisia. Anon. (1989h), "Muslim Pupils." Mandel argues that the "the headscarf itself becomes a locus for many levels of differentiation within the Turkish community and within German society." "Turkish Headscarves," 29.

Girls were also denied the right to attend school wearing the hijab in Trinidad and Tobago in 1994. The debate is said to have begun when three Muslim girls wore the hijab to a Catholic-run school and were refused entry. Rampersad, "Trinidad and Tobago Education." After reaching a decision to ban Muslim students wearing hijabs, secondary schools received death threats and had to institute security measures. Anon. (1994f), "Headwear Flap." Some contend that real fear is of the radical black Muslim sect, which attempted to overthrow the government a few years earlier; one of the girls who was denied entry to class because of her hijab was the daughter of Yasin Abu Bakr, the leader of the Jamaat al Muslimeen, the sect responsible for the attempted coup. Rampersad, "Residents Wary." According to the U.S. Department of State Human Rights Report issued in 1995, a lower court ruled that the Catholic school, which was subsidized by the state, had to admit female students wearing the hijab. I thank Cynthia Muhabir for bringing this issue to my attention.

According to some, the girls reached the decision to remove their headgear after their father received an important message from King Hassan II of Morocco indicating that "his majesty did not appreciate seeing his subjects draw so much adverse attention abroad." Minow, "Identities," 125.

79. See, respectively, Moruzzi, "Headscarves," 653, and Ibrahim, "Head Scarves." In 1994 France had 56 million people, of whom 5 million were Muslims, mostly of Arab descent. Many came from North Africa. For more on the demographics of Muslims in Western Europe, see

Peach and Glevbe, "Muslim Minorities." The headscarf issue generated numerous newspaper articles, some of which (in French) gave accounts of extremist Muslim plots with the foulards being the first step. Beriss, "Scarves," 6.

80. See *Mississippi Employment Security Commission v. McGlothin* (1990). A teacher, who was a member of the African Hebrew Israelite faith, wore a headwrap for its cultural and religious significance. For wearing it, she was dismissed and denied unemployment benefits. The Employment Commission concluded that wearing the headwrap was "misconduct" and dismissed her claim. The Circuit Court disagreed, and the Mississippi Supreme Court also thought the teacher's wearing of religious headwrap was constitutionally protected. For commentary, see Wright, "Constitutional Law."

Janet Cooper wore white clothing and a turban. As the court put it: "If, as a result of her wearing religious dress while teaching, the school district appeared to support her religion, she caused it to violate the establishment clause." *Cooper v. Eugene School District* (1985, 1986), 1165; appeal dismissed 480 U.S. 942 (1987).

81. See, e.g., *Kelley v. Johnson* (1975), which held that a county regulation limiting the length of county policemen's hair did not violate any right guaranteed by the Fourteenth Amendment. Sunni Muslim officers successfully challenged the no-beard policy in federal district court. Smothers, "Beard Ban." For an unsuccessful suit, see *Marshall v. District of Columbia* (1975). African Americans suffer disproportionately from a skin condition known as pseudofolliculitis. Officers have sued in Los Angeles arguing in part that the police department should accommodate "medically justified" beards in accordance with the Americans with Disabilities Act. Corwin, "Lieutenant." For a successful suit, see *University of Maryland at Baltimore v. Boyd* (1992).

82. Lowthian, "Sikhs and Jews."

83. In *Khalsa v. Weinberg* (1986) a Sikh sought an exemption. See also *Sherwood v. Brown* (1980). For an earlier case in which the court held that the air force dress regulation prohibiting yarmulkes did not violate the First Amendment, see *Bitterman v. Secretary of Defense* (1982). *Bitterman* contains a cogent explanation of the rationale for military dress codes. See also Nathan Joseph, *Uniforms*. For background, see Sullivan, "Congressional Response"; Folk, "Military"; Chazin, "*Goldman.*"

84. Sullivan, "Congressional Response," 129.

85. For one reaction, see Dershowitz, "Religion." On not undermining "military readiness," see Sullivan, "Congressional Response," 142. See also Efaw, "Free Exercise." Efaw begins with the example of a Muslim woman who faced a court-martial because she "has chosen to disobey orders and wear her khimar, which is a traditional Islamic scarf, while in uniform." He notes that the British, since colonial times, permitted Sikh and Gurkha service men to wear turbans and long hair in the British military (666). On the accommodation statute, see Sullivan, "Congressional Response," 147.

86. See Lucas, "Protest," and Glionna, "Inmates." As the cases are numerous, in the United States alone, I will refer to only handful of examples. The presumption is that if they are allowed to have long hair, this will make it easier for them to make a drastic change in their appearance should they escape from prison. Moreover, in *Wilson v. Schillinger* (1985) the warden testified "that male inmates with long hair tend to appear more attractive to other male inmates and thereby increase the likelihood of homosexual attacks within the prison." He also asserted that "long hair contributes to unsanitary conditions in prison." (921, 926).

87. Challenges include *Belgard v. Hawaii* (1995), *McKinney v. Maynard* (1991), *Teterud v. Burns* (1975), *Capoeman v. Reed* (1985), and *Standing Deer v. Carlson* (1987). For analytic essays, see Rhodes, "American Tradition"; Holscher, "Sweat Lodges"; Norman, "Inmates."

On dreadlocks, see *Lewis v. Commissioner of Department of Correctional Services of the State of New York* (1986). The highest court in New York held that Lewis, a convicted felon, need not cut his hair, which he had not done for at least twenty years, as this would violate his First Amendment rights. For a case where the court granted no relief, see *Robinson v. Foti* (1981). In one case, *Hall v. Coughlin* (1981, 1982), the court upheld requiring a Rastafarian prisoner to comb his dreadlocks as that was deemed less intrusive than requiring that they be cut. In another case the court thought it was reasonable to remand a question about whether enforcement of short hair policy was justifiable when applied to Rastafarians when it was not enforced against Native Americans. *Reed v. Faulkner* (1988). In one case, *Benjamin v. Coughlin* (1990), the Rastafarians wanted the right to wear loose-fitting headgear known as "crowns," and they objected to limits on where they could be worn; they alleged an equal protection violation, considering that other religious minorities could wear types of hats. See Timothy Taylor's two articles, "Soul Rebels" and "Redemption Song." For the treatment of Rastafarian prisoners in the United Kingdom, see Poulter, *Ethnicity, Law, and Human Rights*, 347–350.

On earlocks, see, e.g., *Moskowitz v. Wilkinson* (1977), *Fromer v. Scully* (1989), and *Goulden v. Oliver* (1979), dissent from denial of cert.

A Muslim prisoner objected to the order to remove his *tarboosh*. *Aqeel v. Seiter* (1991). For cases involving other Muslims suing for the right to wear a prayer cap (*kufi*), see *Rogers v. Scurr* (1982), *Frank "X" St. Claire v. Cuyler* (1979), and *Lloyd-El v. Meyer* (1989). Sikhs have sought to wear turbans in prison, e.g., *Chappell v. Rayl* (1985), and Jews to wear yarmulkes, e.g., *Young v. Lane* (1991).

In the United States, prisoners' rights are evaluated according to the lowest standard of review. The Supreme Court has held that prison regulations that impinge on inmates' constitutions need only be reasonably related to legitimate penological interests. See *Turner v. Safley* (1987).

88. Carpenter, "Dress Codes," 621.

89. This is true of West African cultures such as the Igbo and Yoruba of Nigeria. de Negri, *Adornment*, 12. It is offensive in some cultures to touch the head.

90. "In American experience, ethnic and religious conflicts, with their threat of the submergence of whole systems of values, have plainly been the major focus for militant and suspicious minds of this sort." Hofstadter, "Paranoid Style," 9.

CHAPTER 9

1. On respect for the dead, see Qureshi, *Transcultural Medicine*, 73. See also Poulter, *English Law*, 234–241; Shibles, *Death*; Habenstein and Lamers, *Funeral Customs*; Kalish and Reynolds, *Death and Ethnicity*; Parry and Ryan, *Cross-Cultural Look*. On the afterlife, see Kass, "Thinking"; Feinberg, "Mistreatment"; Csordas, "Body"; Quigley, *Corpse*. Cultural practices concerning the dead vary over time. For a study of changes in the Western tradition, see Aries, *Western Attitudes*. In Anglo-American law, a dead body or corpse "must be the body of a human being, without life, and not entirely disintegrated." Gilligan and Stueve, *Mortuary Law*, 5.

The dearth of scholarship on culture conflict and the legal treatment of the dead might be explained by what has been called the cultural proclivity toward the denial of death. See Ernst Becker, *Denial of Death*, and Kamerman, *Death*, 28–32.

2. Most of the discussion focuses on the United States. The issue arises in other countries, particularly developing countries where there are cultural and religious objections to postmortem examinations. Pesce, "Histopathology." Blasszauer contends that the dead body is considered the property of the state in post-Communist countries, "emerging" democracies, and countries with no democracy. "Autopsy," 19.

3. Criminal cases involving the dead exist. For instance, in *R. v. Noboi-Bosai* (1971–1972), seven natives in Australia were charged with violations of the criminal code provisions that

prohibited improperly or indecently interfering with a corpse when they ate it. Justice Prentice acquitted them for two main reasons: (1) the statute was not intended to and did not cover cannibalism; (2), even if it was applicable to cannibalism, there was the further question of whether the defendants' dealings with the corpse were either "indecent" or "improper."

4. Interestingly, scholarship on social construction of the human body in law ignores the subject of dead bodies. For example, Hyde briefly mentions the corpse only in passing in *Bodies of Law*, 212, 219. See also Gold, *Body Parts*. But see Nelkin and Andrews, "Do the Dead Have Interests?" One issue is whether the dead have any privacy rights. James and Leadbeatter, "Confidentiality." In a famous essay Feinberg acknowledges that the newly dead human body is symbolic of a human person (more so than a fetus) but rejects the idea that it should have rights: "Our sentiments are even more sharply focused on the neomort because it is not only a symbol of human beings generally, but unlike the fetus, it is the symbolic remains of a particular person and his specific traits and history. Moreover, we are not even tempted in rhetoric to ascribe rights and interests to the neomort (with the possible exception of those stemming from testimonial directions he left before he died)." "Sentiment," 20.

5. "The controlling principle is that there exists in our law a right to possess, preserve and bury, or otherwise to dispose of, a dead body, that the right belongs to the surviving spouse, if any, living in the normal relation of marriage, and if none such, then to the next of kin in the order of their relation to the decedent; and that violation of that right is a tort." *Steagall et al. v. Doctors Hospital* (1948), 353.

6. Iserson, *Death to Dust*, 556, 558; Percival Jackson, *Law of Cadavers*, 133; Meyers. *Human Body*, 184, 211 n.16; Gilligan and Stueve, *Mortuary Law*, 5–6. Quotation from Meyers, *Human Body*, 184. Percival Jackson emphasizes that liability will not give rise to damages unless there has been mental anguish, as opposed to mere annoyance. *Law of Cadavers*, 134–138.

7. Souder and Trojanowski, "Autopsy," 135, and Iserson, *Death to Dust*, 114. See also King and Meehan, "History of Autopsy." On early civilizations, see Svendsen and Hill, "Autopsy Legislation," 846. Information on Erasistratus from Souder and Trojanowski, "Autopsy," 135.

8. See, respectively, Svendsen and Hill, "Autopsy Legislation"; Hill and Anderson, *Autopsy*, 112; Souder and Trojanowski, "Autopsy," 135. The 1533 autopsy revealed that each body had a complete set of organs with a fused liver. Although the priest was prepared to baptize each twin separately, the father objected as he was apparently unwilling to pay for more than one baptism. Hill and Anderson, *Autopsy*, 38. For the 1665 autopsy, see Iserson, *Death to Dust*, 116. For discussion of some of the pioneers such as Giovanni Battista Morgagni of Padua, Karl Rokitansky of Vienna, and Rudolf Virchow of Berlin, see Svendsen and Hill, "Autopsy Legislation," and Hill and Anderson, *Autopsy*, chap. 2. See also Iserson, *Death to Dust*, 116.

9. Souder and Trojanowski, "Autopsy," 136. The first medical examiner system established in the United States was in Maryland in 1939. Spitz, *Medicolegal Investigation*, 9. The change to a medical examiner in lieu of a coroner was motivated partly by a desire to insulate the investigator from political pressures. By 1990 many states required a physician to serve as medical examiner or coroner. Among the many exceptions is California, which has a sheriff-coroner system in many counties (10–11).

The term *coroner* is etymologically derived from "crowner," who was the king's representative. This official was responsible for tax collection and convening courts to adjudicate local cases. Hill and Anderson explain that the crowner had to distribute the property of a person found guilty of murder and other crimes, and there "he gradually became identified with matters pertaining to death, thus the 'death investigator.'" *Autopsy*, 113. See also Spitz, *Medicolegal Investigation*, 4–6, and Wecht, "Coroner and Death." Bernard says the office of the coroner predates the period of the Magna Carta in England. *Law of Death*. For overviews of the role of medical examiners, see, e.g., Hanzlick et al., "Death Investigation"; Prahlow and Lantz, "Medical Examiner"; Castiglione and Lomi, "Forensic Autopsies."

10. See Waltz and Inbau, *Medical Jurisprudence*, 203; Hill and Anderson, *Autopsy*, 133–134; Sonder and Trojanowski, "Autopsy," 134; Orlowski and Vinicky, "Conflicting Cultural Attitudes"; Nelkin and Andrews, "Do the Dead Have Interests?" In the late eighteenth and early nineteenth centuries the dissection of cadavers came to be an integral part of medical education. For some time the public abhorred the use of the dead in medicine, considering this shameful, while medical schools were "in their own way obsessed with the dead." "Body snatching" from local graveyards, presumably for dissection, led to public outrage. Laderman, *Sacred Remains*, 81–83, 165–166.

11. See Hill and Anderson, *Autopsy*, 134, 138–139. Insurance companies may refuse to pay insurance death benefits if an autopsy is not performed. Taff and Boglioli, "Practical Approach," 234. On product tampering, see Souder and Trojanowski, "Autopsy," 134.

12. Quotation from Hill and Anderson, *Autopsy*, 160; see also Waltz and Inbau, *Medical Jurisprudence*, 260. With respect to the pro-autopsy stance of the medical profession, see Hill and Anderson, *Autopsy*, 135; Sugiyama and Maeda, "Autopsy Rates"; Rezek and Millard, *Autopsy Pathology*. Much of the medical literature discusses the possible relationship between religious objections and the documented lower rate of autopsies performed in the United States. Some worry about the possible effect of religious objections on organ donation decisions. See, e.g., Orlowski and Vinicky, "Conflicting Cultural Attitudes," 196.

13. In some countries—e.g., Austria, Bulgaria, Hungary, Italy, and Poland—consent is not required for autopsies. Austria has nearly a 100 percent autopsy rate. Iserson, *Death to Dust*, 124–125. On granting authority, see Waltz and Inbau, *Medical Jurisprudence*, 204, and Pearson, "Liability." In Maryland in 1976 the court upheld the constitutionality of autopsies in spite of the expression of religious objections by the "next of kin." Boglioli and Taff, "Religious Objection."

14. Kalish and Reynolds report that one in four Anglos and blacks, and one in three Mexicans and Japanese, would object to an autopsy, suggesting a substantial resistance still remaining to physical violation of the remains. *Death and Ethnicity*, 47. For a scholar rejecting the validity of religious objections in many instances, see Geller, "Religious Attitudes."

On the Hmong, see, e.g., Waters et al., "Health Care," and Beghtol, "Hmong Refugees." Bliatout explains the Hmong view of autopsy: "This is considered one of the most horrible things that can happen to a Hmong person, as it is believed that the person will be born mutilated in the next life. Also, the souls of the person may become unhappy and come back to cause illness to the remaining family members and their descendants." "Hmong Attitudes," 96.

On Jews, see, e.g., works by David Feldman, "Rabbinic Comment"; Geller, "Autopsy"; Green and Green, "Dealing with Death"; Jakobivits, "Dissection," and Jacobovits, "Jewish Laws"; Rosner, "Autopsy." Some deny Jewish law opposes autopsy, e.g., Lauterbach, "Jewish Attitude."

On Mexican Americans, see, e.g., Henry Perkins et al., "Autopsy Decisions." As many Mexican Americans are Roman Catholics, they "may place considerable importance on maintaining the cadaver whole and unmutilated. The basis for this view may be the belief that God wants the human body returned to Him whole after death, that an autopsied patient must live forever in heaven with that same body and its mutilations, or that mutilation of a cadaver is a desecration of a temple of the Holy Spirit." Henry Perkins, "Cultural Differences," 74. See also Gonzalez-Villalpando, "Influence of Culture."

On Muslims, see, e.g., works of Ghanem. According to a ruling of the Prophet Muhammad, "The breaking of a bone of a dead person is like the breaking of the bone of a live person." Ghanem, "Permission," 241, and *Medical Jurisprudence*, 25. See also Hussain," Post-Mortem Examination."

One article stated that a Gypsy objected to an autopsy on the basis of Gypsy custom. Mittleman et al., "Practical Approach," 828.

15. Perkins, "Cultural Differences." Some theorists such as Arnold Van Gennep and Victor Turner consider the recently deceased to be in a liminal state between life and death. Death rituals serve to facilitate the transition between the two states. Lidz, "Death."

16. Henry Perkins et al., "Autopsy Decisions,"153.

17. Acceptable reasons for otherwise prohibited autopsies include, e.g., the willingness of Jewish law to sanction an autopsy to save another life. Also, an autopsy is generally considered justified if there is a "compelling public necessity." In *Rotholz v. The City of New York* (1992), e.g., the court found no such necessity. Because the hospital failed to notify the medical examiner, the court held it responsible for causing an unauthorized autopsy. However, because there was a question as to whether the city exercised sufficient control over the hospital, the court dismissed the motion for summary judgment in favor of the city. The unresolved issue is whether a party that did not perform the unlawful autopsy can be held liable. In some instances there is no apparent need for the autopsies. Many of the documented lawsuits have been filed by Orthodox Jewish individuals when unauthorized autopsies are performed in the absence of any public rationale. See, e.g., *Snyder v. Holy Cross Hospital* (1976); see also Zambito, "Coroner."

18. Pearson, "Liability."

19. In *Ruth Schwartz* (1994), the mother of an Orthodox Jewish state prison inmate who died of AIDS sued after she discovered that her son's body had had an autopsy performed on it, despite her religious objection. The court concluded that even though a state law required autopsies for all inmates for public health reasons, the statute providing for religious objections superseded the correctional law.

20. See the discussion of *You Vang Yang v. Sturner* (1990) later in this chapter for the state justifying policies. "Some states may honor religious objections to medicolegal autopsies, although officials will always conduct an autopsy if they feel it is in the public interest." Iserson, *Death to Dust*, 123–124.

21. *Albareti v. Hirsch* (1993). Case quotes are from this source. On the internal exam, the court stated that it is done "to determine the path and nature of the injuries caused by the bullets, and to rule out other possible contributing factors to the cause of death to a reasonable degree of medical certainty, the standard required for the criminal prosecution of a homicide.". According to some legal definitions, removal of a blood sample might count as a "partial autopsy." Waltz and Inbau, *Medical Jurisprudence*, 205.

22. Quotation from Rispler-Chaim, "Ethics," 167. See also Ghanem, "Permission," 241 and Green and Green, *Dealing with Death*, 209. Sakr says that "autopsy is not recommended unless it is absolutely a must." "Death and Dying," 61. Geller says that "autopsy has not been a controversial issue in most Islamic countries because the orientation of the medical community has not been particularly directed at seeking autopsy." "Religious Attitudes," 496. Geller also predicts that Islamic religious beliefs will not prevent autopsies. Rispler-Chaim summarizes the evolution of thought on the subject: "Although postmortems involve elements unacceptable to Islamic law the benefits they provide are now considered indispensable. The unacceptable elements are excused on the grounds of the pragmatic Islamic legal principle of 'the public benefit' (maslaha). The violation which may befall the body of an individual owing to postmortems is overlooked in order to enable science and justice, and consequently the public good, to prevail." "Ethics," 167.

23. Many Hmong have died in this manner. Adler, "Sudden Death Syndrome." The Yangs told the doctors at the hospital that they were opposed to an autopsy. *Yang* 1990a, 855. See Schriever, "Comparison of Beliefs," 48. The sincerity of the Yangs' religious objection to autopsies was not in dispute. The legal arguments included allegations that the medical exam-

iner violated their First Amendment right to religious freedom and their Fourteenth Amendment rights to due process and equal protection, exceeded the legal authority of his office, and committed a tort against them.

24. Quotation from *Yang* (1990b), 558. Evidently the Hmong worry that their bodies will be a "living cadaver" for surgeons and that after surgery, they may not be recognized by their ancestors in the "spirit" world, that they may not be reborn as a human being, or that their souls will make living family members ill. See Xoua Thao, "Southeast Asian Refugees" and"Cultural Beliefs." On evil spirits, see Beghtol, "Hmong Refugees," 13, and Waters et al., "Health Care," 646. On reincarnation, see Waters et al., "Health Care," 647. On deformity, see Bliatout, "Hmong Attitudes," 26. According to one account, an elderly man died apparently because of brain malfunction. After an autopsy was performed in which the top of his head was cut off in a circular manner, two grandsons were born without heads. Bliatout, "Hmong Attitudes," 26. Quotation from *Yang* (1990b), 558.

25. "Where there may be in its judgment a reasonable belief that the manner of death could be pronounced as:

(1) Death by homicide, suicide, or casualty;
(2) Death due to criminal abortion;
(3) Death due to an accident involving lack of due care on the part of a person other than the deceased;
(4) Death which is the immediate or remote consequences of any physical or toxic injury incurred while the deceased person was employed;
(5) Death due to the use of addictive or unidentifiable chemical agents; or
(6) Death due to an infectious agent capable of spreading an epidemic within the state." *Yang* (1990a), 847.

26. *Yang* (1990a), 856.

27. The court makes an intriguing observation that the autopsy violated the Yangs' religious beliefs to a greater extent than other public policies had burdened individuals in earlier free exercise cases. Among the arguments was a claim that Dr. Sturner had not treated the defendant differently from others. The court took a dim view of that idea: "To say that the medical examiner has performed autopsies in similar situations in the past does no more than admit that he acted in a way that may have violated other individuals' religious beliefs." *Yang* (1990a), 856.

28. *Yang* (1990a), 855.

29. In *Smith* the court held that "generally applicable, religion-neutral laws that have the effect of burdening a particular religious practice need not be justified by a compelling governmental interest." *Smith* (1990a), 1604. Quotation from *Yang* (1990b), 558. On the judge's sympathy, see *Yang* (1990b), 558. His profound regret is often mentioned. See, e.g., Simoneau, "Anomaly," 174. Subsequently, Congress passed the 1993 Religious Freedom Restoration Act, which restored the compelling state interest test, but it was struck down on separation of powers grounds in *City of Boerne v. Flores* (1997). The state settled the case by paying the family $30,000. Polichetti, "ACLU."

30. Adler, "Sudden Death Syndrome," 55.

31. Prosecutors say the exam may show the angle a bullet entered the body and other useful facts.

32. *Montgomery v. County of Clinton, Michigan* (1990). The decision to dismiss was affirmed on appeal in an unpublished opinion (1991). The medical examiner is expected to use "diligent effort" to notify relatives but may order an autopsy, whether or not the next of kin consent.

33. Quotations from *Montgomery* (1990), 1258. The court noted that she was Conservative (rather than Orthodox), that she was not an avid practitioner of her religion, and that her

husband was not Jewish. These observations appear to be designed to call into question the extent to which she identified with the Jewish religion. The court employed the lower standard of review because the *Smith* decision was in effect at the time this case was adjudicated: "The incidental effect upon Joan Montgomery's practice of her religion, though regrettable, does not offend the First Amendment." *Montgomery* (1990), 1260.

34. For a list of selected Rabbinical comments on autopsy, see Geller, "Autopsy." See also Jakobivits, "Dissection," and Wurzburger, "Cadavers." The technical term for autopsy in the Talmud and Codes is *nivul hameth* (dishonoring the dead). Kottler, "Jewish Attitude." See also Rabbi Kranz's statement quoted in *Snyder v. Holy Cross Hospital* (1976), 337. Rabbi Jakobovits explains the traditional view: "All Jewish religious authorities agree that any sanction of dissection can be contemplated solely on the grounds of its immediate, if only potential contribution to the saving of life; that the number and extent of autopsies must be limited to a minimum; that a sense of reverence must be preserved during and after the operation; and that all the remains must be buried as soon as possible with due respect." "Dissection," 212. See also Kottler, "Jewish Attitude"; David Feldman, "Rabbinic Comment"; Cytron, "Honor," 116.

35. The Montgomery family was one of the only Jewish families in the community. This may have affected the way the case was handled by the police and court. John C. Kaplansky, personal communication, 1994.

36. For instance, in San Francisco a Chinese Buddhist family objected to a post-mortem exam for their twenty-year-old daughter because, according to Buddhist tenets, during the seven-day after-death period the spirit remains with the body. Life might be restored to the body, and if not, the mourning facilitates passage to the spiritual realm. Hatfield, "Family"; Henry Lee, "Family Prevails"; Matier and Ross, "Grieving Buddhist Family." The coroner was willing to delay the autopsy for a week, but it turned out that the family was opposed to any autopsy, in principle. Judge Stuart Pollak concluded that there was no need for a postmortem examination. A deputy city attorney worried that the ruling would create an unfortunate precedent. Henry Lee, "Family Prevails." Sometimes courts have enjoined postmortem examinations for Orthodox Jewish bodies where they were deemed unnecessary: *Atkins v. Medical Examiner* (1979), *Weberman v. Zugibe* (1977), and *Wilensky v. Greco* (1973).

37. *Smialek v. Begay* (1986). The New Mexico Supreme Court reversed the decision by the Court of Appeals to reinstate Nelson's siblings as plaintiffs, *Begay v. State* (1985). The facts are taken from the Petition for a Writ of Certiorari to the Supreme Court of New Mexico, Petitioners' Brief, 1986.

38. The authenticity and sincerity of the plaintiffs' religious beliefs were questioned in this case. Petitioners brief, n.2. Other cases where Navajo filed similar challenges include *Kayonnie v. Smialek* (1985), a lawsuit that resulted in a settlement, and *Begay v. Sweeney* (Utah, 1990). Quotation from *Begay v. State* (1985), 256.

39. The New Mexico Supreme Court disagreed with the Court of Appeals, which had reinstated the siblings as co-plaintiffs with the mother. See *Begay v. State* (1985), 259. Some claims were barred by sovereign immunity. The 1983 claim based on the First Amendment failed because the court determined that the state is not a person within the meaning of section 1983. This case stands for the proposition that a medical examiner can be protected by immunity. Pearson, "Liability."Quotation from *Begay v. State* (1986), 258.

40. *Smialek v. Begay* (1986), 1308.

41. The case was dismissed on summary judgment based on a finding that the remaining defendant was not personally involved in the autopsy. Stephen LeCuyer, personal communication, 1991.

42. There is no reason (besides expense) why tribunals could not use the group as the basis for calculating damages. For instance, in the *Aloeboetoe et al.* (1993) decision of the Inter-

American Court of Human Rights, the court used the indigenous concept of family in computing the damages. After the Suriname government accepted responsibility for the massacre to the Saramaca tribe and its failure to investigate the wrongdoing, the only issue adjudicated was that of damages. Compensation was to be based on Saramaca customary law. In another case the Supreme Court of Hawaii ruled that because of the importance of customary adoption within Hawaiian culture, the lack of a blood relationship did not prevent a boy from filing suit for damages when his grandmother was struck and killed by an automobile. *Leong v. Takasaki* (1974), 766. In the Navajo case, the court's analysis was that only the "nearest relative" possesses the property right necessary to have standing to sue. Furthermore, the court relies on statutes that rank kin relationships in order of importance. Thus, the court accepts uncritically the idea that there is a universal hierarchy in the order of next-of-kin relationships, even though this is contrary to fact.

43. In subsequent cases involving the Navajo the same medical examiner's office is the defendant in lawsuits. It is strange that once notified of the religious objections of the Navajo people the office would not have tried to modify its policies.

44. See Goldberg, "Autopsy." Quotation from Gov. C.27491.43-Religious Belief/Autopsy, State of California.

45. One of the problems that arises is that sometimes insurers will not make payments under life insurance policies unless there is a factual determination that the death of the insured was not a suicide. In some instances, unless an autopsy is performed, it may be difficult to establish whether the death was caused by an accident or was a suicide. Individuals whose religious beliefs prohibit autopsies may risk losing the benefits. Furthermore, the law sometimes shields insurers from claims that they should take religious beliefs into account. In California, for example, there is an insurance code provision which states that the insurer cannot be made liable for payment if an autopsy is necessary to establish the cause of death and the autopsy is legally prohibited. Insurance Code, section 10111.5, Insurer Not Liable if 27491–43 Invoked, State of California. So, even if the state permits certificates of religious belief to avoid autopsies for state purposes, private insurance may induce the family to agree to the autopsy.

46. Mittleman et al., "Practical Approach." The committee distinction is "where death is associated with criminal violence, policy custody, gunshot wound injury, prison, poisoning, suspected sudden infant death syndrome, suicide, and when ordered by the State Attorney." "Nonmandated autopsies consist of motor vehicle or aircraft accidents, diseases constituting a threat to public health, drownings, death in state institutions, and otherwise by violence." Mittleman et al., "Practical Approach," 825. For Jewish autopsies, before the autopsy is conducted, a sheet should be placed under the body to trap any escaping bloods or fluids. Instruments used in the procedure should be wiped with a paper towel that is placed with the body. Afterward, the body should be sutured tightly to avoid leakage.

47. With respect to the distinction in (1), a child who has apparently drowned might have died of other causes: "Maybe somebody hit him over the head and dumped him in the pool. Maybe the child has massive internal injuries from being beaten to death, but showed no external evidence of trauma." Di Maio, "Discussion." Item 2: see Di Maio, "Discussion." Item 3: see Taff and Boglioli, "Practical Approach."

48. The New York law passed in 1983 allows autopsies where the death was due to a homicide or to prevent a threat to public health. But where neither applies, the law created a waiting period which gave the family time to object to the autopsy. For a statement in favor of the exemption from the autopsy law, see Stern, "Autopsy Law," 44. Despite the fact that the New York law is considered "onerous," it has not discouraged medical examiners from proceeding without the consent of families. Although the law enabled relatives to win damages, it did not successfully prevent the indignity of desecration. For New York cases, see Spencer,

"State Liable," and Goldman, "Unauthorized." For lawsuits elsewhere, see Curran, "Damage Suits," and Curran, "Religious Objection."

49. Stanley Becker, "Autopsies," 316, and Bogliogli and Taff, "Religious Objection," 7.

50. See Yishai, "Health Policy," and Rosner, "Autopsy," 53–59. Quotation from Yishai, "Health Policy," 438–439. Most autopsies do, in fact, involve persons dying in official health institutions. Svendsen and Hill, "Autopsy Legislation," 847.

51. Quotation from Yishai, "Health Policy," 443. See Yishai, "Autopsy," 12. Yishai contends that the autopsy dispute shows the influence of an "intensive minority" as it was primarily strongly religious groups that lobbied for the restrictions on autopsy. "Health Policy," 443. The issue has a special salience because of the "dual character" of the state. Yishai, "Autopsy," 11.

52. In the United States, medical examiners seem almost completely indifferent to the effect of their work. For instance, a training manual in forensic medicine, *Medicolegal Investigation of Death: Guidelines for the Application of Pathology to Crime Investigation* by Werner Spitz (1993), makes no mention of diverse cultural and religious beliefs about the dead. One physician advised against even discussing religion with family members after the performance of an autopsy. Hirsch, "Talking to Family."

53. Amazingly, even in New York where a specific law known as the Silver Law was enacted, unauthorized autopsies continue to be performed despite religious objections. A particularly glaring error occurred in *Liberman v. Riverside Memorial Chapel* (1996). In the absence of a compelling public necessity, an autopsy was performed on an Orthodox Jew, Philip Braun, by a prestigious Manhattan funeral home that handled almost exclusively Jewish funerals. His daughter, Susan Liberman, sued and won $1.4 million in punitive damages and $75,000 for emotional distress. Goldman, "Unauthorized." On appeal the punitive damages award was dismissed, but the Supreme Court of New York (Appellate Division) reinstated an award of $650,000. The irony was that the deceased had long been a member of Chevra Kadisha, an Orthodox Jewish burial society whose purpose was to ensure that funerals were conducted in accordance with Jewish law. Anon. (1994a), "Unauthorized Autopsy." As Orthodox Jews' appearance is distinctive, it is hard to understand why mistakes continue to be made. Stanley Becker, "Autopsies."

54. When funeral directors do not fulfill their obligations—e.g., the duty not to interfere with burial and the duty to maintain a safe funeral home—they are liable for damages. For an in-depth discussion of tort liability and breach of contract, see Gilligan and Stueve, *Mortuary Law*, 23–35. Sometimes funeral directors are also held liable for participating in unauthorized autopsies.

55. Embalming was seldom used in Europe, and its popularity in the United States may be attributable to "a certain refusal to accept death." Aries, *Western Attitudes*, 98–99. Mitford says embalming became popular because it was perceived as "an essential hygienic measure." *American Way*, 56. The record showed that the Army knew Marc Kohn was Jewish but the Army was "entirely oblivious to the beliefs of that faith that the entire body must be buried and that parts that have been removed by human agency or otherwise should be returned. Nor did the Army attempt to ascertain whether the plaintiffs had such beliefs." *Kohn v. United States* (1984), 573. With respect to the autopsy claim, the court simply deferred to the military (574). According to Kentucky inheritance law, a sister does not inherit if the parents of the deceased are alive. Relying on this notion the court did not award any damages to the sister. Interestingly, the court deferred to the military on the autopsy decision but was quite willing to condemn the embalming decision. Another embalming case in which the court entertained a suit for intentional infliction of emotional distress is *Scheuer v. William F. Howard Funeral Home* (1980). The children of a Jewish mother appealed a summary judgment decision for the funeral home where the home immediately embalmed the mother's body even though they realized she was Jewish.

56. Mrs. Lott was embalmed, put in a coffin with a crucifix and rosary beads, and had make-up applied in accordance with Roman Catholic requirements. Mrs. Tumminelli was placed on a Taharah board, was washed, and had prayers said over her in preparation for an Orthodox Jewish burial. See *Lott v. State and Tumminelli v. State* (1962).

57. *Doersching v. State Funeral Directors Board* (1987), 785.

58. *Doersching*, 791–792.

59. "More Mexicans Americans wished to have a wake than members of other groups." Kalish and Reynolds, *Death and Ethnicity*, 180. They criticize officials who prevented Mexican Americans from staying at a cemetery to grieve after the priest finished saying the prayers (178).

60. There is little evidence to suggest that historically funeral directors have felt that it was incumbent upon them to learn about the traditions of others. For instance, Habenstein and Lamers make no mention of this subject in *The History of American Funeral Directing*. The subject of diverse funeral rites is not a focus of the Funeral Ethics Association, nor of the American Board of Funeral Services Education. However, organizations such as the National Negro Funeral Directors and Morticians Association and the Jewish Funeral Directors of America could serve the needs of some communities.

61. Cremation involves burning a corpse to reduce it to ashes and small bone fragments. For a fuller discussion, see Iserson, *Death to Dust*, chap. 6. Gilligan and Stueve note that cremation is "not technically a method of disposition, but actually one step in a mode of disposition." *Mortuary Law*, 7. They note that the "cremains" are placed in an urn, which can be retained by the family, placed in the niche of a columbarium, or entombed in a cemetery; or the ashes may be taken out and scattered. One of the main reasons cremation was favored in antiquity was to avoid grave robbing and defilement of the body. Ragon, *Space of Death*, 275. A brilliant analysis of cremation can be found in "The Radical Saving of Space by Cremation," chap. 19 of Ragon's book. See also Prothero, *Purified by Fire*. On modern reasons, Ragon quotes the president of the French Federation of Cremation: "The United Kingdom saved in 1967 an area the equivalent of 607 football fields." *Space of Death*, 272. Countries like England and Japan which have high population densities have high rates of cremation. Iserson, *Death to Dust*, 248. More than 97 percent of Japanese are cremated, and in 1998 Japanese developed group graves and burial condominiums that resemble lockers. Magnier, "Squeeze." The Cremation Association of North America projects that by 2010 cremation will be chosen in 42 percent of all deaths in the United States. Emmons, "Funeral Firms," 24. An article in the *Economist* claims that burial in a coffin is still preferred in the "industrialized world." Anon. (1998g), "World's Way."

Cremation spread in northern Protestant countries because Catholicism prohibited cremation until 1964. Ragon, *Space of Death*, 274. Ragon comments on the peculiar fact that cremation spread through Protestant countries except the United States, which "shows the same repugnance for cremation as the Latin countries" where the number of incinerations did not exceed 3.6 percent. Embalming was preferred in the United States. From time to time the Catholic Church considers revising its cremation policy. In 1996 a Committee on the Liturgy composed of bishops recommended that cremated remains not stay outside in the hearse during a funeral Mass. Anon. (1996g), "Catholic Bishops."

The most popular crematorium oven was the gas-burning model designed by an Italian Professor Polli, which was used in Germany in sinister ways. The association of the crematorium ovens of concentration camps may explain why some find the technique repugnant. Gary Laderman's fascinating analysis of deathways, *The Sacred Remains*, explains why embalming became the preferred method of disposing of the dead in the United States: during the Civil War the presence of more bodies to bury than the soldiers could handle created pressure to devise other techniques. In addition, a desire to delay decomposition of the body, so medical institutions would have longer to work on the corpses, thereby minimizing the need for "fresh cadavers," contributed to the popularity of embalming. Another factor was the death industry's promotion of commodities like the coffin.

62. In Miami a funeral home accidentally mixed up the name tags of two babies. One was to be buried, and the other cremated. After discovering that the wrong one, Sunny, had been cremated, and the other buried, the funeral director decided not to reveal the error, hoping the mistake would go undetected. When a former employee disclosed the mistake, one family sued, arguing that cremation was against the family's religion. The Funeral Home explained that it wanted to avoid bad publicity and a second funeral for the family. A jury concluded that the funeral home should pay $276,620. Anon. (1999c), "Dishonesty." In another case in Houston, Texas, Diana Montalvo, a woman whose husband was accidentally cremated due to an error in the medical examiner's office, filed a $1.7 million lawsuit against the funeral home. The allegation was that the magnitude of the error was greater than in other corpse mismanagement suits because the Montalvos were Roman Catholics. Anon.(1999e), "Funeral Home."

In one case a Jewish husband requested that the wife be cremated, and he received a container of ashes six days after her death. Four months later state officials found her body, along with several others, inside a large refrigerator at the crematory. The family sued for physical illness, mental distress and humiliation, and reimbursement for medical expenses. Anon. (1999d), "Get in Line."

Because Illinois law only permitted awarding damages for emotional distress where there was "contemporaneous physical injury," she was not deemed to be "a direct victim of a wrongful cremation." The court held that the exception to the zone of danger rule did not apply in this case.

For an interpretation of an unauthorized cremation suit as commodification of dead bodies, see Brandes, "Cremated Catholic."

63. The problem was that the son's attorney ought not to have waited so long to file the suit.

64. *Singh v. Air Illinois* (1988), 855.

65. I am indebted to Scott Gilligan, general counsel for the National Funeral Directors Association, for mentioning this example to me. Personal communication, 1999. The coffin also contained a banana skin, cigarette butts, and crumpled newspaper. The Jewish burial group was relieved that the mistake was discovered because if she had been buried with the pig, that would have been a desecration to the entire cemetery. The mortuary's explanation was that an employee's wife had dissected the pig for a college project in the mortuary. The embalmer placed the plastic bag containing the fetal pig in the casket, mistakenly thinking it was personal effects. The family's attorney publicly stated that "we are inescapably led to the conclusion that this was not an accidental act." Jonathan Marshall, "Undertaker Sued."

The Book of Leviticus in the Bible prohibits the consumption of pork. For an analysis of the "Judensau," see Dundes, *Like a Chicken Coop*, 119–124.

See also Anon. (1993d), "Jury Hears Mortuary Horror," and Anon. (1993e), "Mortuary Settles Case."

66. The husband said, "With my beliefs, when you do the last blessings, the body is supposed to be there for the whole ceremony, not half. When the [first] casket arrived, the priest blessed it. What if the first blessing is the only one that counts? It's going to be an unanswered question for the rest of my life." Anon. (1997d), "Honest Mistake." Also, Greg Abbott, personal communication, 1999.

67. It is difficult to identify such cases. Even the trade's own case reporter the *Legal Compass*, which is published by the International Cemetery and Funeral Association, provides few

relevant citations. It is an obscure reference, unavailable even at mortuary colleges. Jackie Taylor, personal communication, 1999.

Robert Ninker, director of the Funeral Ethics Association, said it would be "insane" for funeral directors not to pay attention to family needs. Personal communication, 1999. John Carmon, spokesman for the National Funeral Directors Association, said: "People cling to their traditions at the [most difficult] times in their lives. Our job is to create an atmosphere where people can accept the reality of death in whatever way they feel comfortable." Anon. (1996a), "Diverse Customs."

68. See Weber, "New Niches," and Deborah Sullivan, "Funeral Home." The "Diverse Customs" article in *Mortuary Management* (Anon., 1996a) mentions the financial incentive to be culturally sensitive. Weber, in "New Niches," offers an estimate of $4 billion; others claim it is an industry of $25 to $50 billion. Robert Ninker, personal communication, 1999. Information on Paramount, California, from Weber, "New Niches." If a funeral home specialized in one group, the question might arise as to whether it can decline to serve other communities. Such a practice would likely be deemed discriminatory. One mortuary, Malinow and Silverman, catered only to Jewish clients for sixty-five years. But in 1991 when the Muslim Albahri family asked the mortuary to transport or store the body of their deceased child, their request was refused by the company: "We don't pick up Muslim children. We only pick up Jews." Timothy Williams, "Muslim Family," and, "Business Bias." The family filed a $4 million lawsuit against the mortuary alleging unfair business practices, false advertising, and discrimination in violation of the Unruh Civil Rights Act and the Business and Professions Code. The plaintiffs requested an injunction to halt the practice. The Rabbinical Council of California, an association of Orthodox rabbis, condemned the mortuary in a unanimous resolution. Tugend, "LA Rabbis." Apparently nothing happened after the family filed a complaint with the state Board of Funeral Directors and Embalmers until the mother's angry call led to a referral to the state Attorney General's office. Hasemyr, "Pleas." Southern white-owned funeral homes sometimes would not embalm blacks, or if they did, would not allow the wake. Elaine Woo, "Wilbert Oliver."

69. Many cases settle before trial to avoid publicity. Scott Gilligan, personal communication, 1999. Regarding funeral directors with the same background, for example, the Universal Chung Wah Funeral Home in Alhambra, California, caters to Asians. When Rose Hills Cemetery proposed a funeral home in Alhambra with Mandarin- and Cantonese-speaking assistants, members of the community, mostly of Chinese ancestry, reacted with horror. A lawyer, Llewellyn Chin, explained: "Nobody wants to go by or into a mortuary unless they really have to. There is some fear of ghosts impacting the residential neighborhood." Quoted in Romney, "Rose Hills." After discussion, Rose Hills decided against proceeding with the mortuary. It is surprising that Rose Hills made an error of this kind, considering its experience with diverse cultures in Whittier. Wainwright, "Providing Funeral Service."

70. According to Kathie Walczak, research division, National Funeral Directors Association (NFDA), the NFDA provides brief descriptions about the funeral traditions of groups: the Amish, Baha'i, Buddhist, East Orthodox, Hindu, Jewish, Muslim, and Native Americans. Personal communication, 1999. See National Funeral Directors Association, "Cultural Differences." Information on mortuary science colleges from Gordon Bigelow and James Augustine, personal communications, 1999.

71. Tension between medical examiners and funeral directors has existed for decades. See the discussion in *Mortuary Management* (1959, Sept. and Nov.). Funeral directors dislike autopsies as they make it more difficult to prepare bodies for showing at funeral ceremonies. Because of this, they may advise families not to consent to the procedure. Mitford, *American Way*, 59. For an empirical study of whether funeral directors have contributed to low autopsy

rates, see Heckerling and Williams, "Attitudes." In one lawsuit a primary issue was whether the funeral director could have embalmed the body given its condition after Duke University Medical Center had an autopsy performed on it. Gilligan, "Legal Liability." One article published in 2000 gave advice to funeral directors about the "dilemmas" autopsies create for embalmers. Keyser, "Autopsy." In 1972 a committee comprised of members of the NFDA and the College of American Pathologies attempted to resolve differences with "postmortem procedures." Anon. (1985a), "Postmortem Procedures," 6–8.

72. *Otieno v. Ougo* (1991), 1049–1061. For some of the extensive commentary on the case, see Ojwang and Mugambi, *Otieno Case*; Karanja, "Otieno"; Egan, *Otieno*; Stamp, "Burying Otieno"; Alan Goldfarb, "Kenyan Wife's Right"; April Gordon, "Gender"; Howell, "Otieno Case"; Monari, "Burial Law"; Kraft, "Tribal Rites." In the literature the wife is sometimes referred to as Virginia Wambui Otieno. Her book *Mau Mau's Daughter* uses Wambui Waiyaki Otieno; Virginia Edith Wambui Otieno is the name that appears in the appellate decision. The Marriage Act gave couples the ability to choose a monogamous marriage. Goldfarb, "Kenyan Wife's Right," 2 n.6. In a detailed monograph on Luo marriage, Gordon Wilson discusses the fact that European influence has led some to modify Luo customary law: "Examples of these conflicts are numerous and on occasion one or more parties to a dispute will attempt to use what suits them from each culture, that is, the original Luo customary law and the new ideas about law and custom, to their own particular advantage and to the disadvantage of opponents." *Luo Customary Law*, 138. The Luo claimed that because she married a Luo, she should have to follow their customary law. This would have required that she shave her head, wear Otieno's clothes inside out, and marry his younger brother (widow inheritance). Mrs. Otieno objected to these traditions. *Mau Mau's Daughter*, 189.

Otieno repeatedly rejected customary law. Howell, "Otieno Case," 233. In twenty-five years he returned to Luoland only six times, three of which were for funerals of family members. *Otieno v. Ougo*, 1049. See also Kraft, "Tribal Rites," 8. Evidently he recited Shakespeare and enjoyed Perry Mason videos. Howell, "Otieno Case," 232. They raised their children as Kenyans. Some may find it odd that a modern lawyer would not have had a will, particularly if he could anticipate conflict over his burial. Mrs. Otieno's response was that women's inheritance rights were "too easily overturned in courts." April Gordon, "Gender," 884. In her book, she reiterates that Otieno thought written wills could be contested, whereas an oral will would be respected: "For African people, it is a curse to change an oral will left by a deceased person." *Mau Mau's Daughter*, 175. The final court decision explicitly said that a written will might not have settled the question: "It is now clear to us that it is not sufficient to write wills. There often are disputes about burials." *Otieno v. Ougo*, 1061. Harden says it was not adequately explained and said the existence of a written will would have been a determinative factor for the judge. "Battle for Body."

The Court of Appeal decision notes list as one of the questions raised by the case: "Whether a Kenyan African can abandon his tribal origins." *Otieno v. Ougo*, 1049. It concluded that he could not. The deceased's ancestral home was in Nyamila Villega, three hundred miles to the west of Nairobi, and is referred to as Nyalgunga. Karanja, "Otieno," 1, 5. For her account, see Otieno, *Mau Mau's Daughter*. It was not a conflict between Luo and Kikuyu law; Mrs. Otieno would have lost under either system. She maintained that the conflict was about Otieno's "considerable estate," rather than his corpse. April Gordon, "Gender," 884. Stamp says that "Otieno's death represented too important a material opportunity for the lineage to pass up. A significant aspect of the clan's court challenge to Wambui's burial plans was its effort to gain control of Otieno's estate." "Burying Otieno," 837.

73. Howell describes one custom, *tudo lum*, "thing of the grass." "Otieno Case," 23. If the father is deceased, an uncle may substitute. Mrs. Otieno describes the tradition. *Mau Mau's*

Daughter, 188–189. For a synopsis of Luo customary law, see Howell's description of the testimony provided by the expert witness, Professor Henry Odera Ouku, an ethnic Luo and chair of the University of Nairobi philosophy department. "Otieno Case," 238–241. The distinction between "house" and "home" is not mentioned in some ethnographic treatments of burial customs, e.g., Hartmann, "Some Customs."

74. Harden, "African Tradition." See also Hauge, *Luo Religion*, 113.

75. See Monari, "Burial Law." The judge denied the brother and clan standing with regard to burial. Stamp, "Burying Otieno," 818. He was influenced by Otieno's cosmopolitan outlook: "Otieno, therefore, would not have wished to be saddled with ancient customs and superstitions associated with the Luo clan." Van Doren, "Death African Style," 339. The judge relied on the definition of next of kin in the Law of Succession, Act 3. See Karanja, "Otieno," 6, 7.

76. The Justices were J. O. Nyrangi (who wrote the opinion), H. G. Platt, and J. M. Gachuhi. Two were from ethnic groups similar to the Luo; one was Kisii and the other Kikuyu. The third was a white Kenyan. Van Doren obtained this information from his students at the University of Nairobi. "Death African Style," 340. For details, see Karanja, "Otieno," 10–11. Even if there were a duty to bury Otieno in accordance with folk law, Judge Shields did not think it was obvious who had the duty. Karanja emphasizes Shields's distinction between "allowing people to honour their traditions, and forcing them to do so" (24).

77. Stamp says the Court of Appeal limited the case to two questions: whether Otieno was subject to Luo folk law, and what the law required. "Burying Otieno," 818. But Karanja outlines the fifteen issues put to the court. "Otieno," 18–19. Bosire was a Luhya, which like the Kikuyu, is part of the Bantu people. Stamp, "Burying Otieno," 819. Van Doren says the judge was a Kisii. "Death African Style," 340. Monari says Bosire did not base his decision on customary law but, rather, on Otieno's wishes expressed to a gravedigger at his father's burial. "Burial Law," 670. Karanja concurs: "It did not, however, find that the deceased was subject to Luo customary law, it merely found that the reasons given by Judge Shield for finding that he was not were erroneous or insufficient." "Otieno," 14.

For the witnesses, see Karanja, "Otieno," 2. According to Harden, "The verdict was almost certainly fixed by Kenya's president. There is no other credible explanation why the judge would insist on believing the word of one aging gravedigger who loathed Wambui over that of a dozen more credible and disinterested witnesses who said Otieno wanted to be buried in Nairobi." "Battle for Body," 124. A further sign of the president's interest in the case is the fact that a year after Otieno's burial, President Moi appointed the Luo lawyer, Richard Kwach, to Kenya's Court of Appeals (129). Karanja says the mere fact that the judge asked the question about renunciation of Luo law implies that it is possible to do so. Karanja argues that change of domicile should enable a person to "opt out" of customary law. "Otieno," 25, 28. Quotation from Harden, "Battle for Body," 121. Hundreds of police surrounded the courthouse when the decision was handed down. With riot police at every intersection, the city resembled a "war zone." Howell, "Otieno Case," 247.

Mrs. Otieno unsuccessfully objected to the three-judge panel as the judges had ruled against her previously when they overturned Shield's decision. For a detailed description of each motion, see chap. 9, "The Burial Saga," in Otieno, *Mau Mau's Daughter*. See also Monari, "Burial Law."

78. Van Doren explains the hierarchy of laws in Kenya: Constitution, written law (both Kenyan and English), common law, and, if none of these applies, then customary law. His characterization of Bosire's analysis was that as the first three were inapplicable, customary law was controlling. "Death African Style," 341. See also Kraft, "Tribal Rites," 8, and Goldfarb, "Kenyan Wife's Right," 8. See the Constitution of Kenya, section 82 (4)(b). This provision was held not to constitute racial discrimination. Howell, "Otieno Case," 244. According to the

Judiciature Act, courts "shall be guided by African Customary Law in civil cases in which one or more of the parties is subject to it or affected by it so far as it is applicable." Howell, "Otieno Case," 245.

Karanja says that Mrs. Otieno was ill-advised to base her argument on a repugnancy clause because it "led to a lot of unsavory contentions by the plaintiff and some of her witnesses." "Otieno," 70. Karanja thinks it is totally inappropriate in postcolonial Africa (74). Even if common law were to be applied, she would lose because she was not entitled to sue as his husband's personal representative. *Otieno v. Ougo*, 1059. Karanja challenges this point, noting that people often carry out funerals before receiving formal "letters of administration" authorizing them to do so. "Otieno," 79.

79. *Otieno v. Ougo*, 1054. The Luo lawyer, Mr. Kwach said in court: "I too read Shakespeare but I am still a Luo." Stamp, "Burying Otieno," 820.

80. The court supported the national policy of a heterogeneous legal system rather than a uniform law, a policy adopted to avoid ethnic conflict. While there is national law for tort, crime, and contract, customary law is applied for personal law such as marriage, divorce, burial, and inheritance. Goldfarb, "Kenyan Wife's Right," 5. Karanja argues that the case should have been handled using conflict of laws principles. "Otieno," 73.

Quotations from *Otieno v. Ougo*, 1061. The court denies, for instance, that the custom of a widow shaving her head rose to the level of being repugnant. But see Goldfarb, "Kenyan Wife's Right," 1, who argues that the cumulative effect of funeral rites should be considered. The Court of Appeal affirmed on May 15, 1987.

81. On tension, see Howell, "Otieno Case," and Van Doren, "Death African Style." On women's rights, see Howell, "Otieno Case," 246: "Plaintiff (Virginia Wambui Otieno) should have prevailed sub-judice." See, e.g., Goldfarb, "Kenyan Wife's Right." Karanja concludes that the proper criteria should have been those of the Kikuyu or of the urban community in Nairobi. "Otieno," 52. Indeed, Luo customary marriage is extremely sexist. Wilson documents some of the practices in *Luo Customary Law*. Stamp says, "It was evident from the outset that Wambui's case was a major feminist issue." "Burying Otieno," 827.

See the section of Stamp's essay subtitled "When a House Is Not a Home: The Invention of Luo Tradition." "Burying Otieno," 823–824. She uses the term *lineage ideology* as part of her analysis of "ethnic essentialism." Karanja also thinks that the customary law is misinterpreted insofar as it disadvantages women. Referring to one scholar he says, "It seems even he found it impossible not to acknowledge that African customary laws could not have subjugated women to the extent now claimed by the pseudo-traditionalists represented by the defendants in the case before him." "Otieno," 62. The "other critic" is Karanja, "Otieno," 71. For her own thoughts, see Otieno, *Mau Mau's Daughter*, 188–189.

Goldfarb argues thatthe Convention on the Elimination of All Forms of Discrimination against Women (CEDAW) could have served as an interpretive guide for analyzing "repugnancy." "Kenyan Wife's Right," 19. Because the burial law violated Article 5, this might have led the judges to conclude the law was repugnant. On tribal politics, Kraft said in 1987 the 5 million Kikuyu dominated the political scene and the 3 million Luo resented being a subordinate position. "Tribal Rites." See also Howell, "Otieno Case." For an analysis of the enduring relevance of ethnic identity in Kenyan politics but which does not mention the Otieno case, see Ndegwa, "Citizenship and Ethnicity."

On class bias, see April Gordon, "Gender." And on women's rights, see Stamp, "Burying Otieno," 827. She explains that "the leading women's organizations in Kenya have experienced considerable internecine strife over the years" (830). The case did encourage discussions of gender equality in the international human rights community (832). Karanja credits Wambui for providing the inspiration for a successful campaign by the National Council of Women of Kenya to secure the passage of a law giving widows burial rights equivalent to their inheritance rights under the Law of Succession Act. "Otieno," 40.

Karanja attributes the tensions among women to the influence of colonialism. "Otieno," 66–68. On politicization, see Stamp, "Burying Otieno," 833. Van Doren also underscores the importance of funerals because they maintain contact between the living and the spirits of ancestors. "Death African Style," 337, 344.

82. The conflict between the Luo people and Mrs. Otieno is a contest among the living for possession of Mr. Otieno's corpse. There does not seem to be any mention made of the rights per se of Mr. Otieno; his wishes were only presented as part of an argument that Mrs. Otieno should prevail. Stamp refers to the case as Wambui's. "Burying Otieno." Quotation from *Otieno v. Ougo*, 1060.

83. For analysis of NAGPRA, see Marcus Price, *Disputing the Dead*, and the special issue of the *Arizona State Law Journal* 24 (1992) devoted to this topic. A "taking" is the expropriation of property without paying just compensation in violation of the Fifth Amendment. See Hurtado, "NAGPRA," and Ralph Johnson and Haensly, "Fifth Amendment Implications."

84. Ayau, "Restoring," 195–196.

85. Anon. (1998c), "Without Consent."

86. Ragon, *Space of Death*, 16.

87. Iserson uses the term pejoratively to explain the origin of necrophilia. *Death to Dust*, 400. Hovde says the cadaver is feared because it may become an "agent of evil or unsatisfied spirits." "Cadavers."

88. Bry, "Genuinely Distressing," 361. Bry advances an argument for a cause of action for corpse mishandling. Courts in some jurisdictions reject claims that the mishandling of a corpse should give rise to a claim of negligent infliction of emotional distress. "Genuinely Distressing." See, e.g., Anon. (1994c), "Torts."

89. If a decedent has expressed a wish not to have her remains handled according to the religion she was raised in, the court may rule that she has a right not to be treated that way. See, e.g., *Tkaczyk v. Gallagher* (1965) where a daughter preferred to be cremated despite her Catholic parents' objections; the court declined to issue a permanent injunction restraining cremation.

90. Quotations from Andrews, "My Body," 29. She argues that some "have reacted with horror to the idea that body parts may be property. Nevertheless, many legal decisions treat the body as a type of property" (29). See also Matthews, "Whose Body?"; Campbell, "Body"; Horton, "Personhood Analysis."

91. This is reflected in the expression "over my dead body." An individual will fight to the end, but after death will no longer be able to challenge another person.

92. Scholars have noted the symbolic importance of the corpse: "A newly dead human body is a sacred symbol of a real person." Feinberg, "Mistreatment," 32. Feinberg nevertheless rejects the proposition that relatives should have the right to object to the salvaging of the deceased's organs. See also May, "Religious Justifications." On loss of a loved one, see. Mandelbaum, "Funeral Rites."

93. "Kind words cost nothing but mean a lot. It will comfort the bereaved relatives immensely if a health professional were to say to a Christian or a Jewish relative that the deceased died peacefully; to a Muslim that the deceased appeared to say last words as 'Allah'; to a Hindu or a Sikh that a person died reciting 'Bhagwan,' and similar kind words for relatives from other religions." Qureshi, *Transcultural Medicine*, 74. This suggestion indicates that it would be relatively easy to make ethnic minorities feel that they have a stake in the system and would not necessarily involve changes in the law.

94. Even in states with strict rules on autopsy, e.g., New York, medical examiners still fail to comply by obtaining the consent of the next of kin.

CHAPTER 10

1. In U.S. law, this is technically argued as a violation of the Sixth Amendment right to effective assistance of counsel. *Trakulrat* is discussed in chapter 3, note 45.

2. Part of the aim of chapter 11 is to show that such a defense is not only compatible with the principles of pluralism but is necessitated by them.

3. Here I refer to Ronald Dworkin's famous distinction between equal treatment and treatment as equal. *Taking Rights Seriously*, 227. For an illuminating discussion of the concept of equality in the context of the law, see Kay, "Models of Equality."

4. A cultural defense may not always work to the advantage of the defendant. Under the present system a jury may acquit to avoid conviction for a serious offense and its corresponding heavy sentence. If a jury had the option of convicting of a lesser included offense, cultural defendants might wind up with longer sentences in some cases than they receive currently. Nevertheless, as I argue in this chapter, this outcome may very well be preferable from the point of view of the retributive theory of punishment.

5. See, respectively, e.g., Andenaes, "General Prevention" and *Punishment and Deterrence*; Zimring, *Perspectives*; Francis Allen, "Legal Values"; Gardner, "Renaissance of Retribution." Classic analyses of retribution include Kelsen, *Society and Nature*, and Westermarck, "Essence of Revenge."

6. The debate about the relative primacy of one of these over the others is an old one. In the past few decades the "inclusive" theory (which holds that punishment has multiple justifications) has gained favor: "All three elements—justice, deterrence, and reformation—are essential." Hall, "Science and Reform," 796, and *General Principles*, 308.

7. For instance, while some support the use of the death penalty in murder cases, others view it as overly harsh or disproportionate. See, e.g., Lempert, "Desert and Deterrence." In the past there has been controversy over the imposition of capital punishment on rapists. See *Coker v. Georgia* (1977) where the United States Supreme Court held that death is a disproportionate penalty for rape. I have argued that the moral basis of the cultural defense lies in the principle of proportional retribution. It might be argued, however, that a cultural defense contravenes the other justifications of punishment, namely deterrence and rehabilitation. I discuss this here under arguments against the cultural defense

8. Some have argued that retributivism authorizes officials in the criminal justice system to consider the defendants' histories, which would presumably include their cultural background. Monahan, "Prediction," 10. For a cogent argument that motive is relevant to criminal liability, see Husak, "Motive."

9. Originally mens rea was defined as a "guilty mind," which meant a morally guilty mind, but legal thought has evolved so that it has come to be understood as a legally guilty mind. Hall, *General Principles*, 70–83. For the "gray area," see, e.g., Cook, "Act, Intention, and Motive"; Ploscowe, "Examination"; Hitchler, "Motive."

10. See, e.g., Hall, *General Principles*, 88; LaFave and Scott, *Criminal Law*, 227; Perkins and Boyce, *Criminal Law*, 928; Lyman, "Cultural Defense," 99.

11. See, e.g., LaFave and Scott, *Criminal Law*, 443, 229. Motive is also part of the definition of child sexual abuse.

12. Wasik, "Partial Excuses," 516.

13. Wasik, "Partial Excuses," 520.

14. A lesser included offense is one that is closely related to the original charge but which is (a) considered less serious, and (b) more appropriate given the circumstances. To some extent, the law already does this when it allows the prosecutor to charge a defendant with either the felony or misdemeanor version of a crime. But this does not solve the problem at hand, because the misdemeanor charge is for the same offense as the felony charge. Thus, a

defendant would still be charged and convicted of a crime incommensurate with his moral culpability.

15. Indeed, courts seem more willing to permit individualized justice to mitigate a sentence than to excuse a defendant. Fletcher, "Individualization," 1292 n.71. Quotation from Wasik, "Partial Excuses," 531. One astute commentator also objects to this phenomenon: "There is something inescapably odd about a court's simultaneously affirming a conviction and recommending clemency." Fletcher, "Individualization," 1283.

16. The Australian Law Reform Commission twice considered the adoption of a "partial customary law defence" which would reduce "the level of liability in specific cases." After comparing a full customary law defense with a partial one, the commission recommended the latter. In the 1990s, however, the Australian Law Commission apparently lost its enthusiasm for either a complete or a partial cultural defense. Maddock, "Culture and Culpability," 65; Law Reform Commission, *Recognition*, 317, 323, and *Multiculturalism*, 172.

17. *People v. Estep* (1977) illustrates how controversial the decision whether or not to exclude cultural evidence can be. In this case a Korean man, Park Estep, was convicted of several charges including murder, assault, arson, and aggravated robbery. Of the two women who were victims, one was killed, but the other survived. The key witness at the trial was the surviving woman, Miss Lee, who was also Korean. She testified that her assailant did not have a mustache, but the defendant did have one at that time. Estep's attorney tried unsuccessfully to introduce evidence demonstrating the significance of facial hair to Koreans to emphasize the discrepancy. Whether or not the defendant would have been acquitted on the basis of this evidence, it should have been admitted. See Renteln, "Justification."

18. In 1991 in Milwaukee, Wisconsin, jurors had to decide whether or not Jeffrey Daumer, the man who killed, dismembered, and ate several victims, was insane. They were confronted with a difficult decision. If they accepted the insanity defense, he would be committed to a mental institution from which he could be released in a matter of years. If they rejected the defense, he would be incarcerated for decades, if not the rest of his life. The insanity defense proved unsuccessful, and it is difficult to believe that the jury's determination of guilt was made entirely independent of any consideration of the outcome of that decision.

19. The theory known as incapacitation is actually a version of specific deterrence. Specific deterrence refers to both incapacitation and to a defendant's conduct upon his release from prison. Thus, incapacitation is a subcategory of specific deterrence, rather than a separate theory of punishment. If a defendant is not to become a recidivist when he rejoins the community, then some process of transformation must occur during his imprisonment. Hence, it would appear that specific deterrence is not conceptually distinct from rehabilitation.

20. This argument is a variation of the argument that the cultural defense would undermine deterrence. See, for example, Sheybani, "Cultural Defense," 782–783, who says: "We would be living in a state of anarchy if each foreigner's culture and law was the determinant factor of what is right and wrong." See also Choi, "Cultural Defense," 89, and Sherman "Legal Clash."

21. One of the most common criticisms of the cultural defense is the undermining of certain groups. See, e.g., Gallin, "Cultural Defense"; Goldstein, "Cultural Conflicts," 162; Murray, "Battered Woman Syndrome"; Rimonte, "Question of Culture," 1311. It comes as no surprise that most of those who write about the cultural defense are female scholars, many of whom are women of color. Their scholarship reflects ambivalence toward the cultural defense. See, e.g., Chiu, "Cultural Defense," 1112. The main reason most critics reject the defense is that they assume, erroneously in my view, that use of the cultural defense will inevitably condone violence against women. For examples, see Sacks, "Indefensible Defense";

Coleman, "Individualizing Justice," 1337; Cardillo, "Violence," 85; Goldstein, "Cultural Conflicts," 167.

22. Indeed, most articles on the cultural defense reject it on the grounds that the newly arrived should be assimilated as rapidly as possible. James Sing regards the "significant backlash against the cultural defense" as part of the societal trend toward xenophobia. "Culture as Sameness," 1848. For example, see Lyman, who asserts, without argument, that the defense discriminates impermissibly against non-alien defendants. "Cultural Defense," 116 n.189. See also Sams, who contends the policy would be unfair to the "majority who could not use it." "Availability," 337.

23. For a persuasive argument of this kind, see Coleman, "Individualizing Justice." Sing construes Coleman's argument as privileging the interests of immigrant victims over the interests of immigrant defendants. "Culture as Sameness," 1847.

24. On sterotypes, see, e.g., Chiu, "Cultural Defense"; Holmquist, "Cultural Defense"; Koptiuch, "Cultural Defense"; Maeda, "Subject to Justice"; Murray, "Battered Woman Syndrome"; Jenny Rivera, "Domestic Violence"; Sacks, "Indefensible Defense," 549; Suri. "Matter of Principle"; Volpp, "(Mis)identifying Culture" and "Talking 'Culture.'" This type of argument often uses postmodern language, which emphasizes the danger of "essentializing" culture, or presuming that everyone who belongs to an ethnic group accepts a tradition. These analysts are unfamiliar with the anthropological literature, which has long shown that there are always individuals within a group who depart from established patterns of culture, that some traditions are contested, and that culture is dynamic.

Quotation from Volpp, "(Mis)identifying Culture," 100. She nevertheless supports the "informal" consideration of cultural information in court. As I explain later in this chapter, I consider this to be a variant of a cultural defense.

On Asians, see Chiu, "Cultural Defense," 1055, 1096, 1100; Roberts, "Culture Matters," 94, 96; Sams, "Availability," 350–351. Although Roberts favors the consideration of "cultural background" evidence, she is opposed to a formal cultural defense. Part of her critique is that the use of cultural evidence paradoxically benefits foreigners, rather than African Americans and American Indians. The implication seems to be that if cultural bias of judges could be eliminated so that all groups could invoke cultural defenses, she might accept the policy. "Culture Matters," 97.

On characterizing culture, see, e.g., Suri, "Matter of Principle," and Maguigan, "Cultural Evidence."

25. Proving facts about cultures is no more difficult than presenting evidence about mental problems, ballistics, and other types of scientific evidence. Anthropologists and representatives from the ethnic community can confirm the existence of the traditions. This is not to say that the process is without difficulty. For sources on the role of social scientists as expert witnesses, see Connell, "Using Cultural Experts"; Lawrence Rosen, "Expert Witness"; Allen Turner, "Prolegomenon."

26. Chiu argues that the cultural defense might promote deterrence by conveying some measure of respect to immigrant communities for their way of life and facilitating cultural adaptation. "Cultural Defense," 116–118. See also James Sing, "Culture as Sameness," 1850. Critics of the cultural defense cite the *Chen* case (1989) discussed in chapter 3 of this volume, to support their position that the cultural defense condones violence against women. Another case usually cited is *People v. (Kong) Moua* (1986), which I analyzed in chapter 7. Ironically, one critic argues that a leading article supporting the cultural defense begins with *People v. Kimura* (1985) to mitigate the influence of the feminist critique: "It is instructive that the *Harvard Law Review* essay arguing in support of cultural defense takes the *Kimura* case as its first example and paradigmatic case. . . . The author's use of feminine personal pronouns as stand-ins for the generic case has the rhetorical effect of giving a feminine cast to all defendants in cultural

defense criminal cases, when in fact all but one defendant until that time had been men." Koptiuch, "Cultural Defense," 225.

27. The use of other defenses such as insanity also results in differential punishment for defendants, but no one argues that their usage constitutes an equal protection violation of the victims. According to this logic, there could be no individualized justice because any deviation from a designated sentence would violate equal protection.

28. Philosophically, the cultural defense represents another way of trying to achieve the goal of individualized justice, a goal that is well established. To a large extent, many legal systems already accept this approach by tailoring punishment based on the attributes of individuals. The law makes distinctions between adults and children and between the sane and the insane. Having the law adjust punishment in light of cultural characteristics is not a departure from established jurisprudence.

29. This phenomenon is known as cultural hegemony: "The ideas, values, and experiences of dominant groups are validated in public discourse; those of subordinate groups are not, though they may continue to thrive beyond the boundaries of received opinion." Lears, "Cultural Hegemony," 574. See also Swett, "Cultural Bias," and Nunn, "Eurocentric Enterprise."

30. Stereotypes can be true or false. The problem arises with the transmission and reinforcement of false stereotypes. See, e.g., *People v. Rhines* (1978).

31. See, e.g., *People v. Metallides* (1974), discussed in chapter 3, in which a Greek American was prosecuted.

32. See Dundes, "Slurs International," 102–103.

33. For a discussion of their legal relevance, see Metzger, "Exculpatory Group Behavior."

34. See the superb essay on ethnic slurs by Sheri Johnson, "Racial Imagery." Johnson proposes a novel solution, a per se rule: if any reference to an ethnic slur occurs, a reversal would be automatic. This is somewhat persuasive, as there is no way to determine what effect the ethnic slur had on jurors, i.e., whether the jury would not have convicted in the absence of the slur.

35. As the guidelines were presumably designed to avoid punishing minorities more severely than Caucasians, it is arguably an incorrect interpretation of the policy to disallow considerations of culture where this would level the playing field and ensure that courts understand the motivations of defendants from other cultures. Courts tend to say the lawyers have not laid the proper foundation to introduce the information, or even when they have, that the cultural evidence does not affect the disposition of the case. It is difficult to find cases in which cultural factors are dispositive in sentencing because standard tools for legal research have no index for culture and because there is no systematic record kept of sentences. In most of the published decisions even when culture is considered as a possible mitigating factor, the court usually decides against giving it much weight. See, e.g., *U.S. v. Natal-Rivera* (1989) and *U.S. v. Rasag* (1988). For examples where cultural factors are taken into account, see, e.g., *State v. Rodriguez* (1964), *R. v. Hanna* (1982), and *R. v. Ikalowjuak* (1980).

36. See, e.g., Choi, "Application"; Kim, "Cultural Defense"; Maguigan, "Cultural Evidence"; Deborah Taylor, "Paying Attention"; Tomao, "Cultural Defense." Kim characterizes her position as being a "limited use" cultural "defense" advocate. "Cultural Defense," 109. Although Roberts mostly identifies problems with the cultural defense, she is in favor of courts' considering culture: "Cultural background will almost always be relevant to a defendant's state of mind and therefore should be admitted in evidence." "Culture Matters," 95. "This note has expressed a great deal of skepticism over the use of the cultural defense as such. However, not to admit cultural information in some cases, such as crimes where the intent of the defendant is a necessary part of the case, or situations where the context in which the crime was committed would be relevant evidence regardless of the culture of the perpetrator,

would put immigrant defendants on a worse footing than non-immigrant defendants." Sacks, "Indefensible Defense," 548. Some commentators favor the consideration of culture only during sentencing, e.g., Matsumoto, "Plea," 531. Sheybani argues that culture should mitigate, particularly for first-time offenders. "Cultural Defense," 783.

37. Maddock notes that cultural defenses may be justified more easily where a cultural tradition is mandatory, rather than optional. "Culture and Culpability."

38. When legislatures outlaw specific practices, there is a question of whether defendants can raise cultural defenses if they violate the statutes, particularly if the laws explicitly forbid consideration of culture. Occasionally, legislatures exempt religious minorities from general laws, e.g., Jewish and Muslim communities can engage in the ritual slaughter of animals in accordance with *shechita* and *halal*.

39. Some of the legislation on female genital mutilation expressly forbade any consideration of culture during prosecutions.

40. In reality, judges could accept cultural information now since evidence codes generally allow the consideration of relevant evidence. It is the judges who decide that the information is irrelevant. There is nothing in the code that bars its consideration. The mistake many analysts make is assuming that the description of diverse worldviews requires accepting them all. The error is the same as is made in debates about cultural relativism failing to distinguish between descriptive and prescriptive relativism. Renteln, *International Human Rights*.

41. For an analysis of how exemptions afford protection to religious minorities, see Montgomery, "Legislating."

42. Some might think that the ritual sacrifice of animals in religious ceremonies constitutes a cruel and unnecessary use of animals. That view is ethnocentric, of course, as the adherents consider the use necessary. Moreover, from the chicken's point of view, it is probably considered more dignified to die in a religious ritual rather than at a Kentucky Fried Chicken restaurant.

43. Levy characterizes the request in *Reynolds v. United States* (1878), the polygamy case, as a request for immunity from prosecution, i.e., an exemption. Levy, "Classifying Cultural Rights," 55 n.12.

44. Other examples of the use of injunctions are employment discrimination cases in which the person whose employment was terminated is reinstated. Because of the likelihood for repeat occurrences of the culture conflicts, the Sikh community in California tried to obtain a legislative exemption in 1994. This effort failed when the governor vetoed the bill passed by both the Assembly and Senate.

45. The case of *Cha'are Shalom Ve Tsedek v. France* (1995) was discussed in chapter 6.

46. Christian Scientists won statutory exemptions from child neglect laws, which protected them from manslaughter convictions because of their substantial financial resources and political connections.

47. In the employment discrimination cases, the question is whether the employer's action constitutes a "cognizable" form of discrimination under the codes.

48. Although the rules of evidence define relevance broadly enough to permit sympathetic judges to consider cultural information, legislatures should expressly approve its entry into court in case some judges are personally opposed to it. Executive orders could also officially establish this policy.

49. Sometimes when I contacted lawyers about a case reported in the press, they asked me to recommend expert witnesses.

50. For studies that examine the ethical issues associated with the use of social science in the legal system, see, e.g., Monahan and Walker, *Social Science in Law*; Erickson and Simon, *Social Science Data*; Arnold Rose, "Social Scientist"; Kerry Feldman, "Ethnohistory"; Frankena, *Social Science Practitioner*; Hopper, "Research Findings"; Samuelson, "Folklore."

51. Deveney contends that the minority group's understanding of what constitutes an "authentic" tradition is often not considered. "Courts."

52. In fact, ascertainment of the validity of the cultural claim for both the group and the individual remains a major problem for many legal systems. When judges are lax in requiring data to support cultural claims, they are not able to distinguish between accurate and unfounded cultural arguments.

In one Texas case, the judge appears to have been influenced by the cultural argument. See Renteln, "Cultural Defense Detrimental?" It is surprising how little effort seems to have been made to ascertain what child discipline practices actually are in Nigeria. If severe beatings are no longer tolerated in Nigeria, then presumably the cultural argument should have been rejected in Texas. Of course, even if this kind of corporal punishment is still employed, it seems wrong to allow a cultural defense to function as a complete defense in such cases.

One policy recommendation is that lawyers and judges receive instruction in the analysis of culture to help them evaluate cultural claims. Lawyers could study cultural analysis in the required legal ethics class in law school. This sort of training could also be available to judges in their judicial education seminars.

53. As, for example, when a gang member put forward a subcultural defense in a drive-by shooting case. Glover, "Teen Hero Slain" and "Arrested"; Hafferty, "Deadly Clash." Members of gangs may claim that an internal code of conduct requires killing to avenge the death of a member of the group. Although one hopes that juries would decline to mitigate punishment where individuals kill in the name of culture, it would be arbitrary to exclude the arguments. In my view, anyone seeking to raise the cultural defense should be entitled to do so. It is quite likely that presenting an argument of the kind suggested here would result in a more severe punishment rather than a more lenient one. But some insist that the defense should be available to all and that is it unfair to limit its use to immigrants. Dorothy Roberts, for instance, argues that African Americans should be authorized to raise the cultural defense. "Culture Matters." On the latter, see the incisive analysis of the defense by Richard Delgado, "'Rotten Social Background,'" and use of it by Judge Bazelon in *U.S. v. Alexander* (1974).

54. Another variant of the defense is known as the "black rage defense." See Paul Harris, *Black Rage*. There does not appear to be any reasonable way to limit the groups that could use the defense.

55. Ma proposes a five-year time limit but does not justify her proposal. "Cultural Defense."

56. Some might argue that individuals who have no choice but to follow traditions should be treated with greater compassion, but this distinction is not persuasive because individuals should have the right to follow both types of cultural traditions, whether mandatory or voluntary, unless they involve irreparable harm to others.

57. In the final analysis, however, there may be little reason to raise one. If the legislature is culturally sensitive in drafting the provisions applicable to the traditions, there will be no need for a cultural defense as partial excuse, because the concern about proportionality will presumably have been taken into account.

58. In the United States, exclusion of members of an ethnic group has been held not to violate equal protection. In *People v. Hernandez* (1991), the U.S. Supreme Court held that it was not a violation of equal protection to exclude Spanish-speaking jurors. The nexus between language and ethnicity was not close enough as there are Spanish-speaking individuals who are not Latinos, as well as Latinos who do not speak Spanish. Establishing a jury composed entirely of one group might be rejected as an illegitimate form of affirmative action.

59. For potential problems with this type of training, see Klitgaard, "Applying Cultural Theories."

CHAPTER 11

1. There is a distinction between considering the cultural information and giving it weight.

2. See, e.g., Mendus, *Politics of Toleration*; Kymlicka, *Multicultural Citizenship*, chap. 8, "Toleration and Its Limits"; Kukathas "Cultural Toleration"; Addis, "Human Diversity"; Walzer, *Toleration*.

3. Marcuse, "Repressive Tolerance."

4. To be sure, there should be mechanisms that enable individuals to leave. The real issue is not so much whether individuals can leave permanently, i.e., seek asylum elsewhere, as many groups would be perfectly willing to allow the departure of deviants. The real issue is that those who would wish to opt out of particular traditions want to remain in the cultural group and change the tradition in question. Take, for example, the tradition of the get. Orthodox Jewish wives do not want to opt out of Judaism, nor do they wish to opt out of Orthodox Judaism. They want to remain in the group as Orthodox Jewish adherents but want a divorce, so they can remarry within the group. Where the group has not reached the point of wanting to change its own traditions from within, there is the question of whether external forces should be brought to bear to compel the cultural group to change its traditions.

5. The primary reason for protecting cultural rights is that culture so strongly influences identity that not to protect it would be inconsistent with the very idea of human rights. The dignity of the individual is intimately tied to the cultural forces that shaped his or her identity. The literature often presents a false dichotomy between culture on the one hand and human rights on the other. But if the right to culture is itself a basic human right, then this requires that we shift the terms of the debate. If, however, there is a principled basis for the right to culture, then it is not obvious whether the cultural defense can be so easily dismissed.

6. See Prott, "Cultural Rights."

7. There is a large literature on cultural rights. See, e.g., Goulet, "Defense of Cultural Rights"; UNESCO, *Cultural Rights as Human Rights*; van Dyke, "Cultural Rights." One scholar, Vernon van Dyke, lists the components of cultural rights: language, religion, education, and freedom of expression. "Cultural Rights."

8. Furthermore, there has not been any serious attempt to connect the right to culture to the cultural defense, though it is precisely in cases involving the cultural defense that individuals seek to protect some of their cultural rights

9. See, respectively, Nieflc, *Cultural Rights and Wrongs*, and O'Keefe, "'Right to Take Part in Cultural Life.'" Quotation from O'Keefe, "Right to Take Part in Cultural Life," 912.

10. See General Comment No. 23(5), CCPR/C/21/Rev.1/Add5 (April 26, 1994). Many commentators support the protection interpretation. See, e.g., Cholewinski, "State Duty." For an overview of different scholars' views, see Akermark, *Justifications*, 127–131. For a detailed study of the interpretation of Article 27 jurisprudence, see generally the lucid analysis in Akermark. See also Prott, "Cultural Rights"; Burgers, "Cultural Identity"; Stavenhagen, "Cultural Identity."

On the negative formulation, some contend that it was understood that limitations applied. Poulter, *Ethnicity, Law, and Human Rights*, 82. Others deny this, noting the drafters would have included them if they had intended there to be any. In his definitive treatise on the ICCPR, Manfred Nowak rejects the notion that restriction provisions from other articles apply to Article 27. *U.N. Covenant*. The negative formulation makes sense if the right to culture will only be invoked when there is interference with the exercise of the right. Historically there was some question as to whether immigrants, refugees, and those temporarily residing in a country could use this right. Oddly enough, although Article 27 is considered the "minorities' rights" provision, it has mainly been used in disputes involving indigenous groups (though many do not consider themselves "minorities").

11. The Human Rights Committee is only empowered to review complaints against states that have ratified the Optional Protocol to the ICCPR, giving their permission to be subject to the complaints mechanism. For a discussion of the jurisprudence of the Human Rights Committee, see Akermark, *Justifications*; McGoldrick, "Canadian Indians"; Thornberry, *International Law*; Anaya, *Indigenous Peoples*.

12. France ratified the ICCPR with a declaration saying that because of its constitutional provision (Article 2 of the Constitution of the French Republic) guaranteeing nondiscrimination, it would not consider Article 27 applicable. Akermark, *Justifications*, 165–167. Because the Human Rights Committee treated the declaration like a reservation, it declined to review Breton language rights complaints. If the reservation to Article 27 is incompatible with the object and purpose of the ICCPR, it would be invalid.

13. In the context of the present discussion I do not tackle the more challenging problem of skepticism over the enforceability of international law overall.

Most human rights are automatically assumed to be valid. For instance, the right to life, the right against torture, and the right to free and periodic elections are considered self-evident. For some reason, the right to culture requires justification, though the others do not. The explanation for this is that it is perhaps more obvious that the right to culture will conflict with other basic rights. One of the difficulties is the need to reconcile competing rights claims, i.e., to address the "hierarchy" problem.

14. Interestingly, he is uncertain as to whether to claim the presumption as a right. Charles Taylor, "Politics of Recognition," 68.

15. Among the most lucid and eloquent interpretations of cultural rights are those of Baubock, "Cultural Minority Rights for Immigrants"; Levy, "Classifying Cultural Rights"; Parekh, "Minority Practices and Principles of Toleration."

16. Usually immigrants are assumed to have left voluntarily, as compared with refugees who were compelled to flee.

17. I am indebted to Baubock's incisive critique of the "when in Rome" ideology.

18. There is a large literature on minority rights. See, e.g., Rodley, "Conceptual Problems." The culture of the dominant group is often the national identity. This is a social construction. Some consider nations to be "imagined communities." Cf. Benedict Anderson's book by this title.

19. His basic position is laid out in Poulter, "Ethnic Minority Customs, English Law and Human Rights." His defense of the utility of human rights standards was further developed in his last book, *Ethnicity, Law, and Human Rights*.

20. The girls might rely on the right to gender equality or rights embodied in the Convention on the Rights of the Child.

21. On Eurocentrism, see Renteln, *International Human Rights*; Sinha, *Legal Polycentricity*; Beyerly, *Eurocentric International Law*; Anon. (1993b), "Aspiration and Control." Although this debate is an important one, there has been a growing consensus on human rights, despite their European origins. It is intriguing that the right to culture was incorporated in human rights instruments that have come under attack for cultural bias.

22. Follesdal, "Minority Rights." Kymlicka also rejects the use of human rights to achieve what he calls ethnocultural justice. "Human Rights and Ethnocultural Justice," 215.

23. In order for a norm to be designated part of customary international law, there must be state practice, i.e., proof that states adhere to the norm, and *opinio juris*, a sense of binding obligation on the part of the state that it must follow the norm.

24. Article 30 says that "in those States in which ethnic, religious, or linguistic minorities or persons of indigenous origin exist, a child belonging to such a minority or who is indige-

nous shall not be denied the right, in community with other members of his or her group, to enjoy his or her own culture, to profess and practice his or her own religion, or to use his or her own language." Article 24(3) states that "parties [should] take all effective and appropriate measures which a view to abolishing traditional practices prejudicial to the health of children." United Nations, *Human Rights*. On the broader range, see LeBlanc, *Convention on Rights*, 85.

25. Article 2(f) states that parties should undertake "all appropriate measures, including legislation, to modify or abolish existing laws, regulations, customs and practices which constitute discrimination against women." See also Article 5 (a). United Nations, *Human Rights*.

26. See Parekh, "Minority Practices and Principles." In his review of other principles for limiting toleration, he treats moral universalism separately from universal human rights. Quotation from p. 264.

27. "However if the practice deeply offends against its operative public values, it might rightly refuse to be so indulgent." Parekh, "Minority Practices and Principles," 263. In his superb essay, Parekh explains that if the minority practice offends an operative public value, it may deserve disapproval, but he says clearly that that is not necessarily a reason to disallow it (261).But if the minority spokesmen are unable to defend the offensive practice to the satisfaction of the wider society, it must be discarded. It is noteworthy that the operative values can change over time: e.g., accommodating Jewish and Muslim methods of slaughtering animals was acceptable in the 1990s, but that might not be possible if in the future animal rights were to become an operative public value (267).

28. I will not attempt to reconcile this value with practices such as abortion, the death penalty, and war. Suffice it to say that the right to life cannot be construed as an absolute right.

29. Parekh acknowledges this as well: "In light of our discussion it should be obvious that there are no general and foolproof criteria by which to decide whether specific minority practices should or should not be tolerated, let alone to determine the range of permissible diversity." "Minority Practices and Principles," 265.

30. There are traces of countersubversive thinking in much of the writing on the culture wars. In the United States, which is known for having a "paranoid" style in politics, those who are "other" pose a threat to the state. In the United States, anyone who could not be prove he was a "true American" might be subject to sanctions. Other countries experiencing a large influx of immigrants may manifest a similar paranoid reaction.

31. Schlesinger, *Disuniting of America*.

32. Wayland, "Immigration."

BIBLIOGRAPHY

COURT CASES

Abankwah v. INS, 185 F3d 18; 1999 US App LEXIS 15545

Aflalo v. Aflalo, 295 NJ Super 527 (Ch Div, New Jersey 1996)

Albareti v. Hirsch, New York Law Journal 21 (1993, July 7)

Alhaji Mohamed v. Knott, 2 Weekly Law Reports 1446 (1968)

Aloeboetoe et al., Inter-American Court of Human Rights, Reparations, Judgment of Sept. 10, 1993

Aqeel v. Seiter, 781 FSupp 517 (SD Ohio 1991)

Atkins v. Medical Examiner, 418 NYS2d 839 (1979)

Avitzur v. Avitzur, 446 NE2d 136 (1983)

Bankus v. The State, 4 Indiana Reports 114 (1853)

Becher v. Becher, New York Law Journal 29 (1997, Mar. 18)

Becher v. Becher, 245 AD2d 408; 667 NYS2d 50 (1997, Dec. 15)

Becher v. Becher, 91 NY2d 956; 694 NE2d 885 (1998, Mar. 31)

Becher v. Becher, 706 NYS2d 619; 184 Misc2d 138 (2000)

Begay v. Smialek, Petition for Writ of Certiorari to the Supreme Court of New Mexico, Petitioner's brief (1986)

Begay v. State, 723 P2d 252 (NM App 1985)

Belgard v. Hawaii, 883 FSupp 510 (1995)

Benjamin v. Coughlin, 905 F2d 571 (2nd Cir 1990)

Bhatia v. Chevron, 734 F2d 1382 (1984)

Bhinder v. Canadian National Railway Company, Canada Supreme Court Reports 2, 2–157 (1985)

Bitterman v. Secretary of Defense, 553 FSupp 719 (1982)

Bostick v. Florida, 111 S Ct 2382 (1991)

Bowles v. Harjinder Singh, Ohio App LEXIS 3410 (2000)

Breard v. Greene, 523 US 371 (1998)

Bui v. State, 551 So2d 1094 (Ala Cr App 1988)

Canada (Human Rights Commission) v. Canada 3000 Airlines Ltd. (1999) http://www.cmf.gc. ca/en/cf/1999/orig/html/1999fca24508.0.en.html

Cantwell v. Connecticut, 310 US 296 (1940)

Capoeman v. Reed, 754 F2d 1512 (1985)

Carole Dubniczky and Edna Proulx v. Tiffany's Restaurant. Canadian Human Rights Reporter 1, Decision 110 (1981, Sept. 20)

Carswell v. Peachford Hospital, 27 Fair Empl Prac Cas BNA 698, 26 Empl Prac (1981, Dec.) (CCH P32, 012)

Cha'are Shalom Ve Tsedek v. France, 9 Butterworths Human Rights Cases 27 (2000). European Court of Human Rights, Application no. 27417/95) (2000, June 27) http://www.echr.coe. int/eng/Judgments.htm

Chappell v. Rayl, slip opinion (1985, June 27), available on LEXIS

Cheema v. Thompson, 1994 US App LEXIS 24160 (unpublished decision)

Cheema v. Thompson, 67 F3d 883 (1995)

Cheng v. Wheaton, 745 FSupp 819 (D Conn 1990)

Church of Lukumi Babalu Aye v. City of Hialeah, 688 FSupp 1522 (1988, June 10)

Church of Lukumi Babalu Aye v. City of Hialeah, 723 FSupp 1467 (SD Fla 1989, Oct. 5)

Church of Lukumi Babalu Aye v. City of Hialeah, 936 F2d 586 (1991)

Church of Lukumi Babalu Aye v. City of Hialeah, 113 S Ct 2217 (1993)

City of Boerne v. Flores, 521 US 507, 117 S Ct 2157, 138 L Ed2d 624 (1997)

Close-It Enterprises, Inc. v. Weinberger, 407 NYS2d 587 (1978)

Cohen v. Shroman, 231 Cal App2d 1, 41 Cal Rptr 481 (1964)

Coker v. Georgia, 433 US 584, 97 S Ct 2861, 53 L Ed2d 982 (1977)

Commack Self-Service Kosher Meats, Inc. v. New York, 954 FSupp 65 (1997)

Commission for Racial Equality v. Dutton, 1 *All English Reports* 306 (1989)

Commonwealth v. Twitchell, 617 NE2d 609 (1993, Aug. 11)

Cooper v. Eugene School District, 708 P2d 1161 (Or App 1985); 723 P2d 298 (Or 1986)

Dawkins v. Department of the Environment Sub nom Crown Suppliers PSA, Court of Appeal (Civil Division IRLR 284 [1991]; ICR 517 [1993]

Doersching v. State Funeral Directors Board, 405 NW2d 781 (Wis App 1987)

Dumpson v. Daniel M, New York Law Journal 17, col 7 (1974, Oct. 16)

Eddings v. Oklahoma, 455 US 104, 102 S Ct 869, 71 L Ed2d 1 (1982)

Edwards v. County of Arlington, 5 Va App 294 (1987)

EEOC v. Sambo's of Georgia, Inc., 530 FSupp 81 (1981)

Employment Division, Department of Human Resources of Oregon v. Smith, 494 US 872 (1990)

Erika Galikuwa, 18 EACA 175 (Uganda 1951) (East African Court of Appeals)

Fatima v. Secretary of State of the Home Department, AC 527[1986]; 2 All ER 32 [1986]

Ferrell Secakuku v. Albert Hale, 1997 US App LEXIS 4878 (unpublished)

Frank v. State, 604 P2d 1068 (1979)

Frank "X" St. Claire v. Cuyler, 481 FSupp 732 (1979)

Friedman v. State, 282 NYS2d 858 (1967), 54 Misc2d 448

Fromer v. Scully, 874 F2d 69 (2nd Cir 1989)

Gadam v. R., 14 WACA 442 (West African Court of Appeals 1954)

Ger Xiong v. Superior Court of the State of California, County of Fresno, Application requesting stay of the orders of the Superior Court of the State of California pending petition for writ of certiorari. To Justice Sandra Day O'Connor (1990, June 11)

Giahn v. Giahn, New York Law Journal 25 (2000, Apr. 13)

Gibson v. Babbitt, 2000 US App LEXIS 21086

Golding v. Golding, New York Law Journal 21 (1990, June 28)

Goldman v. Weinberger, 472 US 1016 (1985)

Goulden v. Oliver, 442 US 922 (1979)

Grant v. Canada, [1995] FC 158, 1995 CRR LEXIS 95; 31 CRC (2d) 370 (May 31, 1995)

Guttierrez v. State, 920 P2d 987 (Supr Crt Nev 1996)

Ha v. State, 892 P2d 184 (Alaska App 1995)

Hall v. Coughlin (1981, June 24; 1982, Jan. 8). Slip opinions available on LEXIS

Hall v. State, 493 NE2d 433 (1986)

Hermanson v. State of Florida, 570 So2d 322 (Fla App 2 Dist 1990)

Hermanson v. State of Florida, 604 502d 775 (Fla 1992)

Hirani v. Hirani, 4 FLR 232 (1983)

Hoffman v. Allied Corp., 912 F2d 1379 (1990), 1990 US App LEXIS 16912; CCH Prod Liab Rep P12,592

Hothi et al. v. Regina, 3 Western Weekly Reports 256 (1985), 35 Manitoba Reports2d 159 (1985)

Ingraham v. Wright, 430 US 651 (1977)

In re Alameda-Contra Costa Transit District and Amalgamated Transit Union, Local 192, 75 Labor Arbitration Reports, 1273 (1980)

In re Bartha, 134 CalRptr 39 (1976)

In re Fauziya Kasinga v. U.S. Department of Justice, 21 I & N Dec 357 (1996). Interim Decision (BIA) 3278 (1996), 1996 WL 379826 (unpublished)

In re Grady, 61 Cal2d 887, 39 Cal Rptr 912, 394 P2d 728 (1964)

In re Jertrude O., 466 A2d 885 (Md App 1983)

In re Kou X., Reporter's Transcript (1989, Oct. 23)

In re Kou X., Reporter's Transcript (1990, Feb. 20, 21, 22)

In re Kou X., Respondent's Brief. Appeal from the Superior Court of Fresno County sitting as the Juvenile Court (Fresno County Counsel) (1990, Aug. 17)

In re Kou X., Minor's Brief. Appeal from the Judgment of the Juvenile Court of Fresno County (Attorney Howard Hoffman) (1990, Oct. 16)

In re Marriage of Goldman, 554 NE2d 1016 (Ill App Ct, 1st Dist Ill 1990)

In re Marriage of Vryonis, 202 CalApp3d 712; 248 Cal Rptr 807 (1988, June)

In re May's Estate, 110 NYS2d 430 (1952); 1952 NY Nisc LEXIS 2424

In re May's Estate, 305 NY 486, 114 NE2d 4 (1953); 1953 NY LEXIS 791

In re Sampson, 317 NYS2d 641 (1972)

In re Spondre, 162 NYS 943 (Supr Ct 1917)

Izsak v. Izsak, New York Law Journal 25 (1996, Oct. 21)

Jack and Charlie v. R., Canadian Criminal Cases 50 (1979) (2nd series; 1980), 337–345

Jack and Charlie v. R., Dominion Law Reports 139 (1982) (3rd series; 1983), 25–44

Jack and Charlie v. the Queen, 2 SCR 332 Canadian Supreme Court [1985]

Janko v. Illinois State Toll Highway Authority, 704 FSupp 1531 (ND Ill 1989)

Jenkins v. Blue Cross Mut. Hospital Ins., Inc., 538 F2d 164 (7th Cir 1976)

Jones v. Butz, 374 FSupp 1284 (1974), affirmed 419 US 806, 42 L Ed2d 36, 95 S Ct 22

Kelley v. Johnson, 425 US 238 (1975)

Khalsa v. Weinberg, 779 F2d 1393 (9th Cir 1986)

Khan v. UK, 48 Dec and Rep 253 (1986)

Klagsbrun v. Va'ad Harabonim, 53 FSupp2d 732 (1999)

Kohli v. DPI, Brief for Respondents, 34 Appeal Board of the Maryland Commission on Human Relations, 1992

Kohli v. LOOC, Inc., D/B/A Domino Pizza, Inc. (Provisional Order and Opinion, Administrative Law Judge), Mar. 30, 1992

Konkomba v. R., 14 WACA 236 (West African Court of Appeal 1952)

Kohn v. United States, 591 FSupp 568 (1984)

Koykoy Jatta v. Menna Camara, 8 Journal of African Law (1964), 35–36

Krasniqi v. Dallas Cty Child Protective Services, 809 SW2d 927 (Tex Ct App 1991)

Kumwaka Wa Malumbi and 69 Others, 14 KL R 137 (Kenyan Law Reports 1932)

La Rocca v. Lane, 37 NY2d 575, 338 NE2d 606 93 (1975), cert denied, 424 US 968 (1976)

Lawrence v. the State, 20 Texas Court of Appeals (Criminal) 536 (1886)

Leary v. U.S., 383 F2d 851 (1967)

Lee v. State, 423 SE2d 249 (1992); 454 SE2d 761 (1995)

Leonard v. Kurtz, 234 Ill App3d 553, 600 NE2d 896 (1992)

Leong v. Takasaki, 520 P2d 758 (HI 1974)

Lewis v. Commissioner of Department of Correctional Services of the State of New York, 502 NE2d 989 (NY 1986)

Liberman v. Riverside Memorial Chapel, 225 A D2d 283 (1996); 650 NYS2d 194; 1996 NY App Div LEXIS 12299

Lloyd-El v. Meyer, 1989 US Dist LEXIS 8954

Lockett v. Ohio, 438 US 586 (1978), 98 SCt 2954, 57 L Ed2d 973

London Board for Shechita v. The Commissioners, 1 VAT Tribunals Reports (1974)

Lott v. State and Tumminelli v. State, 32 Misc2d 296, 225 NYS2d 434 (1962); 1962 NY Misc LEXIS 3800

Lyng v. Northwest Indian Cemetery Protective Association, 108 S Ct 1319 (1988)

Mahmud v. Mahmud, Scots Law Times (SLT 1994) 599, 4 pp.

Kwai Fan Mak v. Blodgett, 754 FSupp 1490 (WD Wash 1991); 970 F2d 614 (1992), cert denied 507 US 951 (1993)

Malins v. Cole and Attard, Current Law Year Book, 89 (1986). London: Sweet and Maxwell.

Mandla v. Dowell Lee, 2 AC 548 (1983)

Marks v. Clarke, 103 F3d 1012 (9th Cir 1996); 1996 US App LEXIS 37678

Marks v. U.S., 1987 US Dist LEXIS 14869; 87–2 US Tax Cas (CCH) P9556

Marshall v. District of Columbia, 392 FSupp 10120 (1975)

Matter of Gold, 426 NYS2d 504, 74 ad2d 860 (1980), appeal dismissed 50 NYS2d 927 (1980)

McFate v. State of Arizona, American Anthropologist 93 (1961), 1335–1337

McKinney v. Maynard, 952 F2d 350 (10th Cir 1991)

Menora v. Illinois High School Association, 683 F2d 1030 (1982)

Minkin v. Minkin, 80 NJ Super 260 (Ch Div NJ 1981)

Mississippi Employment Security Commission v. McGlothin, 556 So2d 324 (Miss 1990)

Mitchell v. Marriott, Washington, DC Office of Human Rights, No 88–151-P (CN) (1988, Apr. 25)

Montgomery v. County of Clinton, Michigan, 743 FSupp 125 (1990)

Montgomery v. County of Clinton, Michigan, 1991 US App LEXIS 19070 (Unpublished opinion, US Court of Appeals for the Sixth Circuit). Cited as Table Case at 940 F2d 661

Morton v. Mancari, 417 US 535 (1974)

Moskowitz v. Wilkinson, 432 FSupp 947 (1977)

Native American Church of Navajoland, Inc. v. Arizona Corporation Commission, 405 US 901 (1972)

Native American Church of New York v. U.S., 468 FSupp 1247 (1979)

Native American Church v. Navaho Tribal Council, 272 F2d 131 (1959)

New Rider v. Board of Education of Indiana, 480 F2d 693 (1973), cert. denied 414 US 1097

Nguyen v. State, 505 SE 846, 847–848 (Ga App 1998), rev'd 520 SE2d 907 (Ga 1999)

Nhia Bee Vue v. INS, 1995 US App LEXIS 12619 (unpublished decision)

Ohio Veterinary Medical Board v. Harjinder Singh, 1994 Ohio App LEXIS 1818

Ohio Veterinary Medical Board v. Harjinder Singh, 711 NE2d 740 (1998)

Olsen v. Drug Enforcement Administration, 878 F2d 1458 (DC Cir 1989), cert denied 495 US 906 (1990)

Olsen v. Iowa, 808 F2d 652 (1986)

Onyeanusi v. Pan Am, 767 FSupp 654 (ED Pa 1990), 952 F2d 788 (3rd Cir 1992)

Otieno v. Ougo, Kenyan Appeal Reports, 1 (1982–1988). London: Butterworths (1991), 1049–1061.

Pandori v. Peel Board of Education, Canadian Human Rights Reporter 12 (1990), Decision 43, paragraphs 1–235

Panesar v. Nestle Co. Ltd., Industrial Court Reports 144 (CA [1980])

People v. Aphaylath, 499 NYS2d 823 (AD 4 Dept 1986a)

People v. Aphaylath, 502 NE2d 998 (NY 1986b)

People v. Barraza, 23 C3d 675, 153 CalRptr 459, 591 P2d 947 (1979)

People v. Benu, 87 Misc2d 139, 384 NYS2d 222 (1978); 1976 NY Misc LEXIS 2174

People v. Croy, 42 Cal3d 1 (1985)

People v. Croy, Memorandum of Points and Authorities and Declaration in Support of Motion Regarding Admissibility of Evidence in Support of Defendant's Claim of Self-Defense (1988)

People v. Estep, 566 P2d 706 (1977); 583 P2d 927 (1978)

People v. Ezeonu, 155 Misc2d 344, 588 NYS2d 116 (1992); 1992 NY Misc LEXIS 410 Reported in *New York Law Journal* (1992, August 11)

People v. Hernandez, 500 US 352, 111 S Ct 1859, 114 L Ed2d 395 (1991)

People v. Hernandez, Case No A-76761 (1994). Unpublished case

People v. Kimura, Defense Sentencing Report and Statement in Mitigation; and Application for Probation. Case No A 091133 (1985)

People v. Manurasada, Petition for Review of the Decision of the Court of Appeal, Second Appellate District, 17 (1988 Feb. 29)

People v. Metallides, Case No 73–5270 (1974)

People v. Miguel Hernandez, Case No A-76761 (1994)

People v. Natale, 199 CA2d 153, 18 CalRptr 491 (1962)

People v. Palrat Manurasada, Super Ct No 149956 (Santa Barbara County, 1985)

People v. Peck, 52 Cal App 4th 351 (1996)

People v. Poddar, 103 Cal Rptr 84 (1972)

People v. Poddar, 10 Cal3d 750, 111 Cal Rptr 910, 518 P2d 342 (1974)

People v. Rhines, 131 Cal App3d; 182 Cal Rptr 478 (1978)

People v. Rodriguez, 424 NYS2d 600 (1979)

People v. Romero, 69 Cal App 4th 846 (1999); 1999 Cal App LEXIS 78; 81 Cal Rptr2d 823

People v. Schmidt, 110 NE 945 (1915)

People v. Singh, 516 NYS2d 412 (NY City Civ Ct 1987)

People v. Siripongs (1989). 45 Cal3d 548, 247 Cal Rptr 729, 754 P2d 1306 (1988), cert denied 488 US 1019

People v. Superior Court (Soon Ja Du) 7 Cal Rptr2d 177 (Cal Dist Ct App 1992)

People v. Trippet, 56 Cal App 4th 1532 (1997)

People v. Valentine, 28 Cal2d 121 (1946)

People v. Woody, 61 Cal2d 716, 394 P2d 813, 40 Cal Rptr 69 (1964)

People v. Wu, 235 Cal App3d 614, 286 Cal Rptr 868 (1991)

People v. Wu, Order of depublication (1992, Jan. 23)

Peyote Way Church of God, Inc. v. Thornburgh, 922 F2d 1210 (1991)

Peyote Way v. Meese, 698 FSupp 1342 (1988)

Philip Muswi s/o Musele v. R., 23, EACA 622 (East African Court of Appeals 1956)

Prince v. Massachusetts, 321 US 158 (1943)

Pritam Singh v. Workmen's Compensation Board Hospital and Rehabilitation Board, Canadian Human Rights Reporter 2 (103), paragraphs 4144–4223 (1981, Aug. 20)

R. v. Baptiste and Baptiste, 61 Canadian Criminal Cases (2nd), 438–446 (1980)

R. v. Barronet and Allain, 169 English Reports, 169, 633 (QB) (1852)

R. v. Bibi, 1 *The Weekly Law Reports* 1193 (1980)

R. v. Daudi and Daniels, 4 Criminal Appeal Reports (S) 306 (1982)

R. v. Derriviere, Court of Appeal Reports 53 (Criminal Division), 637–639 (1969)

R. v. Dincer, Victorian Reports (Supreme Court of Victoria) Vol 1 (1983), 461

R. v. Hanna, 49 NSR (2d) 176 (Nova Scotia Supreme Court, Appeal Division) (1982)

R. v. Hem, 72 *Criminal Reports* (3d) 233 (1990)

R. v. Ikalowjuak, 27 AR 492 (Northwest Territories Supreme Court 1980). Reported in *Canadian Native Law Reporter* 3 (1982), 12–115

R. v. Immigration Appeal Tribunal ex parte Bhatia, Immigratation Appeal Report 50 [1985]

R. v. Immigration Appeal Tribunal ex parte Kumar, Immigratation Appeal Report 446 [1986]

R. v. Ly, 33 CCC (3d) 31 (1987)

R. v. Machekequonabe, 28 *Ontario Reports*, 309 (1897)

R. v. Mingma Tenzing Sherpa (July 11, 1986, BC Co Ct, Boyle Co Ct J). Synopsis published in 17 WCB (*Weekly Criminal Bulletin*), 461. Unpublished decision, Vancouver County Court

R. v. Noboi-Bosai (Papua New Guina, 1971) (1971–1972). *Papua and New Guinea Law Reports* 271

R. v. Parnerkar, 1 *Western Weekly Reports* 1, 161 (1972)

R. v. Parnerkar, Canada Supreme Court Reports (RCS), 449 (1974)

R. v. Steve Joseph Dallaway, Justice of the Peace, 148 (1984, Jan. 14), 31

Radwan v. Radwan, 3 *All England Reports* 967 (1972) (Family Division)

Radwan v. Radwan (No. 2), 3 *All England Reports* 1026 (1972)

Raminder Singh v. Royal Canadian Legion, Canadian Human Rights Reporter 11, Decision 40, Paragraphs 1–76 (1990, May)

Ran-Dev's County Kosher, Inc. v. New Jersey, 608 A2d 1353 (1992)

Re Aclo Compounders Inc. and United Steelworkers, 25 *Labour Arbitration Cases* 209 (1980)

Reed v. Faulkner, 842 F2d 960 (7th Cir, 1988)

Renee Rogers v. American Airlines, 527 FSupp 229 (1981)

Rex v. Esop, English Reports 173 (Central Criminal Court 1836), 203

Rex v. Williams, 1 Crim App (S) 5 (1979)

Reynolds v. United States, 98 US 145 (1878)

Robinson v. Foti, 527 FSupp 1111 (1981)

Rogers v. Scurr, 676 F2d 1211 (1982)

Rotholz v. The City of New York, 151 Misc2d 613, 582 NYS2d 366 (1992); 1992 NY Misc LEXIS 99 (Supreme Court of New York)

Rupert v. Director, U.S. Fish and Wildlife Service, 957 F2d 32 (1st Cir 1992)

Ruth Schwartz, 162 Misc2d 313, 616 NYS2d 921 (1994); 1994 NY Misc LEXIS 398

Saint Francis College v. Al-Khazraji, 418 US 604 (1987)

Salinas v. Forth Worth Cab and Baggage Co., Inc., 725 SW2d 701 (1987)

Scheuer v. William F. Howard Funeral Home, 385 So2d 1076 (Fla 1980)

Segal v. Segal, New Jersey Lawyer, 27 (1995, Jan. 16)

Sehdev v. Bayview Glen Junior Schools Ltd., Canadian Human Rights Reporter 9, Decision 764, paragraphs 37723–37791 (1988, July)

Sherbert v. Verner, 374 US 398 (1963)

Sherwood v. Brown, 619 F2d 47 (1980)

Singh v. Air Illinois, 520 NE2d 852 (IllApp 1 Dist 1988)

Singh v. Kaur, 11 Fam Law 152 (1981)

Singh v. Singh, 2 All England Reports (All ER) 828 (1971)

Singh v. Singh, 1996 Cal LEXIS 494 (Supreme Court of California)

Siripongs v. Calderon, 35 F3d 1308 (9th Cir 1994), denial of cert 512 US 1183 (1995)

Siripongs v. Calderon, 133 F3d 732 (1998)

Skipper v. South Carolina, 476 US 1, 106 S Ct 1669, 90 L Ed2d 1 (1986)

Smialek v. Begay, Petition for a Writ of Certiorari to the Supreme Court of New Mexico, Petitioners' Brief (1986)

Smialek v. Begay, 721 P2d 1306 (NM 1986)

Snyder v. Holy Cross Hospital, 352 A2d 334 (1976)

Standing Deer v. Carlson, 831 F2d 1525 (9th Cir 1987)

State v. Albee, 847 P2d 848 (1993)

State v. Ali, 613 NW2d 796 (2000), 2000 Minn App LEXIS 713

State v. Ali, Petition for review of decision of the Court of Appeals, July 11, 2000

State v. Berry, 707 P2d 638 (1985)

State v. Billie, 497 So2d 889 (Fla App 2 Distr 1986)

State v. Blake, Case No 99 CR4866 (DeKalb Super Ct) (1999, Nov 15)

State v. Chong Sun France, 379 SE2d 701 (NC App 1989)

State v. Ganal, 917 P2d 370 (1996)

State v. Gurreh, 758 A2d 877 (2000)

State v. Ham, 691 P2d 239 (Wash App 1984)

State v. Haque, 502 NE2d 998 (1999); 726 A2d 205 (Me 1999)

State v. Harjinder Singh, 690 NE2d 917 (1996)

State v. Kargar, 679 A2d 81 (Me 1996)

State v. Mak, 718 P2d 407 (1986), 105 Wash2d 692

State v. Marks, 790 P2d 138 (Wash 1990)

State v. McBride, 955 P2d 133 (Kan Ct App 1998)

State v. Miskimens, 490 NE2d 931 (CP Coshocton 1984)

State v. Rocheleau, 451 A2d 1144 (1982)

State v. Rodriguez, 204 A3d 37 (1964)

State v. Wanrow, 559 P2d 548 (1977)

State v. Welch, 78 Missouri Reports 284 (1880)

State v. Williams, 484 P2d 1167 (1971)

State v. Yi Ching Chou, 981 P2d 668 (1999); 1999 Colo LEXIS 783 (Colo Crt Apps 1999), denial of cert, Colo Supreme Court

State ex rel. Burrell-el v. Autrey, 752 SW2d 895 (Mo App 1988)

State v. McKown, 461 NW2d 720 (Minn Ap 1990); 475 NW2d 63 (1991)

Steagall et al. v. Doctors Hospital, 171 F2d 352 (1948)

Strickland v. Washington, 466 US 558 (1984)

Tarasoff v. Regents of University of California, 118 Cal Rptr 129 (1975)

Tatum and Parahoo v. Hyatt, EEOC Charage Nos 123–87–0384, 123–87–0672. Determination by Dorothy E. Mead, Director, Baltimore District Office, EEOC (1988)

Teterud v. Burns, 522 F2d 357 (1975)

Tkaczyk v. Gallagher, 26 Conn Supp 290, 222 A2d 226, app dismd 153 Conn 744, 220 A2d 163 (1965)

Toledo v. Nobel-Sysco, Inc., 892 F2d 1481 (10th Cir 1989)

Touchette v. Ganal, 922 P2d 347 (1996)

Town v. State ex rel. Reno, 377 So2d 648 (Fla 1979)

Trans World Airlines, Inc. v. Hardison, 432 US 63 (1977)

Trujillo-Garcia v. Rowland, 1992 US Dist LEXIS 6199 (Apr. 28, 1992) US District Court, Northern District of California, 1993 US App LEXIS 30441 (Nov. 10, 1993), US Court of the Appeals for the 9th Circuit. 114 S Ct 2145; 1994 US LEXIS 4219; 128 LEd 873; 62 USLW 3793 (May 31, 1994, cert denied)

Tuan Anh Nguyen v. Reynolds, 131 F3d 1340 (1997)

Tuli v. St. Albert Protestant Board of Education, Canadian Human Rights Reporter 8, Paragraphs 29577–29633 (1987)

Turner v. Safley, 482 US 78 (1987)

Uboh-Abiola v. Abiola, New York Law Journal, part 18, 1A (1992, June 12)

University of Maryland at Baltimore v. Boyd, 612 A2d 305 (Md App 1992)

U.S. v. Abeyta, 632 FSupp 1301 (DNM 1986)

U.S. v. Alexander, 471 F2d 923 (1974)

U.S. v. Ballard, 322 US 78 (1944)

U.S. v. Bauer, 84 F3d 1549 (9th Cir 1996)

U.S. v. Billie, 667 FSupp 1485 (SD Fla 1987)

U.S. v. Boyll, 774 FSupp 1333 (1991)

U.S. v. Carbonell, 737 FSupp 187 (1990)

U.S. v. Carlson, 1992 US App LEXIS 6572 (1992)

U.S. v. Chau Hai Do (a/k/a Do Hai Chau), 1994 US App LEXIS 27389 (9th Cir) (unpublished disposition). Cert denied Feb. 21, 1995, 513 US 1168

U.S. v. Corrow, 119 F3d 796 (1997)

U.S. v. Dion, 476 US 734 (1985)

U.S. v. Dion, 752 F2d 1261 (1985) (en banc); 762 F2d 674 (1985) (panel decision)

U.S. v. Doe, 903 F2d 16 (1990)

U.S. v. Ezeiruaku and Akiagba, 1995 US Dist LEXIS 6037

U.S. v. Fryberg, 622 F2d 1010 (9th Cir 1980)

U.S. v. Gaviria, 804 FSupp 476 (1992)

U.S. v. Gutierrez-Mederos, 965 F2d 800 (1992)

U.S. v. Hoac, 990 F2d 1099 (1993)

U.S. v. Holmes, 26 Fed Cas 360 No 25,484 (CC Pa 1842)

U.S. v. Hsieh Hui Mei Chen, 754 F2d 817 (1985)

U.S. v. Hudson, 431 F2d 468 (5th Cir 1970)

U.S. v. Hugs, 109 F3d 1375 (1997)

U.S. v. Hussein (2002)

U.S. v. Jim, 1995 US Dist LEXIS 8025 (D or Mar. 13 1995)

U.S. v. Joe, 770 FSupp 607 (1991)

U.S. v. Khang, 36 F3d 77 (9th Cir 1994)

U.S. v. Kills Crow, 527 F2d 158 (1975)

U.S. v. Koua Thao, 712 F2d 369 (1983)

U.S. v. Leon, 468 US897 (1984)

U.S. v. Meyers, 95 F3d 1475 (1996)

U.S. v. Middleton, 690 F2d 820 (11th Cir 1982)

U.S. v. Mustapha, 1998 US App LEXIS 10860 (unpublished opinion)

U.S. v. Natal-Rivera, 879 F2d 391 (8th Cir 1989)

U.S. v. Ochoa-Zaragoza, 2000 US App LEXIS 2495 (unpublished decision)

U.S. v. Rasag, 1 *Federal Sentencing Reporter* 1, 200 (1988, Oct.)

U.S. v. Rubio-Villareal, 927 F2d 1495 (9th Cir 1991); 967 F2d 294 (9th Cir 1992)

U.S. v. Ruelas-Altamirano, 463 F2d 1199 (1972)

U.S. v. Rush, 738 F2d 497 (1984)

U.S. v. Sherpa, 110 F3d 656 (1996) (affirmed reduction in sentence)

U.S. v. Sherpa, 99 F3d 1148 (1996) (affirmed his conviction without opinion); 1996 US App LEXIS 26588 (affirmed conviction in an unpublished opinion)

U.S. v. Shrestha, 86 F3d 935 (1996)

U.S. v. Tajeddini, 945 F2d 458 (1991); 996 F2d 1278 (1993)

U.S. v. Takai, 941 F2d 738 (1991)

U.S. v. Thirty Eight Golden Eagles, 649 FSupp 269 (D Nev 1986)

U.S. v. Tomono, US Ct of Appeals, 11th Cir (1998); 1998 US App LEXIS 12660; 143 F3d 1401

U.S. v. Top Sky, 547 F2d 486 (1976)

U.S. v. Villegas, 899 F2d 1324 (1990)

U.S. v. Vongsay, 1993 US App LEXIS 4419 (unpublished decision); 988 F2d 126 (1993) (disposition)

U.S. v. Vue, 13 F3d 1206 (1994)

U.S. v. Wang, 130 FRD 676 (1990); 1990 US Dist LEXIS 5531

U.S. v. Warner, 595 FSupp 595 (1984)

U.S. v. White, 508 F2d 453 (8th Cir 1974)

U.S. v. Yang, 887 FSupp 95 (1995); 1995 US Dist LEXIS 8251

U.S. v. Yusuff, 96 F3d 982 (1996)

U.S. v. Zapata, 997 F2d 751 (1993)

Victor v. Victor, 177 Ariz 231, 866, P2d 899 (1993)

Walker v. Superior Court, 47 Cal3d 112, 253 Cal Rptr 1, 763 P2d 852 (1988)

Warner v. Graham, 845 F2d 179 (1988)

Weberman v. Zugibe, 394 NYS2d 371 (1977)

Weiss v. Goldfeder, New York Law Journal 31 (1990, Oct. 26)

Weiss v. Weiss, 96 CDOS 711 (1996, Jan. 31)

Whitehorn v. State, 561 P2d 539 (1977)

Whyte v. U.S., 471 A2d 1018 DC (1984)

Wilensky v. Greco, 344 NYS2d 77 (1973)

Wilson v. Schillinger, 761 F2d 921 (1985)

Wisconsin v. Yoder, 406 US 205 (1972)

Yellow Cab v. Civil Rights Commission, 570 NE2d 940 (Ind App 2 Dist 1991)

You Vang Yang v. Sturner, 728 FSupp 845 (DRI 1990)

You Vang Yang v. Sturner, 750 FSupp 558 (1990)

Young v. Lane, 922 F2d 370 (7th Cir 1991)

INTERVIEWS AND PERSONAL COMMUNICATIONS

Abbott, Greg (1999, Mar. 18). Abbott and Hast Mortuary, Monterey, California.

Al-Hibri, Azizah Y. (2000, Oct. 19). Professor of Law, University of Richmond.

Augustine, James (1999, Mar. 17). Chair, Curriculum Committee, and Professor of Mortuary Science, Milwaukee.

Beason, Joseph (1992, Oct. 29). Defense attorney in dog-eating case.

Bergeron, Renee (2000, Aug. 16). Defendants' attorney, *State v. Ali.*

Bigelow, Gordon (1999, Mar. 17). American Board of Funeral Services Education.

Brandes, Stanley (1998, Aug. 20). Professor of Anthropology, University of California Berkeley.

Brown, James (1992, June 22). Detective, Los Angeles Police Department, Child Abuse Unit.

Clegern, Jennifer (2000, Sept. 27). Prosecutor in N.Y. scarification case.

Dahle, David S. (1991, Apr. 16). Deputy District Attorney.

Daniel, E. Valentine (1988, Aug. 23). Professor of Anthropology, University of Washington.

Ennis, Scott (2000, Aug. 8). Defense Attorney in kava prosecution case.

Fells, Bob (1999, Mar. 17). International Cemetery and Funeral Association.

Frey, Francesca (1999, Aug. 7). Deputy District Attorney, Los Angeles.

Gilligan, Scott (1999, Mar.17). General Counsel, National Funeral Directors Association.

Goldfarb, Anne (1988, Feb. 15 and Mar. 31). Director, Kempe National Center for Child Abuse, Denver, Colorado.

Herman, Thomas W. (1999, Apr. 21). Defense attorney in *Nguyen v. State.*

Kaplansky, John C. (1994, Mar. 24). Attorney for plaintiff in *Montgomery v. Clinton County of Michigan.*

Kohli, Prabhjot (1992, May 21, and Apr. 7, 1994, June 14, 1994).

Lapin, Harvey (1999, Mar. 17). Attorney in death care industry.

Lazarus, Sarah (1992, Oct. 28). Prosecutor in Long Beach dog-eating case.

LeCuyer, Stephen (1991, Mar. 5 and 27). One of the plaintiff's attorneys in *Begay v. Smialek.*

Levi, Jerome (1998, May 29). Professor of Anthropology, Carleton College.

Liccardo, Cynthia (1996, Apr. 3). Assistant Prosecutor.

McDonald, R. Robin (2000, Apr. 14). Attorney in Harvey homicide case.

McIntire, Betty (1999, Mar. 15). Executive Director, California Funeral Directors Association.

Ninker, Robert (1999, Mar. 17). Director, Funeral Ethics Association.

O'Donovan, Verla (1992, Apr. 8). Fresno County Counsel.

Palumbo, James (2000, Aug. 2). Attorney in Brooklyn khat case.

Powell, Terrell (1993, Dec. 17, and Jan. 31, 1994). Defense attorney in *People v. Miguel Hernandez.*

Scherotter, Gary (1992, June 29). Personal communication regarding the Helen Wu case.

Shaw, Brian (1992, Apr. 8). Pediatric Surgeon, Fresno, California.

Steele, Eric (1993, Dec. 9, and Jan. 6, 1994). Attorney for plaintiffs in braids litigation.

Steffan, Richard (1993, Sept. 17). Assemblywoman Speier's legislative aide.

Taylor, Jackie (1999, Mar. 17). President and Professor, San Francisco College of Mortuary Sciences.

Treppiedi, Rocco (1997, Feb. 1). Attorney for city of Spokane.

Walczak, Kathleen (1999, Mar. 12). National Funeral Directors Association.

Whetstone, Corinne (1988, Mar. 21). Officer. Los Angeles S.P.C.A.

Woo, Michael (1996, Jan. 30). Former legislative aide to Sen. Art Torres.

Yedlin, Bernard (1988, Aug. 4). Attorney for Kostas Metallides.

SOURCES

Aberle, David F. (1966). *The Peyote Religion among the Navaho.* Chicago: Aldine.

Abney, David L. (1986, Aug. 22). "Blocking a Coroner's Autopsy in California based on Religious Preference." *Los Angeles Daily Journal,* S3, col. 1.

Abney, Veronica (1996). "Cultural Competency in the Field of Child Maltreatment." In John Briere et al. (Eds.), *The APSAC Handbook on Child Maltreatment* (409–419). Thousand Oaks, Calif.: Sage.

Abraham, Henry J. (1980). "Religion, Medicine, and the State: Reflections on Some Contemporary Issues." *Journal of Church and State* 22, 423–436.

Abraham, Yvonne, and John Ellement (1999, Apr. 18). "Parents Charged in Genital Mutilation." *Boston Globe,* B4.

Abrams, Richard (1989, Nov. 6). "Ban on Eating Pets Splits Asian-Americans." *Sacramento Bee,* A3.

Abu-Lughod, Lila (1991). "Against Culture." In Richard Fox (Ed.), *Recapturing Anthropology* (134–162). Santa Fe, N.M.: School of American Research Press.

Abu-Nasr, Donna (2000, Mar. 18). "Despite Disapproval, Yemenis Addicted to 'Khat.'" *Gazette* (Montreal), B4.

Abu-Nasr Raydah, Donna (2000, June 12). "Dwindling of Jewish Community Ends in Ancient Culture in Yemen." *Jerusalem Post*, 6.

Abu-Odeh, Lama (1992). "Post-colonial Feminism and the Veil: Considering the Differences." *New England Law Review* 26, 1527–1537.

Acosta, Mark (1992, June 30). "Woman Found Guilty in Son's Death." *Press-Enterprise* (Riverside), B1.

Adams, Emily (1996, July 27). "Leniency Granted to Mother Who Strangled 'Devil' Infant." *Los Angeles Times*, A3.

Addis, Adeno (1992). "Individualism, Communitarianism, and the Rights of Ethnic Minorities." *Notre Dame Law Review* 67, 615–676.

——— (1997). "On Human Diversity and the Limits of Toleration." In Ian Shapiro and Will Kymlicka (Eds.), *Ethnicity and Groups Rights* (112–153). New York: New York University Press.

Adler, Shelley (1991). "Sudden Unexpected Nocturnal Death Syndrome among Hmong Immigrants: Examining the Role of the 'Nightmare.'" *Journal of American Folklore* 104, 54–71.

Adrian, M. (1996). "Substance Abuse and Multiculturalism." *Substance Abuse and Misuse* 31(11–12), 1459–1501.

Ahdar, Rex (1996). "Religion as a Factor in Custody and Access Disputes." *International Journal of Law, Policy and the Family* 10, 177–204.

Ahmed, Leila (1992). *Women and Gender in Islam: Historical Roots of a Modern Debate.* New Haven, Conn.: Yale University Press.

Ahmed, Saeed (2001, Nov. 28). "A Light Buzz for Somalis, Khat Is a Heavy Bust Here." *Atlanta Journal-Constitution*, A1.

Akermark, Athanasia Spiliopoulou (1997). *Justifications of Minority Protection in International Law.* London: Kluwer Law International.

Alem, Atay, and Teshome Shibre (1997). "Khat Induced Psychosis and Its Medico-Legal Implications: A Case Report." *Ethiopian Medical Journal* 35, 137–141.

Alem, A., D. Kebede, and G. Kullgren (1999). "The Prevalence and Socio-demographic Correlates of Khat Chewing in Butajira, Ethiopia." *Acta Psychiatrica Scandinavica* Suppl. 100, 84–91.

al Faruqi, Lois Lamya Ibsen (1985). "Marriage in Islam." *Journal of Ecumenical Studies* 22(4), 55–68.

Al-Issa, Ihsan (Ed.) (1995). *Handbook of Culture and Mental Illness: An International Perspective.* Madison, Conn.: International Universities Press.

Allen, Douglas (Ed.) (1997). *Culture and Self: Philosophical and Religious Perspectives, East and West.* Boulder, Colo.: Westview Press.

Allen, Francis A. (1959). "Legal Values and the Rehabilitative Ideal." *Journal of Criminal Law, Criminology, and Police Science* 50, 226–232.

Allen, Robert (1993, Apr. 17). "Letter: 'Amok' Wasn't Part of Culture." *Honolulu Advertiser.*

Allport, Floyd H. (1930–1931). "Culture Conflict versus the Individual as Factors in Delinquency." *Social Forces* 9, 493–497.

Alonso-Zaldivar, R. (1998). "Agents Arrest Reptile Dealer in Trade Sting." *Los Angeles Times*, A1, 8.

Alston, Pat (1997, Apr. 25). "Man Gets Four Years in Fatal Exorcism: Victim's Husband Also Gets Prison." *Daily Breeze* (Santa Monica).

Alston, Philip (Ed.) (1994). *The Best Interests of the Child: Reconciling Culture and Human Rights.* Oxford: Clarendon Press.

American Academy of Pediatrics, Committee on Bioethics (1988). "Religious Exemptions from Child Abuse Statutes." *Pediatrics* 81(1), 169–171.

American Association of Retired Persons (n.d.). *Customs of Bereavement: A Guide for Providing Cross-Cultural Assistance.* Washington, D.C.: AARP.

American Indian Religious Freedom Act Amendments of 1994 (1994). Pub. L. No.103–344, 2, 108 Stat. 3125 (codified as 42 U.S.C. 1996, 1996a).

Anaya, James (1996). *Indigenous Peoples in International Law.* New York: Oxford University Press.

Andenaes, Johannes (1952). "General Prevention: Illusion or Reality?" *Journal of Criminal Law, Criminology, and Police Science* 43, 176–198.

——— (1974). *Punishment and Deterrence.* Ann Arbor: University of Michigan Press.

Anderson, Benedict (1991). *Imagined Communities.* London: Verso.

Anderson, Cerisse (1992, Mar. 20). "Judge May Weigh Refusal of 'Get' in Dividing Assets." *New York Law Journal* 1.

——— (1992, June 11). "Chief with Many Wives Wins Dismissal of Claim for Equitable Distribution." *New York Law Journal* 1.

——— (1997, Mar. 18). "Consideration of Religious Divorce Upheld: Withholding of 'Get' May Be Weighed in Finances." *New York Law Journal* 1.

Anderson, Edward F. (1996). *Peyote: The Divine Cactus* (2nd ed.). Tucson: University of Arizona Press.

Anderson, Ellen (1994, Sept.–Oct.). "Legislating Cultural Change: Female Genital Mutilation in Minnesota." *Hennepin Lawyer* 16–19.

Anderson, J. (1976). *Law Reform in the Muslim World.* London: Athlone Press.

Anderson, Michael R. (1987). "Law and the Protection of Cultural Communities." *Law and Policy* 9, 125–142.

Andrews, Lori B. (1986, Oct.). "My Body, My Property." *Hastings Center Report* 16(5), 28–38.

Anh, Nong The (1976, Nov. 15). "'Pseudo-Battered Child' Syndrome." *JAMA* 236(20), 2288.

Annin, Peter, and Kendall Hamilton (1996, Dec. 16). "Marriage or Rape? Cultures Clash over Arranged Nuptials." *Newsweek*, 78.

Anon. (1921). "Homicide: Failure to Provide Medical or Surgical Attention." *American Law Reports Annotated* 10, 1137–1152.

Anon. (1959a, Sept.). "What Do You Think?" *Mortuary Management* 46(9), 36.

Anon. (1959b, Nov.). "What Do You Think?" *Mortuary Management* 46(11), 16–17.

Anon. (1974a, July 16). "Mother 'Cut Boys' Faces in Tribal Rituals.'" *Times* (London), 3.

Anon. (1974b, July 17). "Discharge for Mother in Tribal Cuts Case." *Times* (London), 4.

Anon. (1981, Feb. 19). "TV Reporter, Managers in Row over Cornrow Hairdo." *Jet*, 16.

Anon. (1983). "Turban or Not Turban: That Is the Question (*Mandla v. Dowell Lee*)." *Liverpool Law Review* 1, 75–90.

Anon. (1984, Feb. 9). "Charges May Be Refiled in Laotian Baby Case unless Baby Is Returned." *Columbus Dispatch*, 7B.

Anon. (1985a, June). "Postmortem Procedures." *Director* 55(6), 6–8.

Anon. (1985b, Oct. 25). "Profile (Judge Richard Hodge)." *Los Angeles Daily Journal*, 1.

Anon. (1986a). "The Cultural Defense in the Criminal Law." *Harvard Law Review* 99, 1293–1311.

Anon. (1986b, July 6). "Two Australians Hanged by Malaysia for Drug Crimes." *Los Angeles Times.*

Anon. (1987a, June 27–July 3). "Hyatt Hotel Fires Employee over African Style." *Atlanta Voice.*

Anon. (1987b, Oct. 5). "Upbraiding a Hairstyle." *Time* 130(14), 30.

Anon. (1988a, Jan. 25). "Pamela Mitchell Keeps Job and Cornrows in Marriott Hotel Dress Code Dispute." *Jet*, 36.

Anon. (1988b, Jan. 29). "Police Officer Dies as Siege Ends in Polygamists' Arrest." *New York Times,* 7.

Anon. (1988c, May 13). "Thai Sentenced in Slaying." *Los Angeles Times,* Metro, Pt 2, 2.

Anon. (1988d, August 1). "Clerk's Cornrows to Stay: Hotel Pays Her $40,000." *Jet*, 74, 29.

Anon. (1989a, Mar. 20). "Cultural Differences." *Los Angeles Times*, Metro, 4.

Anon. (1989b, May 25). "Anti-Braid Policy Brings $14 Million Lawsuit against Hyatt." *Capital Spotlight*, 17, 23.

Anon. (1989c, June 19). "Kidnap May Have Been Hmong Courting Rite." *Oakland Tribune*, A9.

Anon. (1989d, July 5). "Muslim Jailed for Killing Daughter." *Independent* (London), 3.

Anon. (1989e, July 7). "Life for Father Who Killed 'Convert' Daughter." *New Life*.

Anon. (1989f, July 16). "Briton to Be Hanged." *Sunday Times* (London), A22.

Anon. (1989g, Oct. 20). "Immigrant Sentenced for Rape of 'Betrothed.'" *Los Angeles Times*, B2.

Anon. (1989h, Dec. 3). "Muslim Pupils Will Take off Scarfs [*sic*] in Class." *Los Angeles Times*, A15.

Anon. (1990, Oct. 6). "Must Say No." *Economist* 317 (7675), 25–27.

Anon. (1991a, Oct. 28). "Terror and Death at Home Are Caught in FBI Tape." *New York Times*, A14.

Anon. (1991b, Nov. 7). "Kidnapping or Marriage Tradition?" *Washington Times*, A8.

Anon. (1992a, Apr. 24). "A Gursikh Wins Right to Pizza Job." *World Sikh News*.

Anon. (1992b, Sept. 16). "Gypsies Claim Racial Persecution at Trial." *Olympian*.

Anon. (1993a). "What's Culture Got to Do with It? Excising the Harmful Tradition of Female Circumcision." *Harvard Law Review* 103, 1944–1961.

Anon. (1993b). "Aspiration and Control: International Legal Rhetoric and the Essentialization of Culture." *Harvard Law Review* 106, 723–740.

Anon. (1993c, Apr. 9). "Ganal Case Jury Rightly Rejected 'Amok' Defense." *Honolulu Star-Bulletin*, A10

Anon. (1993d, May 1). "Jury Hears Mortuary Horror." *Washington Post*, A2.

Anon. (1993e, May 4). "Mortuary Settles Case of Pig in Casket." *Phoenix Gazette*, A6.

Anon. (1994a, Mar. 19). "Unauthorized Autopsy Proves Costly." *Houston Chronicle*, 2.

Anon. (1994b, Sept. 13). "Today's Briefing: Cultural Defence." *Australian Business News*, RWE Business News, Sept. 13, 1994 (available on LEXIS).

Anon. (1994c, Sept. 27). "Torts: Emotional Distress." 63 U.S.L.W. 2180.

Anon. (1994d, Nov. 17). "Should Culture Be a Criminal Defence?" *Globe and Mail*.

Anon. (1994e, Sept. 30). "Kirpan Brandishing Alleged in Bay Area High School." *India West*, 41.

Anon. (1994f, Sept. 8). "Headwear Flap." *Miami Herald*, A24.

Anon. (1995a, Mar. 27). "Cockfight Raided: 296 Are Arrested." *Los Angeles Times*, A17.

Anon. (1995b, Sept. 20). "Foreign Minister Says Dutch Businessman Is Due to Hang Friday." Associated Press, AP Worldstream (available on LEXIS /NEXIS , worldnews).

Anon. (1995c, Nov. 3). "Sociologist's Testimony on Culture Is Precluded in Harassment Case: *People v. Jaechoel Yi*, Criminal Court, Part AP-9, Judge Richter." *New York Law Journal*, 25.

Anon. (1995d, Nov. 26). "Death Puts Spotlight on Hmong Customs: Bullet Kills Man with Teen 'Wife.'" *San Francisco Examiner*, C4.

Anon. (1995e, Dec. 19). "Sacrifice of Dog Highlights Clash of Cultures in Central Valley." *San Francisco Chronicle*, A22.

Anon. (1996a, Apr.). "Diverse Customs." *Mortuary Management* 83(4), 32.

Anon. (1996b, May 24). "Diplomas Denied to Three in Ethnic Garb." *San Francisco Chronicle*.

Anon. (1996c June 24). "Singapore: Canadian Avoids Execution." United Press International.

Anon. (1996d, June 10). "Black, Native American High School Students Denied Diplomas for Wearing Ethnic Dress at Graduation." *Jet*, 14.

Anon. (1996e, June 18). "Marriage Dissolves Sex-Abuse Charge." *Los Angeles Times*, A9.

Anon. (1996f, June 21). "Kissing Son's Genitals Wasn't Illegal, Court Says." *San Jose Mercury News*, 9A.

Anon (1996g, June 22). "Catholic Bishops Suggest New Rules on Cremation." *Los Angeles Times,* B5.

Anon. (1996h, June 24). "Singapore: Canadian Avoids Execution." United Press International.

Anon. (1996i, July 6). "Hadassah to Debate Plight of Agunot." *New York Law Journal,* 6.

Anon. (1996j, Aug. 18). "What's A-O.K. in the USA Is Lewd and Worthless Beyond." *New York Times,* E7.

Anon. (1996k, Sept. 5). "Child Mothers and Marriage." *Los Angeles Times,* B12.

Anon. (1996l, Nov. 20). "Minors' Forced Marriages Lead to Three Arrests." *Los Angeles Times,* A30.

Anon. (1997a, spring/summer). "FWS Finds Eagles Are Killed for Profit." *Animal Welfare Institute Quarterly* 46(2 and 3), 12.

Anon. (1997b, Apr. 25). "Two Ministers Sentenced for Fatal Exorcism." *San Francisco Chronicle,* A3.

Anon. (1997c May 22). "Charges Dropped, but Danish Mom Must Leave U.S." *San Francisco Chronicle,* A2.

Anon. (1997d, July/Aug.). "An Honest Mistake." *Mortuary Management* 84(7/8), 23.

Anon. (1997e, July 27). "Serra's Cultural Defense Derided." *Recorder,* 6.

Anon. (1997f, July 28). "'Cultural Defense' Likely in Murder Trial: Blight of Native Americans May Be Cited." *San Francisco Chronicle,* A16.

Anon. (1997g, Aug. 10). "Bloodless Bullfighting a Rage in California." *New York Times,* 15.

Anon. (1997h, Sept. 24). "Iraqis Sentenced for Marrying Minors." *Los Angeles Times,* A13.

Anon. (1997i, Oct. 19, 1997). "Eagle Hunters Cannot Invoke Religion Shield." *New York Times,* A12.

Anon. (1997j, Nov. 27). "Judge Accepts Voodoo Defense in Slaying of Common-Law Wife." *Baltimore Sun,* 24A.

Anon. (1998a). Khat. *Review of Natural Products.* St. Louis, Mo.: Facts and Comparisons, 1–3.

Anon. (1998b). "Monograph: *Piper methysticum.*" *Alternative Medicine Review,* 3(6), 458–460.

Anon. (1998c, Mar.). "Without Consent." *Mortuary Management* 85(3), 23.

Anon. (1998d, Apr. 13). "Indians Jailed for Gathering Peyote." United Press International.

Anon. (1998e, July). "The Schpiel on Getting Divorced under Jewish Law." *Matrimonial Strategist* 16(6), 6.

Anon. (1998f, Nov.). "Jewish 'Get' Controversy Rages On." *Matrimonial Strategist* 16(10), 5.

Anon. (1998g, Nov. 14). "The World's Way of Death." *Economist* 349(8094), 95.

Anon. (1998h, Dec. 20). "NRI Girl Flees After Forced Marriage." *Hindustan Times* (New Delhi).

Anon. (1999a). Kava. *Review of Natural Products.* St. Louis, Mo.: Facts and Comparisons, 1–3.

Anon. (1999b, Apr. 13). "Semi-legal Drugs." *Economist,* 351(8113), 27.

Anon. (1999c, Feb.). "Dishonesty Is a Costly Policy." *Mortuary Management* 86(2), 18.

Anon. (1999d, Feb.). "Get In Line." *Mortuary Management* 86(2), 19.

Anon. (1999e, Apr.). "Funeral Home Blamed for Error." *Mortuary Management* 86(4), 23.

Anon. (1999f, Dec. 23). "Change in Custody Is Denied to Parent Who Seeks More Religious Upbringing: *J.B. v. R.M.*" *New York Law Journal,* 25.

Anon. (1999g, Aug. 25). "School Board Retracts Ruling on Jewish Star." *New York Times.*

Anon. (1999h, Apr. 8). "Guatemala Lets Students Wear Mayan Attire." *New York Times,* A9.

Anon. (2000a, Feb. 5). "Grandma's Report on Elian Stuns Miami." *Times-Picayune,* A12.

Anon. (2000b, Feb. 6). "Cuban's Boy's Relatives File a Complaint." *New York Times,* 20.

Anon. (2000c, Feb. 6). "Elian's Miami Relatives Go to Police over Grandma's Visit." *Atlanta Journal and Constitution,* 4B.

Anon. (2000d, Mar. 17). "Police Arrest Nine People in Restaurant Drug Raid." *New York Times,* B7.

Anon. (2000e, Apr. 23). "$182Gs Khat Bust at Airport." *Toronto Sun,* 22.

Anon. (2000f, June 26). "'Tradition' No Excuse for Child Abuse." *Atlanta Journal and Constitution*, 8A.

Anon. (2000g, July 12). "Mormon Ordered to Stand Trial on Bigamy Charges." *Los Angeles Times*, A14.

Anon. (2000h, Aug. 4). "U.S. Pledges to Resist State's Medical Marijuana Law." *Los Angeles Times*, A24.

Anon. (2000i, Aug. 9). "Customs Seizes Khat Boxes." *Dominion* (Wellington, New Zealand), 18.

Anuakan, Robyn Iset (1993). "Hairpins, Head Raps and Kinky Stories: African American Women in Folklore, and Cornrows as a Mediator of Aesthetics." Masters thesis, University of California, Berkeley.

Aquino, Belinda, and Virginia Miarlao (1993, Apr. 9). "Philippine Culture Used as Scapegoat in Ganal Trial." *Honolulu Star-Bulletin*, A11.

Arax, Mark (1994, Nov. 21). "Cancer Case Ignites Culture Clash." *Los Angeles Times*, A3.

——— (1995, Dec. 16). "Hmong's Sacrifice of Puppy Reopens Cultural Wounds." *Los Angeles Times*, A1, 12.

Areen, Judith (1985). *Cases and Materials on Family Law* (2nd ed.). Mineola, N.Y.: Foundation Press.

Aremu, L.O. (1980). "Criminal Responsibility for Homicide in Nigeria and Supernatural Beliefs." *International and Comparative Law Quarterly* 29, 112–131.

Arenella, Peter (1977). "The Diminished Capacity and Diminished Responsibility Defenses: Two Children of a Doomed Marriage." *Columbia Law Review* 77, 827–865.

Aries, Phillipe (1974). *Western Attitudes toward Death: From the Middle Ages to the Present*. Translated by Patricia M. Ranum. Baltimore: Johns Hopkins University Press.

Arkin, Stanley (1995, Dec. 14). "Criminal Intent and Cultural Dissonance." *New York Law Journal*, 3.

Armour, Robert A., and J. Carol Williams (1980). "Death in Popular Culture." In M. Thomas Inge (Ed.), *Handbook of American Popular Culture* (Vol. 2, 70–104). Westport, Conn.: Greenwood Press.

Arnold, Elaine (1982). "The Use of Corporal Punishment in Child Rearing in the West Indies." *Child Abuse and Neglect* 6, 141–145.

Arocha, Zita, and Jeff Sklansky (1988, Aug. 26). "D.C. Won't Pursue Charges of Bias over Cornrow Policy: Hyatt Hotels Drop Ban on Hair Style." *Washington Post*, C3.

Asante, Molefi Kete (1989) *Afrocentricity*. Trenton, N.J.: Africa World and Press.

——— (1990). *Kemet, Afrocentricity and Knowledge*. Trenton, N.J.: Africa World and Press.

Asher, Brad (1995). "A Shaman-Killing Case on Puget Sound, 1873–1874: American Law and Salish Culture." *Pacific Northwest Quarterly* 86(1), 17–24.

Askari, Ladan (1998). "The Convention on the Rights of the Child: The Necessity of Adding a Provision to Ban Child Marriages." *ILSA Journal of International and Comparative Law* 5, 124–138.

Avakian, Lynne (1986). "*Khalsa v. Weinberger:* No Judicial Review of Army Appearance Regulations." *Golden Gate University Law Review* 16, 1–9.

Ayau, Edward H. (1992). "Restoring the Ancestral Foundation of Native Hawaiians." *Arizona State Law Journal* 24, 193–216.

Ayres, B. Drummon Jr. (1996, Sept. 9). "Marriage Advised in Some Youth Pregnancies." *New York Times*, A10.

Baasher, Taha (1983). "The Use of Khat." In Griffith Edwards, Awni Arif, and Jerome Jaffe (Eds.), *Drug Use and Misuse: Cultural Perspectives* (42–49). London: Croom Helm.

Bahrampour, Firouzeh (1995). "The Caning of Michael Fay: Can Singapore's Punishment Withstand the Scrutiny of International Law?" *American University Journal of International Law and Policy* 10, 1075–1108.

Baines, Cynthia DeBula (1996). "L'Affaire des Foulards: Discrimination or the Price of a Secular Public Education System?" *Vanderbilt Journal of Transnational Law* 29, 303–327.

Balint, G. A., H. Ghebrekidan, and E. E. Balint (1991). "*Catha edulis*: An International Socio-Medical Problem with Considerable Pharmacological Implications." *East African Medical Journal* 68, 555–561.

Balzar, John (1993, Sept. 25). "Creatures Great and—Equal?" *Los Angeles Times*, A1, 30.

Banerjee, Suja (1987, Nov. 24). "Ancient Style for Now: Plaits Can Be Creative, Costly." *Baltimore Evening Sun*, D1.

——— (1987, Nov. 24). "Braids Create Legal Tangles." *Baltimore Evening Sun*, D1, 3.

Banks, Britt (1988). "Birds of a Feather: Cultural Conflict and the Eagle in American Society." *Colorado Law Review* 59, 639–657

Bannon, John Thomas Jr. (1998). "The Legality of the Religious Use of Peyote by the Native American Church: A Commentary on the Free Exercise, Equal Protection, and Establishment Issues Raised by the Peyote Way Church of God Case." *American Indian Law Review* 22, 475–507.

Barber, Carroll G. (1959). "Peyote and the Definition of Narcotic." *American Anthropologist* 61, 641–646.

Barfield, Chet (1995, Mar. 24). "Educators Given Own Lesson on Sensitivity." *San Diego Union-Tribune*, B1, 3.

Barger, W. K. (1980). "Eskimos on Trial: Adaptation, Interethnic Relations, and Social Control in the Canadian North." *Human Organization* 39, 242–249.

Barker, Karlyn (1988, Nov. 6). "Bad Circulation? Try Some Sliced Deer Antlers." *Washington Post* (Sunday, Final Ed.), Metro, B1.

——— (1988, July 8). Marriott, D.C. "Workers Settle Suit: Agent Will Keep Job, Cornrow Hairstyle." *Washington Post*, D5.

Baron, D. N. (1999, Aug. 21). "A Memorable Experience: The Qat Party." *British Medical Journal* 319 (7208), 500.

Barrett, D. C. (1965). "Homicide: Failure to Provide Medical or Surgical Attention." *American Law Reports Annotated* (2nd) 100, 483–519.

Barrett, Leonard (1988). *The Rastafarians: Sounds of Cultural Dissonance*. Boston: Beacon Press.

Barry, Brian (2001). *Culture and Equality: An Egalitarian Critique of Multiculturalism*. Cambridge: Harvard University Press.

Bartels, Lynn (1995, Mar. 9). "Jury Weighs Man's Sanity in '94 Food Court Slaying: 'Teddy' Chou 'Lost Face' after Earlier Beating, Was in Trance during Shooting, Lawyers Say." *Rocky Mountain News* (Denver), 35A.

Barth, Frederik (1969). *Ethnic Groups and Boundaries*. Boston: Little, Brown.

Bartlett, John (1992). *Familiar Quotations* (16th ed.). Boston: Little, Brown.

Bashir, Layli Miller (1996). "Female Genital Mutilation in the U.S.: An Examination of Criminal and Asylum Law." *Journal of Gender and the Law* 4, 415–454.

Basu, Amarendranath (1991). "Hair as Symbol." *Samiksa* 45(2), 45–54, 115–128.

Baubock, Rainer (1996). "Cultural Minority Rights for Immigrants." *International Migration Review* 30, 203–250.

Bauers, Sandy (1990, Mar. 4). "Hair-itage." *Philadelphia Inquirer*, 1-K, 6-K.

Bean, Lowell John (1974). *Mukat's People: The Cahuilla Indians of Southern California*. Berkeley: University of California Press.

Beason, Joseph (1989, Oct. 16). "Overheard." *Newsweek*, 23.

Becker, Ernest (1973). *The Denial of Death*. New York: Free Press.

Becker, Stanley M. (1984, May). "Autopsies and Religious Objection." *Pathologist* 38, 316.

Beeson, Ann (1992). "Dances with Justice: Peyotism in the Courts." *Emory Law Journal* 41, 1121–1184.

Beetham, David (1970). *Transport and Turbans: A Comparative Study in Local Politics*. London: Oxford University Press.

Beghtol, Mary Jo (1988). "Hmong Refugees and the US Health System." *Cultural Survival Quarterly* 12(1), 11–14.

Beigel, Richard (1998, Feb. 1). "Hindu Served Beef at Taco Bell." *Los Angeles Times*, M4.

Beirne, Piers (1983). "Cultural Relativism and Comparative Criminology." *Contemporary Crises* 7, 371–391.

Benhabib, Seyla (Ed.) (1996), *Democracy and Difference: Contesting the Boundaries of the Political*. Princeton, N.J.: Princeton University Press.

Benjamin, Michael J. Major (1998, Nov.). "Justice, Justice Shall You Pursue: Legal Analysis of Religion Issues in the Army." *Army Lawyer*, 1–11.

Berens, Michael J. (1984, Feb. 6). "Laotian Parents May Kill Ill Baby, Selves, Relatives Say." *Columbus Dispatch*, 1A.

Berg, Charles (1936). "The Unconscious Significance of Hair." *International Journal of Psycho-Analysis*, 17, 73–88.

———— (1951). *The Unconscious Significance of Hair*. London: George Allen and Unwin.

Berg, Martin (1987, Nov. 20). "Cultural Defense May Hurt, Help Rights." *Los Angeles Daily Journal*, 5.

Berger, Leslie (1994, Aug. 24). "Learning to Tell Custom from Abuse." *Los Angeles Times*, A1, 16–17.

Berger, Michael S., and Deborah E. Lipstadt (1996). "Women in Judaism from the Perspective of Human Rights." In John Witte Jr. and John D. van der Vyver (Eds.), *Religious Human Rights in Global Perspective: Religious Perspectives* (295–321). The Hague: Martinus Nijhoff.

Beriss, David (1990). "Scarves, Schools, and Segregation: The Foulard Affair." *French Politics and Society* 8(1), 1–13.

Berkovits, Bernard (1990). "*Get* and *Talaq* in English Law and Policy." In C. Mallat and J. Connors (Eds), *Islamic Family Law* (119–146). London: Graham and Trotman.

Berkow, Robert, and Andrew J. Fletcher (Eds.) (1992). *The Merck Manual of Diagnosis and Therapy* (16th Ed.).

Bernard, Hugh Y. (1979). *The Law of Death and Disposal of the Dead* (2nd ed.). Dobbs Ferry, N.Y.: Oceana Publications.

Berquist, Louise M. (1982, July 24). "Peking Duck Legislation Attacked as Dangerous." *Los Angeles Times*.

Berridge, Virginia (1996, Feb. 3). "Drug Policy: Should the Law Take a Back Seat?" *Lancet* 347(8997), 301–305.

Berry, John W. (1980). "Acculturation as Varieties of Adaptation." In Amado M. Padilla (Ed.), *Acculturation: Theory, Models and Some New Findings* (9–25). Boulder, Colo.: Westview Press.

Besharov, Douglas (1981). "Toward Better Research on Child Abuse and Neglect: Making Definitional Issues an Explicit Methodological Concern." *Child Abuse and Neglect* 5, 383–390.

Best, Elsdon (1927). "Notes on Customs, Ritual and Beliefs Pertaining to Sickness, Death, Burial and Exhumation among the Maori of New Zealand." *Journal of the Polynesian Society* 35, 6–30.

Beyer, Lisa (1999, Jan. 18). "The Price of Honor." *Time*, 55.

Beyerly, Elizabeth (1998). *Eurocentric International Law: Contemporary Doctrinal Perspectives*. Buffalo, N.Y.: William S. Hein.

Beyette, Beverly (1998, Feb. 5). "The Complicated (but Lucrative) Business of Keeping Kosher." *Los Angeles Times*, E1, 4.

Bhachu, Amarjeet S. (1996). "A Shield for Swords." *American Criminal Law Review* 34, 197–223.

Bishop, Katherine (1988, Feb. 10). "Asian Tradition at War with American Laws." *New York Times*, A18.

––––––– (1989, Oct. 5). "U.S.A.'s Culinary Rule: Hot Dogs, Yes, Dogs No." *New York Times*, A10.

––––––– (1989, Nov. 26). "18th-Century Law Snares Vietnamese Fishermen." *New York Times*, A1.

Bjorhus, Jennifer (1994, Aug. 1). "School's Knife Ban Angers Sikhs." *San Francisco Chronicle*, A1, 12.

Black, J.A. (1986, Feb.). "Misdiagnosis of Child Abuse in Ethnic Minorities." *Midwife Health Visitor and Community Nurse* 22, 48–53.

Black, John (1987, Aug. 29). "Broaden Your Mind about Death and Bereavement in Certain Ethnic Groups in Britain." *British Medical Journal* 298, 535–539.

Blasszauer, Bela (1998). "Autopsy." In A. Henk, J. J Ten Have, and Jos V. M. Welie (Eds.), *Ownership of the Human Body: Philosophical Considerations on the Use of the Human Body and Its Parts in Healthcare* (19–26). Dordrecht: Kluwer Academic.

Bliatout, Bruce Thowpaou (1988). "Hmong Attitudes towards Surgery: How It Affects Patient Prognosis." *Migration World* 16(1), 25–28.

––––––– (1993). "Hmong Death Customs: Traditional and Acculturated." In Donald P. Irish et al. (Eds.), *Ethnic Variations in Dying, Death, and Grief* (79–100). London: Taylor and Francis.

Bloom, Joseph D., and Jacqueline L. Bloom (1982). "An Examination of the Use of Transcultural Data in the Courtroom." *Bulletin of the American Academy of Psychiatry and the Law* 10, 89–95.

Blum, Deborah (1986). *Bad Karma: A True Story of Obsession and Murder.* New York: Jove Books.

Bock, James (1992, Apr. 2). "Domino's Takes It on Chin." *Baltimore Sun*, 1E, 12E.

Bodovitz, Sandra (1990, Mar. 22). "Indian's Defense Cites Fear of Genocide." *Recorder* (San Francisco), 3.

Bogatyrev, Petr (1971). *The Functions of Folk Costume in Moravian Slovakia.* The Hague: Mouton.

Boglioli, Lauren R., and Mark L. Taff (1990). "Religious Objection to Autopsy: An Ethical Dilemma for Medical Examiners." *American Journal of Forensic Medicine and Pathology* 11(1), 1–8.

Bohannan, Paul (1967). "The Differing Realms of the Law." In Paul Bohannan (Ed.), *Law and Warfare: Studies in the Anthropology of Conflict* (43–56). Garden City, N.Y.: Natural History Press.

––––––– (1973). "Rethinking Culture: A Project for Current Anthropologists." *Current Anthropology* 14(4), 357–372.

Bohlen, Celestine (1989, Apr. 5). "Holtzman May Appeal Probation in the Killing of a Chinese Woman." *New York Times*, B3.

Bolgar, Vera (1967). "The Present Function of the Maxim *Ignorantia Iuris Neminem Excusat*: A Comparative Study." *Iowa Law Review* 52, 626–656.

Bone, James (1999, Dec. 16). "41,000 Pounds for Buggy Mother." *Times* (London).

Booth, Michael (1993, July 22). "Culture Clash Cited in Alleged Illegal Touching: Cambodian Native Charged." *Times* (Trenton, N.J.), A2.

Borek, Jamison S. (1996, July 17). "Testimony before the Senate Committee on Foreign Relations." Federal News Service (available on LEXIS /NEXIS , world news file).

Bossert, Rex (1995, Aug. 2). "Ceremonial Knife Is Allowed in School." *Daily Journal*, 1, 7.

Bott, Elizabeth (1972). "Psychoanalysis and Ceremony." In J. S. La Fontaine (Ed.), *The Interpretation of Ritual* (205–237). London: Tavistock.

Boulware-Miller, Kay (1985). "Female Circumcision: Challenges to the Practice as a Human Rights Violation." *Harvard Women's Law Journal* 8, 155–177.

Bourne, Peter G. (1982). Foreword to Joseph Westermeyer, *Poppies, Pipes, and People: Opium and Its Use in Laos* (xi–xvii). Berkeley: University of California Press.

Bradley, David (1983). "Duress and Arranged Marriages." *Modern Law Review* 46, 499–504.

Brady, Stephen (1980, Feb.). "Insanity as a Defense in Florida." *Florida Bar Journal* 54(2), 163–166.

Braenden, Olav J. (1979). "Research on the Chemical Composition of Khat." In Louis S. Harris (Ed.), *Problems of Drug Dependence, 1979* (320–321). Washington, D.C.: Department of Health, Education and Welfare.

Brain, Robert (1979). *The Decorated Body.* New York: Harper and Row.

Brandes, Stanley (1984). "Animal Metaphors and Social Control in Tzintzuntzan." *Ethnology* 23(3), 207–215.

——— (2001). "The Cremated Catholic: The Ends of a Deceased Guatemalan." *Body and Society* 7, 111–120.

Brandon, Joseph E. (1990). "Sacrificial Practices in Santeria, an Afro-Cuban Religion in the United States." In Joseph E. Holloway (Ed.), *Africanisms in American Culture* (119–147). Bloomington: Indiana University Press.

Brandt, R. B. (1985). "A Motivational Theory of Excuses in the Criminal Law." In J. Roland Pennock and John W. Chapman (Eds.), *Criminal Justice: Nomos 27* (165–198). New York: New York University Press.

Braxton, Greg (1990, Nov. 10). "Challege to Sacrifice Law Blocked: Judge Rules City Ordinance Does Not Infringe on Yoruba Religion." *Los Angeles Times*, B4.

Breitowitz, Irving (1992). "The Plight of the Agunah: A Study in Halacha, Contract, and the First Amendment." *Maryland Law Review* 51, 312–421.

——— (1993). *Between Civil and Religious Law: The Plight of the Agunah in American Society.* Westport, Conn.: Greenwood Press.

Breitung, Barrett (1996). "Interpretation and Eradication: National and International Responses to Female Circumcision." *Emory International Law Review* 10, 657–693.

Brelvi, Farah Sultana (1997). "'News of the Weird': Specious Normativity and the Problem of the Cultural Defense." *Columbia Human Rights Law Review* 28, 657–683.

Brennan, Katherine (1989). "The Influence of Cultural Relativism on International Human Rights Law: Female Circumcision as a Case Study." *Law and Inequality* 7, 367–398.

Brigham, John (1996). "The Other Countries of American Law." *Social Identities* 2, 237–254.

Britt, Donna (1992, May 26). "Kente Cloth's Wiles Have Yet to Unfold." *Washington Post*, B1.

Broder, John (1994, Apr. 30). "Tribal Leaders Meet Clinton, Air Concerns." *Los Angeles Times*, A1, 15.

Bronitt, Simon, and Kumaralingam Amirthalingam (1996). "Cultural Blindness: Criminal Law in Multicultural Australia." *Alternative Law Journal* 21(2), 58–63.

Brooke, James (1996, Nov. 13). "Eight Arrested in Southwest in Crackdown on Trade in Eagle Parts." *New York Times*, A10.

——— (1996, Nov. 25). "Agency Struggles to Meet the Demand for a Sacred Treasure." *New York Times*, A8.

——— (1997, May 7). "Military Ends Conflict of Career and Religion: American Indians Win Ritual Peyote Use." *New York Times*, A12.

——— (1998, Aug. 23). "Utah Being Torn by Swelling Ranks of Polygamists." *San Francisco Examiner*, A4.

Brooks, Robert F., and William H. Wright Jr. (1996, Nov. 4). "States Deny Treaty Rights to Foreign Defendants." *National Law Journal*, B8.

Broom, Leonard, and John I. Kitsuse (1955). "The Validation of Acculturation: A Condition to Ethnic Assimilation." *American Anthropologist* 57, 44–48.

Brown, Bernard (1964). "The 'Ordinary Man' in Provocation: Anglo-Saxon Attitudes and 'Unreasonable Non-Englishmen.'" *International and Comparative Law Quarterly* 13, 203–235.

Brown, David Hilary (1989). *Garden in the Machine: Afro-Cuban Sacred Art and Performance in Urban New Jersey and New York* (2 vols.). Ph.D. dissertation, Yale University.

Brunton, Ron (1989). *The Abandoned Narcotic: Kava and Cultural Instability in Melanesia.* Cambridge: Cambridge University Press.

Bry, Kevin E. (1990). "Genuinely Distressing: Illinois' Failure to Allow a Claim of Action for Emotional Injuries Caused by Negligent Mishandling of a Corpse." *John Marshall Law Review* 23, 353–362.

Bryant, Taimie L. (1990). "Oya-Ko Shinju: Death at the Center of the Heart." *UCLA Pacific Basin Law Journal* 8, 1–31.

Buckley, J. P. et al. (1967). "Pharmacology of Kava." In D. H. Effron et al. (Eds), *Ethnopharmacologic Search for Psychoactive Drugs* (141–151). Washington, D.C.: U.S. Government Printing Office.

Bullis, Ronald K. (1990). "Swallowing the Scroll: Legal Implications of the Recent Supreme Court Peyote Cases." *Journal of Psychoactive Drugs* 22(3), 325–332.

Burgers, J. Herman (1990). "The Right to Cultural Identity." In Jan Berting et al. (Eds.), *Human Rights in a Pluralist World: Individuals and Collectivities* (251–253). Westport, Conn.: Meckler.

Burnett, Arthur L., Sr. (1994). "National Origin and Ethnicity in Sentencing." *Criminal Justice* 9, 26–46.

Burns, John F. (1998, May 11). "Though Illegal, Child Marriage Is Popular in Part of India." *New York Times*, A1, 8.

Burns, Michael (1990, July 7). "State Challenges Domino's Pizza No-Beard Policy." *Baltimore Sun*, 5A.

Burroughs, Catherine B., and Jeffrey David Ehrenreich (Eds.) (1993). *Reading the Social Body.* Iowa City: University of Iowa Press.

Bustillo, Miguel (1994, Apr. 18). "A Question of Culture, or Cruelty." *Los Angeles Times*, A1, 18.

——— (2000, Jan. 23). "Cultures Clash over Sales of Live Turtles, Frogs." *Los Angeles Times*, A22.

Caldwell, Paulette M. (1991). "A Hair Piece: Perspectives on the Intersection of Race and Gender." *Duke Law Journal* 1991, 365–396.

California Committee Analysis (1996, June 5). "Female Genital Mutilation." Senate Committee on Health and Human Services Bill No. AB 2125. Washington, D.C.: U.S. Government Printing Office.

Campbell, Courtney (1992, Sept.-Oct.). "Body, Self, and the Property Paradigm." *Hastings Center Report* 22(5), 34–42.

Canadian Commission for Unesco (1977). "A Working Definition of 'Culture.'" *Cultures* 4(4), 78–83.

Canham, Matt (2002, Nov. 19). "Green's Appeal Says Judge Erred in Calling Him a Married Man." *Salt Lake Tribune*, C4.

Carberry, Charles M., and Harold K. Gordon (1996, Apr.). "Anatomy of an Acquittal: The Cultural Use of Cash." *Money Laundering Law Report* 1.

Cardillo, Cathy C. (1997). "Violence against Chinese Women: Defining the Cultural Role." *Women's Rights Law Reporter* 19, 85–96.

Carens, Joseph H. (2000). *Culture, Citizenship, and Community: A Contextual Exploration of Justice as Evenhandedness.* Clarendon: Oxford University Press.

Carlson, Daryl-Lynn (1994, Nov. 21–22). "Culture, Intoxication as Possible Defences; Ottawa to Study Revamping Part of Criminal Code." *Law Times,* 7.

Carpenter, Dale E. (1988). "Free Exercise and Dress Codes: Toward More Consistent Protection of a Fundamental Right." *Indiana Law Journal* 63, 601–621.

Carstairs, G.M. (1953–54). "The Case of Thakur Khuman Singh: A Culture-Conditioned Crime." *British Journal of Delinquency* 4, 14–25.

Cart, Julie (1998, Aug. 16). "Polygamy Continues in Utah Generating Social, Legal Problems: ACLU Defends the Practitioners' Religious Rights." *San Francisco Examiner,* A-4.

————— (1999, June 4). "Incest Trial Sheds Light on Polygamy in Utah." *Los Angeles Times,* A3, A14

Cassanelli, Lee V. (1986). "Qat: A Quasilegal Commodity." In Arjun Appadurai (Ed.), *The Social Life of Things: Commodities in Cultural Perspective* (236–257). Cambridge: Cambridge University Press.

Castiglione, Andrea Gianelli, and Andrea Lomi (1993). "Forensic Autopsies in Italy." *Journal of Forensic Sciences* 38(3), 622–627.

Cawley, C. C. (1954). "Criminal Liability in Faith Healing." *Minnesota Law Review* 39, 48–74.

Cawte, John (1985). "Psychoactive Substances of the South Seas: Betel, Kava and Pituri." *Australian and New Zealand Journal of Psychiatry* 19, 83–87.

Cha, Yang (1990, June 24). "Letter to Mr. Ernest Velasquez, Director of Social Services in Fresno." Unpublished letter written by Hmong Council President on behalf of Hmong clan leaders.

Chapin, Kristin (1993). "Indian Fishing Rights Activists in an Age of Controversy: The Case for an Individual Aboriginal Rights Defense." *Environmental Law* 23, 971–994.

Charles, Henrietta (1989a) "Judge Chooses Photos in Dog-Slaying Case." *Long Beach Press-Telegram.*

————— (1989b). "Two Men Charged in Dog-Killing Case Sue Long Beach." *Long Beach Press Telegram.*

————— (1989c, Mar. 9). "Court: Killing an Animal for Food Not Illegal." *Long Beach Press-Telegram,* B1.

————— (1989d, Mar. 15). "Judge Dismisses Dog-Killing Case, *Long Beach Press-Telegram,* B1, 2.

————— (1989e, Mar. 27). "Cruelty Law Weighed, L. B. Dog Killing Sparks Outcry." *Long Beach Press-Telegram,* C1–C2.

Charny, Ben (1998, June 4). "No Charges; Sikh's Ceremonial Sword Hidden, but Dull." *Daily Review.*

Chartrand, Sabra (1992, June 19). "A Dispute over Courtroom Attire and Principles." *New York Times,* B8.

Chazin, Daniel D. (1986). *Goldman v. Secretary of Defense:* A New Standard for Free Exercise Claims in the Military. *National Jewish Law Review* 1, 13–40.

Checchio, Michael (1989, Apr. 17). "Racism Claim Brings Capital Case to San Francisco." *Recorder,* 1, 24.

Chen, David (1998, May 13). "City Is Sued by Woman Who Left Baby Outside." *New York Times,* B3.

Chen, Edwin (1999, July 3). "Eagle Lauded with an Eye toward Future." *Los Angeles Times,* A17.

Cheon-Klessig, Young (1988). "Folk Medicine in the Health Practice of Hmong Refugees." *Western Journal of Nursing Research* 10(5), 647–660.

Chevannes, Barry (1994). *Rastafari: Roots and Ideology.* Syracuse, N.Y.: Syracuse University Press.

Chiang, Harriet (1997, Apr. 16). "Suit over Sale of Live Animals for Food: Supervisors, D.A. Ignoring Problem Activists Say." *San Francisco Chronicle*, A15.

Chiba, Masaji (1993). "Legal Pluralism in Sri Lankan Society: Toward a General Theory of Non-Western Law." *Journal of Legal Pluralism and Unofficial Law* 33, 197–212.

Chin, Soo-Young (n.d.). "Bearing Witness: Exorcism, Death, and the Law." Unpublished essay.

Chindarsi, Nusit (1976). *The Religion of the Hmong Njua*. Bangkok: Siam Society.

——— (1983). "Hmong Shamanism." In John McKinnon and Wanat Bhruksasri (Eds.), *Highlanders of Thailand* (187–192). Kuala Lumpur: Oxford University Press.

Ching, Jennifer (1996). "Defending Whose Culture? China, Woman, and the Cultural Defense in the American Legal System. A.B. thesis, Harvard University.

Chiu, Daina C. (1994). "The Cultural Defense: Beyond Exclusion, Assimilation, and Guilty Liberalism." *California Law Review* 82, 1053–1125.

Cho, Aileen (1993, Oct. 28). "Groups Halt Adoption of Black Cats." *Los Angeles Times*, J9.

Cho, Michael (1991). "Animal Appetites." Valencia, Calif.: CalArts School of Film/Video.

Choi, Carolyn (1990). "Application of a Cultural Defense in Criminal Proceedings." *UCLA Pacific Basin Law Journal* 8, 80–90.

Cholewinski, Ryszard (1988). "State Duty to Ethnic Minorities: Positive or Negative?" *Human Rights Quarterly* 10, 344–371.

Christ, H. (1870). "Über *Catha edulis*." *Archiv der Pharmazie* 191, 67–71.

Chukkol, Kharisu Sufiyan (1983). "Supernatural Beliefs and Criminal Law in Nigeria." *Journal of the Indian Law Institute* 25, 444–474.

Claghorn, Kate Holladay (1971). *The Immigrant's Day in Court*. Montclair, N.J.: Patterson Smith. (Originally Published 1923)

Clark, Christine A. (1991). "Religious Accommodation and Criminal Liability." *Florida State University Law Review* 17, 559–590.

Clark, David (1980). "Witchcraft and Legal Pluralism: The Case for Celimo Miquirucama." *Tulsa Law Journal* 15, 679–698.

Clark, Margaret, Sharon Kaufman, and Robert C. Pierce (1976). "Explorations of Acculturation: Toward a Model of Ethnic Identity." *Human Organization* 35, 231–238.

Clarke, Peter V. (1994). *Black Paradise: The Rastafarian Movement*. San Bernardino: Borgo Press.

Clinton, Olabisi L. (1993). "Cultural Differences and Sentencing Departures." *Federal Sentencing Reporter* 5, 348–353.

Clinton, William (1994, Apr. 29). "Memorandum on Distribution of Eagle Feathers for Native American Religious Purposes." *Weekly Compilation of Presidential Documents* 30(17), 935–937.

Cockburn, Alexander (1997, Sept. 28). "Rural Justice for a Man Who Expected None: Native American's Lawyer Says that the White Jury's Action Is a Legacy of the 60's." *Los Angeles Times*, M5.

Cohn, Bernard S. (1989). "Cloth, Clothes, and Colonialism: India in the Nineteenth Century." In Annette B. Weiner and Jane Schneider (Eds.), *Cloth and Human Experience* (303–353). Washington, D.C.: Smithsonian Institution Press.

Cole, Herbert (1990, Oct.). "Kente: A Meaningful Tradition in Cloth." *American Visions* 5(5), 18–23.

Cole, Richard W., and Laura Maslow-Armand (1997). "The Role of Counsel and the Courts in Addressing Foreign Language and Cultural Barriers at Different Stages of a Criminal Proceeding." *Western New England Law Review* 19, 193–228.

Cole, W. Owen, and Piara Singh Sambhi (1994). *The Sikhs: Their Religious Beliefs and Practices*. Brighton, U.K.: Sussex Academic Press.

Coleman, Doriane Lambelet (1996). "Individualizing Justice through Multiculturalism: The Liberals' Dilemma." *Columbia Law Review* 96, 1093–1167.

———— (1998). "The Seattle Compromise: Multicultural Sensitivity and Americanization." *Duke Law Journal* 47, 717–783.

Collocott, E. E. V. (1927). "Kava Ceremonial in Tonga." *Journal of the Polynesian Society* 36, 21–47.

Connell, James G. III (2000). "Using Cultural Experts." In James G. Connell III and Rene L. Valladares (Eds.), *Cultural Issues in Criminal Defense*. Yonkers, N.Y.: Juris.

Connell, James G. III, and Rene L. Valladares (Eds.) (2000). *Cultural Issues in Criminal Defense*. Yonkers, N.Y.: Juris.

Connelly, Sherryl (1995, Mar. 22). "Review of *Guarding the Secrets* by Ellen Harris (Scribner)." *Daily News* (New York), 34.

Cook, Walter Wheeler (1916–1917). "Act, Intention, and Motive in the Criminal Law." *Yale Law Journal* 26, 645–663.

Cooper, Robert, Nicholas Tapp, Gar Yia Lee, and Gretel Schwoerer-Kohl (1991). *The Hmong*. Bangkok: ArtAsia Press.

Cooper, Wendy (1971). *Hair: Sex, Society, Symbolism*. New York: Stein and Day.

Coronado, Ramon (1985, Mar, 29). "Suspect in Voodoo Shooting Found Guilty." *Tribune* (Oakland), B2.

Corrales, Sue (1988, June 25a). "Case Shocks Cambodian Community." *Long Beach Press-Telegram*, A1, A4.

———— (1988, June 25b). "It Began with a Gift." *Long Beach Press-Telegram*, A1, 4.

Correa, Armando (1995, Nov. 28). "Santeria Priest's Trial Begins Today for Sacrifices of 15 Animals." *Miami Herald.*

Corwin, Miles (1988, May 3). "Judge Opens Door to Rare Strategy by Attorney for Campus Protesters." *Los Angeles Times*, Pt. I, 20.

———— (1999, Feb. 11). "Lieutenant with Beard Sues City, LAPD Chief." *Los Angeles Times*, B3, 10.

Cotton, D. W. K., and S. S. Cross (Eds.) (1993). *The Hospital Autopsy*. Oxford: Butterworth/Heinemann.

Council of Europe (1979). *Explanatory Report on the European Convention for the Protection of Animals for Slaughter*. Strasbourg: Council of Europe.

Coven, Phyllis (1995, May 26). "Considerations for Asylum Officers Adjudicating Asylum Claims from Women." INS document reprinted in *San Diego Law Review* 32, 794–714.

Cowling, Wendy E. (1988). "Kava Drinking in Contemporary Tonga." In John Prescott and Grant McCall (Eds.), *Kava: Use and Abuse in Australia and the South Pacific* (40–49). Monograph 5. Sydney, University of New South Wales, National Drug and Alcohol Research Centre.

Coyle, Dennis J., and Richard J. Ellis (Eds.) (1994). *Politics, Policy and Culture*. Boulder, Colo.: Westview.

Coyle, Marcia (1996, May 6). "Case Could Widen Ground for Asylum." *National Law Journal*, A10.

Cramer, Gary C. (1996, Aug. 15). "Cultural Differences." *San Francisco Chronicle.*

Cramer, John D. (1991, July 21). "Rocky US Reception for Ritual." *Fresno Bee*, B1, B4.

Cranfield, Roger, and Elizabeth Cranfield (1983, May). "Female Circumcision: An Assault?" *Practitioner* 227(1379), 816–817.

Cross, Mark (1995, Dec. 31). "Ancient Faiths, Modern Laws Clash over Animal Sacrifices." *Fresno Bee.*

Crossette, Barbara (1995, Dec. 10). "Female Genital Mutilation by Immigrants Is Becoming Cause of Concern in U.S." *New York Times*, 18.

———— (1998, Mar. 23). "Mutilation Seen as Risk for the Girls of Immigrants." *New York Times*, A3.

———— (1999, Mar. 6). "Testing the Limits of Tolerance as Cultures Mix: Does Freedom Mean Accepting Rituals That Repel the West?" *New York Times*, B9; reprinted Mar. 12, as Culture Clash: Courts Increasingly Are Called on to Determine What Is Taboo, *Los Angeles Daily Journal*, 4.

Csordas, Thomas J. (1995). "The Body: Cultural and Religious Perspectives." In Warren Thomas Reich et al. (Eds.), *Encyclopedia of Bioethics* (rev. ed., 305–312). New York: Simon and Schuster.

Cumper, Peter (1996). "Religious Liberty in the United Kingdom." In Johan D. van der Vyver and John Witte Jr. (Eds.), *Religious Human Rights in Global Perspective: Legal Perspectives* (205–241). The Hague: Martinus Nijhoff.

Cunningham, Thomas (1998, Dec. 9–15). "The Culture of Kat." *Nursing Standard* 13(2), 25.

Curran, W. J. (1977a). "Damage Suits against Medical Examiners for Authorized Autopsies." *New England Journal of Medicine* 297, 1220–1221.

———— (1977b). "Religious Objection to a Medical Autopsy: A Case and a Statute." *New England Journal of Medicine* 297, 260–261.

Currie, Elliott P. (1968). "Crimes without Criminals: Witchcraft and Its Control in Renaissance Europe." *Law and Society Review* 3, 7–32.

Curtius, Mary (1995, Mar. 12). "Paying a High Price for Honor." *Los Angeles Times*, A1, A6.

———— (1996, Aug. 12). "Cultures Clash over Sale of Live Animals for Food." *Los Angeles Times*, A1, 21.

Cytron, Barry D. (1993). "To Honor the Dead and Comfort the Mourners: Traditions in Judaism." In Donald P. Irish et al. (Eds.), *Ethnic Variations in Dying, Death, and Grief* (113–124). London: Taylor and Francis.

D'Andrade, Roy G. (1990). "Cultural Cognition." In Michael I. Posner (Ed.), *Foundations of Cognitive Science* (795–830). Cambridge: MIT Press.

Das, Veena (1994). "Cultural Rights and the Definition of Community." In Oliver Mendelsohn and Upendra Baxi (Eds.), *The Rights of Subordinated Peoples* (117–158). Delhi: Oxford University Press.

Davis, Gregory, and Bradley R. Peterson (1996, Nov.). "Dilemmas and Solutions for the Pathologist and Clinician Encountering Religious Views of the Autopsy." *Southern Medical Journal* 89(11), 1041–1044.

Davis, Janice (1987, Dec. 27). "Good Hair/Bad Hair Job Discrimination." *New Pittsburgh Courier.*

Davis, Joseph H. (1991). "Letter to Editor: Religious Objections to Autopsy." *American Journal of Forensic Medicine and Pathology* 12(3), 273.

Dawit, Seble, and Salem Mecuria (1993, Dec. 7). "The West Just Doesn't Get It." *New York Times*, A13.

Dean, Paul (1986, Oct. 5). "Gypsies Are Banding Together to Fight Age-Old Stereotypes." *Los Angeles Times*, Pt IV, 1, 10–11.

———— (1996, Dec. 13). "Cultures at the Crossroads: When Old World Habits Clash with New World Laws, It's Another Sign the Melting Pot Is Bubbling Imperfectly." *Los Angeles Times*, E1, 4.

Deb, Dipanwita (1996). "Of Kirpans, Schools, and the Free Exercise Clause: *Cheema v. Thompson* Cuts Through RFRA's Inadequacies." *Hastings Constitutional Law Quarterly* 23, 877–919.

DeBenedictis, Donald J. (1992). "Judges Debate Cultural Defense." *American Bar Association Journal* 78, 28.

deFiebre, Conrad (1992, Dec. 4). "Two Cousins Accused of Sex Assault on 14-Year-Old." *Star Tribune* (Minneapolis–St. Paul) (Metro ed.), 7B.

Deihl, Joseph R. (1932). "Kava and Kava-Drinking." *Primitive Man* 5(4), 61–68.

Dein, Simon (1997). "ABC of Mental Health: Mental Health in a Multiethnic Society." *British Medical Journal* 315(7106), 473–476.

Deinard, Amos S., and Timothy Dunnigan (1987). "Hmong Health Care: Reflections on a Six-Year Experience." *International Migration Review* 21, 857–865.

Delgado, Ray (1995, Aug. 17). "Cop Killer Suspect Turns Himself In: 'Bear' Lincoln Says That Sheriffs Ambushed Him and That He Fired Back in Self Defense." *San Francisco Examiner,* A6.

Delgado, Richard (1985). "'Rotten Social Background': Should the Criminal Law Recognize a Defense of Severe Environmental Deprivation?" *Law and Inequality* 3, 9–90.

De Meo, Antonia M. (1995). "Access to Eagles and Eagle Parts: Environmental Protection v. Native American Free Exercise of Religion." *Hastings Constitutional Law Quarterly* 22, 771–813.

Demick, Barbara (2002, Jan. 7). "Culinary Flap Dogs S. Korea." *Los Angeles Times,* A1.

De Negri, Eve (1976). *Nigerian Body Adornment.* Lagos: Nigeria Magazine.

Department of Justice Canada (1994). "Reforming the General Part of the Criminal Code: A Consultation Paper." Canada Department of Justice.

Dershowitz , Alan (1985, June 14). "'Marriage by Capture' Runs into the Law of Rape." *Los Angeles Times,* II, 5.

——— (1986, Mar. 30). "Religion, It Seems, Is Fine, Unless It's a Minority One." *Los Angeles Times,* V, 6.

de Turenne, Veronique (2000, May 7). "Kava Tea DUI Case Puts Spotlight on Community Steeped in Tradition." *Los Angeles Times,* A28.

Deukmejian, George (1989, Sept. 15). Letter to the Members of the California Assembly concerning Assembly Bill 1842 [Pet Law Bill].

Deveaux, Monique (2000). *Cultural Pluralism and Dilemmas of Justice.* Ithaca, N.Y.: Cornell University Press.

Deveney, Marie (1992). "Courts and Cultural Distinctiveness." *University of Michigan Journal of Law Reform* 25, 867–877.

Devlin, Mary (1990). "Competent Adult Patient's Religious-Based Refusal of Medical Care." *Journal of Medical Practice Management* 6, 141–145.

——— (1991). "Medical Legal Highlights: Religious-Based Refusals of Medical Care Part II: Children and Impaired Adults." *Journal of Medical Practice Management* 6, 210–214.

Diamond, A. S. (1974, Sept./Oct.). "The Case of Mrs. Adesanya." *RAIN: Royal Anthropological Institute News* no. 4, 2.

Diamond, Bernard L. (1978). "Social and Cultural Factors as a Diminished Capacity Defense in Criminal Law." *Bulletin of the American Academy of Psychiatry and the Law* 6, 195–208.

Dillow, Gordon (1985, Feb. 18). "When Legal System and Culture Collide." *Los Angeles Herald Examiner,* A1, 7.

Di Maio, Vincent J. M. (1993). "Discussion of Practical Approach to Investigative Ethics and Religious Objections to Autopsy." *Journal of Forensic Sciences* 38, 233–234.

Dobkin de Rios, Marlene (1996). *Hallucinogens: Cross-Cultural Perspectives.* Prospect Heights, Ill.: Waveland Press.

Dobkin de Rios, Marlene, and David E. Smith (1977). "The Function of Drug Rituals in Human Society: Continuities and Changes." *Journal of Psychedelic Drugs* 9, 269–275.

Dodes, Ivy (1987). "'Suffer the Little Children . . .': Toward a Judicial Recognition of a Duty of Reasonable Care Owed Children by Religious Faith Healers." *Hofstra Law Review* 16, 165–190.

Doherty, J. F. et al. (1995, Feb. 18). "Fascioliasis due to Imported Khat." *Lancet* 34(8947), 462.

Dolan, Maura (1985, Feb. 24). "Two Cultures Collide over Act of Despair: Mother Facing Charges in Ceremonial Drowning." *Los Angeles Times,* 3, 30, 32.

Dold, Catherine (1995, June 20). "Florida Panthers Get Some Outside Genes." *New York Times,* B1, B7.

Donnelly, Christine (1989, Jan. 23). "Developers, Native Hawaiians Square Off on Cultural Issues: Battle over Ancient Burial Site Halts New Maui Hotel." *Los Angeles Times,* I, 13.

Donoghue, Keith (1996a, Jan. 18). "A Rite of Passage: A Berkeley Lawyer's Client Could Establish Precedent for Asylum Claims based on Female Genital Mutilation." *Recorder,* no. 12, 1, 12.

——— (1996b, Feb. 5). "Cultural Rite Tests Asylum Law: Immigration Judges Ponder Whether Rise of Genital Mutilation Is Grounds for Granting Asylum." *Legal Times,* 1.

Donovan, Dolores, and Stephanie M. Wildman (1981). "Is the Reasonable Man Obsolete? A Critical Perspective on Self-Defense and Provocation." *Loyola of Los Angeles Law Review* 14, 435–468.

Doubleday, Nancy C. (1989). "Aboriginal Subsistence Whaling: The Right of Inuit to Hunt Whales and Implications for International Environmental Law." *Denver Journal of International Law and Policy* 17, 373–393.

Douglas, Mary (1972). "Deciphering a Meal." *Daedalus* 101, 61–81.

——— (Ed.) (1987). *Constructive Drinking: Perspectives on Drink from Anthropology.* Cambridge: Cambridge University Press.

Dowling, Claudia Glenn, and Paul Fusco (1992, Oct.). "Gypsies." *Life* 15(10), 46–54.

Downs, Hugh, and Barbara Walters (1995, Aug. 18). "We Want Our Children Back." *20/20* (ABC 9:00 p.m. EST). Transcript #1533. Available on NEXIS .

Drell, Adrienne (1993, Jan. 24). "Killer to Use Witchcraft as Defense." *Chicago Sun-Times.*

——— (1993, Jan. 29). "Witch Defense Out: Man Guilty." *Chicago Sun-Times.*

——— (1993, May). "Witchcraft Murder Defense Fails." *ABA Journal* 79, 40

Dresser, Norine (1996, July 13). "Luck of the Dial." *Los Angeles Times,* B7.

Drogin, Bob (1994, Dec. 28). "Witch Hunts: The Fatal Price of Fear." *Los Angeles Times,* A1, 8.

Drummond, Tammerlin (1993, Aug. 3). "Kenyan Villagers' Suspicions, Fears Spark Deadly Witch Hunt." *Los Angeles Times,* H3.

Duclos, Nitya (1990). "Lessons of Difference: Feminist Theory on Cultural Diversity." *Buffalo Law Review* 38, 325–381.

Dugger, Celia (1996a, Feb. 29). "Immigrant Cultures Raising Issues of Child Punishment." *New York Times,* A1, 12.

——— (1996b, Apr. 15). "Women's Plea for Asylum Puts Tribal Ritual on Trial." *New York Times,* A1, 12.

——— (1996c, Apr. 25). "U.S. Frees African Fleeing Ritual Mutilation." *New York Times,* A1, 13.

——— (1996d, June 14). "U.S. Grants Asylum to Woman Fleeing Genital Mutilation Rite." *New York Times,* A1, 13.

——— (1996e, Sept. 11). "A Refugee's Body Is Intact but Her Family Is Torn." *New York Times,* A1, 8.

——— (1996f, Oct. 12). "New Law Bans Genital Cutting in U.S.: Violators Could Face Five Years in Prison." *New York Times,* A1, 6.

Dundes, Alan (1984). *Life Is Like a Chicken Coop Ladder: A Portrait of German Culture through Folklore.* New York: Columbia University Press.

——— (1987). "Slurs International: Folk Comparisons of Ethnicity and National Character." In *Cracking Jokes: Studies of Sick Humor Cycles and Stereotypes* (96–114). Berkeley, Calif.: Ten Speed Press.

——— (Ed.) (1994). *The Cockfight: A Casebook.* Madison: University of Wisconsin Press.

——— (1997). *From Game to War and Other Psychoanalytic Essays on Folklore.* Lexington: University Press of Kentucky.

Durand-Prinborgne, Claude (1997, Jan.–Feb.). "Le port des signes exterieurs, de convictions religieuses à l'ecole: une jurisprudence affirmee…, une jurisprudence contestee." *Revue francaise de droit administratif* 1, 151–172

Durham, W. Cole (1999). "State RFRAs and the Scope of Free Exercise Protection." *U.C. Davis Law Review* 32, 665–724.

Dworkin, Ronald (1977). *Taking Rights Seriously.* Cambridge: Harvard University Press.

Dwyer, John (2000). "Spiritual Treatment Exemptions to Child Medical Neglect Laws." *Notre Dame Law Review* 76, 147–177.

Dyers, Bill (1986, Mar. 21). "Moslem Charged with Cruelty in Slaughter of Sheep." *Denver Post.*

Dyssegaard, Elisabeth Kallick (1997, May 17). "The Danes Call It Fresh Air." *New York Times,* 17.

Eaton, Joseph W. (1952). "Controlled Acculturation: A Survival Technique of the Hutterites." *American Sociological Review* 17, 331–340.

Edwards, Griffith, Awni Arif, and Jerome Jaffe (1983). *Drug Use and Misuse: Cultural Perspectives.* London: Croom Helm; New York: St. Martin's Press.

Efaw, Andrew C. S. (1996). "Free Exercise and the Uniformed Employee: A Comparative Look at Religious Freedom in the Armed Forces of the United States and Great Britain." *Comparative Labor Law Journal* 17, 648–669.

Efron, Daniel H. et al. (Eds.). (1967) *Ethnopharmacologic Search for Psychoactive Drugs.* Washington, D.C.: U.S. Government Printing Office.

Egan, Sean (Ed.) (1987). *S. M. Otieno: Kenya's Unique Burial Saga.* Nairobi: National Newspapers Publication.

Egan, Timothy (1992, Apr. 14). "Police Raid and Suit Open Window into Gypsy Life." *New York Times,* A16.

Eggleston, Elizabeth (1976). *Fear, Favour or Affection: Aborigines and the Criminal Law in Victoria, South Australia and Western Australia.* Canberra: Australian National University Press.

Ehrlich, Eugene (1985). *Amo, Amas, Amat and More: How to Use Latin to Your Own Advantage and to the Astonishment of Others.* New York: Harper and Row, 235–236.

Einesman, Floralynn (2000). "Cultural Issues in Motions to Suppress Statements." In James G. Connell III and Rene L. Valladares (Eds.), *Cultural Issues in Criminal Defense* (4-1–4-34). Yonkers, N.Y.: Juris.

Eisenberg, Leon (1981). "Cross-Cultural and Historical Perspectives on Child Abuse and Neglect." *Child Abuse and Neglect* 5, 299–308.

Eisenbruch, Maurice, and Lauren Handelman (1990). "Cultural Consultation for Cancer: Astrocytoma in a Cambodian Adolescent." *Social Science and Medicine* 31, 1295–1299.

El Chingoles: Primer Diccionario del Lenguaje Popular Mexicano (2nd ed.). (1973). Mexico.

Elias, Paul (1999, July 15). "Counsel Criticized in Case Involving Lincoln Manhunt." *Recorder,* 2.

Ellis, Richard, and Michael Thompson (Eds.) (1997). *Culture Matters: Essays in Honor of Aaron Wildavsky.* Boulder, Colo.: Westview Press.

Elon, Menachem, Bernard Auerbach, Daniel D. Chazin, and Melvin J. Sykers (Eds.) (1999). *Jewish Law (Mishpat Ivri): Cases and Materials.* New York: Matthew Bender.

Emmons, Steve (1998, Dec. 7). "Funeral Firms Feel Pressure of New Shoppers." *Los Angeles Times,* A3, 24–25.

Enge, Marilee (2000, June 4). "A Few Cups of Kava Land California Man in Court: Can Traditional Islander Drink Impair Driving?" *Arizona Republic,* A10.

Epps, Garrett (1998). "To an Unknown God: The Hidden History of *Employment Divison v. Smith.*" *Arizona State Law Journal* 30, 953–1021.

Epstein, Edward (1997, Apr. 22). "Supervisor Calls Animal Rights Lawsuits Biased." *San Francisco Chronicle,* A11, 13.

Erickson, Rosemary J., and Rita J. Simon (1998). *The Use of Social Science Data in Supreme Court Decisions*. Urbana: University of Illinois Press.

Erickson, Steve (1983, Mar.). "Ancient Art That's Edible." *PSA Magazine*, 90–91.

Ervin, Alexander (1980). "A Review of the Acculturation Approach in Anthropology with Special Reference to Recent Change in Native Alaska." *Journal of Anthropological Research* 36, 49–70.

Espinosa, Suzanne (1992, July 24). "Resistance to S. F. Ban on Animal Sacrifice." *San Francisco Chronicle*, A28.

Evans, E. P. (1906). *The Criminal Prosecution and Capital Punishment of Animals: The Lost History of Europe's Animals Trials*. London: Faber and Faber. Reissued in 1987.

Evans-Pritchard, Deirdre, and Alison Dundes Renteln (1994). "The Interpretation and Distortion of Culture: A Hmong 'Marriage by Capture' Case in Fresno, California." *Southern California Interdisciplinary Law Journal* 4, 1–48.

Fabrega, Horacio (1989). "Cultural Relativism and Psychiatric Illness." *Journal of Nervous and Mental Illness* 177, 415–430.

Fadiman, Anne (1997). *The Spirit Catches You and You Fall Down: A Hmong Child, Her American Doctors, and the Collision of Two Cultures*. New York: Farrar, Straus, Giroux.

Farhat, Laina (1996, Aug. 13). "Letter to the Editor." *San Francisco Chronicle*, A18.

Farm Animal Welfare Council (1985). *Report on the Welfare of Livestock When Slaughtered by Religious Methods*. London: Her Majesty's Stationery Office.

Faruqi, Anwar (1990, Dec. 16). "Iran's President Presses for Liberalization: Sermon Suggests Sex Really Is OK." *San Francisco Examiner*, A17.

Favazza, Armando R., and Barbara Favazza (1987). *Bodies under Siege: Self-Mutilation in Culture and Psychiatry*. Baltimore: Johns Hopkins University Press.

Favre, David S., and Murray Loring (1983). *Animal Law*. Westport, Conn.: Quorum Books.

Feinberg, Joel (1982). "Sentiment and Sentimentality in Practical Ethics." *Proceedings and Addresses of the America Philosophical Association* 56(1), 19–46.

———— (1985, Feb.). "The Mistreatment of Dead Bodies." *Hastings Center Report* 15(1), 31–37.

Felder, Myrna (1998, Apr. 18). "Are the 'Get' Statutes Constitutional?" *New York Law Journal*, 3.

Feldman, David M. (1984). "Rabbinic Comment: Autopsy." *Mount Sinai Journal of Medicine* 51(1), 82–85.

Feldman, Kenneth W. (1984). "Pseudoabusive Burns in Asian Refugees." *American Journal of Diseases of Children* 138, 768–769.

Feldman, Kerry D. (1980). "Ethnohistory and the Anthropologist as Expert Witness in Legal Disputes: A Southwestern Alaska Case." *Journal of Anthropological Research* 36, 245–257.

Feldman, Marc (1989–90). "Jewish Women and Secular Courts: Helping a Jewish Woman Obtain a Get." *Berkeley Women's Law Journal* 5, 139–169.

Fellner, Jonathan (1990, Mar. 28). "Racism Cited at Trial of 'Hooty' Croy." *Daily Journal* (San Francisco), 2.

———— (1990, Mar. 29). "Croy Details Discrimination: American Indian Testifies about Distrust of Whites during Childhood." *Daily Journal* (San Francisco), 2.

———— (1990, Mar. 30). "Croy, on the Witness Stand, Says He Lied in Earlier Trial." *Daily Journal*, 2.

Fernas, Rob (1995, Jan. 26). "State Sports Official Seeks to Clear Way for Team to Wear Yarmulkes." *Los Angeles Times*, B2.

Fingarette, Herbert (1974). "Diminished Mental Capacity as a Criminal Law Defence." *Modern Law Review* 37, 264–280.

Firmage, Edwin Brown, and Richard Collin Mangrum (1988). *Zion in the Courts: A Legal History of the Church of Jesus Christ of Latter-day Saints, 1830–1900*. Urbana: University of Illinois Press.

Firth, Raymond (1973). "Hair as Private Asset and Public Symbol." In Raymond Firth, *Symbols: Public and Private* (262–298). Ithaca, N.Y.: Cornell University Press.

Fischer, Michael (1998). "The Human Rights Implications of a 'Cultural Defense.'" *Southern California Interdisciplinary Law Journal* 6, 663–702.

Fisher, Douglas (1994, Nov. 16). "A Rock Solid Performance." *Toronto Sun*, 11.

Fiske, Alan Page et al. (1991). "The Cultural Matrix of Social Psychology." In Daniel T. Gilbert et al. (Eds.), *Handbook of Social Psychology* (Vol. 2, 915–981). New York: Oxford University Press.

Fletcher, George P. (1974). "The Individualization of Excusing Conditions." *Southern California Law Review* 47, 1269–1309.

Foblets, Marie-Claire (1998). "Cultural Delicts: The Repercussion of Cultural Conflicts on Delinquent Behaviour. Reflections on the Contribution of Legal Anthropology to a Contemporary Debate." *European Journal of Crime, Criminal Law and Criminal Justice* 6(3), 187–207.

Folk, Thomas R. (1986, Nov.). "The Military, Religion and Judicial Review: The Supreme Court's Decision in *Goldman v. Weinberger.*" *Army Lawyer* 5–10.

Follesdal, Andreas (1996). "Minority Rights: A Liberal Contractualist Case." In Juha Raikka (Ed.), *Do We Need Minority Rights?* (59–83). The Hague: Martinus Nijhoff.

Foster, C. T. (1971). "Annotation: Free Exercise of Religion as Defense to Prosecution for Narcotic or Psychedelic Drug Offense." *American Law Reports*, 3d. Vol. 35, 939–951. Rochester, New York: Lawyers Co-operative Publishing Co. See also Supplement, 143–146.

Fournier, Pascale (2002). "The Ghettoisation of Difference in Canada: 'Rape by Culture' and the Danger of a 'Cultural Defence' in Criminal Law Trials." *Manitoba Law Journal* 29, 81–119.

Fox, Sue (2000, June 10). "Riders Take Center Stage for Mexican Rodeo." *Los Angeles Times*, B4.

Frank, John, Roland Moore, and Genevieve Ames (2000). "Historical and Cultural Roots of Drinking Problems among American Indians." *American Journal of Public Health* 90, 344–351.

Frank, Lesley R. (1990). "Accommodating Religious Drug Use and Society's War on Drugs." *George Washington Law Review* 58, 1019–1043.

Frankena, Frederick (1985, Dec.). *The Social Science Practitioner as Expert Witness: A Bibliography*. Monticello, Ill.: Vance Bibliographies, 1–8.

Franklin, Karen (1985a, Mar. 24). "Man Says He Shot Woman to End Spell." *Daily Review*, 1–2.

––––––– (1985b, Mar. 29). "Jury Finds 'Hexed' Gunman Guilty of Assault." *Daily Review*, 1.

––––––– (1985c, May 12). "Man Who Says He Was Hexed Gets Seven Years for Shooting." *Enterprise*.

Freeman, M. D. A. (1996). "Law, Religion and the State: The Get Revisited." In Nigel Lowe and Gillian Douglas (Eds), *Families across Frontiers* (361–383). The Hague: Martinus Nijhoff.

Freeman, Michael (1995). "The Morality of Cultural Pluralism." *International Journal of Children's Rights* 3, 1–17.

Freud, Sigmund (1965). "Femininity." Lecture 33. *New Introductory Lectures on PsychoAnalysis* (112–135). Translated and edited by James Strachey. New York: Norton. (Originally published 1933.)

––––––– (1959). "Medusa's Head." In *Sigmund Freud: Collected Papers*, Vol. 5. Edited by James Strachey. New York: Basic Books, 105–106. (First published posthumously in 1940.)

Funder, Anna (1993). "*De Minimis Non Curat Lex*: The Clitoris, Culture and the Law." *Transnational Law and Contemporary Problems* 3, 417–467.

Furst, Peter T. (1976). *Hallucinogens and Culture*. San Francisco: Chandler and Sharp.

Gabarino, James, and Aaron Ebata (1983). "The Significance of Ethnic and Cultural Differences in Child Maltreatment." *Journal of Marriage and the Family* 45, 773–783.

Galanter, Marc (1981). "Justice in Many Rooms: Courts, Private Ordering, and Indigenous Law." *Journal of Legal Pluralism* 19, 1–47.

Gallin, Alice (1994). "The Cultural Defense: Undermining the Policies against Domestic Violence." *Boston College Law Review* 35, 723–745.

Gambell, Ray (1993). "International Management of Whales and Whaling: An Historical Review of the Regulation of Commercial and Aboriginal Subsistence Whaling." *Arctic* 46, 97–107

Gans, Herbert J. (1979). "Symbolic Ethnicity: The Future of Ethnic Groups and Cultures in America." In Herbert J. Gans et. al. (Ed.), *On the Making of Americans: Essays in Honor of David Riesman* (193–220). Philadelphia: University of Pennsylvania Press.

Garcia, Irene (1995, Jan. 22). "Team Harassed over Skullcaps." *Los Angeles Times*, B1, 5.

Gardner, Martin R. (1976). "The Renaissance of Retribution: An Examination of Doing Justice." *Wisconsin Law Review* 1976, 781–815.

Garkawe, Sam (1995, Mar.). "The Impact of the Doctrine of Cultural Relativism on the Australian Legal System." Elaw [electronic mail newsletter].

Garron, David C., Paul Thomas, P. J. W. Kersey, and George T. Watts (1988, Feb. 6). "Cupping Brings back Memories." *Lancet* 1, 310.

Gaspard, Francoise, and Farhad Khosrokhavar (1995). *Le Foulard et la Republique*. Paris: Editions La Decouverte.

Gathings, John T. Jr. (1989). "When Rights Clash: The Conflict between a Parent's Right to Free Exercise of Religion versus His Child's Right to Life." *Cumberland Law Review* 19, 585–616.

Gatrad, A. R. (1994). "Muslim Customs regarding Death, Bereavement, Postmortem Examinations and Organ Transplants." *British Medical Journal* 3, 120–122.

Gaw, Albert C. (Ed.) (1993). *Culture, Ethnicity, and Mental Illness*. Washington, D.C.: American Psychiatric Press.

Gearty, Robert (1996, July 9). "Arrested in Ritual Slashing of Boy, 6." *Daily News* (New York), 6.

Gekas, JoAnna A. (1987). "California's Prayer Healing Dilemma." *Hastings Constitutional Law Quarterly* 14, 395–419.

Geller, Stephen (1984a). "Autopsy." *Mount Sinai Journal of Medicine* 51(1), 77–81.

——— (1984b, June). "Religious Attitudes and the Autopsy." *Archives of Pathology and Laboratory Medicine* 108, 494–496.

Gellis, Sydney, and Murray Feingold (1976). "Picture of the Month: Cao Gio." *American Journal of Diseases of Children* 130, 857–858.

Gerstenzang, James (1998, May 6). "Eagle May Fly from Nest of Endangered." *Los Angeles Times*, A1, 25

Ghanem, Isam (1982). *Islamic Medical Jurisprudence*. London: Arthur Probsthain.

——— (1988). "Permission for Performing an Autopsy: The Pitfalls under Islamic Law." *Medical Science and Law* 28(3), 241–242.

Ghodsi, Tamilla F. (1994). "Tying a Slipknot: Temporary Marriages in Iran." *Michigan Journal of International Law* 15, 645–686.

Giannini, A. James, and Sam Castellani (1982). "A Manic-like Psychosis due to Khat." *Journal of Toxicology-Clinical Toxicology* 19, 455–459.

Giannini, A. James, et al. (1986). "Khat: Another Drug of Abuse?" *Journal of Psychoactive Drugs* 18, 155–158.

Gibbs, Walter (1999, Dec. 19). "Ideas and Trends: To Denmark, Something Is Rotten." *New York Times*, IV, 6.

Gilbert, Holley (1992, Jan. 8). "Mother Blamed in Poisonings." *Oregonian* (Portland), A1, 9.

Gilfoy, Peggy Stoltz (1987). *Patterns of Life: West African Strip-Weaving Traditions*. Washington, D.C.: Smithsonian Institution Press.

Gillam, Jerry (1994, Aug.31). "Sacramento File." *Los Angeles Times.*

Gilligan, Scott (1998, June). "Legal Liability for Autopsy and Organ Donation Cases." *Director* 55(6) 68–69.

Gilligan, T. Scott, and Thomas F. H. Stueve (1995). *Mortuary Law* (9th rev. ed.). Cincinnati: Cincinnati Foundation for Mortuary Education.

Gilmore, Norbert (1996). "Drug Use and Human Rights: Privacy, Vulnerability, Disability, and Human Rights Infringements." *Journal of Contemporary Health Law and Policy* 12, 355–447.

Glaberson, William (2003, Jan. 16). "Perjury Conviction in Asylum Case." *New York Times*, B4.

Glassman, Jeffrey (1980). "Free Exercise and the Attorney/Priest: The Clerical Collar in the Courtroom." *Fordham University Law Journal* 9, 51–87.

Gledhill, Lynda (1998, July 23). "Rights Group Loses Animal Cruelty Case: Chinatown Grocers Did Not Violate Laws." *San Francisco Chronicle*, A18.

——— (1998, Oct. 3). "Restrictions Asked on Merchants' Live Food Sales: Permits Would Be Needed from State." *San Francisco Chronicle*, A16.

Glionna, John M.(1995, May 22). "Inmates Demanding Their Rites." *Los Angeles Times*, A1, 8.

Glover, Malcolm (1991a, Jan. 15). "Teen Hero Slain in Drive-by Shooting: Police Suspect S. F. Gang Action." *San Francisco Examiner*, A1.

——— (1991b, Apr. 23). "Two Arrested in Drive-by Slaying." *San Francisco Examiner*, A6.

Gluckman, Max (1961). "Ethnographic Data in British Social Anthropology." *Sociological Review* 9, 5–17.

——— (1966). "The Logic in Witchcraft." In Max Gluckman, *Custom and Conflict in Africa* (81–108). Oxford: Basil Blackwell.

Gold, E. Richard (1996). *Body Parts: Property Rights and the Ownership of Human Biological Materials.* Washington, D.C.: Georgetown University Press.

Goldberg, Charlotte (1985, Dec.). "Autopsy and Religious Belief." *Los Angeles Lawyer* 8(9), 31–34.

Goldberger, Nancy Rule (1996). "Cultural Imperatives and Diversity in Ways of Knowing." In Goldberger et al. (Eds.), *Knowledge, Difference, and Power: Essays Inspired by Women's Ways of Knowing* (335–371). New York: Basic Books.

Golden, Judd (1985, winter). "Non-Indian Peyote Worshipers Acquitted on Drug Charges." *Civil Liberties*, 8.

Golden, Tim (1996, Aug. 26). "Cuisine Raises Debate on Cruelty and Culture." *New York Times*, A1, C8.

Goldfarb, Alan (1990). "A Kenyan Wife's Right to Bury Her Husband: Applying the Convention on the Elimination of All Forms of Discrimination against Women." *ILSA Journal of International Law* 14, 1–21.

Goldman, Ari (1994, Mar. 12). "Unauthorized Autopsy." *New York Times*, Section 1, 27, col. 1.

Goldstein, Beth L. (1986). "Resolving Sexual Assault: Hmong and the American Legal System." In Glenn L. Henricks, Bruce T. Downing, and Amos S. Deinard (Eds.), *The Hmong in Transition* (135–143). Staten Island, N.Y.: Center for Migration Studies of New York Inc. and The Southeast Asian Refugee Studies Project of the University of Minnesota.

Goldstein, Joseph (1977). "Medical Care for the Child at Risk: On State Supervention of Parental Autonomy." *Yale Law Journal* 86, 645–670.

Goldstein, Joseph, and Jay Katz (1963). "Abolish the "Insanity Defense"—Why Not?" *Yale Law Journal* 72, 853–876.

Goldstein, Joseph, Anna Freud, and Albert J. Solnit (1979). *Before the Best Interests of the Child.* New York: Free Press.

Goldstein, Taryn F. (1994). "Cultural Conflicts in Court: Should the American Criminal Justice System Formally Receognize a 'Cultural Defense'?" *Dickinson Law Review* 99, 141–168.

Goldstone, Michael S. (1993, May 19). "'Cat': Methcathinone—A New Drug of Abuse." *JAMA*, 269(19), 2508.

González-Villalpando, Clicerio (1993). "The Influence of Culture in the Authorization of an Autopsy." *Journal of Clinical Ethics* 4(2), 192–194

Gonzalez-Wippler, Migene (1975). *Santeria: African Magic in Latin America*. Garden City, N.Y.: Anchor Books/Doubleday.

Goodman, Ellen (1990, July 12). "Faith vs. Reason in Healing." *San Francisco Chronicle*, A21.

——— (1993, Mar. 5). "At Long Last, Women Are Being Counted as Part of the Human Race." *Los Angeles Times*, B7.

——— (2000, Mar. 23). "'Honor Killings': A Cultural Tradition." *San Francisco Chronicle*, A23.

Goodman, Jordan, Paul E. Lovejoy, and Andrew Sherratt (Eds.) (1995). *Consuming Habits: Drugs in History and Anthropology*. London: Routledge.

Gordon, April (1995, summer). "Gender, Ethnicity, and Class in Kenya: 'Burying Otieno' Revisited." *Signs* 20, 883–912.

Gordon, Larry (1988, May 7). "Jury Deadlocks in Campus Protest Case." *Los Angeles Times*, Pt. I, 28.

Gordon, Lou (1995, Feb. 5). "Anti-Semitism Is Not a Sport: The Valley Torah High Basketball Team Repeatedly Runs into Problems over Wearing Yarmulkes. The Real Issue Is One of Simple Prejudice." *Los Angeles Times*, B17.

Gordon, Milton (1964). *Assimilation in American Life*. New York: Oxford University Press.

Gordon, Neal A. (2001). "The Implications of Memetic for the Cultural Defense." *Duke Law Journal* 50, 1809–1834.

Goulet, Denis (1981). "In Defense of Cultural Rights: Technology, Tradition and Conflicting Models of Rationality." *Human Rights Quarterly* 3, 1–18.

Gourley, Perry (1990, Feb. 27). "Veil 'Fright' Excuse That Didn't Wash." *Lancashire Evening Telegraph*.

Grabmeier, Jeff (1984a, Feb. 22). "Surgeons Remove Laotian Tot's Eyes." *Columbus Citizen Journal*, 1A.

——— (1984b, Feb. 28). "Tot's Dad: 'Nobody Listened.'" *Columbus Citizen Journal*, 1A.

Grace, Bruce R. (1986). "Ignorance of the Law as an Excuse." *Columbia Law Review* 86, 1392–1416.

Graham, Joe S. (1976). "The Role of the Curandero in the Mexican American Folk Medicine System in West Texas." In Wayland D. Hand (Ed.), *American Folk Medicine: A Symposium* (175–189). Berkeley: University of California Press.

Gray, Autumn (1995). "Effects of the American Indian Religious Freedom Act Amendments on Criminal Law: Will Peyotism Eat Away at the Controlled Substances Act?" *American Journal of Criminal Law* 22, 769–807.

Gray, Ellen, and John Cosgrove (1985). "Ethnocentric Perception of Childrearing Practices in Protective Services." *Child Abuse and Neglect* 9, 389–396.

Green, Jennifer, and Michael Green (1992). *Dealing with Death: Practices and Procedures*. London: Chapman and Hall.

Green, L. C. (1975). "'Civilized' Law and 'Primitive' Peoples." *Osgoode Hall Law Journal* 13, 233–249.

Greenawalt, Kent (1998). "Religious Law and Civil Law: Using Secular Law to Assure Observance of Practices with Religious Significance." *Southern California Law Review* 71, 781–843.

Greenberg, Blu (1999). "Feminism, Jewish Orthodoxy, and Human Rights." In Carrie Gustafson and Peter Juviler (Eds.), *Religion and Human Rights: Competing Claims* (145–173). Armonk, N.Y.: M. E. Sharpe.

Greenberg-Kobrin, Michelle (1999). "Civil Enforceability of Prenuptial Agreements." *Columbia Journal of Law and Social Problems* 32, 359–380.

Gregory, R. J., and J. G. Peck (1988). "The Principle of Alien Poisons: Contrasting Psychopharmacology of Kava in Oceania and Australia." In J. Prescott and G. McCall (Eds.), *Kava Use and Abuse in Australia and the South Pacific* (29–39). Sydney: University of New South Wales, National Drug and Alcohol Research Centre.

Gregory, Robert J., Janet E. Gregory, and John G. Peck (1983). "Vanuatu: Kava and Conflicts of Colonialism." In Griffith Edwards, Awni Arif, and Jerome Jaffe (Eds.), *Drug Use and Misuse: Cultural Perspectives* (232–240). London: Croom Helm; New York: St. Martin's Press.

Griffin, Kevin (1992, Apr. 22). "Coin Cure Symbolic of Cultural Challenge." *Vancouver Sun*, B5.

Griffiths, John (1986). "What Is Legal Pluralism?" *Journal of Legal Pluralism* 24, 1–55.

Griffiths, Paul et al. (1997). "A Transcultural Pattern of Drug Use: Qat (Khat) in the UK." *British Journal of Psychiatry* 170(3), 281–284.

Grollman, Earl A. (1974). "The Jewish Way in Death and Mourning." In Earl A. Grollman (Ed.), *Concerning Death: A Practical Guide for the Living* (119–140). Boston: Beacon Press.

Guillermo, Emil (1997, Jan. 10). "Live Food Ban Applies to All of City: Any Chinatown Merchants Playing Race Card." *San Francisco Chronicle*, A27.

Gunby, Phil (1994, Jan. 12). "Could Late Spring Bring an End to US Military Medicine's 'New World Order' Role in Somalia?" *JAMA* 271(2), 92–96.

Gunn, T. Jeremy (1996). "Adjudicating Rights of Conscience under the European Convention of Human Rights." In Johan D. van der Vyver and John Witte Jr. (Eds.), *Religious Human Rights in Global Perspectives: Legal Perspectives* (305–330). The Hague: Martinus Nijhoff.

Gunning, Isabelle (1991–1992). "Arrogant Perception, World-Travelling and Multicultural Feminism: The Case of Female Genital Surgeries." *Columbia Human Rights Law Review* 23, 189–248.

Gunnison, Robert B. (1996, Sept. 24). "Wilson Signs Legislation Forbidding Genital Mutilation of Girls." *San Francisco Chronicle*, A17, A19.

Gurnon, Emily (1998, Mar. 8). "A Messy Food Fight." *San Francisco Examiner and Chronicle*, A1, 14.

Gurza, Agustin (1999, Sept.14). "Charro Spirit Survives and Suits Us Well." *Los Angeles Times*, B1.

——— (2000a, Feb. 29). "Concocting a Cultural Excuse for Child Abuse." *Los Angeles Times*, B1.

——— (2000b, Mar. 31). "Spanking: An Idea Whose Time Has Gone." *Los Angeles Times*, B1.

Gustkey, Earl (1996, June 21). "A Team of Cut-Ups." *Los Angeles Times*, C1, 7.

Gutmann, Amy (1993). "The Challenge of Multiculturalism in Political Ethics." *Philosophy and Public Affairs* 22, 171–206.

——— (Ed.) (1994). *Multiculturalism: Examining the Politics of Recognition*. Princeton, N.J.: Princeton University Press.

——— (Ed.) (1998). *Freedom of Association*. Princeton, N.J.: Princeton University Press.

Habenstein, Robert W., and William M. Lamers (1962). *The History of American Funeral Directing* (rev. ed.). Milwaukee: Bulfin Printers.

——— (1994) *Funeral Customs the World Over* (4th ed.). Revised by Howard C. Raether. Milwaukee: Bulfin Printers.

Haberman, Clyde (1999, Dec. 14). "NYC: Let It Snow, and Put out the Baby." *New York Times*, B1.

Haddad, Lester, Michael Shannon, and James Winchester (Eds.) (1998) "Peyote and Mescaline." In *Clinical Management of Poisoning and Drug Overdose* (3rd ed.). Philadelphia: W. B. Saunders.

Haeri, Shahla (1989). *Law of Desire: Temporary Marriage in Shi'i Iran.* Syracuse, N.Y.: Syracuse University Press.

Hafferty, William (1992, Nov.). "A Deadly Clash of Cultures." *San Francisco Focus,* 39(11), 64–71.

Hager, Philip (1988a, Mar. 6). "Prayer Healing Faces Court Test in Girl's Death." *Los Angeles Times,* 1, 38.

——— (1988b, Nov. 11). "Prosecution OKd in Prayer Healing Case." *Los Angeles Times,* 1, 24.

Hajrizi, Isuf (1995, Aug. 28–30). "Court Takes Children from Family: Experts Blame 'Cultural Misunderstanding.'" *Illyria* (Albanian-American newspaper) 5(427), 1, 7–8.

Halbach, H. (1975). "Khat: The Problem Today." In Louis S. Harris (Ed.), *Problems of Drug Dependence, 1979* (318–319). Washington, D.C.: Department of Health, Education and Welfare.

Haldane, David (1989a, Mar. 13). "Culture Clash or Animal Cruelty? Two Cambodian Refugees Face Trial after Killing Dog for Food." *Los Angeles Times,* Metro, 1, 6.

——— (1989b, Mar. 15). "Judge Clears Cambodians Who Killed Dog for Food." *Los Angeles Times,* Metro, 1, 4.

Hale, Sjarief (1970). "Kente Cloth of Ghana." *African Arts* 3(3), 26–29.

Hall, Jerome (1952). "Science and Reform in Criminal Law." *University of Pennsylvania Law Review* 100, 787–804.

——— (1958). "Culture, Comparative Law and Jurisprudence." In Jerome Hall, *Studies in Jurisprudence and Criminal Theory* (103–118). New York: Oceana Publications.

——— (1960). *General Principles of Criminal Law* (2nd ed.). Indianapolis: Bobbs-Merrill.

——— (1976). "Comment on Justification and Excuse." *American Journal of Comparative Law* 24, 638–645.

Hall, Stuart (1990). "Cultural Identity and Diaspora." In Jonathan Rutherford (Ed.), *Identity, Community, Culture, Difference* (222–237).

Hallpike, C. R. (1978). "Social Hair." In Ted Polhemus (Ed.), *The Body Reader: Social Aspects of the Human Body* (134–146). New York: Pantheon.

Halstuk, Martin (1990a, May 2). "S. F. Retrial Clears Indian in '78 Cop Death." *San Francisco Chronicle,* A1, 10.

——— (1990b, May 31). "Indian Jailed for 12 Years to Be Released Today." *San Francisco Chronicle,* B10.

Hancock, Ian (1992). "The Roots of Inequity: Romani Cultural Rights in Their Historical and Social Context." *Immigrants and Minorities* 11, 3–20.

——— (1996, summer). "American Roma: The Hidden Gypsy World." *Aperture* 144, 14–26.

Handler, Richard, and Jocelyn Linnekin (1984). "Tradition, Genuine or Spurious." *Journal of American Folklore* 97, 273–290.

Hankins, Stephen M. (1990). "The United States' Abuse of the Aboriginal Whaling Exception: A Contradiction in U.S. Policy and a Dangerous Precedent for the Whale." *U.C. Davis Law Review* 24, 489–530.

Hansen, Jane, and Deborah Scroggins (1992, Nov. 15). "Female Circumcision: U.S., Georgia Forced to Face Medical, Legal Issues." *Atlanta Journal,* A1.

Hanzlick, Randy, Debra Combs, R. Gibson Parrish, and Roy T. Ing (1993). "Death Investigation in the United States, 1990: A Survey of Statutes, Systems, and Educational Requirements." *Journal of Forensic Sciences,* 38(3), 628–632.

Harden, Blaine (1987, Feb. 13). "African Tradition and Modern Values: Tribal Loyalties Are Often at Odds with Nationalism." *International Herald Tribune,* 1.

——— (1990). "Battle for the Body." In Blaine Harden, *Africa: Dispatches from a Fragile Continent* (95–129). New York: Norton.

———— (1997, May 14). "Child Parked on New York Sidewalk Causes Stir." *Los Angeles Times*, A27.

Harper, Tom. (1974, Aug. 1). "Travellers' Tales." *New Law Journal* 124, 708.

Harris, Harry (1988, May 9). "Ancient Healing Practice or Child Abuse? Southeast Asian Coining Custom Alarms School Officials, Police." *Oakland Tribune*, A1–2.

Harris, Louis S. (Ed.) (1979). *Problems of Drug Dependence, 1979*. Washington, D.C.: Department of Health, Education, and Welfare.

Harris, Michael (1985, Apr. 30). "Insult." Proprietary to United Press International (a.m. cycle, NEXIS).

Harris, Paul (1997). *Black Rage Confronts the Law*. New York: New York University Press.

Harris, Scott (1988, July 21). "Ban Urged on Religious Sacrificing, Maiming of Animals." *Los Angeles Times*, 1, 18.

Harris-Abbott, Deborah (1994, Apr.). "Variations in Cultural Atittudes toward Autopsies." *Second Opinion*, 19(4), 92–95.

Hart, H. L. A. (1958). "Legal and Moral Obligation." In A. I. Melden (Ed.), *Essays in Moral Philosophy* (82–107). Seattle: University of Washington Press.

———— (1968). *Punishment and Responsibility: Essays in the Philosophy of Law*. New York: Oxford University Press.

Hart, Jonathan, and Richard Bauman (Eds.) (1996). *Explorations in Difference: Law, Culture, and Politics*. Toronto: University of Toronto Press.

Hartmann, Rev. H. (1928). "Some Customs of the Luwo (or Nilotic Kavirondo) Living in South Kavirondo." *Anthropos* 23, 263–275.

Hasemyr, David (1992, Dec. 10). "Pleas to State Boards often Unheeded." *San Diego Union-Tribune*, A11.

Hassman, Phillip E. (1978). "Unemployment Compensation: Eligibility as Affected by Claimant's Refusal to Comply with Requirements as to Dress, Grooming, or Hygiene." *American Law Reports* 3d Cases and Annotations 88, 150–171.

Hatfield, Larry D. (1995, June 14). "Family Seeks to Block Autopsy: Fears Endangering Soul of Daughter Who Drowned." *San Francisco Examiner*, A2.

Hauge, Hans-Egil (1974). *Luo Religion and Folklore*. Oslo: Universitetsforlaget.

Hays, Tom (2000, Apr. 26). "Yemeni Drug Makes Its Way to U.S.: Police Cracking Down on Khat, Stimulating Leaf Chewed Like Tobacco." *San Francisco Chronicle*.

Hayter, K. (1984). "Female Circumcision: Is There a Legal Solution?" *Journal of Social Welfare Law* 323–333.

Hazard, John N. (1962). "Furniture Arrangement as a Symbol of Judicial Roles." *ETC: A Review of General Semantics* 19, 181–188. Reprinted in Renteln and Dundes (1994).

Heckerling, Paul, and Melissa Williams (1992, Nov.). "Attitudes of Funeral Directors and Embalmers toward Autopsy." *Archives of Pathology and Laboratory Medicine* 116, 1147–1151.

Heimmel, Jennifer P. (1996, Dec. 2). "Husband and Wife: Court Has No Authority to Order a Party to Grant Jewish Divorce." *New Jersey Lawyer*, 35.

Heller, Kevin Jon (1998). "Beyond the Reasonable Man? A Sympathetic but Critical Assessment of the Use of Subjective Standards of Reasonableness in Self-Defense and Provocation Cases." *American Journal of Criminal Law* 26, 1–120.

Hellmich, Nanci (2000, July 19). "Foods with Kava, Gingko Are Labeled 'Snake Oil': FDA Ban Sought on Such 'Functional Foods.'" *USA Today*, 1D.

Hendricks, Glenn L., Bruce T. Downing, and Amos S. Deinard (Eds.) (1986). *The Hmong in Transition*. Staten Island, N.Y.: Center for Migration Studies of New York Inc. and the Southeast Asian Refugee Studies Project of the University of Minnesota.

Hepple, Bob, and Erika M. Szyszczak (Eds.) (1992). *Discrimination: The Limits of Law.* London: Mansell.

Herskovits, Melville J. (1937). "The Significance of the Study of Acculturation for Anthropology." *American Anthropologist* 39, 259–264.

Herzog, Harold, and Gordon Burghardt (1988). "Attitudes toward Animals: Origins and Diversity." In Andrew Rowan (Ed.), *Animals and People Sharing the World* (75–94). Hanover, N.H.: University Press of New England.

Hill, C. M., and A. Gibson (1987). "The Oral and Dental Effects of Q'at Chewing." *Oral Surgery, Oral Medicine, Oral Pathology* 3, 433–436.

Hill, Rolla B., and Robert E. Anderson (1988). *The Autopsy: Medical Practice and Public Policy.* Boston: Butterworths.

Hinch, Ronald (1987). "Cultural Deviance and Conflict Theories." In Rick Linden (Ed.), *Criminology: A Canadian Perspective* (177–198). Toronto: Holt, Rinehart and Winston.

Hirsch, Charles S. (1984, June). "Talking to the Family after an Autopsy." *Archives of Pathology and Laboratory Medicine* 108, 513–514.

Hitchler, Walter Harrison (1931). "Motive as an Essential Element of Crime." *Dickinson Law Review* 35, 105–118.

Hobsbawm, Eric, and Terence Ranger (Eds.) (1984). *The Invention of Tradition.* Cambridge: Cambridge University Press.

Hofstadter, Richard (1996). *The Paranoid Style in American Politics and Other Essays.* Cambridge: Harvard University Press.

Hogbin, H. Ian (1935). "Sorcery and Administration." *Oceania* 6, 1–32.

Hoge, Warren (1997, Oct. 18). "Women Marked for Death, by Their Own Families." *New York Times,* A4.

Holder, Angela R. (1985). *Legal Issues in Pediatrics and Adolescent Medicine* (2nd ed.). New Haven, Conn.: Yale University Press.

——— (1987). "Minors' Rights to Consent to Medical Care." *JAMA* 257, 3400–3402.

Holding, Reynolds (1996, Feb. 3). "Rastafarian Pot Could Be Legal." *San Francisco Chronicle,* A14.

Holmes, Lowell (1967). "The Function of Kava in Modern Samoan Culture." In Daniel H. Efron, et al. (Eds.), *Ethnopharmacologic Search for Psychoactive Drugs* (107–118). Washington, D.C.: U.S. Government Printing Office.

Holmquist, Kristen L. (1997). "Cultural Defense or False Stereotype? What Happens When Latina Defendants Collide with the Federal Sentencing Guidelines?" *Berkeley Women's Law Journal* 12, 45–72.

Holscher, Louis M. (1992). "Sweat Lodges and Headbands: An Introduction to the Rights of Native American Prisoners." *New England Journal on Criminal and Civil Confinement* 18, 33–62

Holzer, Henry Mark (1995). "Contradictions Will Out: Animals Rights vs. Animal Sacrifice in the Supreme Court." *Animal Law* 1, 79–102.

Homola, Victor (2002, Jan. 16). "Germany: Muslim Animal Slaughter Approved." *New York Times,* A9.

Hooker, M.B. (1975). *Legal Pluralism: An Introduction to Colonial and Neo-Colonial Law.* Oxford: Clarendon Press.

hooks, bell (1988) *Black Looks: Race and Representation.* Boston: South End Press.

Hopewell, Lynda K. (1987). "Appropriate Attire and Conduct for an Attorney in the Court Room." *Journal of the Legal Profession* 12, 177–189.

Hopper, Kim (1990). "Research Findings on Testimony: A Note on the Ethnographer as Expert Witness." *Human Organization* 49, 110–1113

Horn, Marilyn J., and Lois M. Gurel (1981). *The Second Skin: An Interdisciplinary Study of Clothing* (3rd ed.). Boston: Houghton Mifflin.

Horowitz, David (1989, July 5). "Moslem Father Kills Daughter for His Faith." *Jerusalem Post.*

Horton, Jennifer (1994). "A Personhood Analysis of Property Rights in the Human Body." *Revue Canadienne de Propriete Intellectuelle* 11, 213–231.

Houlberg, Marilyn Hammersley (1979). "Social Hair: Tradition and Change in Yoruba Hair-styles in Southwestern Nigeria." In Justine M. Cordwell and Ronald A. Schwarz (Eds.), *The Fabrics of Culture: The Anthropology of Clothing and Adornment* (349–397). The Hague: Mouton.

Houlgate, Laurence D. (1967). "Ignorantia Juris: A Plea for Justice." *Ethics* 78, 32–41.

Hovde, Christian A. (1978). "Cadavers: General Ethical Concerns." In Warren T. Reich (Ed.), *Encyclopedia of Bioethics* (Vol. 1, 139–143). New York: Free Press.

Howard, Colin. (1961) "What Colour Is the 'Reasonable Man'?" *Criminal Law Review* 41–48.

Howard, James H. (1962). "Peyote Jokes." *Journal of American Folklore* 75, 10–14

Howe, Kevin (1997, Mar. 27). "Cockfight Raid Second in Month." *Monterey County Herald,* C1.

Howell, Roy Carleton (1989). "The Otieno Case: African Customary Law Versus Western Jurisprudence." *Southern University Law Review* 16, 231–248.

Howenstein, Mark S. (1997). "Law, Identity and Difference in Multicultural America." *Legal Studies Forum* 21, 73–86.

Howman, Roger (1948). "Witchcraft and the Law." *Nada* 25, 7–18.

Hubler, Shawn (1987, Nov. 1). "Foreign Customs, Abuse Laws Clash in Schools." *Los Angeles Herald Examiner,* A1, 10.

Huelsman, B.R. (1976). "An Anthropological View of Clitoral and Other Female Genital Muti-lations." In T. P. Lowry and T. S. Lowry (Eds.), *The Clitoris* (111–161). St. Louis: Warren H. Green.

Hugh-Jones, Stephen (1995). "Coca, Beer, Cigars, and Yage: Meals and Anti-meals in an Amerindian Community." In Jordan Goodman, Paul E. Lovejoy, and Andrew Sherratt (Eds.), *Consuming Habits: Drugs in History and Anthropology* (47–66). London: Rout-ledge.

Hughes, Karen (1995). "The Criminalization of Female Genital Mutilation in the U.S." *Journal of Law and Policy* 4, 321–370.

Hultkrantz, Ake (1997). *The Attraction of Peyote: An Inquiry into the Basic Conditions for the Diffusion of the Peyote Religion in North America.* Stockholm: Almqvist and Wiksell Int'l.

Human Rights Committee (1994). "General Comment no. 23(5)." CCPR/C/21/Rev.1/Add5 (Apr. 26, 1994).

Humphrey, Norman Daymond (1943). "On Assimilation and Acculturation." *Psychiatry* 6, 343–345.

Huntington, Samuel (1997). *The Clash of Civilizations and the Remaking of World Order.* New York: Touchstone.

Hurd, Heidi Margaret (1988). "Relativistic Jurisprudence: Skepticism Founded on Confu-sion." *Southern California Law Review* 61, 1417–1509.

Hurtado, Daniel J. (1993). "Native American Graves Protection and Repatriation Act: Does It Subject Museums to a 'Taking'?" *Hofstra Property Law Journal* 6, 1–83.

Husak, Douglas N. (1989). "Motive and Criminal Liability." *Criminal Justice Ethics* 8, 3–14.

Hussain, Wajid (1992). "Post-Mortem Examination: The Qur'anic View." *Hamdard Islamicus* 15(3), 85–92.

Hyde, Alan (1997). *Bodies of Law.* Princeton, N.J.: Princeton University Press.

Ibrahim, Youssef M. (1994, Sept. 11). "Muslim Girls' Head Scarves Banned in French Schools." *New York Times,* 4.

Ima, Kenji, and Charles F. Hohm (1991). "Child Maltreatment among Asian and Pacific Islander Refugees and Immigrants." *Journal of Interpersonal Violence* 6, 267–285.

Irish, Donald P., Kathleen F. Lundquist, and Vivian Jenkins Nelsen (Eds.) (1993). *Ethnic Variations in Dying, Death, and Grief: Diversity in Universality.* London: Taylor and Francis.

Iserson, Kenneth V. (1994). *Death to Dust: What Happens to Dead Bodies.* Tucson: Galen Press.

Ives, Laurel (2000, Jan. 23). "Make Mine a Kava." *Sunday Times* (London).

Jackson, Cath (1991). "Should Angels Fear to Tread?" *Health Visitor* 64(8), 252–253.

Jackson, Percival E. (1950). *The Law of Cadavers and of Burial and Burial Places* (2nd ed.). New York: Prentice Hall.

Jackson, Robert (1996, May 3). "Unusual Asylum Case May Lead to New U.S. Guidelines." *Los Angeles Times,* A12.

Jacob, Marvin (1995). "The Agunah Problem and the New York State Get Law: A Legal and Halakhic Analysis." In Jack Nusan Porter (Ed.), *Women in Chains: A Source Book on the Agunah* (159–184). Northvale, N.J.: Aronson.

Jacobs, Paul (1989). "Governor Signs Pet Protection Bill but Opposes Penalties." *Los Angeles Times,* 3, 23.

Jacobsohn, Francoise (1989, May 9). "Letter to Gerald Stern, State of New York Commission on Judicial Conduct."

Jain, Harish C., and Peter J. Sloane (1981). *Equal Employment Issues: Race and Sex Discrimination in the United States, Canada, and Britain.* New York: Praeger.

Jakobivits, Immanel (1960). "The Dissection of the Dead in Jewish Law." *Hebrew Medical Journal* 2, 212–221.

———— (1969). "Jewish Law Faces Modern Problems." In Leon D. Stitskin (Ed.), *Studies in Torah Judaism* (395–401). New York: Yeshiva University Press.

James, D. S., and S. Leadbeatter (1996, Jan.). "Confidentiality, Death, and the Doctor." *Journal of Clinical Pathology* 49(1), 1–4.

Jayaratnam, Neelakanthi (1979). "Irresistible Impulse." *Colombo Law Review* 5, 103–114.

Jeter, Jon (1999, Jan. 20). "Arab Family Feels Cultural Crunch as State Removes Children." *Washington Post,* A3.

Jiobu, Robert M. (1988). *Ethnicity and Assimilation.* Albany: State University of New York.

Johnson, Dirk (1994, June 6). "Last-Chance Sale Lets Tough Horses Buck the Butcher." *San Jose Mercury News.*

Johnson, Ralph W., and Sharon I. Haensly (1992). "Fifth Amendment Takings Implications of the 1990 Native American Graves Protection and Repatriation Act." *Arizona State Law Journal* 24, 151–173.

Johnson, Sally J. (1992). "Honoring Treaty Rights and Conserving Endangered Species after *U.S. v. Dion.*" *Public Law Law Review* 13, 179–192.

Johnson, Sheri Lynn (1993). "Racial Imagery in Criminal Cases." *Tulane Law Review* 67, 1739–1805.

Johnstone, Diana (1990, Jan. 24–30). "In 'Great Kerchief Quarrel' French Unite against 'Anglo-Saxon Ghettos.'" *In These Times* (Chicago), 10, 11.

Jones, Richard, and Welhengama Gnanapala (2000). *English Minorities in English Law.* Oakhill, Stoke on Trent, U.K.: Trentham Book.

Jones, Terril (1994, Dec. 4). "Family Sentenced for Killing 'Disrespectful Daughter.'" *San Francisco Examiner and Chronicle,* A13.

Jones, Wanda, Jack Smith, Burney Kieke, Jr., et al. (1997). "Female Genital Mutilation/Female Circumcision: Who Is at Risk in the United States?" *Public Health Reports* 112, 368–377.

Joppke, Christian, and Steven Lukes (Eds.) *Multicultural Questions.* Oxford: Oxford University Press.

Joseph, Cathy (1996). "Compassionate Accountability: An Embodied Consideration of Female Genital Mutilation." *Journal of Psychohistory* 24, 2–17.

Joseph, Nathan (1986). *Uniforms and Nonuniforms: Communication through Clothing.* New York: Greenwood Press.

Joseph, Sarah (1996). *Interrogating Culture: Critical Perspectives on Contemporary Social Theory.* New Delhi: Sage.

Joy, Janet E., Stanley J. Watson Jr., and John A. Benson Jr. (Eds.) (1999). *Marijuana and Medicine: Assessing the Science Base.* Washington, D.C.: National Academy Press.

Judicial Studies Board (1994). *Handbook on Ethnic Minority Issues.* London: Judicial Studies Board.

Jung, Carolyn (1996, Jan. 14). "Female Circumcision Scars Bodies, Lives." *San Jose Mercury News,* 1A, 1H.

Kadish, Sanford H., and Stephen J. Schulhofer (1989). *Criminal Law and Its Processes: Cases and Materials* (5th ed.). Boston: Little, Brown.

Kalish, Richard A., and David K. Reynolds (1976). *Death and Ethnicity: A Psychocultural Study.* Los Angeles: Ethel Percy Andrus Gerontology Center, University of Southern California.

Kalix, Peter (1984). "The Pharmacology of Khat." *General Pharmacology* 15, 179–187.

——— (1987). "Khat: Scientific Knowledge and Policy Issues." *British Journal of Addiction* 87, 47–53.

——— (1988). "Khat: A Plant with Amphetamine Effects." *Journal of Substance Abuse and Treatment* 5, 163–169.

Kalland, Arne, and Brian Moeran (1990). *Endangered Culture: Japanese Whaling in Cultural Perspective.* Copenhagen: Nordic Institute of Asian Studies.

Kallen, Horace M. (1924). *Culture and Democracy in the United States: Studies in the Group Psychology of the American Peoples.* New York: Boni and Liveright.

Kamerman, Jack B. (1988). *Death in the Midst of Life: Social and Cultural Influences on Death, Grief, and Mourning.* Englewood Cliffs, N.J.: Prentice Hall.

Kandela, Peter (2000, Apr. 22). "Women's Rights, a Tourist Boom, and the Power of Khat in Yemen." *Lancet* 355(9213), 437.

Kang, Connie K. (1996, Aug. 8). "They've Got Luck All Figured Out." *Los Angeles Times,* E1, 3.

Kang, Connie K., and Miles Corwin (1996, July 9). Three Men Charged with Murder in Exorcism Death." *Los Angeles Times,* B3.

Kanter, Andrew M. (1995). "The Yenaldlooshi in Court and the Killing of a Witch: The Case for an Indian Cultural Defense." *Southern California Interdisciplinary Law Journal* 4, 411–454.

Karanja, Minneh M. (1987). "Otieno versus Ougo and Omolo: A Case Study of Conflict in Modern Kenya." L.L.M. thesis, Harvard University.

Karch, Steven B. (1996). *The Pathology of Drug Abuse* (2nd ed.). Boca Raton, Fla.: CRC Press.

Karibi-Whyte, A. G. (1977). "Cultural Pluralism and the Formulation of Criminal Policy." In Adedokun A. Adeyemi (Ed.), *Nigerian Criminal Process* (9–25). Lagos: University of Lagos.

Karst, Kenneth (1986). "Paths to Belonging: The Constitution and Cultural Identity." *North Carolina Law Review* 64, 303–377.

——— (1989). *Belonging to America: Equal Citizenship and the Constitution.* New Haven, Conn.: Yale University Press.

——— (1993). *Law's Promise, Law's Expression: Visions of Power in the Politics of Race, Gender, and Religion.* New Haven, Conn.: Yale University Press.

Karsten, Ian G.F. (1969). "Child Marriages." *Modern Law Review* 32, 212–217.

Kass, Leon R. (1985, Feb.). "Thinking about the Body." *Hastings Center Report* 15(1), 20–30.

Kass-Annese, Barbara (2000, Mar.). "Alternative Therapies for Menopause." *Clinical Obstetric and GYN* 43(1), 162–183.

Kassindja, Fauziya, and Layli Miller Bashir (1998). *Do They Hear You When You Cry?* New York: Delta.

Kassman, Martin (1997, July 9). "Unfree Exercise." *Recorder*, 4.

Kawanishi, Yuko (1990). "Japanese Mother-Child Joint Suicide: The Psychological and Sociological Implications of the Kimura Case." *UCLA Pacific Basin Law Journal* 8, 32–46.

Kay, Herma Hill (1985). "Models of Equality." *University of Illinois Law Review* 1985, 39–88.

Keedy, Edwin R. (1952). "Irresistible Impulse as a Defense in the Criminal Law." *University of Pennsylvania Law Review* 100, 956–993.

Keefe, J. E. Jr. (1950). "Failure to Provide Medical Attention for Child as Criminal Neglect." *American Law Reports, Annotated* (2nd) 12, 1047–1051.

Kehres, Kevin (1984, Feb. 26). "Laotian Baby out of Hospital." *Columbus Dispatch*, C3.

Keller, Bill (1994 Oct. 2). "Witch Burning South African Style." *San Francisco Chronicle*, 5.

Keller, Eugene L., and James Apthorp (1977). "Folk Remedies vs. Child Battering." *American Journal of Diseases of Children*, 131, 1173.

Kellner, Nancy Irene (1993). "Under the Knife: Female Genital Mutilation as Child Abuse." *Journal of Juvenile Law*, 14, 118–132.

Kelly, Nancy (1993). "Gender-Related Persecution: Assessing the Asylum Claims of Women." *Cornell International Law Journal* 26, 625–674.

Kelman, Mark (1991). "Reasonable Evidence of Reasonableness." *Critical Inquiry* 17, 798–817.

Kelsen, Hans (1946). *Society and Nature: A Sociological Inquiry*. London: Kegan Paul.

Kelson, Gregory A. (1995). "Granting Political Asylum to Potential Victims of Female Circumcision." *Michigan Journal of Gender and Law* 3, 257–298.

Kennedy, John G. (1987) *The Flower of Paradise: The Institutionalized Use of the Drug Qat in North Yemen*. Dordrecht: D. Reidel.

Kenworthy, Tom (1998, Aug. 9). "Spotlight on Utah Polygamy: Teenager's Escape from Sect Revives Scrutiny of Practice." *Washington Post*, A3

Kenyatta, Jomo (1965). *Facing Mount Kenya: The Tribal Life of the Gikuyu*. New York: Vintage.

Keysèr, Steven (2000, Aug.). "Autopsy: A Fact of Life." *Director* 72(8), 34–36.

Khan, Inayat, and Patrick H. Hughes (1979). "Assessment of Public Health and Social Problems associated with Khat Chewing." In Louis S. Harris (Ed.), *Problems of Drug Dependence, 1979* (316–317). Washington, D.C.: Department of Health, Education, and Welfare.

Khan, Shahnaz (1995). "Race, Gender, and Orientalism: Muta and the Canadian Legal System." *Canadian Journal of Women and Law* 81, 249–261.

Kilborn, Peter T. (2000, June 6). "The Rural Enclaves of U.S.: Cockfights Are Flourishing." *New York Times*, A1.

Kilham, Chris (1996). *Kava: Medicine Hunting in Paradise*. Rochester, Vt.: Park Street Press.

Kim, Nancy S. (1997). "The Cultural Defense and the Problem of Cultural Preexemption: A Framework for Analysis." *New Mexico Law Review* 27, 101–139.

King, Lester S., and Marjorie C. Meehan (1973). "A History of the Autopsy." *American Journal of Pathology*, 73(2), 514–544.

King, Nicole A. (1999). "The Role of Culture in Psychology: A Look at Mental Illness and the 'Cultural Defense.'" *Tulsa Journal of Comparative and International Law* 7, 199–225.

Kisliuk, Bill (1997, June 12). "In Brief." *Recorder*, 6.

Kitayama, Shinobu, Hazel Rose Markus, and Cary Lieberman (1995). "The Collective Construction of Self Esteem: Implications for Culture, Self, and Emotion." In J. A. Russell et al. (Eds.), *Everyday Conceptions of Emotion* (523–550). The Hague: Kluwer Academic.

Kleinman, Arthur, Leon Eisenberg, and Byron Good (1978). "Culture, Illness, and Care: Clinical Lessons from Anthropologic and Cross-Cultural Research." *Annals of Internal Medicine* 88, 251–258.

Klingshirn, A. (1971). "The Trial of a Witch: A Document from Ghana." *Africana Marburgensia* 4(1), 19–26.

Klitgaard, Robert (1997). "Applying Cultural Theories to Practical Problems." In Richard Ellis and Michael Thompson (Eds.), *Culture Matters: Essays in Honor of Aaron Wildavsky* (191–202). Boulder, Colo.: Westview Press.

Kluckhohn, Clyde, and William H. Kelly (1980). "The Concept of Culture." In Ralph Linton (Ed.), *The Science of Man in the World Crisis* (78–106). New York: Octagon Books.

Kolm, Richard (1980). *The Change of Cultural Identity: An Analysis of Factors Conditioning the Cultural Integration of Immigrants*. New York: Arno Press.

Konker, Claudia (1992). "Rethinking Child Sexual Abuse: An Anthropological Perspective." *American Journal of Orthopsychiatry* 62, 147–153.

Koptiuch, Kristin (1996). "'Cultural Defense' and Criminological Displacements: Gender, Race, and (Trans)nation in the Legal Surveillance of U.S. Diaspora Asians." In Smadar Lavie and Ted Swedenburg (Eds.), *Displacement, Diaspora, and Geographies of Identity* (215–233). Durham, N.C.: Duke University Press.

Korbin, Jill (1977). "Anthropological Contributions to the Study of Child Abuse." *Child Abuse and Neglect* 1, 7–24.

——— (1979). "A Cross-Cultural Perspective on the Role of the Community in Child Abuse and Neglect." *Child Abuse and Neglect* 3, 9–18.

——— (1980). "The Cross-Cultural Context of Child Abuse and Neglect." In C. Henry Kempe and Ray E. Helfer (Eds.), *The Battered Child* (3rd ed., 21–35). Chicago: University of Chicago Press.

——— (Ed.) (1981). *Child Abuse and Neglect: Cross-Cultural Perspectives*. Berkeley: University of California Press.

——— (1982). "What Is Acceptable and Unacceptable Child-Rearing: A Cross-Cultural Consideration." In Kim Oates (Ed.), *Child Abuse: A Community Concern* (256–265). New York: Brunner/Mazel.

——— (1987). "Child Maltreatment in Cross-Cultural Perspective: Vulnerable Children and Circumstances." In Richard J. Gelles and Jane B. Lancaster (Eds.), *Child Abuse and Neglect: Biosocial Dimensions* (31–55). New York: Aldine de Gruyter.

——— (1991). "Cross-Cultural Perspectives and Research Directions for the 21st Century." *Child Abuse and Neglect* 15(Supp. 1), 67–77.

Korbin, Jill, and Maxene Johnston (1982). "Steps toward Resolving Cultural Conflict in a Pediatric Hospital." *Clinical Pediatrics* 21, 259–263.

Koso-Thomas, Olayinka (1987). *The Circumcision of Women: A Strategy for Eradication*. London: Zed Books.

Kottler, Aaron (1952). "The Jewish Attitude on Autopsy." *New York State Journal of Medicine* 57, 1649–1650.

Kousser, J. Morgan (1990). "Are Expert Witnesses Whores? Reflections on Objectivity in Scholarship and Expert Witnessing." In Theodore J. Karamanski (Ed.), *Ethics and Public History: An Anthology* (31–44). Malabar, Fla.: Robert E. Krieger.

Kraft, Scott (1987a, Mar. 2). "Tribal Rites, Western Ways Clash in Kenya Burial Case." *Los Angeles Times*, 1, 8.

——— (1987b, Sept. 22). "Modern-Day African Turns to Old Magic." *Los Angeles Times*, 1, 12.

Krajewski-Jaime, Elvia R. (1991). "Folk-Healing among Mexican-American Families as a Consideration in the Delivery of Child Welfare and Child Health Care Services." *Child Welfare* 70, 157–167.

Kraut, Alan M. (1990). "Immigrant Attitudes toward the Physician in America: A Relationship in Historical Perspective." *JAMA* 263(13), 1807–1811.

Kressel, Gideon M. (1981). "Sororicide/Filiacide: Homicide for Family Honour." *Current Anthropology* 22, 141–152.

Krikorian, Abraham D. (1984). "Kat and Its Use: A Historical Perspective." *Journal of Ethnopharmacology* 12, 115–178.

Kroeber, A. L., and Clyde Kluckhohn (1952). *Culture: A Critical Review of Concepts and Definitions.* Cambridge, Mass.:The Museum.

Kukathas, Chandran (1992a). "Are There Any Cultural Rights?" *Political Theory* 20, 105–139.

——— (1992b). "Cultural Rights Again: A Rejoinder to Kymlicka." *Political Theory* 20, 674–680.

——— (1997). "Cultural Toleration." In Ian Shapiro and Will Kymlicka (Eds.), *Ethnicity and Groups Rights* (69–104). New York: New York University Press.

Kuper, Hilda (1973). "Costume and Identity." *Comparative Studies in Society and History* 15, 348–367.

Kymlicka, Will (1991). "Liberalism and the Politicization of Ethnicity." *Canadian Journal of Law and Jurisprudence* 4(2), 239–256.

——— (1992). "The Rights of Minority Cultures: Reply to Kukathas." *Political Theory* 20, 140–146.

——— (1995a). *Multicultural Citizenship.* Oxford: Clarendon Press

——— (1995b). *The Rights of Minority Cultures.* Oxford: Oxford University Press.

——— (1998a). "Ethnic Associations and Democratic Citizenship." In Amy Gutmann (Ed.), *Freedom of Association* (177–213). Princeton, N.J.: Princeton University Press.

——— (1998b). "Human Rights and Ethnocultural Justice." *Review of Constitutional Studies* 4, 213–238.

La Barre, Weston (1957). "Mescalism and Peyotism." *American Anthropologist* 59(4), 708–710.

——— (1960). "Twenty Years of Peyote Studies." *Current Anthropology* 1(1), 45–60.

——— (1980). "Obscenity: An Anthropological Appraisal." In Weston La Barre, *Culture in Context* (258–268). Durham, N.C.: Duke University Press.

——— (1989). *The Peyote Cult* (5th ed.). Norman: University of Oklahoma Press.

Lacayo, Richard (1993). "The 'Cultural' Defense." *Time* 142(21), 61.

Laderman, Gary (1996). *The Sacred Remains: American Attitudes toward Death, 1799–1883.* New Haven, Conn.: Yale University Press.

LaFave, Wayne R., and Austin W. Scott Jr. (1986). *Criminal Law* (2nd ed.). St. Paul: West.

La Fontaine, J. S. (Ed.) (1972). *The Interpretation of Ritual.* London: Tavistock.

Lait, Matt (1996, Sept. 2). "Agency's Role in Teen Weddings to Be Reviewed." *Los Angeles Times,* A3, 18.

Lam, Andrew (1989, Aug. 9). "Cuisine of a Pragmatic Culture." *San Francisco Chronicle,* A17.

Lam, Anh (1993). "Culture as a Defense: Preventing Judicial Bias against Asians and Pacific Islanders." *Asian American and Pacific Islands Law Journal* 1, 49–68.

Lane, Sandra D., and Robert A. Rubinstein (1996 May-June). "Judging the Other: Responding to Traditional Female Genital Surgeries." *Hastings Center Report,* 31–40.

Langenfeld, Christine (2003). "Developments: Germany." *International Journal of Constitutional Law* 1, 144–147.

Larson, Lori Ann (1996). "Female Genital Mutilation in the United States: Child Abuse of Constitutional Freedom." *Women's Rights Law Reporter* 17, 237–257.

Larson, Sven R. (1999, Dec. 20). "Danish Child Care." *New York Times,* A36.

Latimer, Leah Y. (1988, Jan. 19). "Union Assails Policies on Cornrows: Some Hotel Rules Said to Discriminate against Blacks." *Washington Post,* B3.

Laughran, Catherine W. (1975). "Religious Beliefs and the Criminal Justice System: Some Problems of the Faith Healer." *Loyola of Los Angeles Law Review* 8, 396–431.

Laurence, Robert (1988). "The Bald Eagle, the Florida Panther and the Nation's Word: An Essay on the 'Quiet' Abrogation of Indian Treaties and the Proper Reading of *U.S. V. Dion.*" *Journal of Land Use and Environmental Law* 4, 1–21.

Lauterbach, Jacob Z. (1970). "The Jewish Attitude toward Autopsy." In Jacob Z. Lauterbach *Studies in Jewish Law, Custom, and Folklore* (247–251). New York: KTAV Publishing. Originally published in *Central Conference of American Rabbis Year Book*, 35, 1925.

Lawless, Elaine J. (1986). "'Your Hair Is Your Glory': Public and Private Symbology of Long Hair for Pentecostal Women." *New York Folklore* 12, 3–4, 33–49.

Law Reform Commission (1986). *The Recognition of Aboriginal Customary Laws.* Vols. I and II. Canberra: Australian Government Publishing Service.

——— (1992). *Multiculturalism and the Law.* Sydney: Australian Government Publishing Service.

Lawrence, Elizabeth Atwood (1982). *Rodeo: An Anthropologist Looks at the Wild and the Tame.* Knoxville: University of Tennessee Press.

——— (1990). "Symbol of a Nation: The Bald Eagle in American Culture." *Journal of American Culture* 13, 63–69.

Laycock, Douglas (1990). "The Remnants of Free Exercise." *Supreme Court Review* 1990, 1–68.

Laymon, Lana (2001). "Valid-Where-Consummated: The Intersection of Customary Law Marriages and Formal Adjudication." *Southern California Interdisciplinary Law Journal* 10, 353–384.

Lazarus, Elizabeth (1988, Jan. 15). "Ease of Care, Cultural Identity Woven into Hair Styles." *Washington Post*, E1, 2.

Le, Tony (1997, Apr. 22), "Letter to the Editor: Cultural Bias." *San Francisco Chronicle*, A16.

Leach, Edmund (1964). "Anthropological Aspects of Language: Animal Categories and Verbal Abuse." In Eric H. Lenneberg (Ed.), *New Directions in the Study of Language* (23–63). Cambridge: MIT Press.

——— (1972). "The Structure of Symbolism: Kava Ceremony in Tonga." In J. S. La Fontaine (Ed.), *The Interpretation of Ritual* (239–275). London: Tavistock.

Leader-Elliott, Ian (1996, Apr.). "Sex, Race, and Provocation: In Defense of Stingel." *Criminal Law Journal* 20, 72–96.

Lears, T. J. Jackson (1985). "The Concept of Cultural Hegemony: Problems and Possibilities." *American Historical Review* 90, 567–593.

LeBlanc, Lawrence J. (1995). *The Convention on the Rights of the Child: United Nations Lawmaking on Human Rights.* Lincoln: University of Nebraska Press.

Lebot, Vincent, Mark Merlin, and Lamont Lindstrom (1992). *Kava: The Pacific Drug.* New Haven, Conn.: Yale University Press

Lee, Henry K. (1995, June 15). "Family Prevails—No Autopsy for Drowning Victim: Judge Rules against S. F. Coroner." *San Francisco Chronicle*, A23.

——— (1996, Nov. 15). "Preliminary Ban on Sale of Animals: Chinese Residents Call It an Attack on Their Culture." *San Francisco Chronicle*, A21, 23.

——— (1998, June 2). "Sikh to Contest Citation for Ceremonial Knife." *San Francisco Chronicle*, A15, 16.

Lee, Henry, and Stephen Schwartz (1996, Oct. 3). "Faithful Worship in Pace at Troubled Sikh Temple." *San Francisco Chronicle*, 18.

Lee, Nella (1995). "Culture Conflict and Crime in Alaskan Native Villages." *Journal of Criminal Justice* 23, 177–189.

Leeson, Fred (1992, Feb. 11). "Mental Defense Seen in Poisoning Case." *Oregonian* (Portland), D6.

——— (1992, Sept. 23). "Mother Who Killed Two May Get 20 Years." *Oregonian* (Portland), B1.

Leichter, Alexandra (1998, July). "The Problem of Getting the 'Get'; Impact of Jewish Divorce Law on Matrimonial Litigation." *Matrimonial Strategist* 16(6), 4.

Leikind, Robert (1986). "Regulating the Criminal Conduct of Morally Innocent Persons: The Problem of the Indigenous Defendant." *Boston College Third World Law Journal* 6, 161–184.

Lemert, Edwin M. (1967). "Secular Use of Kava in Tonga." *Quarterly Journal of Studies on Alcohol* 28, 328–341.

Lemoine, Jacques (1986). "Shamanism in the Context of Hmong Resettlement." In Glenn L. Henricks, Bruce T. Downing, and Amos S. Deinard (Eds.), *The Hmong in Transition* (337–348). Staten Island, N.Y.: Center for Migration Studies of New York Inc. and the Southeast Asian Refugee Studies Project of the University of Minnesota.

Lempert, Richard (1981). "Desert and Deterrence: An Assessment of the Moral Bases of the Case for the Death Penalty." *Michigan Law Review* 79, 1177–1231.

Lenihan (1995). "A Physician's Dilemma: Legal Ramifications of an Unorthodox Surgery." *Santa Clara Law Review* 35, 953–1231.

Leong, Gregory B., and J. Arturo Silva (1989). "Asian American Forensic Psychiatrists." *Psychiatric Annals* 19, 629–632.

Leung, Alexander K. C. (1986). "Ecchymoses from Spoon Scratching Simulating Child Abuse." *Clinical Pediatrics* 25(2), 98.

Leusner, Jim, and Susan Jacobson (Aug. 17, 1997). "Two Dealers of Reptiles Go to Jail." *Orlando Sentinel.*

Levy, Jacob (1997). "Classifying Cultural Rights." In Ian Shapiro and Will Kymlicka (Eds.), *Ethnicity and Groups Rights* (22–66). New York: New York University Press.

Lewis, Justin (1958). "The Outlook for a Devil in the Colonies." *Criminal Law Review* 661–675.

Lewis, Rita (1992a, June 16). "Wu Testifies Shame Played Part in Slaying: Chinese Mother Wanted to Escape Unhappy Marriage." *Desert Sun* (Palm Springs), A5.

———— (1992b, June 18). "Chinese Culture Used as Defense during Wu Trial." *Desert Sun*, A9.

———— (1992c, June 19). "Culture Shaped Decision to Kill, Expert Testifies." *Desert Sun*, A5.

———— (1992d, July 25). "Wu Sentencing Postponed; Officials to Evaluate Case." *Desert Sun*, A3.

Li, Jisheng (1996). "Culture as a Defense: An Ignored Factor in Determining the Application of the Cultural Defense." *University of Hawaii Law Review* 18, 765–796.

Lidz, Victor (1995). "Death: Anthropological Perspectives." In Warren Thomas Reich (Ed.), *Encyclopedia of Bioethics* (rev. ed.; vol. 1, 477–487). New York: Simon and Schuster/ Macmillan.

Lindsay, Sue (1995, June 2). "Killer Gets Life for Slaying at Food Court." *Denver Rocky Mountain News*, 30A.

Lindstrom. Lamont (Ed.) (1987). *Drugs in Western Pacific Societies: Relations of Substance.* New York: University Press of America.

Linton, Ralph (1961). *The Tree of Culture.* New York: Alfred A. Knopf.

Linzey, Andrew (1991) *Christianity and the Rights of Animals.* New York: Crossroad.

Littman, Rachel J. (1997). "Adequate Provocation, Individual Responsibility, and the Deconstruction of Free Will." *Albany Law Review* 60, 1127–1170.

Lloyd, Peter (1974, Sept./Oct.). "The Case of Mrs. Adesanya." *RAIN: Royal Anthropological Institute News*, No. 4, 2.

Lobenz, Leo (1994, May 15). "Letter." *Los Angeles Times Magazine*, 5.

Lock, Margaret M. (1978). "Scars of Experience: The Art of Moxibustion in Japanese Medicine and Society." *Culture, Medicine, and Psychiatry* 2, 151–175.

Lockwood, William G., and Sheila Salo (1994). *Gypsies and Travelers in North America: An Annotated Bibliography.* Publication 6.Cheverly, Md.: Gypsy Lore Society.

Lolli, G, et al. (1958). *Alcohol in Italian Culture: Food and Wine in Relation to Sobriety among Italians and Italian Americans.* New Haven, Conn.: Yale Center of Alcohol Studies.

Louisna, Gariot (1998, Aug. 31). "Discipline, Abuse Meet Head-on in Culture Clash." *Caribbean Today* 9(9), 31.

Lowie, Robert H. (1955). "Peyote Rite." In James Hastings (Ed.), *Encyclopaedia of Religion and Ethics* (vol. 9, 815). New York: Scribner's.

Lowthian, Annie E. (1994, Sept./Oct.). "Sikhs and Jews Face 'Disheartening Struggle' against Canadian Legion Rules Banning Religious Headgear." *Human Rights Tribune* 2(4).

Lucas, Greg (1994, Aug. 30). "Now It's a Crime to Trip a Horse." *San Francisco Chronicle.*

———— (1997, Dec. 13). "Sikhs, Muslims, American Indians Protest Prison Hair Rules." *San Francisco Chronicle,* A18.

Luqman, Wijdan, and T. S. Danowski (1976). "The Use of Khat (*Catha edulis*) in Yemen: Social and Medical Observations." *Annals of Internal Medicine* 85, 246–249.

Ly, Choua (2001). "The Conflict between Law and Culture." *Wisconsin Law Review* 2001, 471–499.

Lyman, John C. (1986). "Cultural Defense: Viable Doctrine or Wishful Thinking." *Criminal Justice Journal* 9, 87–117.

Lynch, April (1996, Nov. 16). "Supervisors Unlikely to Stop Animal Sales: S. F. Board Shows Little Interest in Ban." *San Francisco Chronicle,* A1, 15.

Lyons, Harriet (1981). "Anthropologists, Moralities and Relativities: The Problem of Genital Mutilations." *Canadian Review of Sociology and Anthropology* 18, 499–518.

Ma, Veronica (1995). "Cultural Defense: Limited Admissibility for New Immigrants." *San Diego Justice Journal* 3, 461–484.

MacCannell, Dean (1979). "Ethnosemiotics." *Semiotica* 27(1/3), 149–171.

MacGregor, Hilary (1998, Jan. 25). "Faith and Food." *Los Angeles Times,* A3.

MacInnes, Nicole (1988, Aug. 22). "Letter to Deputy District Attorney, Seattle."

Mackay, R. D. (1983). "Is Female Circumcision Unlawful?" *Criminal Law Review,* 717–722.

Macklem, Timothy (1987). "Provocation and the Ordinary Person." *Dalhousie Law Journal* 11, 126–156.

Maddock, Kenneth (1992, July). "Culture and Culpability: Notes towards a Belated Response." *Commission on Folk Law and Legal Pluralism Newsletter* 21, 64–67.

Maeda, Donna K. (2000). "Subject to Justice: The 'Cultural Defense' and Legal Constructions of Race, Culture, and Nation." In C. Richard King (Ed.), *Postcolonial America* (81–100). Urbana: University of Illinois Press.

Magnarella, Paul J. (1991). "Justice in a Culturally Pluralistic Society: The Cultural Defense on Trial." *Journal of Ethnic Studies* 19, 65–84.

Magnier, Mark (1998, Nov. 5). "Putting the Squeeze on the Dead." *Los Angeles Times,* A1, 13.

Maguigan, Holly (1995). "Cultural Evidence and Male Violence: Are Feminist and Multicultural Reformers on a Collision Course in Criminal Courts?" *New York University Law Review* 70, 36–99.

———— (1999). "Will Prosecutions for 'Female Genital Mutilation' Stop the Practice in the U.S.?" *Temple Political and Civil Rights Law Review* 8, 391–423.

Maharaj, Davan (1999, Feb. 11). "Taco Bell Settles Suit with Hindu over Meal Order." *Los Angeles Times,* C1, 2.

Maier, Silvia (2001). "Multicultural Jurisprudence: A Study of the Legal Recognition of Cultural Minority Rights in France and Germany." Ph.D. diss., University of Southern California.

Malecha, Wayne F. (1985). "Faith Healing Exemptions to Child Protection Laws: Keeping the Faith versus Medical Care for Children." *Journal of Legislation* 12, 243–263.

Malinowski, Bronislaw (1937). "Culture." In Edwin R. A. Seligman (Ed.), *The Encyclopedia of the Social Sciences* (621–645). New York: Macmillan.

Mandel, Ruth (1989). "Turkish Headscarves and the 'Foreigner Problem': Constructing Difference through Emblems of Identity." *New German Critique* 46, 27–46.

Mandelbaum, David. G. (1965). "Social Uses of Funeral Rites." In Herman Feifel (Ed.), *The Meaning of Death* (189–217). New York: McGraw-Hill.

Mandell, Louise (1987). "Native Culture on Trial." In Sheilah L. Martin and Kathleen E. Mahoney (Eds.), *Equality and Judicial Neutrality* (358–365). Toronto: Carswell.

Manson, Bill (1993, Dec. 12). "For Cockfighters, 'It All Comes Down to This Moment.'" *Los Angeles Times*, E4.

Marcosi, Richard (1998a, Dec. 3). "Attorney Has Case of a Lifetime." *Los Angeles Times*, B1, 6.

———— (1998b, Dec. 15). "Siripongs Gets New Execution Date: Will Take Appeal to Davis." *Los Angeles Times*, A3.

Marcosi, Richard, and Greg Hernandez (1999 Feb. 9). "Convicted Killer Siripongs Put to Death." *Los Angeles Times*, A1, 18.

Marcosi, Richard, and Daniel Yi. (1998, Nov. 15). "Friends and Foes Offer Conflicting Pictures of Killer." *Los Angeles Times*, A34.

Marcuse, Herbert (1969). "Repressive Tolerance." In Robert Paul Wolff (Ed.), *A Critique of Pure Tolerance* (81–123). Boston: Beacon Press.

Marimow, Ann E. (2000, Nov, 27). "DA Targets Kava Plant." *San Jose Mercury News*.

Markman, Ronald, and Dominick Bosco (1989). *Alone with the Devil.* New York: Doubleday.

Markus, Hazel Rose, and Shinobu Kitayama (1991a). "Culture and the Self: Implications for Cognition, Emotion, and Motivation." *Psychological Review* 98, 224–253.

———— (1991b). "Cultural Variation in the Self-Concept." In J. Strauss and G. R. Goenthals (Eds.), *The Self: Interdisciplinary Approaches* (18–48). New York: Springer-Verlag.

Markus, Hazel Rose, and Leah Lin (1999). "Conflictways: Cultural Diversity in the Meanings and Practices of Conflict." In Deborah Prentice and Dale Miller (Eds.), *Cultural Divides: Understanding and Overcoming Group Conflict* (302–333). New York: Russell Sage.

Marriott, Michel (1992, July 5). "Kente Cloth." *New York Times*, V8.

Marsack, C.C. (1959). "Provocation in Trials for Murder." *Criminal Law Review*, 697–704.

Marsh, Wallace W., and Kae Hentges (1988). "Mexican Folk Remedies and Conventional Medical Care." *American Family Physician* 37(3), 257–262.

Marsh, Wallace W., and Mary Eberle (1987). "Curanderismo Associated with Fatal Outcome in a Child with Leukemia." *Texas Medicine* 83(2), 38–40.

Marshall, Jonathan (1990, Dec. 17). "Undertaker Sued over Pig in Coffin: Mortuary Accused of Anti-Semitism." *San Francisco Chronicle*, A3.

Marshall, Lawrence (1986). "The Religion Clauses and Compelled Religious Divorces: A Study in Marital and Constitutional Separations." *Northwestern University Law Review* 80(1), 204–258.

Marshall, Mac (1987). "An Overview of Drugs in Oceania." In Lamont Lindstrom (Ed.), *Drugs in Western Pacific Societies: Relations of Substance* (1–49). New York: University Press of America.

Martin, Nina (1992). "When Cultures Collide: Immigrants, Prosecutors and Social Workers Can't Decide How Old-Country Customs Fit into the New World's Order." *California Lawyer* 12(11), 22–25.

Martinez, Don (1985, May 9). "Ethiopian Gets Seven Years for Voodoo Shooting but No Deportation." *San Francisco Examiner*, B4.

Matier, Phillip, and Andrew Ross (1995, June 14). "Grieving Buddhist Family Clashes with Coroner." *San Francisco Chronicle*, A1.

Matsuda, Mari J. (1991) "Voices of America: Accent, Antidiscrimination Law, and a Jurisprudence for the Last Reconstruction." *Yale Law Journal* 100, 1329–1407.

Matsumoto, Alison (1995). "A Plea for Consideration of Culture in the American Criminal Justice System: Japanese Law and the Kimura Case." *Journal of International Law and Practice* 4, 507–538.

Matthews, Paul (1983). "Whose Body? Whose Property?" *Current Legal Problems* 38, 194–239.

May, William (1972). "Attitudes toward the Newly Dead." *Hastings Center Studies* 1(1), 3–13.

——— (1985). "Religious Justifications for Donating Body Parts." *Hastings Center Report*, 14, 38–42.

Mazur, Eric Michael (1999). *The Americanization of Religious Minorities: Confronting the Constitutional Order*. Baltimore: Johns Hopkins University Press.

McCaghy, Charles, and Arthur Neal (1974). "The Fraternity of Cockfighters: Ethical Embellishments of an Illegal Sport." *Journal of Popular Culture*, 557–569. Reprinted in Dundes (1994).

McCarthy, Michael (1999, Mar. 27). "New Antidepressants No Better Than Old." *Lancet* 353(9158), 1073.

McCaslin, Megan (1985, Sept. 5). "Immigrant's Suicide Attempt Marks Death of a Dream, Birth of a Cause: Japanese American's Trial Widely Followed in Homeland." *Washington Post*, A12.

McClean, Scilla, and Stella Efua Graham (1985). *Female Circumcision, Excision, and Infibulation* (2nd rev. ed.). Report no. 47. London: Minority Rights Group.

McClintock, Pam (1987, Dec. 18). "EEOC Asked to Act in Cornrow Dispute." *Washington Times*, D3.

——— (1988a, Jan. 7). "Hotel's Hair Stand Grows Less Certain." *Washington Times*, A1, 11.

——— (1988b, Jan. 12). "Cornrow Hairstyle Has Ancient Roots." *Washington Times*, E1, 2.

——— (1988, Apr. 7). "Smithsonian Retreats in Cornrows Skirmish." *Washington Times*, A1, 10.

——— (1988c, Apr. 14). "Coiffeurs of Cornrow Win Official Approval." *Washington Times*, C1, 12.

——— (1988d, Jul. 8). "Marriott Stung for $40,000 in Settling Cornrows Episode." *Washington Times*, A1, 10.

——— (1988e, Aug. 26). "D.C. Drops Its Probe of Hair Policy at Hyatt." *Washington Times*, C1.

McConnell, Michael W., and Richard A. Posner (1989). "An Economic Approach to Issues of Religious Freedom." *University of Chicago Law Review* 56, 1–60.

McCormick, Susan (1999, Dec. 15). "Leaving Baby Outside: Not in New York." *New York Times*, A26.

McCrossin, G. Michael (1980). "General Laws, Neutral Principles, and the Free Exercise Clause." *Vanderbilt Law Review* 33, 149–174.

McCullough, Marie (1995, May 30). "Medical Conditions Can Look Like Child Abuse." *Chicago Tribune*, Tempo section, 3.

McDonald, R. Robin (2000, Mar. 8). "Harvey: Client in Altered State When Ex-Lover Was Murdered." *Fulton County Daily Report*.

McElroy, Ann, and Patricia K. Townsend (1989). *Medical Anthropology in Ecological Perspective* (2nd ed.). Boulder, Colo.: Westview Press.

McGillivray, Anne (1992). "Reconstructing Child Abuse: Western Definition and Non-Western Experience." In M. Freeman and P. Veerman (Eds.), *The Ideologies of Children's Rights* (213–236). The Hague: Kluwer.

McGoldrick, Dominic (1991). "Canadian Indians, Cultural Rights, and the Human Rights Committee." *International and Comparative Law Quarterly* 40, 658–669.

McInnis, Kathleen (1991). "Ethnic-Sensitive Work with Hmong Refugee Children." *Child Welfare* 70, 578.

McLeod, W.H. (2000). *Exploring Sikhism: Aspects of Sikh Identity, Culture, and Thought.* New Delhi: Oxford University Press.

McMillan, Penelope (1989, Mar. 28). "Pets Are Not Food in U.S.: S.P.C.A. Will Advise Immigrants." *Los Angeles Times*, Pt. II, 3.

McNamara, Joseph D. (1996, May 19). "A Former Police Chief's Plea to Clinton's New Drug Czar." *Washington Post*, C3.

McPhail, Beverly (1996, Feb. 26). "Unacceptable in Any Culture and in Any Country." *Houston Chronicle*, 17.

McPhatter, Anna R. (1997). "Cultural Competence in Child Welfare: What Is It? How Do We Achieve It? What Happens without It?" *Child Welfare* 76, 255–278.

McQuiston, John T. (1986, Dec. 28). "Jewish Divorce Law Plagues Wives." *New York Times*, B35.

Mead, Margaret (1963). "Socialization and Enculturation." *Current Anthropology* 4(2), 184–188.

Mendelsohn, Oliver, and Upendra Baxi (Eds.) (1994). *The Rights of Subordinated Peoples.* Delhi: Oxford University Press.

Mendus, Susan (Ed.) (2000). *The Politics of Toleration in Modern Life.* Durham, N.C.: Duke University Press

Mengel, Reiner et al. (1996). "Peridontal Status of a Subject Sample of Yemen." *Journal of Clinical Periodontology* 23(95), 437–443.

Mercer, Kobena (1990). "Black Hair/Style Politics." In Russell Ferguson et al. (Eds.), *Out There: Marginalization and Contemporary Cultures* (247–264). New York: New Museum of Contemporary Art; Cambridge: MIT Press.

Merry, Sally Engle (1988). "Legal Pluralism." *Law and Society Review* 22, 869–896.

Merwin, W. S. (1989, Aug. 6,). "The Sacred Bones of Maui." *New York Times*, VI, 21.

Messito, Carol M. (1997–1998). "Regulating Rites: Legal Responses to Female Genital Mutilation in the West." *In Public Interest* 16, 33.

Metzger, Michael (1988, July). "Exculpatory Group Behavior Patterns, or, 'If My Client Wasn't Involved in a Drug Deal, Why Was He Carrying a Gun?' " *Champion*, 18–19, 36.

Mews, Alastair (1985, Wint.). "Religious Slaughter: Rite or Wrong?" *RSPCA Today*, 19.

Meyerhoff, Barbara G. (1974). *Peyote Hunt: The Sacred Journey of the Huichol Indians.* Ithaca, N.Y.: Cornell University Press.

Meyers, David (1990). *The Human Body and the Law* (2nd ed.). Stanford, Calif.: Stanford University Press.

Miller, Bruce G. (1998). "Culture as Cultural Defense." *American Indian Quarterly* 22, 83–97.

Miller, Carol (1975). "American Rom and the Ideology of Defilement." In Farnham Rehfisch (Ed.), *Gypsies, Tinkers and Other Travellers* (41–54). London: Academic Press.

Miller, Jessica Davidson (1997). "The History of the Agunah in America: A Clash of Religious Law and Social Progress." *Women's Rights Law Reporter* 19, 1–15.

Miller, Robert J. (2000). "Exercising Cultural Self-Determination: The Makah Indian Tribe Goes Whaling." *American Indian Law Review* 165–197.

Milloy, Courtland (1988, Jan. 7). "Curbing a Centuries-Old Fad." *Washington Post*, J1.

Miner, Jeffrey (1994). "*U.S. v. Zapata:* The Tenth Circuit Rejects Cultural Background and Nationality as Part of Fourth Amendment Seizure Analysis." *Journal of Contemporary Law* 20, 236–244.

Minow, Martha (1990). *Making All the Difference: Inclusion, Exclusion, and American Law.* Ithaca, N.Y.: Cornell University Press.

———— (1991). "Identities." *Yale Journal of Law and the Humanities* 3(1), 97–130.

———— (1995). "Rights and Cultural Difference." In Austin Sarat and Thomas R. Kearns (Eds.), *Identities, Politics, and Rights* (347–365). Ann Arbor: University of Michigan Press.

Minow, Martha, and Todd Rakoff (1998). "Is the "Reasonable Person" a Reasonable Standard in a Multicultural World?" In Austin Sarat et al. (Eds.), *Everyday Practices and Trouble Cases* (40–67). Evanston, Ill.: Northwestern University Press.

Mitchell, Rick (1988, Feb. 7). "Power of the Orishas: Santeria, an Ancient Religion from Nigeria, Is Making Its Presence Felt in Los Angeles." *Los Angeles Times Magazine*, 16–21, 30.

Mitford, Jessica (1998). *The American Way of Death Revisited*. New York: Alfred A. Knopf.

Mittleman, Roger E., Joseph H. David, Warren Kasztl, and Wallace M. Graves (1992, May). "Practical Approach to Investigate Ethics and Religious Objections to the Autopsy." *Journal of Forensic Sciences* 37(3), 824–829.

Monahan, John (1984, Jan.). "The Prediction of Violent Behavior: Toward a Second Generation of Theory and Policy." *American Journal of Psychiatry* 141, 10–15.

Monahan John, and Laurens Walker (1998). *Social Science in Law* (4th ed.). Westbury, N.Y.: Foundation Press.

Monari, Evans (1988). "Burial Law: Reflections on the S. M. Otieno Case." *Howard Law Journal* 31, 667–674.

Montgomery, Jonathan (1992). "Legislating for a Multi-Faith Society: Some Problems of Special Treatment." In Bob Hepple and Erika M. Szyszczak (Eds.), *Discrimination: The Limits of Law* (193–213). London: Mansell.

Moody-Adams, Michele M. (1994). "Culture, Responsibility, and Affected Ignorance." *Ethics* 104, 291–309.

Moore, Joanne I. (Ed.) (1999). *Immigrants in Courts*. Seattle: University of Washington Press.

Morales, Dan (1994, Dec. 21). "Attorney General, Letter Opinion No. 94–095, 1994 Texas AG LEXIS 444.

Morgan, Edward M. (1984). "The Defence of Necessity: Justification or Excuse?" *University of Toronto Faculty Law Review* 42, 165–183.

Morgan, Jenny (1997). "Provocation Law and Facts: Dead Women Tell No Tales, Tales Are Told about Them." *Melbourne University Law Review* 21, 237–276.

Morgan, Melissa (1997). "Female Genital Mutilation: An Issue on the Doorstep of the American Medical Community." *Journal of Legal Medicine* 18, 93–115.

Morin, Tina (1992). "Indians, Non-Indians, and the Endangered Panther: Will the Indian/Non-Indian Conflict Be Resolved before the Panther Disappears?" *Public Land Law Review* 13, 167–178.

Morlin, Bill (1992a, Sept. 16). "Police Accused of Dumping Urn during Gypsy Raid." *Spokesman-Review* (Spokane), B4.

——— (1992b, Sept. 17). "Expert Says Raids Were 'Catastrophic' to Gypsy Families." *Spokesman-Review*, 2.

——— (1992c, Nov. 17). "Ill Judge Asks New Schedule in Gypsy Case." *Spokesman-Review*, A1, 7.

——— (1992d, Dec. 6). "New Judge Takes over Gypsy Case: McNichols Too Ill to Continue." *Spokesman-Review*, B1.

——— (1993, Jan. 28). "Judge Hopes Gypsies Case Won't Go to Jury Trial." *Spokesman-Review*, A1, 4.

——— (1994, Jan. 26). "Searches Violated Gypsy Rights: City Now May Face Punitive Damages." *Spokesman-Review*, B1, 4.

——— (1996, Dec. 24). "City Loses Again in Gypsy Search Case." *Spokesman-Review*, B4.

——— (1997a, May 23). "Celebrating a Gypsy's Life: Romani Hold Traditional Wake to Mark the Death of Grover Marks." *Spokesman-Review*, A1.

——— (1997b, July 1). "Gypsies, City Apparently Settle Lawsuit: Judge's Gag Order Squelches Settlement Details." *Spokesman-Review*, A1.

——— (1997c, July 2). "City Settles Gypsy Suit for $1.43 Million: Deal Ends 11-Year Battle over Police Raid of Homes." *Spokesman Review*, A1.

Morlin, Bill, and Rebecca Nappi (1992, Nov. 18). "Gypsy Daughters Say 1986 Search Violated Culture." *Spokesman-Review* (Spokane), A1, A4.

Morris, Norval (1951). "Somnambulistic Homicide: Ghosts, Spiders, and North Koreans." *Res Judicatae* 5, 29–33.

Morse, Stephen (1979). "Diminished Capacity: A Moral and Legal Conundrum." *International Journal of Law and Psychiatry* 2, 217–298.

———— (1984). "Undiminished Confusion in Diminished Capacity." *Journal of Criminal Law and Criminology* 75, 1–55.

———— (1985). "Excusing the Crazy: The Insanity Defense Reconsidered." *Southern California Law Review* 38, 777–836.

Moruzzi, Norma Claire (1994). "A Problem with Headscarves: Contemporary Complexities of Political and Social Identity." *Political Theory* 22, 653–672.

Moskos, Charles C. (1989). *Greek Americans: Struggle and Success* (2nd ed.). New Brunswick, N.J.: Transaction Publishers.

Mowatt, Raoul V. (1992, Nov. 2). "Man Sues Ex-Wife for Allegedly Filing Phony Personal Ad." *Houston Chronicle*, A9.

Mrozek, Thom (1993, May 7). "Accused Wife Killer to Claim Mental Abuse." *Los Angeles Times*, B1,6.

———— (1994a, Mar. 4). "Cultural Defense in Wife's Death." *Los Angeles Times*, B3.

———— (1994b, Mar. 18). "Prosecutor Says Accused Killer Lied." *Los Angeles Times*, B4.

———— (1994c, Mar. 26). "Jury Finds Wife-Killer Acted in Heat of Passion." *Los Angeles Times*, B1.

Mulick, Chris (1997, July 2). "City, Marks Family Reach Settlement." *Columbian*, B2.

Mullin, Sue (1988, July 1–7). "The Braiding Bunch." *City Paper* (Washington, D.C.), 14–16. 18, 20.

Mumford, S. E. (1998). "The Judicial Resolution of Disputes Involving Children and Religion." *International and Comparative Law Quarterly* 47, 117–148.

Munro, Donald, John F. Schumaker, and Stuart C. Carr (Eds.) (1997). *Motivation and Culture*. New York: Routledge.

Murcott, Anne (1996). "Food as an Expression of Identity." In Sverker Gustavsson and Leif Lewin (Eds.), *The Future of the Nation State: Essays on Cultural Pluralism and Political Integration* (49–78). London: Routledge.

Murdock, George P. et al. (1965). *Outline of Cultural Materials.* (4th rev. ed.). New Haven: Human Relations Area Files, i–x.

Murphy, Joseph (1993). *Santeria: African Spirits in America*. Boston: Beacon Press.

Murray, Yxta Maya (1995). "The Battered Woman Syndrome and the Cultural Defense." *Federal Sentencing Reporter* 7, 197–200.

Mutungi, O. K. (1971). "Witchcraft and the Criminal Law in East Africa." *Valparaiso University Law Review* 5, 524–555.

———— (1977). *The Legal Aspects of Witchcraft in East Africa with Particular Reference to Kenya*. Nairobi: East African Literature Bureau.

Mylonas-Widdall, Michael (1988). "Aboriginal Fishing Rights in New Zealand." *International and Comparative Law Quarterly* 37, 386–391.

Nafziger, James A. R. (1984). "Some Remarks on the Writing Style of the International Court of Justice." In Thomas Buergenthal (Eds.), *Contemporary Issues in International Law* (325–345). Kehl, Germany: N. P. Engel.

Najera-Ramirez, Olga (1996). "The Racialization of a Debate: The Charreada as Tradition or Torture." *American Anthropologist* 98, 505–511.

Nash, Marian (1997). "Contemporary Practice of the United States Relating to International Law." *American Journal of International Law* 91, 103.

National Association of Colleges of Mortuary Science, Inc. (1994). *Funeral Services and Ceremonies.* Dallas: Professional Training Schools.

National Funeral Directors Association (1997, Oct.). "Cultural Differences in the U.S." Special issue of the *Director* 69(10), 1–104.

Native American Church (2003). 21 C.F.R. Section 1307.31 Code of Federal Regulations, Title 21, Vol. 9, Parts 1300 to end. Available on the government printing office website.

Ndegwa, Stephen N. (1997). "Citizenship and Ethnicity: An Examination of Two Transition Moments in Kenyan Politics." *American Political Science Review* 91, 599–616.

Neely, David E. (1989, June). "Conditions of Employment: From Grooming Codes to Polygraph and Drug Testing." *CBA Record* (Chicago Bar Association) 3(6), 18–25.

Nelkin, Dorothy and Lori Andrews (1998). "Do the Dead Have Interests? Policy Issues for Research after Life." *American Journal of Law and Medicine* 24, 261–291.

Nencini, Paolo, and Abdullahi Mohamed Ahmed (1989). "Khat Consumption: A Pharmacological Review." *Drug and Alcohol Dependency* 23, 19–29.

Nencini, Paolo et al. (1988). "Khat Chewing Spread to the Somali Community in Rome." *Drug and Alcohol Dependency* 23, 255–258.

Newell, W. W. (1892). "Conjuring Rats." *Journal of American Folk-lore* 5, 23–82.

New York Times Regional Newspapers (1990, Apr. 20). "Religion Rejected as Murder Defense." *New York Times* (Late City Final Ed.), Section A, 17.

Nguyen, Maj Duong (1985). "Culture Shock: A Review of Vietnamese Culture and Its Concepts of Health and Disease." *Western Journal of Medicine* 142(3), 409–412.

Nhu, T. T. (1989, Aug. 25) "Most Asians Are Not Doggie Diners." *San Jose Mercury News.*

Nieflc, Halina (Ed.) (1998). *Cultural Rights and Wrongs.* Paris: UNESCO.

Nieves, Evelyn (1995, Mar. 7). "Blood Sport Moves to the Suburbs." *New York Times,* A9.

Norman, William (1993). "Native American Inmates and Prison Grooming Regulations: Today's Justified Scalps—Iron Eyes v. Henry." *American Indian Law Review* 18, 191–225.

Norton, S. A., and P. Ruze (1994). "Kava Dermopathy." *Journal of the American Academy of Dermatologists* 31, 89–97.

Nowak, Manfred (1993). *The U.N. Covenant on Civil and Political Rights: CCPR Commentary.* Kehl, Germany: N. P. Engel.

Nunez, Ann E., and Mark L. Taff (1985). "A Chemical Burn Simulating Child Abuse." *American Journal of Forensic Medicine and Pathology* 6(2), 181–183.

Nunn, Kenneth B. (1997). "Law as a Eurocentric Enterprise." *Law and Inequality* 15, 323–371.

Oberg, Kalervo (1960). "Cultural Shock: Adjustment to New Cultural Environments." *Practical Anthropology* 7, 177–182.

O'Brien, James (1989, July 4). "Moslem Cut Throat of Daughter in Row over Christianity." *Daily Telegraph,* 3.

Ojito, Mirta (1997a, May 18). "They're Not in Denmark Anymore." *New York Times,* 2.

——— (1997b, June 29). "Culture Clash: Foreign Parents, American Child Rearing." *New York Times,* E3.

Ojo, J. D. (1981). "Supernatural Powers and Criminal Law: A Study with Particular Reference to Nigeria." *Journal of Black Studies* 11(3), 327–348.

Ojoade, J. O. Olowo (1978/1979). "'When in Rome, Do as the Romans Do': African Parallels." *Midwestern Language and Folklore Newsletter* 1/2, 13–18.

Ojwang, J., and J. N. K. Mugambi (Eds.) (1989). *The S. M. Otieno Case: Death and Burial in Modern Kenya.* Nairobi: Nairobi University Press.

O'Keefe, Roger (1998). "The 'Right to Take Part in Cultural Life' under Article 15 of the ICESR." *International and Comparative Law Quarterly* 47(4), 904–923.

Okin, Susan (1999). *Is Multiculturalism Bad for Women?* Princeton, N.J.: Princeton University Press.

Oliver, Myrna (1988, July 15). "Cultural Defense: A Legal Tactic." *Los Angeles Times*, 1, 28–30.

Oltman, David (1989, July 26). "Bloody History of Whites and Indians Being Retried with Accused Murderer." *Daily Journal*, 1, 7.

Omi, Michael, and Howard Winant (1986). *Racial Formation in the United States: From the 1960s to the 1980s*. New York: Routledge and Kegan Paul.

O'Neill, Ann (1997, Apr. 17). "Two Missionaries Guilty in Fatal Exorcism Case." *Los Angeles Times*, B3.

O'Regan, R. S. (1972). "Ordinary Men and Provocation in Papua and New Guinea." *International and Comparative Law Quarterly* 21, 551–557.

Orlowski, James P., and Janicemarie K. Vinicky (1993, summer). "Conflicting Cultural Attitudes about Autopsies." *Journal of Clinical Ethics* 4(2), 195–197.

Ortiz, Almudena (1996, Nov. 9). "Re-evaluate Tradition." *San Francisco Chronicle*, 20.

Ortner, Sherry B. (1978). *Sherpas through Their Rituals*. Cambridge: Cambridge University Press.

Otieno, Wambui Waiyaki (1998). *Mau Mau's Daughter: A Life History*. Boulder, Colo.: Lynne Rienner.

Padilla, Amado M. (Ed.) (1980a). *Acculturation: Theory, Models and Some New Findings*. Boulder, Colo.: Westview Press.

———— (1980b). "The Role of Cultural Awareness and Ethnic Loyalty in Acculturation." In Amado M. Padilla (Ed.), *Acculturation: Theory, Models and Some New Findings* (47–84). Boulder, Colo.: Westview Press.

Pankratz, Howard (1995, Mar. 10). "Jury Rejects 'Loss of Face' Insanity Plea." *Denver Post*, B1.

Paradysz, Amy H. (1995, Aug. 18). "U.M. Professor Testifies in Molestation Case." *Massachusetts Daily Collegian* (Amherst), A1, 3.

Parekh, Bhikhu (1994). "Cultural Pluralism and the Limits of Diversity." *Alternatives* 20(3), 431–457.

———— (1996). "Minority Practices and Principles of Toleration." *International Migration Review* 30, 251–284.

———— (2000). *Rethinking Multiculturalism: Cultural Diversity and Political Theory*. Cambridge: Harvard University Press.

Parish-Pixler, Michele (1990, summer). "Polygamy: Practicing What They Preach." *Civil Liberties* no. 370, 6, 10.

Parke, Ross D., and Candace Whitmer Collmer (1975). *Child Abuse: An Interdisciplinary Analysis*. Chicago: University of Chicago Press.

Parker, Sandra (1992). "Conviction Voided in Case Raising Cultural Defense." *Los Angeles Daily Journal*, 1, 10.

Parry, Aaron (1995, Jan. 29). "Referee's Reaction to Players' Skullcaps Is Disturbing." *Los Angeles Times*, Pt. B, 14.

Parry, Joan K., and Angela Shen Ryan (Eds.) (1995). *A Cross-Cultural Look at Death, Dying, and Religion*. Chicago: Nelson-Halls.

Partington, Angela (Ed.) (1996). *The Oxford Dictionary of Quotations* (rev. 4th ed.). Oxford: Oxford University Press, 10, 679.

Passmore, John (1975). "The Treatment of Animals." *Journal of the History of Ideas* 35, 195–218.

Pate, H., Shabbir A. Wadee, and P. Lingham (1995, Nov.). "Muslim Customs regarding Autopsies [Letters to the Editor]." *South African Medical Journal* 85(11), 1198–1199.

Paul, Jordan (1989). "'You Get the House. I Get the Car. You Get the Kids. I Get Their Souls.' The Impact of Spiritual Custody Awards on the Free Exercise Rights of Custodial Parents." *University of Pennsylvania Law Review* 138, 583–613.

Paul, Robert A. (1997). "Act and Intention in Sherpa Culture and Society." In Lawrence Rosen (Ed.), *Other Intentions* (15–45). Santa Fe: School of American Research Press.

Paz, Octavio (1961). "The Sons of La Malinche." In Octavio Paz, *The Labyrinth of Solitude: Life and Thought in Mexico* (65–89). Translated by Lysander Kemp. New York: Grove Press.

———— (1972). "Eroticism and Gastrosophy." *Daedalus* 101, 67–85.

Peach, Ceri, and Gunther Glevbe (1995). "Muslim Minorities in Western Europe." *Ethnic and Racial Studies* 18, 26–45.

Pearl, David (1986). *Family Law and the Immigrant Communities*. Bristol: Jordan and Sons.

Pearson, James O. Jr. (1981). "Liability for Wrongful Autopsy." *American Law Reports* (1998 Supp.) 18, 858–000.

Pelton, Tom (1994, Sept. 11). "Faither Jailed in Spanking." *Chicago Tribune*, B1–2.

Pepping, Joseph (1999, May 15). "Kava: *Piper methysticum.*" *American Journal of Health-System Pharmacy* 56(1), 957–958, 960.

Perkins, Henry S. (1991, May). "Cultural Differences and Ethical Issues in the Problem of Autopsy Requests." *Texas Medicine* 87(5), 72–77.

Perkins, Henry S., Josie D. Supik, and Helen P. Hazuda (1993). "Autopsy Decisions: The Possibility of Conflicting Cultural Attitudes." *Journal of Clinical Ethics* 4(2), 145–154.

Perkins, Rollin M., and Ronald N. Boyce (1982). *Criminal Law* (3rd ed.). Mineola, N.Y.: Foundation Press.

Pesce, Carlo M. (1986, July). "Histopathology in Tropical Medicine: A Perspective." *Public Health Reports*, 101, 417–419.

Peters, Jacquelin C. (1990a, winter). "Braids, Cornrows, Dreadlocks, and Hair Wraps: An African Continuum." *Folklife Center News*, 8–10.

———— (1990b). "Affirming an Ancient Aesthetic: The Revival of Hair Braiding among African-Americans." *World and I*, 646–657.

Piccalo, Gina (2000, Feb. 17). "Attorneys to Cite to Similar Incident in Drowning Case Defense." *Los Angeles Times*, B11.

Pimentel, Benjamin (1994a, Feb. 12). "Culture Clash Ends in Death of 5-Week-Old." *San Francisco Chronicle*, A1, 15.

———— (1994b, Feb. 19). "Grieving Laotian Family Mourns Infant." *San Francisco Chronicle*, A19.

Pine, Donald W. (1993, Jan. 10). "Local Hedges Harbor a Stash: Reports from Somalia Put Spotlight on Ornmental Plant That Has a Kick." *Oakland Tribune*, A1, 9.

Pittler, Max, H., and Edzard Ernst (2000, Feb.). "Efficacy of Kava Extract for Treating Anxiety: Systematic Review and Meta-Analysis." *Journal of Clinical Psychopharmocology* 20(1), 84–89.

Pittman, Jennifer (1994, Jan. 14). "No 'Defective Bride.' So No Damages." *Daily Journal*, 2, 11.

Ploscowe, M. (1930). "An Examination of Some Dispositions Relating to Motives and Character in Modern European Penal Codes." *Journal of Criminal Law and Criminology* 21, 26–40.

Polichetti, Barbara (1995, Apr. 17). "ACLU: Its Cause Is the Bill of Rights." *Providence Journal-Bulletin*, 1C.

Polman, Dick (1989, July 2). "Controversial 'Cultural Defense' Creeps into Courts." *Philadelphia Inquirer*, 1A, 4A.

Polyhemus, Ted (Ed.) (1978). *The Body Reader: Social Aspects of the Human Body*. New York: Pantheon.

Pomorski, Stanislaw (1997). "On Multiculturalism, Concepts of Crime, and the "De Minimis" Defense." *Brigham Young University Law Review* 1997, 51–99.

Poulter, Sebastian (1975). "Foreign Customs and the English Criminal Law." *International and Comparative Law Quarterly* 24, 136–140.

———— (1986). *English Law and Ethnic Minority Customs*. London: Butterworths.

———— (1987a). "African Customs in an English Setting: Legal and Policy Aspects of Recognition." *Journal of African Law* 31, 207–225.

———— (1987b). "Ethnic Minority Customs, English Law and Human Rights." *International and Comparative Law Quarterly* 36, 589–615.

———— (1989). "The Significance of Ethnic Minority Customs and Traditions in English Criminal Law." *New Community* 16(1), 121–128.

———— (1990) *Asian Traditions and English Law: A Handbook*. Stoke-on-Trent: Runnymede Trust, with Trentham Books.

———— (1998). *Ethnicity, Law and Human Rights: The English Experience*. Oxford: Clarendon Press.

Powers, Dorothy (1972, July 16). "'Genuine' Gypsies Are Born That Way." *Spokesman Review* (Spokane), 1, 4f.

Powers, William K. (1987). "North American Indians: Indians of the Plains." In Mircea Eliade (Ed.), *The Encyclopedia of Religion* (vol. 10, 497–499). New York: Macmillan.

———— (1995). "The Peyote Road: A Text in Search of a Context." *American Anthropologist* 97, 768–773.

Prahlow, Joseph A., and Patrick E. Lantz (1995). "Medical Examiner/Death Investigator Training Requirements in State Medical Examiner Systems." *Journal of Forensic Sciences* 40(1), 55–58.

Prentice, Deborah, and Dale Miller (Eds.) (1999). *Cultural Divides: Understanding and Overcoming Group Conflict*. New York: Russell Sage Foundation.

Prescott, J., and G. McCall (Eds.) (1988). *Kava Use and Abuse in Australia and the South Pacific*. Sydney: University of New South Wales, National Drug and Alcohol Research Centre.

Price, H. Marcus (1991). *Disputing the Dead: U.S. Law on Aboriginal Remains and Grave Goods*. Columbia: University of Missouri Press.

Price, Maurice T. (1930–31). "The Concept 'Culture Conflict': In What Sense Valid?" *Social Forces* 9, 164–167.

Primosch, Robert E., and Stephen Kent Young (1980, July). "Pseudobattering of Vietnamese Children (Cao gio)." *JADA* 101, 47–48.

Probst, Jane E. (1990). "The Conflict between Child's Medical Needs and Parents' Religious Beliefs." *American Journal of Family Law* 4, 175–192.

Prothero, Stephen R. (2001). *Purified by Fire: A History of Cremation in America*. Berkeley: University of California Press.

Prott, Lyndel V. (1988). "Cultural Rights as Peoples' Rights in International Law." In James Crawford (Ed.), *The Rights of Peoples*. Oxford: Clarendon Press.

Pulaski, Alex (1990a, Jan. 1). "Judge Will Decide Fate of Hmong Child Caught in Cultural Vise." *Fresno Bee*, A1

———— (1990b, Jan. 5). "Eastern Beliefs Meet Western Law: Hmong Father Insists on Ritual before His Son Has Operation." *Fresno Bee*, A12.

———— (1990c, Jan. 9). "Surgery Dispute Going to Trial: Settlement Falls Apart." *Fresno Bee*, B1.

———— (1990d, Feb. 11). "Hmong Healers in US: A Cultural Clash?" *Fresno Bee*, A1, 10.

———— (1990e, Feb. 21). "On Trial: Beliefs of Family, Boy's Needs." *Fresno Bee*, B1, 4.

———— (1990f, Feb. 22). "Judge Will Rule on Surgery for Hmong Boy." *Fresno Bee*, B1, 3.

———— (1990g, June 13). "Hmong Suit Heads for High Court: Family Appeals to Stop Surgery on Son's Clubfeet, Hip." *Fresno Bee*, B1, 4.

———— (1990h, June 28). "Hmong Plea: Leave Boy Alone: Clans Ask Change of Ruling on Surgery." *Fresno Bee*.

———— (1990i, July 7). "Another Lawyer in Hmong Battle to Avoid Surgery." *Fresno Bee*, B1, 2.

———— (1990j, Sept. 20). "Hmong Boy Appears Safe from Surgery." *Fresno Bee*, B1, 6.

———— (1990k, Sept. 22). "Psychiatrist Named to Help Hmong Boy." *Fresno Bee.*

———— (1990l, Dec. 19). "Doctor's View: Let Hmong Boy Decide." *Fresno Bee*, A1.

———— (1990m, Dec. 21). "No Hmong Surgery—Judge." *Fresno Bee*, B1, 8.

Quigley, Christine (1996). *The Corpse: A History.* Jefferson, N.C.: McFarland.

Qureshi, Bashir (1988). "Cultural Aspects of Child Abuse in Britain." *Midwife, Health Visitor, and Community Nurse* 24(10), 412–413.

———— (1994). *Transcultural Medicine: Dealing with Patients from Different Cultures* (2nd ed.). Dordrecht: Kluwer.

Rafalko, Walter (1967/68). "Sociological Evidence as a Criminal Defence." *Criminal Law Quarterly* 10, 77–98.

Ragon, Michel (1983). *The Space of Death: A Study of Funerary Architecture, Decoration, and Urbanism.* Translated by Alan Sheridan. Charlottesville: University Press of Virginia.

Rahav, Giora (1981). "Culture Conflict, Urbanism, and Delinquency." *Criminology* 18, 523–530.

Rainey, James (1993, May 25). "Banner of Roasting Dog at City Hall Art Exhibit Is Removed." *Los Angeles Times*, B1, 8.

Rampersad, Sheila (1994a, Sept. 22). "Trinidad and Tobago: Residents Wary of Hard-Line Muslim Assault." *Inter Press Service.*

———— (1994b, Oct. 7). "Trinidad and Tobago Education: The Politics of Learning." *Inter Press Service.*

Randall, Teri (1993, Jan. 6). "Khat Abuse Fuels Somali Conflict, Drains Economy." *JAMA* 269(91), 12, 15.

Randolph, Mary (1997). *Dog Law* (3rd ed.). Berkeley: Nolo Press.

Randrianame, Maurice et al. (1983). *The Health and Socio-Economic Aspects of Khat Use.* Lausanne: International Council on Alcohol and Addictions.

Rattray, R. S. (1959). *Religion and Art in Ashanti.* London: Oxford University Press.

Rayman, Graham (1996, July 9). "Grandma Jailed in Cut Ritual." *Newsday* (New York).

Raz, Joseph (1994, winter). "Multiculturalism: A Liberal Perspective." *Dissent*, 67–79.

Regan, Tom (1983). *The Case for Animal Rights.* Berkeley: University of California Press.

Regan, Tom, and Peter Singer (Eds.) (1989). *Animal Rights and Human Obligations* (2nd ed.). Englewood Cliffs, N.J.: Prentice Hall.

Reid, Betty (1993, Sept. 19). "Witchcraft 'Very Much Alive.'" *Arizona Republic/Phoenix Gazette*, NV6.

Renteln, Alison Dundes (1987/88). "Culture and Culpability: A Study in Contrasts." *Beverly Hills Bar Association Journal*, 17–27. Reprinted in Renteln and Dundes (1994).

———— (1988). "Relativism and the Search for Human Rights." *American Anthropologist* 90, 56–72.

———— (1990). *International Human Rights: Universalism versus Relativism.* Newbury Park, Calif.: Sage.

———— (1993). "A Justification of the Cultural Defense as Partial Excuse." *Southern California Review of Law and Women Studies* 7, 437–526.

———— (1994). "Is the Cultural Defense Detrimental to the Health of Children?" *Law and Anthropology* 7, 27–106.

———— (2000). "Raising Cultural Defenses." In James G. Connell III and Rene L. Valladares (Eds.), *Cultural Issues in Criminal Defense.* Yonkers, N.Y.: Juris.

———— (2002). "In Defense of Culture in the Courtroom." In Rick Shweder, Martha Minow, and Hazel Rose-Markus (Eds.), *Engaging Cultural Differences: The Multicultural Challenge in Liberal Democracies* (194–215). New York: Russell Sage.

Renteln, Alison Dundes, and Alan Dundes (Eds.) (1994). *Folk Law: Essays in the Theory and Practice of Lex Non Scripta.* New York: Garland; Madison: University of Wisconsin Press, 1995.

Retter, David E. (1979). "The Rise and Fall of Title VII's Requirement of Reasonable Accommodation for Religious Employees." *Columbia Human Rights Law Review,* 11, 63–86.

Rezek, Philipp R., and Max Millard (1963). *Autopsy Pathology: A Guide for Pathologists and Clinicians.* Springfield, Ill.: Charles C. Thomas.

Rhodes, John (1991). "An American Tradition: The Religious Persecution of Native Americans." *Montana Law Review* 52, 13–72.

Rimonte, Nilda (1991). "A Question of Culture: Cultural Approval of Violence against Women in the Pacific-Asian Community and the Cultural Defense." *Stanford Law Review* 43, 1311–1326.

Rispler-Chaim, Vardit (1993). "The Ethics of Postmortem Examinations in Contemporary Islam." *Journal of Medical Ethics* 19, 164–168.

Rivera, Carla (1995, Apr. 19). "Supervisors Ban Horse Tripping." *Los Angeles Times,* B2.

Rivera, Jenny (1994). "Domestic Violence against Latinas by Latino Males: An Analysis of Race, National Origin, and Gender Differentials." *Boston College Third World Law Journal* 14, 231–251.

Rivko, Harriet (1988). "The Emergence of Modern Pet-Keeping." In Andrew N. Rowan (Ed.), *Animals and People Sharing the World* (13–31). Hanover, N.H.: University Press of New England.

Roan, Shair (1997, Aug. 20). "Spank Your Kid, Go to Jail?" *Los Angeles Times,* E1, 6.

Roberts, Dorothy E. (1999). "Why Culture Matters to Law: The Difference Politics Makes." In Austin Sarat and Thomas R. Kearns (Eds.), *Cultural Pluralism, Identity Politics, and the Law* (85–111). Ann Arbor: University of Michigan Press.

Robeson, George (1989, Oct. 6). "Governor Pleads for Softer Law." *Press-Telegram,* F5.

Robinson, Paul H. (1980). "A Brief History of Distinctions in Criminal Culpability." *Hastings Law Journal* 31, 815–853.

——— (1982). "Criminal Law Defenses: A Systematic Analysis." *Columbia Law Review* 82, 199–291.

——— (1985). "Causing the Conditions of One's Own Defense: A Study in the Limits of Theory in Criminal Law Doctrine." *Virginia Law Review* 71, 1–63

Robinson, Shelli Dawn (1991). "*Commonwealth v. Twitchell:* Who Owns the Child?" *Journal of Contemporary Health Law and Policy* 7, 413–432.

Rodley, Nigel (1995). "Conceptual Problems in the Protection of Minorities: International Legal Developments." *Human Rights Quarterly* 7, 48–71.

Rohde, David (1999, July 23). "Court Ruling Favors Two Who Left Baby Outside." *New York Times,* B3.

Rollin, Bernard (1981). *Animal Rights and Human Morality.* Buffalo, N.Y.: Prometheus.

Romano, Lois (1996, May 24). "Diplomas Denied Three Students Who Wore Cultural Symbols." *Washington Post,* A3.

Romney, Lee (1993, Dec. 9). "Rose Hills Withdraws Plan for Mortuary." *Los Angeles Times,* J1, 4.

Root, Waverley (1968). *The Cooking of Italy.* New York: Time-Life Books, 38, 110, 137–138, 187.

Rosato, Jennifer L. (1994). "Putting Square Pegs in a Round Role: Procedural Due Process and the Effect of Faith Health Exemptions on the Prosecution of Faith Healing Parents." *University of San Francisco Law Review* 29, 43–119,

Rose, Arnold (1956). "The Social Scientist as an Expert Witness." *Minnesota Law Review* 40, 205–218.

Rose, David James (1994, Apr. 17). "Ride 'Em, Charro." *Los Angeles Times Magazine,* 18–21.

Rosen, Lawrence (1977). "The Anthropologist as Expert Witness." *American Anthropologist* 79, 555–578.

——— (1979). "Response to Stewart." *American Anthropologist* 81, 111–112.

——— (1991). "The Integrity of Cultures." *American Behavioral Scientist* 34, 594–617.

Rosen, Ruth (2000, Aug. 13). "Ending a Murderous Custom: Jordan's King Wants to Punish 'Honor' Killers with Life in Prison." *San Francisco Examiner and Chronicle*, 7.

Rosner, Fred (1971, spring). "Autopsy in Jewish Law and the Israeli Autopsy Controversy." *Tradition* 11(4), 43–63.

Rostain, Tanina (1987). "Permissible Accommodations of Religion: Reconsidering the New York 'Get' Statute." *Yale Law Journal* 96, 1147–1171.

Roth, Hans Ingvar (1999). *The Multicultural Park: A Study of Common Values at School and in Society*. Stockholm: Skolverket.

Rotstein, Arthur (1998, May 10). "Girl Tells Police Gypsy Parents Sold Her—Twice." *Spectrum*, A9.

Rowland, Debra (1988a, May 7). "D.C. Human Rights Office Rules against Marriott in Row over Cornrows." *New Pittsburgh Courier*, A-4.

———— (1988b, May 18). "Second Landmark Decision in 'Cornrow Dispute.'" *New Pittsburgh Courier*.

Royce, Anya Peterson (1982). *Ethnic Identity: Strategies of Diversity*. Bloomington: Indiana University Press.

RSPCA (1985). *The Slaughter of Food Animals*. Horsham: Royal Society for the Preventin of Cruelty to Animals.

Rubel, Arthur J., and Michael R. Hass (1990). "Ethnomedicine." In Thomas M. Johnson and Carolyn F. Sargent (Eds.), *Medical Anthropology: A Handbook of Theory and Method* (115–131). New York: Greenwood Press.

Rubin, Vera (Ed.) (1978). *Cannabis and Culture*. The Hague: Mouton.

Rubin, Vera, and Lambros Comitas (1975). *Ganga in Jamaica: A Medical Anthropological Study of Chronic Marihuana Use*. The Hague: Mouton.

Rudgley, Richard (1993). *The Alchemy of Culture: Intoxicants in Society*. London: British Museum Press.

———— (1994). *Essential Substances: A Cultural History of Intoxicants in Society*. New York: Kodansha International.

Rule, Sheila (1985, July 29). "Female Circumcision Is Debated in Third World." *New York Times*, A12.

Rushby, Kevin (1998). *Eating the Flowers of Paradise: A Journey through the Drug Fields of Ethiopia and Yemen*. London: Constable.

Rushing, Andrea Benton (1988). "Hair-Raising." *Feminist Studies* 14(2), 325–335.

Rutherford, Jonathan (Ed.) (1990). *Identity, Community, Culture, Difference*. London: Lawrence and Wishart.

Rutledge, Paul James (1992). *The Vietnamese Experience in America*. Bloomington: Indiana University Press.

Sacks, Valerie L. (1996). "An Indefensible Defense: On the Misuse of Culture in Criminal Law." *Arizona Journal of International and Comparative Law* 13, 523–549.

Sagatun, Inger, and Leonard P. Edwards (1995). *Child Abuse and the Legal System*. Chicago: Nelson-Hall.

Sagay, Esi (1983). *African Hairstyles: Styles of Yesterday and Today*. Portsmouth, N.H.: Heinemann Educational.

Sahagun, Louis (1994, June 13). "American Album: Peyote Harvests Face Supply-Side Problems." *Los Angeles Times*, A5.

Sakr, Ahmed H. (1995). "Death and Dying: An Islamic Perspective." In Joan K. Parry and Angela Shen Ryan (Eds.), *A Cross-Cultural Look at Death, Dying, and Religion* (47–73). Chicago: Nelson-Hall.

Salopek, Paul (1996, Aug. 28). "Korean Exorcism, Bare-Knuckle Style." *Chicago Tribune*, 1.

Salsgiver, Richard O. (1990, July 17). "Editorial on Crippled Hmong Child Draws Dissent." *Fresno Bee*, B11.

Saltman, Michael (1991). *The Demise of the 'Reasonable Man': A Cross-Cultural Study of a Legal Concept*. New Brunswick, N.J.: Transaction Publishers.

Sams, Julia P. (1986). "The Availability of the 'Cultural Defense' as an Excuse for Criminal Behavior." *Georgia Journal of International and Comparative Law* 16, 335–354.

Samuels, Alec (1971). "Excusable Loss of Self-Control in Homicide." *Modern Law Review* 34, 163–171.

——— (1981). "Legal Recognition and Protection of Minority Customs in a Plural Society in England." *Anglo-American Law Review* 10, 241–256.

Samuelson, Sue (1982). "Folklore and the Legal System." *Western Folklore* 41, 139–144.

Sanderson, Lillian Passmore (1986). *Female Genital Mutilation: Excision and Infibulation (A Bibliography)*. London: Anti-Slavery Society for the Protection of Human Rights.

Sandler, Alan P., and Vincent Haynes (1978). "Nonaccidental Trauma and Medical Folk Belief: A Case of Cupping." *Pediatrics* 61(6), 921–922.

Sands, Barbara (1994, May 4). "Horse Treatment in Charreadas." *Los Angeles Times*, B6.

Sands, Jon M. (1996, Nov./Dec.). "Departure Reform and Indian Crimes: Reading the Commission's Staff Paper with "Reservations." *Federal Sentencing Reporter*, 144–148.

Sands, Kathleen Mullen (1993). *Charreria Mexicana: An Equestrian Folk Tradition*. Tucson: University of Arizona Press.

Sarat, Austin, and Roger Berkowitz (1994). "Disorderly Differences, Recognition, Accommodation, and American Law." *Yale Journal of Law and the Humanities* 6, 285–316.

Saunders, R. N. S. (1983). "Ethnic Origins and Religious Discrimination: The *Mandla* Case." *Trent Law Journal* 7, 23–40.

Savage, David (1990, Apr. 18). "Won't Shield Religions from Law, Court Says." *Los Angeles Times*, A1, 16.

——— (1992, Nov. 1). "Justices Revisit Unsettled Issue in Santeria Case." *Los Angeles Times*, A22.

——— (1993, June 12). "Justices Affirm Religion's Right to Sacrifice Animals." *Los Angeles Times*, A1, 19.

Savane, Marie-Angelique (1979). "Why We Are Against the International Campaign." *International Child Welfare Review* 40, 37, 39.

Schacter, Jim (1988a, Mar. 12). "Perfect Fit: The '80s and Dress Codes." *Los Angeles Times*, IV, 1–2.

——— (1988b, May 17). "EEOC Says Hyatt Showed Bias in Its Ban on Cornrows." *Los Angeles Times*, 1, 3.

Schaefer, Stacy B. (1996). "The Crossing of Souls: Peyote, Perception, and Meaning among the Huichol Indians." In Schaefer and Furst (Eds.), *People of the Peyote* (141–144). Albuquerque: University of New Mexico Press.

Schaefer, Stacy B., and Peter T. Furst (Eds.) (1996). *People of the Peyote*. Albuquerque: University of New Mexico Press.

Schaffner, Eva Matter (2002, June 26). "'Freed from a Mental Yoke': Denmark Tightens Its Immigration Laws." *Neue Zurcher Zeitung*.

Schlei, Barbara Lindemann, and Paul Grossman (1983). *Employment Discrimination Law* (2nd ed.). Washington D.C.: Bureau of National Affairs.

Schlesinger, Arthur M. Jr. (1993). *The Disuniting of America*. New York: Norton.

Schreiber, Ariane M. (1996). "States That Kill: Discretion and the Death Penalty: A Worldwide Perspective." *Cornell International Law Journal* 29, 263–327.

Schriever, Silvia H. (1990). "Comparison of Beliefs and Practices of Ethnic Viet and Lao Hmong Concerning Illness, Healing, Death and Mourning: Implications for Hospice Care with Refugees in Canada." *Journal of Palliative Care* 6(1), 42–49.

Schroeder, Patricia (1994). "Female Genital Mutilation: A Form of Child Abuse." *New England Journal of Medicine* 331(11), 739–740.

Schutze, Jim (1995, Sept. 17). "Albanian Cleared of Crime but Loses Kids Anyway: Clash of Cultures Catches Couple." *Houston Chronicle*, A1, 28.

Schuyler, Nina (1991, Sept. 25). "Cultural Defense: Equality or Anarchy?" *San Francisco Weekly* 10(30), 1, 12.

Schwartz, Stephen (1993). "Family Awarded $750,000: Dead Pig in Woman's Casket." *San Francisco Chronicle*, A13.

———— (199, Apr. 1). "Accord Reached on Killing of Live Animals for Food." *San Francisco Chronicle*, A13.

Sciolino, Elaine (2000, Oct. 4). "Love Finds a Way in Iran: 'Temporary Marriage.'" *New York Times*, A3.

Scrivener, Leslie (1999, Apr. 11). "Standing Tall: Sikhs Mark Third Century." *Toronto Star*, 1.

Scull, Andrew, and Diane Fabreau (1986). "The Clitoridectomy Craze." *Social Research* 53, 243–260.

Seedat, O. H. (1995, Aug.). "Muslim Customs Regarding Autopsies." *South African Medical Journal* 85(8), 789–790.

Seidman, Robert B. (1965a). "Witch Murder and Mens Rea: A Problem of Society under Radical Social Change." *Modern Law Review* 28, 46–61.

———— (1965b). "The Inarticulate Premise." *Journal of Modern African Studies* 3, 565–587. Reprinted in Renteln and Dundes (1994), 805–826.

Sellers, John (1978). "Mens Rea and the Judicial Approach to "Bad Excuses" in the Criminal Law." *Modern Law Review* 41, 245–265.

Sellin, Thorsten (1938). *Culture Conflict and Crime.* New York: Social Science Research Council.

Serpell, James A. (1988). "Pet-Keeping in Non-Western Societies: Some Popular Misconceptions." In Andrew N. Rowan (Ed.), *Animals and People Sharing the World* (33–52).

Serrano, Barbara A. (1991, Aug. 30). "Cultures Clash in Rearing Children: State Acts when Abuse Is Feared—Parents Follow Custom in Laotian Boy's Case." *Seattle Times*, A1.

Sevilla, Charles (2000). Preface to James G. Connell III and Rene L. Valladares (Eds.), *Cultural Issues in Criminal Defense*. Yonkers, N.Y.: Juris.

Shachar, Ayelet (1998). "Reshaping the Multicultural Model: Group Accommodation and Individual Rights." *Windsor Review of Legal and Social Issues* 8, 83–111.

———— (1999). "The Paradox of Multicultural Vulnerability." In Christian Joppke and Steven Lukes (Eds.), *Multicultural Questions* (87–111). Oxford: Oxford University Press.

———— (2000a). "Group Identity and Women's Rights in Family Law: The Perils of Multicultural Accommodation." *Journal of Political Philosophy* 6, 285–305.

———— (2000b). "The Puzzle of Interlocking Power Hierarchies: Sharing the Pieces of Jurisdictional Authority." *Harvard Civil Rights–Civil Liberties Law Review* 35, 385–426.

———— (2000c). "On Citizenship and Multicultural Vunerability." *Political Theory* 28, 64–89.

———— (2001). *Multicultural Jurisdictions: Cultural Differences and Women's Rights.* Cambridge: Cambridge University Press.

Shadid, W. A., and P. S. van Koningsveld (1992). "Legal Adjustments for Religious Minorities: The Case of the Ritual Slaughtering of Animals." In W. A. R. Shadid and P. S . van Koningsveld (Eds.), *Islam in Dutch Society: Current Developments and Future Prospects* (2–25). Kampen, The Netherlands: Kok Pharos Publishing House.

Shapiro, Stephanie (1998, Sept. 20). "A Little Cake to Sweeten the Verdict." *Sun* (Vancouver) , 2A.

Sharif, Khadijah F. (1997). "Female Genital Mutilation: What Does the New Federal Law Really Mean?" *Fordham Urban Law Journal* 24 409–426.

Sharp, Saundra (1993). *Black Women for Beginners*. New York: Writers and Readers Publishing.

Sheleff, Leon (1995, Aug. 1–4). "The Right to a Cultural Defense in the Criminal Law." *Legal Culture: Encounters and Transformations*. Proceedings of the Annual Meeting of the Research Committee on Sociology of Law, International Sociological Association. Tokyo, 1–15.

——— (2000). *The Future of Tradition: Customary Law, Common Law and Legal Pluralism*. London: Frank Cass.

Shemonsky, Natalie Kaplin (1987). "Medical Examiner's Prerogative: Consent for Autopsy Not Always Required. *Legal Aspects of Medical Practice* 15, 4, 8.

Sherman, Rorie (1989, Apr. 17). "Cultural Defenses Draw Fire." *National Law Journal* 3, 28.

Sherman, Spencer (1985, Aug. 5). "Legal Clash of Cultures." *National Law Journal* 1, 26–27.

——— (1986). "When Cultures Collide." *California Lawyer* 6(1), 33–36, 60–61.

Sherratt, Andrew (1995). "Alcohol and Its Alternatives: Symbol and Substance in Pre-industrial Cultures." In Jordan Goodman, Paul E. Lovejoy, and Andrew Sherratt (Eds.), *Consuming Habits: Drugs in History and Anthropology* (11–46). London: Routledge.

Sheybani, Malek-Mithra. (1987). "Cultural Defense: One Person's Culture Is Another's Crime." *Loyola of Los Angeles International and Comparative Law Journal*, 9, 751–783.

Shibles, Warren (1974). *Death: An Interdisciplinary Analysis*. Whitewater, Wisc.: Language Press.

Shimahara, Nobuo (1970). "Enculturation: A Reconsideration." *Current Anthropology* 11, 143–154.

Shipp, E.R. (1987, Sept. 23). "Braided Hair Style at Issue in Protests over Dress Codes." *New York Times*, C1, 14.

——— (1988, Feb.). "Are Cornrows Right for Work?" *Essence*, 9–10.

Shoham, Shlomo (1962). "The Application of the 'Culture-Conflict' Hypothesis to the Criminality of Immigrants in Israel." *Journal of Criminal Law, Criminology, and Police Science* 53, 207–214.

Shore, Bradd (1996). *Culture in Mind: Cognition, Culture, and the Problem of Meaning*. New York: Oxford University Press.

Short, Christy A. (1999). "The Abolition of the Death Penalty." *Indiana Journal of Global Legal Studies* 6, 720–756.

Shulman, Ericka (1996, Aug. 27). "Letter to Editor: Not Clean and Shiny." *New York Times*, A18.

Shweder, Richard A. (1991). *Thinking through Cultures: Expeditions in Cultural Psychology*. Cambridge: Harvard University Press.

Shweder, Richard A., and E. J. Bourne (1982). "Does the Concept of the Person Vary Cross-Culturally?" In Anthony J. Marsella and G. M. White (Eds.), *Cultural Conceptions of Mental Health and Therapy* (65–81). Dordrecht: D. Reidel.

Shweder, Richard A., and Robert A. LeVine (1984). *Culture Theory: Essays on Mind, Self, and Emotion*. Cambridge: Cambridge University Press.

Shyllon, F. O. (1971). "Immigration and the Criminal Courts." *Modern Law Review* 34, 135–148.

Sikora, Damian (2001). "Differing Cultures, Differing Culpabilities: Using Circumstances as a Mitigating Factor in Sentencing." *Ohio State Law Journal* 62, 1695–1728.

Silverman, H. I., and Leon Shargel (1986). "Phenylpropanolamine." *American Family Physician* 34(4), 39–42.

Silvestre, Nathalie (1991, Sept./Oct). "Can Genital-Mutilation Fugitive Win Political Asylum?" *Ms.*

Simkins, Anna Atkins (1982). "The Functional and Symbolic Roles of Hair and Headgear among Afro-American Women: A Cultural Perspective." Ph.D. diss., University of North Carolina, Greensboro.

Simon, Peter (1994, July 19). "Man Convicted in Beating Death of Son." *Buffalo News*, 8.

Simoneau, Susan E. (1992). "An Anomaly: Religious Freedom Protected through Political Process Rather Than First Amendment." *Bridgeport Law Review* 13, 155–181.

Simons, Marlise (1993, Nov. 23). "Mutilation of Girls' Genitals: Ethnic Gulf in French Court." *New York Times*, A4.

Simons, Marlise (1999, Feb. 18). "Eight-Year Sentence in France for Genital Cutting." *New York Times*, A3.

Simoons, Frederick (1962). *Eat Not This Flesh*. Madison: University of Wisconsin Press.

Simpson, George Eaton, and J. Milton Yinger (1985). *Racial and Cultural Minorities: An Analysis of Prejudice and Discrimination* (5th ed.). New York: Plenum Press.

Sing, James J. (1999). "Culture as Sameness: Toward a Synthetic View of Provocation of Culture in the Criminal Law." *Yale Law Journal* 108, 1845–1884.

Sing, Lillian (1989, Nov.). "Sexual Bias or Cultural Sensitivity." *Courts and Commentary*, 4.

Singh, Yadhu N. (1986). *Kava: A Bibliography*. Suva, Fiji: University of the South Pacific.

Singh, Yadhu N., and Mark Blumenthal (1997). "Kava: An Overview." *Herbalgram (Journal of the American Botanical Council and the Herb Research Foundation)* 39, 36–55.

Sinha, Surya Prakash (1996). *Legal Polycentricity and International Law*. Durham, N.C.: Carolina Academic Press.

Skolnick, Andrew (1990a Sept. 12). "Religious Exemptions to Child Neglect Laws Still Being Passed Despite Convictions of Parents." *JAMA* 264(10), 1226, 1229, 1233.

Slack, Alison (1988). "Female Circumcision: A Critical Appraisal." *Human Rights Quarterly* 10, 437–486.

Slonim, Maureen B. (1991). *Children, Culture, and Ethnicity: Evaluating and Understanding the Impact*. New York: Garland.

Smelser, Neil J. (1992). "Culture: Coherent or Incoherent." In Richard Munch and Neil J. Smelser (Eds.), *Theory of Culture* (3–28). Berkeley: University of California Press.

Smith, Robert J. (1989). "Culture as Explanation: Neither All nor Nothing." *Cornell International Law Journal* 22, 425–434.

Smith, Shea Clark (1975). "Kente Cloth Motifs." *African Arts* 9(1), 36–39.

Smothers, Ronald (1998, June 26). "Beard Ban Dispute Turns into Constitutional Debate." *New York Times*, 85.

Snyder, George (1995, Apr. 27). "Indian Reservation Alleges Police Misconduct; Mendocino County Board Backs Idea of Federal Probe." *San Francisco Chronicle*, A15.

——— (1996, June 1). "Families Sue Cops over Manhunt on Reservation." *San Francisco Chronicle*, A19

——— (1997, Oct. 3). "Mendocino Acquittal Explained: Juror Said Cop Shooting Was in Self Defense." *San Francisco Chronicle*, A17.

Sochart, Elise A. (1988). "Agenda Setting, the Role of Groups and the Legislative Process: The Prohibition of Female Circumcision in Britain." *Parliamentary Affairs* 41(4), 508–526.

Sollors, Werner (1986). *Beyond Ethnicity: Consent and Descent in American Culture*. New York: Oxford University Press.

——— (Ed.) (1989). *The Invention of Ethnicity*. New York: Oxford University Press.

Souder, Elaine, and John Q. Trojanowski (1992, June). "Autopsy: Cutting away the Myths." *Journal of Neuroscience Nursing* 24(3), 134–139.

Spatz, Melissa (1991). "A 'Lesser' Crime: A Comparative Study of Men Who Kill Their Wives." *Columbia Journal of Law and Social Problems* 24, 597–638.

Spencer, Gary (1994, Sept. 19). "State Liable for Ordering Autopsy of Jewish Inmate." *New York Law Journal*, 1.

Spicer, Edward (1968). "Acculturation." In David L. Sills (Eds.), *International Encyclopedia of the Social Sciences* (vol. 1, 21–27). New York: Macmillan and Free Press.

Spiro, Melford E. (1955). "The Acculturation of American Ethnic Groups." *American Anthropologist* 57, 1240–1252.

Spitz, Werner U. (Ed.) (1993). *Medicolegal Investigation of Death: Guidelines for the Application of Pathology to Crime Investigation* (3rd ed.). Springfield, Ill.: Charles C. Thomas.

Spivak, C. D. (1914, June 13). "Post Mortem Examinations among the Jews." *New York Medical Journal*, 1185–1189.

Spores, John C. (1988). *Running Amok: An Historical Inquiry.* Athens: Ohio University Center for International Studies

Stamp, Patricia (1991, summer). "Burying Otieno: The Politics of Gender and Ethnicity in Kenya." *Signs* 16, 808–845.

Stannard, Matthew B. (2000, Oct. 28). "Mistrial in Kava Case: San Bruno Man Arrested on Road." *San Francisco Chronicle*, A17.

Stavenhagen, Rodolpho (1990). "The Right to Cultural Identity." In Jan Berting et al. (Eds.), *Human Rights in Pluralist World: Individuals and Collectivities* (255–258). Westport, Conn.: Meckler.

Steinmetz, Paul B. (1998). *Pipe, Bible, and Peyote among the Oglala Lakota: A Study in Religious Identity.* Syracuse, N.Y.: Syracuse University Press.

Stern, Marc (1984). "N.Y. Autopsy Law and Religious Concerns." *Patterns of Prejudice* 18(1), 44.

Stewart, M. J., Venessa Steenkamp, and Michele Zuckerman (1998, Oct.). "The Toxicology of African Herbal Remedies." *Therapeutic Drug Monitoring* 20(5), 510–516.

Stewart, Omer C. (1956). "Peyote." *The Encyclopedia Americana*, vol. "P," 700.

——— (1961). "Peyote and the Arizona Court Decision." *American Anthropologist* 63, 1334–1337.

——— (1973). "Anthropologists as Expert Witnesses for Indians: Claims and Peyote Cases. In James Officer (Ed.), *Symposium on Anthropology and the American Indian* (35–42). San Francisco: Indian Historial Press.

——— (1979). "An Expert Witness Answers Rosen." *American Anthropologist* 81, 108–111,

——— (1987). *Peyote Religion: A History.* Norman: University of Oklahoma Press.

——— (1991). "Peyote and the Law." In Christopher Vecsey (Ed.), *Handbook of American Indian Religious Freedom* (44–59). New York: Crossroads.

Storke, Frederic P. (1964). "The Incestuous Marriage: Relic of the Past." *University of Colorado Law Review* 36, 473–499.

Stratton, Lee (1984, Feb. 5). "Ailing Baby Hard to Find." *Columbus Dispatch*, 7B.

Strijbosch, Fons (1985). "The Concept of Pela and Its Social Significance in the Community of Moluccan Immigrants in the Netherlands." *Journal of Legal Pluralism* 23, 177–208.

Stumbo, Bella (1988, May 13). "Polygamists: Tale of Two Families." *Los Angeles Times*, 1, 24–25.

Subotnik, Dan (1995). "Sue Me, Sue Me, What Can You Do Me? I Love You—A Disquisition on Law, Sex, and Talk." *Florida Law Review* 47, 311–409.

Sugiyama, T. Fujimori, and S. Maeda (1991). "Autopsy Rates in Medical Schools and Hospitals in Japan." In E. Riboli and M. Delendi (Eds.), *Autopsy in Epidemiology and Medical Research* (245–252). Lyon: International Agency for Research on Cancer.

Suh, Matthew (1980). "Psychiatric Problems of Immigrants and Refugees." In Elliot L. Tepper (Ed.), *Southeast Asian Exodus: From Tradition to Resettlement—Understanding Refugees from Laos, Kampuchea and Vietnam in Canada* (207–217). Ottawa: Canadian Asian Studies Association.

Sullivan, Charles A., Michael J. Zimmer, and Richard F. Richards (1988). *Employment Discrimination*, Vol. I (2nd ed.). Boston: Little, Brown.

Sullivan, Deborah (1994, Dec. 8). "Funeral Home Fills Need by Catering to Asians." *Los Angeles Times*, 6(S).

Sullivan, Dwight H. (1988). "The Congressional Response to *Goldman v. Weinberger.*" *Military Law Review* 121, 125–152.

Sullivan, Meg (1988, May 5). "Charreadas: Unspoiled by Glitter, Bucking for Tradition, Mexican Rodeo Fights Critics and Carries On." *Los Angeles Times,* Pt. 9, 1.

Sungaila, Mary-Christine (1995). "Taking the Gendered Realities of Female Offenders into Account: Downward Departures for Coercion and Duress." *Federal Sentencing Reporter* 8, 169–172.

Suri, Sharan K. (2000). "A Matter of Principle and Consistency: Understanding the Battered Woman and Cultural Defenses." *Michigan Journal of Gender and Law* 7, 107–139.

Sussman, Erika (1998). "Contending with Culture: An Analysis of the Female Genital Mutilation Act of 1996." *Cornell International Law Journal* 31, 193–250.

Sutherland, Edwin H. (1947). *Principles of Criminology* (4th ed.). Chicago: Lippincott.

Svendsen, Einar, and Rolla B. Hill (1987, Sept.). "Autopsy Legislation and Practice in Various Countries." *Archives of Pathology and Laboratory Medicine* 111, 846–850.

Swain, Jon (1982, Aug. 1). "Curbing 'Matrons from Mali.'" *Sunday Times* (London), 8.

Sward, Susan (1996, Aug. 7). "No Sex Charges in Case of Minor's Marriage: S. F. DA Won't Tread on Culture Difference." *San Francisco Chronicle,* A11, 14.

Swett, Daniel (1969). "Cultural Bias in the American Legal System." *Law and Society Review* 4, 79–110.

Swindell, Bill (1996, May 31). "Three Students Can Pick Up Transcripts." *Tulsa World,* A13.

Symonides, Janusz (2000). "Cultural Rights." In Janusz Symonides (Ed.), *Human Rights: Concept and Standards* (175–227). Paris: UNESCO.

Szabad, George M., and Gary E. Rubin (1992). "The Newest Americans: Reports of the American Jewish Committee's Task Force on the Acculturation of Immigrants to American Life." In Michael D'Innocenzio and Josef P. Siefman (Eds.), *Immigration and Ethnicity: American Society—"Melting Pot" or "Salad Bowl"?* (281–308). Westport, Conn.: Greenwood Press.

Szapocznik, Jose, and William Kurtines (1980). "Acculturation, Biculturalism and Adjustment among Cuban Americans." In Amado M. Padilla (Ed.), *Acculturation: Theory, Models and Some New Findings* (139–157). Boulder, Colo.: Westview Press.

Taff, Mark L., and Lauren R. Boglioli (1993). "Discussion of Practical Approach to Investigative Ethics and Religious Objections to Autopsy." *Journal of Forensic Sciences* 38, 234.

Tager, Esther (1999). "The Chained Wife." *Netherlands Quarterly of Human Rights* 17(4), 425–457.

Talbot, David (1990, July 8). "The Best Defense: Image." *San Francisco Examiner,* 6–12. (Reprinted from *Los Angeles Times,* June 24, 1990).

Talbot, Margaret (1997, Aug. 11 and 18). "Baghdad on the Plains: A Melting Pot Meltdown." *New Republic* (4,308 and 4,309), 18–22.

Talton, Jana Meredyth (1992, Jan./Feb.). "Asylum for Genital-Mutilation Fugitives: Building a Precedent." *Ms.,* 17.

Tam, Bill (1996, Nov. 19). "Slaughtering Practices: East vs. West." *San Francisco Chronicle,* A22.

Tamaki, Julie (1998, July 13). "Cultural Balancing Act Adds to Teen Angst." *Los Angeles Times,* A1, 8–9.

Tamanaha, Brian (1993). "The Folly of the 'Social Scientific' Concept of Legal Pluralism." *Journal of Law and Society* 20, 192–217.

Tambiah, Stanley (1969). "Animals Are Good to Think and Good to Prohibit." *Ethnology* 8, 452–453.

Tanji, Edwin (1990, July 12). "Dog's Death Cruel, Judge Rules." *Honolulu Advertiser,* A3.

Tarpley, John (1988, summer). "The Law and the Golden Eagle." *Barrister* 15(2), 16–17.

Taylor, Brendon (1998). "Kansas Denies Religion-Based Defense to Rastafarians on Marijuana Charges [*State v. McBride,* 955 P.2d 133 (Kan. Ct. App. 1998)]." *Washburn Law Journal* 38, 307–325.

Taylor, Charles (1994). "The Politics of Recognition." In Amy Gutman (Ed.), *Multiculturalism: Examining the Politics of Recognition.* Princeton, N.J.: Princeton University Press.

Taylor, Deborah M. Boulette (1998). "Paying Attention to the Little Man behind the Curtain: Destroying the Myth of the Liberal's Dilemma." *Maine Law Review* 50, 446–470.

Taylor, Timothy R. (1984). "Soul Rebels: The Rastafarians and the Free Exercise Clause." *Georgetown Law Journal* 72, 1605–1635.

———— (1988). "Redemption Song: An Update on the Rastafarians and the Free Exercise Clause." *Whittier Law Review* 9, 663–682.

Taylor, Todd (1997). "The Cultural Defense and Its Irrelevancy in Child Protection Law." *Boston College Third World Law Journal* 17, 331–364.

Tempelman, Sasja (1999). "Constructions of Cultural Identity: Multiculturalism and Exclusion." *Political Studies* 47, 17–31.

Tempest, Rone (1989, Nov. 7). "Muslim Schoolgirl Scarves Banned; France in a Furor." *Los Angeles Times,* A7.

———— (1993). "Ancient Traditions vs. the Law." *Los Angeles Times,* A1, 10.

Terhune, Cassandra (1997). "Cultural and Religious Defenses to Child Abuse and Neglect." *Journal of the American Academy of Matrimonial Lawyers* 14, 152–192.

Terry, Don (1996, Dec. 2). "Cultural Tradition and Law Collide in Middle America: Arranged Marriage Leads to Rape Charges." *New York Times,* A6.

Teske, Raymond H. C. Jr. and Bardin H. Nelson (1974). "Acculturation and Assimilation: A Clarification." *American Ethnologist* 1, 351–367.

Thao, T. Christopher (1987, Oct.). "Torn between Cultures: Southeast Asian Immigrants in Minnesota." *Bench and Bar of Minnesota,* 21, 24–26.

Thao, Xoua (1984). "Southeast Asian Refugees of Rhode Island: The Hmong Perception of Illness." *Rhode Island Medical Journal* 67, 323–330.

———— (1986a). "Cultural Beliefs and Surgical Procedures." *JAMA* 255(23), 3302.

———— (1986b). "Hmong Perception of Illness and Traditional Ways of Healing." In Glenn L. Henricks, Bruce T. Downing, and Amos S. Deinard (Eds.), *The Hmong in Transition* (365–378). Staten Island, N.Y.: Center for Migration Studies of New York Inc. and The Southeast Asian Refugee Studies Project of the University of Minnesota.

Tharp, Roland G. (1991). "Cultural Diversity and Treatment of Children." *Journal of Consulting and Clinical Psychology* 39, 799–812.

Thomas-Osborne, Valerie, and Carla Brown (1992). *Accent African: Traditional and Contemporary Hairstyles for the Black Women* (3rd ed.). New York: Cultural Expressions.

Thompson, Mark (1985a, June 6). "Immigrants Bring the Cultural Defense into U.S. Courts." *Wall Street Journal,* 28.

———— (1985b, Sept.). "Cultural Defense." *Student Lawyer* 14(1), 24–29.

Thornberry, Patrick (1991). *International Law and the Rights of Minorities.* Oxford: Clarendon.

Titcomb, Margaret (1948). "Kava in Hawaii." *Journal of the Polynesian Society* 57(3), 105–171.

Titunik, Vera (1987, July 20). "Women Sues over Loss of Job: Says Hyatt Was Insensitive to Her Black Culture, Tradition." *Arlington Journal,* A1, 4.

———— (1992, May 1–7). "When Worlds Collide: In Their Homeland, Bride-Capture Was a Hmong Tradition; Here, It's Called Kidnapping and Rape." *Isthmus* (Madison), 17(18), 1, 8.

Todd, T. Wingate (1930–1931). "Culture Conflict and Physical Inadequacy as Bases for Misconduct." *Social Forces* 9, 497–499.

Tomao, Sharon M. (1996). "The Cultural Defense: Traditional or Formal?" *Georgetown Immigration Law Journal* 10, 241–256.

Toomey, Sheila (1985, Feb. 4). "Eskimo Erotica? Traditional-Conduct Plea Wins Sex-Charge Acquittal." *National Law Journal*, 6.

Torry, William (1999). "Multicultural Jurisprudence and the Cultural Defense." *Journal of Legal Pluralism* 44, 127–161.

——— (2000). "Culture and Individual Responsibility: Touchstones of the Culture Defense." *Human Organization* 59, 58–71.

Toubia, Nahid (1995). "Female Genital Mutilation." In Julie Peters and Andrea Wolper (Eds.), *Women's Rights, Human Rights: International Feminist Perspectives* (224–237). New York: Routledge.

Trescher, Robert L., and Thomas N. O'Neill Jr. (1960). "Medical Care for Dependent Children: Manslaughter Liability of the Christian Scientist." *University of Pennsylvania Law Review* 109, 203–217.

Trevison, Catherine (1993). "Sexual Assault Law and the Hmong." *Indiana Law Review* 27, 393–414.

Trimarchi, Anthony (1989, May–June). "U.S. Judge Refuses to Jail Wife-Killer." *Asian Outlook* 24(3), 29–30.

Tsai, Rose (1997, Jan. 10). "Animal Groups Got 'Their Ban.'" *San Francisco Chronicle*, A27.

Tugend, Tom (1992, Nov. 22). "LA Rabbis Blast Jewish Mortuary for Refusing to Assist Moslems." *Jerusalem Post*.

——— (1994, Mar. 29). "'Cultural Defense' Plea Gets Sentence Lowered." *Jerusalem Post*, 3.

Tung, Tran Minh (1980). *Indochinese Patients: Cultural Aspects of the Medical and Psychiatric Care of Indochinese Refugees.* Washington, D.C.: Action for South East Asians.

Turner, Allen C. (1992). "Prolegomenon to a Forensic Cultural Anthropology." *American Journal of Trial Advocacy* 16, 391–415.

Turner, James W. (1986). "'The Water of Life': Kava Ritual and the Logic of Sacrifice." *Ethnology* 25, 203–214.

Tyler, Tom R., Robert J. Boeckmann, Heather J. Smith, and Yuen J. Huo (1997). *Social Justice in a Diverse Society.* Boulder, Colo.: Westview Press.

Uberoi, J. P. S. (1967). "On Being Unshorn." *Transactions of the Indian Institute of Advanced Study*, 87–100.

——— (1996). *Religion, Civil Society and the State: A Study of Sikhism.* Delhi: Oxford University Press.

UNESCO (1970). *Cultural Rights as Human Rights.* Paris: UNESCO.

United Nations (1981). "Special Issue Devoted to *Catha edulis* (Khat)." *Bulletin on Narcotics* 32(3).

——— (1994). *Human Rights: A Compilation of International Instruments.* Vol. 1. New York: United Nations.

United States Sentencing Commission. (1995). *Federal Sentencing Guidelines Manual.* St. Paul, Minn.: West Publishing.

U.S. Department of State (1995, Nov.). "Travel Warning on Drugs Abroad." Publication 10307. Washington, D.C.: U.S. Department of State, Bureau of Consular Affairs.

U.S. Department of State (1996). "Trinidad and Tobago Human Rights Practices, 1995." Dispatch, vol. 7. Washington, D.C.: U.S. Department of State.

U.S. Fish and Wildlife Service (1997, Jan 31). "Eagle Permit Instructions." Atlanta, Ga.: National Eagle Repository.

Valladares, Rene (2000). "Cultural Issues in Fourth Amendment Motions to Suppress." In James G. Connell III and Rene L. Valladares (Eds.), *Cultural Issues in Criminal Defense.* Yonkers, N.Y.: Juris.

van Dijk, Theo (1996). "Democracy and Minority Rights." *Howard Journal* 35, 148–160.

Van Doren, John (1988, Spr.). "Death African Style: The Case of S. M. Otieno." *American Journal of Comparative Law* 36, 329–350.

van Dyke, Vernon (1980). "The Cultural Rights of Peoples." *Universal Human Rights* 2, 1–21.

Vang, Ka (1997, Dec. 13). "Judge Rules out Courtroom Hmong Ceremony." *Saint Paul Pioneer Press*, B1, 3.

Vang, Tou-Fu (1984, Nov.). "Clash of Cultures." *Bridge* 1(6), 5.

Van Praagh, Shauna (1997). "Religion, Custody and a Child's Identities." *Osgoode Hall Law Journal* 35, 309–378.

Van Tuong, Nguyen (1997, 10 Mar.). "Le Port du Foulard Islamique n'est pas par lui'meme incompatible avec le principe de laicite de 1'enseignement public." *Les Petites Affiches,* no. 30, 10–12.

van Velsen, J. (1967). "The Extended-Case Method and Situational Analysis." In A. L. Epstein (Ed.), *The Craft of Social Anthropology* (129–149). London: Tavistock.

Vasdev, Krishna (1961). "Ghosts, Evil Spirits, Witches and the Law of Homicide in the Sudan." *Sudan Law and Reports,* 238–244.

——— (1968). "Provocation as a Defense in Sudan Criminal Law." *Sudan Law Journal and Reports,* 167–229.

Vecoli, Rudolph (1985). "Return to the Melting Pot: Ethnicity in the United States in the Eighties." *Journal of American Ethnic History* 5, 7–20.

Viele, Lawrence (1999, Oct. 4). "Court Expands Self Defense Claims." *National Law Journal,* A6.

Vigh, Michael (2000, Sept. 20). "Prosecutor Rebuts Polygamist's Time-Limit Challenge." *Salt Lake Tribune,* B3.

Villarreal, Carlos (1991). "Culture in Law Making: A Chicano Perspective." *University of California Davis Law Review* 24, 1193–1242.

Volpp, Leti (1994). " (Mis)identifying Culture: Asian Women and the 'Cultural Defense.'" *Harvard Women's Law Journal* 17, 57–101.

——— (1996). "Talking 'Culture': Gender, Race, Nation, and the Politics of Multiculturalism." *Columbia Law Review* 96, 1573–1617.

——— (2000). "Blaming Culture for Bad Behavior." *Yale Journal of Law and the Humanities* 12, 89–116.

von Ehrenfels, Iset (1979). "Clothing and Power Abuse." In Justine M. Cordwell and Ronald A. Schwarz (Eds.), *The Fabrics of Culture: The Anthropology of Clothing and Adornment* (399–403). The Hague: Mouton.

Vu-Duc Vuong (1989, June). "A Position Paper Opposing Assembly Bill 1842." San Francisco: Center for Southeast Asian Refugee Resettlement.

Vuoso, George (1987). "Background, Responsibility, and Excuse." *Yale Law Journal* 96, 1661–1686.

Wadlington, Walter, Whitebread, Charles H., and Samuel M. Davis (1983). *Cases and Materials on Children in the Legal System.* Mineola, N.Y.: Foundation Press.

Wagner, Frank D. (1974). "Enforcement of Preference Expressed by Decedent as to Disposition of His Body after Death." *American Law Reports* 3d, Vol. 54 (Aug. 1998 Supplement).

Wah, Carolyn (1995). "The Custodial Parent's Right to Control Religious Training: Absolute or Limited?" *American Journal of Family Law* 9, 207–217.

Wainwright, Dessie (1997, Oct.). "Providing Funeral Service in a Culturally Diverse Market." *Director,* 69(10), 46–48.

Waldman, Mitchell J. (1988). "Dead Bodies." *American Jurisprudence* (2nd ed.), 22A.

Waldron, Jeremy (2002). "One Law for All? The Logic of Cultural Accommodation." *Washington and Lee Law Review* 59, 3–34.

Walker, Alice (1988, June). "Oppressed Hair Puts a Ceiling on the Brain." *Ms.*, 16(12), 52–53.

Walker, Jana L. (1986). "On Reservation Treaty Hunting Rights: Abrogation v. Regulation by Federal Conservation Statutes—What Standard?" *Natural Resources Journal* 26, 187–196.

Wallace, Charles (1990, May 25). "American on Trial: Can U.S. Urge Mercy?" *Los Angeles Times*, A5.

Walsh, James (1918). "The Priest and Post-Mortem Examinations." *Ecclesiastical Review* 58(4), 396–405.

Waltz, Jon R., and Fred E. Inbau (1971). *Medical Jurisprudence.* New York: Macmillan.

Walzer, Michael (1997). *On Toleration.* New Haven, Conn.: Yale University Press.

Wanderer, Nancy A., and Catherine R. Connors (1999). "Culture and Crime: *Kargar* and the Existing Framework for a Cultural Defense." *Buffalo Law Review* 47, 829–873.

Wang, Hans (1999). "The Nadia Case: From Oslo to Nador, and Back Again." Unpubl. manuscript.

Wasik, Martin (1982). "Partial Excuses in the Criminal Law." *Modern Law Review* 45, 516–533.

Watanabe, Teresa (1994, Aug. 30). "Sparing the Rod in S. Korea." *Los Angeles Times*, A1, 12–13.

Waters, David A., Rama B. Rao, and Helen E. Petracchi (1992, Nov.). "Providing Health Care for the Hmong." *Wisconsin Medical Journal* 91, 642–651.

Watson, Alan (1986). "The Justice of the U.S. Constitution." *International Journal of Moral and Social Studies* 1, 21–30.

Wayland, Sarah (1997a). "Immigration, Multiculturalism, and National Identity in Canada." *International Journal on Minority and Group Rights* 5, 33–58.

———— (1997b). "Religious Expression in Public Schools: Kirpans in Canada, Hijab in France." *Ethnic and Racial Identities* 20(3), 545–561.

Weber, Tracy (1994, Aug. 29). "New Niches for Funeral Marketers." *Los Angeles Times*, A1, 11.

Wecht, Cyril H. (1974). "The Coroner and Death." In Earl A. Grollman (Ed.), *Concerning Death: A Practical Guide for the Living* (177–185). Boston: Beacon Press.

Weihofen, Henry, and Winfred Overholser (1947). "Mental Disorder Affecting the Degree of Crime." *Yale Law Journal* 56, 959–981.

Weil-Curiel, Linda (1990, May). "France: A Lawyer's View on Female Circumcision Performed among Immigrants." *Newsletter* (Inter-African Committee on Traditional Practices Affecting the Health of Women and Children) no. 9, 8–9.

———— (1992, June). "Story of a Courageous Girl [Aminata D.]." *Newsletter* (Inter-African Committee on Traditional Practices Affecting the Health of Women and Children) no. 12, 10–11.

Weiner, Annette B., and Jane Schneider (Eds.) (1989). *Cloth and Human Experience.* Washington, D.C.: Smithsonian Institution Press.

Weir, Richard (2000, Apr. 3). "Drug-War Aim: Nip Khat in the Bud." *Daily News* (New York), 6.

Weiser, Benjamin (1999, Dec. 15). "Danish Mother's Claim of False Arrest Is Rejected." *New York Times*, B1.

Weiss, Martin, and Robert Abramoff (1992). "The Enforceability of Religious Upbringing Agreements." *John Marshall Law Review* 25, 655–725.

Wells, Tom (1998, Feb. 14). "Coffee Windows Steamed: Miami Cafe Owners Feuding with State Health Inspectors." *San Francisco Chronicle*, D2.

Westermarck, Edward (1924). "The Essence of Revenge." *Mind* 7, 289–310.

Westermeyer, Joseph (1982). *Poppies, Pipes, and People: Opium and Its Use in Laos.* Berkeley: University of California Press.

Westermeyer, Joseph, and Xoua Thao (1986). "Cultural Beliefs and Surgical Procedures." *JAMA* 255(23), 3301–3302.

Weyrauch, Walter Otto, and Maureen Anne Bell (1993). "Autonomous Lawmaking: The Case of the 'Gypsies.'" *Yale Law Journal* 103, 323–399.

Wheeler, Linda (1988, Jan. 5). "Hotel Worker Fights to Keep Cornrows. *Washington Post*, D3.

Wheeler, Timothy (2000, Jan. 4). "Domino's Pizza Drops Ban on Facial Hair for Workers." *Baltimore Sun*, 1B, 4B.

White, George (1991, Nov. 13). "Hmong Case to Be Settled with Pleas This Afternoon." *Louisville Times/Lafayette News*, 1, 16.

White, L. A. (1948). "The Definition and Prohibition of Incest." *American Anthropologist* 50, 416–535.

Wiersinga, Hermine C. (2002). *Nuance in benadering: Culturele factoren in het strafproces.* Boom: Juridische uitgevers.

Wikan, Unni (1999a). "Debate: Culture in the Nation and Public Opinion—A Norwegian Case." *Social Anthropology* 7(2), 57–64.

——— (1999b)."Parents' Rights, the Rights of the Child, and Citizenship: The Case of Nadia." Unpublished manuscript.

——— (2000). "Citizenship on Trial: The Case of Nadia. *Daedalus* 129, 55–76.

——— (2001). *Generous Betrayal: Politics of Culture in the New Europe.* Chicago: University of Chicago Press.

——— (2002). "Citizenship on Trial: Nadia's Case." In Rick Shweder, Martha Minow, and Hazel Rose-Markus (Eds.), *Engaging Cultural Differences: The Multicultural Challenge in Liberal Democracies* (128–143). New York: Russell Sage.

Wilkinson, Charles F., and John M. Volkman (1975). "Judicial Review of Indian Treaty Abrogation: 'As Long as Water Flows, or Grass Grows upon the Earth'—How Long a Time Is That?" *California Law Review* 63, 601–661.

Williams, Brett (Ed.) (1991). *The Politics of Culture.* Washington, D.C.: Smithsonian Institution Press.

Williams, Charles (1977). "Utilization of Persisting Cultural Values of Mexican-Americans by Western Practitioners." In Philip Singer (Ed.), *Traditional Healing: New Science or New Colonialism? Essays in Critique of Medical Anthropology* (108–122). Owerrir, Nigeria: Conch Magazine.

Williams, Glanville (1949). "Homicide and the Supernatural." *Law Quarterly Review* 65, 491–503.

——— (1954). "Provocation and the Reasonable Man." *Criminal Law Review*, 741–754.

Williams, Nick (1986, July 5). "Malaysia Standing Firm on Tough Drug Law." *Los Angeles Times.*

Williams, Timothy (1992a, Oct. 1). "Muslim Family Sues, Claiming Jewish Mortuary Disciminates." *Los Angeles Times*, B4.

——— (1992b, Oct. 4). "Business Bias or Service to a Community?" *Los Angeles Times*, J4.

Wilson, Gordon (1961). *Luo Customary Law and Marriage Laws Customs.* Kenya: Government Printer.

Wilson, Marshall (2000, Apr. 29). "Driver Busted for Kava Tea: San Mateo County Case First of Its Kind in State." *San Francisco Chronicle*, A17.

Winkelman, Michael (1996). "Cultural Factors in Criminal Defense Proceedings." *Human Organization* 55(2), 154–159.

Winston, Kimberly (1996, Oct. 3). "Most People around Temple Find Sikhs Good Neighbors." *Daily Review.*

Winter, Bronwyn (1994). "Women, Law, and Cultural Relativism in France: The Case of Excision." *Signs* 19, 939–974.

Wirth, Louis (1930–1931). "Culture Conflict and Delinquency." *Social Forces* 9, 484–492.

Wong, Charmaine M. (1999). "Good Intentions, Troublesome Applications: The Cultural Defence and Other Uses of Cultural Evidence in Canada." *Criminal Law Quarterly* 42(2 and 3), 367–396.

Woo, Deborah (1989). "The People v. Fumiko Kimura: But Which People?" *International Journal of the Sociology of Law* 17, 403–428.

Woo, Elaine (1999, Aug. 25). "Wilbert Oliver: Sued to Halt Mortuary Discrimination." *Los Angeles Times,* A16.

Wright, Douglas M. Jr. (1991). "Constitutional Law." *Mississipppi Law Journal* 61, 223–236.

Wright, Hugh (1988, July 8). "Father Sentenced to Jail for Torturing Son." *Stockton Record,* B1.

——— (1991, Oct. 29). "Parents of Teen Bride Face Trial: Couple Forced Her to Wed, Girl Says." *Stockton Record.*

——— (1992, Jan. 15). "Man Gets Probation in Forced Marriage Case." *Stockton Record.*

Wudunn, Sheryl (1997, Jan. 2). "Where a Dog Can Be a Pet, or a Dining Experience." *New York Times,* A4.

Wurzburger, Walter S. (1978). "Cadavers: Jewish Perspectives." In Warren T. Reich (Ed.), *Encyclopedia of Bioethics* (vol. 1, 144–145). New York: Free Press.

Wyman, James H. (1997). "Vengeance Is Whose? The Death Penalty and Cultural Relativism in International Law." *Journal of Transnational Law and Policy* 6, 543–570.

Yeatman, W., and Viet Van Dang (1980). "Cao Gio (Coin Rubbing): Vietnamese Attitudes toward Health Care." *JAMA* 244(24), 2748–9.

Yeatman, W. et al. (1976). "Pseudobattering in Vietnamese Children." *Pediatrics* 58, 616–618.

Yeats, Mary Ann (1991). "Cultural Conflict in Community-Based Corrections." *Criminal Law Forum* 2, 341–354.

Yee, Phoebe (1981, Nov. 23). Task Force on Chinese Food, Minutes.

Yen, Marianne (1989, Apr. 10). "Refusal to Jail Immigrant: Judge Ordered Probation for Chinese Man, Citing 'Cultural Background.'" *Washington Post,* A3.

Yeo, Stanley M. H. (1987). "Provoking the 'Ordinary' Ethnic Person: A Juror's Predicament." *Criminal Law Journal* 11, 96–104.

——— (1990–1991). "Recent Australian Pronouncements on the Ordinary Person Test in Provocation and Automatism. *Criminal Law Quarterly* 33, 280–297.

Yi, Daniel (2000, Sept. 6). "Health Codes Often at Odds with Ethnic Tastes." *Los Angeles Times,* A3, 17.

Yinger, J. Milton (1976). "Ethnicity in Complex Societies." In Lewis A. Coser and Otto N. Larsen (Eds.), *The Uses of Controversy in Sociology* (197–216). New York: Free Press.

——— (1981). "Toward a Theory of Assimilation and Dissimilation." *Ethnic and Racial Studies* 4, 249–264.

Yishai, Yael (1979). "Autopsy in Israel: Political Pressures and Medical Policy." *Ethics in Science and Medicine* 6, 11–20.

——— (1980). "Health Policy and Religion: Conflict and Accommodation in Israeli Politics." *Journal of Health Politics, Policy and Law* 5(3), 431–446.

York, Michael (1989, Oct. 12). "Dismissal of Bias Suit over Braids Overruled." *Washington Post,* B5.

Young, Cathy (1992a, July 8). "Feminists' Multicultural Dilemma." *Chicago Tribune,* 15.

——— (1992b). *Equal Cultures or Equality for Women? Why Feminism and Multiculturalism Don't Mix.* Washington, D.C.: Heritage Foundation.

Young, Iris (1990). *Justice and the Politics of Difference.* Princeton, N.J.: Princeton University Press.

Yourse, Robyn-Denise (1988, Jan. 16). "Cornrow Wearers Told to 'Obey the White Man.'" *Washington Afro-American,* 1, 14.

Yousif, Ahmad (1994). "Family Values, Social Adjustment and Problems of Identity: The Canadian Experience." *Journal of the Institute of Muslim Minority Affairs* 15(1 and 2), 108–119.

Zack, Margaret (2000, July 12). "Khat Tests Needn't Be Quantitative, Court Rules." *Star Tribune,* 3B.

Zambito, Thomas (1995, Oct. 3). "Coroner over Son's Autopsy." *Record,* 3.

Zane, Maitland (1997, May 6). "Minister in Fatal Exorcism Ordered to Leave U.S." *San Francisco Chronicle,* A18

Zangwill, Israel (1914). *The Melting Pot: Drama in Four Acts.* New York: Macmillan.

Zimring, Franklin E. (1971). *Perspectives on Deterrence.* Chevy Chase, Md.: National Institute of Mental Health, Center for Studies of Crime and Delinquency.

Zwigoff, Terry (1996, Nov. 19). "Letter to Editor: Animal Protection." *San Francisco Chronicle,* A22.

Zybrzycki, J. (1957, July/Sept.). "Immigration and Culture Conflict." *REMP Bulletin* (Research Group for European Migration Problems) 5(3), 71–77.

INDEX